CM01603782

This publication
is made possible by

FONDATION
elf

Monet

Richard Thomson

with an essay by Michael Clarke

to Matisse

Landscape Painting in France 1874–1914

National Gallery of Scotland

Edinburgh 1994

Published by the Trustees
of the National Galleries of Scotland
for the exhibition held at the
National Gallery of Scotland, Edinburgh
11 August – 23 October 1994

© Richard Thomson and the Trustees
of the National Galleries of Scotland 1994
All rights reserved

ISBN 0 903598 51 5 *cloth*
ISBN 0 903598 47 7 *paper*

Designed by Dalrymple and typeset in
W. A. Dwiggins's Caledonia and Electra types
Printed by BAS Printers Ltd, Over Wallop
on 150 gsm Consort Satin supplied
by Donside Paper Company

Foreword 6

Lenders to the Exhibition 8

Sponsor's Foreword 9

Acknowledgements 10

LANDSCAPE PAINTING IN FRANCE 1874–1914
Richard Thomson

1 Pictures of Progress, Nationalism and Tradition 13

2 The Suburbs of Paris 27

3 Notre-Dame and the Eiffel Tower 39

4 The Channel Coast 53

5 The Mediterrean Coast 65

6 Reinventing the Pastoral Ideal 77

7 Incidents in the Landscape 89

8 Landscape as Vision and Metamorphosis 99

9 The Nocturne 109

10 The Panoramic Landscape 121

11 Landscape as Decoration 131

12 Landscapes in Series 141

13 The Seasons 149

14 Tour d'horizon 161

Notes and References 163

Explication de texte: Critical Writings on Landscape 1874–1914 169
Michael Clarke

CATALOGUE SECTION

Bibliography 179

Chronology 186

Artists' Biographies and List of Works in the Exhibition 189

Illustration Acknowledgements 196

Index of People and Places 197

Foreword

MONET TO MATISSE continues the series of distinguished exhibitions on French art mounted by the National Gallery of Scotland to coincide with the Edinburgh International Festival. In particular, it follows on from *Lighting up the Landscape; French Impressionism and its Origins*, held in 1986, which examined Impressionist landscape up to the first great 'Impressionist' exhibition of 1874. The subtitle of *Monet to Matisse*, that is *Landscape Painting in France 1874–1914*, defines the parameters of our present show. It only hints, however, at the unexpected riches of Dr Thomson's exploration of this enormous subject. The familiar names such as Gauguin, van Gogh, Matisse, Monet, Picasso, Pissarro and Seurat are juxtaposed with lesser-known masters such as Aman-Jean, Dulac, Lacombe, Ponson, Ségé and Tauzin. Organised thematically, *Monet to Matisse*, offers the first in-depth survey of this critical period in French landscape painting.

We are only too aware of the enormous debts we have incurred to many lenders (some of whom wish to remain anonymous) and individuals throughout the world in bringing this ambitious undertaking to fruition. We would like to thank: Véronique Alemany-Dessaint, Jean Aubert, Joseph Baillio, Dr Felix Baumann, Jacques Beauffet , Mr & Mrs J. Benatoff, Heinz Berggruen, Paula D. Berry, René Le Bihan, Dr Bengt von Bonsdorff, Emmanuel Bréon, Steven L. Brezzo, Thérèse Burollet, Peter Burton, Françoise Cachin, Richard Calvocoressi, Stéphane Colsenet, Drs D. A. S. Connegieter, Henry-Claude Cousseau, Jack Cowart, Pierre Curie, Barbara Dawson, Agnès Delannoy, Marina Ducrey, Philippe Durey, Professor Folke Edwards, Everett Fahy, Claire Frèches, Josette Galiegue, Dr J. van Gogh, Yannick Guin, Vivien Hamilton, Theresa Harley-Wilson, Arnaud d'Hauterives, Robert Henning Jr, Grant Holcomb, Prof. Dieter Honisch, Sona Johnston, Sue Johnston, Dr David Josefowitz, Ellen Josefowitz, Paul Josefowitz, Samuel Josefowitz, Laurence B. Kanter, Dr Christian Klemm, Dr Z. Kolks, Professor Clive C. Kuenzle, Geneviève Lacambre, Ellen W. Lee, Dr Ronald de Leeuw, Arnold L. Lehman, John Leighton, Nathalie Leleu, Tomás Llorens, Jacques Lugand, Neil MacGregor, Prof. Cyrille Martin, Peter C.

Marzio, Caroline Mathieu, Peter Mitchell, Jean-Paul Monery, Philippe de Montebello, Bernard de Montgolfier, Mme Ossant, Merribell Parsons, Dr Nicholas Penny, Paul N. Perrot , Professor M. Piotrovsky, Earl A. Powell III, Gérard Regnier, M. Rérolle, Joseph Rishel, Kathryna Ritchie, Cora Rosevear, Antoine Salomon, Marie-José Salmon, George T. M. Shackelford, Dr Angela Schneider, Didier Schulmann, Dr Dieter Schwarz, David Scrase, Nicholas Serota, Julian Spalding, Björn Springfeldt, David W Steadman, Hollister Sturges, Dr Peter C. Sutton, Belinda Thomson, Sally B. Thornton, Louis van Tilborgh, Gary Tinterow, Mäithé Vallès-Bled, Kirk Varnedoe, Maria Via, Germain Viatte, Jeanne Villeneuve, Malcolm Warner, Dr Christopher White, Dr Catherine Whistler, Mrs John Hay Whitney, Dr Robert A. Yassin.

The exhibition has been devised by Dr Richard Thomson, Senior Lecturer in the History of Art at the University of Manchester, who is an international authority in this field of study. The Gallery is greatly indebted to him for his imaginative scholarship and the dedication he has given to all aspects of this enterprise. The organisation and administration of the exhibition has been undertaken by Michael Clarke, Keeper of the National Gallery of Scotland.

Ambitious loan exhibitions place heavy burdens on our colleagues. Sheila Scott has efficiently dealt with the extensive correspondence. The Registrar's Department, in particular Margaret Mackay, has handled the complex transport problems inevitably generated by such an international exhibition. In this context we are happy also to acknowledge a contribution towards transport costs from Momart. Victoria Keller has nobly supervised the ordering of photographic material for the catalogue, which has been seen to press by Janis Adams, edited by Susie Leiper and designed, with his customary flair, by Robert Dalrymple. The exhibition installation has been devised by Zoë Hall.

The National Galleries receive no exhibition grant, so sponsorship for shows such as *Monet to Matisse* is absolutely essential. In this respect, we have been especially fortunate to have received the generous support of Fondation Elf, in particular that of its President, François de Wissocq. It gives us particular pleasure to acknowledge such an international collaboration. From its inception, the exhibition has engaged the keen interest and knowledgeable support of Pierre Provoyeur, Director of Cultural Affairs at Fondation Elf and Michel Romieu, Managing Director of Elf Petroleum UK. The administration of the sponsorship has been assisted by the participation of Fiona McGhie and John Gourley, in collaboration with our own sponsorship consultant, Dianne Stein.

However our greatest debt, organisers and visitors alike, is surely to those described by the French critic Jules Castagnary as that 'great army of landscape painters' who have celebrated the interest and variety afforded by the landscape of the beautiful and (in both senses) *cultivé* country of France.

TIMOTHY CLIFFORD

Director, National Galleries of Scotland

MICHAEL CLARKE

Keeper, National Gallery of Scotland

Lenders to the Exhibition

Amsterdam
Fridart Stichting
Rijksmuseum Vincent van Gogh

Baltimore
Baltimore Museum of Art

Beauvais
Musée départemental de l'Oise

Berlin
Staatliche Museen Preussischer Kulturbesitz

Béziers
Musée des beaux-arts

Boston
Museum of Fine Arts

Boulogne-Billancourt
Musée municipal de Boulogne-Billancourt

Brest
Musée de Brest

Cambridge
Private Collection on loan to the Fitzwilliam Museum

Chartres
Musée des beaux-arts

Columbus
Columbus Museum of Art

Courbevoie
Musée Roybet-Fould

Dublin
Hugh Lane Municipal Gallery of Modern Art

Edinburgh
National Gallery of Scotland
Scottish National Gallery of Modern Art

Enschede
Rijksmuseum Twenthe

Glasgow
Glasgow Museums & Art Galleries

Göteborg
Göteborgs Konstmuseum

Helsinki
Private Collection on loan to Amos Andersonin Taideomuseo

Houston
Museum of Fine Arts Houston

Indianapolis
Indianapolis Museum of Art

London
The Berggruen Collection, on loan to the National Gallery
National Gallery
Tate Gallery

Los Angeles
The Armand Hammer Museum of Art & Cultural Center

Lyon
Musée des beaux-arts

Madrid
Fundación Colección Thyssen-Bornemisza

Nantes
Musée des beaux-arts

New York
Metropolitan Museum of Art
Museum of Modern Art
Mrs John Hay Whitney

Oxford
Ashmolean Museum

Paris
Musée Carnavalet
Musée Marmottan
Musée Gustave Moreau
Musee national d'art moderne
Musée d'Orsay
Musée du Petit Palais
Musée Picasso

Philadelphia
Philadelphia Museum of Art

Poitiers
Musées de la ville

Reims
Musée des beaux-arts

Rennes
Musée des beaux-arts

Rochester
Rochester Memorial Art Gallery

Santa Barbara
Santa Barbara Museum of Art

San Diego
San Diego Museum of Art

Saint-Etienne
Musée d'art moderne

Saint-Germain-en-Laye
Musée départemental du Prieuré

St Petersburg
The Hermitage Museum

Saint-Tropez
Musée de l'Annonciade

Springfield
Springfield Museum of Fine Arts

Stockholm
Moderna Museet

Toledo
Toledo Museum of Art

Washington
Corcoran Gallery of Art
National Gallery of Art

Winterthur
Kunstmuseum

Zurich
Kunsthaus

Mr & Mrs J. Benatoff

Josefowitz Collection

Private Collections

Sponsor's Foreword

Over the last few years Fondation Elf has established its reputation as a contributor to the arts in the UK by making possible two major cultural events in London. Following its successful patronage of a new production of Mozart's *Don Giovanni* at the Royal Opera House, Covent Garden in 1992, Fondation Elf supported the first retrospective exhibition of the work of Alfred Sisley at the Royal Academy of Arts.

In 1994 Fondation Elf is marking its first contribution to the arts in Scotland by supporting the National Gallery of Scotland's initiative to bring together a collection of the works of landscape painters active in France during the first 40 years of the modern movement (1874–1914). Fondation Elf has lent its full support to the Keeper of the National Gallery of Scotland, Michael Clarke, and Exhibition Curator, Dr Richard Thomson, both of whom expressed a wish to take a fresh look at Impressionism, Fauvism, Cubism and Symbolism and stimulate new ideas and thinking.

It is worth noting that this innovative collection of paintings will be hosted exclusively at the National Gallery of Scotland in Edinburgh, attracting visitors from all over Europe to the Scottish capital. Similarly, in 1993 Fondation Elf was involved outside Paris when it supported a successful exhibition of Russian Avant-Garde art at the Musée des beaux-arts, Nantes.

A great deal of the Fondation's patronage can be seen throughout Europe, of which Edinburgh is undoubtedly one of the great historical capitals. Scotland's historical and economic importance to France and Elf's UK North Sea activities make us proud participants in this Franco-Scottish alliance.

This unique exhibition is a new creation which challenges traditional ways of thinking and aims to provoke new methods of analysis. We hope the exhibition will attract thousands of visitors who will be enlightened and inspired by paintings of such beauty.

FRANÇOIS DE WISSOCQ
President, Fondation Elf

Acknowledgements

Over the long period of this project's gestation I have been fortunate to have been able to discuss it with or receive helpful information from a number of friends and colleagues, among them Françoise Cachin, Nicolas Cendo, Elizabeth Cowling, Claire Frèches-Thory, Vivien Hamilton, John House, Dr David Josefowitz, Paul and Ellen Josefowitz, Richard Kendall, Geneviève Lacambre, John Leighton, Peter Mitchell, Anne Roquebert, Richard Shone and Malcolm Warner. I thank them all, as well as any others I may impertinently have forgotten. My wife Belinda has been a constant source of stimulating advice and support, not least in her patient and acute reading of the manuscript. I have been warmly received by collectors and by curators in many museums in Europe and the United States while working on the selection, and I would like to express my gratitude to them all. The staff of various libraries have been most co-operative, among them the Bibliothèque Nationale and the Documentation of the Musée d'Orsay, Paris, the History of Art Department Library, Oxford, the Courtauld Institute and Witt Libraries, London, and the John Rylands University Library, Manchester. I owe a particular debt of thanks to the most welcoming curators and staff who were my temporary colleagues when I was Guest Scholar in the Departments of Painting and of Education and Academic Affairs at the J. Paul Getty Museum during the summer of 1993; it was there, and in particular in the Getty Center Library, that I was able to advance my research significantly. In Pierre Provoyeur of the Fondation Elf I have had a sponsorship officer who was not only sympathetic but who, rarely for that *métier*, could also suggest pertinent comparative illustrations. The efficient staff of the National Galleries of Scotland have been unfailingly helpful, and I would like to thank in particular Sheila Scott, Victoria Keller the picture-researcher, and Janis Adams who has seen the publication to press. I knew of old that Michael Clarke would prove the ideal colleague: a stimulating fellow-scholar, a trustworthy eye, a serenely effective administrator, and mischievous company.

RICHARD THOMSON
Heaton Moor

Richard Thomson

Landscape Painting in France 1874–1914

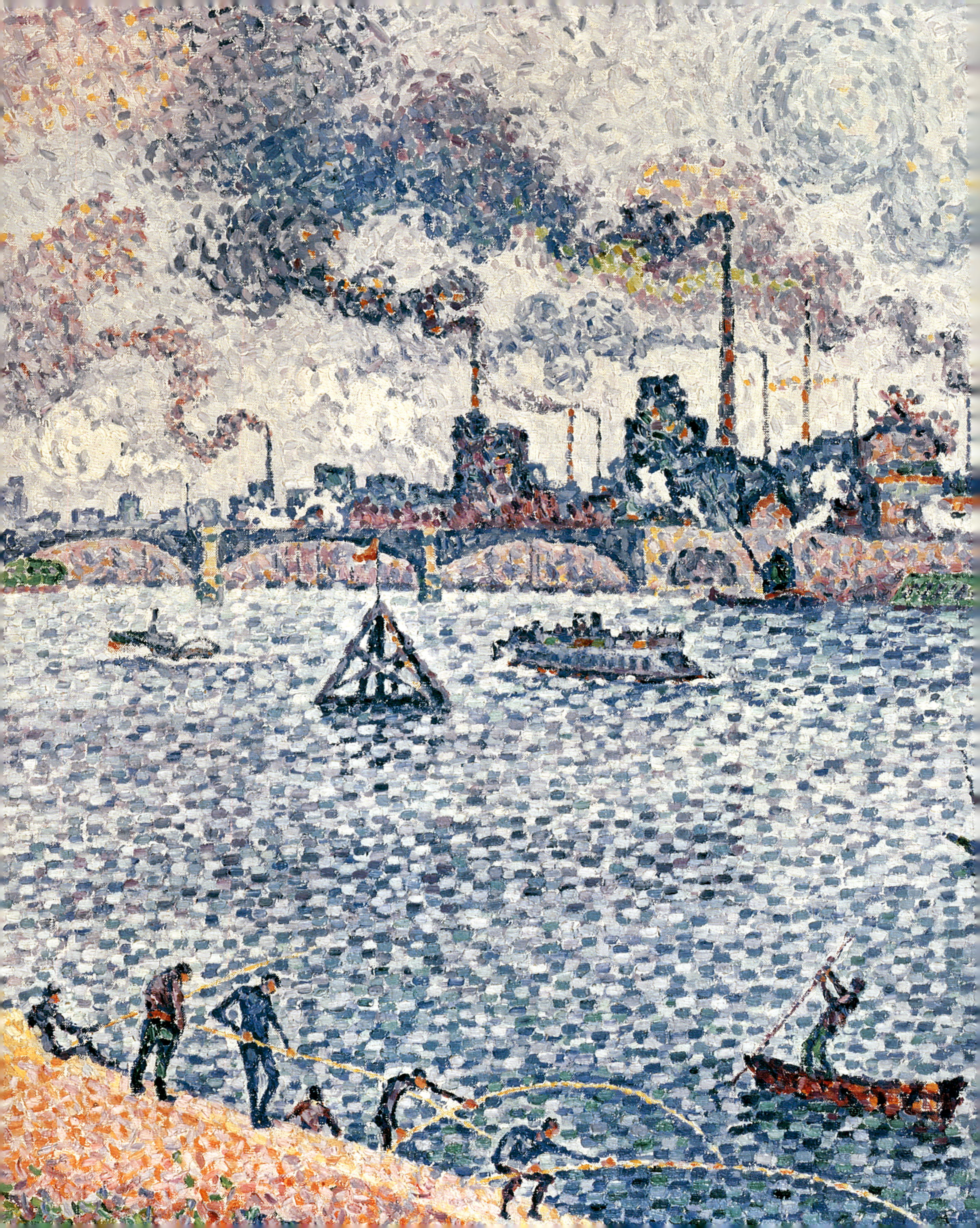

1

Pictures of Progress, Nationalism and Tradition

The aim of this book and the accompanying exhibition is to investigate various themes that, I believe, were matters of vital aesthetic and intellectual importance in the practice of landscape painting in France between 1874 and 1914. Painting at this time witnessed the most radical and exciting transformations since the Renaissance, and the landscape genre was at the core of both experimentation and reaction. The period begins with the first Impressionist exhibition of 1874 and closes with the start of the First World War – on the one hand an artistic event and on the other a political one. These events themselves are enough to suggest that the painting of landscape needs to be considered within wide and contrasting contexts.

The strategy of juxtaposing landscape images by artists not usually considered together is intended to overhaul old assumptions and prompt new lines of enquiry. It should come as a surprise to see together, for example, panoramic views by both a Salon painter such as Ségé and the Impressionist Sisley, or cityscapes by artists of different generations and groupings, for example the Neo-Impressionist Signac and the Orphic Cubist Delaunay. The purpose of such juxtapositions is to use the representation of landscape to challenge our preconceptions about painting in France a century ago, to explore unexpected interrelationships and consistencies, and to offer alternatives to the cumbersome and outdated division of this period into sequential 'movements'.

Three broad categories draw together the book and the exhibition: representations of contrasting regions and sites, the use of landscape motifs as a vehicle for the artist's imagination, and different types of 'landscape'. Within this tripartite structure particular themes have been pursued, to the inevitable exclusion of others. Thus in discussing representations of the French regions, my choice of the Channel and Mediterranean coasts necessitated the omission of, say, images of Brittany. For this project is no all-encompassing, chronological survey. It is based on certain pivotal and provocative themes, the paths of which have been followed using crucial images as landmarks. These paintings form the pictorial arguments in the exhibition (inevitably dependent to an extent on the availability of loans) and shape the discussion in the book. The choice of themes and the selection of works are inevitably personal; another guest curator would have made different decisions, and individual pictures could equally well have been considered within one group as another. However, after the themes had been chosen and loan requests dispatched, I came upon the *musée imaginaire* drawn up by Raymond Bouyer, one of the most important contemporary writers on landscape, in his *Le Paysage dans l'art*, published in 1894 – exactly midway through this period. Bouyer envisaged galleries grouped thematically, among them 'a single eternal effect, hour or season', such as Night; 'a single site represented by several artists'; and 'a single landscape treated by the same artist in its multiple physiognomies', such as Monet's *Grainstacks* or *Poplars*.[1] Perhaps the structure of this exhibition is not so arbitrary after all.

The landscape paintings explored here were made during a period of immense change and controversy in the fabric of French life; as the poet Charles Péguy wrote, not long before his death in the First World War, the world had changed more in his lifetime than since the time of Jesus.[2] Those forty years had been fraught with Franco-German rivalry. Humiliating military defeat in the war of 1870–1 and the cession of Alsace and much of Lorraine in the east had necessitated economic rebuilding, encouraged the restoration of national pride under the flag of *revanche* (revenge), and led ultimately to the outbreak of world war. Social change in France – burgeoning industrialisation and the rise of the Left, agricultural depression and rural depopulation – had been paralleled by political instability, the Third Republic precariously balancing under the pressures of short-lived governments, threatened coups, establishment corruption and above all the Dreyfus Affair, which so sharply polarised French society during the later 1890s.

One might question the validity of such historical outlines in the discussion of landscape painting. But the painting of landscape is not just a question of visual experience, of the artist making an image in response to natural phenomena, and of the spectator responding in turn to the colours and composition of

opposite
1
P. Signac ***Seine, Grenelle*** 1899 (detail)
Helsinki, private collection on loan to the Amos Andersonin Taideomuseo

that representation. Making and reading landscape pictures involves complex sets of rules, expectations and values, brought by painter or viewer to the motif in nature and to the created image. In looking at paintings made over a span of barely two generations, we will be considering very different styles of representation, from the meticulous naturalism of Tauzin to the strident naïvety of Chagall, from the tonal subtlety of Berthe Morisot to the fragmented colour planes of Sonia Delaunay. Such diversity demonstrates the range of expression and association inherent in landscape painting at this time, and surely requires an equivalent pluralism of interpretative approach. My text thus deliberately brings into play a divergent and perhaps surprising variety of perspectives – religious beliefs, techniques of pictorial composition, issues concerning nationalism or touching on music, the approaches of social history – the better to suggest the complex patterns with which landscape painting interwove with the fabric of contemporary French cultural life.

The aim is to enrich the study and enjoyment of landscape painting between 1874 and 1914, and to question and discard clichés. Among such *idées reçues* is the notion that the Universal Exhibition of 1855 saw the acceptance of landscape as a major force in French painting, no longer a lesser genre than history painting, and the establishment of artists such as Corot, Théodore Rousseau and Millet as leading figures in the art market. A younger generation, such an account would continue, developed the practice of *plein air* oil sketching into finished work, their brighter colour and broken surfaces more naturalistically recording atmospheric and light effects. Smeared by an unsympathetic press at their first exhibition in 1874 as 'Impressionists', artists such as Monet, Pissarro and Sisley had won only partial, and often American rather than national, recognition even by the 1890s. In their wake, the modernist account continues, emerged other avant-garde groups, notably in the 1880s the Neo-Impressionists with their pointillist touch and ordered division of tone, and individuals such as Cézanne, Gauguin and van Gogh with their varied means of highly personal brushwork, synthetic drawing and exaggerated colour. After 1900 yet another generation tested, combined and discarded these possibilities, the avant-garde settling in the years prior to 1914 for experiments with Cubist fragmentation.

That modernist litany of conservatism versus successive avant-gardes presents far too simple a picture. Landscape painting had a complex and somewhat paradoxical status in the French art world. On the one hand it was perhaps the chief commodity on the art market, offering a rich variety of styles and subjects popular with a bourgeois clientele desirous of appealing images which sustained the values and expectations to be discussed shortly.[3] On the other hand, landscape painting could hardly be considered central to the artistic establishment when the first *paysagiste* to take a major official position was Louis Cabat, who served as Director of the French School in Rome from 1879 to 1885, and the first to win the Medal of Honour at the annual Salon was François-Louis Français as late as 1890.[4] That there was a sense of continuity and rivalry among progressive painters is evident; one needs only to think of Derain's doleful recollection, whilst on military service, of the 1901 van Gogh show – 'his memory haunts me ceaselessly' – or his painting campaigns in London in 1905 and 1906 made in frank competition with Monet's work.[5] Impressionism did not long keep its radical reputation, gradually entering the mainstream. After six years of independent exhibiting, Renoir and Monet showed again at the Salon, the former in 1879, the latter in 1880, and their work began to sell; of the 145 canvases shown by Monet at the exhibition shared with Rodin in 1889, some eighty were lent from private collectors and at least ten by dealers.[6] Even Jules Breton, reactionary painter of rural life, found the Impressionist paintings at the 1889 Universal Exhibition unexceptionable,[7] and by the early years of the century not only the Impressionists but also artists such as Signac and Denis, who had emerged in the late 1880s and early 1890s respectively, were considered increasingly established figures. This was not merely a case of the market's predominantly middle-class taste absorbing innovation. For at a time when critics complained that 'landscape has invaded everything',[8] when defining different and shifting categories of *paysages* and groupings of *paysagistes* was a convoluted task, a degree of controversy was essential to maintain identity in public debate and on the market. To paint landscapes differently from one's contemporaries and antecedents was often taken as a necessary strategy to promote one's individuality, though beneath this jockeying for exclusivity lay continuities and consistencies which are fascinating to explore.

CONSTRUCTIONS OF 'LANDSCAPE'

This initiative to investigate more varied patterns and explore some neglected areas of landscape painting in France between 1874 and 1914 is based on two foundations. First, it is necessary to site the making of landscape pictures within a wide cultural framework. One needs to examine different constructions and categories of landscape, or *paysage*, to question the different forms it might take, and to analyse how images of landscape might be socially formed, taking their place within patterns of social change. There are very complex issues and forces at play here, which a single exhibition and text can only begin to develop, but it is surely time to shift the debate away from artistic movements to the broader socio-cultural matrix of the first forty years of the Third Republic. Second, implicit within this is the hypothesis that this period saw the rebirth of *paysage* as a vehicle for the artist's imagination. Within the history of European painting, landscape has served as a theatre in which artists could stage events echoed or dominated by nature; one thinks of Mantegna, Rubens, Rembrandt. From Poussin and Claude in the seventeenth century, through to Watteau and Fragonard in the eighteenth, the notion of landscape as an imaginative genre had been a unifying current in French painting, the withering of which Baudelaire lamented in his review of the Salon of 1846.[9] His was an early voice in the chafing against the predominance of naturalism in landscape which by the final quarter of the century had become insistent, with critics uncomfortable about excessive surface detail, 'bourgeois beauties' and too much 'respect for realities'.[10] By the 1890s relieved enthusiasm for more imaginative representations of landscape was being voiced not only by young independents such as Denis and Signac but also by conservative curators such as Georges Lafenestre and *juste milieu* theorists such as Bouyer who could simultaneously sustain a cult of Corot and admiration for Monet.[11] The resurgence of landscape as an imaginative vehicle which I am positing was due not only to critical pressure but to a number of forces: the very prevalence of landscape which gave it ample scope for artistic manipulation; the emergence of Symbolism which stressed the emotive and spiritual; and the avant-garde's desire for innovation. One might even risk a sweepingly subversive conjecture that the naturalism of much French landscape painting between 1830 and 1890, in the work of Rousseau or Dupré, Pissarro or Monet, is an aberration in the history of the genre, which would involve asking under what circumstances naturalism flourished. Both starting-points, then, return us to the cultural formation of 'landscape', to which we should now turn.

Notions of 'landscape' are complex and overlapping; the attentive reader will have noticed that I have already used that single word to carry several mean-

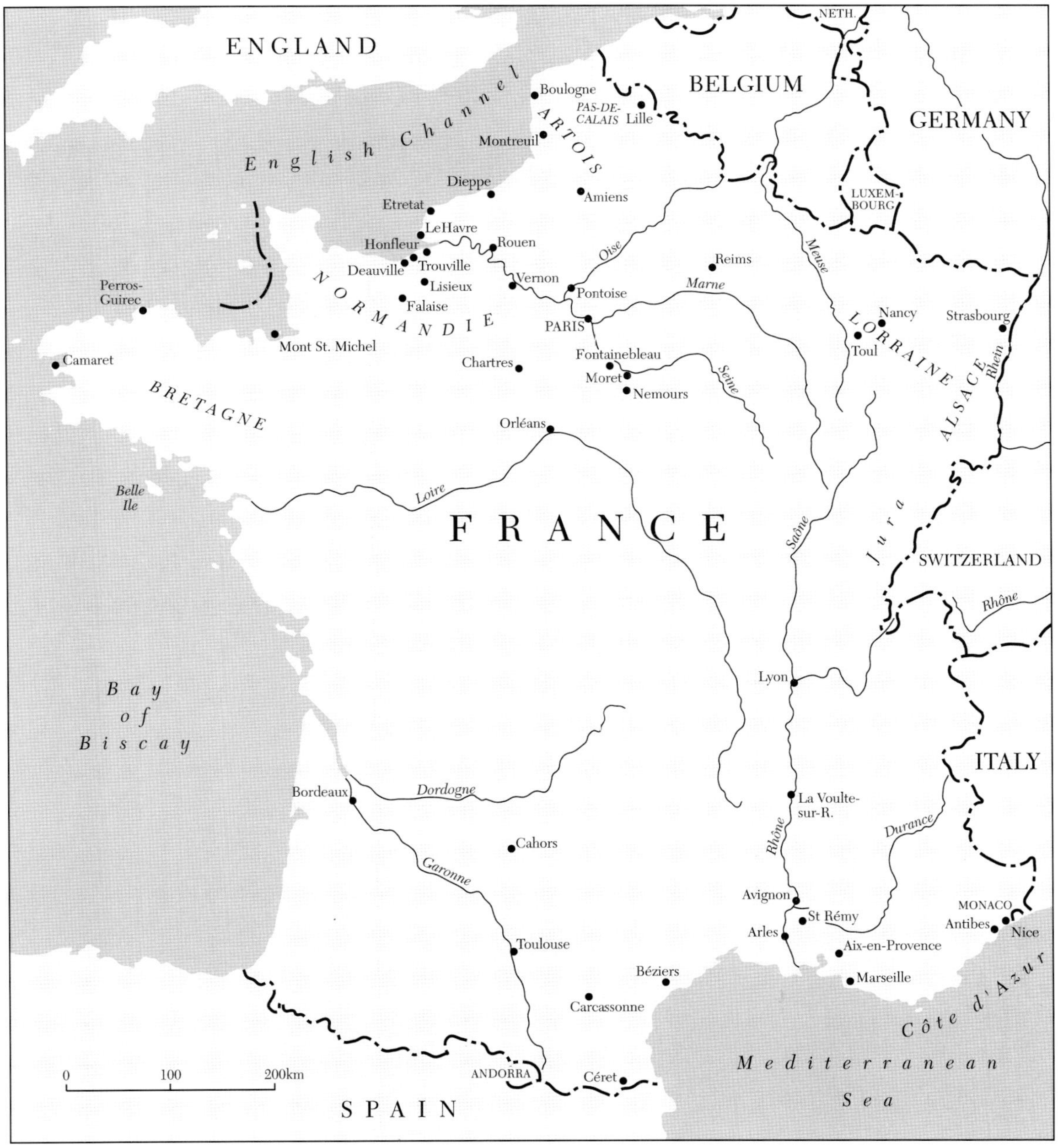

ings. In French the word *paysage* can mean, as can the English 'landscape', both landscape as a physical environment, an aspect of nature, and as a category of artistic representation. Significantly, the French word has its root in *pays*, meaning both country in a generic sense and also homeland or native region, as does *paysan*, peasant, one who works on and is perhaps tied to that land, a term at this period not without pejorative connotations. Thus in terms of language alone associations of space, nature, visual culture, national or regional identity, agricultural labour and social class all come into play. The third of these – visual culture – specifically concerns us here, and one needs to be clear that of course an individual's experience of nature, of a site, will be different from one's experience of a representation of that location. As Frédéric Paulhan insisted in his *L'Esthétique du paysage* of 1913, an image of a landscape is not exact, but is a transformation by artistic means.[12] In the nineteenth century visual culture had terms for different categories of representation. Neo-Classical theorists such as Valenciennes [**154**] had been responsible for defining the *paysage historique*, in which the landscape was structured according to Italianate formulations derived from the examples of Claude and Poussin and served as a theatre for small-scale figures involved in usually mythological narratives in the manner of the supreme genre of history painting. A less elevated category of landscape painting was the *paysage rustique*, representing the active landscape and its agriculture, *la vie agreste* as it was commonly termed at the end of the century. Both these, though particularly the *paysage historique*, might be covered by the term *paysage composé*, which refers less to the content than to the making of the image, ordering the raw materials of nature into a disciplined picture. The *effet* and *impression* identified other levels of making, the rapid notation in paint of effects observed in nature. These might be kept as independent studies, useful in the honing of the painter's eye, or might be quoted in more finished state, in a *paysage composé*. In the last third of the century, as working *en plein air* became more prevalent and even acceptable as the basis for a finished painting, tastes in landscape began, broadly speaking, to shift away from more contrived motifs towards those which were more banal and by their apparent immediacy gave the spectator a sense of sharing the painter's response to nature. Central to this was the notion of *sensation*, crucial to the practice of Monet, Pissarro and Cézanne, and meaning both the artist's immediate optical and emotional response to the landscape and the particular individual means of transcribing that response in paint.[13] Despite this shift, artists never ceased to order their landscape images, however discreetly. Even a *plein air* canvas as apparently spontaneous as Sisley's *Bend in the Seine at Saint-Cloud* [**195**], with its breeze-swept panorama and lack of salient features, balances the pictorial weight of sky and landscape and orders the view in zones of different value.

But landscape is not just a question of aesthetic formulation and artistic rendering. Courbet's claim that 'landscape is just about tones' is the *reductio ad absurdum* of a complex and developing debate about the rôle of the artist in the transcription or interpretation of nature. In 1865 Zola's definition of naturalism as 'nature seen through a temperament' had insisted upon the importance of individuality, and by the turn of the century this theory was being extended. Landscape, argued Paul Flat in 1893, quintessentially articulated 'the painter's own sensibility', 'the intimacy of his being'.[14] Here was the notion of making landscape images turned around, with the emphasis being taken off the business of the painter's recording of external nature and placed on the landscape image as an expression of the artist's inner life. This attitude was neatly articulated in the nostrum 'A landscape is a state of the soul' coined by the Swiss philosopher Henri-Frédéric Amiel whose *Journal*, published posthumously in 1882–4, was widely read. His almost ubiquitous definition was extensively cited in debates about landscape at the *fin-de-siècle* and beyond, whether denounced as pretentious by Degas in 1892, used approvingly about the paintings of Denis in 1907, or criticised by Paulhan in 1913 for its assumption that a landscape has a mood of its own, independent from that of the spectator.[15] By the end of our period *paysage* could still refer to a natural environment or a representation of one, but it had taken on another dimension. At the very beginning of Alain-Fournier's *Le Grand Meaulnes*, published in 1913, the narrator reflects on how the presence of Meaulnes transformed '*tout ce paysage paisible* – the school, *père* Martin's field with its three nut trees, the garden', as well as 'our whole adolescence';[16] the concept of landscape was no longer limited to visible place and image of place but could encompass the inner geography of psychology and soul.

By the end of the nineteenth century the experience of nature had long been codified. Following the Enlightenment ideas of Jean-Jacques Rousseau, the rural walk or the country holiday signified calm, the human's tranquil reimmersion in timeless nature. Amiel once again is typical; his *Journal* often reports after solitary walks: 'I felt myself soothed, grateful, melted; a mood of serenity and contemplation took possession of me'.[17] Such sensations were by no means the exclusive experience of the introverted philosopher. The astute social commentator Octave Uzanne was among many voicing what were now clichés, writing in 1889: 'Country life makes us healthy, gives us new strength, and purifies our mind; it sweeps away all germs of disease'.[18] Such clichés both emerged from and fuelled shared social experience. The rapid expansion of the seaside holiday from chic diversion to bourgeois commonplace is perhaps the pivotal example of the nineteenth century's growing appetite for a nature understood as wholesome and calming. Painters, most of them of bourgeois stock and catering for a middle-class market, could generally be expected to subscribe to these notions of nature restoring a natural harmony. In 1874 Daubigny referred to the countryside as a 'tuning-fork' for an integrated existence while a quarter of a century later the usually city-based Vuillard expressed the topos in a letter to Vallotton: 'Going to bed early, getting a good night's sleep, not seeing too many people, living in a pleasant landscape, understanding little by little its objects and silhouettes, having those around you who care for you, without fuss or complication, is an ideal lot'.[19] Given the currency of such attitudes to nature, responses to the physical landscape spilled over into responses to the painted *paysage*. This is clear from critical writing, in which reviewers of exhibitions slid knowingly from one to the other. 'Let's escape into the fields for a moment', urged André Michel in 1888, before going on to discuss the paintings of rural life, and the following year Georges Lafenestre claimed that the Salon signalled the spring because 'the prisoners of the city, while they await their country holidays or suburban strolls, can have a foretaste of the open air, peace and health thanks to the painters'.[20] Representing a landscape on canvas and going on a seaside holiday, looking at a landscape painting and walking in the countryside, are all social activities which, however different, share common notions about nature as a repository of positive values such as peace and harmony, health and repose. Indeed, throughout our period commentators drew attention to the way nature had come to embody moral and spiritual values, Victor Champier's irony that 'our sceptical, irreligious era ... has created the religion of sun and greenery' was echoed thirty-five years later, in 1913, by Paulhan.[21]

Notions of landscape may have been based on those generalities, but they could also be manipulated in many ways. We need to recover some of the tensions, polarities and dialogues which moulded the way painters worked and in which landscape images were read.

Landscape painting was an ideal vehicle for nationalist ideologies. The late nineteenth and early twentieth centuries witnessed a shift from solid nationalism to the fervent chauvinism of 1914. At the Universal Exhibition of 1889, when the country was suffering an agricultural slump, over 200 of the 650 French paintings on view represented rural France, articulating a low-key patriotism in their images of the beauties of the national *paysages* and their reassuring representations of the fecundity of the land.[22] That very year the danger that Millet's *Angélus* [**2**], a landscape painting held as a national icon, would be exported to the United States caused a public furore, the picture being saved from such a fate by the department store magnate Alfred Chauchard.[23]

Patriotism could be far less discreet in its use of landscape imagery. Anti-German feeling amongst those seeking *revanche* and the recovery of the eastern provinces was frequently voiced in terms of the homeland – 'the sacred contours of your ancient territory'[24] – and when French artists contributed to an international exhibition in Berlin in 1891 their submissions included several landscapes loaded with patriotic references to the Franco-Prussian War or the ceded regions: *The Church at Bourget*, *Landscape with Ruins (Saint-Cloud)*, *Landscape in the Vosges*, *The Rhine* and so on.[25]

If nationalism implicit or extreme was one way of colouring landscape after 1871, another was of longer standing. The division of painters into those from the north – the *septentrionaux* – and the south – the *méridionaux* – dated back at least to the beginning of the nineteenth century. Under this classification the combination of environment, character and aesthetic created among the former a tendency towards a more sombre, melancholy and realistic art, typified by artists such as Ruysdael and Watteau, and among the latter greater illumination, harmony and idealism, typified by Poussin and Claude. These broad distinctions were still active in debates about landscape painting a century later; in 1914 Segard, in his volumes on decorative pictures, felt obliged to define them.[26] The north-south polarity, a means of placing artists within traditions and establishing differences between painters' work, was deployed frequently by critics and subscribed to by certain artists. There was hardly an obituary after the death in 1901 of Cazin [**82**], born in the Pas-de-Calais, which did not refer to him as *'homme du nord'*, and Vlaminck always insisted on his northern temperament and how his work was 'warped' when he tried to work in the south.[27] Such generalisations only set up rules to be broken, however. For a number of reasons northern painters were increasingly attracted to the south, as we shall see; Vlaminck's friend and fellow Parisian, Derain, wrote to his dealer Kahnweiler in 1914 of his need for 'that delicious crack of the whip which the Midi gives me every year'.[28] This opening up of new sites and associations in the southern landscape undermined what validity there might have been in the north-south polarity. After all, Poussin and Claude, whose idealised Mediterranean landscapes were once again so admired around the turn of the twentieth century, may have spent their careers in Rome but were both northerners by birth. Poussin, like Othon Friesz, came from Les Andelys in Normandy. However, to claim as André Salmon did in 1912 that Friesz's recollection of Les Andelys coloured his Mediterranean motifs as Poussin's had his Roman paintings was to subvert the notion of regional characteristics by trying to combine them.[29]

The notion absolutely central to our understanding of landscape painting at this period is that of the city and the country. As Raymond Williams has

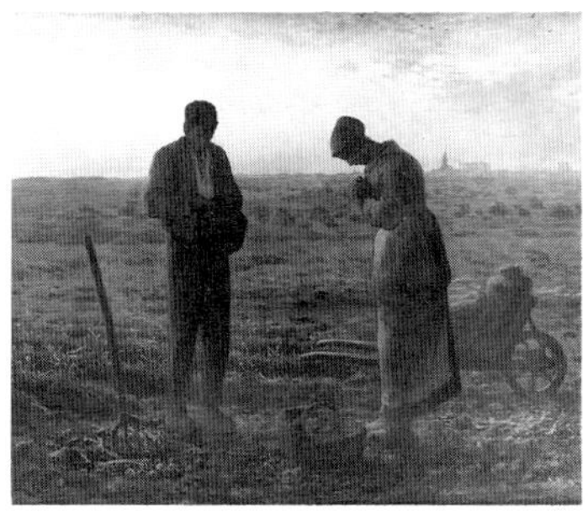

2
J.-F. Millet *L'Angélus* 1857–9
Paris, Musée d'Orsay

shown, they are complex terms which can be constructed in various ways. The city can be seen as the hub of order, administration and intellectual activity, the country as backward, wild, untameable. Alternatively, the city can be held up as unnatural, corrupt and worldly, the country as natural, healthy and pure.[30] City and country are not absolute polarities; rather they are flexible and interdependent. Any snapshot of France between 1874 and 1914 reveals this. Rural depopulation was caused by agricultural crises and the growth of urban industry. The countryside was transformed by the construction of roads, railways and canals intended to link built-up areas. There was also an increasingly felt need to get out of the city, whether on holiday or to the rural camps set up by charities and churches from the 1880s for impoverished city children. City and country involved contrast, dialogue, exchange, a cross-fertilisation nowhere clearer than in patterns of urbanisation, for the growth of suburbs saw the city infiltrate the country, and the creation of parks established a rural element in the urban environment. That dialogue or exchange was repeated in the visual arts. For the urban middle-class populations, many of whom were first or second generation city dwellers, faced with the social complexities, sprawling growth, increasing industrialisation, and potential for civic disorder which kept the modern metropolis in constant agitation, images of landscape could serve as icons of reassurance: timeless, changeless, calm. Making landscape pictures might well mean making images which embodied such values. This was not necessarily opportunism, for landscape painters themselves felt the pressures of the modern condition. Van Gogh voiced them in a letter to his sister of January 1890: I have been forcing myself to forget Paris as much as possible on account of the trouble and excitement a prolonged stay there causes me. As far as painters are concerned it is right to say one works better in the country; there everything speaks a distinct language, everything is firm, everything explains itself. And in the big city, when one is tired, one cannot understand anything, and feels lost'.[31]

This was a common opinion. Vuillard ended his encomium of the countryside to Vallotton with the words: 'I've scarcely been back to Paris for three weeks'; Vlaminck, who at the outset of his career worked by night as a violinist at sordid urban nightclubs, remembered: 'On the banks of the Seine I would forget everything. I painted to restore my peace of mind, to calm my desires, and, above all, to purify myself a little'; and Henri Martin raged: 'I'm furious still to be in Paris when the poplars are budding at Labastide-du-Vert', his home near Cahors.[32] Adulation of nature in face of a changing and increasingly urban world preoccupied the bourgeoisie, among whom were painters who shared these values and anxieties and made images of landscape which reinforced that adulation. Such was the cycle that dominated landscape painting in France between 1874 and 1914.

Painting landscape had a moral as well as an ideological dimension; it was a matter of values, whether it was the purification that Vlaminck sought or the patriotic evocation of the lost Rhenish frontier. That landscape was central to the ethos of the Third Republic is apparent from the decoration that Martin was commissioned to paint in 1913 for the Grande Salle du Conseil d'Etat in the Palais Royal in Paris [3]. The central panel represents the place de la Concorde being repaved by toiling workers, the left-hand panel the quayside and busy port of Marseille, and the right-hand one an open field somewhere in rural France being harvested by peasants under a blazing sun. Martin set up a dense but legible complex of contrasts symbolic of the nation's life: city and country, trade and agriculture, sea and land, north and south, and tradition and modernity, for harvesting machine and pneumatic drill help out the manual workers.

MODERNITY IN THE LANDSCAPE

The French landscape was in the process of change, brought about by modern demands and developments which threatened a natural and social fabric centuries old. In a lecture given at Nancy in 1876 the landscape painter and critic Emile Michel argued that middle-aged people would be aware of how much the countryside had changed since their youth, how hills had been opened up for quarries or mines, plains punctured by salt mines or marked with factory chimneys and slag heaps, forests exploited, rivers polluted, canals and tenements constructed in monotonous uniformity.[33] This was perhaps the first generation in France to have complained of changes so familiar to us today, changes which inevitably affected landscape painters. Jules Breton, for example, made his reputation in the 1850s with wholesome images of

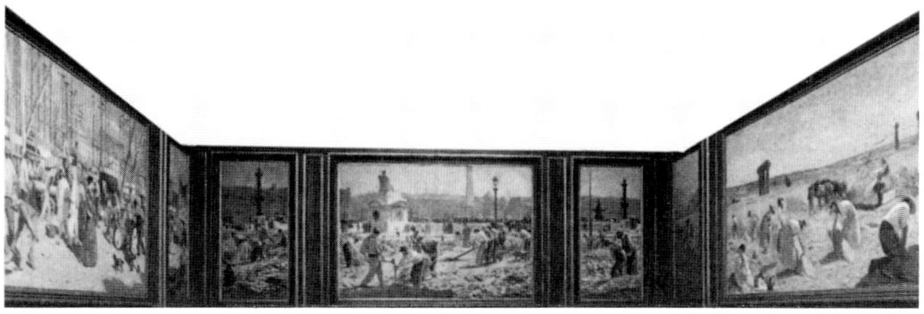

3
H. Martin
Grande Salle du Conseil d'Etat 1913–24
Paris, Palais Royal

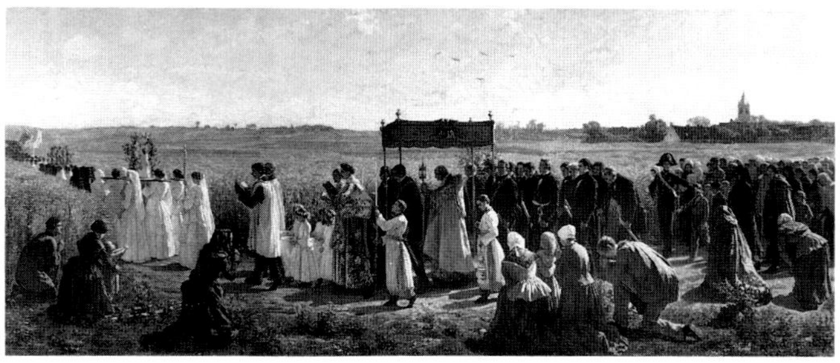

4
J. Breton
Blessing the Wheat in Artois 1857
Paris, Musée d'Orsay

ordered, time-honoured rural life around his home village of Courrières, just south of Lille [4]. Plentiful coal seams had been discovered in this part of northern France in the 1840s, and production started at Courrières in 1861.[34] Breton could no longer sustain the fiction he had constructed of his *pays*, and by 1865, with his first visit to Brittany, was searching further afield for unspoilt landscapes in which to set his rural idylls.

If Breton retreated, others sought to preserve. The poet André Theuriet and Léon Lhermitte, a younger painter of peasant life, collaborated on *La Vie rustique*, published in 1888, in order to record the traditional agricultural tasks and communal activities of Lhermitte's native Mont-Saint-Père, near Reims, before these disappeared in the face of what the authors identified as 'the transformation or rather the degeneration of country life'.[35] Voices were raised against change. When a causeway was proposed in 1883 to link to the mainland Mont-Saint-Michel – 'a granite jewel, a colossus in lace, an incomparable marvel set in a landscape of unbelievable beauty' – Maupassant was so infuriated that he made a blunt recommendation on the grounds of public benefit: 'If you see an engineer near your property, kill him'.[36] In Great Britain anxiety to protect the landscape had resulted in the creation in 1895 of the National Trust. Similar appeals for conservation in France began to be unified in the years preceding the First World War, led by the *Société pour la protection des paysages*, which held an international congress in Paris in October 1909. The authors of the *Compte-rendu* published the following year were Fernand Cros Mayrevieille, scion of a distinguished family from Carcassonne and author of *De la Protection des monuments historiques ou artistiques des sites et des paysages* (1907), and Raoul de Clermont, a lawyer, agronomist and diplomat from the Doubs who in 1905 was on the staff of Dujardin-Beaumetz, the Minister of Fine Arts.[37] In the very decade before 1914, when avant-garde painters subjected landscape motifs to extremes of chromatic experimentation and formal fragmentation, paradoxically conservation of the natural landscape was being advanced by regional notables with connections in the cultural establishment.

Painters of rural life only occasionally seem to have wanted to disturb the fiction of field labour's changeless rhythms by the introduction of modern agricultural machinery. Although such machinery was being introduced, albeit gradually, from the 1850s, it remained a rarity in imagery even at the end of the century; in the early 1890s the British critic Hamerton thought it worthy of note that 'a few of the younger [French] painters are introducing the steam-engine into their agricultural pictures', ironically recollecting a painting of a 'new fangled iron plough, very neat, and drawn with the same careful accuracy that a Parisian painter of street scenes will put into a perambulator'.[38] Modernity of aesthetic and ideology was not necessarily a stimulus to the introduction of images of the 'new fangled'. Loyal Impressionist and committed anarchist as he was, Pissarro included farm machinery in only four of over 1,300 canvases,[39] and even as late as 1912 Gleizes's *Harvest Threshing* [250] may have included steam-driven equipment but it is well hidden in the Cubist faceting and the naturally undulating movements of figures and landscape.

If the imagery of the modern was seen to disturb the idealised representation of rural labour there were other categories of landscape in which it did have a significant place. At the first Impressionist exhibition in 1874 Guillaumin showed *Sunset at Ivry* [5], a canvas painted shortly before in the suburbs to the south-east of the city. It is still recognisably a river landscape of towpath and trees illuminated by the glow of a splendid sunset, but those conventions are brought up to date by the line of factory chimneys silhouetted along the skyline, their spreading fumes tinged with violet in the orange light. We need to be careful how we interpret such images today. Our late twentieth-century instincts might react negatively to what is, in our terms, the pollution of nature; 125 years ago such a motif might have been read as industry's remarkable capacity to harness the forces of nature, Guillaumin's imposition of the fumes upon the sunset giving some kind of parity between man and the elements. Motifs such as the suburbs gave the painter a licence to experiment with the modern which the agricultural scene, with its intricate cultural associations rooted in both biblical and classical, Virgilian, sources, did not. If Pissarro or even Gleizes was constrained by the social values imputed to rural life, by artistic convention and by the expectations of the market, the modern industrial subject allowed the landscape painter more room for manoeuvre. During the 1890s Maximilien Luce undertook a number of painting campaigns in the coalfields around Charleroi, just across the Belgian border. As one would expect of an artist committed to anarchism and the proletarian cause, some of the canvases he made there are celebrations of the heroic miners and steel workers, but the majority of Luce's paintings were landscapes. *Factory Chimneys, Couillet* of 1898–9 [6] seems at first sight a straightforward view. But that 'landscape' did not exist a generation before. Then it would have looked like the Artois meadows that Breton painted in the 1850s [4]. If Breton worked to create a fiction of changelessness, Luce represented nothing but change. Everything in his painting is new and indebted to man's activity, except for the bare armature of sky and horizon; not only the chimneys, mills and factories, the street and the miserable tenements, but also the very valley which shelters the mining village, for the flat land of Artois has been reshaped by the slag heaps to whose soilless sides cling scrub which gives a feeble impression of ver-

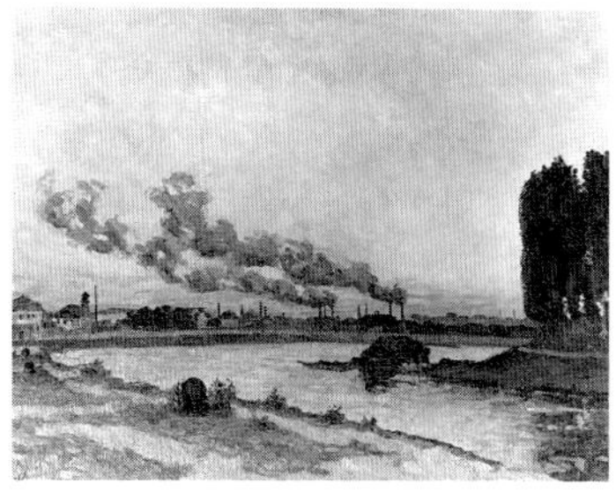

5
A. Guillaumin ***Sunset at Ivry*** 1873
Paris, Musée d'Orsay

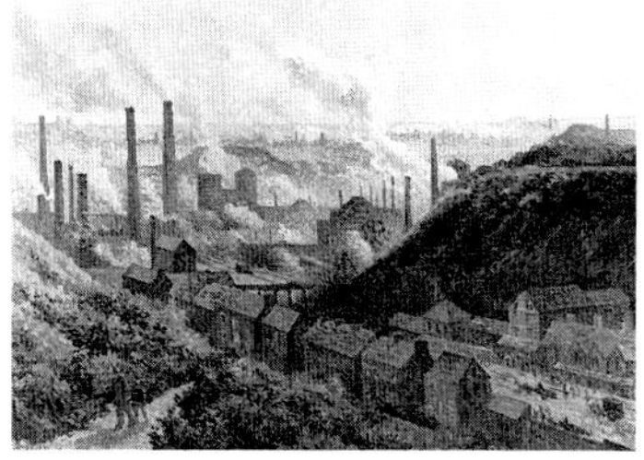

6
M. Luce
Factory Chimneys, Couillet 1898–9
USA, Robert Rice Gallery

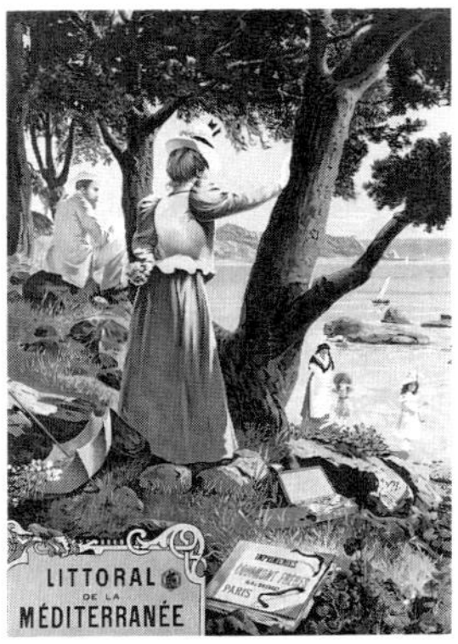

7
H. Gray
Paris-Lyon-Marseille 1897

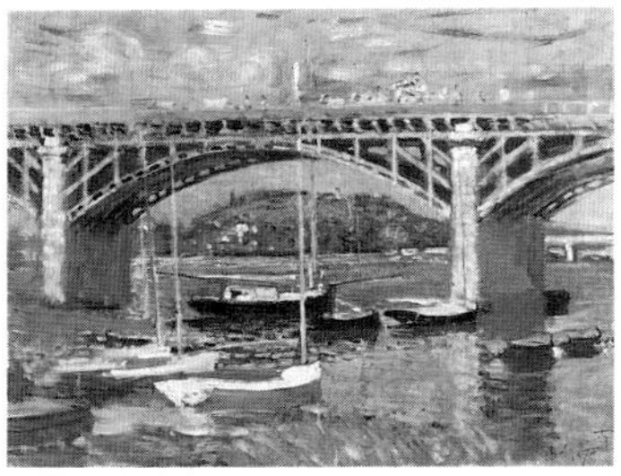

8
C. Monet
The Bridge at Argenteuil 1874
Munich, Neue Pinakothek

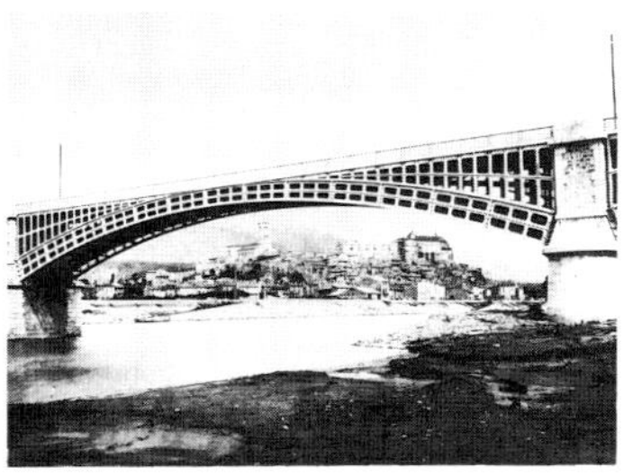

9
E. Baldus
The Viaduct at La Voulte c.1855
Private Collection

dancy, of nature's will to reclaim. Here new landscape painting – Luce's pointillist touch and division of tone – represented an entirely new landscape environment.

If sprawling suburb or burgeoning industry changed many a landscape, it was the railway which joined them. The development of the railway in France was rapid. The first trunk routes – from Paris to Rouen and Orléans – had been opened in 1843, and between 1850 and 1870 track had increased ninefold, from 2,000 to 18,000 kilometres. This momentum was sustained under the Third Republic, with politicians taking up railway development as a cause which demonstrated their commercial initiative and progressive republicanism.[40] The effects of the railway on people's perceptions of landscape were multiple, effects which – one way or another – had an impact on the representation of landscape. Spreading railway networks increased passenger traffic throughout France, shifting patterns not only of commerce and demography but also of tourism. The train facilitated mass travel, especially for the bourgeoisie, formalising the early nineteenth-century notion of the *voyage pittoresque*, the discovery of the architectural and natural delights of historic regional France, as well as opening up new areas and modern pleasures.

The final third of the nineteenth century saw the development, as we shall see, of first the Channel and then the Mediterranean coasts as tourist venues, a process aided by the smoothing of transfers between regional lines negotiated by Thomas Cook in 1875.[41] Painters had easier access to new sites, and the physical extension of the middle class's experience of landscape encouraged a wider taste in landscape imagery; a count of Mediterranean motifs at the Salon of 1874 in comparison with the Salons of 1894 would surely show a substantial difference. All this is conveniently articulated in Henri Gray's 1897 poster advertising the Paris-Lyon-Marseille railway [7]. Here the male tourist is identified as a painter who can enjoy the Mediterranean motifs while his wife gathers wild flowers on the unspoilt shores and their children play on the beach, tended by a local woman in regional costume. Differences are established – between costumes both chic and vernacular, between transitory tourists and untouched nature, thus city and country – but set in healthy sunlit harmony; the landscape motif conveys a tourist ideal, all made possible by the railway.

A second aspect of railway development was that the environment was altered by the intrusion of technology and engineering: marshalling yards and stations, cuttings and embankments, bridges and viaducts. Much as such things annoyed proto-conservationists like Maupassant, they inevitably found their way into landscape painting; even Cézanne's poised canvases of Mont-Sainte-Victoire [19] made in the late 1880s include the viaduct which, built in the 1840s, led the railway across the valley of the Arc. Other images made more of the new landscape furniture. The paintings Monet executed during his first years at Argenteuil frequently represented the road and railway bridge, which have been interpreted as symbols of France's recovery after the Franco-Prussian War, in which they had been destroyed, and of the artist's commitment to a 'modern' *paysage*.[42] The modernity of Monet's paintings lies not just in how they are made – in gestural strokes and dabs implying immediate observation and spontaneous record – or in what they represent – the bridge rebuilt with parts from Argenteuil's own ironworks; they are modern in how they are composed. The *Bridge at Argenteuil* [8], for instance, spans the picture surface with the bridge, a single arch, alone commanding the space; denied steadying banks other than the nearby tuft which defines our viewpoint and the strip of the far shore, the magisterial bridge seems to reach a huge distance. Normally salient features of a landscape such as the sky or a hill are dominated by the piers and trelliswork which allow – as does the railway bridge beyond – the passage of sailing boats below and traffic across it, the two emblematic of Argenteuil's identity as suburban town geared to both leisure and commerce. Monet's construction was not entirely novel. Commissioned in the mid-1850s to produce an album celebrating the extension of the railway from Paris to the Mediterranean, the photographer Baldus had employed the same composition, also using a low riverside viewpoint to present the new iron viaduct overarching the landscape and the town of La Voulte [9], between Valence and Montélimar, manipulating the landscape in order to subjugate the traditional *pittoresque* to the modern.

The railway's third effect was to change people's perception of landscape. As Wolfgang Schivelbusch has pointed out, the velocity of the train – all the more disconcerting for being such a novel experience – diminishes visual perception and distorts the passing landscape.[43] The viewer's constant progress at speed through a landscape which appears to move is quite the opposite to looking at the still image of a landscape painting for an extended period. Contemporaries were well aware of this. Artists who set store by the use of memory and its ability to simplify and transform claimed that their landscapes stemmed from what they had seen from the train window; Puvis de Chavannes, Degas and Carrière [**210**, **156**, **167**] all made this claim as they sought to use the experience of rapid transit to distance their work from close observation of nature.[44] But even painters working in the landscape might adapt their motif in response to the new perception of speed. Monet's *Railway Bridge at Argenteuil* [**10**] can be read as a record of light, and as the equation of leisure and business we have already described, but it also insists on the velocity of the train by the sharply angled perspective of the bridge which pitches the train into the picture space.[45] By the turn of the century the railway was no longer a novelty, but the transport revolution continued, again with ramifications for perceptions of landscape. The Parisian Métro, begun in 1898 and opened for the Universal Exhibition in 1900, carried only 15 million cautious passengers in its first year, the number spiralling to 312 million by 1909.[46] By taking railway technology below ground, the Métro denied its passengers any experience of the landscape or cityscape under which they were carried. Another new invention returned the traveller to the physical surroundings of nature and at a pace conducive to experiencing the landscape: the bicycle. The bicycle and soon its motor-powered variant brought the countryside to a wide, popular public, carrying on the train's penetration of the landscape. Steinlen's 1899 poster for *Motocycles Comiot* [**11**] neatly encapsulated this, with the geese surprised and the peasants awed by the intrusion of the chic woman from the city into the country. Many artists were keen cyclists – Forain, Bonnard, Denis and Vlaminck among them – and in the summer of 1905 the Signac and Manguin families bicycled together along the Côte d'Azur, the hardy Manguins making it as far as Nice.[47]

That autumn Signac bought a Peugeot in Marseille.[48] Although colleagues like Luce laughed at him, Signac was convinced of the car's advantages for the landscape painter; unrestricted by rail-track, it could travel and stop wherever the artist wished.[49] Car travel caught on quickly among those like Signac, Manguin and Monet with the means to afford it. At its foundation in 1895 the Touring Club de France had 25,000 members, a number quadrupled in the next half-decade. The Automobile Club de France, founded the same year, and Michelin both brought out their first annual guides for the new century.[50] Reading the preface to the 1900 *Guide Michelin* one comes across a list of travellers' requirements, most of which would have been unheard of half a century before; alongside hotels and post offices, there are mechanics, petrol stations, tram lines, telephone connections to the big cities, recommended dealers in spare parts and of course Michelin tyres.[51] The car's speed caught the imagination. Reporting in 1906 the visit to Giverny of the rich, dashing Prince de Wagram, cavalry officer and art collector, Alice Hoschedé-Monet gushed: 'He is stationed at St. Michel and can reach Paris in four hours with his 120 horse power Itala. No one dares accompany him, not even Fournier, the racing car driver'.[52] Octave Mirbeau, close friend of landscape painters like Monet, Pissarro and Raffaëlli, published a semi-fictional travelogue about driving in 1908, illustrated by Bonnard [**12**] and titled after his car's number-plate, *La 628–E8*. Mirbeau emphasised velocity's distortion of the driver's perception: 'The speed of travel confuses impressions, batters the mind and upsets one's balance … Life comes hurtling at him and buffeting him from every direction, as in a mad cavalry charge, only to melt flickeringly away like a film or like the trees, hedges and walls that line the road'.[53]

The period 1874–1914 saw a transport revolution; following the train came the bicycle and the car, and then in 1909 powered flight across the Channel. Human perception of landscape had been irrevocably changed in terms of both time and space, and it is interesting that Mirbeau compared car travel to film. The year 1895 had seen not only the advent of motoring organisations but also the Lumière brothers' 'cinematographic device', and by 1900, under the aegis of entrepreneurial film-makers such as Georges Méliès, French cinema was in rapid growth. Connecting travel and cinema is essential to any understanding of representations of landscape at the beginning of the twentieth century. Train, car and film made movement a cultural phenomenon, the axis of modern society. Movement was central to modern philosophy, for instance to Henri Bergson's notions of dynamism and universal flux and to Jules Romains's *unanimisme*, which saw life, especially in the city, as a collective, interrelating experience. The ideal of landscape imagery embodying timeless values in a changeless rural scene became all the more difficult to sustain, for artist and critic alike. A canvas such as Gleizes's *Landscape at Toul* [**13**] of 1913 exemplifies one response to ideas of perceptual flux, its man-made environment rendered 'modern' by its imagery of railway viaduct and road, its rushing perspectives, its interpenetrating Cubist facets standing as a pictorial metaphor for the fragmentation of time in human perception and memory. When the critic Roger Marx came to write about Monet's water-garden paintings [**218**] four years earlier, he argued that whereas art in the past had tried to eternalise the transitory, Monet, 'smitten by the vertigo of speed', did not try to fix what remains but to seize what passes.[54] By this account, then, the artist did not have to use the most avant-garde means to make images *au courant* with the latest metaphysics. Indeed, nor was it only the avant-garde who painted landscapes which came to terms with modernity of composition, subject, or even perception, as Billotte's paintings of the suburbs or Devambez's of flight amply prove [**45**, **203**]. This is not to say that representing landscape was transformed overnight, that old certainties and expectations just disappeared; the 1900 *Guide Michelin*, for all its modernity, hoped to provide motorists with a *voyage pittoresque*.[55] But the traditional notions of landscape, as physical environment and aesthetic experience, as restful and revivifying, encapsulating values of continuity and harmony, standing for some kind of idyll, values so strong in 1874, by 1914 had become increasingly difficult to sustain and many artists felt called to use their imagination to recreate a lost world.

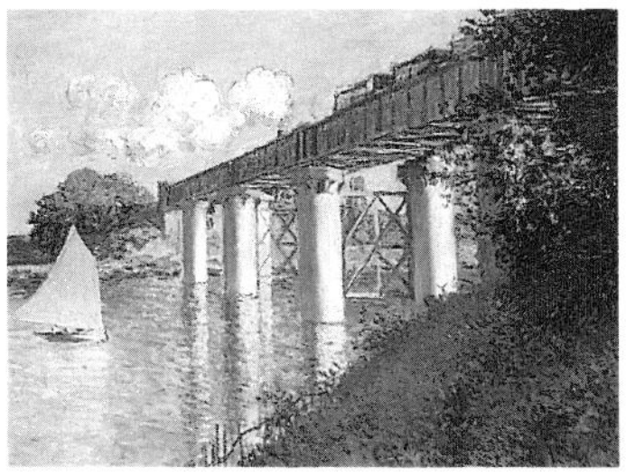

10
C. Monet
The Railway Bridge at Argenteuil 1874
Philadelphia Museum of Art, John G. Johnson Collection

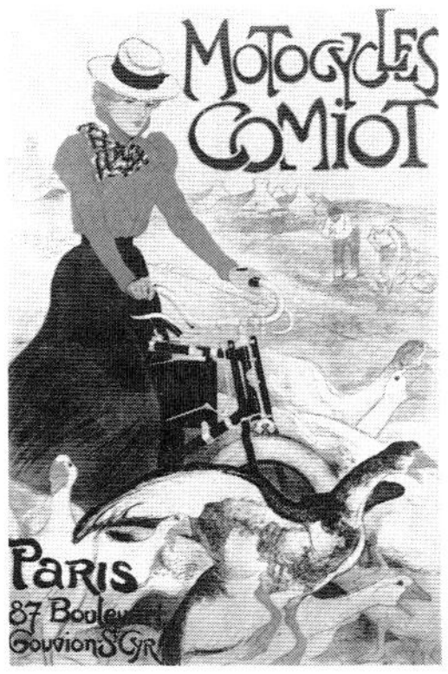

11
T. Steinlen
Motocycles Comiot 1899
Private Collection

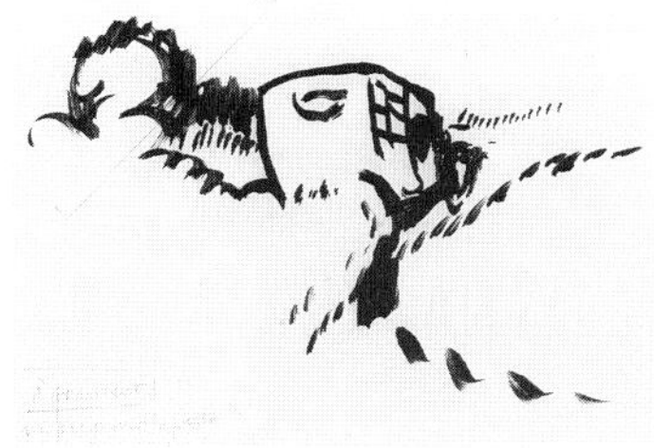

12
P. Bonnard
La 628-E8 1908
London, Richard Nathanson

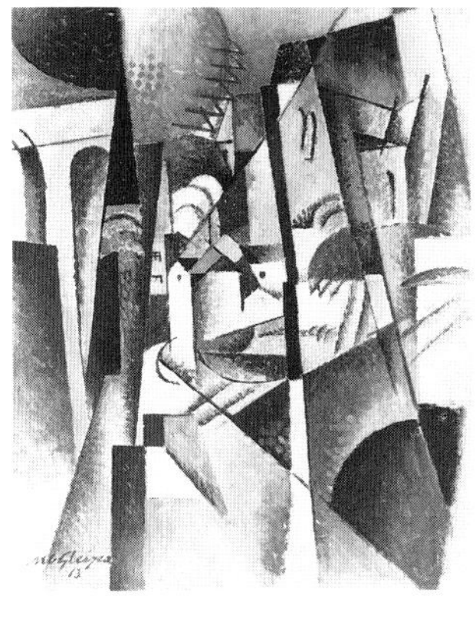

13
A. Gleizes ***Landscape at Toul*** 1913
Ohio, Columbus Museum of Art, Gift of Ferdinand Howald

In the end you are tired of that world of antiquity.
O Eiffel Tower shepherdess the bridges this morning are a bleating flock
You have had enough of living in Greek and Roman antiquity
Here even the motorcars look like antiques
Only religion is still quite new religion
Remains as simple as the airfield hangars [56]

Those opening lines from *Zone*, the first poem of Apollinaire's collection *Alcools*, published in 1913, mingle many cultural patterns and allusions. They simultaneously elide and contrast city and country, modernity and the pastoral, and suggest that twenty-five years after its completion in 1889 the Eiffel Tower, symbol of engineering innovation, has been surpassed in the rampant momentum of modernity by the new technologies of car and aircraft and has already achieved 'classic' status. The pairing of progress and the pastoral in *Zone* had been anticipated half a century earlier in a quirky canvas by the sculptor Bartholdi, in which a train speeds through a landscape scaring fauns and nymphs [**14**]. In their interweaving of a fascination with the modern and a nostalgia for the past both poem and painting highlight two currents – each, in their different ways, ideals – crucial to French culture at the time and to one of its pivotal manifestations: images of landscape.

If one account of landscape painting in France emphasises the development of modern subjects and styles, it should be paralleled and interleaved with another, seeking to trace artists' and their audiences' responses to past traditions of representing landscape. Taking a view from 1900 and looking back over the past century of French landscape painting one could set up a pattern something like this. The Neo-Classical *paysage historique* codified by Valenciennes had been worthy but dull, formulaic, given to 'debauches of erudition'.[57] The gradual decline of the Italianate ideal on which it had been founded could be traced with a collage of responses to Rome, from Michel-Martin Drölling's encomium of 1811–12: 'I am writing to you from Paradise because I don't believe there exists a more beautiful place than Rome', via Chassériau's ambivalence of 1840: 'the place on earth where there are the greatest number of sublime things, but also a tomb', to Whistler's dismissal of 1899: 'a bit of an old ruin alongside of a railway station where I met Mrs. Potter Palmer'.[58] The *paysage rustique* of the so-called Barbizon group that had displaced Neo-Classical landscape in mid-century may have focused painters on nature again, but the Forest of Fontainebleau itself was condemned as theatrical and the Chauchard collection, rich in Rousseaus and Millets, which entered the Louvre in 1909, was written off by young lions like Apollinaire as mediocre.[59] To the exhibition-going public around 1900 Impressionism represented the new wave with which landscape painters had to come to terms. Even a defender such as Holl, who could argue that its influence had changed the character of landscape painting and the public's appreciation of it by freeing artists' *sensations* and celebrating light, feared that the emulation of Monet threatened stagnation.[60]

But if past styles and conventions were questioned, challenged and surpassed, it would be an exaggeration to say that they were discounted, for at a number of levels landscape painting in France between 1874 and 1914 was deeply involved in dialogues with the past. Painting on the Channel coast in 1883 Monet was conscious of Courbet's activity there before him. He wrote to Alice Hoschedé: 'I'm plan-

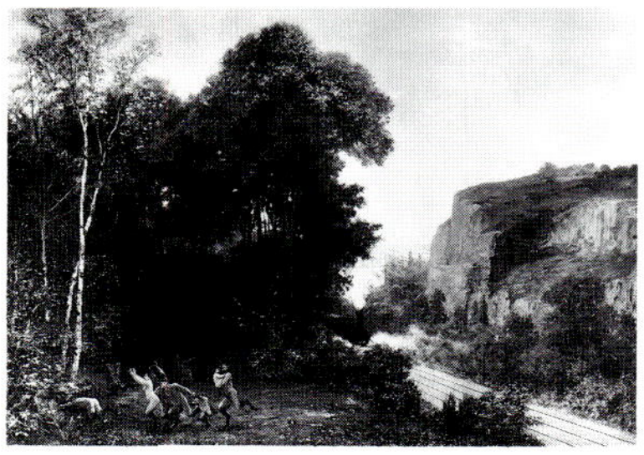

14
F.-A. Bartholdi
Fauns and Nymphs Frightened by a Train 1860s?
Colmar, Musée Bartholdi

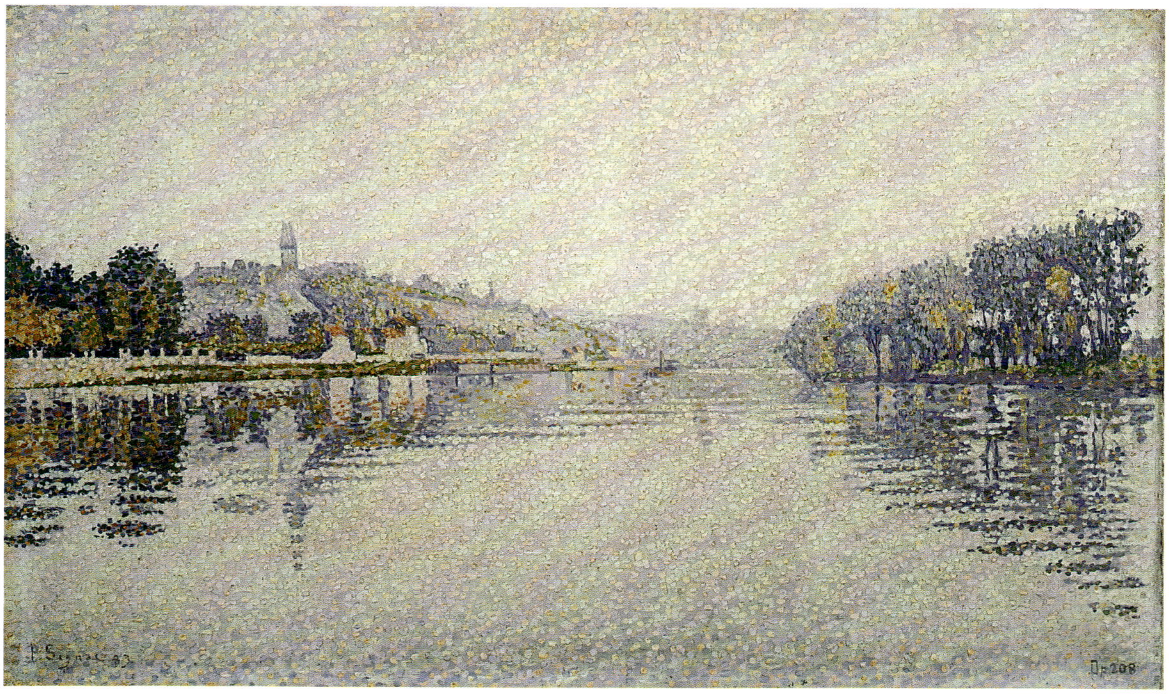

15
P. Signac
Banks of a River, the Seine at Herblay 1889
Paris, Musée d'Orsay

ning to paint a large canvas of the cliff at Etretat, even though it would be very audacious on my part to do so after Courbet did it so admirably'.[61] Monet's desire to measure himself against an artist he had known and admired as a young man is perhaps less surprising than an incident in Signac's career. In 1889, working with Luce at Herblay on the Seine to the west of Paris, Signac painted a motif which closely recalls one captured there by Daubigny thirty years before [**15**, **16**]. We do not know whether Signac was emulating a canvas he had seen – Daubigny had painted this motif more than once [62] – or whether he chose an identical viewpoint by accident; both artists worked from boats and the conspicuously sited church makes an appealing focus. The point is that Signac, a leading painter and apologist of Neo-Impressionism, the most advanced style of the day, *persona grata* of Symbolist poets and critics, opted for a frankly *pittoresque* motif and an open riverscape composition of a kind pioneered by Daubigny. Why should he have painted such an ostensibly *retardataire* canvas? Perhaps as a diversion from the unremittingly modern subjects drawn from the harshly man-made suburbs of north-western Paris [**44**] which he had been painting for some years, though Signac did not avoid the new elements installed in the Herblay environment since Daubigny's painting, notably the embanked riverside. But Daubigny, modern in his own terms, had balanced the picturesque with the new by including a steam-tug on the river, which Signac repeated. Perhaps Signac deliberately wanted to pit his novel divisionist technique against a motif typical of mid-century naturalism, to replace the 'verities' of Daubigny's local colour with a more synthetic, harmonious surface attuned to Symbolism's new aesthetic of suggestiveness. Whatever the case, Signac's *Seine at Herblay* reveals a painter conscious of his avant-garde status deliberately reworking conventions established by a painter two generations before his own. This was not exceptional, however. A painting such as Sauzay's *The Blue Washing Barges, Villeneuve-la-Garenne* [**17**], shown at the Salon des artistes français in 1890, couched its grimly naturalist portrayal of the squalid outer suburbs of Paris in a Daubignyesque composition, just as Simonnet reworked a Corot motif in 1893 and van Gogh copied a Millet landscape in 1890 [**233**, **234**, **235**, **237**]. Just this small cross-section taken from the middle of our period reveals that, in the early 1890s at least, both members of the avant-garde and exhibitors at the Salons felt the need to reconsider the touchstones of mid-century *paysage*.

Impressionism did not have the defused standing of the generation of Corot, Millet and Daubigny, who had died in the 1870s. It was still an active and widespread current in French landscape; whereas Morisot and Sisley died in the 1890s and Pissarro in 1903, Monet, Renoir and Guillaumin lived beyond the First World War. Although by the turn of the century Impressionism had gained a degree of established respectability, following the acceptance of the Caillebotte bequest by the Musée du Luxembourg, the state's museum of modern art, and the showing of a significant body of work at the Universal Exhibition of 1900, it could hardly qualify as a modern 'tradition'. It was commonplace in the 1880s and 1890s for critics to argue that any painter who tackled a contemporary subject with a broad brush qualified as 'impressionist'.[63] Nothing changed this view in the early years of this century; although Monet and Renoir in particular set distinct examples, and one might identify Maufra, Moret and Loiseau as followers of one and André, Valtat and d'Espagnat of the other, the identification of any light-filled, loosely painted canvas as broadly

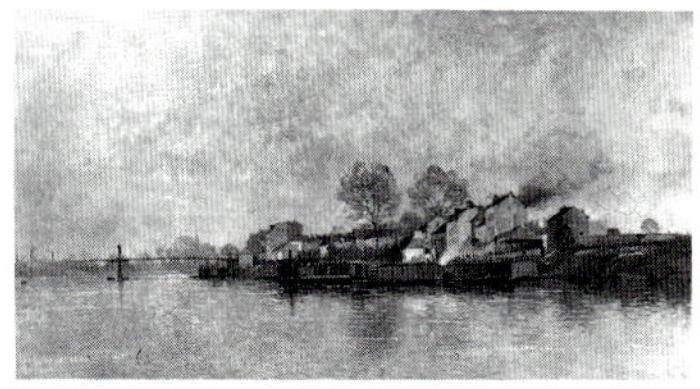

17
A. Sauzay
The Blue Washing Barges. Villeneuve-la-Garenne 1890
Paris, Musée d'Orsay

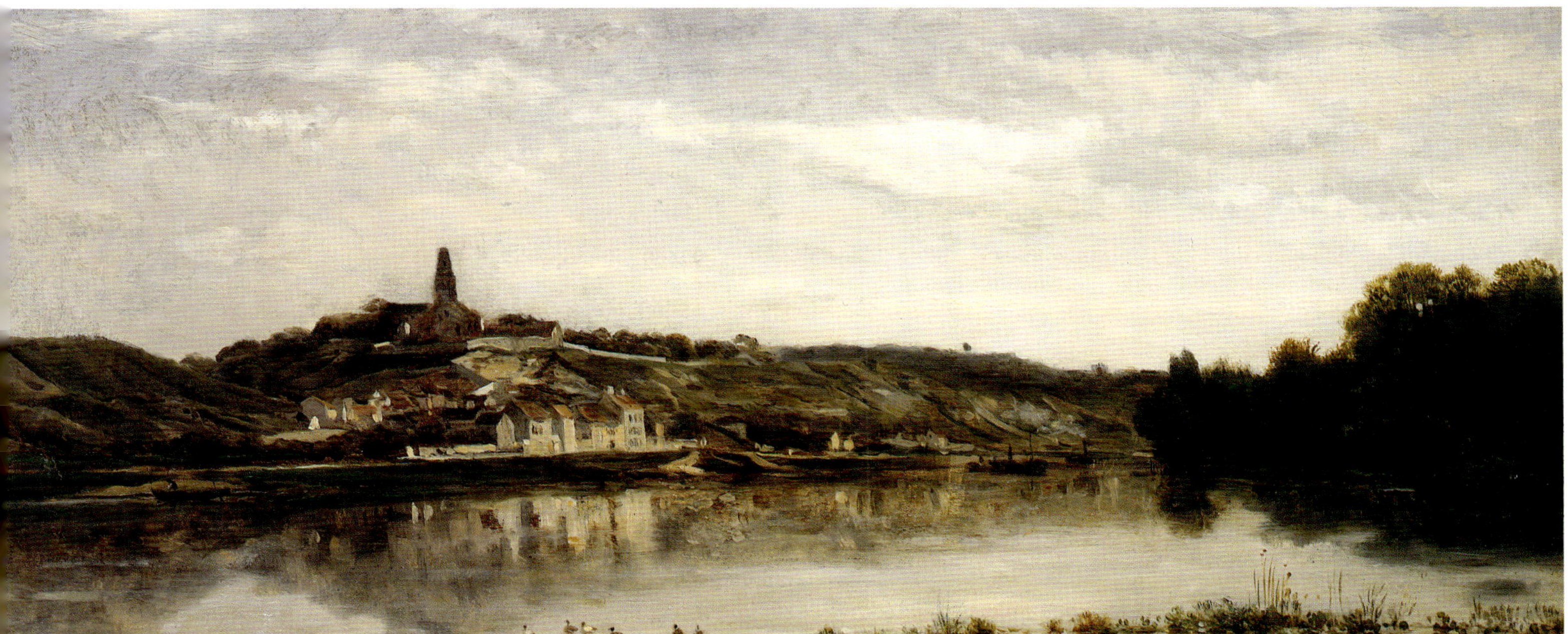

16
C. Daubigny
The Seine at Herblay c.1858–60
London, Agnew's

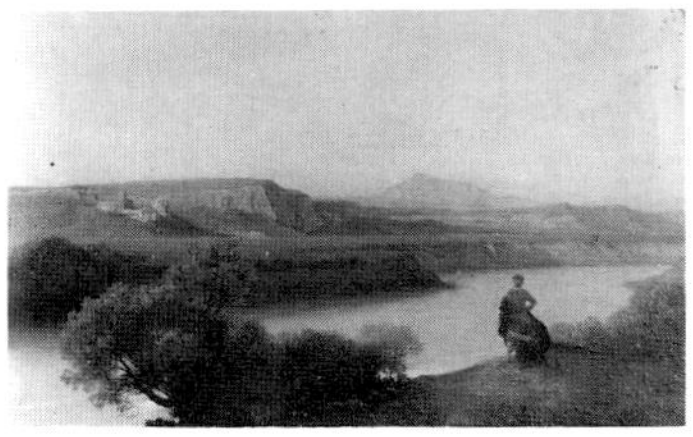

18
A. de Curzon *L'Aqua Acetosa: Poussin and Claude Drawing on the Banks of the Tiber* 1886
Formerly Poitiers, Musées de la ville

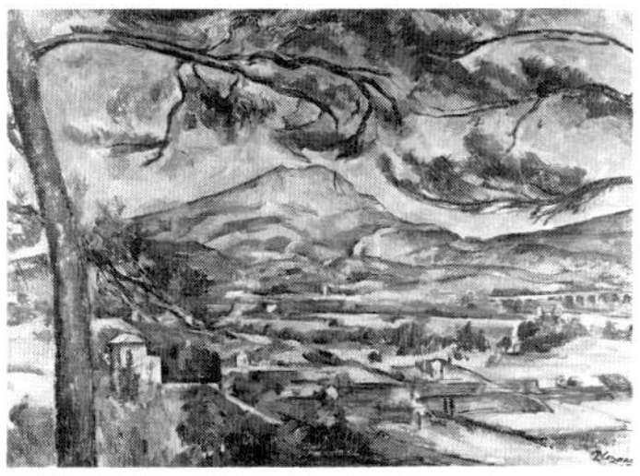

19
P. Cézanne *Mont-Sainte-Victoire* c.1887
London, Courtauld Institute Galleries

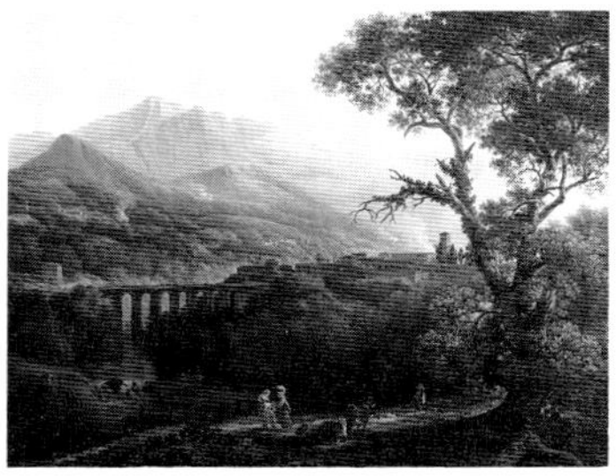

20
F. de Barrigue de Fontainieu *View of Cava dei Tirenni* 1816
Marseille, Musée des beaux-arts

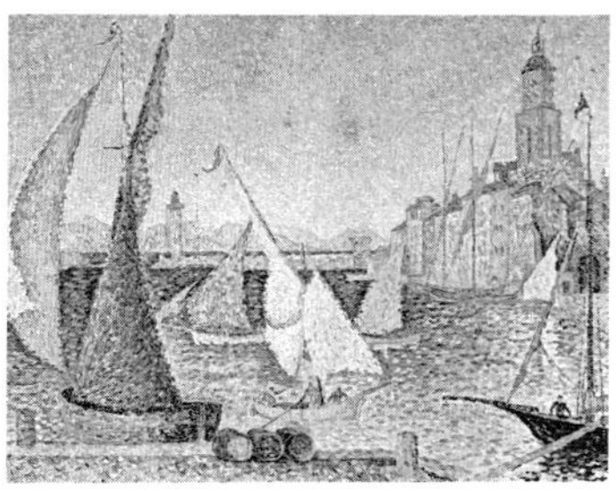

21
P. Signac *St Tropez, the Quay* 1899
St Tropez, Musée de l'Annonciade

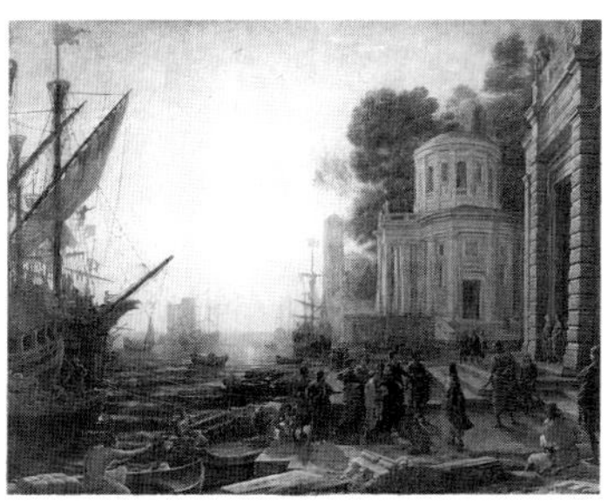

22
Claude Gellée (le Lorrain) *The Disembarkation of Cleopatra at Tarsus* 1647
Paris, Musée du Louvre

speaking 'impressionist' lingered.[64] If one consistent element linked the commonly understood definition of Impressionism from the first exhibition in 1874 to the outbreak of the First World War, it was that such painting, with its emphasis on the spontaneous recording of the fall of light, was by its very nature sketchy, approximate, lacking in structure.[65]

Increasingly prevalent but frustratingly diffuse, Impressionism's importance, one might argue, lay as much in its provocation of external reactions against its perceived lack of structure as in its inherently radical rethinking of the representation of landscape. Recent scholarship has done much to explore the classical 'revival' in French landscape in the 1890s and 1900s, looking at the work of painters as diverse as Ménard and Matisse, Picasso and Denis [**140**, **128**, **131**, **136**] as well as the writings of Bouyer, Mauclair and others.[66] That classicism in various guises reasserted itself during that period is without question, as we shall see, but it is perhaps an exaggeration to talk of a 'new' classicism at the turn of the century. After all, in a review of the 1879 Impressionist exhibition Henry Havard had reacted against work that he called 'indecisive and badly defined' on the grounds that, as a Frenchman, he had an innate appreciation of 'clarity, precision, frankness' and, as a republican, of the 'simplicity, purity, logic' of classical philosophy.[67] Although Havard did not pursue this line, he might have posited that these were qualities promoted in the traditional *paysage composé* or *paysage historique*, based on the 'classicism' of Poussin and Claude. That kind of painting had never disappeared as a cultured taste or as an artistic criterion. When in 1872 Ernest Renan compared the Roman landscape favourably to the Greek it was because Poussin had painted there; when in 1875 Flaubert admired a sunset he called it 'a real Claude Lorrain'.[68] The classicising *paysage composé* of Poussin and Claude was still actively painted – in 1886 Alfred de Curzon even produced *Poussin and Claude Drawing on the Banks of the Tiber* [**18**] – and was appreciated not only by conservative critics such as Emile Michel, who praised Français at the Salon of 1880 for his now unusual ability to bring off a *paysage composé*, but also by the avant-garde; in 1886 the Symbolist poet Laforgue praised the elderly Paul Flandrin for the way his canvases allied a 'modern' realism with 'noble classical poetry'.[69]

The definition of classicism outlined by Havard in 1879 remained substantially the same twenty-five years on. The qualities that critics such as Emile Michel and Bouyer saw embodied in Poussin in particular were logic, harmony, the ability to organise a landscape into a noble unity at once responsive to nature, expressive of emotion, and articulating notions of intellectual and moral order.[70] These were qualities found in the tradition of the *paysage historique* which were held to be particularly true to French culture, and they came to be increasingly promoted by critics and developed by painters as pressures within France to redefine national identity grew from the 1890s onwards. The reasons behind this were manifold and need to be sought outside the immediate forum of the visual arts. In the 1890s and 1900s a number of forces stimulated a resurgence of nationalism and the Right in French public life, among them the growing strength of the Left, of Syndicalism and proletarian unrest, a vociferous Catholic revival objecting in particular to the secularisation of education, and the polarisation of support for the army during the Dreyfus Affair. French nationalism centred on *revanche* against Germany, and French culture needed to be defined accordingly. This could take outright anti-German form, as in the composer Vincent d'Indy's claim that it was no wonder the Germans could not appreciate the French qualities of César Franck's music – 'balanced proportion and good style' – given their admiration for 'the abstruse canvases of Böcklin and the over-lengthy symphonic poems of Richard Strauss'.[71] Less confrontationally, it could highlight cultural characteristics which could be construed as specifically French and consistent with the ideology of the Right: clarity, logic, discipline, order.[72] These were notions that could be traced back to the seventeenth century, the *grand siècle* which saw French political, cultural and military hegemony in Europe; thus it is no surprise to find Poussin, 'the most *French* of our masters' compared to his literary contemporaries such as Corneille and Descartes.[73] They could be traced back further, as Havard avowed, to Greek and Roman antiquity, thus accrediting French culture with sustaining the values of the great Mediterranean civilisations of Athens and Rome. It was not only the visual arts which could be construed in this way; Jean Moréas's Ecole romane, initiated in 1891, aimed to revive the Latin qualities of French poetry by going back to the forms of the seventeenth century and the Provençal tradition, which Frédéric Mistral and his fellow Midi writers also sought to promote.[74] Such arguments and aesthetic posturing, in sum, sought to define French culture as classical, Latin and Mediterranean, as ordered in form, continuous in tradition, and southern in character.

This was such a common construction that it belonged neither to Left nor Right, establishment or avant-garde. When André Michel wanted to praise Puvis de Chavannes or André Salmon to eulogise Friesz the stock comparison was with Poussin.[75] And with the currency of such a classicising aesthetic it is no wonder that landscape painters drew once more on the conventions of the *paysage historique*. Cézanne's images of Mont-Sainte-Victoire painted in the late 1880s, for instance, follow very closely the prescriptions of Neo-Classical landscape, with their *repoussoir* tree, ordered recession of planes and distant focal point, and one wonders whether they were not quite consciously made in emulation of paintings of this kind that he would have known, such as Barrigue de Fontainieu's *View of Cava dei Tirenni* which had been in the Marseille museum since 1817 [**19**, **20**]. And in the next generation one finds canvases such as Signac's *Saint-Tropez, the Quay* or Cross's *View of Menton* which seem to recall in their general distribution of forms and attention to structural order compositions by Claude or Poussin which they would have known from the Louvre [**21**, **22**, **23**, **24**]. Although Cézanne's views of Mont-Sainte-Victoire would have been made *en plein air* and those of Signac and Cross made up in the studio as genuine *paysages composés*, differences in their making do not contradict the classical character which these images impose upon their motifs. Nor too did differences in ideology. Cézanne's politics seem to have become increasingly conservative in his later years and Maurice Denis – a devotee of the classicising landscape [**136**] – was a reactionary Catholic and anti-Dreyfusard, while Signac and Cross were committed anarchists. All painted *paysages composés*. A modernist explanation would characterise this consistency in terms of a reaction against Impressionism and the interest of artists from the later 1880s in pictorial synthesis and unity. However that would not explain the position of a painter such as René Ménard, a constant creator of *paysages historiques* who surely saw his career less as a response to Impressionism than as a continuation of the grand tradition of French art. We have seen how landscape painting had to come to terms with the modern, and yet its relations with tradition remind us once again of how landscape painting is a cultural receptacle constantly remoulded to accommodate external values. When we look at the *paysages composés* of Corot or Denis, Ménard or Cross [**116**, **25**, **139**, **111**], we do well to remember not only the aesthetic considerations of *paysage* but also the wider connotations of *patrie*.

CODA: 1914

Given the emotional ramifications of painting nature and the patriotic associations of the landscape it is no wonder that the outbreak of war in August 1914 drew a metaphorical line under an era of representing the French *paysage*. Vlaminck later claimed to have had an almost visionary premonition: 'On the 14th July, 1914, … I escaped from my village and the fireworks of the kids to work on the edge of the forest. Stretching out before me, the plain descended as far as Reuil. In the dark blue distance the Eiffel Tower thrust skywards above the line of the horizon. All at once, the sky became a sulphrous yellow; the air grew thick. In the field nervous cattle became restive and noisy, and began to run around without purpose. Frightened birds hid themselves and chirped in the bushes. The immense plain was as sad as could be'.[76] Here are several familiar constructions – nature as escape from society and haven of peace, the juxtaposition of city and country, the intrusion into the timeless natural panorama of modern technology – thrown out of joint by the unexpected, the unnatural: an omen of apocalypse. When war came and *la patrie* was invaded by the Germans, *paysage* was central, for soldiers fight over land, their language is landscape-based: trying to capture the high ground, digging in, clearing fields of fire. Landscape imagery remained pivotal for painters too. For Signac it was a metaphor for emotional blockage; he wrote to van Rysselberghe: 'Are you working, Théo? I try a bit but I scarcely succeed. How can one respond to a sunset when one's just seen a train of wounded pass?'[77] Others managed to find forms. Denis used the *paysage historique* for *The Princess in the Tower* [**25**], transforming the terrace of his Brittany holiday villa with his wife and son into a place of shelter for the Christian family while knights combat the dragon below, using allegory and a conventional idiom to address, and yet distance himself from, events. Vallotton faced up to the battlefield with images which ironically lock into stable compositions the very antitheses of landscape's customarily tranquil ideal [**26**]; here the *repoussoir* is a blazing farm, the distance a shell-wracked wasteland, the sky coloured by explosions. Matisse, no longer able to sustain the Mediterranean landscape in the image of Fauve energy or Claudian harmony, painted the view from his Collioure window [**27**] as nothingness. For four years after 1914, *paysage* was either hell or void.

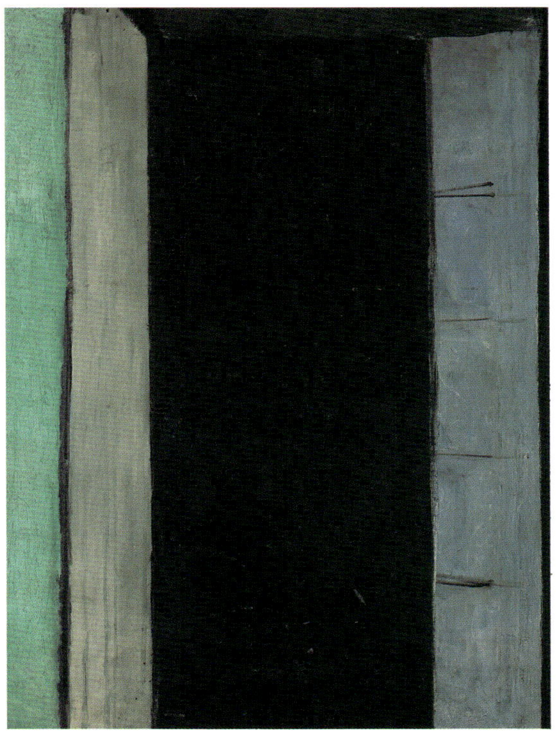

27
H. Matisse ***French Window at Collioure*** 1914
Paris, Musée national d'art moderne, Centre Georges Pompidou

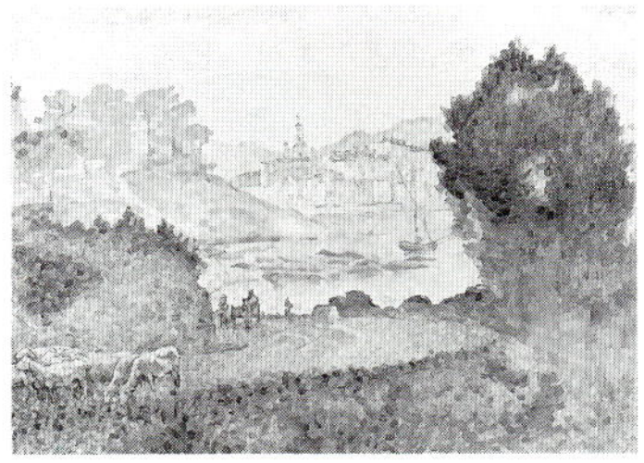

23
H. -E. Cross
View of Menton *c.*1899–1900
Private Collection

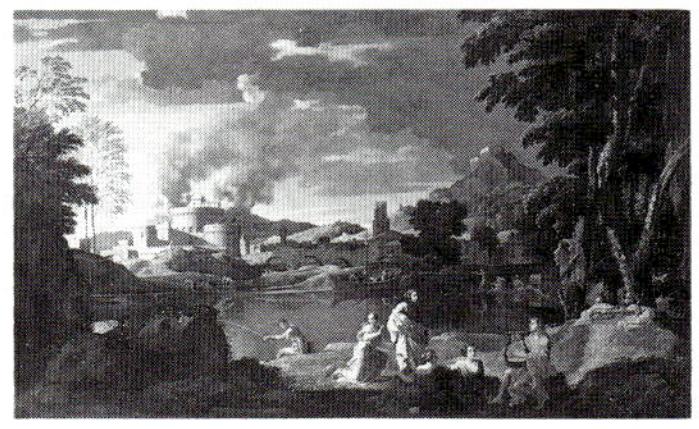

24
N. Poussin ***Orpheus and Eurydice*** 1659
Paris, Musée du Louvre

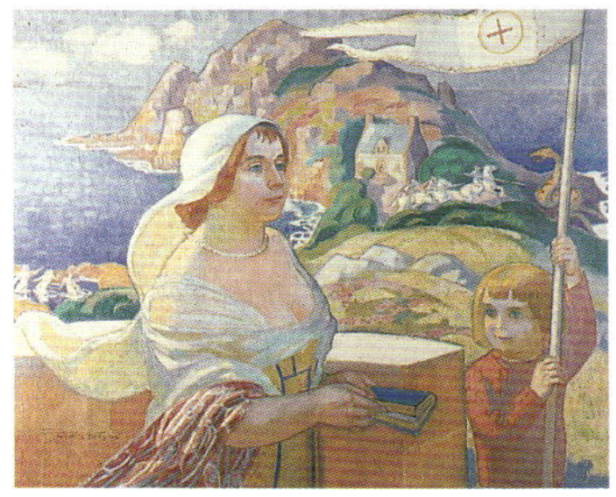

25
M. Denis
The Princess in the Tower 1914
Saint Germain-en-Laye, Musée départemental du 'Prieuré'

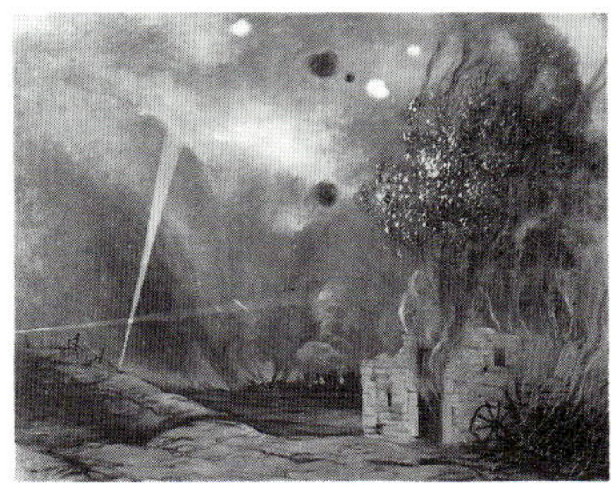

26
F. Vallotton
1914 … Landscape with Scorched Ruins 1915
Bern, Kunstmuseum, Emil Bretschger Collection

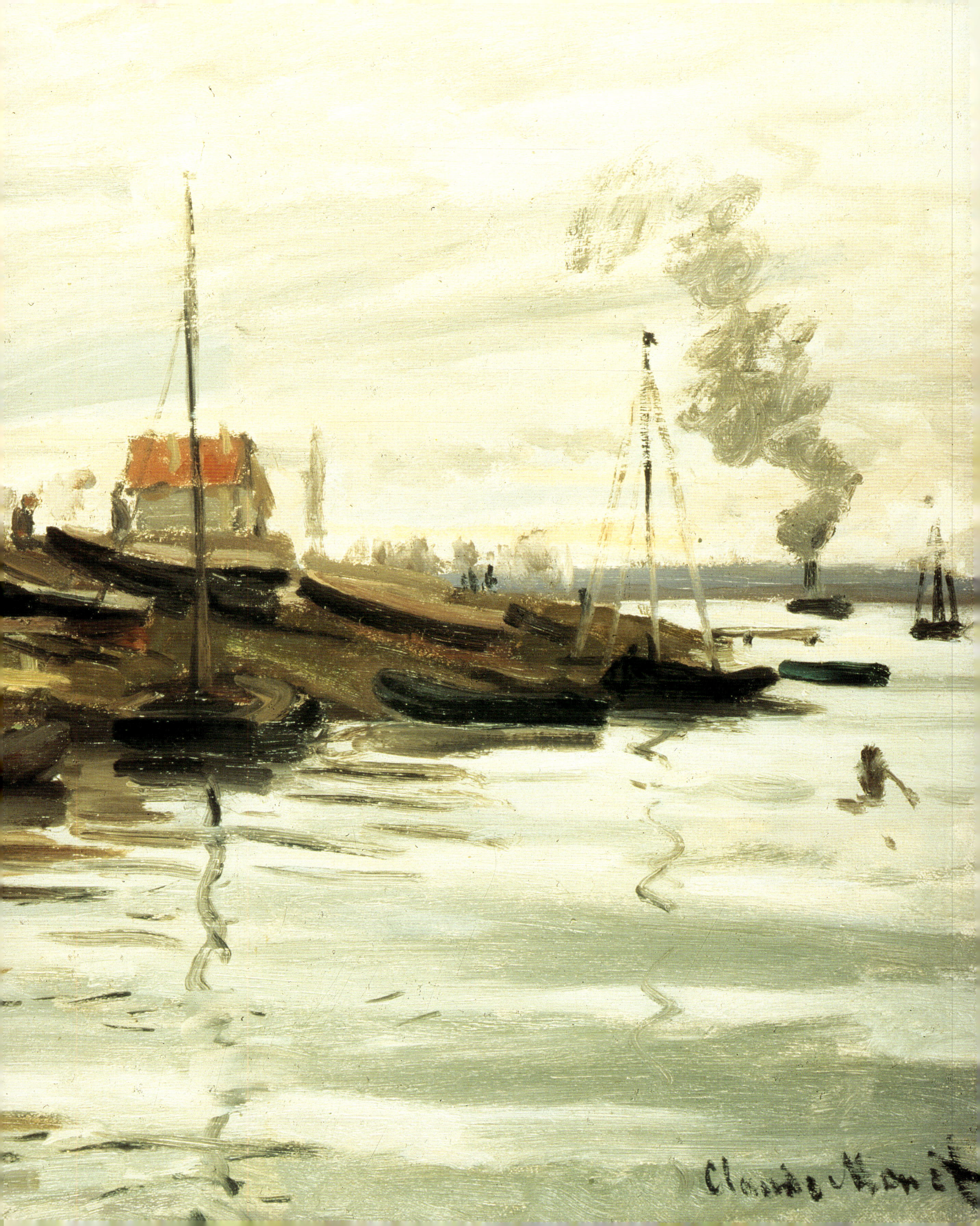
Claude Monet

2 The Suburbs of Paris

It might seem paradoxical to begin a survey of images of landscape in France with Paris and its environs. The idea of landscape immediately conjures up scenes of meadow and mountain, forest and stream, rather than streets and houses. But the capital city makes an appropriate beginning. In such a centralised country as France, Paris acts as lodestone, and at the end of the nineteenth century and the beginning of the twentieth this was no less true for the art world than for the country's political, economic and administrative machinery. The major art schools were in the capital, as well as the exhibition forums where reputations were to be made and clients won. These included the annual Salon, which was divided into two organisations from 1890, the radical co-operative known as the Salon des Indépendants from 1884, and the chic Salon d'Automne from 1903. These were the main places for showing work, and were paralleled by the increasing number of picture dealers, with whom one might associate a particular painter; thus to buy a landscape by Monet one would first visit Durand-Ruel; by Harpignies, one would go to Arnold and Tripp. In these circumstances it is understandable that artists, however committed they felt to their regional home, usually retained a dwelling or studio in the capital or set up within convenient distance of the city. Thus while Lhermitte might summer at Mont-Saint-Père on the Marne to the north-east of the city, and Redon at Peyrelebade in Les Landes near Bordeaux, they would winter in Paris, and when in 1883 Monet settled at Giverny and Pissarro at Eragny both chose these villages to the north-west of the capital for ease of communication. Paris also proffered visual delights which could stimulate the eye of the landscape painter. 'With what resources, what an abundance of subjects, does this privileged city furnish painters!', over-enthused a writer in the *Revue des deux mondes* in 1876; 'Not only does it have the beauty of its proportions and perspectives, but also the incomparable softness of its sky, the gentlest, the most graceful, the most vaporously lively, the most coquettishly artistic of all skies'.[1]

To commercial necessity, career platform, and natural spectacle, Paris could add to its inviting inventory the powerful attraction of modernity. For it was a rapidly changing city, one which had increased its population from 1 million in 1850 to 1.8 million in 1870 and over 2.5 million by the turn of the century. The city saw constant physical change too; following the massive urbanisation undertaken by Haussmann during the Second Empire, in which the city's fabric of roads, buildings, sewers and parks had been drastically overhauled, further developments continued, be they new structures – the Eiffel Tower, the Sacré-Coeur, or the Samaritaine department store – or new facilities such as the Métro or the Renault factory on the île Séguin. But in the four decades before the outbreak of the First World War it was the suburbs of the city that were transformed more than the central *quartiers*.

The growth of the surrounding suburbs was due to a number of factors, not all of which were acknowledged or given equal weight by contemporaries. An important element had been the rise in inner city rents which had followed Haussmann's rebuilding programme, forcing the lower strata of Parisian society out of the capital itself. Haussmann had encouraged this drift by subsidising large industrial concerns such as the Say and Cail ironworks to set up their factories in the suburbs, in this case northern Saint-Denis, thus concentrating the work-force in the vicinity. A further factor was the fortifications built to encircle Paris in the 1840s. While no longer serving as an effective strategic defence, they remained a tax-barrier, so that food and goods were cheaper outside them.[2] Such disparate, fluctuating social and economic forces meant that the suburbs grew haphazardly and with minimum regulation. One element controlling the expansion – and an effective indicator of it – was the railway. Take the example of Asnières. A small village to the north-west of the city centre, on the far bank of the Seine, it had a population of 450 in 1837, the year a bridge was built there, carrying the first railway in France, which linked Paris to the river-port of Le Pecq, south-west of Asnières. Within a decade its population had doubled; by 1872 it stood at over 6,000, and that in turn tripled by 1890, by which time Asnières was completely absorbed in the urban sprawl.[3] In 1883 workers' season tickets were introduced on the railways and for the next three decades

opposite
28
C. Monet
The Seine at Petit-Gennevilliers 1872
(detail)
John M. and Sally B. Thornton Trust

ticket prices were 40 per cent lower than they had been in the 1860s and 1870s, convenience and economy combining to fix a pattern of commuting from the suburbs.[4]

As railway lines, factories and tentacular conurbations spread across what had been fields and woodland the physical appearance of the landscape around the city continuously changed. Artists' growing consciousness of this is evident in Raffaëlli's *Paris 4 km*, exhibited at his first one-man exhibition in 1884 [**29**], in which the road-sweeper sits in what at first sight is countryside but on closer inspection is terrain bordering the advancing frontiers of the suburbs. The suburb then was no longer defined by signs of 'country' – the agricultural, perhaps, or the picturesque – but by its relation to the city. The suburb was definable too by its state of perpetual transformation. Outlying regions could no longer rely on their role of providing fresh produce for the city when as early as November 1871 cut flowers were sped to Paris by train from the Côte d'Azur to be sold at Les Halles, the central market. Foreign competitors greatly admired the ability of the market gardeners in the Parisian region to force commercially viable crops such as asparagus in confined spaces, but this was adaptation with a limited future. By the turn of the century such production was limited to the north- and south-east fringes of the city, liable to be consumed by the next wave of suburban building, a precarious situation which between 1904 and 1907 gave rise to growing political radicalism in those districts.[5] Constant change rendered the outskirts of the city often illegible. In his 1886 guide *Les Environs de Paris* Louis Barron complained that to call one vicinity the Forest of Bondy no longer bore any resemblance to the truth, as it was an incoherent jumble of smallholdings, weekend cottages, bars, workshops and thickets marked *chasse réservée*.[6]

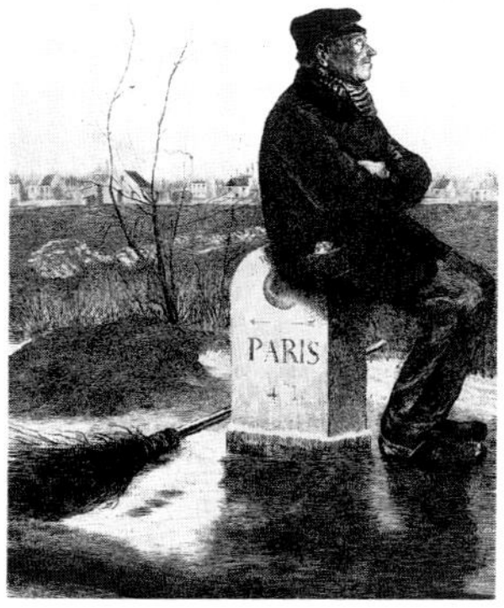

29
J. -F. Raffaëlli
Paris 4km c.1884
Location unknown

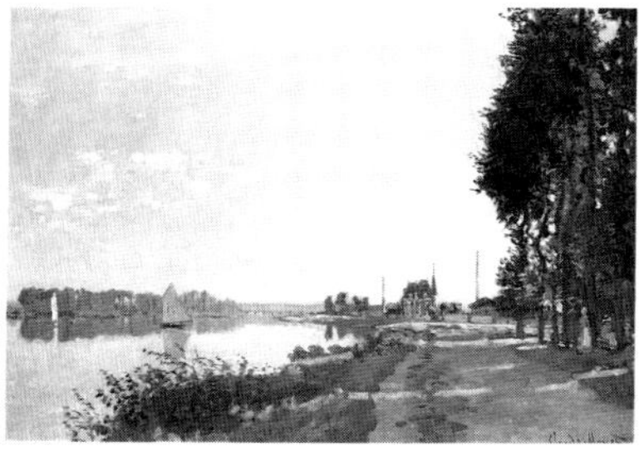

30
C. Monet
Argenteuil c.1872
Washington, National Gallery of Art, Ailsa Mellon Bruce Collection

Why were artists drawn to these areas in which the make-up of the landscape was in perpetual redefinition? At one level, they were influenced in the same way as their fellow citizens; living or working in the suburbs allowed convenient access to Paris, market and cultural hub. At another they followed a tradition of landscapists working on the outskirts of the city, a tradition going back at least to the eighteenth century and including in the first half of the nineteenth Georges Michel around Montmartre, Troyon at Sèvres, and Corot at Ville-d'Avray. Such painters had, however, tended to emphasise the landscape painter's conventional concerns and so edit out the evidence of the nearby city, to reduce its traces to a steamer on the river or a dome on a distant horizon. After 1870 pressing public debate about suburban expansion brought the issue into the artist's focus. The suburban motif was perhaps of all landscapes the one most quintessentially modern, and the painter had to confront and find forms for change. Given the flux of the subject, representations of the suburbs could take on many associations. The canvases that Monet painted at Argenteuil, where he settled for six years in 1871, can, for example, be read as images of national reconstruction after the Franco-Prussian War, as Paul Tucker has pointed out.[7] The suburbs had been the front-line during the siege of Paris and during the early 1870s their streets and bridges were often being rebuilt, but a landscape did not have to show this to be an image of French resurgence, for a picture of leisure along the suburban Seine could equally be taken to imply prosperity and stability regained [**30**]. By contrast, in the hands of Raffaëlli, who established his career in the early 1880s with scenes of the shanty-towns and impoverished populations of the north-western suburbs and the *zone* surrounding the fortifications, a wasteland kept bare as a field of fire [**29**, **33**], this raw material could be taken to address

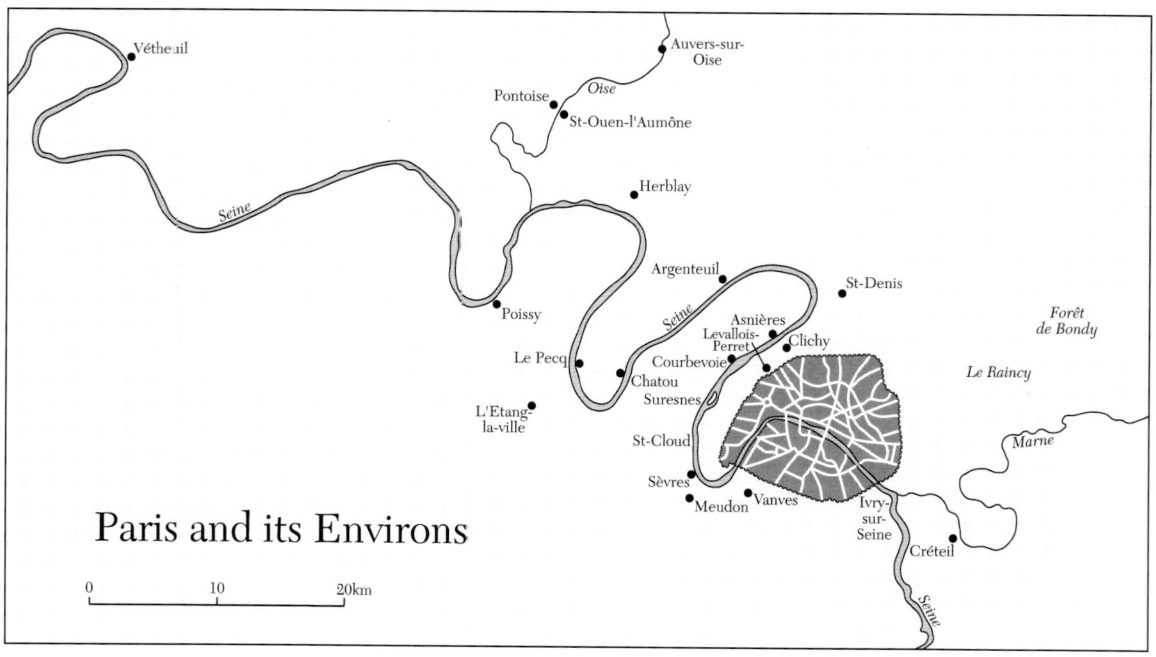

directly the *question sociale*, one of the dominant issues in Third Republic politics. It comes as no surprise that paintings were lent to his 1884 show by prominent left-of-centre deputies such as Clemenceau and Antonin Proust. And the suburban motif could also be taken up in images which sought to promote the social virtues of Republican France. This period saw an intense programme of decoration in the town halls of the Parisian *arrondissements* and the suburban *communes*. For instance, the scheme for the *mairie* at Vanves, to the south of the city, completed in 1902 by Henry Darien, tackled each of the four requisite allegories – *Studia*, *Labor*, *Pax* and *Pro Patria* – with landscapes of the area. *Labor* [**31**] shows work in one of the local limestone quarries.[8]

We have seen that the suburb provided a range of landscape motifs ripe for modern treatment and potent with conflicting associations; the question facing the painter was how to make sense of the social flux and visual incoherence of the city's outskirts. Writers tended to draw broad social distinctions, no doubt following and fuelling common prejudices and oversimplifications, classifying the northern districts as more squalid and industrial, the southern as neater and more 'bourgeois'.[9] And they also commonly stratified different kinds of suburb in bands surrounding Paris like ripples emanating from a central point of impact. Barron made a distinction between inner localities such as Clichy and Levallois-Perret, industrial and proletarian areas, and Asnières across the river from them, petit-bourgeois and relatively prosperous.[10] Often the writer would take the view towards the city from the outskirts, Jean Lorrain for one describing in layers the 'uncultivated suburban wasteland', the 'tall factory chimneys and the leprous slopes of the fortifications', with the 'distant cupolas of the Val-de-Grâce and the Panthéon' above them.[11]

This was a structure, a hierarchy, which painters also deployed. It came quickly enough to Monet in representing the outlying suburban town of Argenteuil. In one painting of 1873 [**32**] he adopted a distinctly layered composition. Standing in an open field he arrayed across his canvas first a rank of saplings marking the end of the meadow and the beginning of gardens, next a line of newly erected houses, then a bank of well established trees, and finally the medieval spire of the local church. Thus he marked out, one by one, the edge of the country, contemporary suburban construction, and the old town, a visual classification in which is inherent the notion of past, present and future: the perfect pictorial structuring, one might say, of suburban flux. It was a strategy

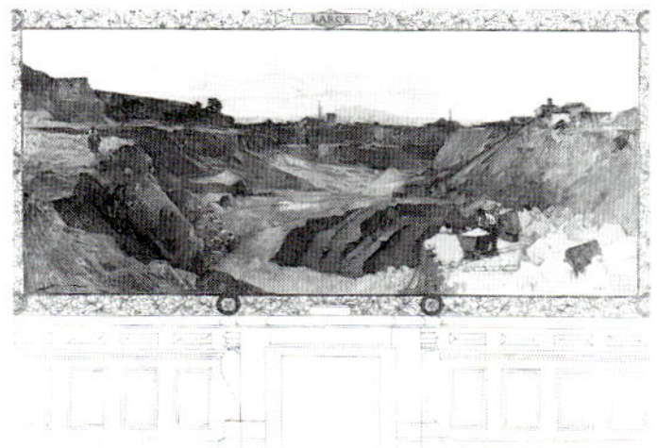

31
H. Darien
Study for 'Labor'
Paris, Musée du Petit Palais

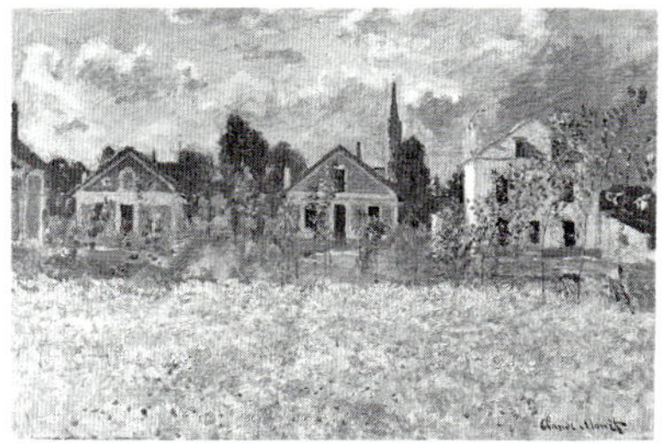

32
C. Monet
Houses at Argenteuil 1873
Berlin, Neue Nationalgalerie

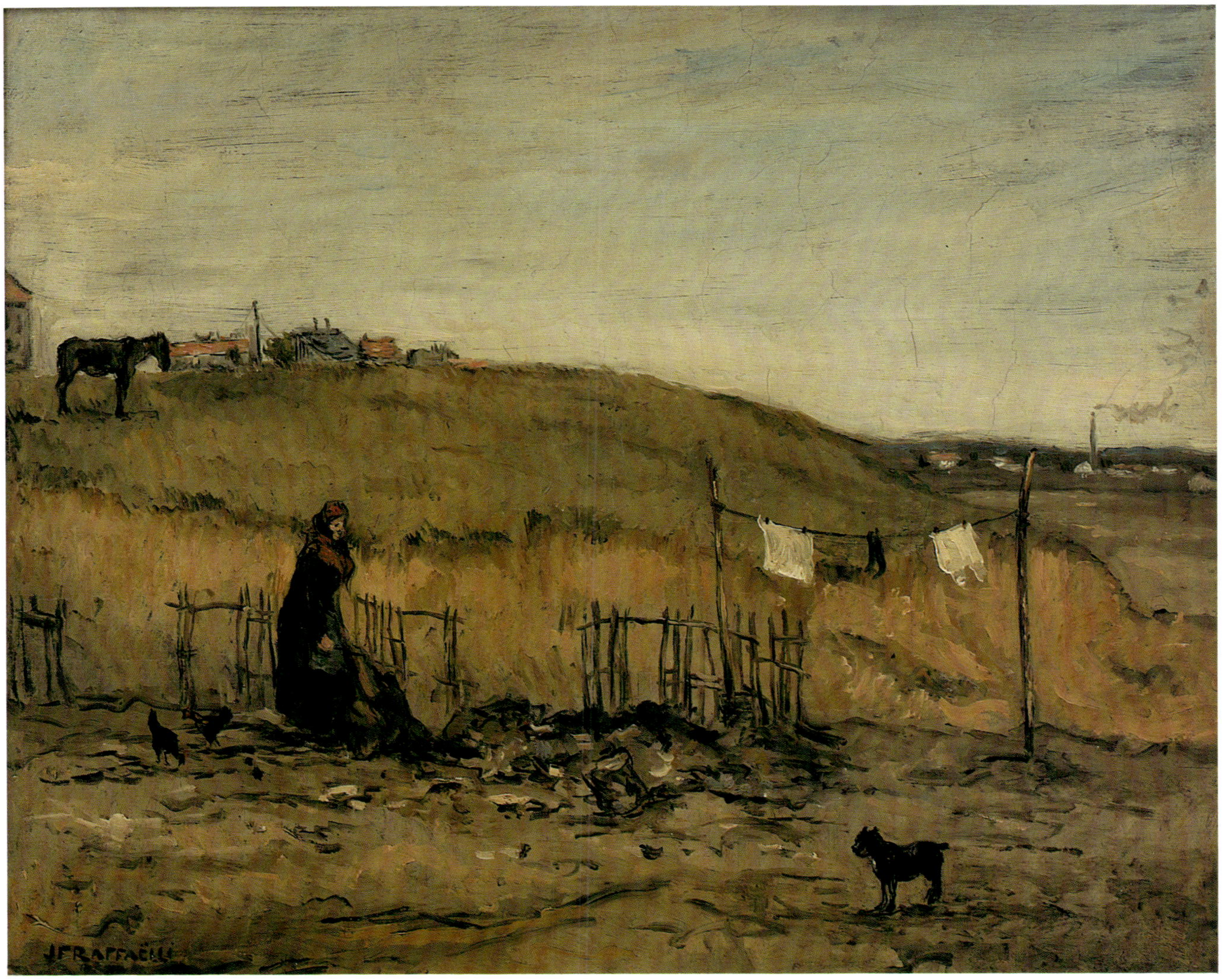

33
J. -F. Raffaëlli
The Gipsy Woman
*c.*1880–4
Paris, Musée Marmottan

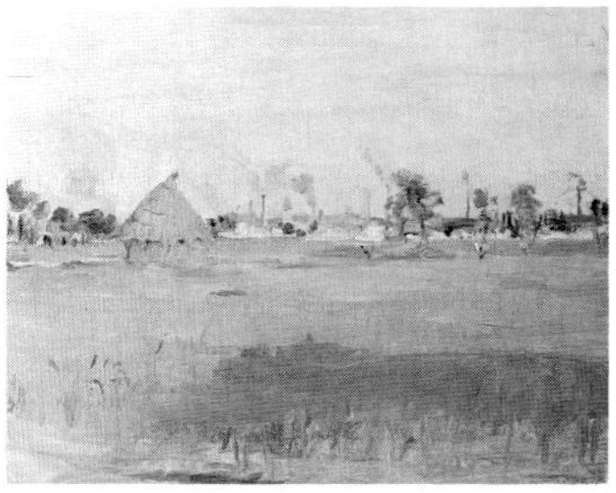

34
B. Morisot
Landscape at Gennevilliers 1875
London, J. P. L. Fine Arts

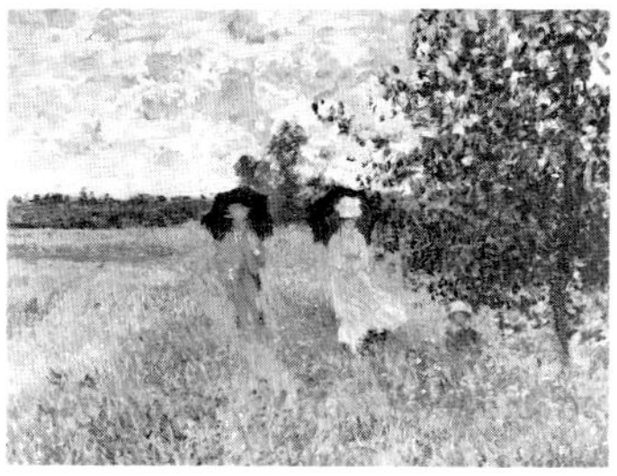

35
C. Monet
Promenade near Argenteuil 1873
Paris, Musée Marmottan

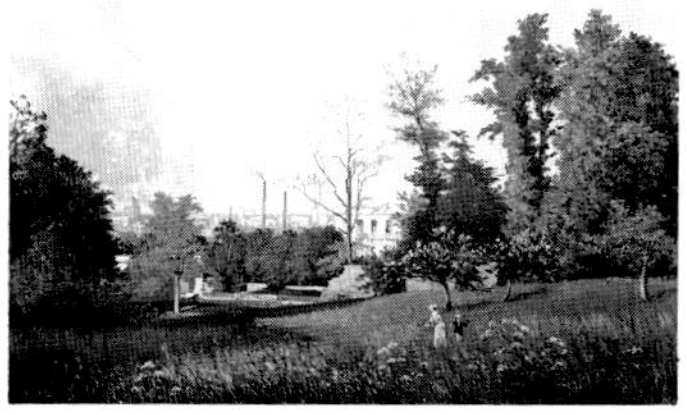

36
P. Galerne
In the Park of Issy-les-Moulineaux 1876
Sceaux, Musée de l'île de France

shared with other artists. During the late spring of 1875 Berthe Morisot spent some time at the family property at Gennevilliers, in the loop of the Seine as it flows from Asnières to Argenteuil. Here she produced three canvases that adopt much the same formula: all look across an expanse of open countryside to a horizon lined with the haphazard construction of the modern suburb. In the sparsest and most spontaneous of them [**34**] the eye is drawn to a haystack left of centre, but this apparently rural motif is but a decoy, for behind it lurk more than half-a-dozen factory chimneys. The others also gradually reveal the thin veneer of rurality, for in one the boy in the cornfield looks on close inspection to be a suburban stroller rather than a peasant and the second looks over a group of women hanging out so much laundry as to register a commercial, not merely domestic, operation.[12] Almost surreptitiously one learns from these fresh and verdant pictures, and from the paintings Monet also made there of smartly dressed bourgeois families taking walks [**35**], that the plain of Gennevilliers was a landscape in thrall to the city. Naturally poor land of pebbles and sand, its cultivable quality was being enhanced even as Morisot and Monet painted their canvases by the building of irrigation channels and liberal dousing with Parisian sewage.[13]

Critics of the 1870s recognised that in their landscapes the Impressionists were exploring a new territory, modern and suburban. Writing of their 1877 exhibition Charles Bigot regretfully contrasted them with the previous generation of landscapists such as Corot and Daubigny who had painted '*la campagne*': 'not only the poetry, but also the truth of nature'. Morisot, Monet and their colleagues did not paint '*la véritable nature*' but 'above all nature as one sees it by fits and starts in the city or its outskirts, where the brash accents of houses, of white walls, ... mingle with the foliage of the trees and create violent contrasts with them'.[14] The insinuation here was that as the suburb is not true countryside, so representation of the suburb cannot be a true landscape painting. But the challenge posed by the suburban environment to the traditional status of landscape was one of the primary motives for artists to paint it, to make sense of it. By the use of strategies such as banding – and there were others in their compositional repertoires – Monet and Morisot produced images which rendered the suburb stable and tame. It was an ideal construction arrived at by others. Their little-known contemporary Prosper Galerne produced an image in 1876 of the park at south-eastern Issy-les-Moulineaux [**36**], which also operates in less insistent strips that begin with the middle-class mother and boy strolling in a meadow filled with cow-parsley, zigzags back past villas and gardens, then a line of factories whose smog fouls the cloudless sky, to the golden dome of Les Invalides in the far distance. One senses in Galerne, as much as in Morisot or Monet, a desire to find ways to structure the haphazard nature of suburban expansion, and in each case the elements of the landscape are ordered in such a way as to harmonise apparent opposites: city and country, meadow and factory, locus of capitalist prosperity and middle-class tranquillity.

If that construction was a necessary myth for the Third Republic's bourgeoisie in the decade after the Franco-Prussian War and the suppression of the Paris Commune in 1871, by the 1880s the image of the suburbs shifted. The increasingly apparent failure of the Republic to deal with *la question sociale* – conditions of employment, housing supply, urban deprivation and so on – coupled with the growing importance of the organised Left in French politics led to sharper public debate about social issues, a debate which included artists and concerned the Parisian suburbs. At a time when the prospective demolition of the fortifications was hotly argued in the press, when anarchists were arrested in Levallois-Perret, it was inevitable that representations should take on a sharper, less comfortable edge.[15] What a contrast there is between Galerne's *Park at Issy-les-Moulineaux* and Raffaëlli's *Gipsy Woman* [**33**], an inventory of decrepitude – rubbish tip, spavined nag, flimsy clothes-line – and what an apt parallel to the strictures of sociologist and reformist politician.

How, then, do we read Seurat's *Field of Alfalfa, Saint-Denis*, painted in the mid-1880s [**37**]? It is a difficult painting, not least because the insistently flecked surface arrests the eye and complicates the articulation of space and form. One's gaze moves from shadow into light, across a field of alfalfa sprinkled with scarlet poppies, but beyond this it is uncertain whether one makes out a low wall and then another broad field or a track beyond which is a high wall.[16] The confusion is not aided by Seurat's still experimental touch or by the absence of any spatial marker before the somewhat apologetic tree, but one wonders whether this degree of visual uncertainty is not in some way symptomatic of difficulties of definition. *Field of Alfalfa* once again uses the system of stratification, setting up a relatively direct contrast between *campagne* – the foreground crop – and suburb – the scattered buildings and factories on the high horizon. If on the one hand it rehearses the landscape painter's concerns, with its sunlight falling on the dominant, verdant green and its loyalty to aerial perspective, it also registers the equivocal, in Bigot's terms 'untrue', character of this view of 'nature', for this too is landscape in thrall to the city, with the field of alfalfa, cultivated as feed for Paris's equine workforce, shoved up against the sprawl of industrial Saint-Denis. Seurat's image allows this vicinity a more palatable identity than that offered by a fellow-painter's description a few years later: 'a lamentable landscape, [its] unpleasing plains sliced by factory walls a kilometre long looking like ragpickers' shanties hastily thrown together; the countryside

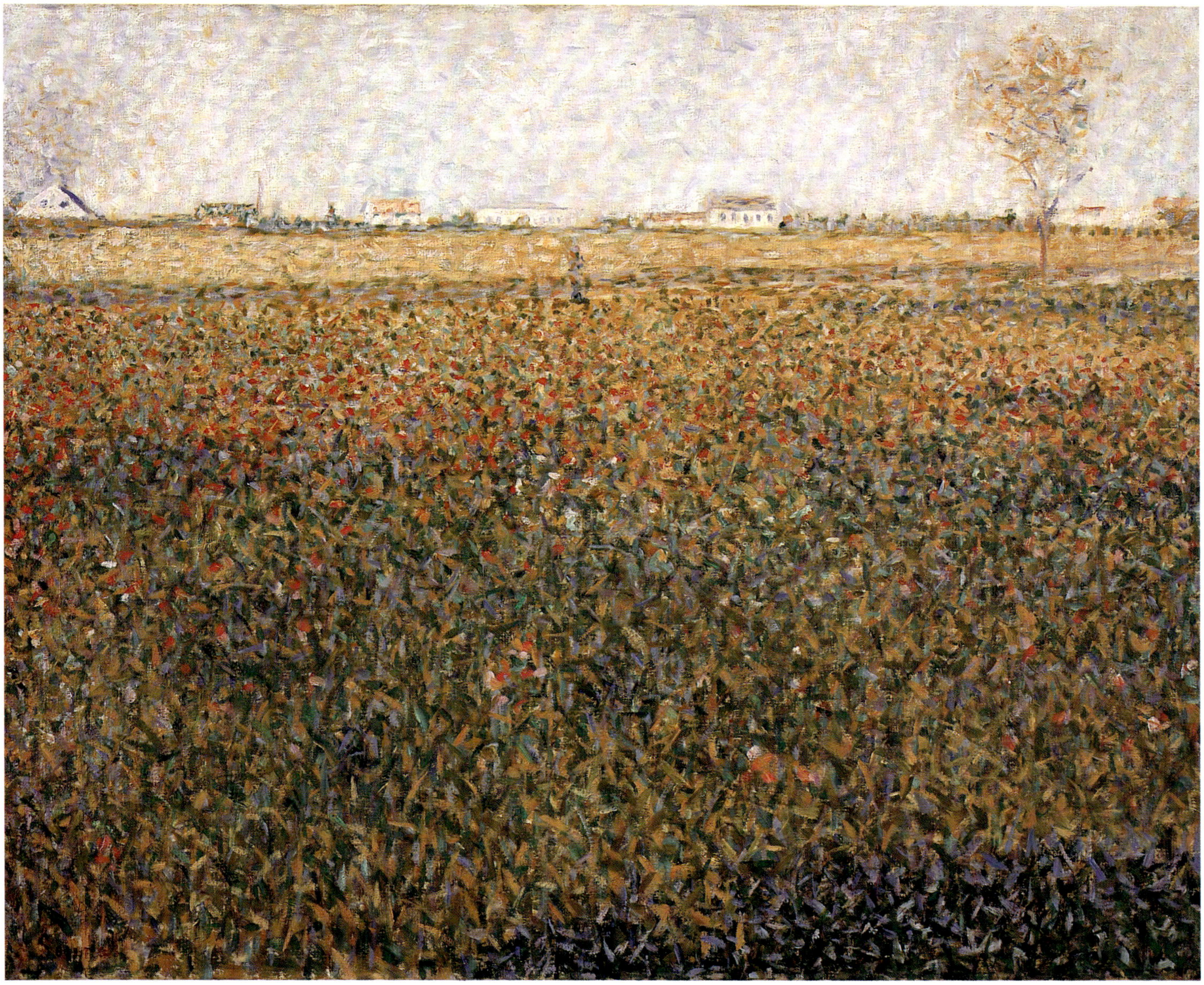

37
G. Seurat
Field of Alfalfa, Saint-Denis c.1884–5
Edinburgh, National Gallery of Scotland

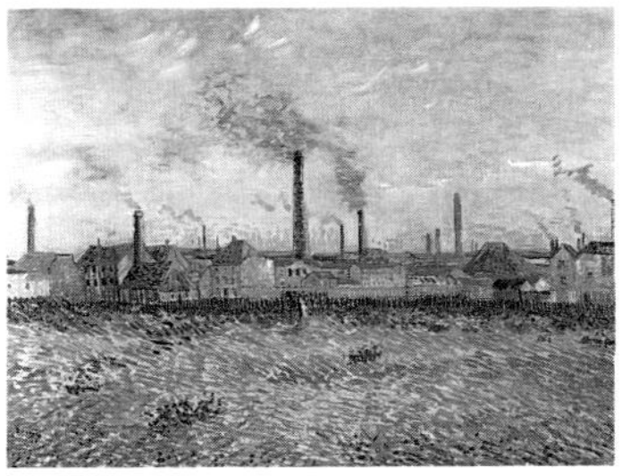

38
V. van Gogh
Hüth Factory, Asnières 1887
Saint Louis Art Museum,
Gift of Mrs Mark C. Steinberg

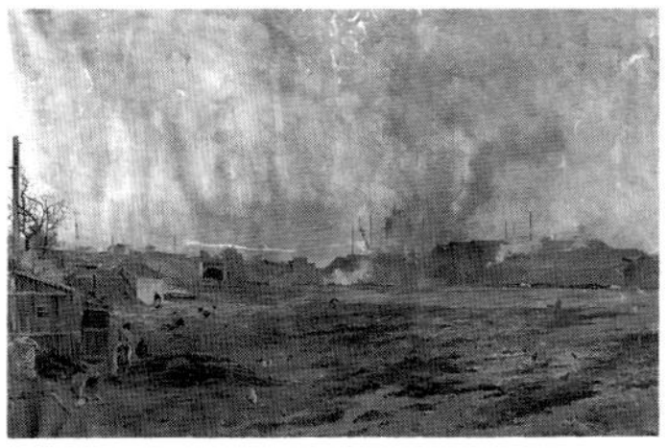

39
P. Vauthier
Saint-Denis: la Fosse-aux-Anglais 1889
Paris, Musée d'Orsay

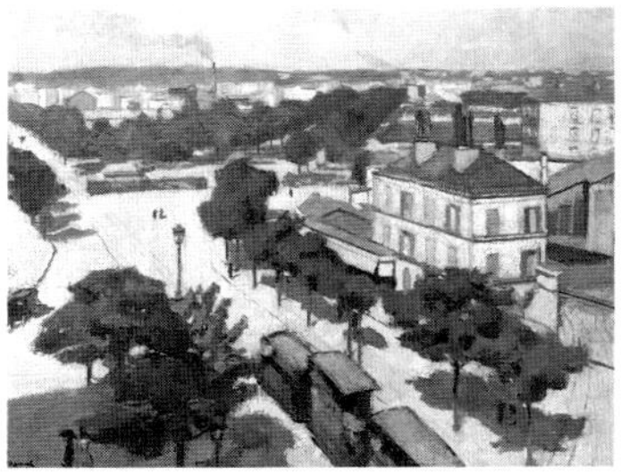

40
A. Marquet
The Porte de Saint-Cloud 1904
Cleveland Museum of Art,
Gift of Mr and Mrs Lewis B. Williams
from the Blair Trust

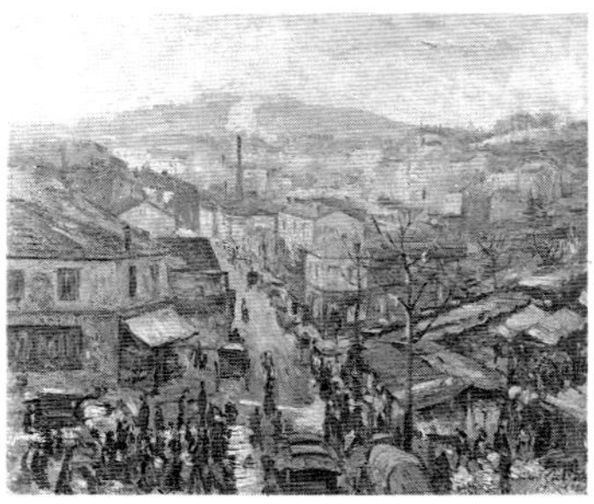

41
A. Gleizes
The Market at Courbevoie 1905
Lyon, Musée des beaux-arts

[*campagne*] seems like an immense pile of garbage'.[17] This was the image of the industrial suburb shared by van Gogh in his *Hüth Factory, Asnières* [**38**], a stark confrontation of capitalist production and ersatz landscape, or by Pierre Vauthier's large and dramatically sparse *Saint-Denis: la Fosse-aux-Anglais* [**39**]. Both these paintings articulate their representation of dreary suburb in definable strips, a strategy which had never been the exclusive prerogative of the avant-garde. Nor had the pictorial probing of the shifting realities of these suburbs, and in contemporary debate about these problems such images had a public rôle to play. Vauthier's painting was shown at the Salon des artistes français in 1890 and bought by the state; it was dispatched to the museum at Bourges, whether as prudent exile to provincial obscurity after token display of concern or for more laudable motives we do not know.

After 1900 stratification as a device seems to have fallen into abeyance. Both Marquet's *Porte de Saint-Cloud* of 1904 and Gleizes's *Market at Courbevoie* painted the following year [**40, 41**], while still views of the western suburbs, do not look in towards the centre of Paris but rather look out. They no longer register definable areas, but envisage the suburbs as an undifferentiated panorama of dense population. And, crucially, landscape concerns now function entirely within the limitations imposed by the city. Trees are where they have been planted, set in lines in pavements; the sky is banished by the high horizon; only the far, generalised band of hills provides a natural accent, marking – for now – the edge of the city.

One can identify another consensus in the representation of the suburban landscape: emphasis on the starkly man-made character of the grim environment. This too was not exclusive to painter, writer or social commentator; it emerged from a common desire to categorise the perceived modernity of the suburban environment. One sees it emerging in Monet's paintings made at Argenteuil during the mid-1870s. These images are much more diverse in mood and motif than is often acknowledged, for it is too easy to envisage them as a middle-class artist's construction of a suburban idyll of blooming gardens and promenades along the Seine on whose sunlit waters skim sailing boats. Such motifs were part of Monet's construction of the suburban town, but there was also a tougher edge to his vision. One of the earliest canvases he painted on arriving in Argenteuil gave notice of his willingness to come to terms with the less picturesque aspects of the area. The *Seine at Petit-Gennevilliers* [**42**] shows the bank opposite Argenteuil. It was from here that the leisurely weekend sailing and amateur regattas were serviced, that boats could be moored, rented, made and repaired. Monet's painting has all the vivacity of a *plein air* picture, and it was in all probability executed entirely from his *botin*, the boat that he had fixed up as a floating studio following the example of Daubigny. From this vantage point he could work off shore, as he did here, looking westward towards the sun setting downstream, under an overcast autumnal sky. Monet was concerned to catch the nuances of this sombre but still warm light, registering it in the browns and aubergines with which he defined the structures on the shoreline and the mushroom-coloured sky reflected in the rippling water. There are sharp, even daring accents in this tonal structure – notably the single green dab which indicates a boat to the right – and the whole canvas is marked by a sense of spontaneity: in the confidence with which a single stroke marks out a form, in the use of brushstrokes – perhaps blocky, or linear, or wavering – to indicate the space between objects. The vitality of the canvas, then, comes from its chromatics and touch, for the motif itself is unremittingly dreary, with its functional buildings under scaffolding, its beached boats, and the detritus of planks, shafts and freshly sawn timber. Even the sky is grubbied by the foul smoke of a passing steamer.[18] A painting such as this not only counterpointed Monet's other, more immediately appealing, images of Argenteuil, but it also began to identify another formula for the representation of the suburbs.

During the following decade a number of painters of the younger generation also focused, for a relatively short but extremely fruitful time, on representing the suburbs. Their experience was markedly different from Monet's. Monet, born in 1840, had undergone the rites of passage conventional for a landscape painter in mid-century – the campaigns in the Forest of Fontainebleau and on the Channel coast at the ferme Saint-Siméon – and had settled at Argenteuil with the specific undertaking of painting the suburbs. However, young artists such as Seurat, Signac and Bernard, the generation of the 1860s, seem to have considered the suburban experience almost as a cultural and artistic birthright. Seurat's father owned a 'country' property at Le Raincy, to the north-east of the city, and both Bernard and Signac lived at Asnières. All three cut their teeth as landscape painters on local motifs. And Seurat, the eldest, most ambitious and thoroughly trained of the three, surely had an eye to the modern, vernacular themes increasingly being treated in commissions for the *mairies* when he devoted his first two exhibition paintings to large-scale compositions of the suburban populations in their physical environment: *Une Baignade, Asnières*, rejected from the Salon but hung at the Indépendants in 1884, and *Un Dimanche à la Grande Jatte (1884)*, shown at the eighth Impressionist exhibition in 1886.[19]

The controversy caused by the *Grande Jatte* in 1886 – debating for and against its starkly outlined, even ridiculous, figures; dividing the avant-garde *pro* and *contra* its innovative division of tone – did not immediately stem the younger generation's fascination with suburban motifs. In fact the following year

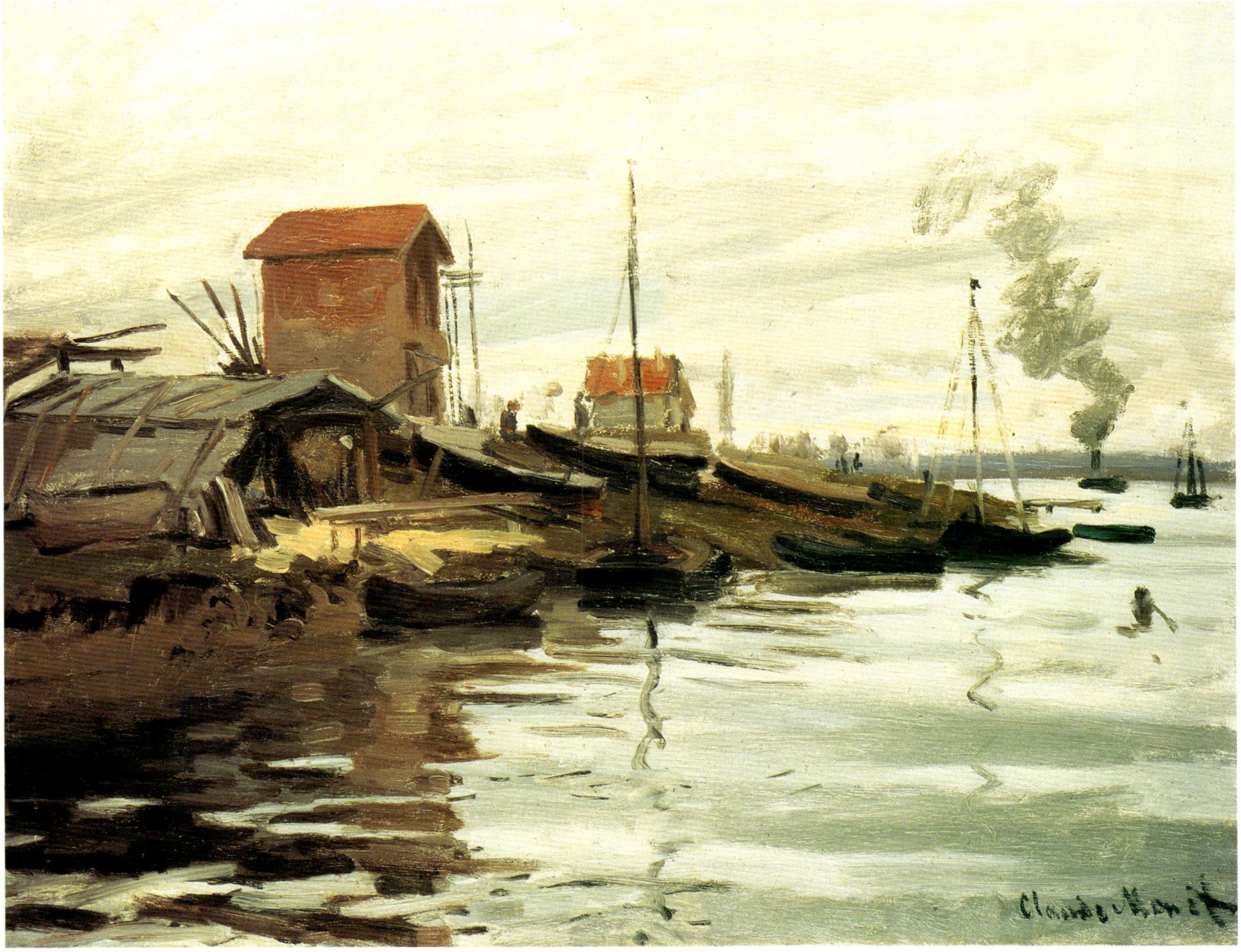

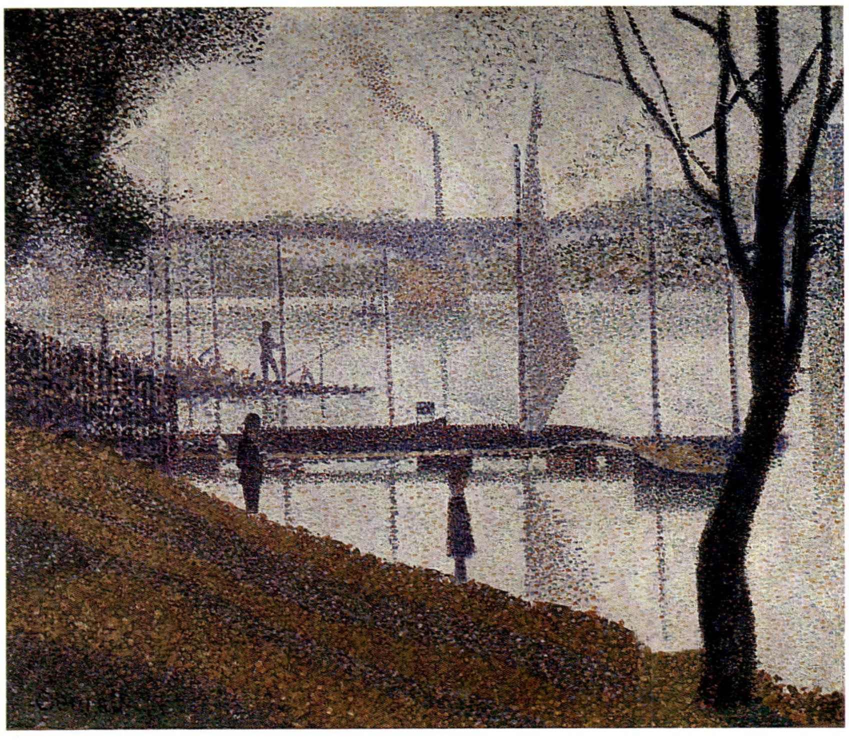

42
C. Monet
The Seine at Petit-Gennevilliers 1872
John M. and Sally B. Thornton Trust

43
G. Seurat
The Bridge at Courbevoie 1886
London, Courtauld Institute Galleries

saw a remarkable concentration on them. In March 1887 Seurat himself exhibited at the Indépendants *The Bridge at Courbevoie* [**43**], a canvas he may have completed the previous autumn.[20] Returning to more conventional proportions for a landscape painting, this canvas once again depicts the island of La Grande Jatte, looking southwestwards towards the Courbevoie bank. But whereas in his grand composition Seurat was concerned with orchestrating, or subverting, the relationships between the figures, in *The Bridge at Courbevoie* he reverted to the landscapist's consideration of light and atmosphere by honing his pointillist touch as a vehicle for his divisionist colour. But to consider *The Bridge at Courbevoie* simply as a technical exercise founded on a landscape motif is surely to underestimate its eerieness: the unnatural imbalance between verdant and skeletal trees to left and right; the reduction of the figures to doll-like cyphers; and the canvas's almost programmatic orientation around the two secondaries of green and purple, an apparently minimal palette which nevertheless exudes a subtle chromatic sensuality. It is a painting which has given rise to varying interpretations, considered on the one hand a poetic evocation of monotony and alienation and on the other a tranquil image of harmony and coexistence.[21] Perhaps comparison with contemporaneous images of this stretch of the Seine might help characterise this inscrutable painting.

Both Signac and Bernard worked in the vicinity in 1887, Signac before he travelled south late in May and Bernard during the second half of the year, after his return from Brittany at the end of July. Signac had been working around Clichy and Asnières since the beginning of the decade, but it was only in 1886–7 that a consistency of vision appeared in his work. This can be traced from a drawing of the quai de Clichy facing downstream dated 1886, via a canvas of the same site looking upstream in overcast weather,[22] to another motif of the *quai*, further south and opposite Asnières, which he must have painted in late spring as it is strongly sunlit and the trees are in leaf [**44**]. Confidently executed in a variously dotted touch laid over more broadly applied tones, the saturated corals, oranges and contrasting blues of Signac's *Quai de Clichy* effectively convey the even warmth of a May day. Bernard, who had experimented with pointillism but not found it to his satisfaction, turned late in the year to the same motif as Signac's 1886 drawing, a coincidence no doubt as the two painters were not in contact at this time. Bernard's *Quai de Clichy* [**46**], like Signac's, is one of a cluster of images of this restricted vicinity made over a short period of time.[23] It represents the *quai* as it passes beneath the huge

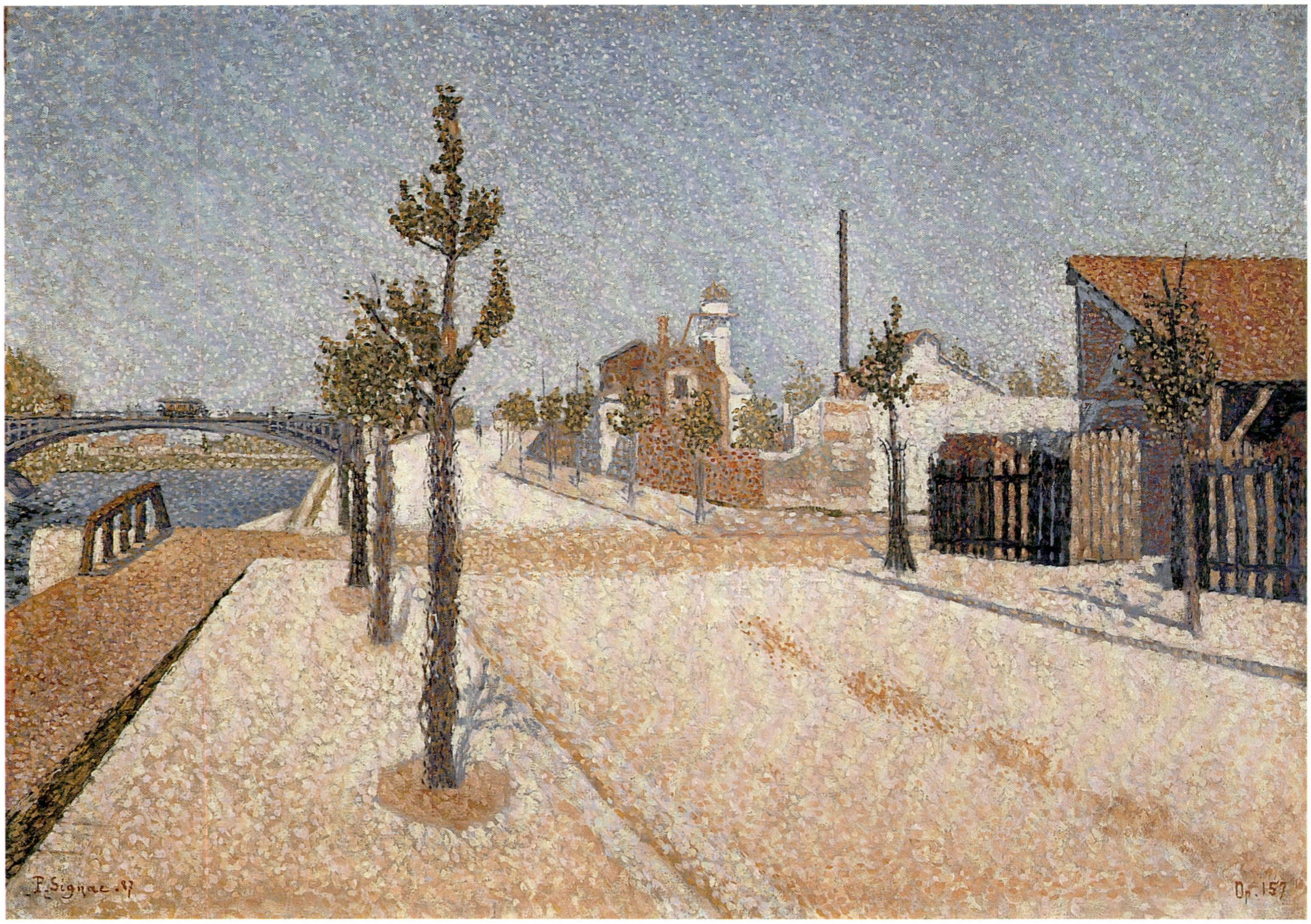

44
P. Signac
Quai de Clichy 1887
Baltimore Museum of Art,
Gift of Frederick H. Gottlieb

iron pier erected to carry trains out over the river where a steam crane loaded them with coal from barges below, just upstream from the île de Robinson which is visible to the upper left. Bernard worked the canvas in a manner almost contradictory to the controlled chromatics of Signac. The painting is based on a grey ground, over which Bernard brushed rapidly, scrubbing on the 'white' snow of the *quai* and creating the sludgy tone of the right-hand wall by mixing blue and red over the initial grey ground. This rather cursory, almost amateurish, immediacy is offset by the careful crafting of the figures, whose position in the design was decided early and around whom the white was applied.

Seurat's *Bridge at Courbevoie* and the two representations by Signac and Bernard of the quai de Clichy at first sight seem remarkably different. If the Neo-Impressionist paintings share a dotted touch and stand quite apart from Bernard's coarser, more gestural surface, the exuberance of Signac's colour contrasts with Seurat's sobriety. And yet there are consistencies. Despite the difference in seasons, all three painters were sensitive to atmospheric conditions: Seurat to autumnal overcast, Signac to spring sunshine, Bernard to wintry mists. More than that, in each canvas human presences, such as they are, are rendered subservient to the suburban environment, and that environment is represented as insistently man-made, far more starkly so than in Monet's *The Seine at Petit-Gennevilliers*. Trees are planted in orderly lines along the *quais*, in Signac's image caged to protect their growth; Seurat's skeletal tree stands in mute opposition to the regimented forest of vertical masts, mooring poles and factory chimneys which regulate its environs. The landscape is dictated by the engineers' and planners' desiderata of efficiency and access, marked by road junctions, loading piers, and bridges; natural elements – the île de Robinson in Bernard's picture, the foreground bank in Seurat's – make little impact on the dominant order. All three painters resorted to a similar compositional ploy, the use of a forceful perspective counterpointed by vertical and, to a lesser extent, horizontal accents, making design the determinant in the representation of the modern suburb as harshly unbending to atmospheric change, man-made but inhuman, an environment where nature has so restricted a presence that the image almost beggars the term 'landscape'.

This was an impromptu consensus arrived at by artists of contrasting stylistic inclinations moving in different circles: Bernard's close colleagues in late 1887 were van Gogh, Anquetin and Toulouse-Lautrec, not the Neo-Impressionist group. They were also of different politics: Bernard was a devout Catho-

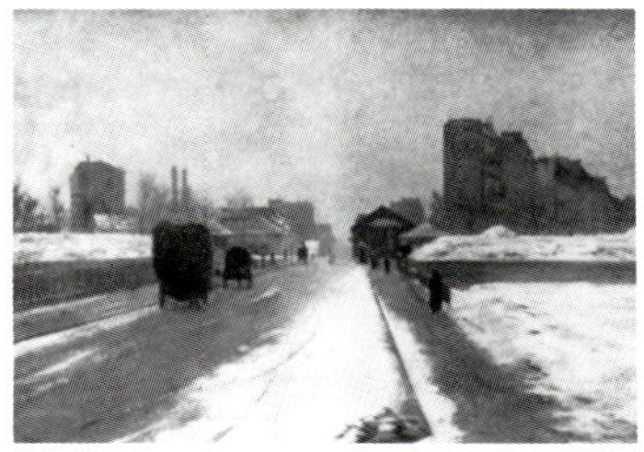

45
R. Billotte
Snow at the Porte d'Asnières 1890
Location unknown

46
E. Bernard
Quai de Clichy 1887
Paris, Musée d'Orsay (on deposit to the Musée départemental du 'Prieuré', Saint-Germain-en-Laye)

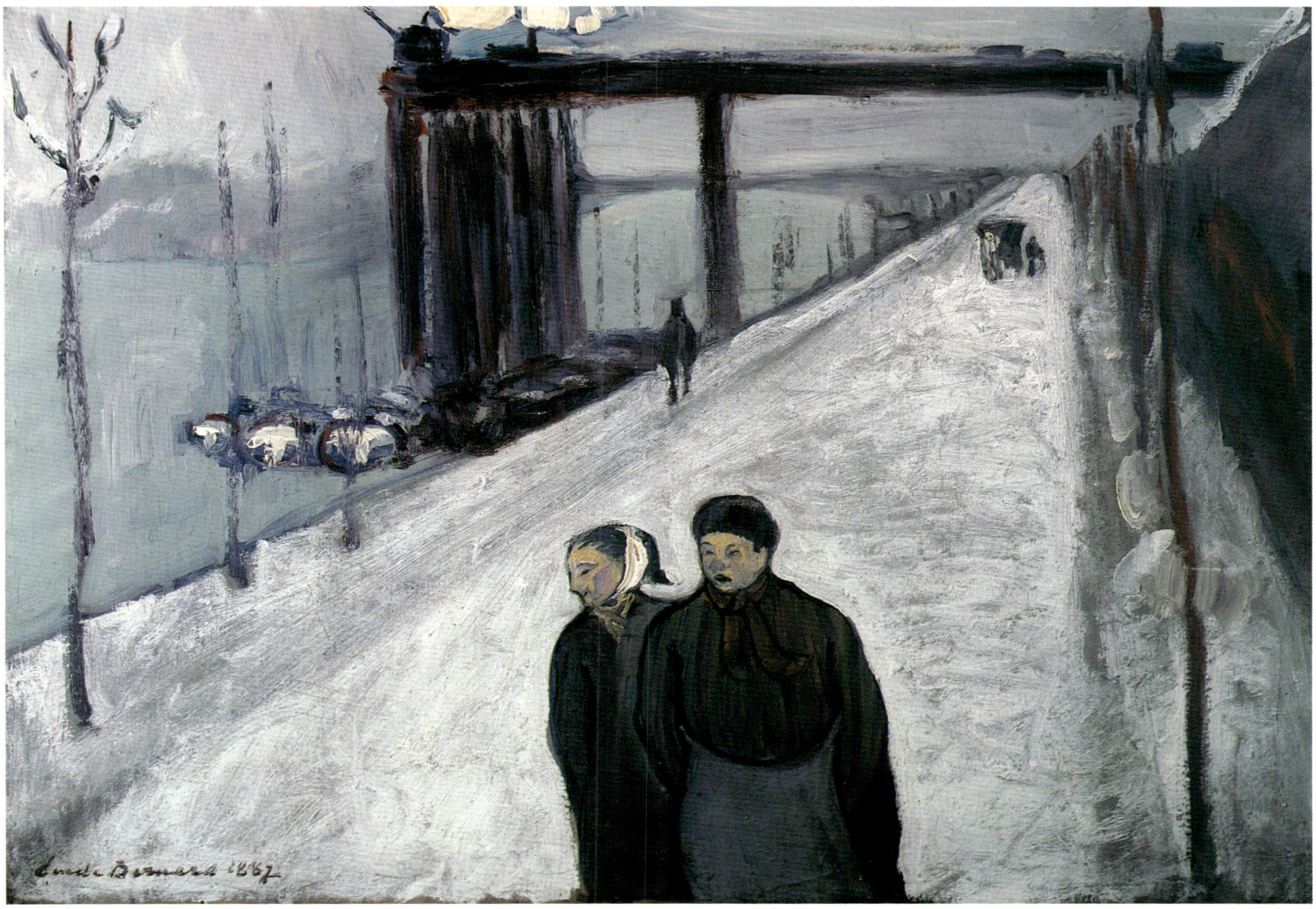

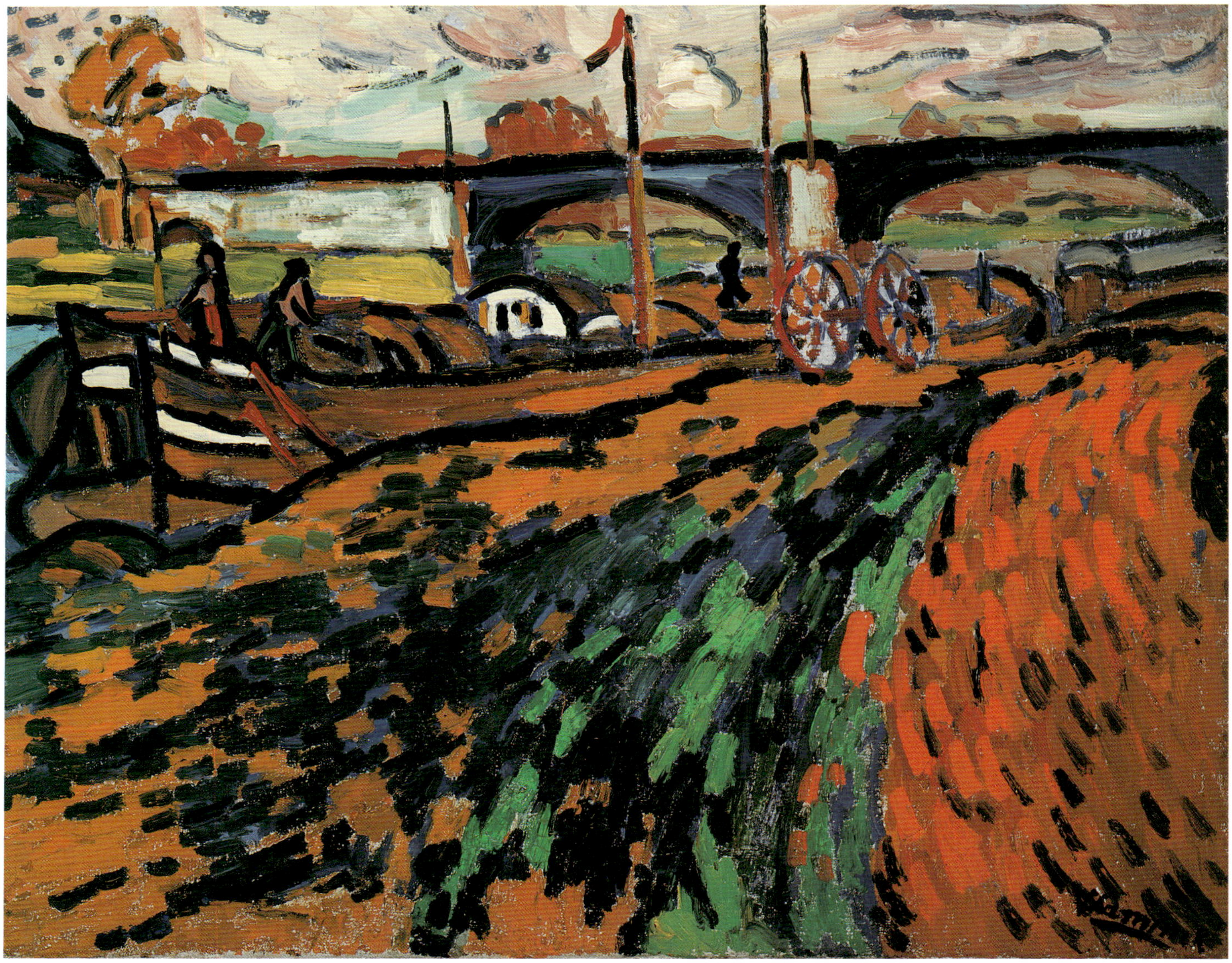

47
M. Vlaminck
Barges at Le Pecq c.1905–6
Houston, Museum of Fine Arts,
Gift of Oveta Culp Hobby

48
A. Derain
The Seine at Le Pecq c.1904
Paris, Musée national d'art moderne,
Centre Georges Pompidou

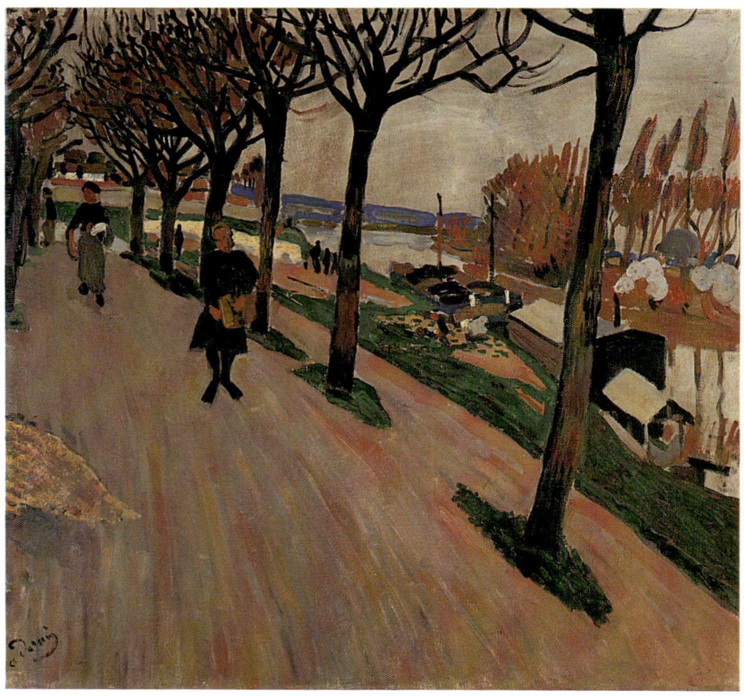

lic, Signac a man of the Left, Seurat mute but probably not indifferent. The consistency of vision is of particular interest not only because of its temporary but insistent identity in the ranks of the avant-garde – by 1888 these painters had all but abandoned suburban motifs – but also because it had been come upon independently by others. René Billotte, for example, showed two canvases of the fortifications at the 1890 Salon de la nationale, *Snow at the Porte d'Asnières* [**45**] and *Winter Fog at the Porte de Courcelles*, both of which revolve around a sharply perspectival axis which emphasises the harsh suburban environment. But by the end of the century that was a dominant construction of the suburbs. One finds it voiced in journalistic accounts such as Barron's description of Bois-Colombes as 'conceived and laid out by engineers, … a vast and flat symmetry, monotonous and dry' [24] and in literature. Writers such as J.-K. Huysmans, Jean Ajalbert and François Coppée all wrote about the suburbs in similar terms, but perhaps none more forcefully than Emile Verhaeren, whose poems about *les villes tentaculaires* demonstrated that, as one contemporary put it, he sees 'the landscape as Signac and Seurat paint it'.[25]

Seurat's representation of the suburbs was still provoking comment in 1914, Apollinaire approvingly quoting Lucie Cousturier's article on his drawings, in which she described how 'Seurat dusts off the ground, sets the wall straight, shears the grass, and sharpens the angles'.[26] That construction of Paris's environs, that topos, survived until the First World War, and the paintings made by Derain and Vlaminck in the western suburbs in the first half-dozen years of the century need to be considered in this light. It has been suggested that Vlaminck's brightly coloured and decoratively textured pictures represent an image of the suburbs which lingers on the myth of unspoilt rusticity, the cherished belief of the dweller in the dormitory town. Despite being vehemently anti-bourgeois in his rhetoric, Vlaminck seems to have adopted this image inadvertently on canvas.[27] While many of his paintings could be read in this way perhaps as many adopt the harshly structured formula. *Barges at Le Pecq* [**47**], for instance, catches the eye by its energetically arcing marks, patterned as if seized in a magnetic field, and its striking zones of blue and green, red and orange. But beneath the painterly pyrotechnics is an emphatic structure – the sweeping perspective of the tow-path, the restraining horizontal of the bridge, supported upon two geometric arches – which invokes the man-made nature of this environment. However decorative and dynamic the hues, this is at base an image of commercial river traffic. At one level style and subject are at odds, and yet the underlying pictorial order relies on that by now customary visual metaphor for the modern suburb. It was appropriate for Vlaminck to deploy a variety of means of representing the western outskirts of the city given the diverse characters of the suburbs he frequented. His beat included Le Pecq, a busy river port described by a contemporary American visitor as a 'forbidding settlement, … a sordid collection of grey houses', and the contrasting Chatou, more residential and superficially rural.[28]

As well as diversity there is ambivalence in Vlaminck's images of the suburbs. Contributor to anarchist periodicals, he painted middle-class dormitory 'villages' nestling in trees; fierce detractor of the railways ('a gaping sore which admits infection')[29] he represented the comings-and-goings of the industrialised Seine; wishing to protect as changeless the locality in which he had been brought up, he produced images of diversity and modernity. His colleague Derain did much the same, switching from motifs which seem to be rural hamlets to paintings such as *The Seine at Le Pecq* [**48**], which pits the thrust of its perspective against the dreary regimentation of autumnal trees.

When André Michel claimed in 1897 that the appetite for painting the suburbs was disappearing he was wrong, as proven by the activities of Vlaminck and Derain, Gleizes [**41**, **124**] and Léger. Throughout the four decades under consideration here the outskirts of Paris were a crucial gauge for painters striving to find some kind of equation between notions of landscape and of modernity. The challenge of the suburbs was not of interest to all – Matisse and Martin are cases in point – nor was it all-consuming; Monet and Derain, Seurat, Signac and Bernard, all moved on to other motifs, other sites. As we have seen, the varied and changing character of the suburb allowed for multiple possibilities of interpretation. Indeed, those that we have analysed resulted in somewhat unwelcoming images which are instantly put into relief when set against an alternative, optimistic type of suburban painting, such as Lepère's *Descending Balloon – Sunday at the Pré-St.Gervais* [**49**], shown at the Salon in 1912, with its soft, sunlit landscape and hurrying crowd, excited and *bon enfant*. But perhaps precisely because the suburbs represented such a shifting, diverse subject, the painter or writer needed to establish some certainties, to find some formulae. The compositional strategy of deploying the landscape in distinctly stratified bands and of insisting upon its man-made, perspectival hardness proved lasting and flexible possibilities.

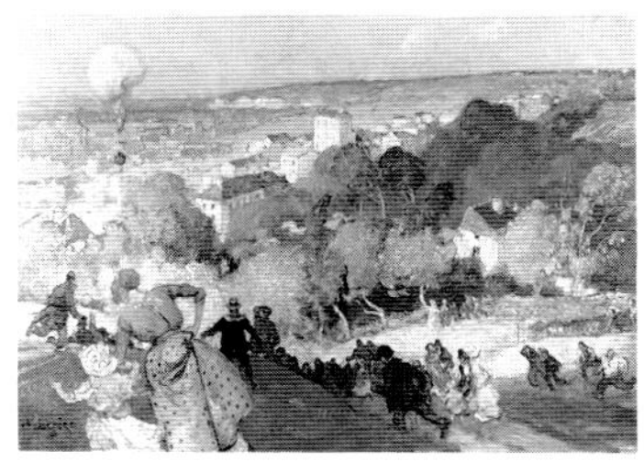

49
A. Lepère
The Descending Balloon – Sunday at the Pré-Saint-Gervais, Paris 1908
Sceaux, Musée de l'île de France

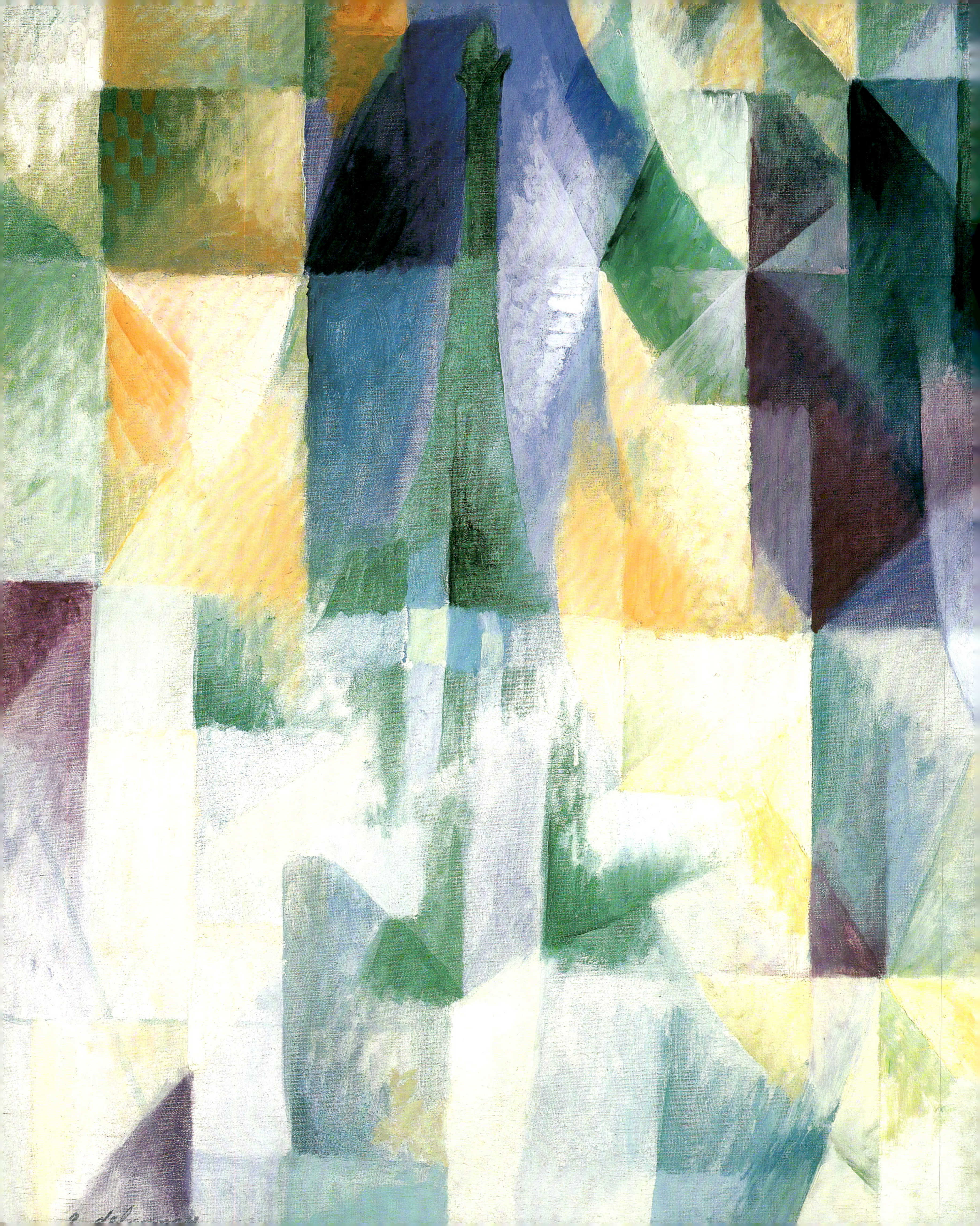

3

Notre-Dame and the Eiffel Tower

To contrast the numerous painted images of Notre-Dame and the Eiffel Tower is an illuminating way of analysing how painters represented the inner city of Paris. Each great building is not only a topographical feature, a monumental object dominating the urban spaces around it, but it is also steeped in values and associations, those intended by its constructors and those which have since accrued. Notre-Dame, the metropolitan cathedral of Paris, can be seen as the embodiment of eternal spiritual values, as an image of historical continuity, rock solid since the Middle Ages and witness to the human dramas of centuries. By contrast, the Eiffel Tower proffers different values, those of modernity and technology, the triumph of human design and engineering skills over the natural forces of wind and gravity. The cathedral was constructed over three centuries, between about 1150 and 1450, the gradual erection and embellishment of natural materials, of wood and stone, decorated with glass. By contrast, the tower was put up in just over two years, its iron skeleton scrupulously designed and manufactured in advance, the foundations begun on 28 January 1887 and the tricolour hoisted at the pinnacle on 31 March 1889.[1]

Archetypes of religion and tradition on the one hand and industry and progress on the other, Notre-Dame and the Eiffel Tower nevertheless shared for the painter and scanner of the urban panorama the status of landmark in the grey sea of the Parisian roofscape. Notre-Dame had gradually lost the dominance it must have had in the Middle Ages over the city's skyline, to the towers of the Louvre, to Soufflot's Panthéon, most recently to Garnier's Opéra, opened in 1875, but it was Eiffel's tower, some four kilometres away and almost exactly due west, that most insistently challenged the cathedral's authoritative presence, not least because its single thrust of criss-cross ironwork contrasted so abruptly with the squat stone volumes of the church. What concerns us here is the significance of each building for painters and the extent to which the values they embodied might be articulated on canvas. Were such values inevitably suggested by images of cathedral or tower, or could they be avoided, abbreviated, even replaced by purely pictorial concerns?

During the Second Empire, immediately preceding our period, Notre-Dame had featured regularly in the urban views of independent painters concerned with the modern urban scene. Both the Dutchman Jongkind and Stanislas Lépine painted the cathedral on a number of occasions. In their images, often showing the east end seen from upriver, Notre-Dame is both given a prominence with its unmistakable silhouette set against the skyline and yet also elided with the city by the tonal scheme of the painting. They are images of the ancient cathedral within the modern changing city; a Jongkind canvas of 1864 shows Notre-Dame itself undergoing alteration, clad in the scaffolding of Viollet-le-Duc's renovations,[2] and his views, like Lépine's **[51]**, couch the great cathedral in a cityscape of busy quays and river traffic, balancing its spiritual solidity against the momentum of modern commerce.

The cathedral was an inevitable focal point in any history or guidebook, and the tone of descriptions was conventionally reverential. 'One would be powerless to translate the intimate union of emotion and matter with which the pious and artistic genius of the Middle Ages composed this perfect ensemble', wrote Saint-Juirs typically in 1890. 'In this exceptional edifice, everything rises towards God. It is a sculpted hymn, it is a canticle, a chorus both gentle and powerful in strophes of perfect pitch. There is not a detail of its architecture which does not unite in this triumphant effect and add to its harmony'.[3] This emphasis on Notre-Dame as a religious monument was of special significance to Catholic artists towards the end of the century, especially given the long drawn-out struggle between Church and State over education, successive Third Republic governments trying to wrest influence over future generations from the ecclesiastical authorities.[4] For a Jesuit-educated *dévot* such as Edmond Aman-Jean the cathedral could only be an image of spiritual significance. At the Salon of 1886 he exhibited *Sainte Geneviève*, representing the patron saint of Paris dressed in blue and holding the city's emblem of a white barque, standing before a Notre-Dame silhouetted against the warm intensity of an evening sky **[56]**. Executed in a touch and adventurous colour range developed from earlier

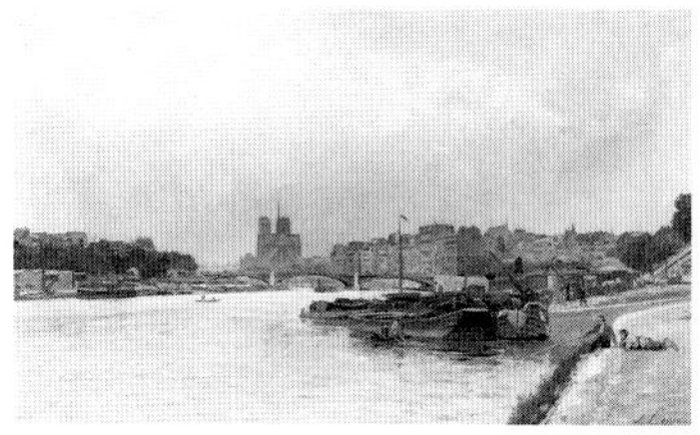

51
S. Lépine ***The Seine at the Pont d'Austerlitz*** **c.1865**
Paris, Musée Carnavalet

opposite
50
R. Delaunay
The Windows, No.3 **1912**
Winterthur, Kunstmuseum, Bequest 1973 of Clara and Emil Friedrich-Jezler

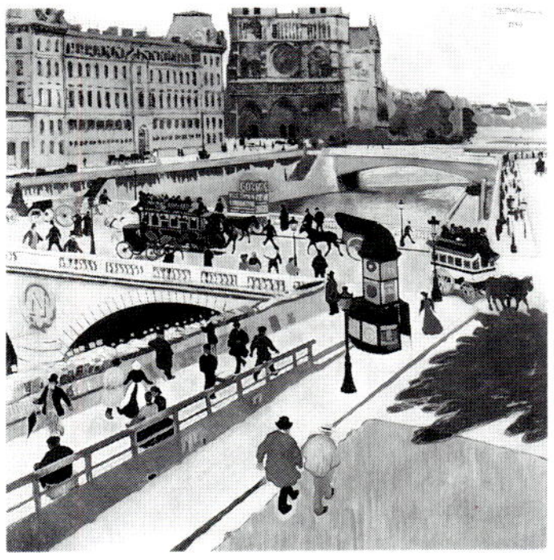

52
J. F. Willumsen
Notre-Dame and the Quais 1890
Frederikssund, Willumsens Museum

53
L. Lévy-Dhurmer
Notre-Dame in Winter c.1900? (detail)
Private Collection

experimental essays with his fellow student Seurat, *Sainte Geneviève* has a consciously *naïf* quality to the drawing reminiscent of Puvis de Chavannes. Aman-Jean did not neglect the quotidian, the commercial, in a view taken from much the same vantage point as that used by Lépine, but the assimilation of the barges into the unified simplicity of his cityscape is surely intended to suggest the protection of modern Paris under the eternal aegis of her patron saint. Such a deployment of Notre-Dame in an allegory of moral and spiritual import was by no means a new development; Aman-Jean's and Seurat's teacher at the Ecole des beaux-arts, Henri Lehmann, had used the motif in his mural *Law prevailing over Force*, painted for the Faculty of Law at the Sorbonne in 1872–3.[5] Notre-Dame appears also in the fictional painting by Claude Lantier, the tragic artist-hero of Zola's novel *L'Oeuvre*, published in 1886. Against a historic roofscape of the île de la Cité Lantier sets a female nude signifying modern Paris, an imaginary composition similar in design to Aman-Jean's actual canvas, though evidently more sensual than spiritual in allusion.

If images such as those by Lépine and Aman-Jean required Notre-Dame to be easily identifiable as part of a modern cityscape or religious allegory, it could also function quasi-legibly. As early as the Salon des Indépendants of 1884 Dubois-Pillet exhibited a pastel, now lost, of 'great delicacy with the carcase of Notre-Dame scarcely indicated in the background'.[6] This was probably a naturalistic study of fog, but for other artists of the Symbolist generation such a device was used less to study atmospheric effects than to conjure up a mood of mystery. Lucien Lévy-Dhurmer represented the cathedral shrouded in mist on a number of occasions [**53**]. Notre-Dame's very celebrity allowed it to be recognised despite its reduction almost to a cipher in an exquisite play of close values. Apse, *flèche* and towers rise above the fog, but the river and quays are scarcely visible to provide a plinth for the great building. The spectator's position is undefined, and modern elements make no intrusion; thus Notre-Dame is rendered as a timeless and ethereal presence. Such effects were also sought in representations of the cathedral's interior; in 1893 Paul Helleu, for one, was praised in the Symbolist press for his *Notre-Dame de Paris*, 'mysteriously lit by the soft, diffuse light which filters through the rose-windows'.[7]

Parallel to this consciously evocative mode ran an apparently more documentary vein. If painters in the 1870s and 1880s had made little of the cathedral – it has no place, for instance, in the Impressionist canon – during the 1890s it gained a new prominence. Notre-Dame was represented by foreigners and Frenchmen alike. The Dane Willumsen chose it for his first major canvas on settling in Paris in 1890, and the Norwegian Thaulow for one of his submissions to the Salon du Champ-de-Mars in 1893 [**52**, **54**]. Willumsen elected for a vantage point looking down on two promenaders on the quai des Grands Augustins, a motif which draws one's eye in a zigzag

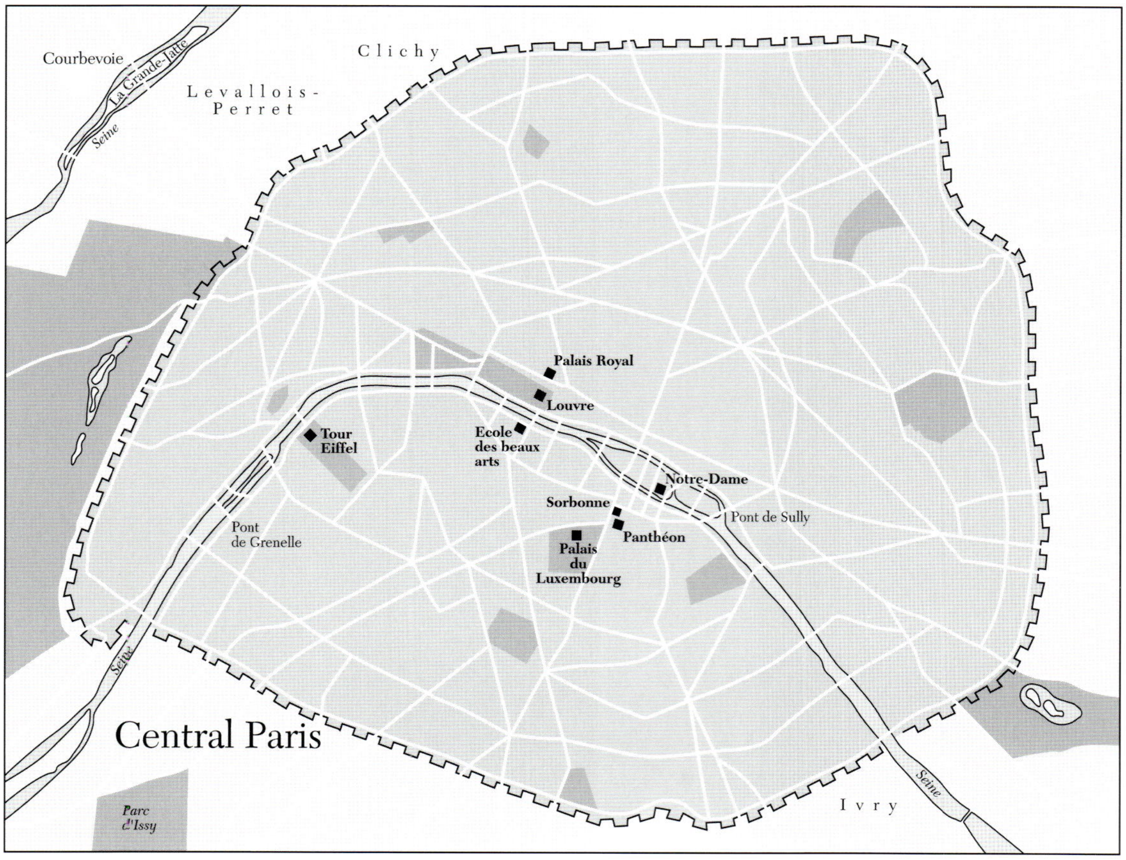

up the *quai*, across the pont Saint-Michel, along the opposite *quai* to the foot of Notre-Dame, the towers of which are cropped by the upper edge of the canvas. Thaulow took an exciting vantage point upstream, looking over the dangerous currents of a swollen Seine and along the piers of a wooden footbridge which linked the quai Henri IV and the île St Louis.[8] The perspective carries up the quai de Béthune to terminate abruptly with the silhouette of the cathedral against the grey December sky. Viewing Notre-Dame from opposite cardinal points, both pictures use its mass as a pictorial buffer, as the culmination of their composition's trajectory. Whether these painters considered it significant that they brought their images of the people and pacey perspectives of modern Paris to an end at the great cathedral or whether it was merely convenient to lead the eye towards a recognisable landmark remains open to question, though certainly Notre-Dame was a commercial motif. In 1896 Jean-François Raffaëlli painted a number of views from different angles, all on the same size canvas. Two from the south-east were bought immediately by the Musée du Luxembourg, the French national collection of modern art, and by the Musées royaux des beaux-arts in Brussels.[9] Another of this group viewed the *parvis* in front of the western façade [**55**] from street level, perhaps the Republican artist's tactic to incorporate the diverse Parisian citizenry and the various elements of modern street furniture – gas lamp and public urinal – as a secular, even democratic, presence in contrast to the monument.

Possibly the most frequently used viewpoint was that from the *quais* on the left bank, looking over the river to the twin towers, three great windows and triple portals of the west façade. The American draughtsman Joseph Pennell, for one, commissioned by the *Century Magazine* in 1893 to produce drawings of French religious architecture, specifically chose the quai des Grands Augustins 'because of the view of the Cathedral'.[10] Dubois-Pillet had taken a studio at 19 quai Saint-Michel in 1884; Matisse moved into the same building in February 1899, staying until 1907, while Marquet lived there too.[11] Whether any of these painters chose the location specifically for the view of Notre-Dame we do not know. The first to devote a significant group of canvases to the view was Maximilien Luce, hitherto associated with very different views of Paris's proletarian *quartiers*. The dozen he produced in 1899–1900 were made as he was gradually shifting from strict Neo-Impressionism to a looser touch. This freer play of the brush encouraged Luce to experiment with different effects of light and atmosphere. As he wrote to Henri-Edmond Cross in late 1899: 'It's incredibly beautiful. I'm doing piles of studies and will try to make use of them for some larger canvases'.[12] Luce responded particularly to changes in the lighting of the motif, using shadow and illumination literally to order his compositions. The largest of these [**57**] is seen in late afternoon light, the sun's last rays only catching the cathedral and the upper storeys of the surrounding houses. The shadow in which the

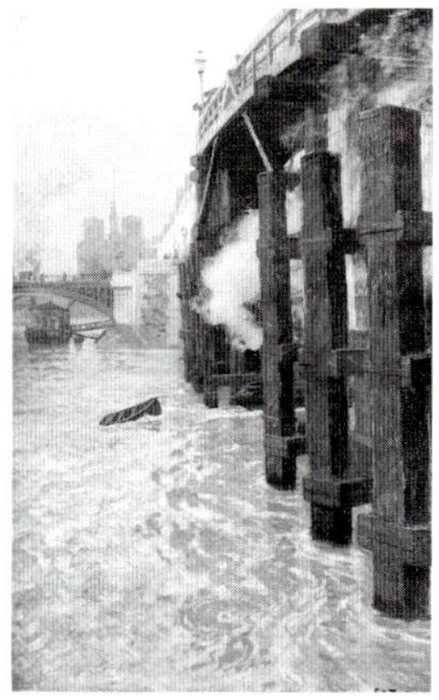

54
F. Thaulow
The Seine in December 1893
Sweden, Per Wästberg

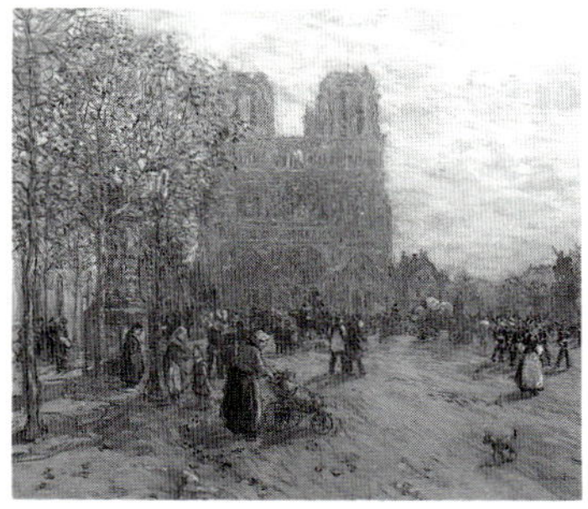

55
J. -F. Raffaëlli
Place du Parvis, Notre-Dame *c.*1896
Boston, Museum of Fine Arts,
The Henry C. and Martha B. Angell Collection

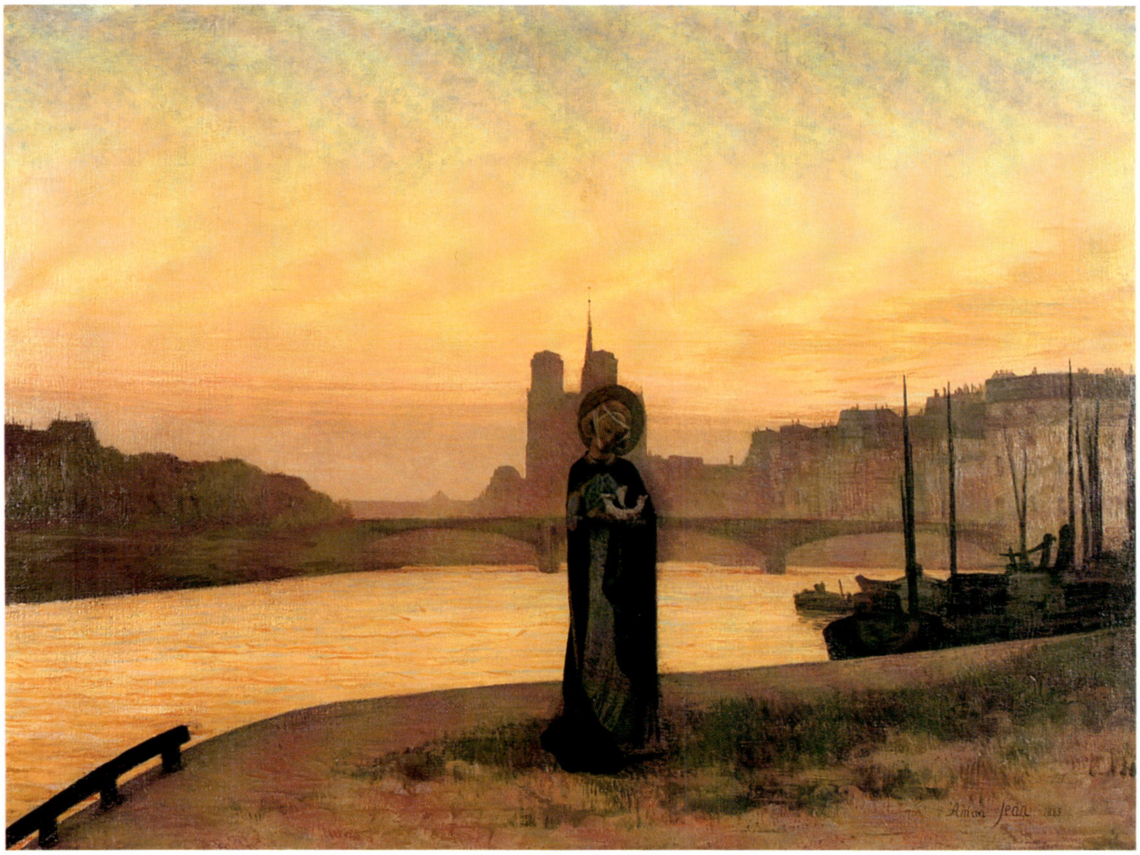

56
E. Aman-Jean
Sainte Geneviève before Paris 1885
Brest, Musée municipal

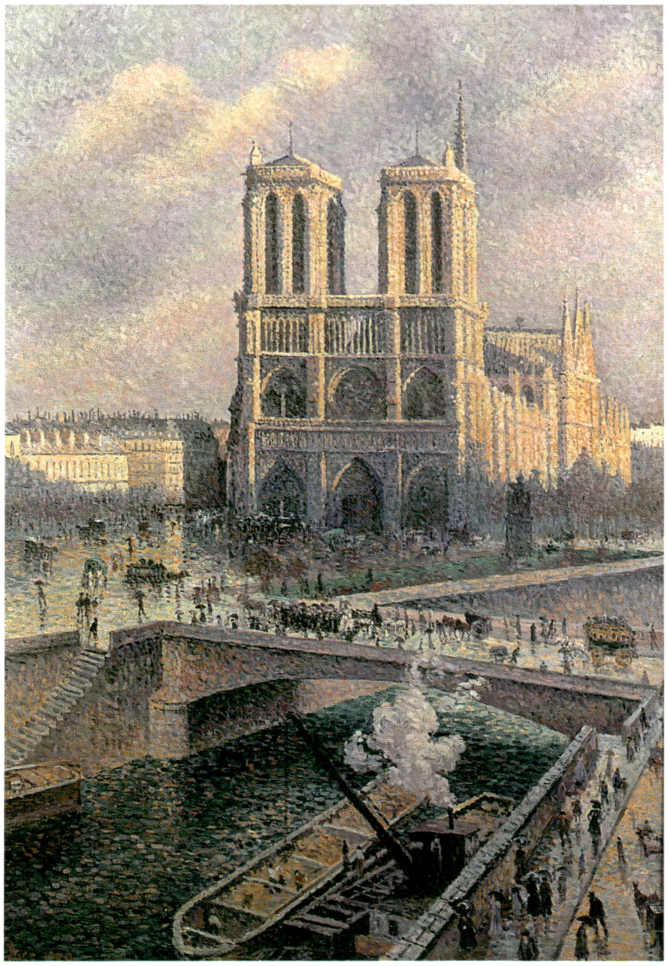

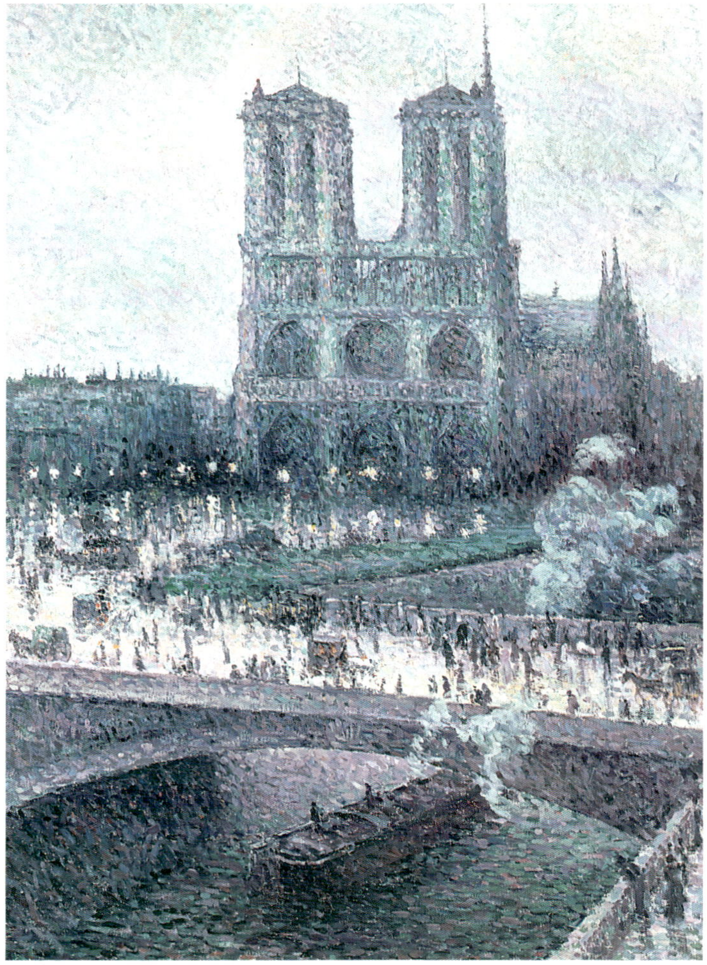

colour plates left to right

57
M. Luce
Notre-Dame 1900
Private Collection

58
M. Luce
Notre-Dame *c.*1900
San Diego Museum of Art, Gift of Ambassador & Mrs Maxwell Gluck

59
H. Matisse
Notre-Dame *c.*1900
London, Tate Gallery

60
A. Marquet
Notre-Dame under Snow *c.*1910
Paris, Musée Carnavalet

rest of the composition is couched covers the lower half of the canvas, starting at the doors of Notre-Dame. It thus serves as an implicit base of secondary violets and greens, above which stands the sculptural mass of the cathedral, starkly modelled in the strong light. In another version Luce chose a later hour [**58**], but still divided the composition along the base of Notre-Dame, here using the illumination of a gently irregular line of gas-lamps, their glow reflected on the rainy paving, to suggest the division. In another letter to Cross, written in early 1900, Luce explained: 'I'm still grinding away at Notre-Dame. I would like to do ceremonies, marriages, people coming and going, the crowd, in a word – Paris'.[13] Luce's fascination with the *parvis* of Notre-Dame as a stage on which the spectacle of modern urban life was performed is evident in both these canvases. If this is more immediately apparent in the late afternoon picture, with its steam crane, omnibuses, and the funeral procession making its slow way across the Petit Pont, it is still evident in the other; even as twilight falls crowds continue to mill and a barge makes its way up river. As one would expect from a working-class artist deeply committed to the Left, Luce's eye for the social activity of the city never allows these paintings to give way to visual atmospherics or reverie. And yet for all his anarchist ideology, these images centre on Notre-Dame, with its associations of ecclesiastical hierarchy; the zigzag play of the *quais* and the tense arch of the bridge exert pictorial pressure up towards the cathedral, which dominates the skyline. Perhaps this was not a contradiction on Luce's part. He clearly found the motif visually satisfying to his own *sensation*, and he may have shared with his friend and fellow anarchist Camille Pissarro a fascination with the Gothic, which he saw as truly French and full of '*sensation vitale*'.[14]

It is more difficult to determine why Matisse and Marquet chose Notre-Dame as a motif. Matisse seems to have used it as a vehicle for experimentation with touch and colour. Thus the version in the Tate Gallery [**59**], made about 1900, contrasts the dense facture and deep tones of the river with the brushier, warmer sky; the larger Buffalo painting of 1902 [**61**] explores broad planes and a more gestural handling; Stockholm's canvas made about 1904–5 plays off a dabbed touch against insistent scarlet scaffolding, and so on. It would seem that Notre-Dame supplied a verity with which Matisse could essay painterly procedures, and that his interest in it as a monument was minimal. Indeed, in such paintings the building itself is scarcely identifiable, but merely rendered as three blocks, two vertical and one horizontal. Nor does Matisse give much attention to the traffic of the city.

Although they were long-standing colleagues and working from the same building, Marquet chose to paint Notre-Dame in a manner significantly different from Matisse. Marquet tackled the *quai* motif over a number of years. The view of the cathedral now in Pau was exhibited at the Salon des Indépendants of 1905, and by 1913 the critic of *Art et décoration* was complaining of the 'monotony' of such motifs.[15] Over the years Marquet took various viewpoints, perhaps looking down sharply on the motif or representing it from a lower position but on a canvas of horizontal format. What these paintings have in common is a wintry austerity, suggesting that it was Marquet's habit to make such images cyclically over the winter months, before setting out on provincial campaigns in the spring and summer. Images of flood [16] and snow, they deploy starkly simplified forms and subdued tones of ochre and grey. But for all their apparent dearth of colour and animation, the best of these paintings – such as that in the Musée Carnavalet [**60**] – have an economy of touch and daring use of bare canvas which effectively conjure up the damp luminosity of a northern European winter. Such pictures won him a substantial reputation for 'his urban landscapist's vision'.[17] J.-C. Holl, in an important survey of recent painting published in 1912, chose to see Marquet less as a painter of city life – 'man is nothing but a shadow and a statistic' – than as a painter of mood: 'these large surfaces, this murky green water, these buffed, velvety *quais*, and these skies speak an intense, doleful language'.[18] To take such an essentially Symbolist line may underestimate Marquet's eye for the urban scene; his views are always populated, however discreetly, with an appropriately purposeful staffage, bringing them closer to those of Lépine or Luce than to those of Matisse. Marquet's images of Notre-Dame seem subtly to occupy a middleground between the modern, the painterly, and the mysterious. They show that such a position was tenable even in the climate of intense pictorial experimentation during the early 1910s.

Then Matisse, returning to the Notre-Dame motif, reduced the cathedral to geometric blocks, rendered translucent by scraped and textured surfaces, and the urban architecture to simple angles and arcs [**62**]. At much the same time Dunoyer de Segonzac represented the motif with similar simplicity but markedly contrasting opacity, building up the volumes in dense textures and sonorous abuttments of browns and blacks [**63**]. Yet even with images treated with such apparent painterly concern, one wonders whether the painters were entirely ignoring the symbolic associations of Notre-Dame, hovering 'over the city like an emanation of its past', as Holl put it. It was a site, he continued, resonant with 'the restless atavism of our equivocal modernity where love of the past combines with the provocative image of modern ostentation'.[19] By so ruthlessly reducing their motif, Matisse, Segonzac and to a lesser extent Marquet played down the momentum of the modern metropolis the better to concentrate on creative concerns. But may it not have been the very nature of that motif, a building so axiomatically Parisian, so redolent of continuity and the highest human values,

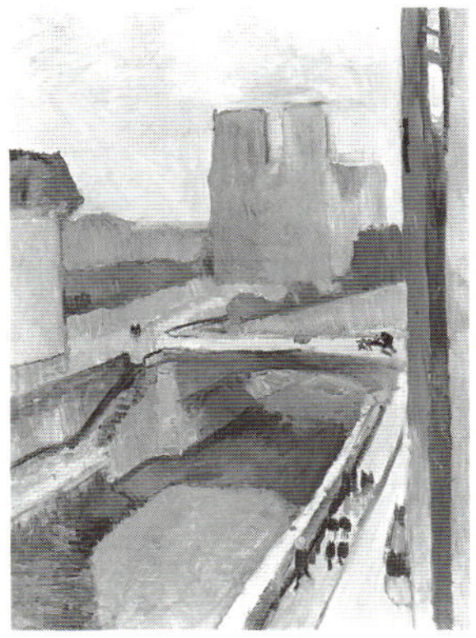

61
H. Matisse
Notre-Dame, Late Afternoon 1902
Buffalo, Albright-Knox Art Gallery, Gift of Seymour H. Knox

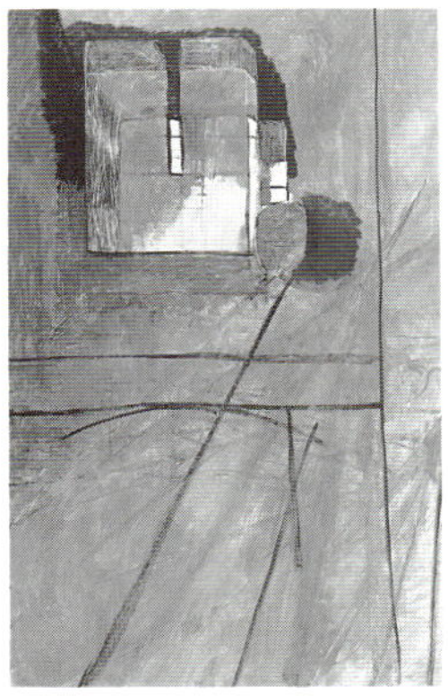

62
H. Matisse
Notre-Dame 1914
New York, Museum of Modern Art

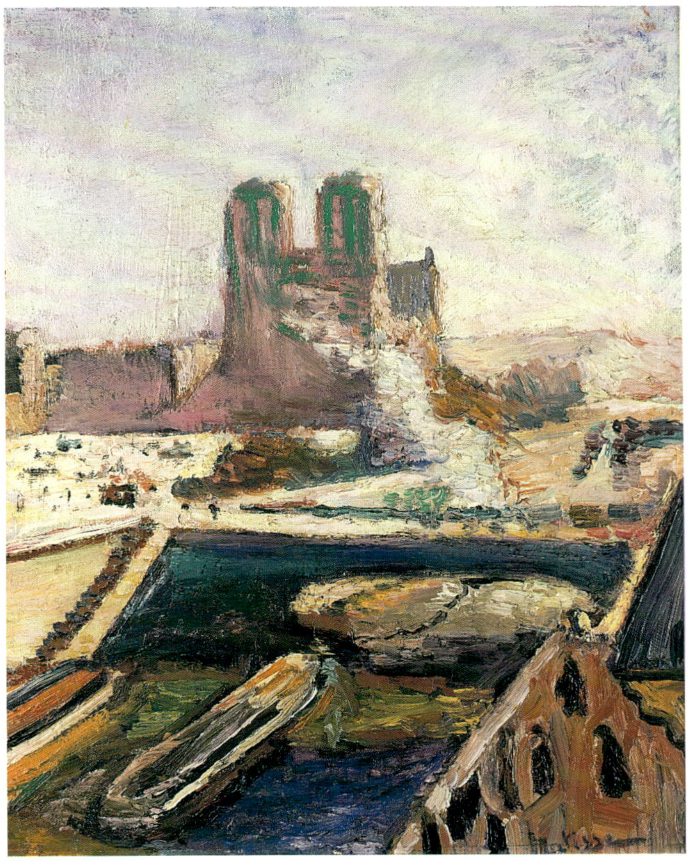

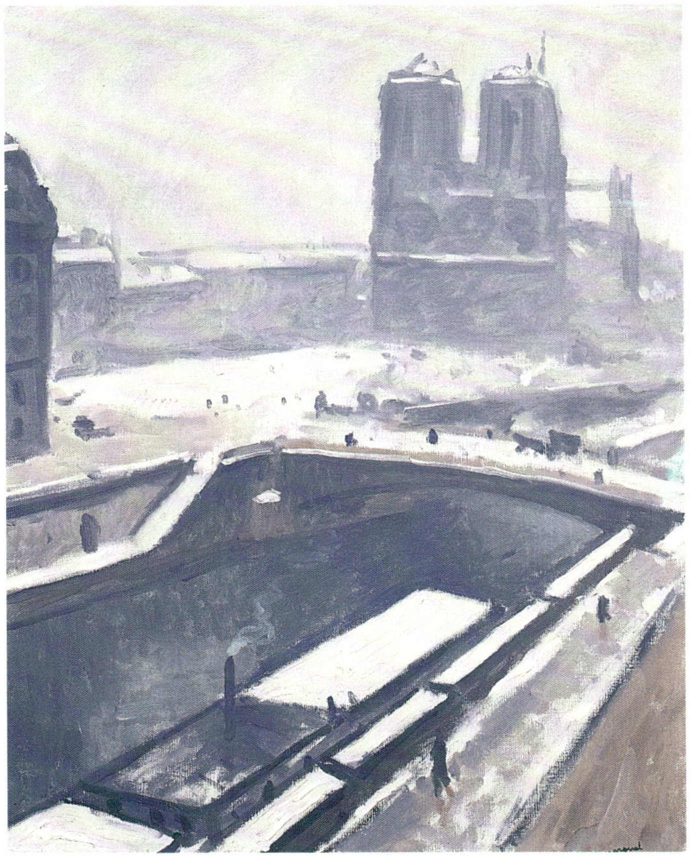

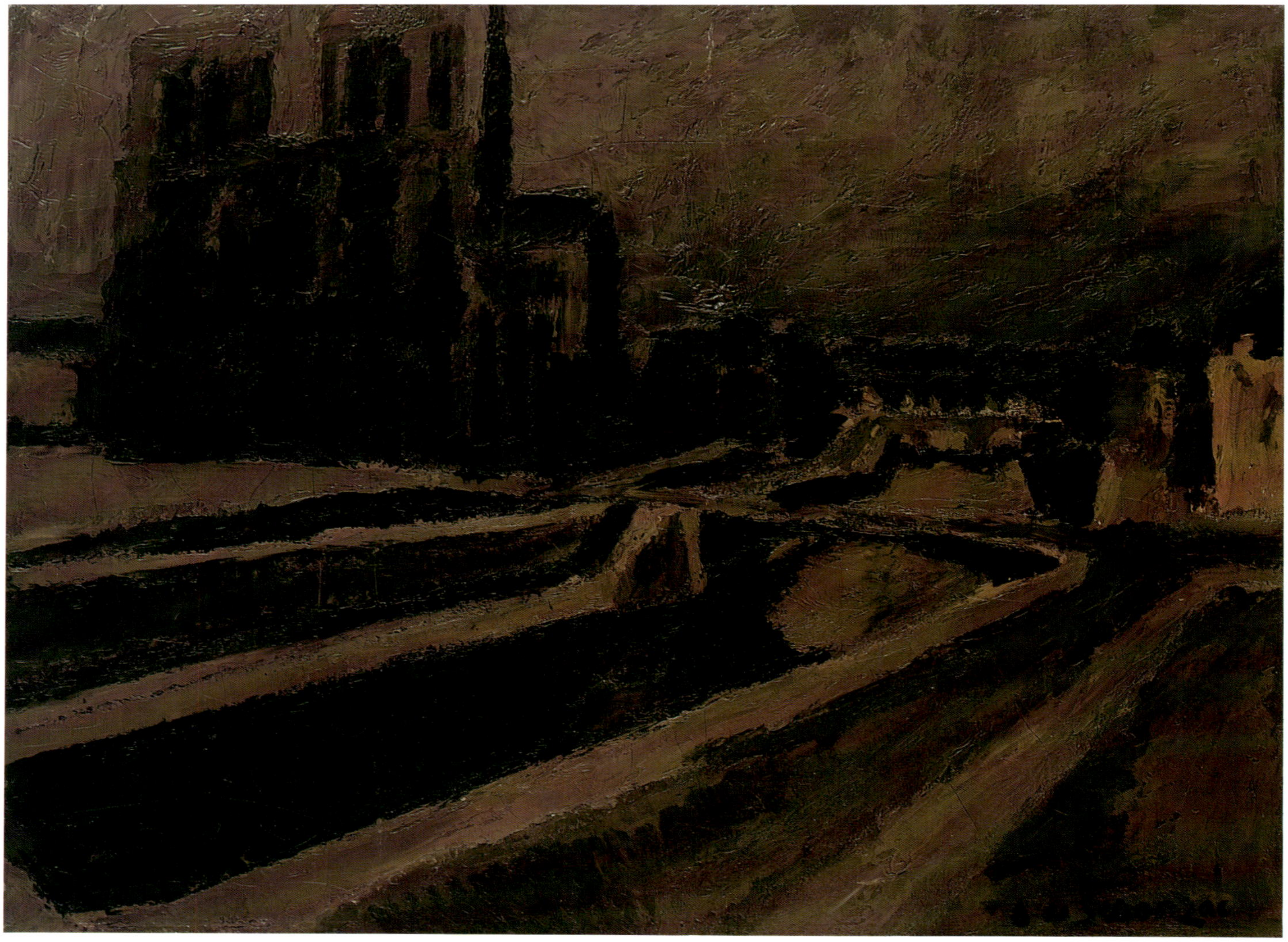

63
A. Dunoyer de Segonzac
Notre-Dame 1913
Ohio, Columbus Museum of Art,
Gift of Howard D. and Babette L. Sirak

that permitted such an unflinching focus and, paradoxically, such liberties?

Notre-Dame served different generations of artists as a foil against more modern buildings not only when represented as a motif within the cityscape but also when it was used as a vantage point for panoramas over Paris. The famous sculptures and gargoyles on the twin towers easily identified the spectator's position. Auguste Lepère placed them at his left shoulder in a view to the east [**64**], overlooking the wharves and warehouses of commercial Bercy. Etienne Moreau-Nélaton, great collector of Delacroix, Corot and the Impressionists but also a talented painter, chose to work on the towers of Notre-Dame during the winter of 1897-8 at a time when he was mourning the disastrous deaths of both his wife and mother in the fire at the charity bazaar on the rue Jean Goujon the previous May.[20] One of these paintings looks westwards, over the quai Saint-Michel, past identifiable landmarks such as the unequal towers of Saint-Sulpice and the dome of Les Invalides, to the distant Eiffel Tower silhouetted against the dusk [**65**]. We can only guess whether this sombre cityscape was simply a therapeutic diversion during his bereavement, or whether the pious Moreau-Nélaton's faith was so shaken by this tragedy

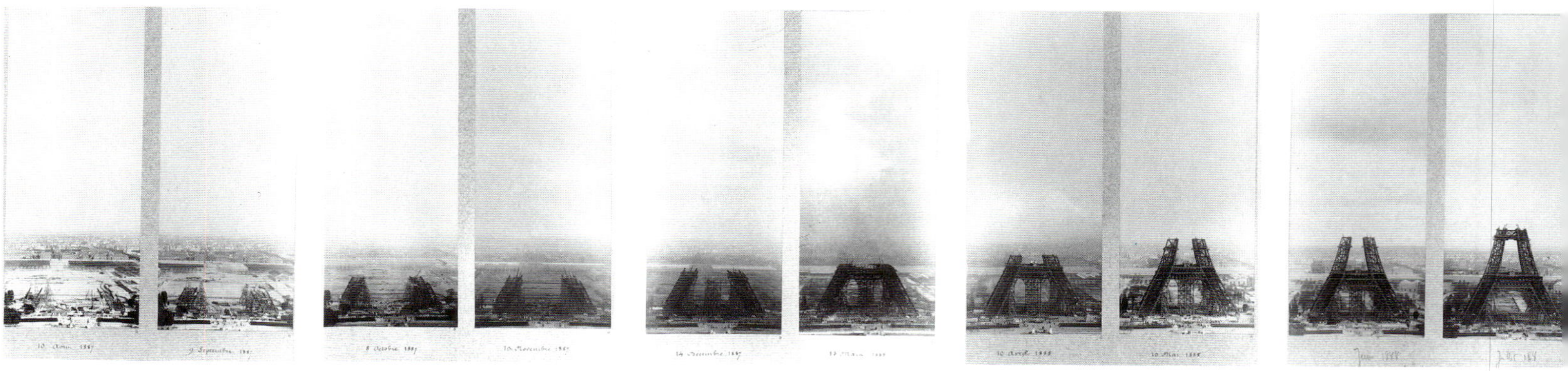

that his seclusion on the towers of Notre-Dame and his meditation on the rivalry between the churches and that secular totem on the Parisian skyline formed part of the reshaping of his inner world. Certainly it was a commonplace in guidebooks to compare the greater height of the Eiffel Tower to the cathedral spires of Ulm, Cologne or Rouen,[21] and the pitting of Notre-Dame against the 300 metre tower was by no means just a physical rivalry.

Parisians a century ago debated the merits or otherwise of new buildings in various styles and materials intruding upon the familiar and elegant fabric of the city as fiercely as they do today. In 1905, for instance, Camille Mauclair pleaded for pluralism and diversity in urban buildings; while he argued against certain contemporary tastes, notably pseudo-classicism and polychromy, he wondered why people were upset by the contrasts visible during the twenty-minute ride from the boulevard des Italiens to Notre-Dame, rather than being stimulated by the architectural antitheses.[22] The cathedral thus typified a building of timeless, unquestioned beauty against which new monuments must be judged. That it stood too for spiritual values is clear from an illustration by Heidbrinck in the *Courrier français* of 1888 [**66**]. The precise meaning is not quite clear; perhaps the *savant* is attempting to explain Christian belief by the same rational procedures which built the tower, while the Virgin looks down unperturbed. Nevertheless, the image establishes a polarity, a rivalry indeed, between cathedral and tower, before the latter had even been completed. Nowhere is that challenge clearer than in an article, published as Eiffel's tower was opened to the public in 1889, by Melchior de Vogüé, aristocrat, intellectual and translator of Tolstoy and Dostoyevsky. Here the Eiffel Tower makes an imaginary speech challenging and ridiculing the ancient church monuments of Paris: 'Old abandoned towers, nobody listens to you any longer. Don't you understand that the world has changed its pole and that now it turns on my iron axis? ... You were ignorance, I am science ... I no longer have need of your God, invented to explain a creation of which I know the laws. These laws suffice for me, they suffice for the spirits I have conquered from you and who will never turn back'.[23] The new giant of the Parisian skyline stood, by that account, four-square for science against religion.

The idea for the tower was not originally Eiffel's but that of two of his professional staff, Maurice Koechlin and Emile Nouguier. In 1884 they conceived the project as the centrepiece for the Universal Exhibition which, following the eleven year pattern eventually established by its predecessors of 1855, 1867 and 1878, would take place in 1889 and would have the particular purpose of celebrating the centenary of the French Revolution. Given a rival project by the architect Jules Bourdais, an official competition was held in 1886, and the site on the Champ-de-Mars was handed over to Eiffel and his winning team on 1 January 1887.[24] The scheme was not without significant opposition. On 14 February that year *Le Temps* published a letter signed by a distinguished group of cultural heavyweights, among them the composer Gounod, the architect Garnier, the writers Sardou, Coppée, Leconte de Lisle and Maupassant, and the artists Gérôme, Bonnat, Bouguereau and Meissonier. It argued that 'the Paris of sublime Gothic' should not be defaced by 'a vertiginously ridiculous Tower, like a gigantic black factory chimney', fearing that for 'twenty years we will see stretching over the entire city, still quivering with the genius of many centuries, ... the odious shadow of the odious column of bolted ironwork'.[25] These objections, made on the grounds of taste, pitted intangible cultural, and implicitly spiritual, values against the physical presence of the new construction and its explicit modernity. A younger generation was inclined to sympathy for the new aesthetic embodied by the tower. The poet Jules Laforgue defended it under the banner *'Place aux jeunes!'*, countering – with ironic punctuation – in March 1887 that 'it will acquire its beauty (?) like the other *machines* of Paris', while, on its completion two years later the theatrical impresario Antoine acknowledged 'the grandeur of this first realization of the aesthetic of iron. There are some days when the tower takes on an admirable lightness and elegance in the Parisian atmosphere'.[26]

One of the objections of *Le Temps*'s correspondents was that the Eiffel Tower had no function. They miscalculated its effect on the public of the Universal Exhibition. There were thirty-two million visitors over

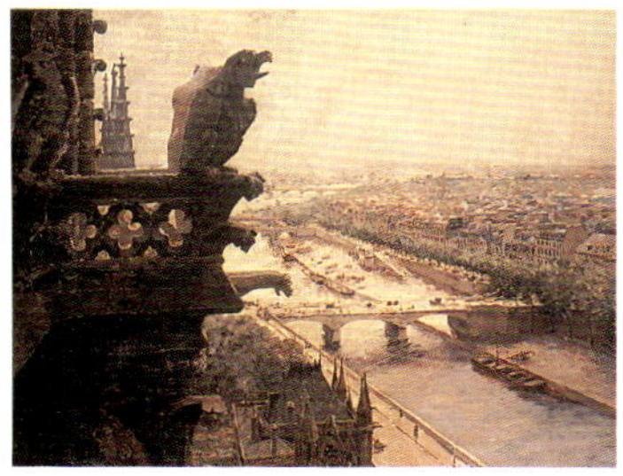

64
A. Lepère
View of Paris from the Gargoyles of Notre-Dame c.1900
Fontenay-le-Comte, Musée Vendéen

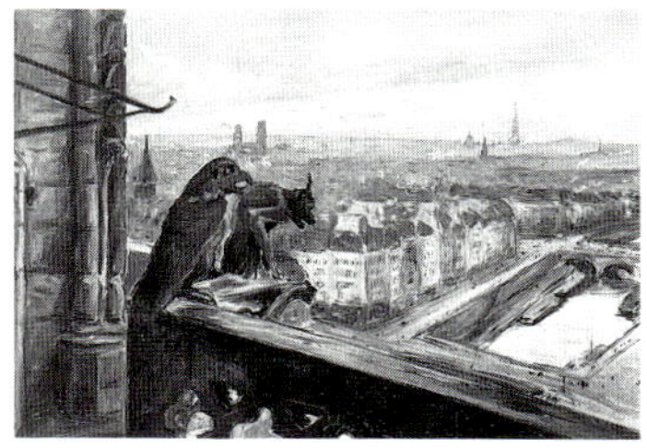

65
E. Moreau-Nélaton
The Great Beasts of Notre-Dame 1898
Private Collection

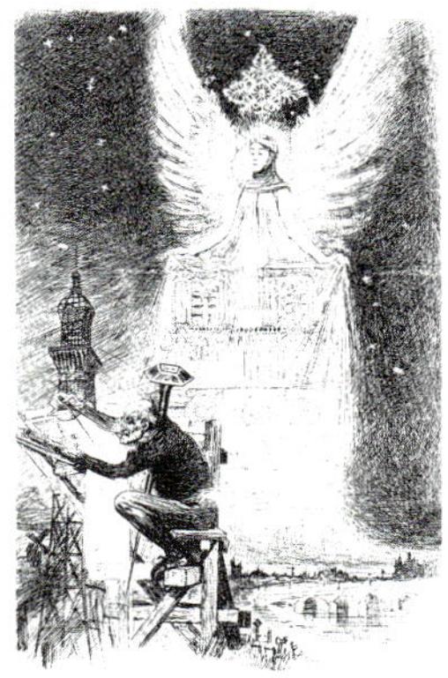

66
Heidbrinck ***Pauvre Savant!***
Drawing reproduced in *Le Courrier français*, 9 September 1888

67
Photo-sequence of the erection of the Eiffel Tower, 1887–9

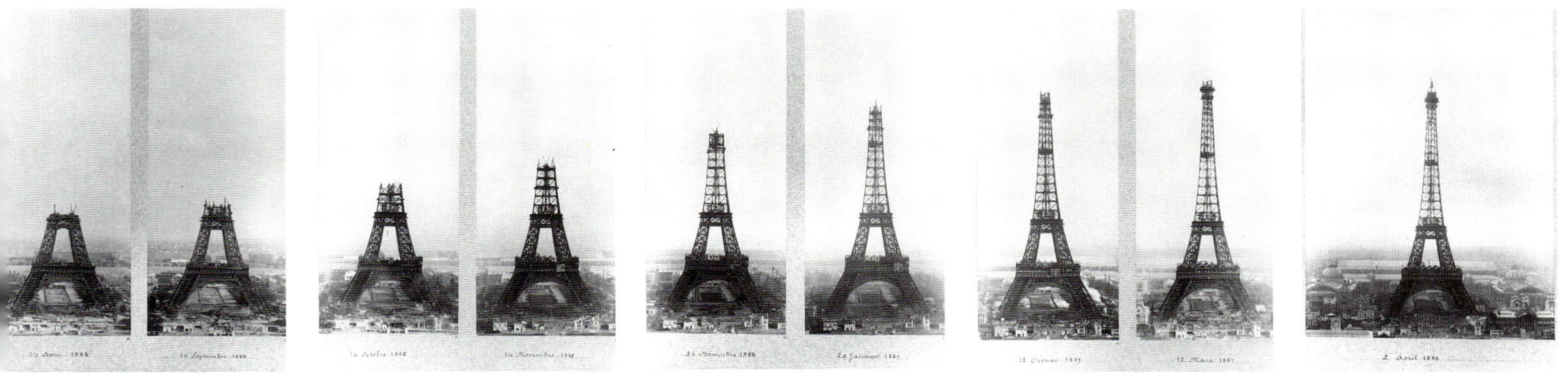

the summer of 1889, and two million of them ventured up the new construction to enjoy the exceptional new view it gave over the city; these visitors – 12,000 per day – all but paid for the building costs during the official exhibition period. Even for those who did not make the ascent the Eiffel Tower was unforgettable, the centrepiece, the talisman of the Exhibition. Miniature versions became the junk gift of the year: 'the *bibelot-roi*, what all the foreigners and provincials take home', it was reported, 'is the Eiffel Tower, the famous tower that illuminates Paris – immense or miniscule'.[27]

Artists too were fascinated by the Eiffel Tower. From the outset they recorded its elevation [**67**], responding to public curiosity by charting its growth in drawings for the illustrated press; the fashionable fortnightly *La Vie moderne*, for instance, published a drawing by Louis Moreno of one of the four supporting piles in October 1887 and the following February another by Louis Hayet showing the completion of the first platform.[28] As well as this business of documenting, artists also painted the tower's construction, for, as well as being something entirely new, it was a fascinating object visually, both when seen from a distance because of the way it altered the Parisian skyline, and from close to because of its intricate trellis-work of iron. It comes as no surprise that a painter of an older generation such as Lépine should choose to represent it from a distance in a more conventionally 'landscape' mode, while a younger painter – Hayet again – should focus on the building work itself.[29] Paul Delance's large painting of the Eiffel Tower nearing completion [**68**], signed in January 1889, and exhibited at the Universal Exhibition, succeeded in combining both approaches. Delance brushed his canvas broadly, his painterly energy echoing the industry of his motif. The winter atmosphere is subtly conveyed in the pearly blue-grey sky, with the clouds just breaking up, and the warm russets, pinks and browns of the stark cityscape. Trees have no presence here, and the painter's concern for the general effect led him to discount details such as figures. Nevertheless, Delance's canvas gives a powerful impression of business in hand, of unresolved work, with the rising steam from the machinery and the scaffolding around the buildings. The tower is set off-centre, its unfinished summit threatening to push out of the picture frame, giving a sense of its imminent completion and ultimate majesty, but also showing it as integral to its surroundings: an industrial achievment in a man-made environment. Nature, and the conventional raw materials of landscape such as sky and water, play second fiddle to technology.

The Eiffel Tower was inevitably a central image in artists' representations of the Universal Exhibition. In Jean Béraud's image of the Exhibition entrance [**69**]

68
P. Delance
The Champ-de-Mars, Paris, in January 1889 1889
Paris, Musée Carnavalet

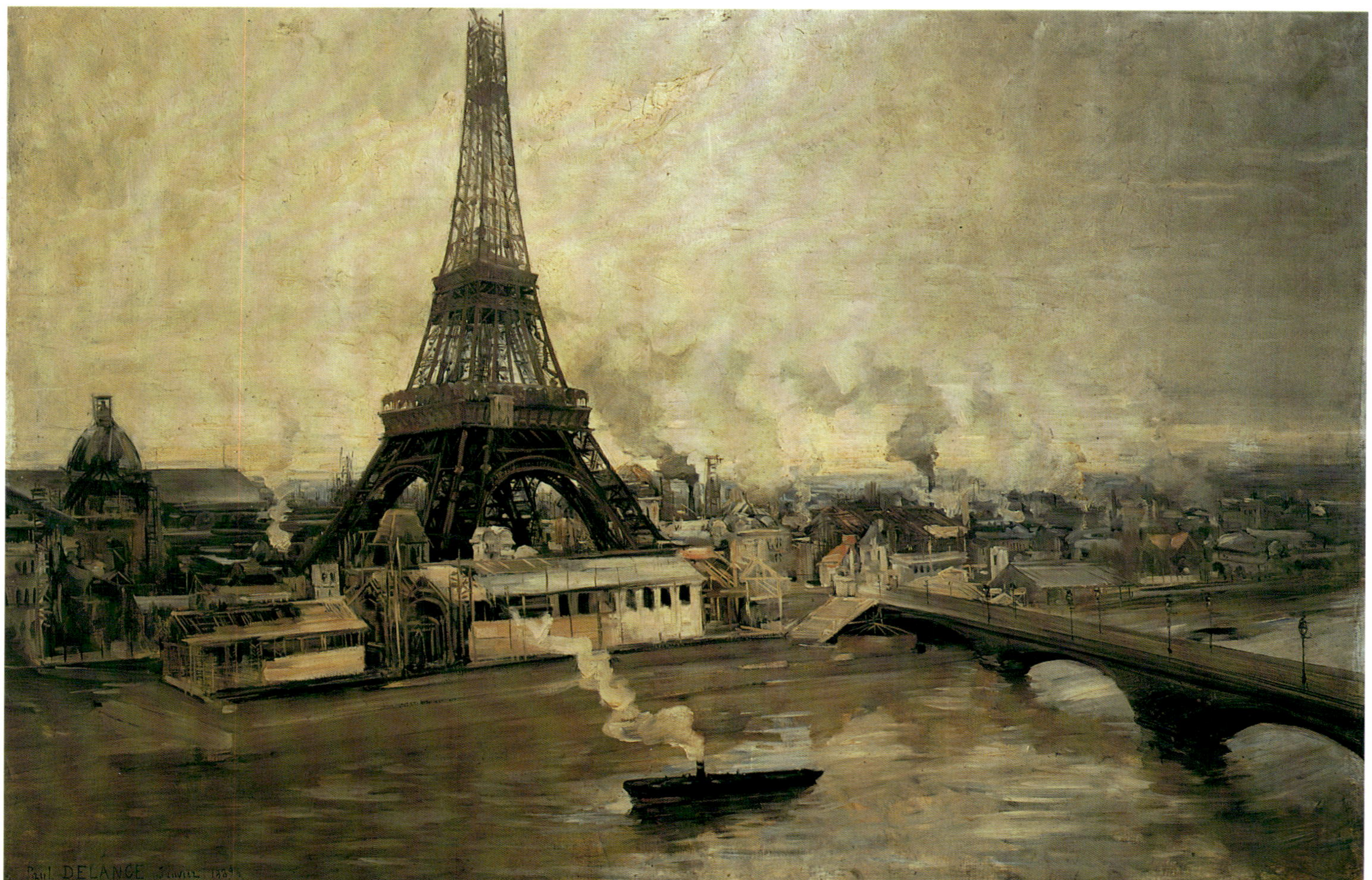

it is used as the salient vertical accent, thrusting up from an unbroken horizon of heads. The tower seems to be the magnet that draws in the crowd, while the bustling figures serve as a vibrating counterpoint, almost a plinth, to the suave and disciplined edifice. In fact Béraud carefully orchestrated this apparently spontaneous image, selecting his types to indicate a cross-section of the visitors: peasant couple accompanying rural *curé*, chic Parisian bourgeois, pestering urchins, the wealthy in their carriages, all following the new tramlines and the directions of the gendarme. It is an image of social harmony and shared purpose, under the aegis of the totemic Eiffel Tower flanked by tricolours.

This was a soothing fiction, for in fact the early months of 1889 had witnessed major political and economic problems. Popular support for General Boulanger, coming somewhat incoherently from both Right and Left, had almost led to a *coup d'état* that spring, but fortunately for the Republic the general's political sang-froid did not match his charisma, and the crisis defused with his self-exile to Brussels in April. The previous month had seen the suicide of Denfert-Rochereau, a leading financier, which led to panic-stricken crowds besieging the Bourse, fearful of a stockmarket crash.[30] The success of the Universal Exhibition, opened by President Carnot on 6 May, served the Third Republic well, as it diverted attention from the régime's precarious stability. By implication, then, Béraud's painting – ordered as an image of unanimity across the classes and of France's prosperity and progress – can be read as a demonstration of the artist's support for the Republic.

But if Béraud's painting adopted the tower as a unifying symbol, Camille Pissarro treated it, privately but explicitly, as an emblem of the negative power of the bourgeoisie. Like his friend Luce, Pissarro was an anarchist; he believed that the individual's innate goodness and talents were repressed by the essentially urban organisation of government, class and capitalism and would best prosper in freely structured rural co-operatives. This ideologically-based polarisation of city and country came to the fore in his work during 1889. That summer he visited the Universal Exhibition and was initially impressed by the site and buildings, writing to his English niece Esther Isaacson in July: 'When are you coming to Paris? … You must see the Eiffel Tower, which grabs everyone's attention!'.[31] But his attitude seems to have changed as he reflected on what he took the Exhibition to stand for. During the later months of 1889 Pissarro prepared an album of twenty-eight pen-and-ink drawings, executed in an unusually resolved and caricatural style, which he entitled *Turpitudes sociales*. At the end of the year Pissarro sent these images, attacking the greed and oppression of the capitalist middle-classes, to Esther, whom he was trying discreetly to inculcate with his anarchist views. The Eiffel Tower appears on the title page [**70**], and Pissarro describes the intended allegory to Esther: 'The first drawing represents a poor old philosopher … [who] gazes ironically at the sleeping city; he watches the radiant sun rising and by concentrating sees written in luminous letters the word Anarchy; the Eiffel Tower tries to hide the sun from the philosopher's view, but it is neither high nor large enough to disguise the star which illuminates us.'[32] For Pissarro the Eiffel Tower stood for the oppressive forces of capitalism and the bourgeois Republic; its domination of the cityscape echoed their domination of French society. If the *Turpitudes sociales* drawings represent the city as locus of corruption and oppression, the paintings which Pissarro was making of rural subjects in 1889 are sun-drenched landscapes in which peasant figures work in co-operative harmony within a bountiful nature. In 1889 Pissarro could only construct his ideal around rural imagery, while Paris, symbolised by the Eiffel Tower, represented its negative counterpart.[33] Thus the very symbol of unity for Béraud was the symbol of division for Pissarro.

The predominant associations of the Eiffel Tower were ones of modernity and progress. Eiffel himself, naturally enough, held it to be 'a symbol of power and difficulties overcome'.[34] Even the eccentric writer Villiers de l'Isle-Adam could not avoid that notion, although his fantasy of a second tower alongside the original, with a 25 metre high sculpture of a bourgeois in frock-coat and top-hat spanning them like a modern Colossus of Rhodes, representing Progress, was laced with heavy irony.[35] Most painters seem to have adopted the positive view, from Seurat's sparkling little panel made before the tower was completed [**74**] to Douanier Rousseau's canvas of a decade or so later [**73**]. Seurat's vision of the tower has it rising from the emphatically urban geometry below, a more distilled but ultimately similar conception to that of Delance. Rousseau too set it squarely above the illuminated nocturnal city, flanked by that other image of modernity to which the tower had been so unflatteringly compared in *Le Temps*, the factory chimney, and as the *point de vue* at the end of an embanked stretch of the Seine – a view that does not exist. Both Seurat and Rousseau were prepared to doctor the cityscape to have the Eiffel Tower read centrally, head on, as an icon of symmetry and order over the city.

Other images made in the tower's first decade or so – Signac's *Seine, Grenelle* of 1899 [**72**], Vallotton's *Yellow Sand and the Eiffel Tower* of two years later [**75**], Henri Rivière's panorama from Montmartre, one of the album of *Thirty-six Views of the Eiffel Tower* published in 1902 [**71**] – push it into a corner of the composition.

Such images raise ambiguities. One questions whether the tower was losing its fascination, being demoted, almost edited from the artist's image of Paris, or whether it remained – however marginal and insinuating – the dominant Parisian monument.

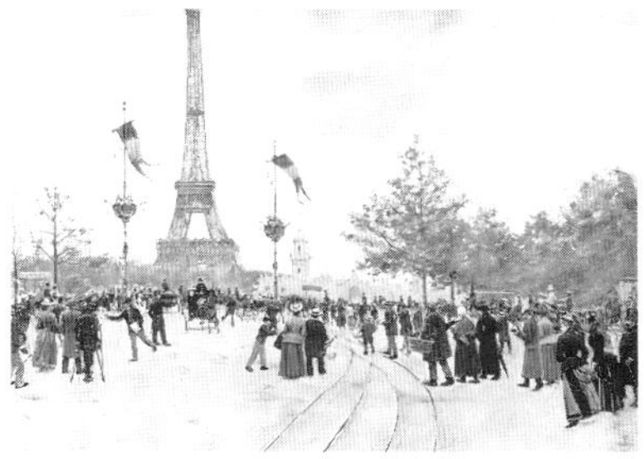

69
J. Béraud
The Entrance to the Universal Exhibition 1889
Paris, Musée Carnavalet

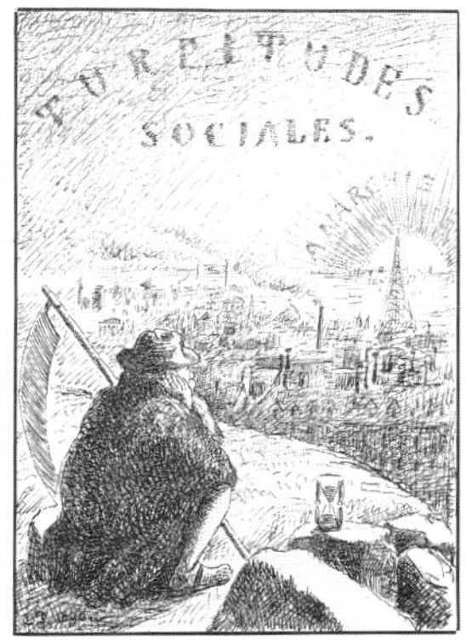

70
C. Pissarro
Turpitudes sociales: title page 1889
Geneva, Private Collection

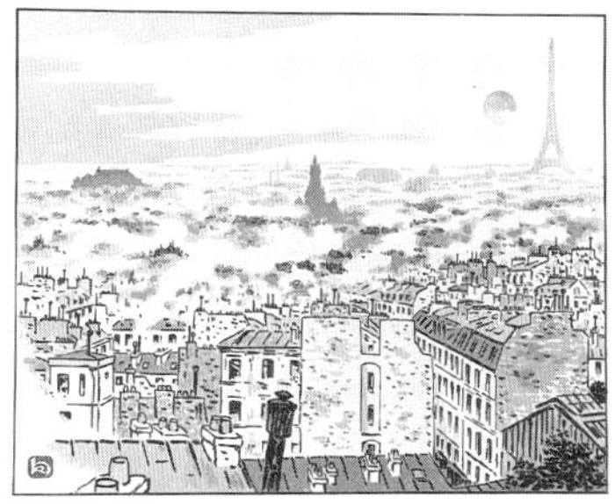

71
H. Rivière
Thirty-six Views of the Eiffel Tower 1902
New Brunswick, Jane Vorhees Zimmerli Art Museum

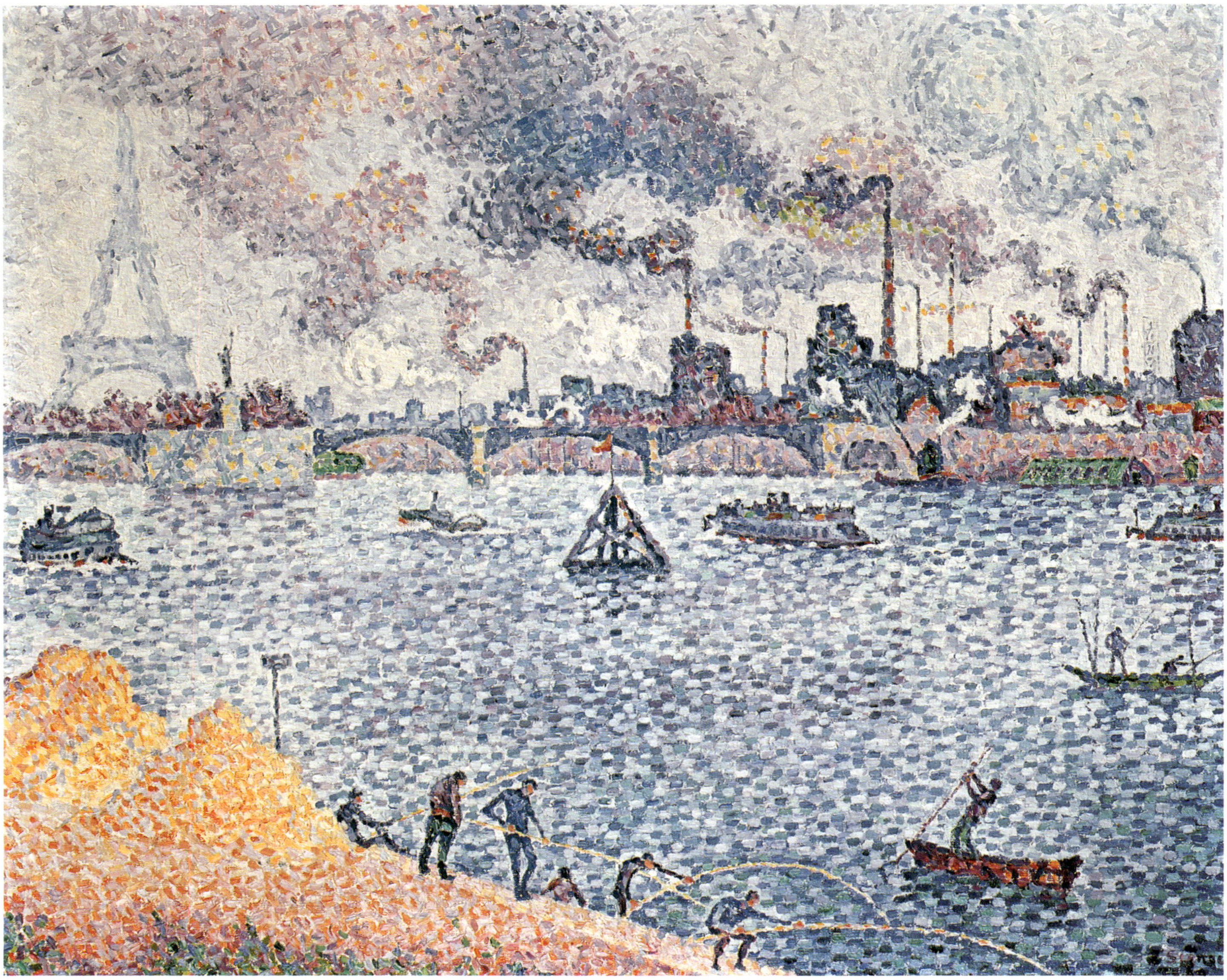

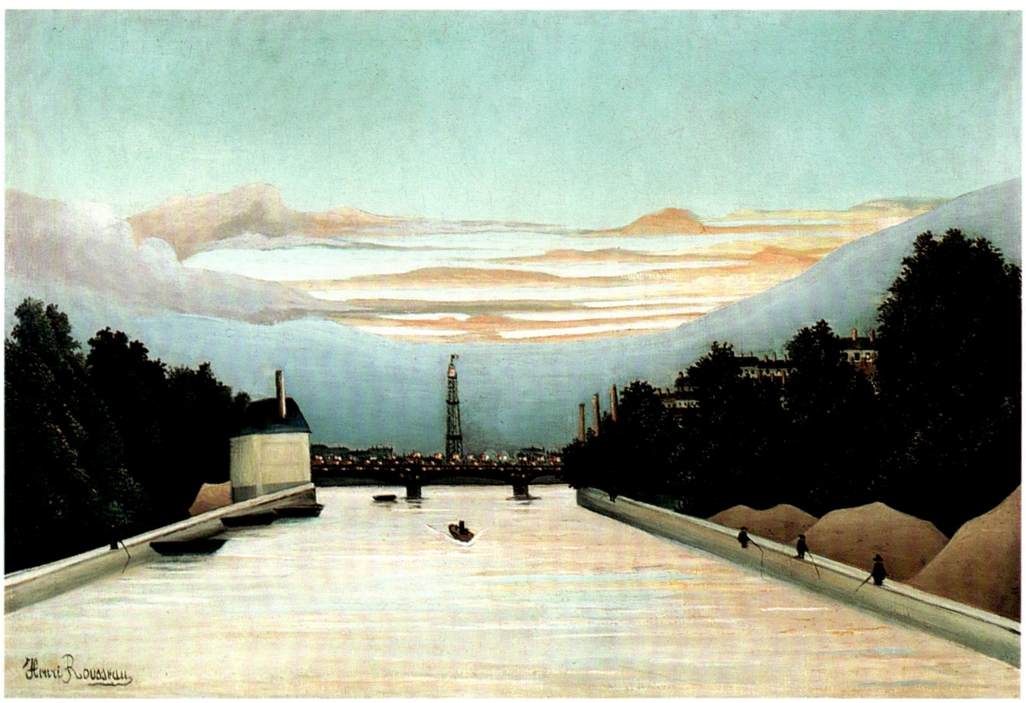

above
72
P. Signac
Seine, Grenelle 1899
Helsinki, private collection on loan to the Amos Andersonin Taideomuseo

right
73
H. Rousseau
The Eiffel Tower *c.*1898
Houston, Museum of Fine Arts, The John A. and Audrey Jones Beck Collection

opposite above
74
G. Seurat
The Eiffel Tower 1889
San Francisco, Fine Arts Museums William H. Noble Bequest Fund

opposite below
75
F. Vallotton
Yellow Sand and the Eiffel Tower 1901
Private Collection

There is ambiguity, too, in the relation of the tower to nature in such images. On the one hand nature might appear to be a mollifying force, curbing the tower's presence by the beauty of its effects, simplifying it in aerial perspective, shrouding it in mist, blurring it in haze. On the other it might appear that the 300 metre tower still protrudes emphatically but incongruously into the landscape artist's view, still imposes its vertiginous identity. But then these images are not strictly landscapes. They are cityscapes, and Signac, Vallotton and Rivière deliberately concerned themselves with views of houses, quays, roofs and bridges. Knowing that Signac and Vallotton shared Pissarro's anarchist beliefs, one might interpret their paintings as representations of the heartless man-made city. Signac's in particular, with its thicket of chimneys all but blotting out the sky with their blue smoke and its sluggish river punctuated by hurrying tugs and *bateaux-mouches*, could be read in such a light, not least given an entry in his journal the year before this canvas was painted. Writing in December 1898 on his return to the capital from the Mediterranean, Signac dispiritedly employed the north-south polarity: 'What a sad awakening in Paris this morning. It's seven-thirty and it's not yet light; rain's falling and from our window I can only see miserable rooves and chimneys. And I remember waking up to lovely days at Saint-Tropez. In the beautiful golden light, the town appeared between the yellow leaves of the trees in the place des Lices and the gentle blue of the sea, the hills still in shadow covered with light mist … And instead of this Eiffel Tower, desolate in the rain, the spruce silhouette of Grimaud, bathed in sunlight, dominating the hazy plain'.[36] And yet his *Seine, Grenelle* may be read quite differently, and still consistently, with an anarchist position. For Signac offsets the backdrop of urban industry with a foreground scene of workmen fishing, suggesting that there is scope for individual interests, for community, within the city, that industry and its attendant machinery – so evident in this painting – have at least a positive outcome by permitting the proletariat leisure time and a degree of freedom. Such a reading might gather credence in view of Signac's juxtaposition of the Eiffel Tower and the reduced Statue of Liberty, sited at the end of the île des Cygnes just in front of the pont de Grenelle and inaugurated on 4 July 1889, a date of double significance for the United States and France.[37] But unresolved questions such as whether Signac planned that juxtaposition of the image of progress with the image of freedom or whether their alignment in his canvas was just a matter of topographical coincidence serve pertinently to remind us of the ambivalences involved in reading the motifs of the cityscape.

The Eiffel Tower remained the talisman of the Parisian skyline until the First World War. Chagall, arriving in Paris from Vitebsk in 1911, was immediately struck by the tower. One of his paintings from

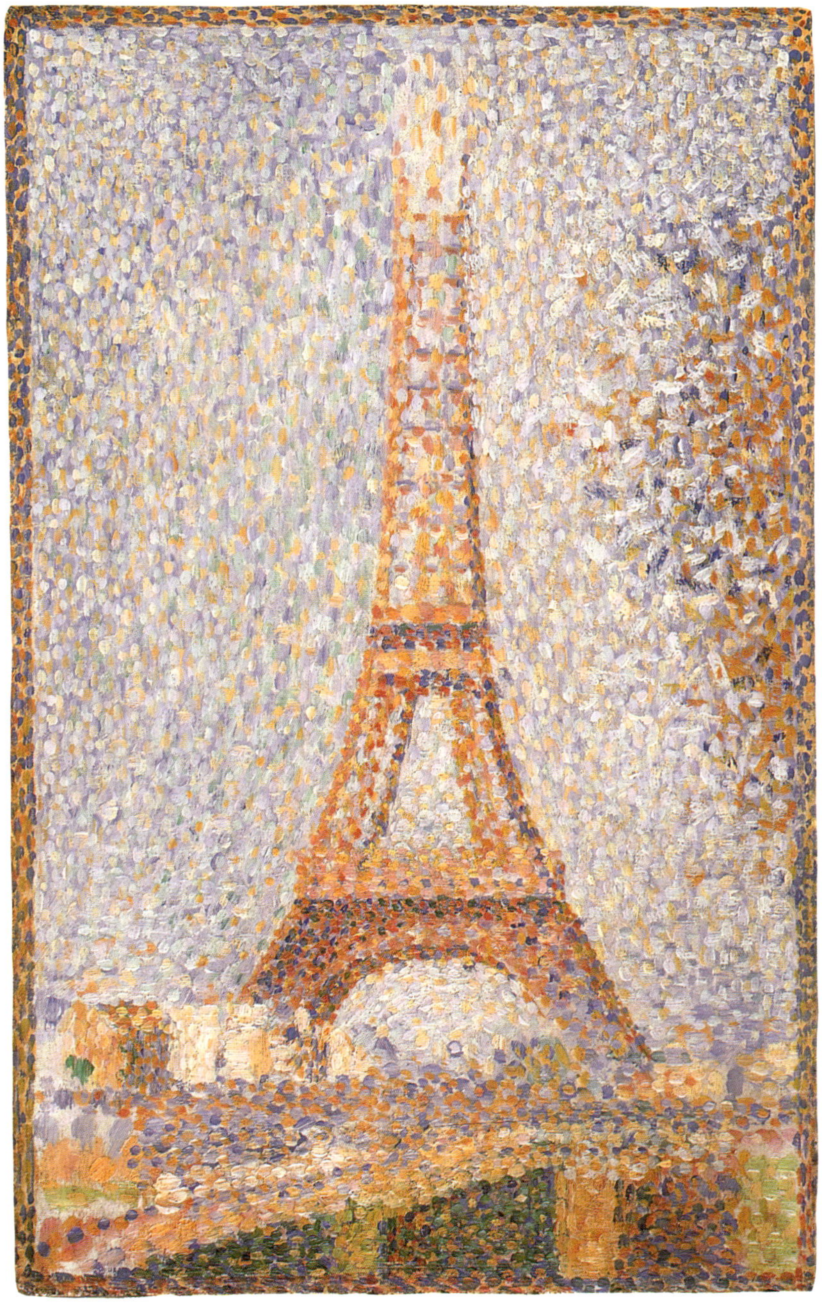

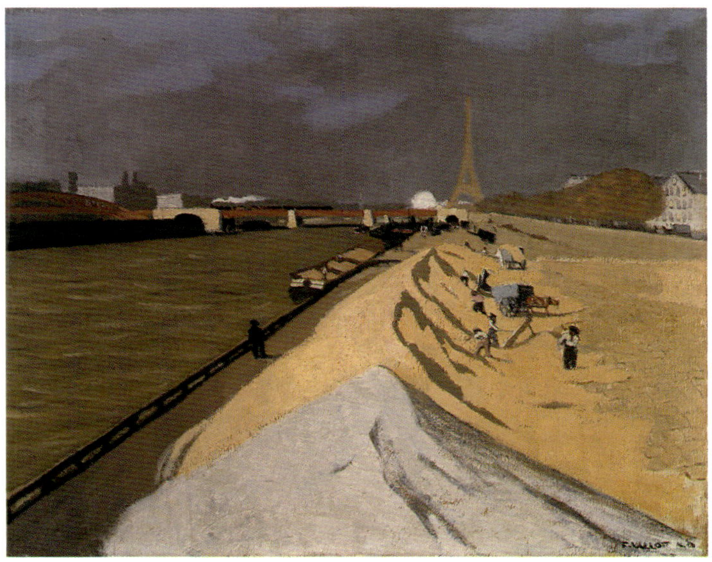

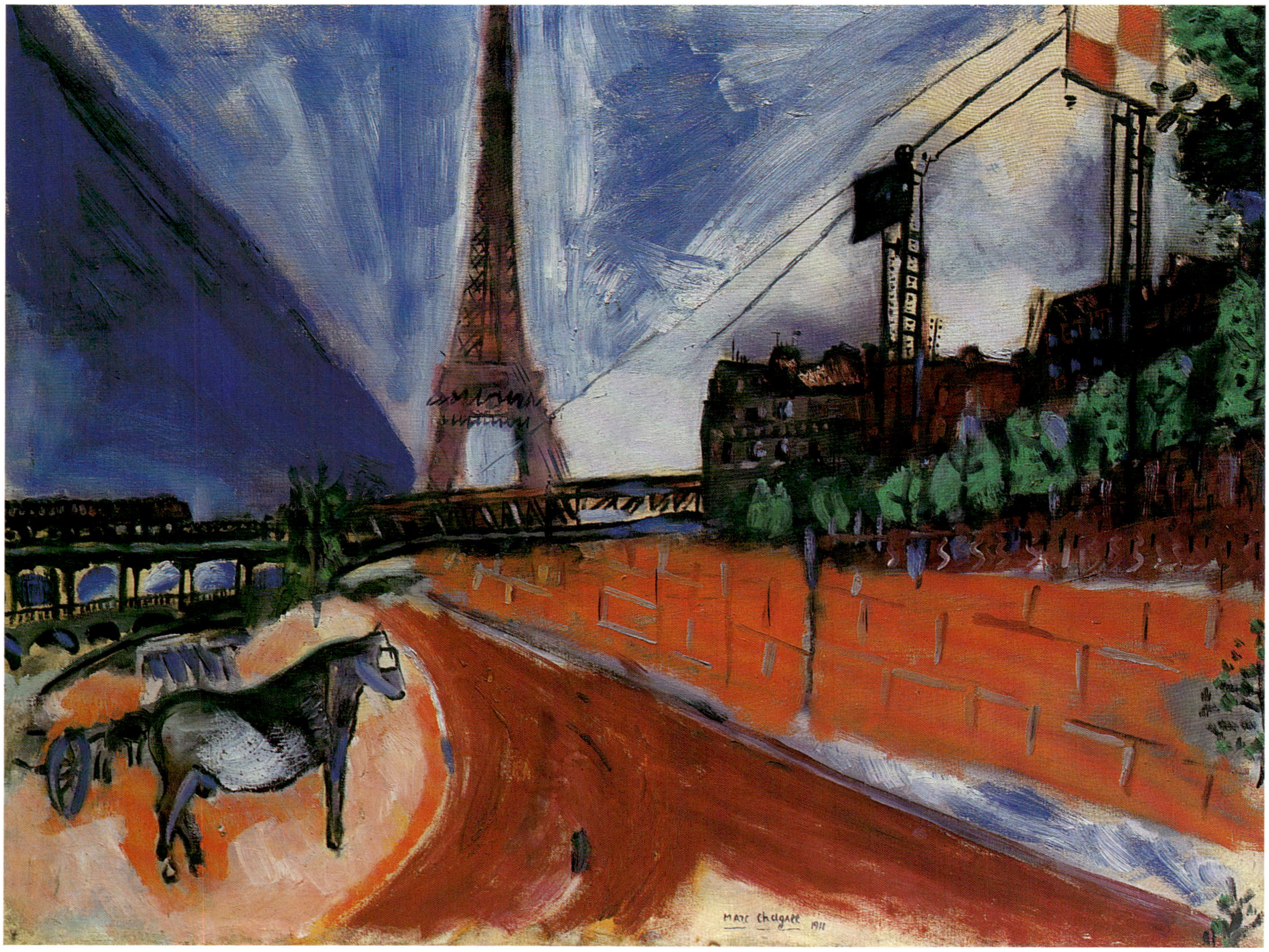

76
M. Chagall
The Pont de Passy and the Eiffel Tower
1911
New York, Metropolitan Museum,
Robert Lehman Collection, 1975

this first visit took a vantage point similar to that in Vallotton's *Yellow Sand*, but from nearer to the tower and the railway bridge crossing the Seine at the île des Cygnes [**76**]. Chagall's representation is more than an inventory of the modern – Eiffel Tower, girdered bridge, train signals and telegraph wires – because it generates its sense of modernity by its equation of those elements of urban furniture with startling construction and execution. The eye is wrenched up the speeding diagonal of the quai de Grenelle, Chagall like Signac, Vallotton and others before him recognising perspectival rush as an essential pictorial metaphor for the dynamic of the modern city. This sense of velocity is compounded by the consciously tart and vulgar conjunctions of colour, notably the maroon road and vermilion parapet surmounted by acid green foliage, and by the spontaneous attack of the brush. Beside this vortex which sweeps the eye to the foot of the tower stands a horse and cart, providing an almost *naïf* accent, a still, timeless surety among the totems of modern communication. For Chagall, Paris meant both artistic stimulus and a challenge to the certainties of a Russian provincial.

Chagall was quickly taken up by the poet and critic Apollinaire, who was also writing about the work of Robert Delaunay. Apollinaire's account of the latter's recent pictures, published in March 1912, could almost apply to Chagall's image of the tower: 'Delaunay's art is full of movement and does not lack power. Rows of houses, architectural views of cities, especially the Eiffel Tower – these are the characteristic themes of an artist who has a monumental vision of the world, which he fragments into powerful light'.[37] Apollinaire was referring here to the canvases Delaunay was showing at the Galerie Barbazanges, in which Cubist fragmentation was employed in celebration of the tower. As in 1889 modern pictorial experimentation was once again pitting itself against the still most emphatically modern building in the city [**77**]. That summer Delaunay, in an intense bout of work, developed his style, with the Eiffel Tower again the pivot. As he began the series that became known as *Les Fenêtres* (*The Windows*), he wrote to Kandinsky in Munich of his 'search for pure painting'. Delaunay had read the treatise *De la loi du contraste simultané des couleurs* by the nineteenth-century chemist Chevreul, as well as Signac's book *From Eugène*

Delacroix to Neo-Impressionism, published in 1899, in which the law concerning the simultaneous contrast of colours is described in relation to modern painting. A canvas such as *The Windows, No.3* [**50**], in which Delaunay uses colour to evoke a sense of light, derives from the scientific theory that 'a clear blue will make an adjoining yellow appear more orange or ... a darker blue will make the same yellow appear more green'.[38] *The Windows* show a view through a curtained window towards the Eiffel Tower, which is in turn seen through shifting facets of colour light. What appears a semi-abstract painting remains vitally concerned with light, the quintessential ingredient of landscape painting. These magical pictures are not just painterly experiments. They were made in casual collaboration with the poets of Apollinaire's circle, all fascinated by the modern. Apollinaire wrote in June 1912: 'I once heard the following exchange between two painters standing on the pont d'Iéna: "How ugly the Eiffel Tower is! It has no style at all!" "Excuse me, but its style is pure Louis XIV." The Eiffel Tower does indeed have a style. It may even be Louis XIV but it is above all modern, ... [and] the masterpieces of the modern style are made of cast iron, steel, sheet metal',[39] precisely the industrial ingredients emphasised in Delaunay's first series on the tower. The painter showed several of *The Windows* with Der Sturm in Berlin in early 1912, and Apollinaire was asked to write the catalogue introduction. He contributed a poem of the same title, either – the legend differs – composed in Delaunay's studio or slung together in a café with other poets lobbing in lines.[40] Whatever its genesis, the poem is an analogue to the paintings. Its staccato lines, imagery and obsession with coloured light are indebted, like the paintings' luminescent facets constantly refracting, to the current notions of the simultaneity of thought, perception and experience derived from the philosophy of Bergson.[41]

Raise the blind
And now see how the window opens
If hands could weave light this was done by spiders ...
An old pair of yellow shoes under a window
Towers
Towers are streets
Wells
Wells are squares.[42]

For painter and poet alike, the Eiffel Tower remained the inescapable archetype in the Parisian cityscape.

The Eiffel Tower had never been a simple architectural element for the painter to insert into a representation of the city. Whether represented symmetrically and iconically, as in Delaunay's *The Windows* or the images of Seurat and Rousseau, or introduced into the urban panorama perhaps aggressively, as in Chagall's canvas, or even surreptitiously, as in Rivière's print, the tower was inescapably the symbol, albeit polyvalent and ambiguous, of the modern. Most interestingly, many artists represented the completed tower without showing the very top. From Béraud to Chagall, the decision to stunt the tower was a pictorial ploy to add to its visual excitement, to give a sense of its then awesome height, for that yearning verticality, that reaching into the clouds, gave the Eiffel Tower, modern rival to the ancient status of Notre-Dame, something of the identity of a secular spire.

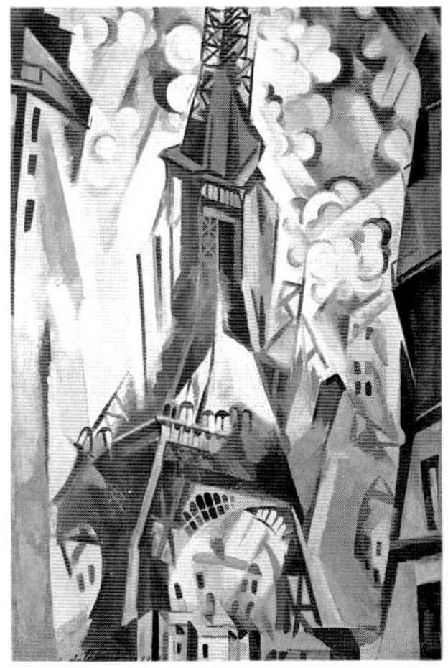

77
R. Delaunay
The Eiffel Tower 1910–11
Basel, Kunstmuseum, Emanuel Hoffman Foundation

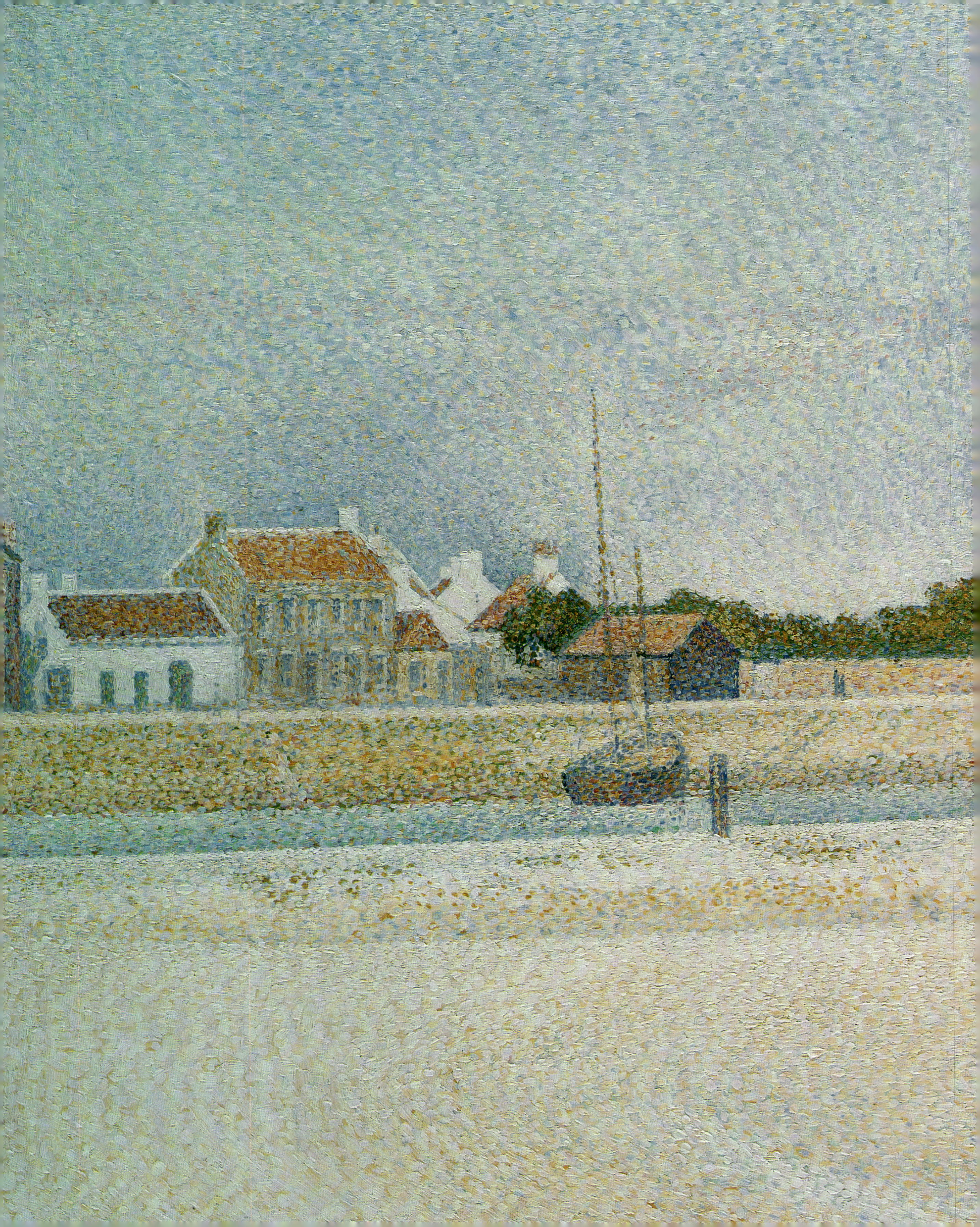

4 The Channel Coast

The varied coastlines of France, a maritime nation surrounded on three sides by sea, provide alluring prospects for painters. But with few exceptions such as the royal commission of Joseph Vernet to record the nation's great ports in 1754 it was not until the early nineteenth century that the French shores began to be visited regularly by artists. As the vogue for Italian landscape sites began to wane and the publication of Baron Taylor's illustrated *Voyages pittoresques*, commencing in 1819, drew attention to the beauties and curiosities of their native land, artists turned their attention to French motifs. The Mediterranean had its painters, and Brittany and the Biscay coast too, but it was Normandy and the Channel which first drew painters in large numbers. A painting by Xavier Le Prince of cattle being loaded in the port of Honfleur was bought from the Salon for the Louvre as early as 1824, and in that decade a number of other landscapists worked at Honfleur, among them Isabey, Huet and Corot.[1] The Channel coast retained its popularity with painters. In mid-century the ferme Saint-Siméon, among the orchards on the high slopes overlooking Honfleur and the expanse of the Seine estuary, was a rendezvous for landscape painters of many stamps, from established figures such as Troyon through *petits-maîtres* like Cals to a younger generation of independents, among them Monet and Bazille. At the turn of the century onè could almost define a characteristic 'Channel' painting, close to the melancholy tranquillity typical of the work of Boulogne-born Cazin, in the pictures of an informal group including Le Sidaner, Henri Duhem and Louis-Antoine Leclercq. And a number of the important young artists who emerged around 1905 were Normans and worked on the shores of their *pays*: Braque, Dufy and Friesz. This is not to say that painters were exclusive to one region. All those young northerners worked on the Mediterranean coast and elsewhere prior to 1914, and so did older native or adoptive Normans such as Boudin and Monet. Seurat was relatively unusual in restricting his landscape painting forays from his Parisian base to the Channel. Similarly his Neo-Impressionist colleague Charles Angrand could never be prised south, despite the enthusiastic efforts of his friends Signac and Cross to lure him to Saint-Tropez.

The contrasts between Angrand's native Normandy and Signac's adopted Mediterranean form a *leitmotif* in the two painters' correspondence. 'I see that you don't want to be unfaithful to the Blue sea in favour of the Green sea', Angrand wrote in 1901, forgetting that Signac had worked extensively on the northern shores earlier in his career. 'So the Mediterranean will have all the honours ... I must go and see it with my own eyes', he temporised, continuing that, to judge from the postcards Cross and Signac had sent him, Mediterranean houses seemed 'built in the opposite way to those in the *pays de Caux*. Here they are designed to let in the sun; with you to keep it out'.[2] The light of the Channel coast that Angrand so loyally favoured was one of the region's great attractions for painters. Recording his different experiences of watching Corot, Courbet and Monet at work, another Norman, Guy de Maupassant, sang the praises of the Channel light, as varied – he claimed – as the wines of Bordeaux: 'Here the light is striking without being harsh; everything is clear without being brutal, and is nuanced in an admirable way'.[3] This watery marine light, constantly changing under the clouds and winds that shift across the face of the Channel, illuminated a landscape which was more appealing to painters, claimed one art critic in another regional comparison, than that of Brittany: 'Nature in Normandy is richer but much less strange than in Brittany. Lines are more abbreviated, masses are heavier, the horizon is more confined. Even with a storm approaching, the Channel is slower, thicker.'[4] Normandy provided a landscape of great diversity: expansive beaches bordered by cliffs or dunes; watermeadows in the estuary plains, the *bocage* with its hamlets and farms cramped within tight valleys and high hedgerows, and the windswept moorland surmounting the cliff-wall. Above all it had the changeable sea – 'deliciously hypocritical', as Debussy put it.[5]

By 1875 or so the natural and visual attractions of the Channel coast had been nourishing the landscape painter for fifty years. Ways of representing the region had become codified; not only had certain sites or phenomena come to be taken as typical, but certain categories of landscape motif constituted an informal canon. The picturesque was one of these.

opposite
78
G. Seurat
The Channel of Gravelines, Grand Fort-Philippe 1890 (detail)
The Berggruen Collection on loan to the National Gallery, London

Traceable back to first generation painters of the region such as Isabey, picturesque images might include both motifs of historic or quaint buildings – churches, *châteaux*, ramshackle fishing ports – and the salient natural features of the Norman shore. These very characteristics had since mid-century drawn increasing numbers of tourists to the Channel, a development which itself gave rise to another category. For painters had swiftly shown themselves ready to represent the summer visitors, who provided a ready market for pictures of holiday-makers, a taste Boudin [**86**] cultivated to his advantage in the 1860s. A third category of subject consisted of working images, representations of the local populations, perhaps the inland farms but more likely the fishing fleets unloading or trawling offshore, women gathering shellfish along the beaches, or the ports, from the pretty old harbours to the hectic transatlantic docks of Le Havre. These categories were by no means mutually exclusive, but they formed the broad parameters within which a landscape painter could expect to work.

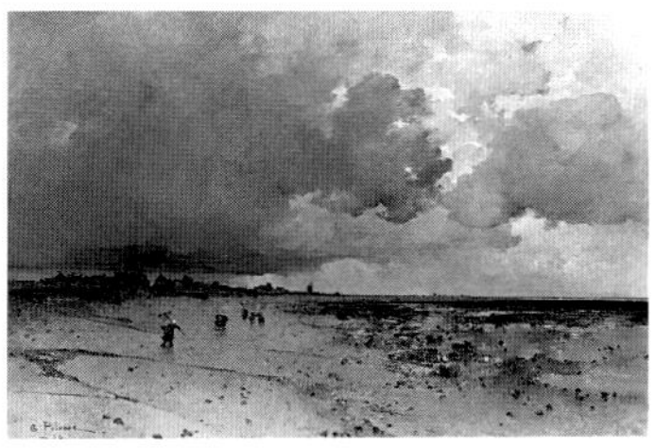

79
L. -G. Pelouse
Low Tide at Grandcamp 1884
Carcassonne, Musée des beaux-arts

All of them, of course, were subject to the vagaries of the weather. Changes in atmospheric conditions can affect the mood of a picture and the sensations it arouses in the spectator, just as they can one's response to nature itself. At the Salon of 1889 Antoine Guillemet showed *Wreck at Villerville* [**80**], which represents the remains of a boat washed up on the beach some fifteen kilometres west of Honfleur. Sensibly, it seems, he paid little attention to the place itself, a fishing village of a thousand inhabitants with no distinguished architectural features which stands on a low cliff and had failed to establish itself as a bathing resort due to its unappealing strip of highwater pebbles and shallow sea.[6] Guillemet pitched his horizon line low the better to focus on the rain clouds massing over the western Channel. His rich tones and fluid facture give a powerful sense of the moisture underfoot and the pearly dampness of the incoming front. Vast space and typical weather thus compensate for the absence of the picturesque, the atmospheric standing in for the quaint. Villerville is in Lower Normandy, whose coastline alternates between steep cliffs and easier, sloping access to the shore. Others worked along this stretch, among them in the 1880s painters as different as Pelouse, one of the most successful contemporary landscapists, and Seurat. Pelouse's submission to the 1884 Salon, *Low Tide at Grandcamp* [**79**], shared a similar format to Guillemet's, and most of Seurat's canvases made at the same modest fishing village the following year show the flat, rather dreary shoreline and use quite a low horizon to indicate, if not the vastness conveyed by Guillemet or Pelouse, at least a great expanse of sky and water. An exception to this pattern is Seurat's painting of the Bec du Hoc [**81**], an extraordinary chalk horn to the east of Grandcamp now much reduced in grandeur due to the aerial and naval

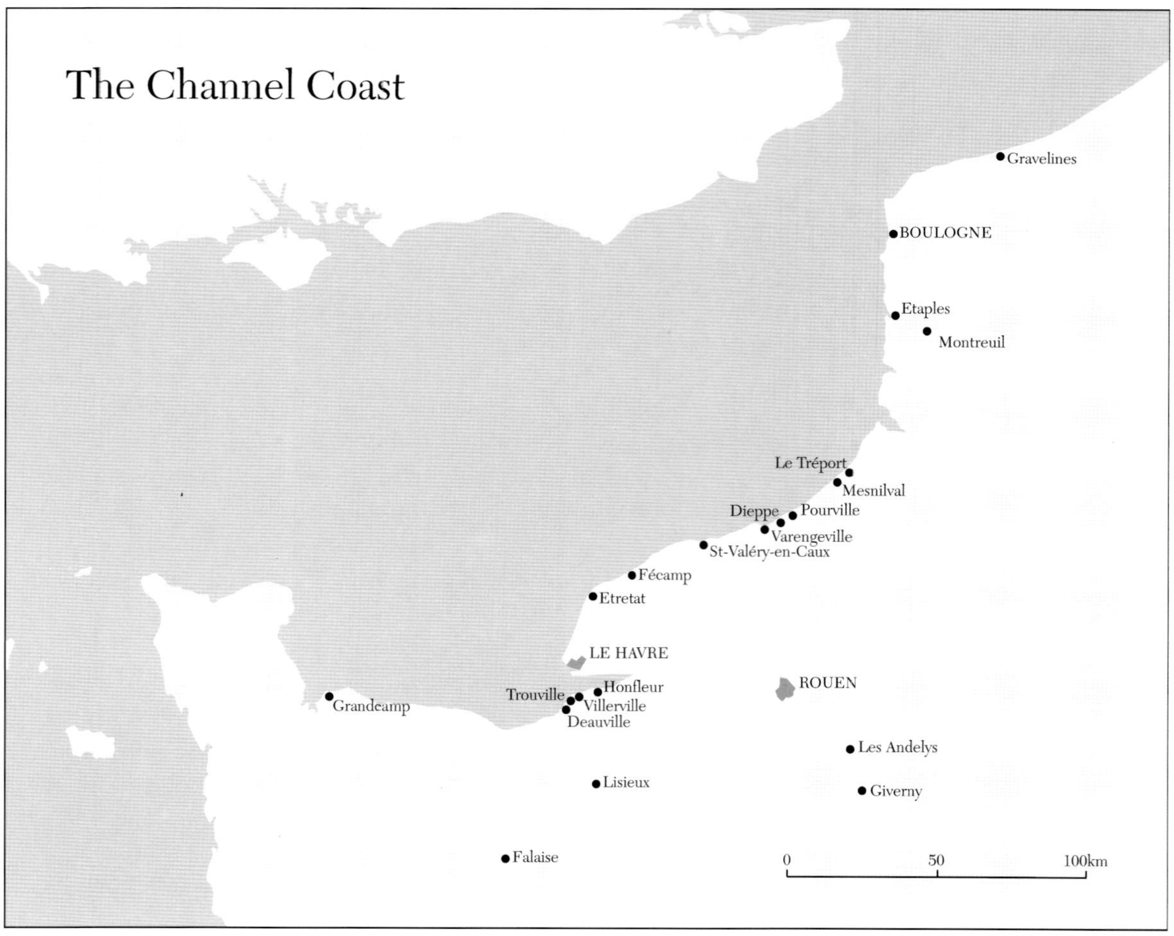

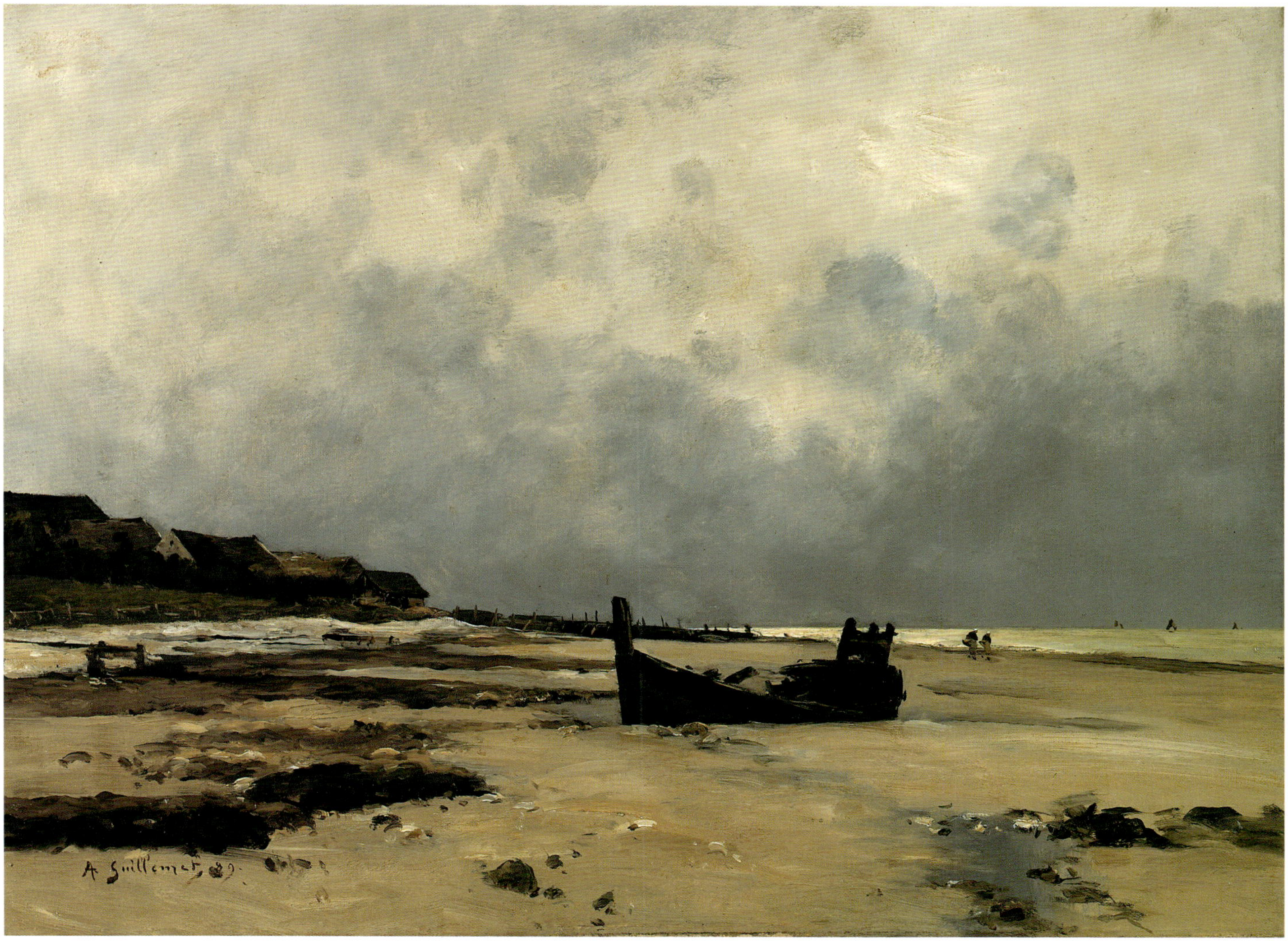

80
A. Guillemet
Wreck at Villerville 1889
USA, Private Collection, Courtesy of John Mitchell and Son

bombardment of the battery behind it prior to D-Day. Seurat's painting displays an entirely different touch to Guillemet's. Instead of employing a broad brush to map out areas of tone and generalise the fall of light, Seurat used his marine subjects of 1885 to experiment with different kinds of touch in an attempt to find a method of applying paint that could best approximate to the vibration of light on physical objects. Conscious that this meant keeping coloured marks separate, the better to contrast with each other, he employed in *Le Bec du Hoc* a variety of touches: quite wide strokes in the sky, horizontal dashes on the sea, and criss-cross flecks on the grass. Although Seurat showed this canvas three times in 1886–7, including at the 1886 Impressionist exhibition, he later felt it necessary to rework the original surface, and probably in early 1888 he added the dotted marks to the edges of the canvas and around the Bec itself, as well as the painted border.[7] These two phases of work have produced a surface which the eye may find too hectic and pocked, the all too apparent artifice of mark-making seeming at odds with the sensitive observation of natural colours: sandy yellow, the meagre greens of grass growing in poor soil, the nuanced blues and greens of the undulating sea. For *Le Bec du Hoc*, despite being so evidently different from the work of Guillemet or Monet, shows Seurat's response to the same problem as that faced by his contemporaries: how to tally touch and colour to convey the light and atmosphere of one's chosen motif.

To the north of Le Havre and the Seine estuary lies Upper Normandy, walled with a massive bulwark, 'one great cliff carved out, indented and grand', as the bore M. Roland puts it in Maupassant's novel *Pierre et Jean* of 1888, 'making an immense white wall all the way up to Dunkirk, every dent in which has a village or a port – Etretat, Fécamp, Saint-Valéry, Le Tréport, Dieppe'.[8] These huge cliffs had consistently featured in Normandy landscapes, and as archetypal emblems of the Channel coast they remained essential to the painter's repertoire and the public's expectations. How inevitable then, that a canvas of the cliffs at Mesnilval [**82**], just south of Le Tréport, by Cazin, one of the most esteemed painters of the 1880s and 1890s and strongly identified with the Pas-de-Calais, was the landscape purchased to represent him in the collections of the city of Paris. It was selected from the Salon de la nationale of 1894, and re-exhibited in the survey of the finest paintings of the last decade at

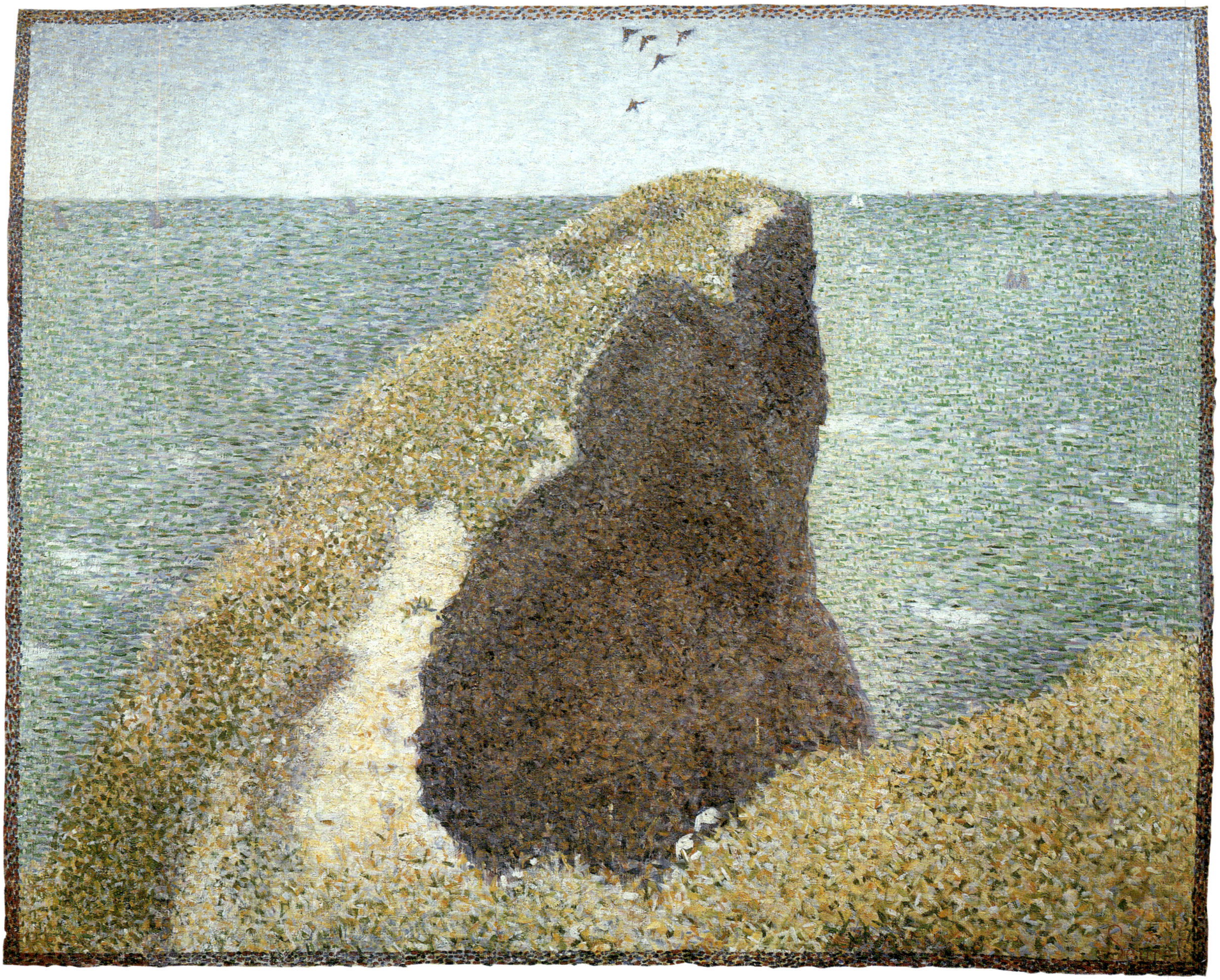

81
G. Seurat
Le Bec du Hoc 1885
London, Tate Gallery

the Universal Exhibition of 1900. *Mesnilval* is an expansive, rhythmic painting. The dipping wall of cliff faces is seen across a tract of beach exposed by the low tide, great blocks caught between the reflections in the sodden sand and the tattered veil of cloud cover. Cazin subtly balanced colours, setting the deep grey rocks tinged with green against the buff-grey of the cliffs, rendering them with brushstrokes of great delicacy. The horizon tinged with the subdued violet rays of the fading sun, *Mesnilval* encapsulates Cazin's qualities: the ability to choose a moment and motif of great tranquillity, even melancholy, and a sensitivity for the moist Channel light that drenches his image of beach and cliffs. It was in such a vein that the painting was received, Raymond Bouyer writing in 1894 that with *Mesnilval* Cazin 'seems a classic' and 'remains poet of the North, as delicate and measured as ever, very moving, a little cold, a little dim, a little faint, romantic in his greys'.[9]

In 1882 Monet, then living at Poissy to the northwest of Paris, undertook a major campaign on the shores of Upper Normandy. He had never entirely neglected his native region, making forays there from Argenteuil during the 1870s and in 1880 producing a substantial body of work at Petites-Dalles. But his return to the Channel coast in 1882 took place at a highly significant stage in Monet's career. He was trying to recast himself as a landscape painter, seeking fresh motifs after his ultimately disillusioning attempts in the previous decade to represent the modern suburban or inner-city scene and having recently discovered that Poissy's motifs did not stimulate his *sensations*. He was also attempting to win himself an individual identity on the market in response to his growing anxieties about Impressionist group shows. And above all he was striving to develop his eye's sensitivity to changes of light in nature and his ability to transcribe them. Early that year he visited Dieppe,

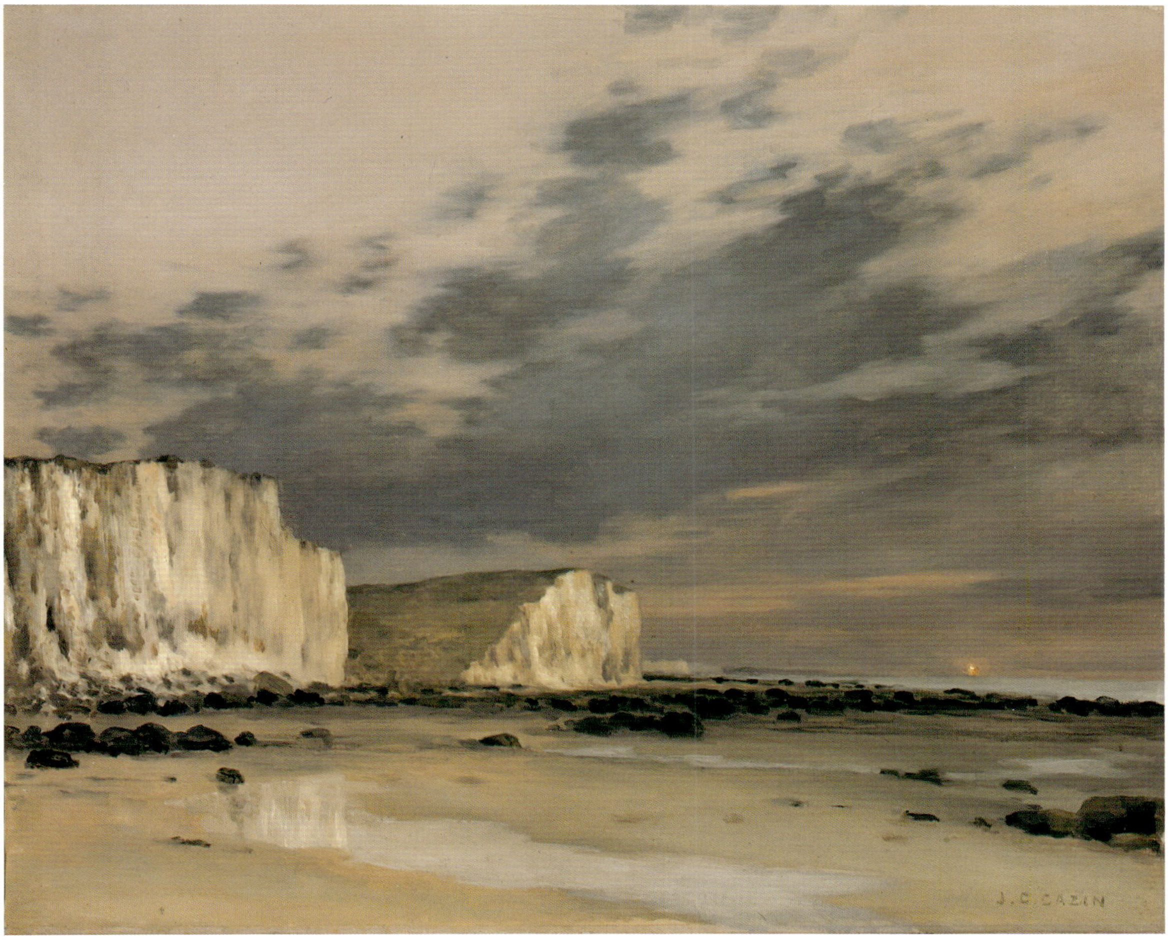

82
J. -C. Cazin
Mesnilval c.1894
Paris, Musée du Petit Palais

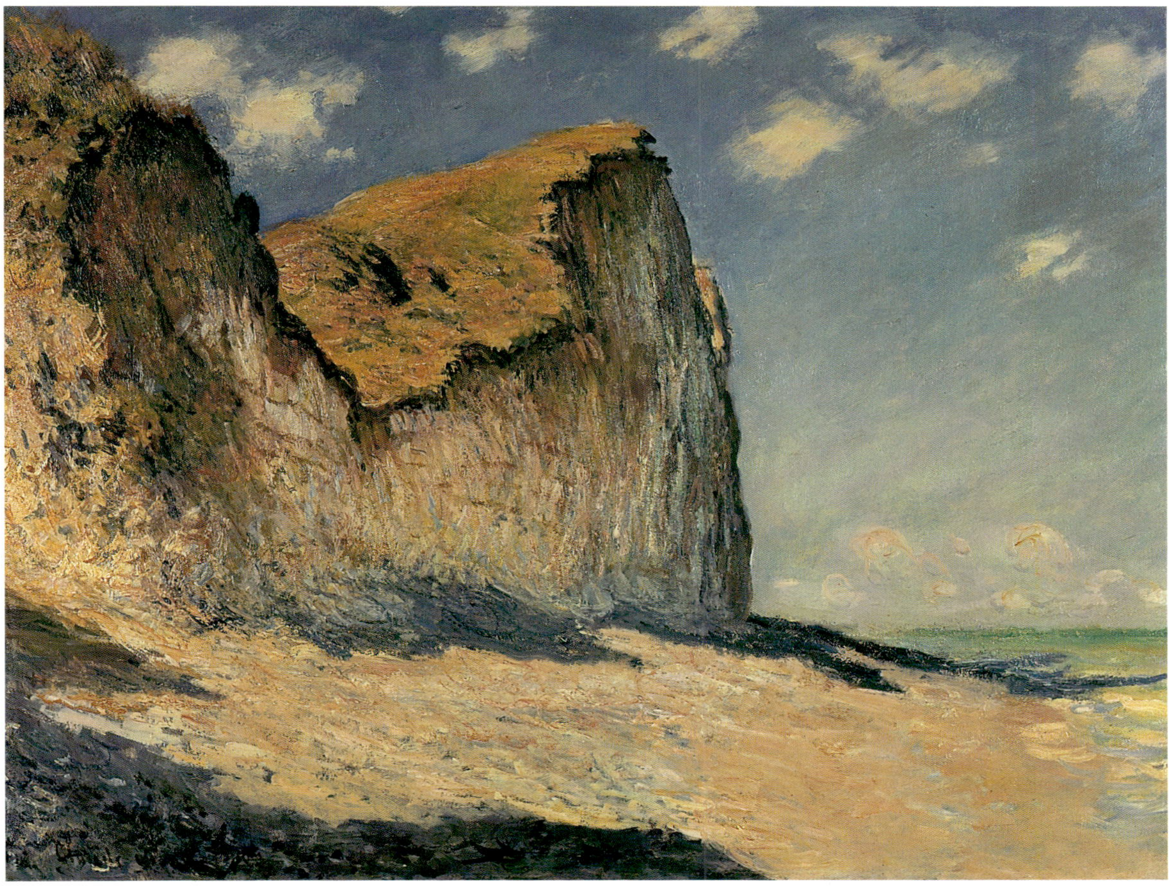

83
C. Monet
Cliffs at Pourville 1882
Enschede, Rijksmuseum Twenthe

but disliked it; by 5 February, however, he had settled in the small fishing community of Pourville, just to the west. Except for a short trip to Paris at the beginning of March when the seventh Impressionist show opened, he remained at Pourville until mid-April. On 17 June he went back, this time with his whole family, and they stayed until 5 October. This overall campaign of more than six months resulted in almost a hundred canvases.[10] The motifs Monet chose at Pourville form various groups. A fifth of the paintings are views over the Channel taken from the top of the cliffs; others were made at sea-level, a dozen looking along the beach, ten concentrating on the cliff-faces, and a smaller cluster looking out to sea. Monet's letters home from his first trip are full of the woes of the *plein air* painter – a gnat-bite has made his hand too swollen to work; he has lost an afternoon's painting because the local who carries his canvases is dead-drunk [11] – but they centre, inevitably, on the weather which determined the natural light and therefore the chromatics of his canvases. Without the appropriate light he was unable to complete pictures, writing home on 6 April that he could not yet return because 'to do well I must still have two days of sun and two or three overcast',[12] a typical instance of his enslavement to the unpredictable Channel climate.

One of the finest paintings of this campaign is *Cliffs at Pourville* [**83**], a startling combination of stillness and movement. The cliff seems massive, dominant, solid. It faces another elemental force, the rich turquoise-green sea we glimpse to the right. The cliff has grandeur but also momentum, provided by both the rhythm of the grassy edge, precarious and staccato, and the dashes of ochre and pink that mark horizontal strata on the chalk-face and lure the eye into the picture-space. As well as creating a formidable sense of mass, Monet also managed to imply the invisible element of the wind at work on the cliff, especially in the flecked grasses on the left-hand bank, a very animated passage compared to the more matted, flatter textures on the cliff top. The clouds too are in patches blurred at the edges to suggest the wind's direction, which would appear to move across the diagonal formed by the cliffs, Monet using natural resources to imply an invisible compositional counterpoint to the huge dominant block. The clouds also seduce the eye upward, making the spectator look up to the sublime mass of the cliff. As in *Mesnilval* there is no human presence, which also adds to the grandeur of nature's monolith. But whereas Cazin settled, notwithstanding his subtlety, for an immediately naturalistic colour range, Monet challenged conventional expectations; the cliff itself, for instance, he painted using deep coral and blue streaks in the shadows, with the great bluff reflecting the turquoise of the sea against a meaty red.

84
A. Marquet
The Beach at Fécamp 1906
Paris, Musée national d'art moderne, Centre Georges Pompidou

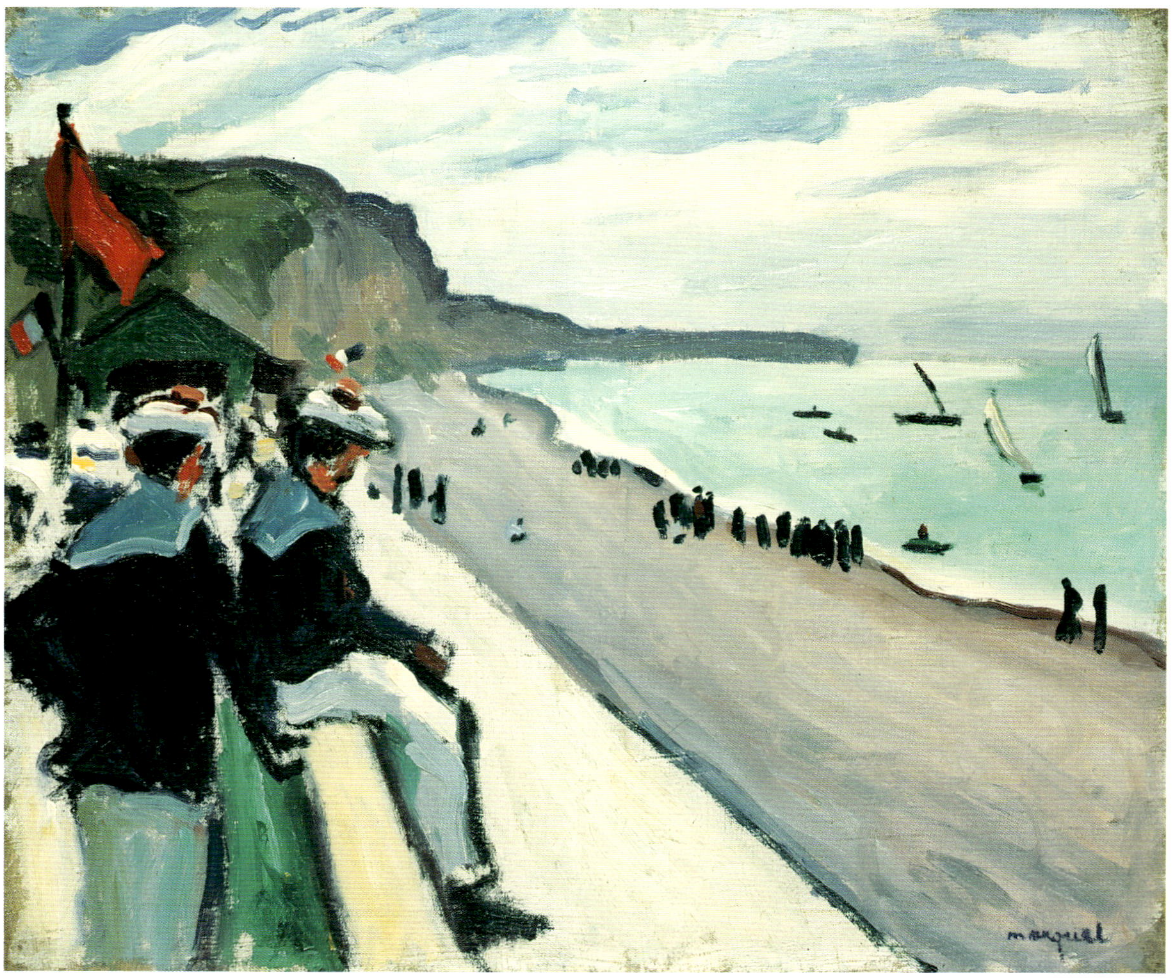

The cliffs of Upper Normandy continued to feature in landscapes of the coast in the twentieth century. Marquet, who hailed from Bordeaux, was introduced to the Channel in 1904 by his Norman friend Dufy, when they worked together at Fécamp. Marquet painted there again in 1906, when his canvases included *The Beach at Fécamp* [**84**]. For all Marquet's association with the Fauves, his work here, as in Paris, is characterised by the scrupulous control of tone, though the paintings are not without verve and risky decisions. *The Beach at Fécamp* has a high-key tonality set by the pink-mauve underlayer. The wedge of beach was applied in dull grey-violet, marked with deep blue strokes, which towards the cliffs darken to a brown-pink. Towards the horizon the cliffs deepen in their violet-blue tone, as does the aquamarine sea, and where they meet at the far point a white horizon indicates the reflection of the sun's light, low in the sky. The sky has streaks of *lapis lazuli* to the upper left, gradually dimming into paler blues and grey-white to register the overcast settled over the Channel. Marquet's handling of tone was sure – a point made by Paul Jamot in his review of the painting at the 1906 Salon d'Automne [13] – but *Beach at Fécamp* is not without daring and spontaneity, the artist leaving the left edge audaciously uncertain and pitching the vermilion safety flag against the deep green cliff-top.

These paintings of the Normandy cliffs could at one level be taken to typify different approaches, different stylistic 'movements': Cazin's sensitive naturalism, Monet's high Impressionism, Seurat's incipient Neo-Impressionism, Marquet's discreet Fauvism. But such a litany, however functional, would mask important underlying consistencies. Seurat wished to offer a corrective to Monet's gestural, 'romantic' touch; Cazin might have found Marquet's canvas unfinished. But whether the artists chose a flecked handling to allow diversity of colour marks or preferred a more broadly brushed, tonal approach, all were concerned with the moist, pearly light of the Channel coast. And they were concerned with it as an ambient atmosphere around the cliff motif. The *Bec du Hoc* and the *Cliffs at Pourville* deal not only with massive form, invoking a sense of the sublime, but also with the invisible space implicit behind it, Seurat and Monet responding to the cliffs as sculptural forms. By viewing the cliffs at Mesnilval and Fécamp from a distance, as part of a shoreline panorama, Cazin and Marquet made less rhetorical images, representing the great chalk wall as a noble element in a picturesque panorama. All four painters were fascinated by the imposing presence of the Channel cliffs, that definition of national frontier, whose historical associations and elemental timelessness made them, coupled of course with the challenging climatic conditions of the Norman coast, such an irresistible motif.

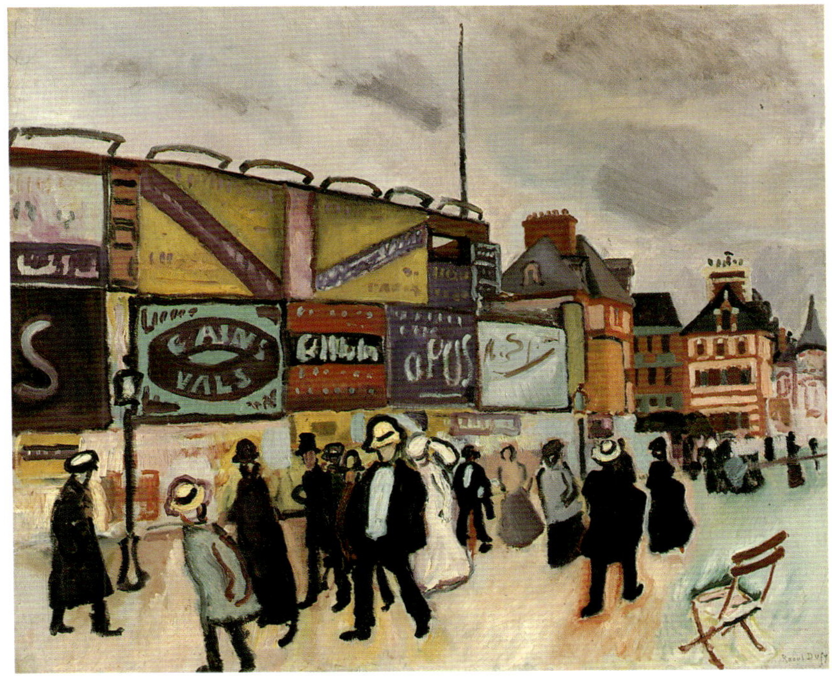

85
R. Dufy
Les Affiches à Trouville 1906
Paris, Musée national d'art moderne, Centre Georges Pompidou

Painters were not alone in responding to the picturesque views and bracing weather of the Channel coast. In Marquet's *Beach at Fécamp* the cliffs serve as a compositional anchor to a foreground scene of off-duty sailors and promenaders on the shore; here the eternal verities of nature meet the temporary presence of the tourist. The nineteenth century had seen the continuous expansion of tourism along the Channel coast. As the closest seashore to the capital it was inevitable that Normandy would be the first to be exploited by the new appetite for – successively – regional visits for culture or cures, 'hygienic' sea-bathing, and finally the middle-class holiday. The spread of the railways made this possible. Trouville is an excellent example of this process. During the 1840s a number of aristocrats began to buy property there, gradually elevating a humble fishing village to the status of smart retreat. The arrival of the railway at inland Lisieux in 1855 and finally at Trouville in 1863 established the place as a full-blown popular resort, and from 1870 to 1914 it catered for 150,000 visitors or more each year.[14] As the poet Stéphane Mallarmé ironically put it, during the summer season Normandy belonged to the Western Railway Company.[15] Trouville's transformation at the hands of entrepreneurs and the tourists they brought there was consistently noted by painters: Boudin's view of the Casino [**86**], made the year the railway arrived, and Dufy's motif of a wall of posters [**85**] executed along with similar images by Marquet in 1906, treat adjacent stretches of the promenade in essentially the same way. Both are concerned with the atmospheric treatment of the sky, while the seafront serves as a stage for crowds and commercialism. Here, then, in images neither of grandeur nor of the picturesque but of the raw urbanisation of the Normandy coast, we see painters trying to negotiate this transformation and the temporary summer populations of the sea-

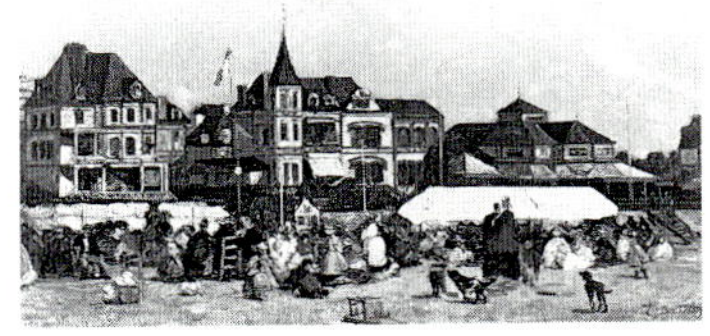

86
E. Boudin
The Casino at Trouville 1863
Private Collection

87
R. Dufy
Old Houses Along the Honfleur Basin
1906
Amsterdam, Fridart Stichting

88
C. Monet
The Museum at Le Havre 1873
London, National Gallery

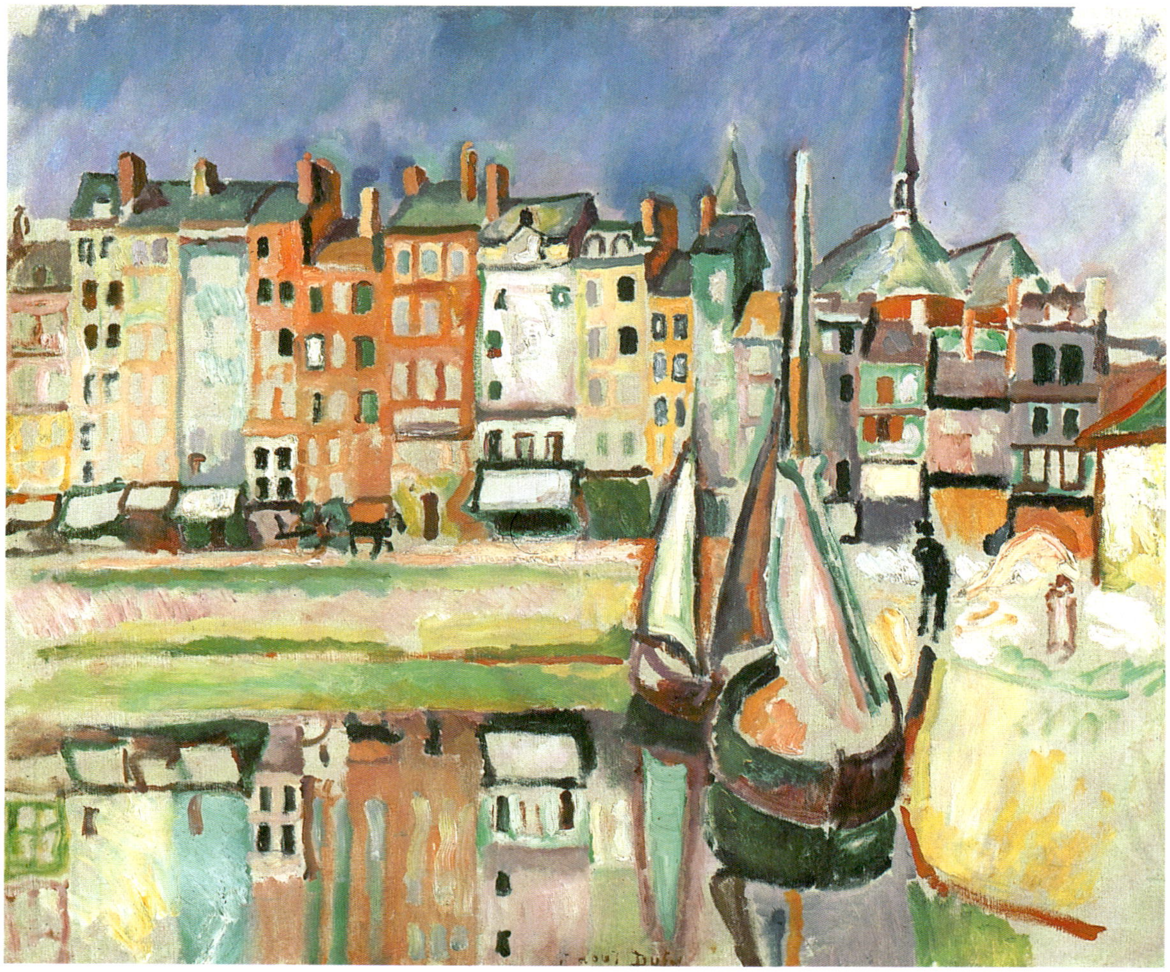

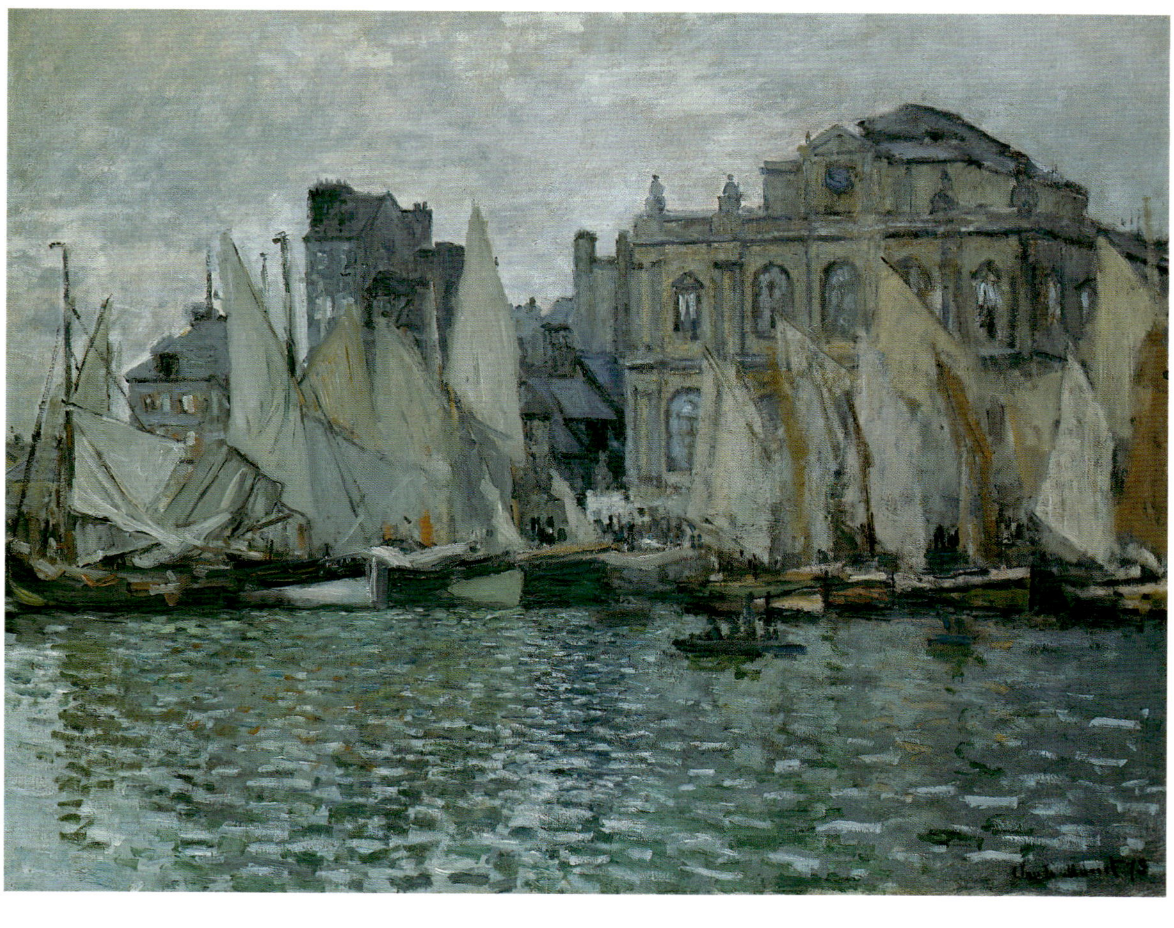

side. An alternative solution – that taken by Cazin and Guillemet – was to ignore them, to adhere to a notion of 'pure' landscape. Another was to divide one's production into the 'pure' and the 'modern', an option taken by both Monet and Boudin at different stages. Yet another was to arrive at some kind of accommodation. Marquet's *Beach at Fécamp* shows the natural shape of the beach constrained by the concrete of the promenade, and the motif is populated and to an extent man-made; indeed, one is reminded of the use of forceful perspective as a metaphor for modernity in images of city and suburb. But if it serves that rôle in the foreground of this image of an urbanised resort, it is surely balanced by the tranquillity of the distant horizon, mollified by the way Marquet's nacreous tones and fluid handling evoke the watery Channel light. Monet essayed such an assimilation in his 1882 paintings. *Cliffs near Dieppe* [**89**] takes a vertiginous, plunging view down the chalk bluff which is surmounted by modern buildings: a large villa or hotel and three identical summer houses, all no doubt recently built and sited for the view. Monet thus juxtaposed the elemental and the modern, and one might ask how comfortable a painting he has made of it, suggesting precariousness both anecdotally – the crazy railing – and pictorially, with the rough, assertive visual presence of the great cliff reduced in representation to the all-too-evident fabrication of the painter's marks. Compared to his images of the church at Varengeville [**90**], proud atop the cliff, an almost organic part of nature, the villas seem exposed and ridiculous, [16] as if Monet here found the equation of the sublime and the commercial infelicitous.

Another established category of images of the Channel coast was the representation of work. Such subjects focused on the local populations rather than the tourists – though, again, combinations were an option – and were open to great variation, as one can gauge from images of channel ports. Dufy's splendid canvas *Old Houses Along the Honfleur Basin* [**87**] uses the full rich range of his Fauve palette, balancing the almost pastel secondaries of pinks and greens in the reflections against the deep-toned moss-greens and aubergines of the fishing smacks, the terracottas and buttery yellows of the quayside façades, and the saturated blue of the sky. It is a most successful essay in the ability of intense colour and suave touch to represent strong light, with the buildings seeming to dissolve in the midday sun. It is also an image of the working port in a tradition that goes back to Le Prince's painting of almost a century before. The boats are in the inner harbour used for the local fishing fleet, bordered by the quay lined with the awnings of shops and cafés and along which a horsedrawn cart passes. But Dufy scarcely drew attention to Honfleur's working port, unlike, say, Seurat, whose paintings made there in 1886 concentrated chiefly on the harbour and its nautical commerce.[17] Dufy seems to have relished the characteristic tall thin houses bunched irregularly along the quay and topped by the fifteenth-century timber church of Ste Catherine, celebrated in all the guidebooks.

The paintings Monet made of Le Havre in the first half of the 1870s are substantially different. Honfleur had been an important port, and still retained a significant commerce with England, but by the late nineteenth century it had ceded the position of major Channel seaport to Le Havre. Sharing with Marseille the status of France's most important port, by the end of the century Le Havre handled a quarter of the country's overseas trade as well as being the chief harbour for transatlantic traffic. It was also a growing conurbation, with a population of some 90,000 in 1881 increasing to 120,000 by the turn of the century,[18] and decidedly metropolitan in character, its centre laid out on a system of impressively straight boulevards like Haussmann's Paris. A new photographic journal, advising holidaymakers on the prospects for their hobby in Normandy, dismissed Le Havre rapidly before recommending its readers – perhaps, in 1891, still quite imaginatively – to get off the beaten track. Visitors to Normandy cannot avoid the port any more than visitors to Provence can Marseille, opined *Photo-Journal*, but if the latter gives the flavour of the south, Le Havre has hardly any Norman character; 'it's the extension of Paris by the sea'.[19] The British devotee of historic architecture Augustus Hare remarked sourly of the panorama over the harbour that 'no one will agree with Casimir Delavigne (who was born on the quay which is named after him) – "Except for Constantinople, there is nothing as beautiful"'.[20] But Monet, whose youth had been spent there, evidently found considerable fascination in the hectic port during the early 1870s, no doubt seeing Le Havre as a continuation of his current interest in the 'modern' landscape of Paris and its suburbs. His *Museum at Le Havre* [**88**] shows the building erected in 1845 to house the town's library and art collections. The viewpoint is similar to that taken by Dufy at Honfleur, but Monet masks the irregular façades at the left behind fishing boats' tall sails, only revealing the imposing civic structure to the right, sacrificing the picturesque for the productive and the municipal. The weather is dreary, and the steely-toned painting has a character – solid and frontal, busy but drab – well suited to an industrial port.

Gravelines, or more particularly its adjacent seaward environs Petit and Grand Fort-Philippe, was painted by two important artists: Seurat in 1890 and Le Sidaner in 1902. We do not know why Seurat opted to summer at this modest little harbour on the canalised river Aa close to the Belgian border, though Le Sidaner, who came from the region, may have discovered it on journeys to Bruges where he had recently worked. On the face of it Gravelines had little to offer the painter: no spectacular natural

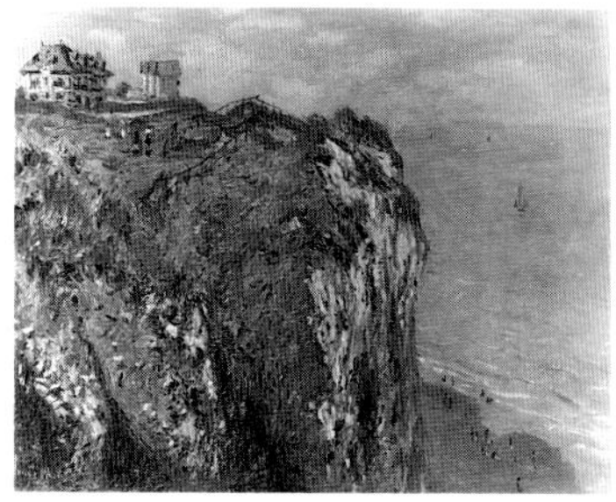

89
C. Monet
Cliffs near Dieppe 1882
Zürich, Kunsthaus

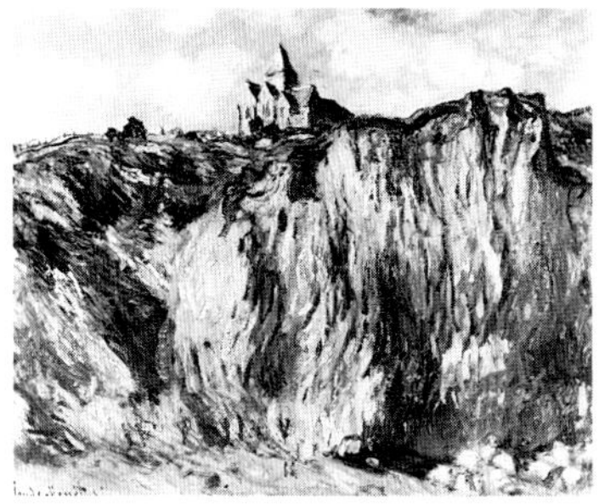

90
C. Monet
Church at Varengeville 1882
Private Collection

phenomena such as cliffs, only sand dunes and the river channel, no lively tourist centre or flourishing port, no historic or quaint buildings. Perhaps, though, their absence was to its advantage, for it was quiet, a virgin site, and in the flat landscape of the northern Pas-de-Calais it offered clear light under a huge sky. Seurat revelled in this, and the four canvases he completed in 1890 represent Petit Fort-Philippe to the north of the waterway and Grand Fort-Philippe to the south at four different times of the day.[21] Both the paintings of morning [**91**] and evening light [**174**] represent Grand Fort-Philippe and the same large house with its semaphore mast. The view in the morning painting is taken from the northern beach, looking across an expanse of sand bared by the low tide towards the river channel. The motif presented a pictorial challenge, with the three-dimensional forms crowded into a thin band of middle-ground between the close-toned sand and the overarching sky. Seurat solved this by fixing the lower corner with a patch of grass and leading the eye across the beach with a medley of pale yellows mixed with white and punctuated by etiolated blues and greens, a harmony which effectively renders light falling on soggy sand. The central band of Grand Fort-Philippe allowed Seurat to play with shape – the blocky, low-slung, strictly-windowed houses typical of the region softened by stunted shoreline trees – and greater contrasts of value and colour, the sunlit greens of the foliage sharpening the pinks and reds of brick and tile. This fastidious harmonisation of chromatics and composition takes place under a sky which gently pales over the sea itself, that great reflector of light.

It is possible that Le Sidaner might have seen *Grand Fort-Philippe*, either when it was first shown at the Indépendants in 1891 or later at the Seurat retrospective held by the cultural monthly *La Revue blanche* in 1900. However, as a native of Etaples, he would have been familiar with by-waters such as Gravelines and one need not necessarily see his decision to paint there in 1902 as a riposte to the late Neo-Impressionist. On the other hand, by this time Le Sidaner was painting in a discreetly divisionist manner which owed something to Seurat and his colleagues, and their motifs make an instructive comparison. Perhaps Le Sidaner's finest painting from this trip was *The Square at Petit Fort-Philippe*, a view of the *place publique* by twilight [**92**]. As Seurat did for his evening view of the river channel,[22] Le Sidaner produced an oil sketch [**93**] of the dusk motif. The finished painting adheres closely to the sketch both in composition and colour, with dabbed warm mushroom-greys emanating from the cloud-cover over the subdued russets, pinks and blanched lichen-greens of the village. Le Sidaner also opted for an extensive foreground which he anchored with a gaslamp and block of stone not to be found in the original sketch and unified with a surface of suggestive pale violet, olive green and aubergine complementaries. Be it the clarity of the morning or the nuances of the dusk, both painters were extremely conscious of the play of light. But does one's reading of these pictures stop at their record of atmospheric conditions? Le Sidaner's painting more immediately evokes a sense of mystery often associated with twilight. This is enhanced by the group of gloomy figures by the doorway of the large building whose lower windows are darkly hollow above their shutters and from whose upper floor blazes the welcome of bright lights. Viewing this from across the *place publique*, the spectator feels excluded, as he does from Seurat's image, in which even more remote figures pass along the far quay. Distance sets up a degree of emotional dislocation, as both painters must have been aware. One becomes conscious, particularly in the context of other images of the Channel coast, that neither of these two paintings of seaside villages, for all their apparent respect for topography, presents us with a working port or lively habitation. Petit and Grand Fort-Philippe are constructed not as places of collaboration or community but as locales strange, sparse and mysteriously forbidding.

Although Seurat and Le Sidaner were both painters of the same age, class and academic training they were both inevitably affected by and working within the Symbolist aesthetic that so coloured their generation, with its disdain of description and its fascination with suggestion and the emotive. It might be said that Le Sidaner, a successful Salon painter, was more obviously playing to this gallery than Seurat, who made his way among the avant-garde. And yet the notion of both the making of and the looking at landscape paintings as an emotional, evocative experience was commonplace at this time, particularly in

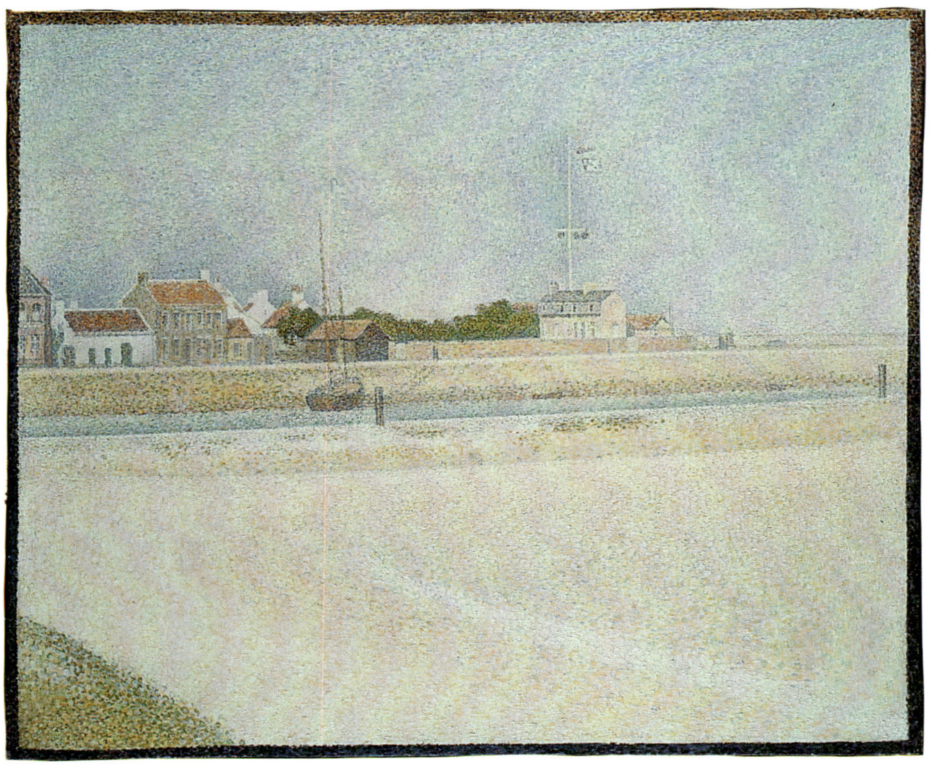

91
G. Seurat
The Channel of Gravelines, Grand Fort-Philippe 1890
The Berggruen Collection on loan to the National Gallery, London

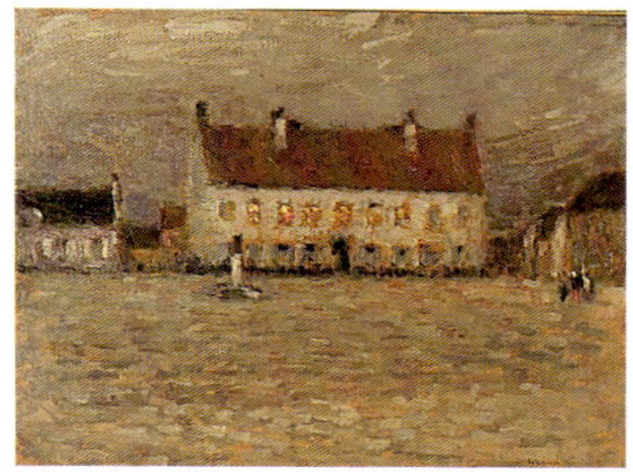

93
H. Le Sidaner
Study for 'The Square at Petit Fort-Philippe' 1902
Paris, Musée Marmottan

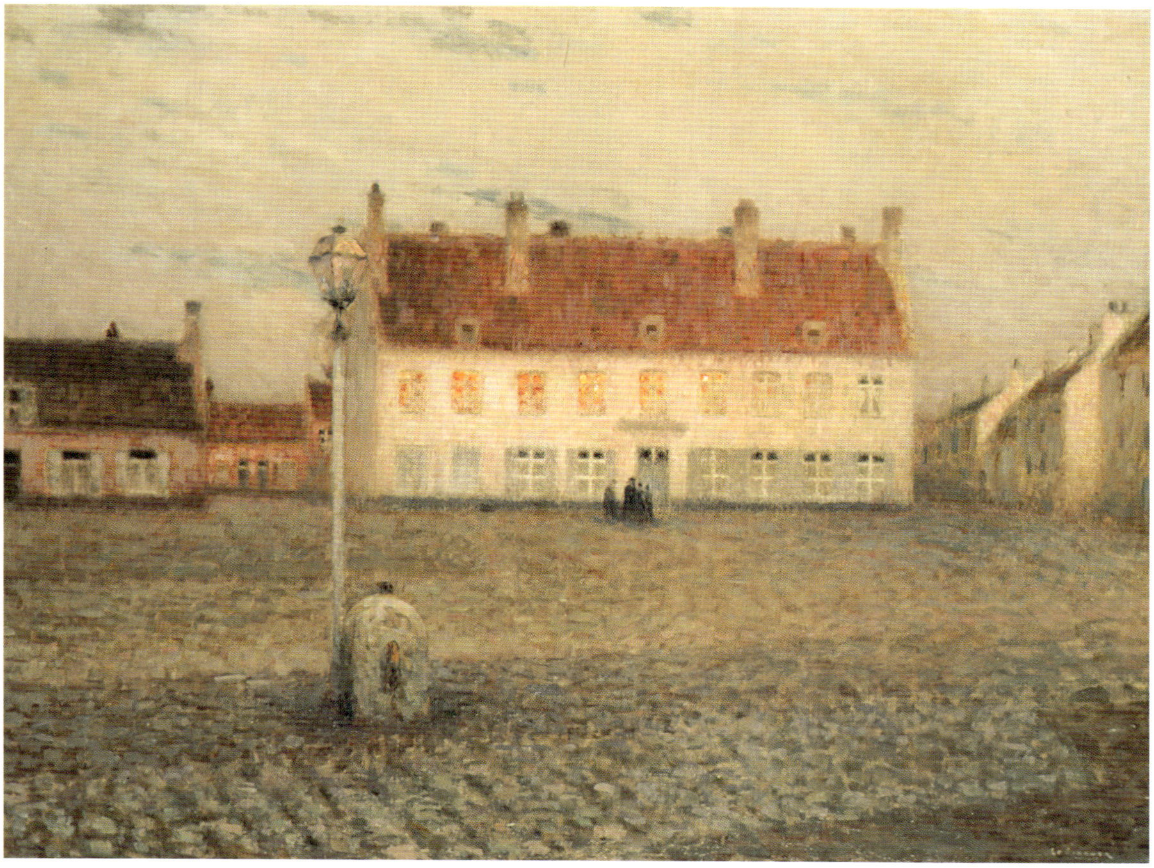

92
H. Le Sidaner
The Square at Petit Fort-Philippe 1902
Dublin, Hugh Lane Municipal Gallery of Modern Art

the case of images of the Channel coast, and not necessarily in relation to Symbolism. The association of certain aspects of light with moods of melancholy and loss was commonplace in nineteenth-century culture. For instance a book on comparative physiognomy, of all the unlikely subjects, had spoken in these terms in 1885: 'In proportion to the clouds becoming denser and darker, the mood turns towards sadness and everything appears sad and dismal under the sky's grey light: such is the sky on the shores of the Channel'.[23] Zola's novel *La Joie de vivre* of 1884 uses a dreary fishing village in Lower Normandy and the leaden Channel weather as a backdrop for a story of cramped emotion, self-sacrifice and unrequited love. Such pathetic fallacy is employed pictorially by his close friend Guillemet in his *Wreck at Villerville* [**80**], painted the year his wife died after a long illness and interpretable as a metaphor of loneliness and desolation.[24] Monet certainly saw landscape in emotional terms. Before settling at Pourville in 1882 he was frustrated because he could not find sites which had any impact on his *sensations*: 'nothing seizes me'.[25] It was a difficult time. He left his two sons by his wife Camille, who had died in 1879, with Alice Hoschédé, with whom he was living; while Monet was at Pourville, money was short, the baby was ill, he was deeply anxious that Hoschédé was going to claim his wife back. In these highly charged circumstances the Pourville paintings might well be considered not only as a response to light or as social iconography but also, as other groups of paintings have,[26] as emotional expression. The Pourville pictures, especially those made early in the year, generally take the viewpoint of the solitary; more specifically, the sense of pictorial and physical precariousness in *Cliffs near Dieppe* [**89**] might be taken to have a personal dimension. Others appear optimistic; one could read *Cliffs at Pourville* [**83**], for instance, as a cathartic submission to the immensities of nature, a renunciation of human care in face of the elemental. Certainly Monet's work at his one-man show in 1883, which included Pourville paintings, was interpreted affectively; 'he's an artist who is moved and who moves one', commented Alfred de Lostalot in his review in the influential *Gazette des beaux-arts*, 'the feelings he aims at and conveys are refined, poetic'.[27] Cazin, too, was commonly accounted a landscape painter of emotion and melancholy.[28]

The Channel coast may have given rise to certain formulaic categories – images of the picturesque, even the sublime, of the touristic or the working port – and to certain ways of seeing, certain allusions: the celebration of its light, the association with melancholy. Yet the painters we have seen here did not allow themselves to be entirely subject to these constructions, but used, discarded or imaginatively blended them.

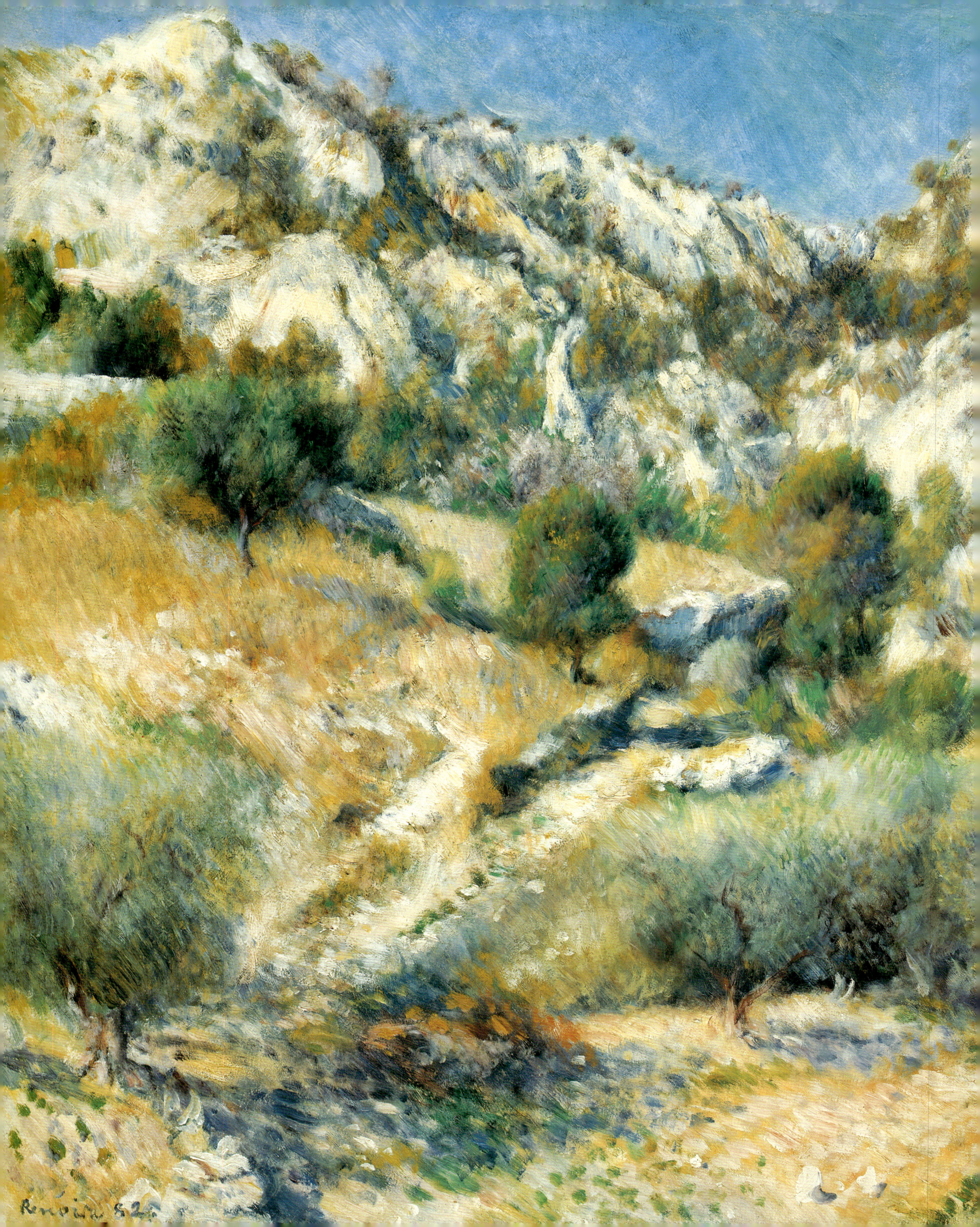
Renoir 82

5 The Mediterranean Coast

Tracing painters' responses to the landscapes of the Mediterranean coast and the southern *départements* – the Midi – throws up some different patterns to the representation of the Channel coast. The Midi had a distinguished tradition of native painters of the regional landscape. Notable among them were François-Marius Granet, who had retired from a career spent largely in Rome and Paris to his family property of Malvalat near Aix-en-Provence in 1847, and the important cluster of artists – Aiguier, Grésy, Engalière, Guigou – who had emerged during the 1850s and 1860s in the orbit of Emile Loubon [**101**], the influential director of the Ecole des beaux-arts in Marseille.[1] Northern painters had worked in the Midi in mid-century, but perhaps more often by force of circumstances than by choice, as in the case of Paul Huet who in 1838–9 painted motifs in the south [**95**] where he was staying for the health of his wife. As the Mediterranean coast began to play an increasingly important role within the economic and social fabric of France, it opened up a new set of possibilities for painters, who were both following and creating market taste. The Paris-Lyon-Marseille railway had been constructed between 1843 and 1848, but seems to have served in its early decades primarily as a commercial route. It was not until the later years of the century that it serviced the burgeoning tourist traffic now accustomed to train journeys and increasingly persuaded of the delights of sunshine; that revenue from the door-and-window tax in Nice tripled between 1884 and 1904 is an index of both new building and the promotion of sunlight and fresh air as tourist commodities.[2] If, due to its greater distance from Paris, the Mediterranean coast was slower than Normandy to gain popularity as a holiday destination, from the eighties it developed rapidly, and the landscape painters followed.

Artfully or not, Apollinaire was being highly disingenuous when he wrote in June 1914 that 'artists today are being drawn to the Midi. Instead of spending their vacations in Brittany or in the area around Paris, as many artists of the previous generation did, painters are now heading for Provence'.[3] Painters had been travelling south in numbers for three decades; indeed, the Brussels-based society La Libre esthétique had recognised this in 1913 by organising a retrospective exhibition entitled 'Interprétation du Midi' and the following year the Parisian dealers Bernheim Jeune staged a 'Paysages du Midi' survey.[4] There was ample material for such shows. Successful Salon landscapists worked there; Harpignies, for instance, wintered on the Riviera from 1885, usually at Beaulieu. Monet and Renoir had scouted the Côte d'Azur together in December 1883, the former's first trip to the south as a mature painter, though his colleague had painted there the year before. In other cases it was not just a question of visiting but of settling in the Midi: Cross bought a house at Cabasson in 1891; Signac visited St Tropez regularly from 1892, building a villa in 1897; Valtat came upon Agay that year, and built there in 1899; while Renoir, who had known the region for more than twenty years, finally had his own house constructed at Cagnes in 1907–8. Building one's own property, of course, was not only a commitment to the landscape as painterly motif, but also to the land as capital investment. Such painter-proprietors were no longer peripatetic landscapists in search of motifs, the artist equivalent of the tourist, but as investors in the Midi *paysage* as a saleable commodity they more closely paralleled – one might argue – hoteliers and travel agents who profited from marketing the idea of the Mediterranean.

The motives for this colonisation of the Mediterranean coast were not just artistic – Signac was a passionate sailor, Renoir needed a warm climate for his arthritis – but also fit inescapably within the broader socio-cultural fabric. Perhaps the greatest initial attraction of the Midi was that it was relatively undiscovered. Whereas 'Normandy is trodden by as many pedestrians as the boulevard des Italiens' and 'Brittany hides … an odious tourist behind every menhir', the Montagnes des Maures inland of Saint-Tropez had not yet been reached by the railway, enthused Maupassant in 1884, so its beautiful wild valleys were unspoilt by the villas which already defaced Cannes and Menton.[5] As late as 1912 the composer Gabriel Fauré was experiencing the thrill of discovering the Var, writing to his son from Hyères after he had passed through the landscape by train: 'I've never

opposite
94
A. Renoir
Rocky Crags at L'Estaque 1882 (detail)
Boston, Museum of Fine Arts,
Juliana Cheney Edwards Collection

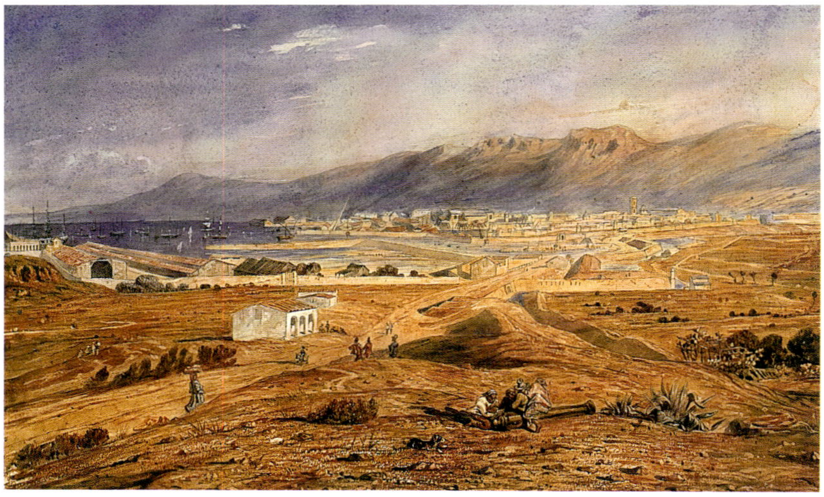

95
P. Huet
View of Toulon 1838–9
Edinburgh, National Gallery of Scotland

seen anything more delightful than the scenery of this region, mountainous and maritime at the same time'.[6] This thrill of discovery was echoed by painters. After his reconnaissance with Renoir, Monet returned swiftly to the Mediterranean early in 1884, begging their dealer Durand-Ruel (while asking him to pay for the railway ticket) not to tell his friend where he was going; Monet wanted to work alone on the new motifs.[7] The perceptions of the Midi as wild, off the beaten track, waiting to be explored by the intrepid painter, combined with geographical distance to establish a key characteristic in constructing images of the Mediterranean; they were not tarred by Paris's brush.

The perils of proximity to the city had driven Félix Ziem south years earlier. About 1860 Ziem, who had settled at Martigues to the west of Marseille, tried to persuade Théodore Rousseau to join him, explaining that Barbizon had become intolerably *touristique* and listing the attractions of the Bouches du Rhône. Having inventoried the trees and the lie of the land – 'forgotten by civilizers' – he continued: 'The sky is gentle and warm. It's a blue habitat'.[8] Motifs, light and colour were the landscape painter's preoccupations, and the Mediterranean climate provided them along with the promise of long summer seasons and reliable weather. Manguin's complaint about unpredictable weather written enviously from Normandy to Matisse in Saint-Tropez in August 1904 is only one of a litany of such moans, though Matisse riposted in turn that the intense heat was hindering his work.[9] One of the key issues for the painter working in the southern heat was how the light and atmosphere of the Midi affected colour. Light flooding from a strong sun in a cloudless sky gave the initial impression of strong colour, especially blue. Monet noted this laconically on returning to the Mediterranean in 1884 – 'as for the blue of sea and sky, it's impossible' – while van Gogh regaled his sister with his observations of 'the deepest royal blue of the water to the blue of the forget-me-nots, cobalt, particularly clear, bright blue – green-blue and violet-blue'.[10] But painters usually came to see that the intense light had a softening, harmonising effect and that strong colours and harsh contrasts were dissolved. Several weeks into his 1884 campaign Monet had realised that the Riviera light tended to have a dominant pink tone,[11] and a decade later Signac was furious when the Symbolist writer Adolphe Retté published some travel notes in *La Plume* which compared his Mediterranean canvases unfavourably to those of van Gogh [**246**], whose paintings Retté argued had caught the 'harsh colours' and 'brusque contrasts' of the Midi whereas Signac's Neo-Impressionism tended to grey the landscape. Signac objected in his journal: 'Everywhere reflected light eats up the local colours and greys the shadows.Because they are in the Midi people expect to see red, blue, green, yellow. On

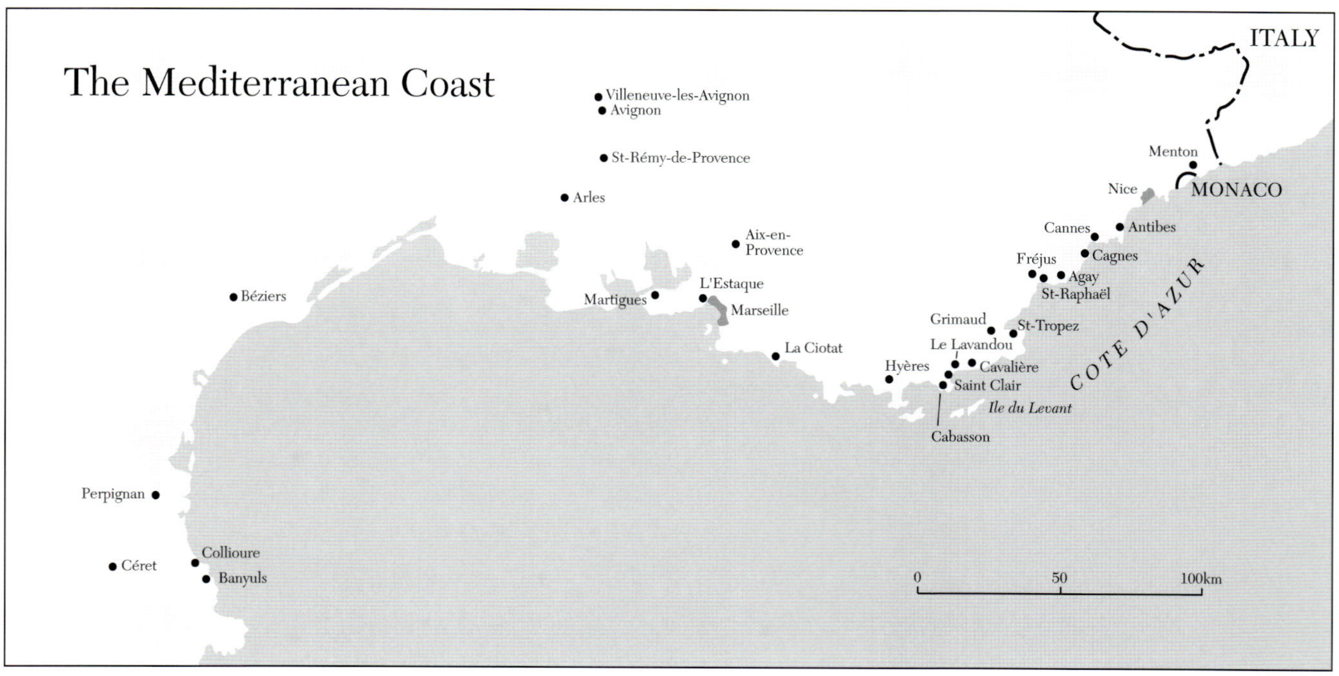

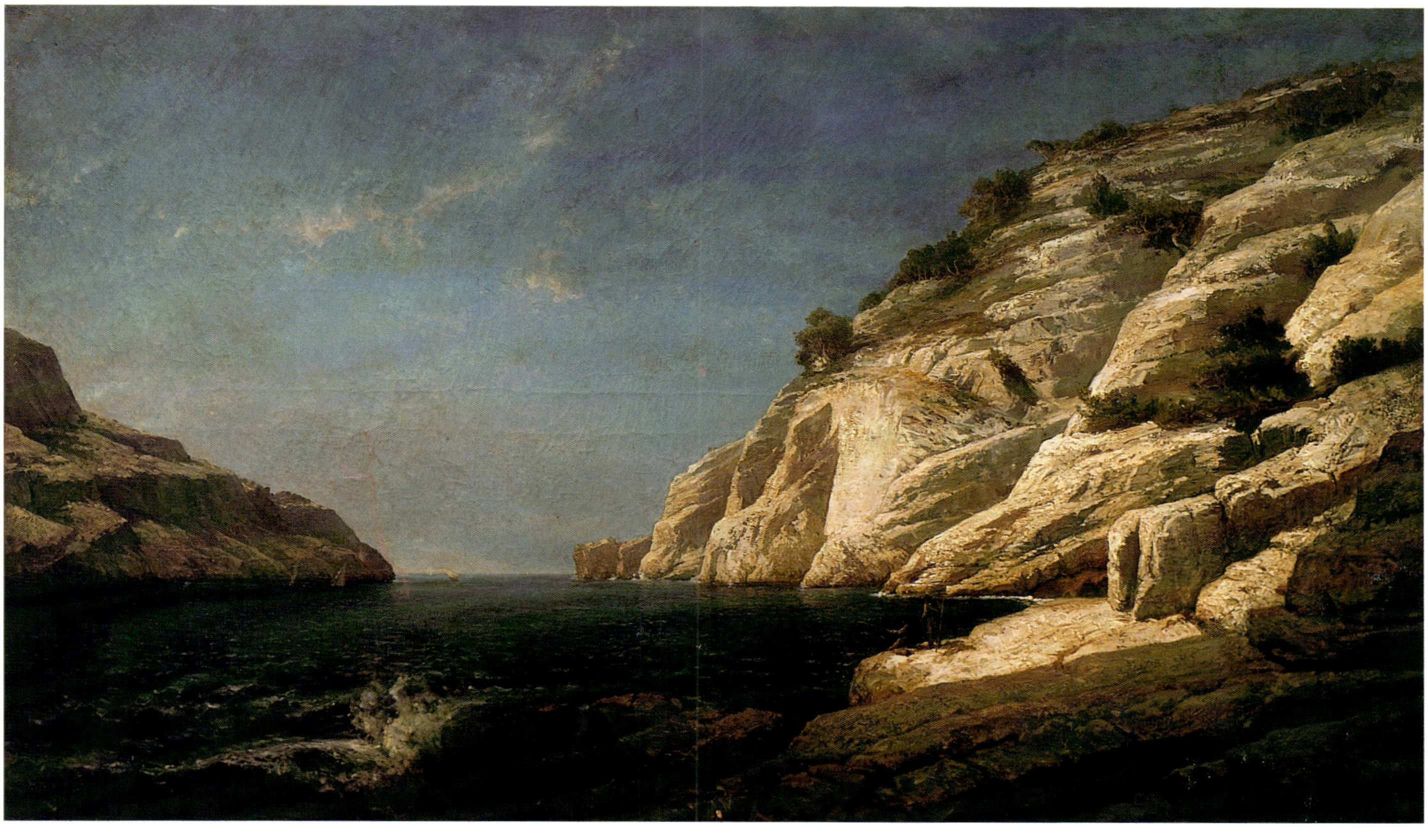

the contrary, it's the north – Holland, say – which is "coloured" (local colour), whereas the Midi is "luminous"'.[12] Derain agreed exactly, writing back to Vlaminck from Collioure in 1905 that he was grappling with 'a blonde, gold light which suppresses the shadows'.[13]

Although by the last quarter of the nineteenth century the Mediterranean coast had not been exploited as much by landscape painters as the Channel, this did not mean that there were not certain established motifs and modes of representation. The perceived wildness of the Midi had been promoted by regional painters. Raphaël Ponson's major canvas of 1874, *The Calanque de Port-Pin Near Cassis* [**96**], is a fine example of this. Its very title is expressly local, not only identifying a particular location on the coast south-east of Marseille but also using Midi *patois*, for *calanque* is a vernacular term for the rocky inlets along these shores. Ponson clearly delighted in the intense blues and blanched ochres of his native terrain, and he used scale effectively, both in setting small figures against the vast stark rocks and in representing his motif in a large format. By these means the spectator is given a sense of the *calanque* as an environment – hot, hard, parched, inhospitable – and as an experience: natural, grand, sublime. The construction of the Midi landscape as wild and harsh was used consistently by regional painters, whether they were Salon exhibitors such as Ponson or independent figures like Monticelli. Cézanne too produced landscapes which promote this image of Provence. In *Rocks Near L'Estaque* [**97**] he edited out all human presence except for the roof which appears almost apologetically over the horizon, out of place in this harsh, barren coastline. Such a manipulation of the motif to emphasise wild grandeur to the exclusion of the modern – the thriving port of Marseille is just over the rocky ridge to the left – was surely a conscious decision here, and it followed the precedent of painters such as Ponson, responding and contributing to this construction of the Mediterranean coast.

Inevitably the image of Provence's wild grandeur was one echoed by visitors, both in verbal and pictorial terms. Enthusiastically describing the steep fall of pine-covered rocks down to the sea near Cabasson, Cross, in a letter to Signac of 1891, could not resist punctuating his account with 'oh Gustave Doré!', referring self-consciously to the artist celebrated for his exaggeratedly dramatic landscapes.[14] On his way back from a trip to Italy early in 1882, Renoir visited Cézanne at L'Estaque where he was very taken by the landscape. Although he succumbed to pneumonia he completed a substantial canvas of the hilly scrubland behind the small town [**94, 98**]. While working on a much smaller scale than that of Ponson's picture, Renoir seems to have chosen the motif to convey an impression of the physical authority of the bluffs, which spread across the field of view, towering uninvitingly over the painter's vantage point. *Rocky Crags at L'Estaque* discreetly represents a frontier, where land fit to cultivate a cluster of hardy olive trees gives way to barren rock and dry scrub, *garrigue* in Midi vernacular, of the kind often painted by natives such as Monticelli, Guigou and Cézanne. Renoir

96
R. Ponson
The Calanque de Port-Pin Near Cassis
1873
Béziers, Musée des beaux-arts

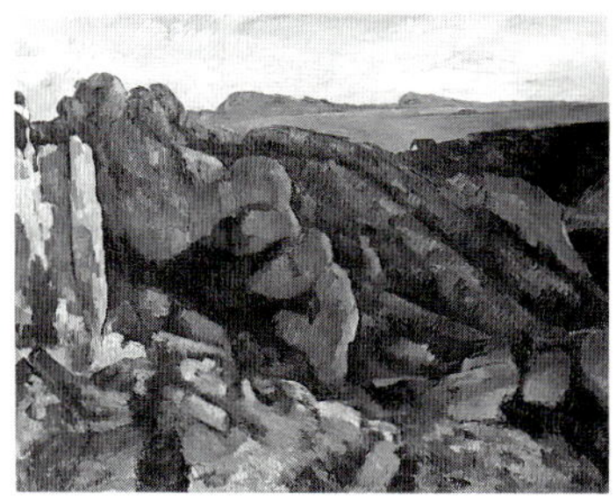

97
P. Cézanne
Rocks Near L'Estaque c.1884
São Paulo, Museu de Arte
Assis Chateaubriand

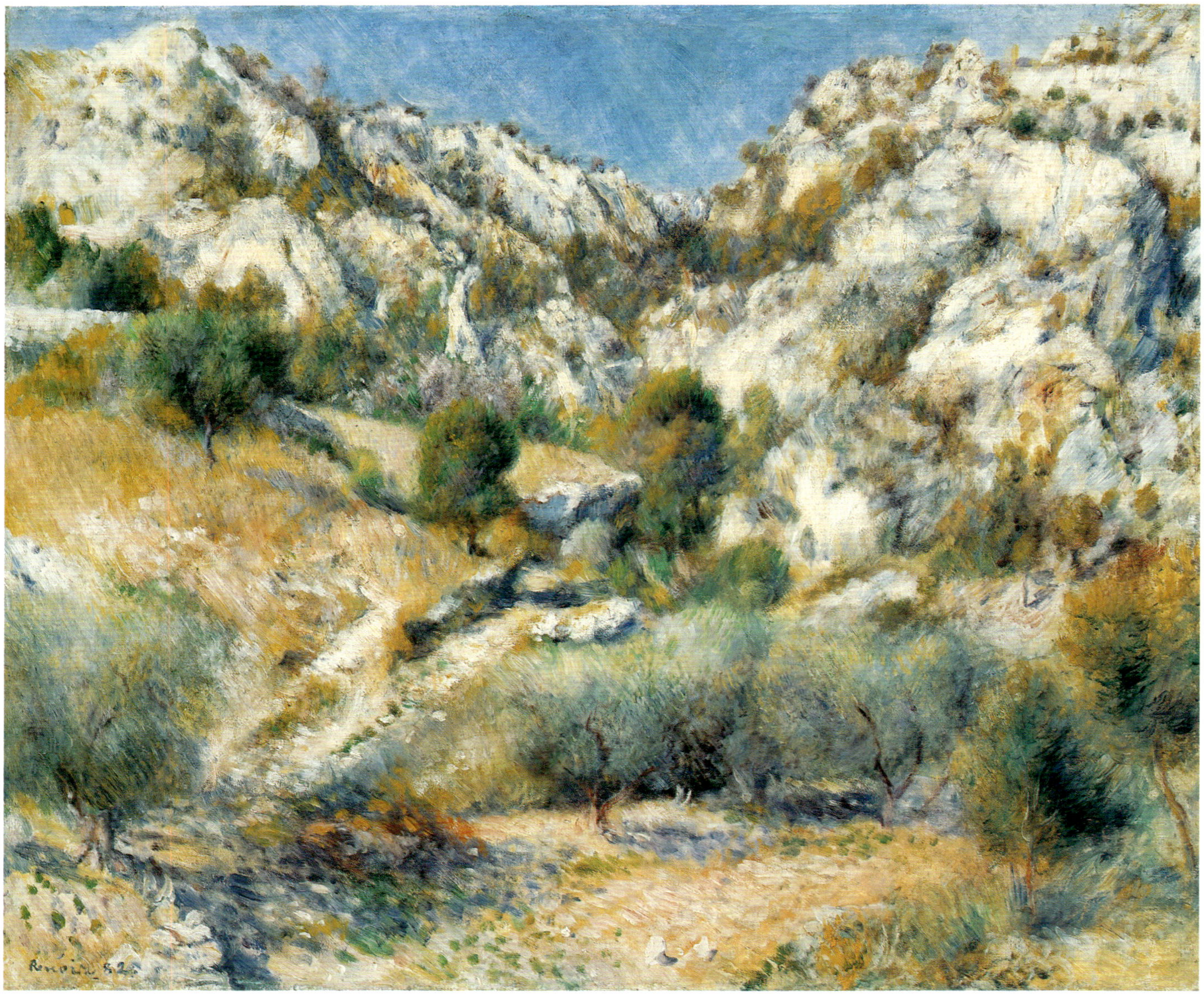

98
A. Renoir
Rocky Crags at L'Estaque 1882
Boston, Museum of Fine Arts,
Juliana Cheney Edwards Collection

charted this in his colour range, allowing more verdant greens on the lower slopes to contrast with the dessicated tones of the stony heights. Pitching the horizon high also allowed him to limit the sky to a band of rich modulated blue, but restricting it did not reduce the intensity of light, which he too saw as a unifying force in the Mediterranean atmosphere. The ample admixture of white pulls together the dry ochres, lively greens and occasional sappy browns of a landscape which, in January, still held some moisture. As he wrote back to Mme Charpentier, wife of one of his Parisian collectors: 'I've ended up by only seeing large harmonies without any longer bothering with little details which diminish the sunlight rather than stoke it up'.[15]

The poet Jean Moréas, travelling along the Mediterranean coast in the early years of the century, complained that he had seen nothing sublime in the landscape from St Raphaël to Menton.[16] It is unlikely that Valtat would have agreed, for his base at Agay on that very coast allowed him not only dramatically plunging views down to the sea close to where the famous red rocks of Anthéor butt out of the waves but also views inland to the forbidding terrain of the massif de l'Estérel. Valtat was seen at this time very much as a 'Midi' painter, and he was admired by contemporaries, Signac owning one of his Estérel landscapes.[17] In another view of the *massif*, made about 1903 [**99**], Valtat celebrates the ruggedness of this range by choosing a rough, thick-weave canvas and applying the paint in uncompromising patches of colour blocked in warm and cool in a manner reminiscent of Cézanne. But for all the energy of Valtat's picture it is surprisingly subtle; despite abandoning traditional aerial perspective he managed to give a sense of atmospheric recession by applying the medium densely in the foreground but more thinly and sparsely behind. Colour is used to evoke space, the deep purple-blue shadow to the right defining the pine-filled gorge over which we look towards the rippling orange-red rocks in the centre. Behind this we imagine another dipping valley, rising steeply through a zone of heather and petrol-blue marks to the surmounting towers of coral and orange rock. Texture of canvas, vivid paint surface and density of colour combine with motif in an energetic yet harmo-

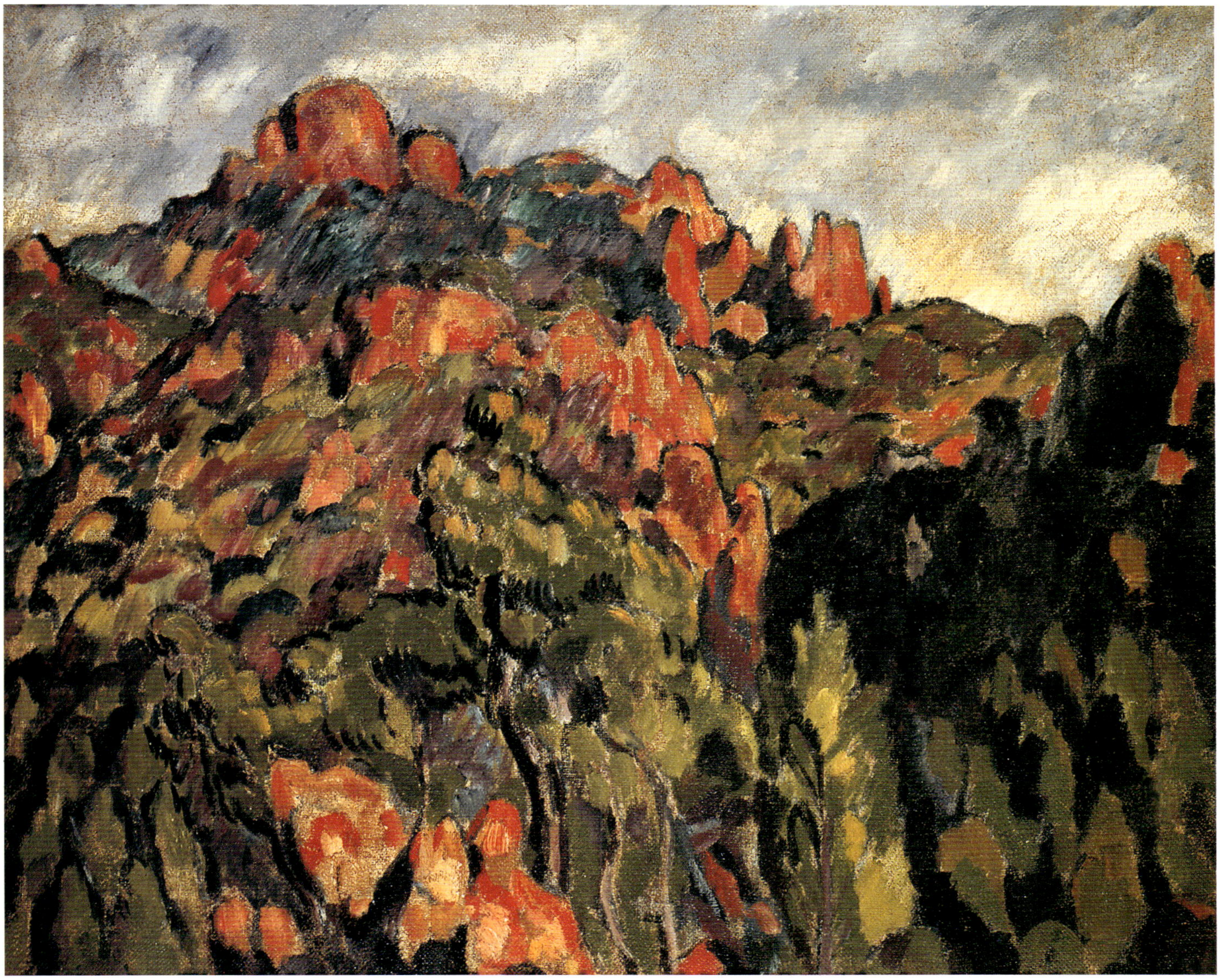

99
L. Valtat
The Estérel 1903
Saint-Tropez, Musée de l'Annonciade

nious ensemble to create a powerful image of a feral landscape, unpeopled and uncultivated.

The Mediterranean coast also provided landscape painters with sites of a picturesque character, time-honoured ports, ruined castles and the like [**114**]. This was the kind of motif that Monet sought out on his second extended trip to the Mediterranean in 1888, for while he seems to have had an eye for viewpoints and foci which caught the salient aspects of a place he probably also had 'assistance from local inhabitants or guidebooks'.[18] By keying his images to the pre-ordained and the picturesque Monet was furnishing his landscapes, painted in a technique which was still not universally approved, with an advantage on the market. This must have been on his mind at Antibes, for about half of the thirty-six canvases he made there represent the town's blanched ramparts and the medieval towers of the church and the château Grimaldi against the distant spectacle of the snow-capped Maritime Alps.[19] It is the view looking north from the Cap d'Antibes, which guidebooks recommended as a vantage point.[20] Four of his paintings were taken from the Salis gardens and employ the same composition: the right half of the design, with its *repoussoir* tree filling the foreground space with its reaching branches and light-filtering foliage, is balanced by the view in the left-hand side across the sea to the ancient town. These canvases [**100**] are each carefully harmonised, the local colour moderated by softening, almost pastel tones which give the landscape motifs far and near the sense of being dissolved in the warm ambient light. Their pleasing colour and picturesque motifs made the Antibes group a commercial success when they were shown at Théo van Gogh's Boussod et Valadon Gallery in Paris in June–July 1888, the four Salis paintings all finding buyers in short order. But to the critic Félix Fénéon, supporter of the younger generation, the Antibes work displayed 'excessive bravura' and 'brilliant vulgarity', a remark aimed surely not just at their execution but at their subject, which Fénéon's concluding barb about the New York art market insinuated was overtly commercial.[21] Monet's choice of the picturesque Mediterranean site was hardly exclusive or unprecedented, for local artists such as Contini [**114**] had set the tone, and they in turn were

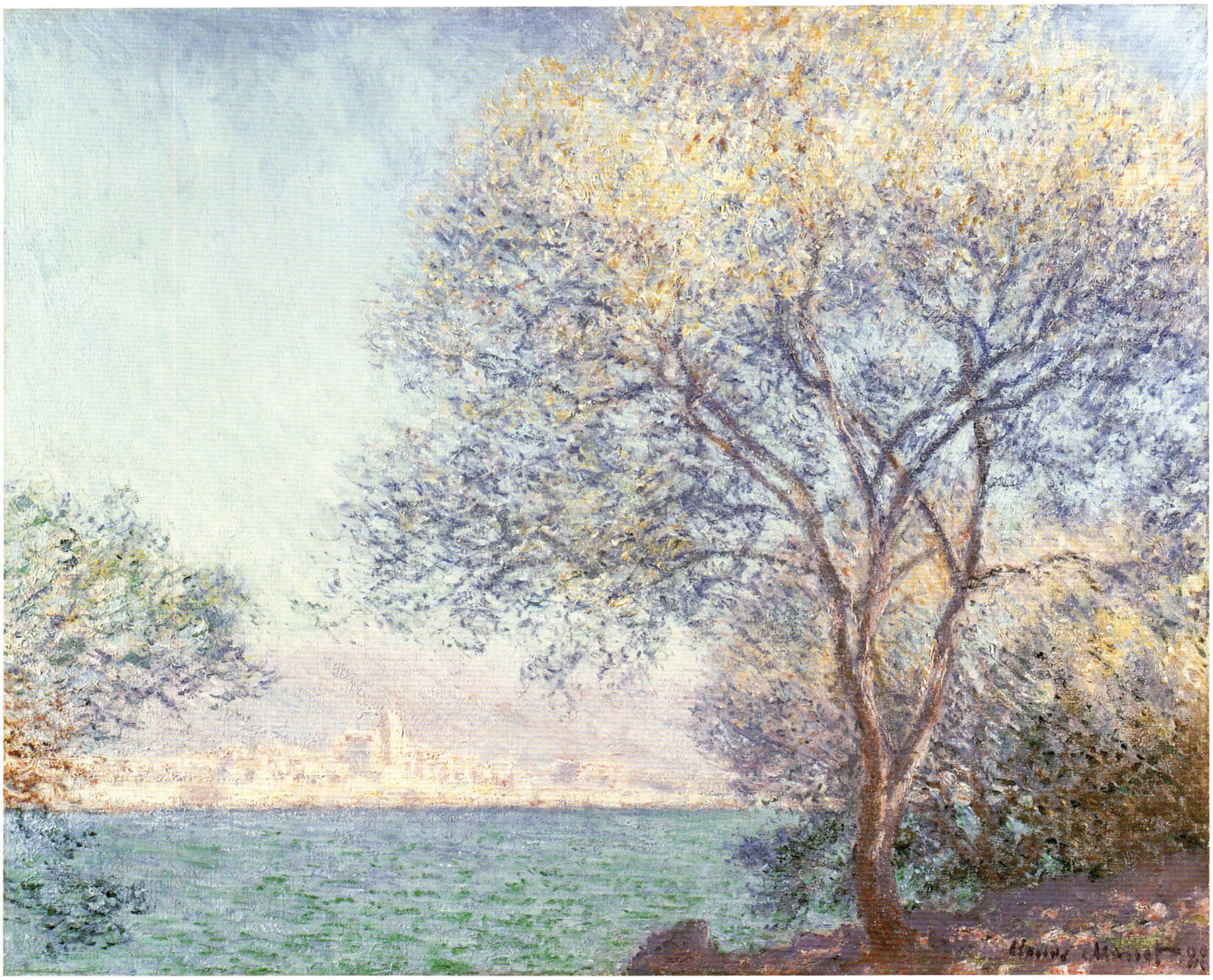

100
C. Monet
Antibes Seen From the Salis 1888
Philadelphia Museum of Art, Bequest of Charlotte Dorrance Wright

following an existing taste for the *pittoresque*. In an unpublished letter of about 1907–8 Signac wrote to Théo van Rysselberghe in Paris asking him to procure a photograph of one of Monet's views from the Salis. Signac explained why he needed it: 'It's not that I want to filch the motif, but out of curiosity because I've looked in vain for where it could have been done from – the Cap has been so parcelled up that the motif might have disappeared'.[22] Signac's letter points to a continued propensity for the picturesque as well as suggesting that he was aware of working within some kind of tradition, albeit recent, of representing Mediterranean motifs, an awareness that Monet would likely have felt far less strongly twenty years before. But it raises another issue, one reinforced by Signac's succeeding remark that while he had been drawing pines on the Cap they were being chopped down to clear space for the cables of a new tramway. The wild, unspoilt shores of the Mediterranean and their picturesque sites were increasingly under threat from encroaching modernity.

The forty years from 1874–1914 saw substantial changes in the social and commercial structures of the Mediterranean coast. Regional trade developed following the opening of the Suez Canal in 1869, Marseille expanded on the profits of commerce with France's colonies in north Africa and elsewhere, and the tourist industry burgeoned.[23] This process of modernisation was a regional variation on a national pattern, and it involved changes to the physical character of particular areas, notably around large towns and cities. It was for the painter to make individual decisions about how to highlight, accommodate, or avoid such shifts in the way a landscape might look. The ways in which painters might order or eliminate elements from their natural or man-made surroundings to make a landscape painting which would read in a certain way can be followed by comparing representations of a single vicinity: L'Estaque.

L'Estaque lies to the north of the Bay of Marseille, some seven kilometres from the city centre. Of ancient origin, with one landmark – the tour Sommati – first recorded in 1298, it was an active fishing port, producing catches principally of sardine. The 11 a.m. train from Marseille regularly stopped to take on cases of fish for Avignon and Paris. The construction of the Paris-Lyon-Marseille railway in the 1840s had necessitated the digging of the long Tunnel de la Nerthe under the hills to the west of L'Estaque, the first of a series of intrusions into the local landscape. In 1857 a factory was built up one of the inland valleys to produce cement from the indigenous limestone, and in 1884 the mining conglomerate Rio Tinto set up a large facility. The conditions at L'Estaque were particularly propitious for the production of tiles, and in the 1870s some 200,000 tons were exported from local works. As well as being a growing industrial area, L'Estaque retained its pleasant shoreline conveniently close to the city, a distinction recognised by the inhabitants in 1872 when they petitioned the mayor of Marseille to build two new roads, one along the coast to serve the restaurants and seafront pleasures and another inland for commercial traffic. The coast road was not finally built until 1900, though the extension of the city's steam-tram service along the littoral eight years earlier indicates how L'Estaque, like Asnières, was gradually becoming absorbed into the conurbation.[24]

The changes that were taking place in the environs of Marseille had been suggested two decades before our period in Loubon's large painting *View of Marseille from Les Aygalades* of 1853 [**101**]. This panorama from the north shore of the bay represents the port as the junction of open land, mountain and sea. But these natural features carry further associations. Marseille is envisaged as an active port, its wharves and shoreline buildings picked out, with boats plying the bay. It is the destination of the herdsmen, bringing in their cattle for market or export, and thus essential to the exchange between city and country implicit on Loubon's image. Contrasting with the timeless motif of the herd are the smoking factory chimneys, perhaps of L'Estaque's tile works, which, silhouetted against the bay and bissected by a quay, mark modernity's intrusion. It is a subtle intrusion, however, mollified by Loubon's generally unassertive working of the city into its natural environment and his equally discreet depiction of picturesque incidents such as the hilltop ruin and the Château d'If on its harbour island. All this is set against the massif de Marseilleveyre, rising sternly in the sunlight, and its continuation in the rocky islands, notably the abrupt flanks of the île Maire, the scale of which Loubon exaggerated. In this large exhibition painting, shown at the Salon of 1853, Loubon presciently orchestrated almost the whole gamut of issues and polarities to be found in later landscape painting: city and country, the timeless and the modern, the agricultural and the industrial, the picturesque and the sublime.

Cézanne never produced a landscape painting that was as intentionally ambitious as this in its iconography. However, to consider his paintings of L'Estaque solely in terms of stylistic achievement, without assessing how he selected and ordered his landscape imagery – as has hitherto been the case – is seriously to underestimate them. Undoubtedly painting at L'Estaque was important to Cézanne's understanding of his work and the direction it was taking. This is clear from the famous letter to Pissarro of July 1876, in which he explained that the Bay of Marseille is 'like a playing card, red roofs over the blue sea. The olive and pine trees always keep their leaves. The sun here is so tremendous that it seems to me as if the objects were silhouetted not only in black and white, but in blue, red, brown and violet. I may be mistaken, but this seems to me to be the opposite of modelling'.[25] Cézanne evidently responded to the light and climate of the locale, and in painting landscapes under those conditions he arrived at the results he elucidated to Pissarro. In a canvas such as *View of Mont*

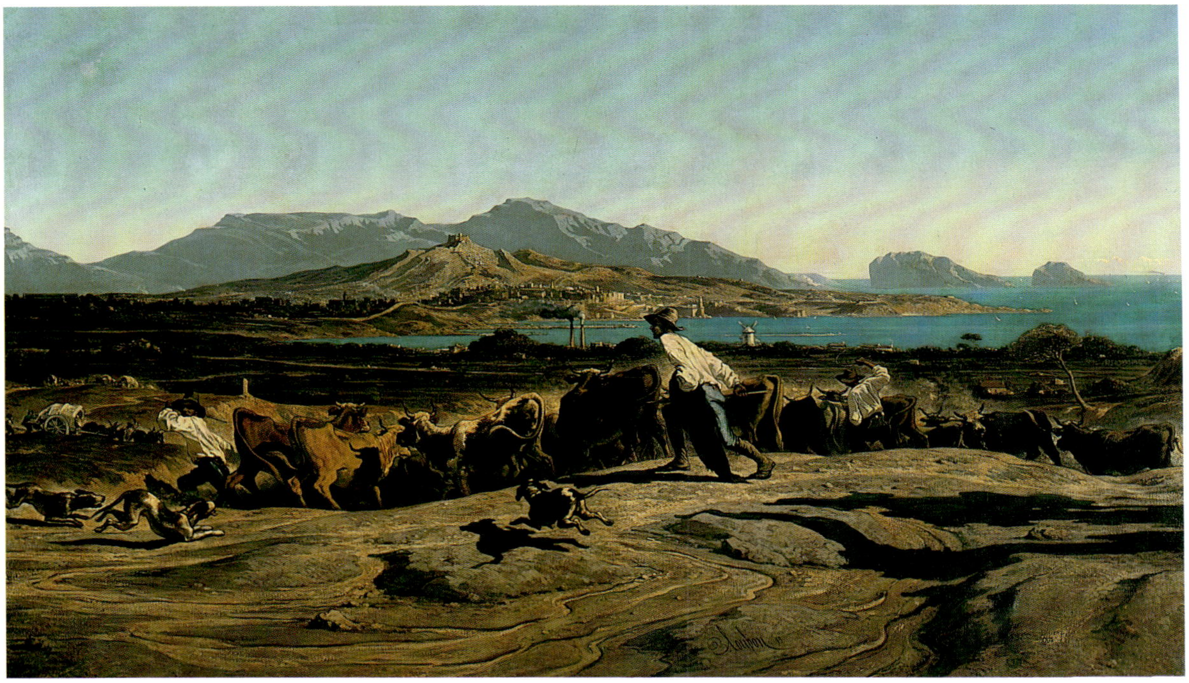

101
E. Loubon
View of Marseille from Les Aygalades
1853
Marseille, Musée des beaux-arts

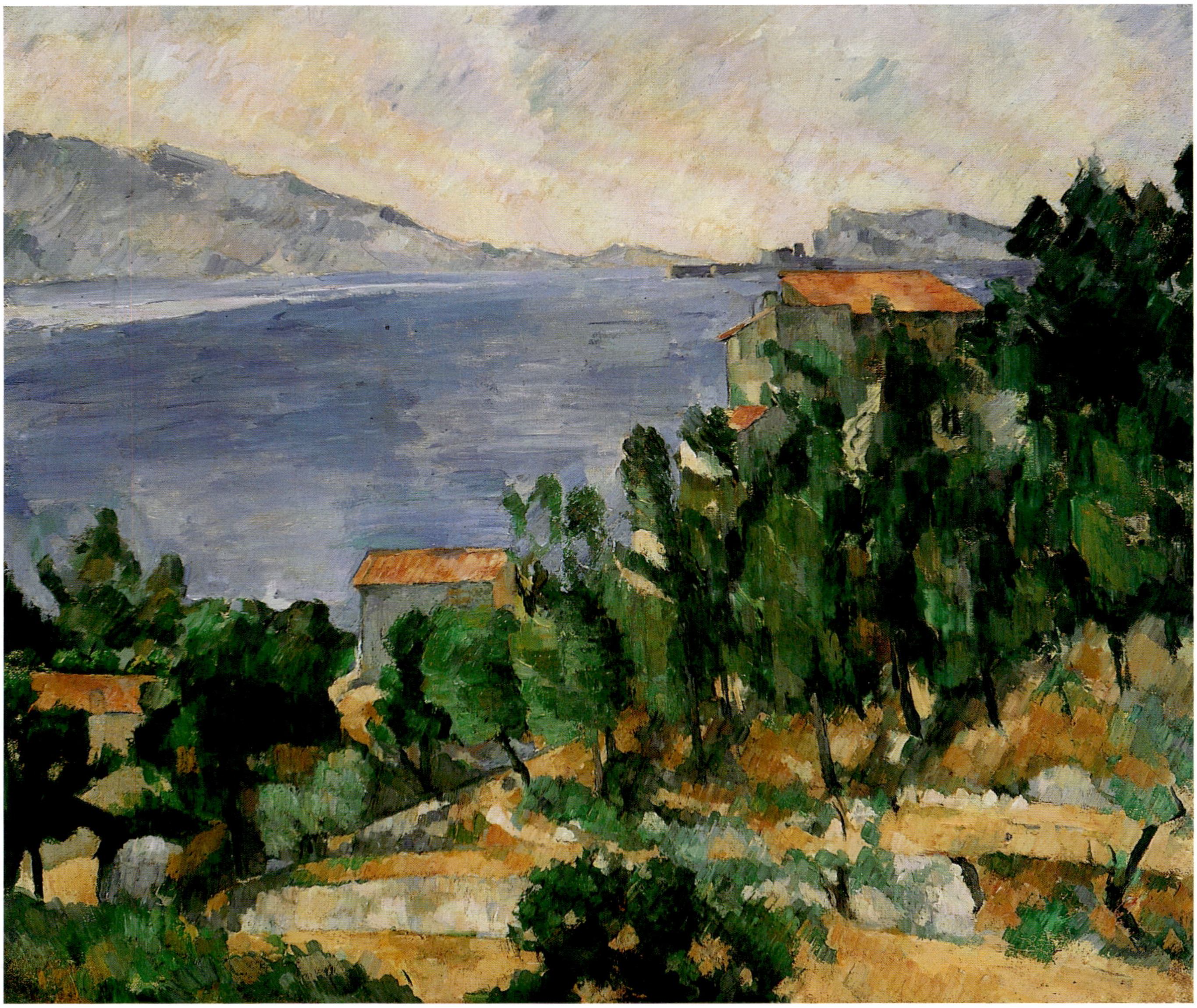

102
P. Cézanne
View of Mont Marseilleveyre and the île de Maire c.1878–82
Memorial Art Gallery of the University of Rochester, anonymous gift in tribute to Edward Harris and in memory of H. R. Stirlin of Switzerland

Marseilleveyre and the île de Maire [**102**], made a few years after that letter, the warms of the tiled roofs and sun-soaked soil are contrasted with the cool greens and blues of foliage and sea to produce a chromatic push-and-pull which evokes space. But what does Cézanne actually represent here? There are no chimneys or tile works, no distant view of Marseille and its port. Modernity is excluded, and *View of Mont Marseilleveyre* presents us with an image of L'Estaque as an unchanged hamlet on an unspoilt littoral. One might expect Cézanne to have favoured such a construction of the landscape given his opinions on the development of L'Estaque, for in 1902 he complained to his god-daughter about the 'once so picturesque banks of L'Estaque. Unfortunately what we call progress is nothing but the invasion of bipeds who do not rest until they have transformed everything into hideous *quais* with gas lamps – and, what is worse – with electric illumination!'[26] Cézanne had first painted at L'Estaque while dodging conscription during the Franco-Prussian War of 1870–1, though the bulk of his work there was made on a succession of visits between the mid-1870s and the mid-1880s. His neglect of the area after that might be taken as evidence of his disgruntlement with L'Estaque's modernisation, but as we have seen this was well under way during the period of his most intense work there. And in those paintings modernity is not necessarily denied. The famous panoramas across the bay, now in Paris and Chicago, both show factory chimneys in the foreground and in the distance the jetties and blocky urban sprawl of Marseille,[27] while a canvas such as *Saint-Henri and the Bay of L'Estaque* [**103**] looks along the shoreline and presents an image neither of the elemental sublimity of the São Paulo painting [**97**] nor of the tranquil rurality of the Rochester picture [**102**] but of change and industrialisation. The church's identity as the hub of the villages now challenged by the insistent vertical accents of the tile works' chimneys, especially that of the *tuilerie* Amadée Pierre which broaches the horizon. Cézanne may not have emulated Loubon's complex interplay of images and values within a single landscape, but his paintings of L'Estaque go beyond painterly response to natural phenomena and articulate a variety of responses to a changing landscape.

Various were the ways younger painters too read L'Estaque, when they visited the locality early in the twentieth century. Braque in 1906, for instance, painted the same motif [**104**] as Cézanne's *Saint-Henri*, which for all its bright decorative surface registers the further modernisation of L'Estaque, the tall chimneys now joined in their rigidifying of the landscape by a new jetty and the embankment of the recently completed coastal road. Yet other paintings from Braque's same campaign represent houses, hills and trees, motifs uncluttered by modernity.

That, of course, was the construction of the Midi as changeless, uncivilised, different, the topos Maupassant voiced when he enthused about the Montagnes des Maures and the Saint-Tropez peninsula: one can walk for a day and meet nobody; the railway has not reached here; it is almost like a wild island separated from the continent.[28] West of the Rhône the countryside became even more remote. Visiting Béziers in 1900 for the staging of his opera *Prométhée*, Fauré went down to the coast, where, he reported to his wife, 'there are fishermen's huts, with thatched roofs, separated by enormous clumps of maize, giving the illusion of landscapes from central Africa, near Lake Chad or Oubangui!' [29] Such comments, slipping easily into the language of the explorer although each writer was describing his own country, stress the differences visitors were astonished and delighted to find. That sense of the unexplored, the alien, increased the further west one travelled along the Mediterranean coast into the Languedoc, through relatively impoverished *départements* such as the Hérault and into the Pyrénées. Here there were few large population centres, no established resort towns on the lines of Nice or Cannes, but a sun-parched land supporting humble agricultural and fishing communities along the ancient Roman road to Spain, with its dramatic coastline where the mountain chain tumbles into the sea. It was local painters who first made the most of this landscape. Daniel de Monfried, for example, follower and friend of Gauguin, came from a family with estates in the Pyrénées orientales, and his early canvases celebrate the harsh land beaten by the sun; in his *Roussillon Landscape* of 1889 [**105**] the long rectangle of sky, flecked but unbroken, acts as a metaphor for the weight of the heat in this barren environment. Among those who – like Gauguin – benefited from Monfried's generosity with his private means was the sculptor Aristide Maillol, a native of Banyuls, only a few kilometres from the Spanish border. In the 1890s Maillol still painted regularly, and his *Village in the Pyrénées orientales* [**106**] represents a community in his native region. It is an image concerned with the effect of strong sunlight falling from a stark blue sky on to the ochres, corals and pinks of the weathered stone houses. It articulates, too, the picturesque construction so savoured by visitors such as Maupassant: the structures dating back to the Moors and beyond, the low doors, the crudely formed arches. But notation of climate and observation of architecture surely add up to something more. Such ancient villages were formed by building houses cheek-by-jowl in order to create shelter and shade, as Maillol insists with his strong contrasts of value which give the structures such a

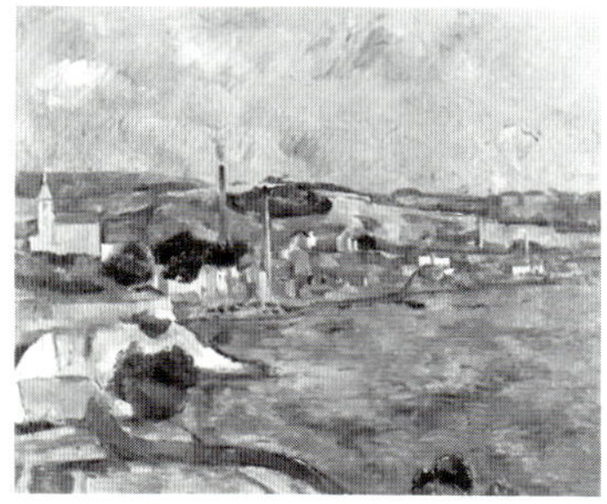

103
P. Cézanne
Saint-Henri and the Bay of L'Estaque
*c.*1877–9
Philadelphia, Museum of Art,
Mr and Mrs Carroll S. Tyson

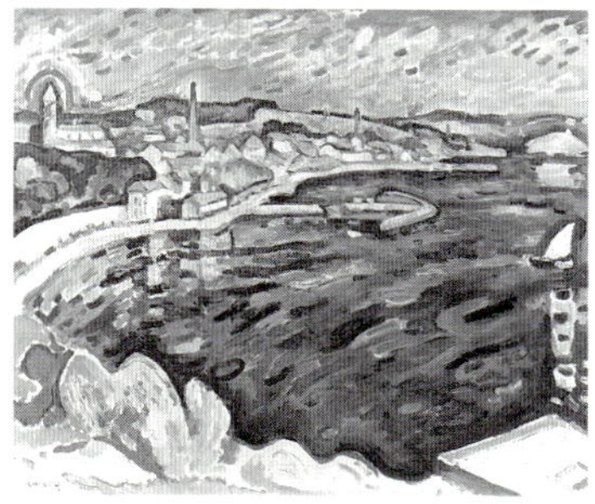

104
G. Braque
The Port of L'Estaque 1906
Copenhagen, Statens Museum for Kunst

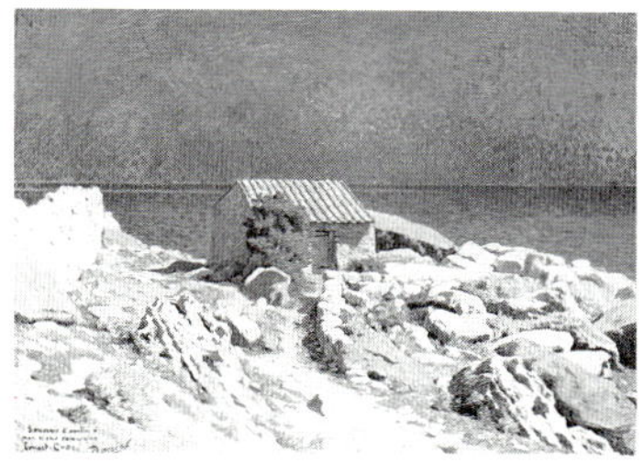

105
D. de Monfried
Roussillon Landscape 1889
Indianapolis Museum of Art,
Gift of the Alliance of the Indianapolis
Museum of Art

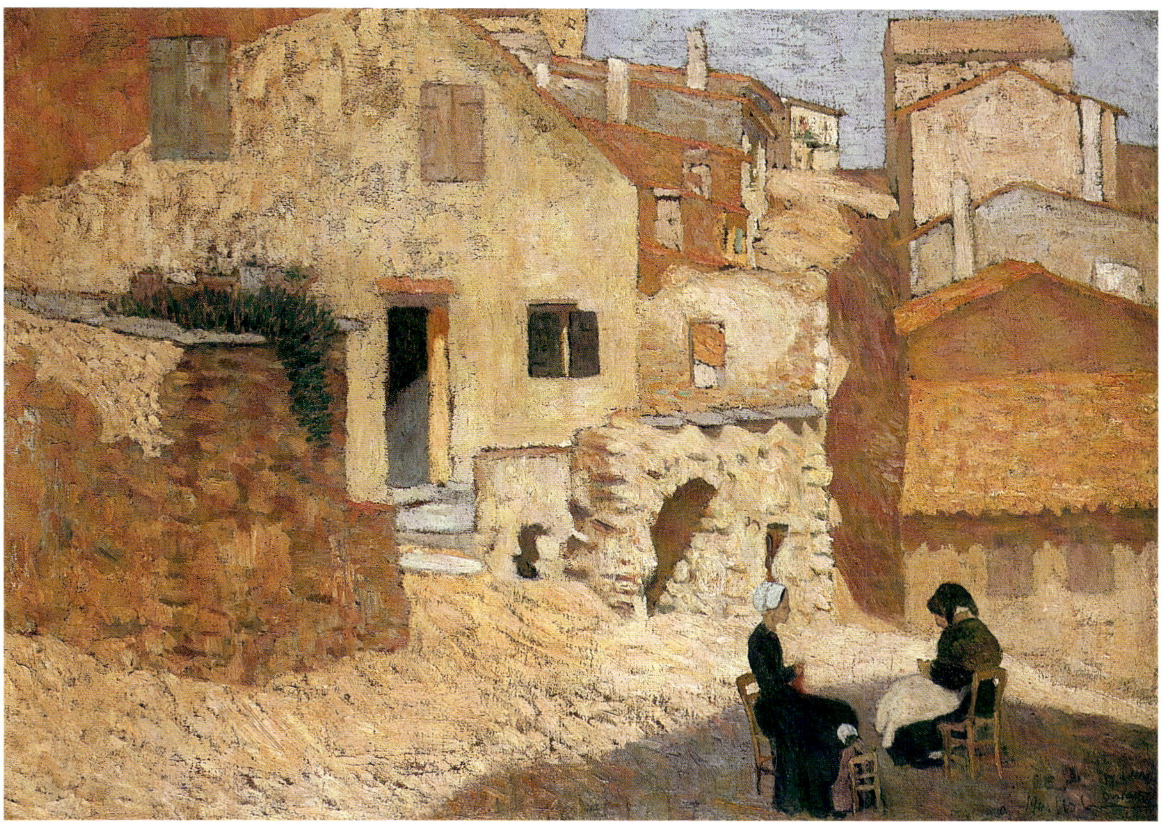

106
A. Maillol
Village in the Pyrénées orientales
*c.*1895
Oxford, Ashmolean Museum

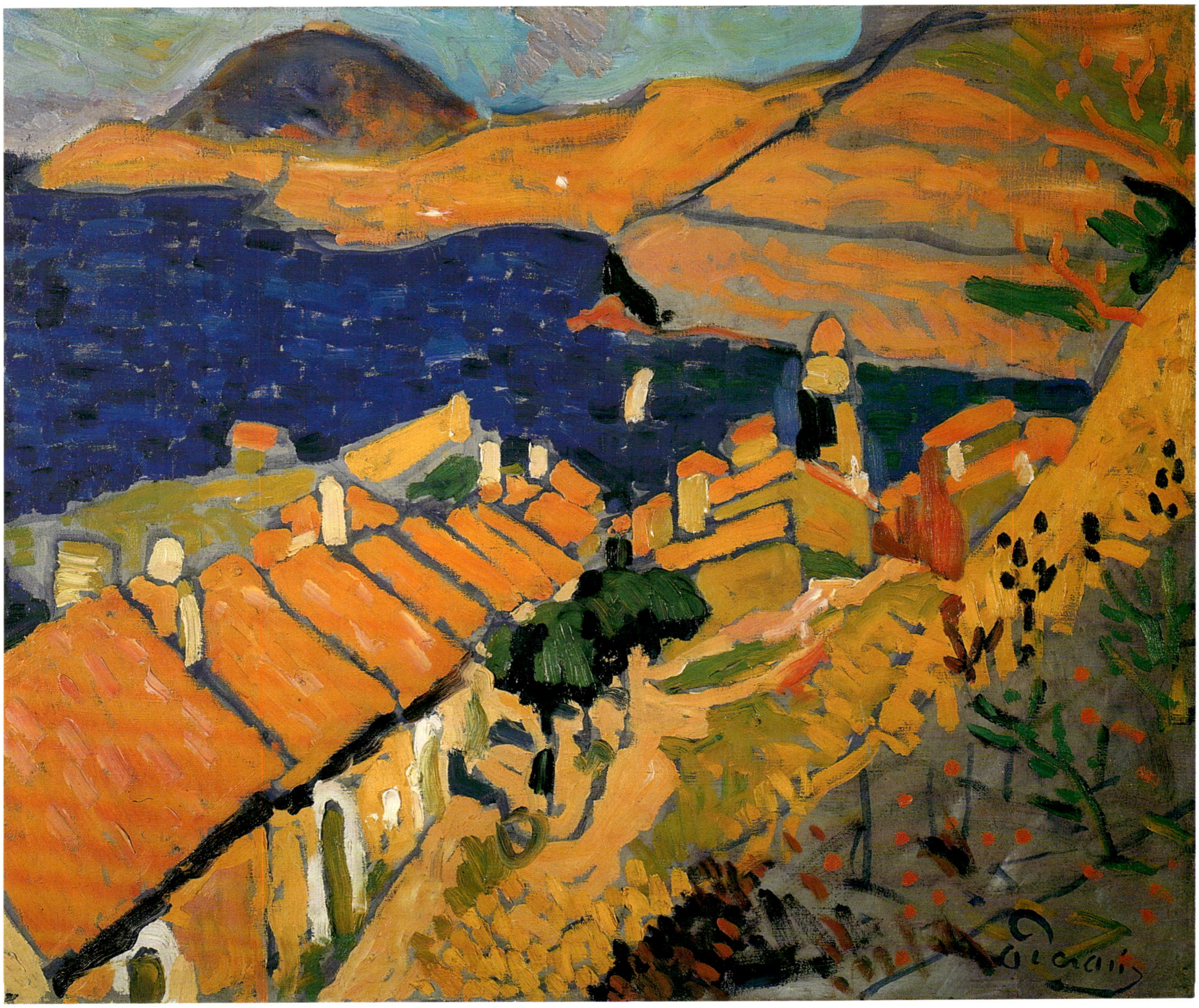

107
A. Derain
Collioure, the Village and the Sea
1905
Edinburgh, Scottish National
Gallery of Modern Art

108
H. Matisse *View of Collioure*
1905
St Petersburg, The Hermitage
Museum

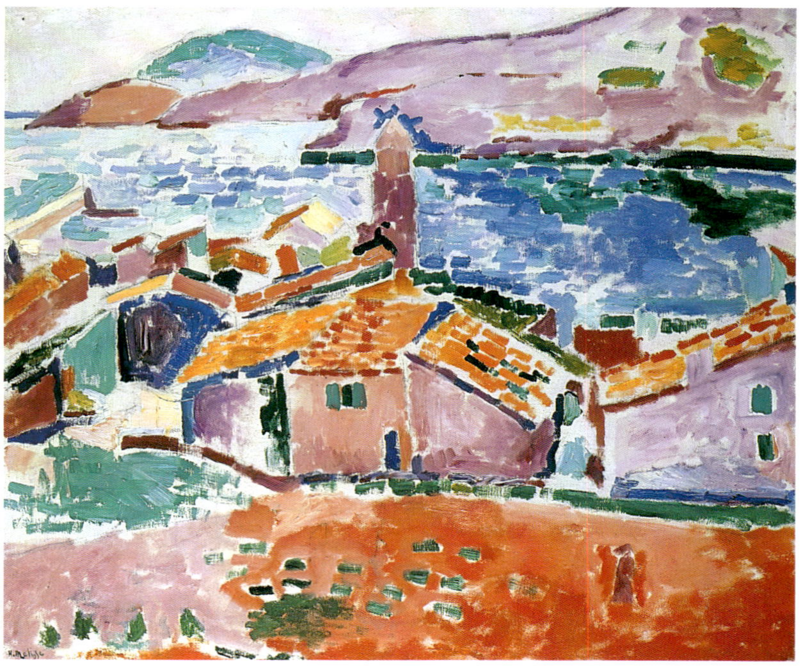

blocky, interlocking character. These villages are thus environments made by man to defeat the climate, to defend against the inhospitable local landscape. In Maillol's representation the village is at once protecting habitat and yet – given its age, its formation from the very stones which surround it – almost a landscape itself: timeless, a quasi-organic feature of the Pyrenean terrain.

When Derain arrived at Collioure, very near Banyuls, to spend the summer of 1905 painting with Matisse, he rattled off his first excited impressions in a letter to Vlaminck. The villages, their churches and wooden carvings; the rocks, fish and reptiles; the multicoloured boats and pottery; the tanned men and graceful women – amounted to a drastically different experience, and led Derain to an emphatic recommendation: 'one must get the hell out of Paris'.[30] The paintings made by Derain and Matisse at Collioure that summer 'present a vision of town and landscape intertwined'.[31] In this they were party to an existing construction of the Mediterranean, an idea already used by Maillol and even insinuated in Loubon's representation of Marseilles, but a construction which – for Paris-based painters using their season's campaign to forward their pictorial researches into the play between flat and actively marked zones of colour – served as a useful iconographical topos, and allowed for certainty of association. Paintings of the fishing port by both artists suggest an easy, 'natural' relationship either between the fisherfolk, boats and sea, or between village and surrounding landscape. Take the two artists' similar views over the roofs of Collioure to the bay beyond. Matisse [**108**] allowed blank canvas an active role, bringing light through from behind the painted surface, building the coloured forms up from an essentially graphic understructure, whereas Derain prepared his canvas [**107**] overall in a battleship grey, covered thickly with the only slightly modulated indigo of the sea, from which the rich oranges of buildings and distant shore emerge resonantly. Despite their different pictorial means, both represented Collioure essentially unpeopled, Derain including a single sail in the bay and Matisse what may be a figure in the foreground. Again, both used strokes of equivalent weight or texture and similar colours for both village and landscape, pictorially linking the natural and the man-made. Matisse implied this by those methods alone, Derain by more complex means. The latter's more distant viewpoint allowed greater use of the perspective formed by the valley which sets the cottages, marching regularly towards the Mediterranean, against the hillside scrub. If Derain counterpointed the uniformity of the village against the diversity of nature, he still represented the village as another quasi-organic entity, absorbed into the folds of the landscape. For all this, both painters registered a distance between the spectator and the village, Matisse by an open expanse and Derain by a visually chaotic central section whose blues and greens prevent the eye from penetrating the village itself. It is as if both artists were conscious of their temporary relationship with this community and landscape, aware of the fiction with which they were colluding.

The construction of the Mediterranean village as a tranquil locale assimilated into its landscape surroundings continued to be used by painters of different stylistic affiliations up to the First World War. A painting by Braque [**109**] said to represent La Ciotat, between Marseille and Toulon, where he worked during the summer of 1907, shows an identical solution to that of Derain and Matisse at Collioure in 1905. The sloping line of houses is paralleled by the rank of tilted trees, while the rich violets and pinks of the trunks are echoed in the walls and roofs. Again, motif, chromatics and touch work together to produce an image of harmony and shelter on the Mediterranean shore. It was a construction sustained by Cubism. For all its self-evident stylistic differences, Braque's 1911 painting of the *Rooftops, Céret* [**110**], another town in the Pyrénées orientales, adopts essentially the same fiction of the community – huddled, changeless, sharply shadowed, organically textured – as Maillol had done and as Juan Gris was to do in another Céret motif painted two years later.[32]

The attraction of such places was their remoteness, their difference from the north in terms of climate and environment, their relative freedom from industrialisation and tourism; as Matisse reassured Manguin about Collioure in 1906: 'it's just a village, whose only regular visitors are some lower middle-class people from Perpignan'.[33] Mediterranean motifs, just as much as those on the Channel coast, could be constructed in a variety of ways. They might be represented as modern, shifting with the rhythms of technology and commerce, or as wild, perhaps starkly sublime or quaintly changeless. Painters' options may have been diverse, but they fell into patterns, and dominating these was a central mythology about the Midi. It was voiced by Derain in an undated reply to an *enquête* about the Mediterranean, probably held between the Wars. While in his youth, Derain remembered, he had been attracted by the light and colour of the region; latterly he had come to appreciate the Midi for the way in which, while adapting to the modern, it was characterised by 'the preservation of a moral purity', a 'Provençal sociability and civility'.[34] This appealing combination of physical environment and social order was at the core of a myth, a nostalgia, which painters were able to manipulate in their landscapes of the Mediterranean, whether observed or imagined.

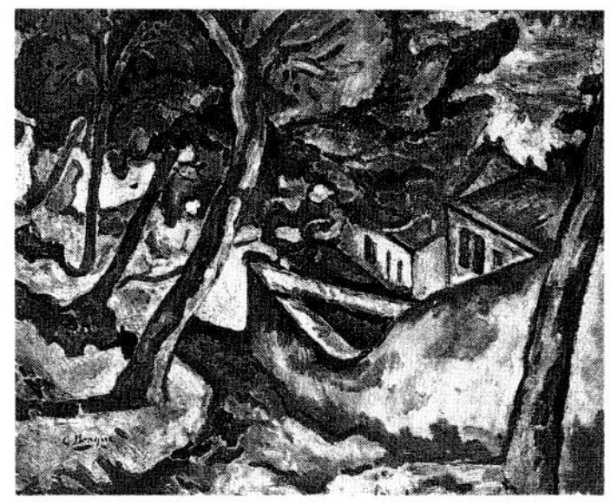

109
G. Braque
Landscape at La Ciotat 1907
Chicago, Art Institute

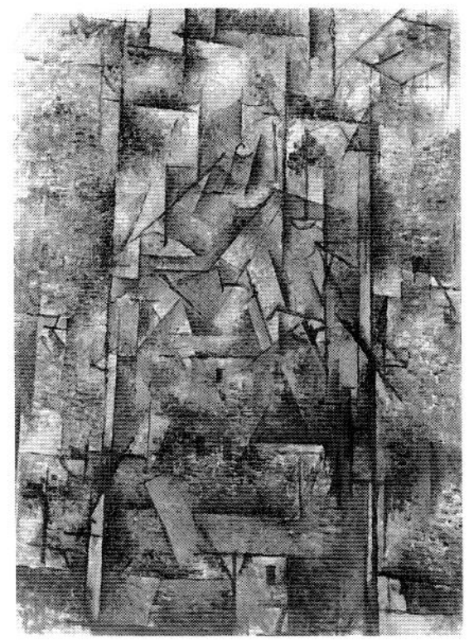

110
G. Braque
The Rooftops, Céret 1911
Private Collection

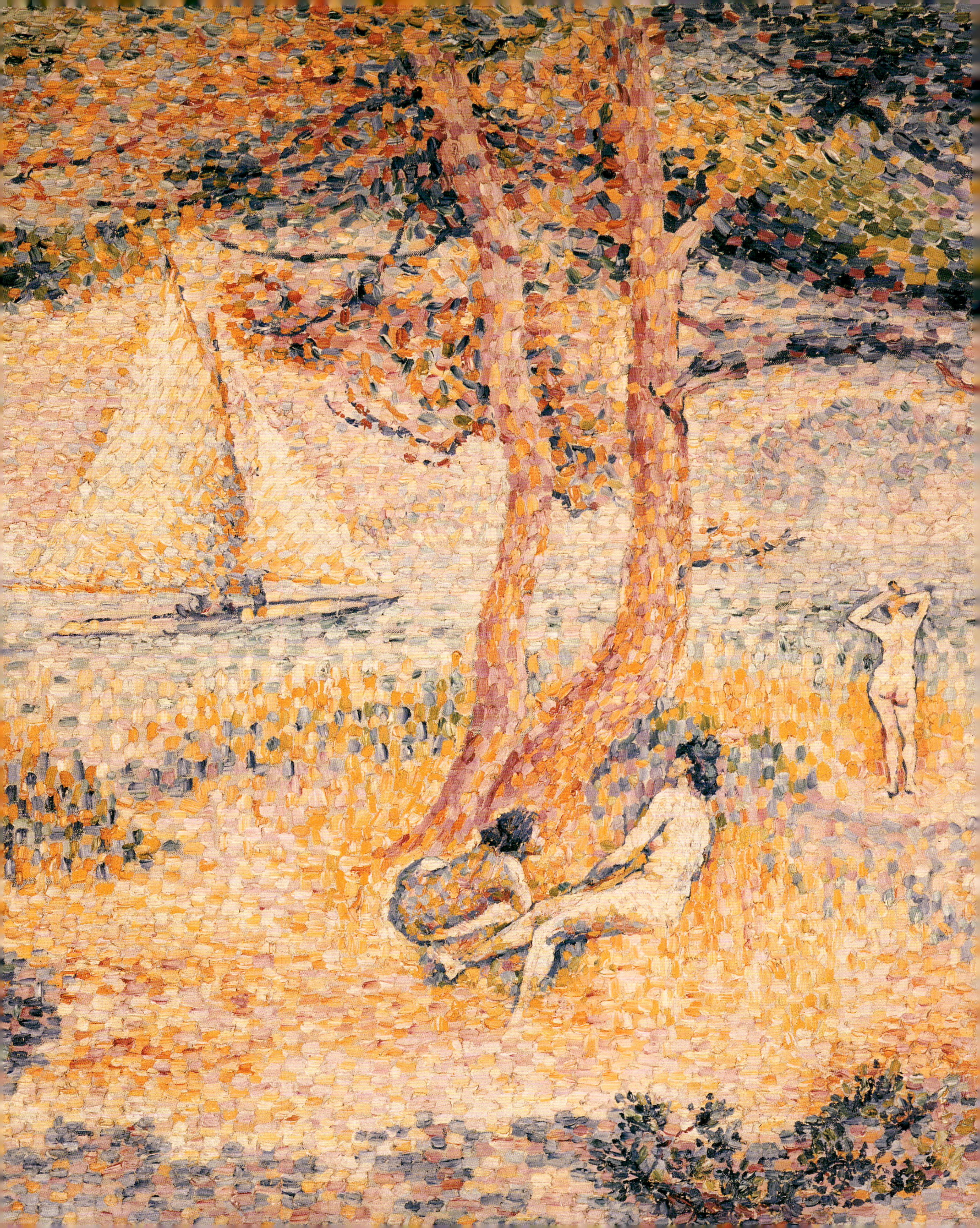

6 Reinventing the Pastoral Ideal

The *Prix de Rome de paysage historique* had been established in 1817 under the auspices of Neo-Classical landscape painters such as Valenciennes [**154**]. Awarded every four years, it allowed a young artist the opportunity to study in Italy alongside his history painting colleagues and was instigated in order to sustain the Italianate, Poussinesque *paysage composé* with its emphasis on mythological and historical subjects. The Prix was abolished in the reforms of the Ecole des beaux-arts in 1863, and replaced in 1869 by the Prix Troyon, named in honour of the late animal painter, which was awarded biennially and did not insist on the traditional idiom of the *paysage historique*; the first subject set in the competition was merely *A Landscape Crossed by a Torrent*.[1] Such a development would seem to show the decline of traditional values in the face of the mid-century's dominant naturalism. However, that would be an over-simplification; as the introductory chapter argued, the conventions of the *paysage composé* continued, if not vigorously then at least consistently, throughout the 1870s and 1880s. The increasing pressures of nationalism and the desire for social order in the 1890s and after provided fertile cultural ground for those conventions to gather fresh momentum.

A vital link in that continuity was Corot and his reputation. Corot, who died in 1875, had been a pupil in the 1820s of Michallon, first winner of the *Prix de Rome de paysage historique*, as well as being a friend of Millet, Rousseau and the naturalist landscape painters who had come to prominence in the 1850s and 1860s. His work covered both camps; his career stood for both tradition and transformation. If Corot's reputation never dipped after his death, twenty years on it was at a highpoint. In 1895 there was a large retrospective of his work, and progressive painters such as Monet and Signac expressed their admiration.[2] Corot's work could be taken to uphold varied values. To the establishment critic Lafenestre, writing in 1893, his example stood behind the survival of the *paysage composé* and in particular his staffage of nymphs encouraged the fanciful canvases of young Symbolist painters.[3] And with the hindsight of another fifteen years Corot's contribution could be seen as combining the virtues of classical composition and modern *poésie*, thus influencing more recent giants of French painting such as Puvis de Chavannes and Cazin [**119**, **143**], as well as acting as an antidote to Impressionist improvisation.[4] The *paysage composé*, of which Corot's work was a paradigm, answered the call for form in art – itself part of a wider call for nationalist definition – desired by many at the *fin-de-siècle*. Opinions from widely different quarters in the visual arts formed a degree of consensus. In 1896 the middle-of-the-road critic André Michel judged that, although the lessons of *plein air* painting had been fruitful, a reaction in favour of form was under way, exemplified in the pictures of René Ménard [**139**, **140**]; his argument found a close echo in a letter by Derain of 1903, which decried the attempt to paint 'the effect of a moment in nature' and spoke of his search for 'order and logic'.[5]

This promotion of a 'classical' ideal, although it had an identifiable and important presence in French culture at the time, is difficult to define as it took on such diverse forms. In this chapter alone we will be discussing artists as different as Corot and Gleizes, Denis and Picasso [**116**, **124**, **131**, **136**]. The word *classique* itself had varied connotations. André Michel, writing of Millet, defined it in terms of structured composition to articulate a dominant pictorial idea, to which details should be subordinated.[6] For Michel, as for Maurice Denis, perhaps the most important young theorist on the Right, Poussin was the key exemplar. Praising Roussel [**130**, **214**] in 1903 for organising his 'love of French soil' and mythological figures in a unified composition, Denis could think of no higher praise than to compare his colleague's painting with Poussin's.[7] Not only seventeenth-century but more recent, even living, artists could be considered under the rubric *classique*. Denis's friend Paul Jamot did just this in his review of the 1906 Salon d'Automne; he characterised the work of Maillol and Denis as sharing 'an ideal of classical serenity' and that of Cézanne as representing a 'return to classical simplicity, to unity of effect', a usage apparently contradicted by his description of Courbet's technique as 'classical' when he surely meant conventional.[8] These variations and Jamot's

opposite
111
H. -E. Cross
The Beach at Saint-Clair 1901 (detail)
Paris, Private Collection

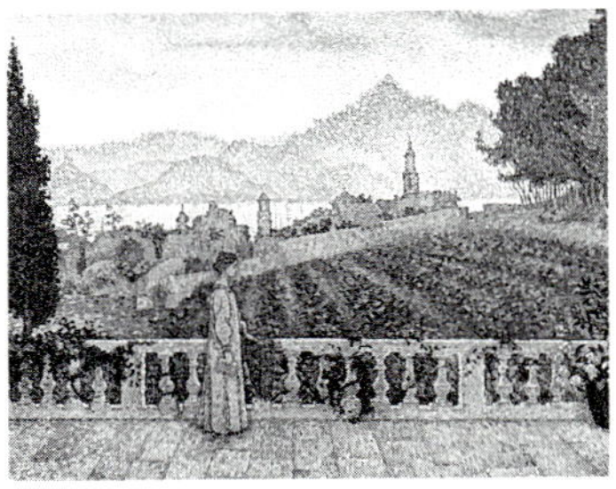

112
P. Signac
Lady on the Terrace 1898
Dublin, National Gallery of Ireland

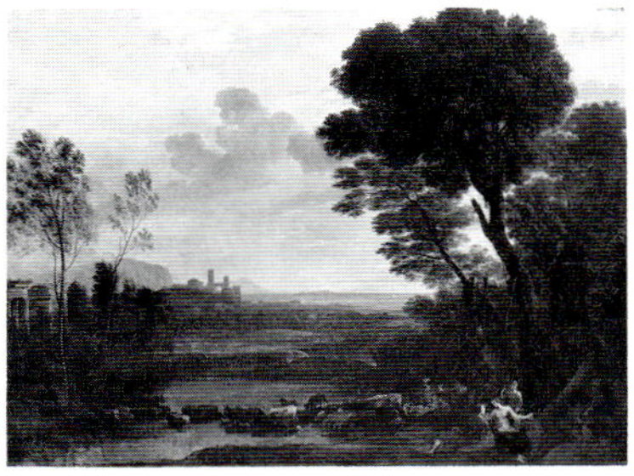

113
Claude Gellée (le Lorrain)
Landscape with Paris et Oenone (The Ford) c.1647–8
Paris, Musée du Louvre

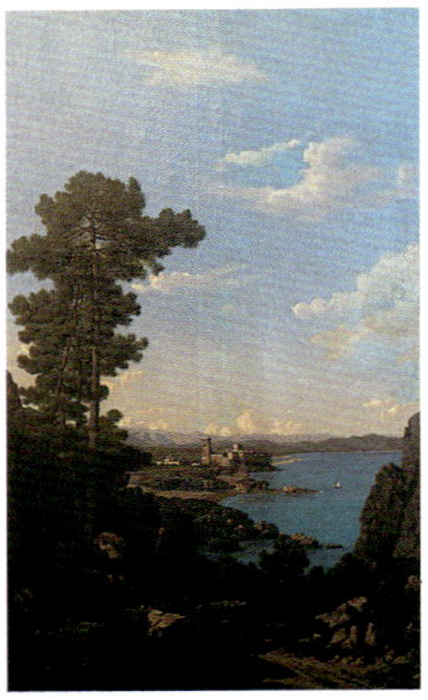

114
J. Contini
The Château de la Napoule 1877
Cannes, Musée de la Castre

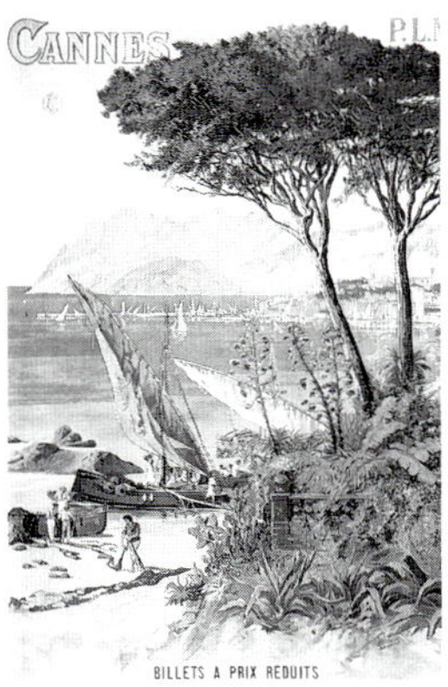

115
Tanconville *Cannes*
c.1900

inconsistencies go some way to indicating the fluid notions of classicism at the time, a diversity matched by the paintings themselves.

The Mediterranean landscape was all but an absolute in discourse about classicism. After all, it was at the very foundations of current French notions of the classical: arena of the gods and heroes of ancient mythology and history, cradle of Greek and Roman civilisation, inspiration for the ideal *paysages* of Poussin and Claude, opposite pole to the northern, Germanic culture against which modern France wished to define her traditions. The imaginary elision of the Midi with Italy was not a *fin-de-siècle* phenomenon; in 1865 Théophile Gautier had prompted: 'Provence is almost Italy, Avignon is almost Rome'.[9] But by the turn of the century it had become a commonplace. Reporting his delighted arrival at Saint-Tropez in 1892 Signac spontaneously compared the scene to Naples and Capri,[10] and six years later he painted a vista of the gulf of Saint-Tropez [**112**] which recalls the Tuscan panoramas of quattrocento panels and perhaps teasingly echoes the views from Fiesole Denis had made in emulation of them the year before. For the French to feel at one with the common Latin character of the southern landscape, then, was natural, unlike for the Germans. This was the assumption voiced by the poet Moréas, a Greek naturalised French, when he visited Agay on the Côte d'Azur. He opined that whereas Goethe, 'born under an inhuman sky', could only gush on seeing Lake Garda he himself experienced the Mediterranean 'to the depths of [his] soul'.[11] Moréas's exclusive nationalism may have been pompous, but it echoed an active cultural construction that was being enhanced by the growth of Mediterranean tourism: the roots of French culture were in southern, Latin soil.

If the Mediterranean and the classical amounted to an ideal, how might artists find forms to articulate it? The seventeenth-century paradigms of Poussin and Claude provided the answer. With their soft light and open views the landscapes of Claude [**113**], rather than those of the graver Poussin, offered particularly adaptable formulae. Claude's reputation was high throughout the century – in 1876 Fromentin had lauded him as 'very French albeit very Roman, very much a poet' [12] – and his example was evident throughout. Given that the native painters of the Mediterranean in the 1860s and 1870s tended to represent their region as a serene, sunlit environment, it is no surprise that Claude was a touchstone for them. The soft yet intense light of the Toulonais painter Auguste Aiguier's marines shows a debt to Claude,[13] but it was Claude's compositional characteristics which had more general impact. Joseph Contini's large canvas of the château de la Napoule, on the coast to the west of Cannes, painted in 1877 [**114**], is an impressive example of a Midi-born painter adopting Claudian formulae two decades before calls for classical order became habitual. The whole composition – well defined foreground with *repoussoir* tree, focus of ruins in the central planes, panoramic view towards distant mountains – follows the Claudian pattern. What Claude had developed in the seventeenth century to evoke an ideal of the ancient mythological Mediterranean could be redeployed to articulate a nineteenth-century ideal of France's southern coast, the picturesque changelessness that garnered greater authenticity by its Claudian inflection. That appealing fusion of ideal composition and ideal nature suited another pictorial form: the railway poster designed to sell the delights of the Mediterranean to tourists from the north. A poster by Tanconville advertising Cannes for the Paris-Lyon-Méditerranée railway company [**115**] utilised essentially the same components as Contini's painting in its presentation of the Mediterranean coast as a paradise of age-old tranquillity. Something of the interplay between such configurations of the ideal can be traced in the genesis of Matisse's *Luxe, calme et volupté* [**118**], painted over the winter of 1904–5. The idea originated during the previous summer, which Matisse and his family spent at Saint-Tropez at the invitation of Signac. The design Matisse used in painting his wife and one of their children on a beach [**117**] – vertical format, panorama of mountains and sea, bourgeois figures contentedly relaxing, and once again the *repoussoir* tree – recall contemporary railway posters [**115**] and their Claudian ancestry. Developing the initial idea into the exhibition painting Matisse changed to a more Poussinesque horizontal format and introduced nude bathing figures. The making of *Luxe, calme et volupté*, then, involved a clutch of transformations: from *plein air* study to *paysage composé*, Impressionist *sensation* to Neo-Impressionist *décor*, Claude to Poussin, and from the modernity of the poster to the intemporality of Puvis de Chavannes [**119**].

Corot's late paintings had consciously claimed affinities with Claude's work. *Pastorale: Souvenir d'Italie* [**116**], shown at the Salon of 1873 just two years before his death, with its dancing nymphs or shepherds, its framing trees, its classical buildings and soft, diffuse light, is an elegant reminder of the poetic characteristics of Claude's work. Corot had been mining that seam for quarter of a century; *Pastorale* is close in composition to the *Italian Goat-Herd*, a cartoon commissioned by the State in 1848 for a Beauvais tapestry which was never executed.[14] These late paintings by Corot had a mixed reception when he exhibited them. Their traditional qualities could be seen as either reassuring or repetitious, their loose handling and subdued tones poetic or facile. But what such a painting as *Pastorale* did embody was continuity of the Claudian landscape which combined pastoral myth, mood of reverie or nostalgia, and 'elegance of composition', as one critic put it in 1873.[15]

That Claudian design of framing trees remained a stock composition long after Corot's death. At the

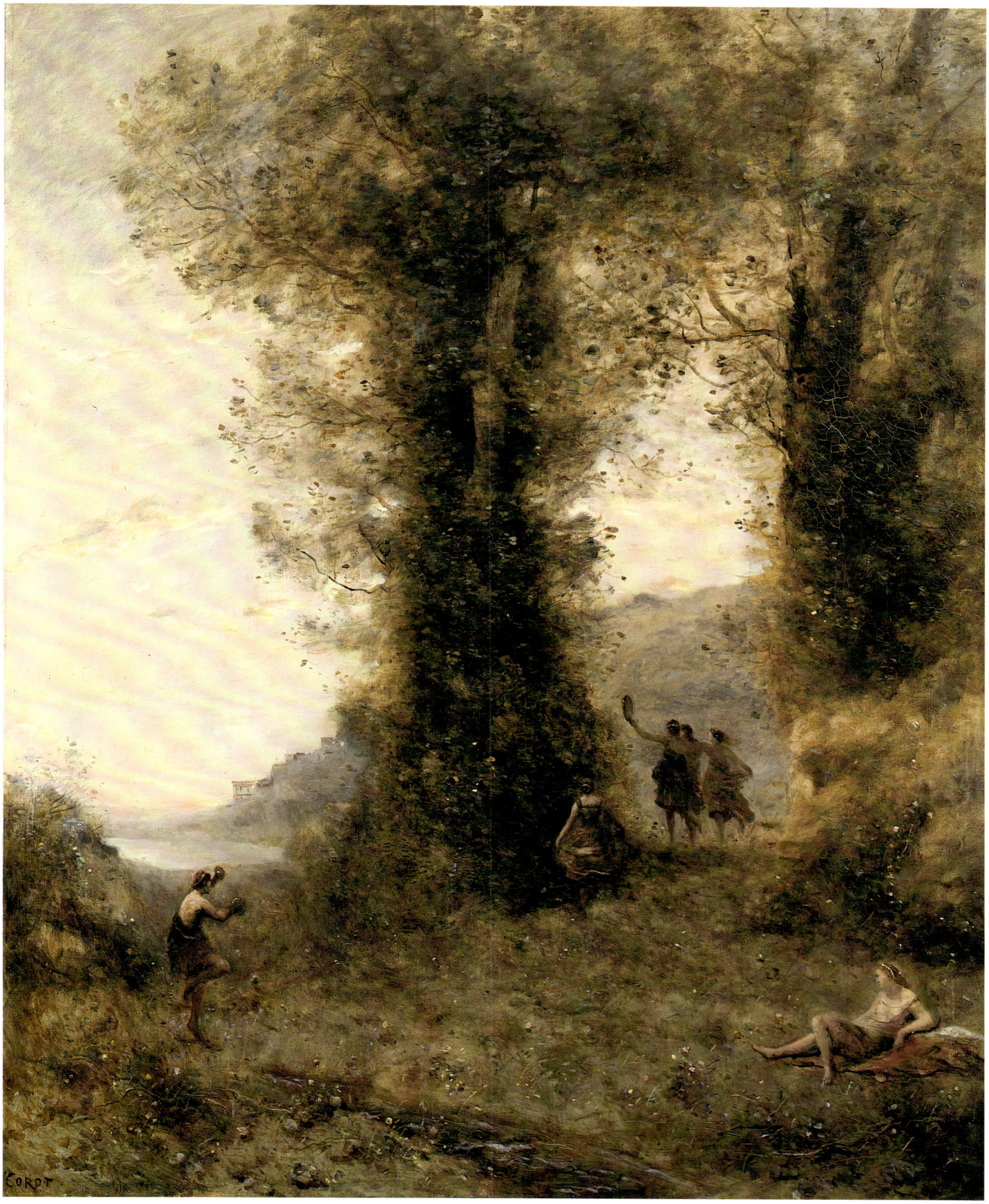

116
C. Corot
Pastorale: Souvenir d'Italie 1873
Glasgow, Glasgow Art Gallery
and Museum, Kelvingrove

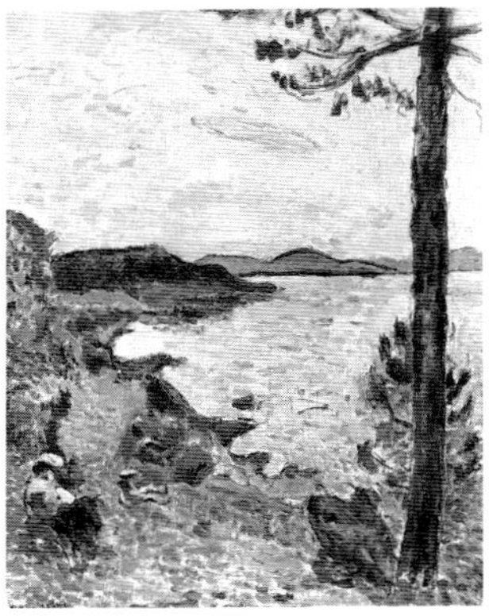

117
H. Matisse
Gulf of St Tropez (Le Goûter) 1904
Düsseldorf, Kunstsammlung Nordrhein-Westfalen

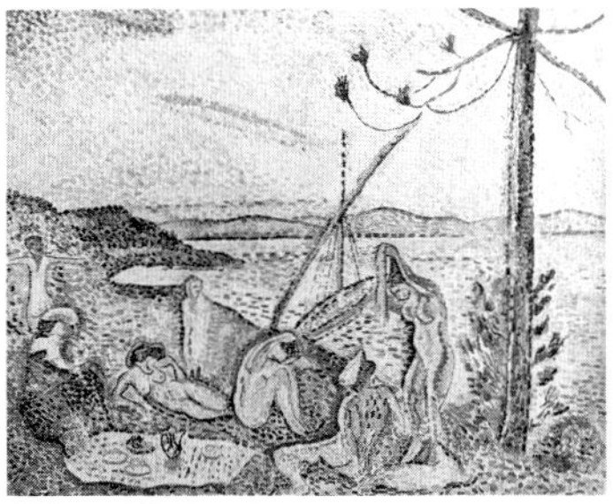

118
H. Matisse
Luxe, calme et volupté 1904–5
Paris, Musée d'Orsay

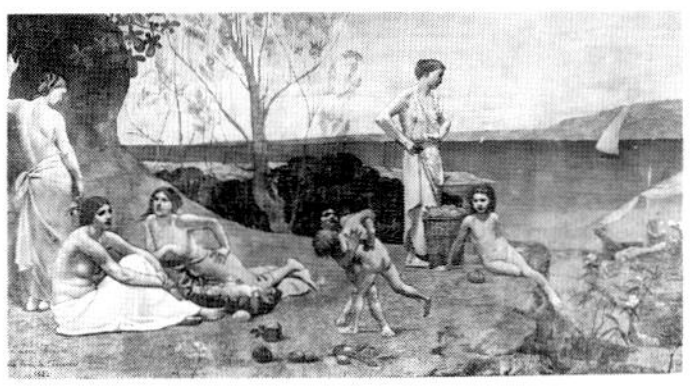

119
Puvis de Chavannes
Doux pays 1882
Bayonne, Musée Bonnat

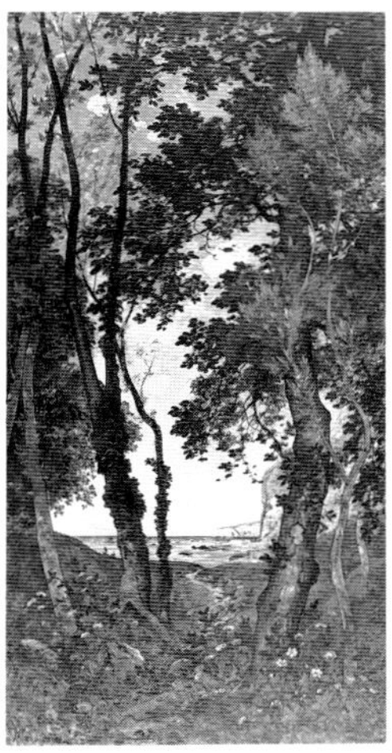

120
H. Harpignies
The Cliffs 1880
Paris, Musée d'Orsay

Salon of 1880, for example, Harpignies exhibited a large decorative panel entitled *The Cliffs* [**120**], commissioned as a design for a Gobelins tapestry to hang on the staircase of the Senate. Its composition closely followed that convention, and may well have been chosen because its ideal, Italianate configuration was apt for such an élite location. Indeed, in 1887 Harpignies's canvas was sent to Rome where it hung for almost a century in the Palazzo Farnese.[16] Harpignies's Claudian credentials were regularly praised, and often linked to the 'constructive' qualities of his compositions. In his review of the 1899 Salons, Desjardins claimed that Harpignies alone among contemporary landscape painters demonstrated 'the unbroken line' which ran from Claude.[17]

But Harpignies was far from the only painter to compose landscapes in a vertical format echoed by trees which frame an image of sheltered and untroubled nature. Furthermore, Claude's ideal formula was not echoed only by the *retardataires*. The chapter on representations of the Mediterranean suggested that among the paintings Cézanne made at L'Estaque in the late 1870s and early 1880s he set up some as wild, others as bucolic, still others as modern. One of these, dating from about 1882–5 [**121**], has a vertical configuration, the design edged by trees, with the landscape lapping back between them in controlled planes of rocky foreground, rooves, and marine vista, with the île Maire on the far horizon. To the viewer it is an image of stability and serenity, responses which are substantially preordained by the compositional structure. In 1883 Cézanne wrote to Zola from L'Estaque: 'I am still busy painting – I have some beautiful views but they do not quite make *motifs*'.[18] The comment suggests that the natural beauty of the site had yet to be ordered by the painter into a configuration which suited both the character of the landscape and the response of his *sensations* to it, and that in the case of the single vertical view of L'Estaque it was Claudian convention to which Cézanne turned for the appropriate artifice. That he was aware of such convention has been shown in the comparison made recently by Richard Verdi of *L'Estaque* of 1883–5 and one of the mural paintings Cézanne had made over twenty years previously at his parents' house near Aix, the Jas de Bouffon.[19] This mural by the young Cézanne trotted out all the Claudian ingredients in a pattern-book manner. By the mid-1880s these were integrated with his orchestrated tension between warm and cool colours and his brushwork, which, although applied in his personal system of parallel strokes, nevertheless has an energy and agitation also present in the structural composition. By ordering the motif in this way Cézanne arrived at another representation of L'Estaque, transforming it here into a haven of pastoral serenity.

During the summer of 1887 Gauguin travelled with fellow painter Charles Laval to the West Indies. After a grim period navvying on the Panama Canal, they settled for four months on Martinique, a French colony. Despite sickness, Gauguin produced a number of impressive canvases of the landscape and native life which indicate how enthusiastically he had responded to the rich vegetation of the Caribbean. He called Martinique a 'Paradise' compared to Panama, describing the hut he and Laval shared: 'below us the sea with a sandy beach for bathing, and all around coconut palms and other fruit trees of all kinds admirable for the landscape painter'.[20] The most important landscape Gauguin painted there is a view over the bay of St Pierre with Mont Pelée (a volcano which erupted disastrously in 1902) in the distance [**122**]. The view Gauguin chose was not only common in postcards and travel books of the period, but also he edited out aspects that displeased him, notably the town of St Pierre itself.[21] Both were common strategems among landscapists; witness Monet's practice at Antibes, and Cézanne's at L'Estaque. In fact, *Martinique Landscape* bears comparison with Cézanne on a number of points. Gauguin had admired the older painter's work since about 1880, buying Cézanne's pictures for his collection, making copies of specific examples, and even rather unscrupulously aping Cézanne's characteristic parallel stroke, an affront to his *sensation* much resented by the touchy Aixois. The tapestry-like handling of the foliage in *Martinique Landscape* strongly recalls Cézanne's handling, despite Gauguin's highly personal palette, in which succulent greens and sensuous pinks are offset in an exaggerated chromatic medley that seems to stretch local colour beyond the frontiers of plausibility. Above all, Gauguin's motif is reminiscent of Cézanne's vertical canvas of L'Estaque.[22] Perhaps this is coincidence, and Gauguin stumbled upon the Martinique motif independently or because it was indicated to him. On the other hand, one might argue that Gauguin constructed his Martinique view along Claudian lines, reaching back for a formula associated with the ideal in landscape with which to represent his Caribbean paradise.

At the turn of the century critical debates about landscape often hinged on design. We have heard Desjardins's claim in 1899 that Harpignies alone, with his 'constructive' qualities, represented the Claudian tradition, and in his review of the 1905 Salon d'Automne François Monod cited Corot, as well as the ancestral Poussin and Claude, as 'architect-artists' in contrast to the absence of 'construction' in Impressionism.[23] Part of the Right's call for order and traditional values in contemporary art, such views ignored the continuity of idealising composition in progressive painting. After 1905 these currents began to coalesce. Celebrated in retrospectives at the Salon d'Automne, the work of artists such as Cézanne and Gauguin, hitherto considered experimental, began to be assimilated into the mainstream, while the new avant-garde swung into line as the stylistically radical flank of the broad march towards an art based on convention and discipline.

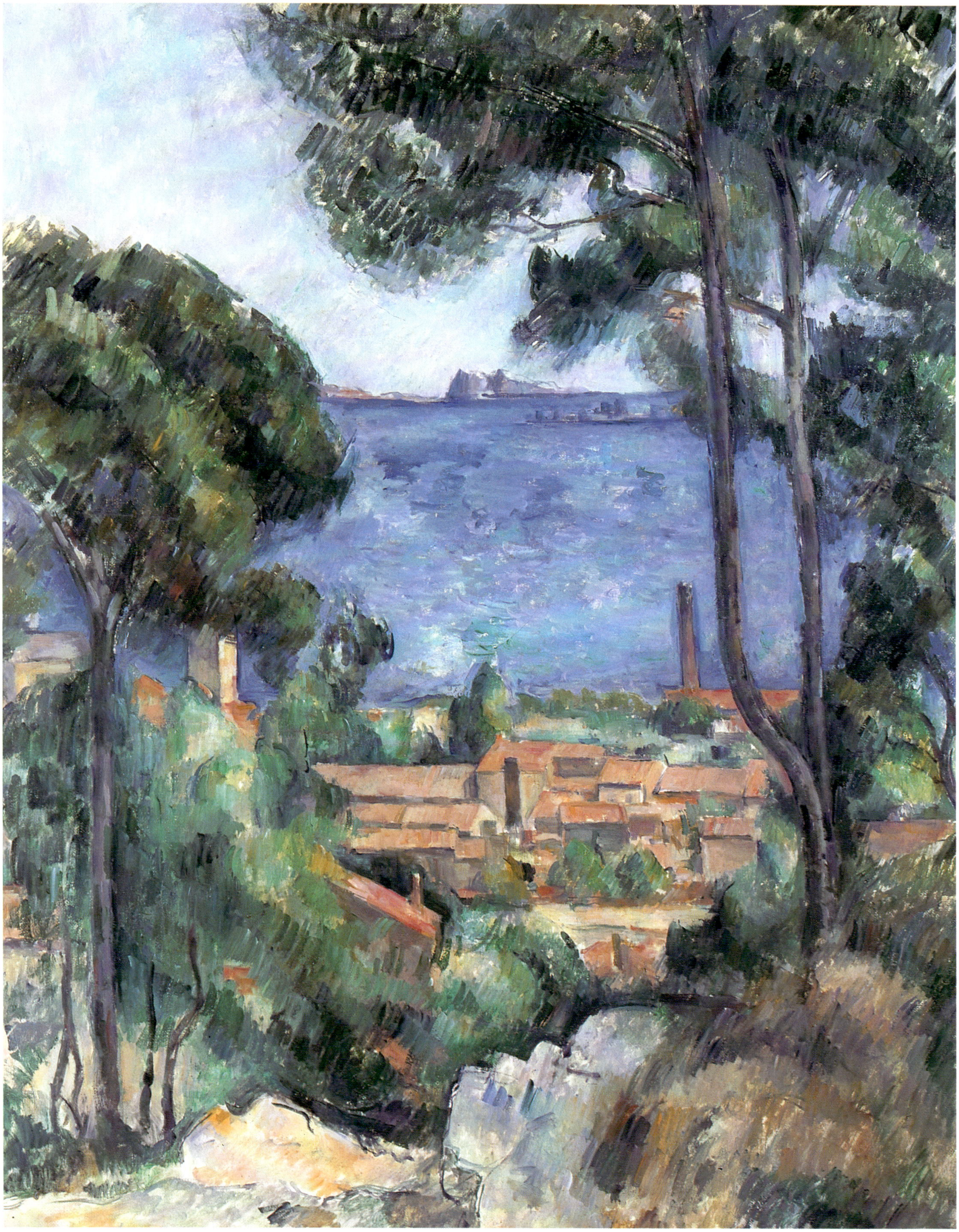

121
P. Cézanne
The Sea at L'Estaque c.1885
Private Collection, on loan to the Fitzwilliam Museum, Cambridge

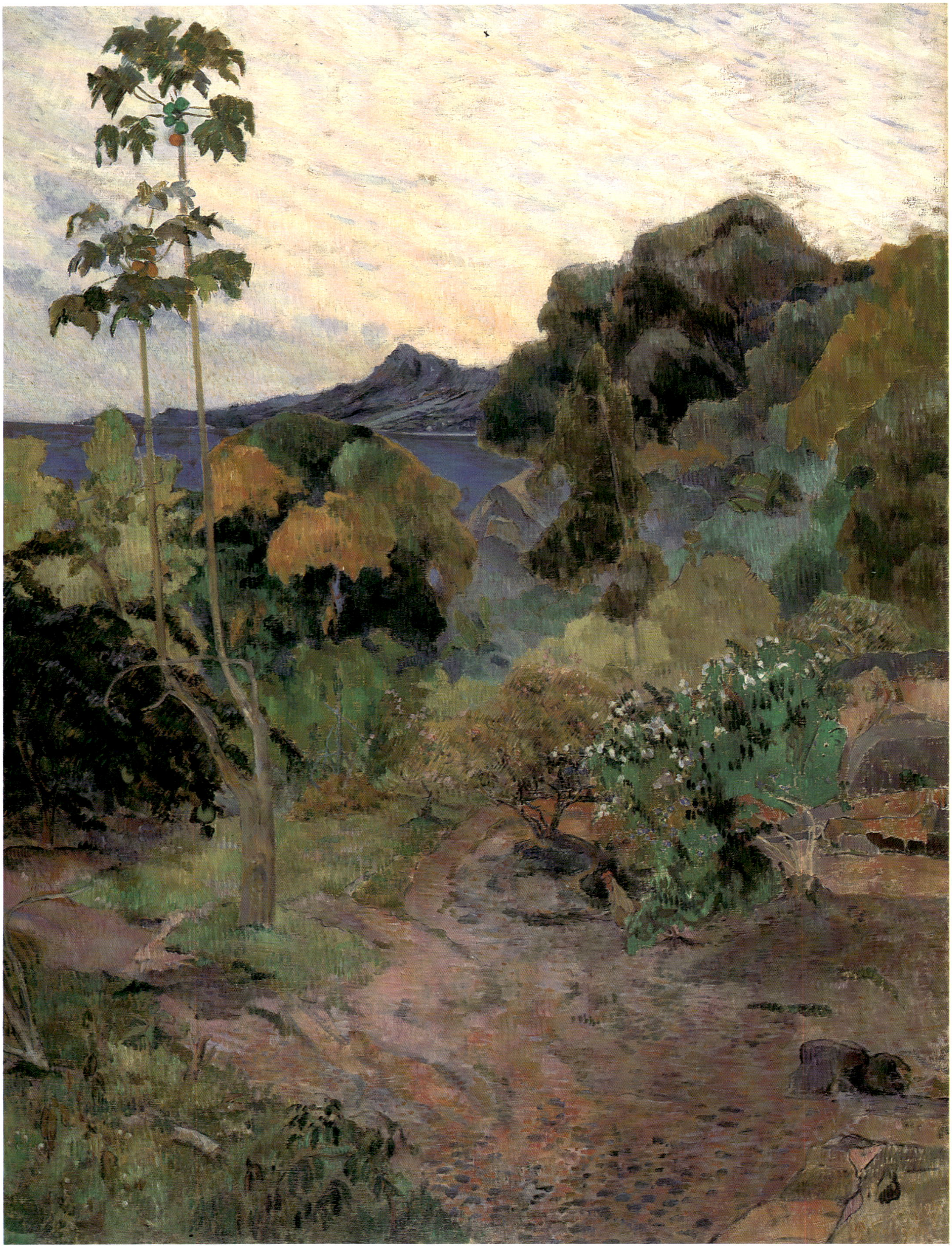

122
P. Gauguin
Martinique Landscape 1887
Edinburgh, National Gallery of Scotland

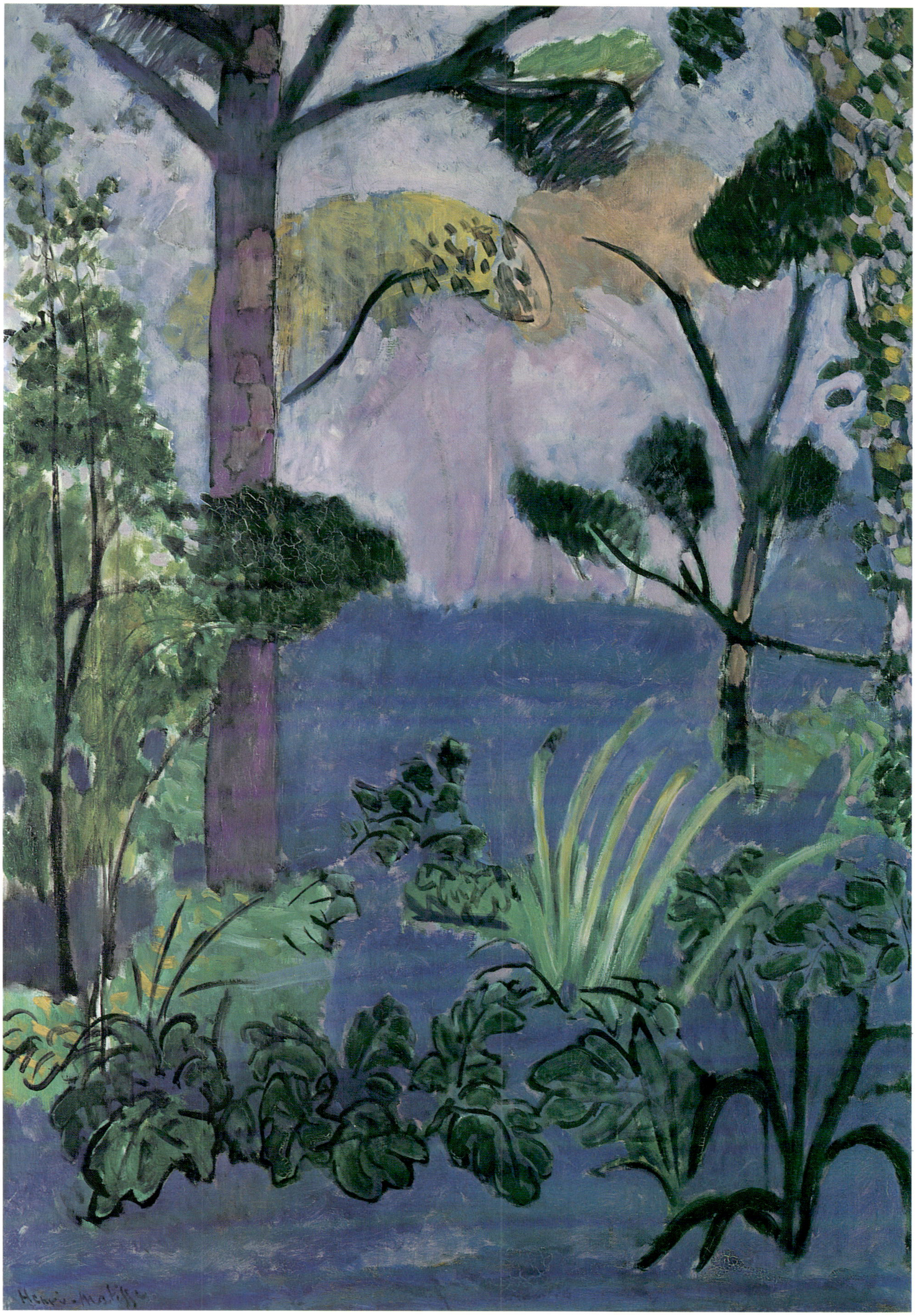

123
H. Matisse
Acanthus 1912
Stockholm, Moderna Museet

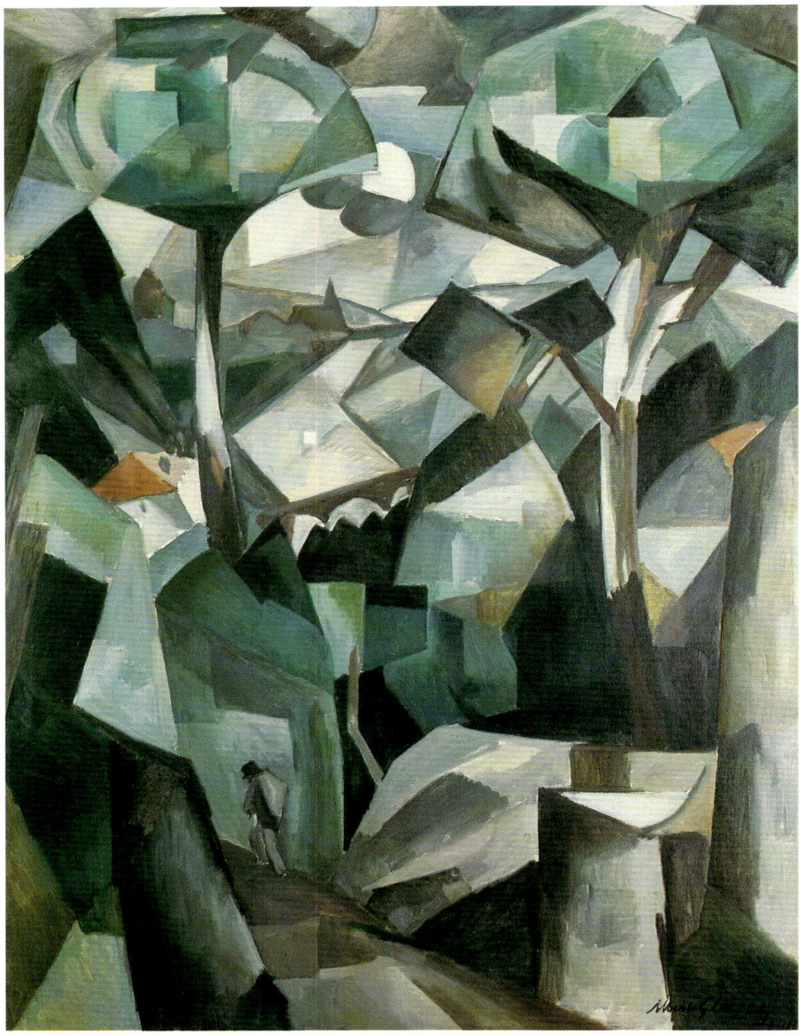

124
A. Gleizes
Landscape (Meudon) 1911
Paris, Musée national d'art moderne, Centre Georges Pompidou

Gleizes's *Landscape (Meudon)* of 1911 [**124**] is typical of his work at this period. A heavily faceted landscape in greys, browns and silvery greens, it is perhaps closer to the example of late Cézanne than fully Cubist as the forms themselves are not fragmented. Within the facets one can make out a house, a steeple, a bridge over a river, a man carrying a sack along a road. At first sight its austerity makes a sharp contrast with a canvas made by Matisse on his first trip to Morocco the following year, *Acanthus* [**123**]. Matisse painted this canvas over about six weeks from early March to mid-April 1912. He worked in the garden of the Villa Brooks, near his hotel in Tangier. 'I worked in a part which was planted with very large trees, whose foliage spread very high,' he recalled in an interview of 1941. 'The ground was covered with acanthus. I had never seen acanthus. I knew acanthus only from the drawings of Corinthian columns that I had made at the Ecole des beaux-arts. I found the acanthus magnificent, much more interesting, green, than those at the Ecole! My spirit was exalted by these great trees, very tall, and below the rich acanthus provided a no less important focus of interest through their sumptuousness.'[24] Stimulated by this enclosed but fecund corner of nature, Matisse worked rapidly and spontaneously. The surface of *Acanthus* is a complex interplay of drawing, animating the decorative leaves and structural branches, and painted passages laid down in a variety of zones, patches and marks. Pentimenti and overpainting are left visible. When Matisse returned to Tangier later in 1912 for the winter he intended to rework *Acanthus*, but on reconsidering the painting alongside the motif he left it as it is, perhaps concluding that the artist's visible activity on the canvas combined with the textures and succulent, sappy greens, pinks and violets to convey the natural luxuriousness of this North African garden.[25] Yet that sense of fertility and flux is held by the composition which Matisse chose for this painting; once again its vertical format, framed view, and recession articulated by *repoussoir* elements all derive ultimately from the Claudian repertoire.

One could argue that here Matisse opted for those conventions because they suited his vision of the colonial garden as an earthly paradise and place of retreat and contemplation. To promote landscape as an ideal environment meant choosing a representational idiom which in itself had ideal associations. The same might be said of Gleizes's *Landscape (Meudon)*. It represents the south-western suburbs of Paris, and for all the painting's experimental Cubist surface it is ordered around the conventional Claudian composition, from bracketing trees right down to the distant monument. Gleizes had recently been involved in the artists' commune known as the Abbaye de Créteil. This group had affiliations with the Left-wing idealism of the anarchists and included the poets Henri-Martin Barzun and Jules Romains, whose respective volumes of 1907, *La Terrestre Tragédie* and *La Vie unanime*, explored modern themes such as the city and the crowd. The latter's *unanimisme* in particular emphasises the absorption of the individual into all-encompassing consciousness.[26] Gleizes's painting, with its solitary figure locked into the harmonious tones and unifying surface, suggests the unanimity of man and nature, values given implicit credence by the composition.

The avant-garde could thus make fruitful use of the conventions of ideal landscape. Apollinaire might condemn the establishment Salon de la nationale in 1910 on the grounds that 'the influences of Poussin, of the Italian masters, of Corot, give this Salon a praiseworthy air of timid nobility',[27] but he was somewhat missing the point. To return finally to the Claudian formula, its 'influence' may have been peripheral in the late nineteenth century – sustained by the likes of Harpignies, found useful on occasion by Cézanne or Gauguin – but by 1910 it was prevalent. Braque's *La Roche-Guyon: the Castle* of 1909, Matisse's *View of Collioure and the Sea* of 1911, Derain's *View of Martigues* of 1913 [**125, 126, 127**] – in many ways three very different paintings – all rehearse pictorial conventions we have seen employed by Corot, Cézanne and Contini.

The classical tradition embodied both by Claude and Poussin involved the integration of figure and landscape, perhaps the use of nature as a theatre for some mythological or historical event or for the evocation of some pastoral scene. The pastoral had many attractions. A representation of a timeless past, calling up images of the ancient Mediterranean as described by such classical poets as Virgil and Theocritus and with a noble tradition in western art, it appealed to the sense of tradition and order. With its stock staffage of flocks, shepherds and nymphs, the pastoral suggested man's closeness to the land, and its mood was conventionally tranquil, nostalgic, yet not without sensuality, thus at one with escapist constructions of changeless landscape. Such characteristics – at once delightful, cultured and complacent – guaranteed the survival of the pastoral in the modern momentum of late nineteeth- and early twentieth-century society. Corot's *Morning Dance of the Nymphs* had been bought by the state for the Salon of 1850–1 for the Musée du Luxembourg, but in 1874 was transferred to the Louvre.[28] In his lifetime, therefore, Corot's work was represented in the pantheon by a pastoral. In one form or another, for it is a flexible idiom,[29] pastoral had a continuous presence in French painting of the period. It might surface specifically in an academic canvas such as Georges Bretegnier's *Idyll – The Poetic Contest, after an Idyll by Theocritus*, shown at the Salon of 1883, or more generally in the diaphanous nymphs who peopled so many Symbolist fantasies at the *fin-de-siècle* and whose ancestry was traced back via Corot.[30] Matisse's *Bonheur de vivre* of 1905–6 [**128**], one of the decade's key avant-garde canvases, displayed its innovatory fluid chromatic planes and sinuous arabesques on the scaffolding of pastoral.

If pastoral took on fresh prominence in painters' imaginations in the quarter century before 1914 this was due to the broad socio-cultural forces behind the resurgence of classicism outlined in the introductory chapter. That artists felt part of this pattern of thought is evident from their comments and interests. Renoir defined his late work in those terms, telling the poet Gasquet: 'What admirable beings the Greeks were. Their existence was so happy that they imagined that the Gods came down to earth to find their paradise and to make love. Yes, the earth was the paradise of the Gods ... That is what I want to paint'.[31] The pagan gods had a lively, even self-conscious, place in painters' fantasy. In 1906 Denis thought it worthy of note in his journal that Valtat had a little marble deity in his garden, and two years earlier Signac wrote to Angrand that while he had been building a sailing boat at Saint-Tropez Roussel had read aloud to him from the *Odyssey*.[32] Creating pictures around these fantasies required populating scenes of the 'earthly paradise' with the shepherds and nymphs of the mythic past. For minds formed around a classical education the echoes rang in the imagination. Taking an evening walk at Hyères in 1875 Amiel felt 'it was like an expedition into Arcadia. Here was a wild and woodland corner, ... which reminded me of an ode of Horace or a drawing of Tibur. I felt a kind of certainty that the landscape had much that was Greek in it. And what made the sense of resemblance the more striking was the sea, which one feels always to be near ... We found a little tower with an overgrown garden, of which the owner might have been taken for a husbandman from the *Odyssey*'.[33] By the 1900s such responses were commonplace. In his early years by the Mediterranean Cross had painted local figures in his landscapes, but by the turn of the century had abandoned them. He explained his 'insensitivity towards the peasant' in a letter to van Rysselberghe written about 1905, arguing that the rustic figure now seemed to him insignificant, whereas by contrast 'on the rocks, on the sand of the beaches, under the clumps of pine, nymphs and naiads appear to me, a whole world born of beautiful light. These beautiful forms have circulated in my vision too long for me not to attempt to render them perceptible by painting'.[34] Cross's imagination was fuelled not only by the classical authors but also by Nietszche, a volume of whose writings he owned and whose ideas he mulled over in his *carnets*.[35] Despite their German origin, Nietszche's ideas were current among French painters and intellectuals early in the century; Roussel and Derain were also admirers. The appeal of Nietszche lay in his belief in the self and in the artist's creative capacities. Nietszche's persistent evocation of a sensual pagan past added a modern, piquant, even disruptive quality to pastoral images whose figures might in some hands have been made anaemically nostalgic. If those stimuli for the inclusion of figures were positive and imaginative, Friesz offered a more practical reason when he described the Mediterranean landscape as 'arid and wholly intellectual ..., where the only expression of vegetation is the pine and the cypress'. In such circumstances, he continued, 'we need the human presence, even though it would be quite superfluous in a pasture in Normandy, or on the banks of a river in Brittany where nature is sufficient in herself'.[36] Friesz was stressing difference, using the old polarities of the *méridionaux* and *septentrionaux* to insist that Mediterranean landscapes needed nude figures to make it clear that they were 'classical', and not northern.

How did artists contrive to incorporate these imaginary figures in Mediterranean scenes? Manguin preferred the *plein air* convention of posing his wife Jeanne naked in the landscape, but this had its drawbacks! Painting at La Cavalière in 1906 he complained to Matisse that 'despite the isolation of this wretched village, there are always some bloody fishermen in the rocks'.[37] Cross, on the other hand, developed his figures from drawings made independently; studies from the nude drawn while visiting van Rysselberghe's studio in Paris made their way into a

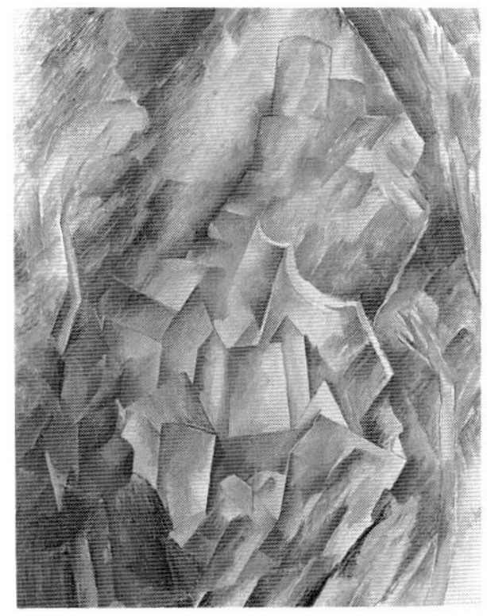

125
G. Braque
La Roche-Guyon: the Castle 1909
Eindhoven, Stedelijk van Abbemuseum

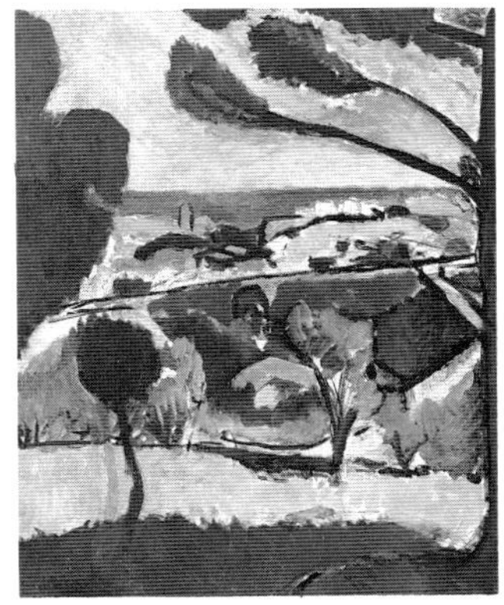

126
H. Matisse
View of Collioure and the Sea 1911
New York, Museum of Modern Art, Nelson A. Rockefeller Bequest

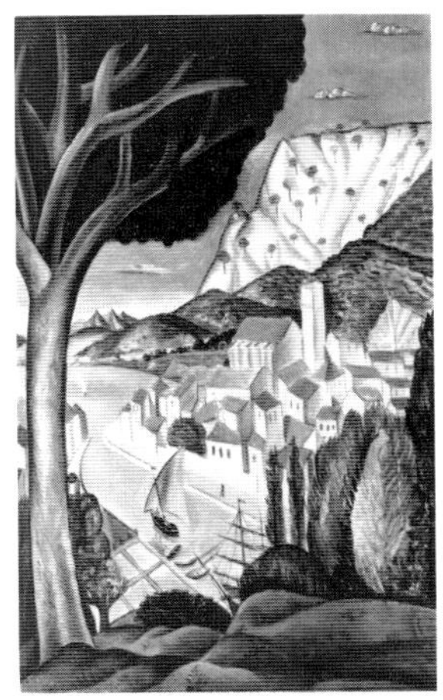

127
A. Derain ***View of Martigues*** 1913
St Petersburg, The Hermitage Museum

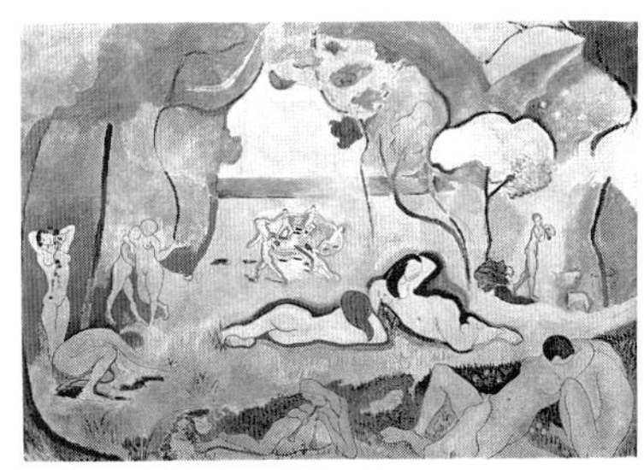

128
H. Matisse ***Le Bonheur de vivre*** 1905–6
Merion, Pennsylvania, Barnes Foundation

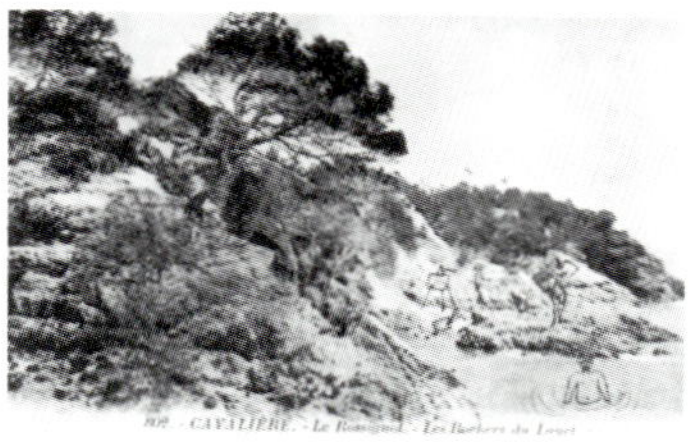

129
H. Matisse
Postcard sent to Manguin *c.*1905
Private Collection

Mediterranean pastoral of 1902.[38] Manguin's and Cross's admissions of their problems and artifices reveal the painters' consciousness of imposing a fictional 'classicism' on the modern Mediterranean shores, a consciousness given amusing visual form on a postcard sent by Matisse [**129**]. Over the 'reality' of the photograph the artist sketched himself, his painting gear and model, their *naïf* absurdity pointing to the artificiality of such imaginative figure compositions.

During the 1900s the *paysage composé* peopled with fantasy figures flourished, and painters of very different styles and ambitions felt pressed to explore the genre. In the years around the turn of the century Roussel, whose early works had been chiefly interiors and decorative panels influenced by his brother-in-law and fellow-Nabi Vuillard, changed direction, settling on loosely brushed and sumptuously coloured landscapes with a pastoral or mythological staffage, an idiom which he explored for the rest of his career. *The Embrace* [**130**] may date from this transitional period, or even from later in Roussel's career for a similar landscape appears in a pastel of 1925, *Orpheus and Eurydice*.[39] Roussel's emotive and highly personal use of colour is evident in the *Embrace*. The sky was originally a conventional pale blue, which he overpainted with an extraordinary green-aubergine tone. Its density constricts the picture space, already compressed by the glowering foliage, creating an aura of warm intimacy around the couple which the eye gradually discerns making love in the deep shadows. Roussel does not seem to have intended any specific classical reference here, though the tenebrous figures may be fauns. Certainly, they sink into the shadows and the soil as if they have a natural place in this glade protected from the fierce Mediterranean light; as his friend the painter and critic Lucie Cousturier suggested, 'his nymphs and fauns are trees, the movements of the earth are incarnated in them'.[40] That metaphoric elision of figure and landscape, which invokes an atavistic ideal of human harmony with nature even if it does not illustrate any ancient myth, attracted other artists. During the summer of 1908 Picasso painted an unusual canvas in which landscape plays a major part. In *Landscape with Two Figures* [**131**] natural forms are contrived to create a theatrical space, the two massive trees flanking the rocky escarpment behind. It is a powerfully sculptural image with its blocky, simplified forms. One senses that Picasso was carving out the very structural essence of the landscape beneath the soily sonorous browns, summarising the fecund energy of nature in the ruthlessly reductive trees with their clumsy leaves reminiscent of Rousseau's jungle pictures. Two figures lurk in this landscape. One reclines along the foreground and the other leans against the right-hand tree. The pose of the former recalls the conventional Venus typified by Giorgione's famous painting in the Dresden Gemäldegalerie[41] while the latter takes up a pose used frequently by Cézanne in his late bather paintings. Picasso's landscape is thus a fusion of modern 'primitive' starkness with 'classical' allusion both traditional and avant-garde. Yet for all the associations

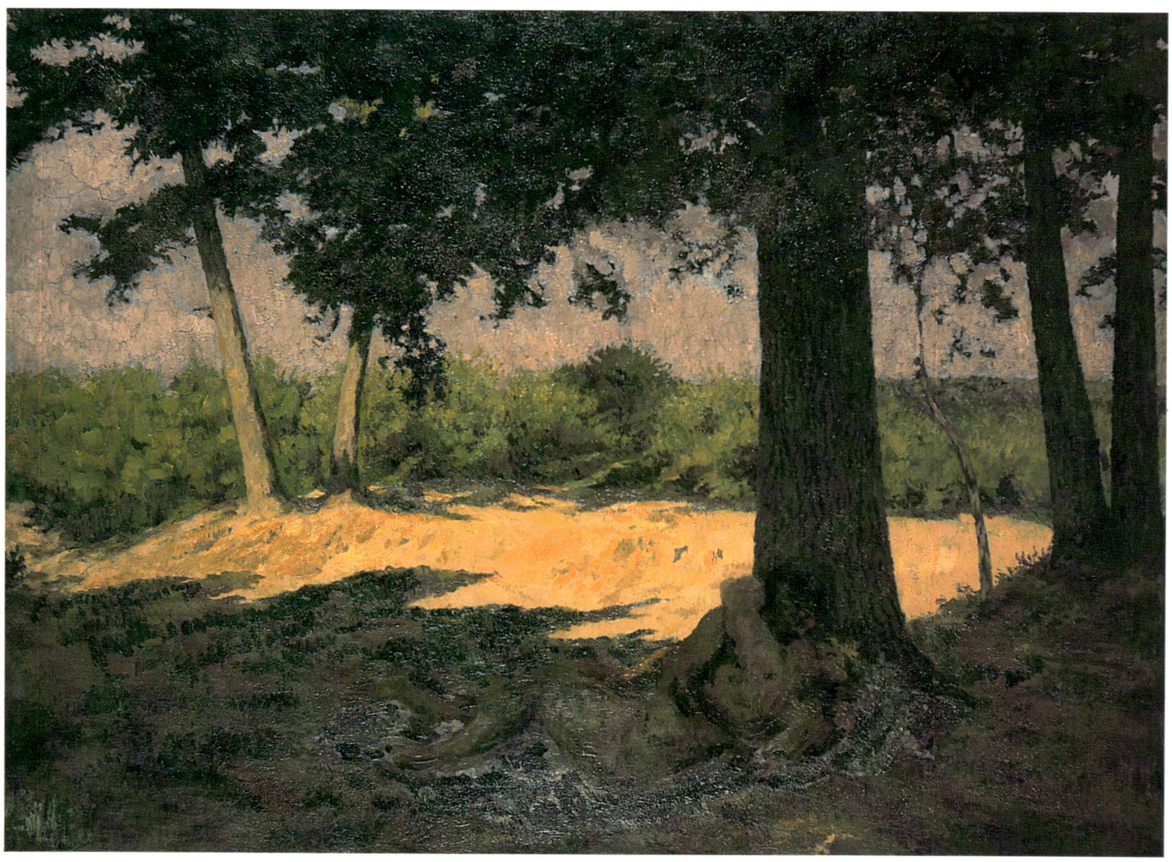

130
K.-X. Roussel
The Embrace c.1900–5
Saint-Tropez, Musée de l'Annonciade

of their poses the two figures deny the sensual aspect of pastoral. Sexless and separated, stripped to forms as simple as the natural surroundings with which their colours blend them, they elide with the roots and trunk of the trees. De-eroticised and dehumanised, in Picasso's image they fuse almost effortlessly with nature, reincarnations in the most radical style of the mythological dryad.

Whereas Roussel and Picasso envisaged their figures as part of nature, Cross, in his *Beach at Saint-Clair* [**111**] of 1901, seems to make the female nudes float freely from their natural environment. Their conventional flesh tone outlined in deep blue, the figures stand out from Cross's decorative mosaic-like surface which exudes a light-filled glow with its passages of yellow and pink, violet and blue. The artificiality of these extraordinary chromatics is matched by the treatment of light, for the figure at the left is in full sun but most deeply shaded. Cross's compositions with nude figures were arbitrary and flexible in subject. Some deal with everyday motifs of women undressing to bathe; others have generalised classical titles such as *Faun* and *Fleeing Nymphs*; still others are fantasies with nudes dancing and draped incongruously in trees.[42] The *Beach at Saint-Clair* belongs within the last group. Its 'classical' allusions are even more understated than Roussel's fauns or Picasso's dryads, especially given the intrusion of a modern yacht. In Cross's painting of arbitrary decorative colour and fanciful, floating nudes, the insistence is on the image as an act of the imagination, the vision of an ideal.

These three paintings by Roussel, Picasso and Cross play with notions of the pastoral, the imaginative, the metaphoric; they are not strictly mythological, but have vestigial parallels with the Poussinesque *paysage historique*. Equally, while Corot may have been conscious of the Claudian ancestry of major compositions such as *Pastorale* [**116**], it is unlikely that the same could be said of Gauguin, Matisse, Cézanne or Gleizes. Their retrieval of a 'classical' composition was at one level the deployment of a stock design to stabilise their experimental chromatics and surfaces, and yet perhaps also acted to convey an ideal of order and tranquillity in the landscape. References to the paradigms of the seventeenth century – however tangential or allusive – may have become more common after 1890 as debates about 'classicism' and Frenchness intensified, but they had never been entirely absent from French landscape painting. Those debates may have centred on nationalism, but order and ideal in images of nature were as fascinating for painters of Leftist sympathies such as Cross as for the reactionary Catholic Denis. The *paysage composé* consistently proved itself a pictorial vehicle imaginatively adaptable in both style and ideology.

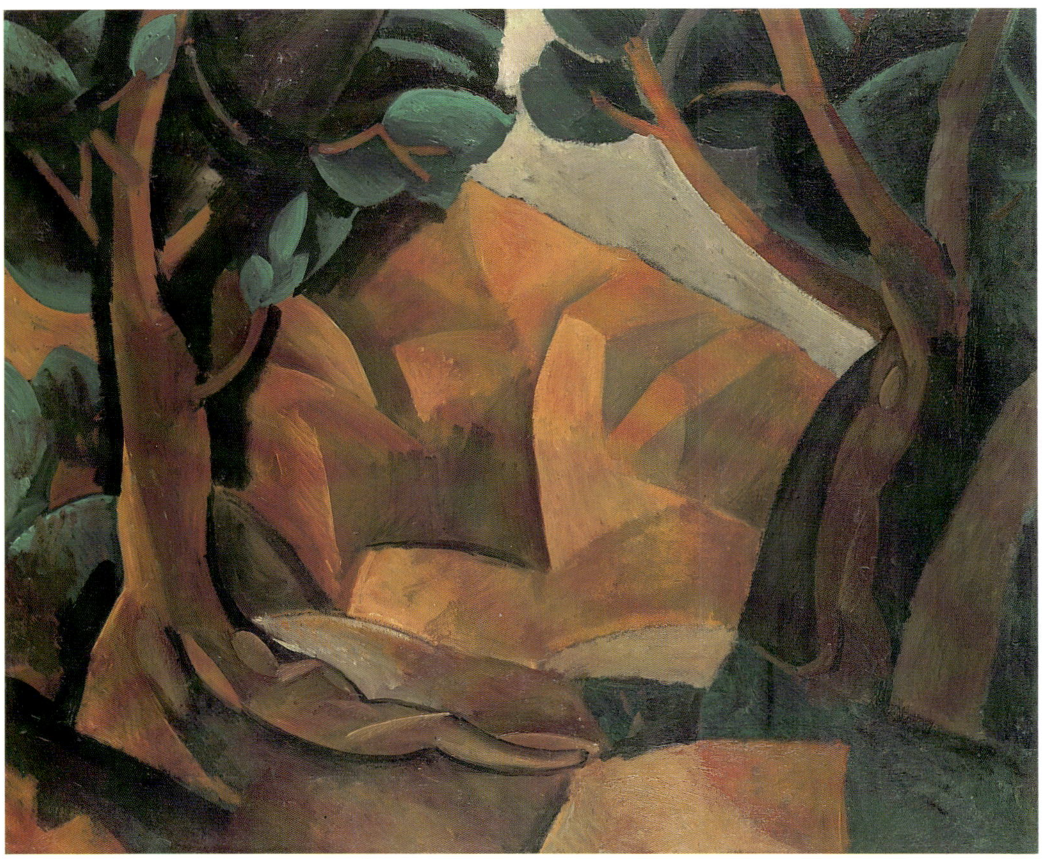

131
P. Picasso
Landscape with Two Figures 1908
Paris, Musée Picasso

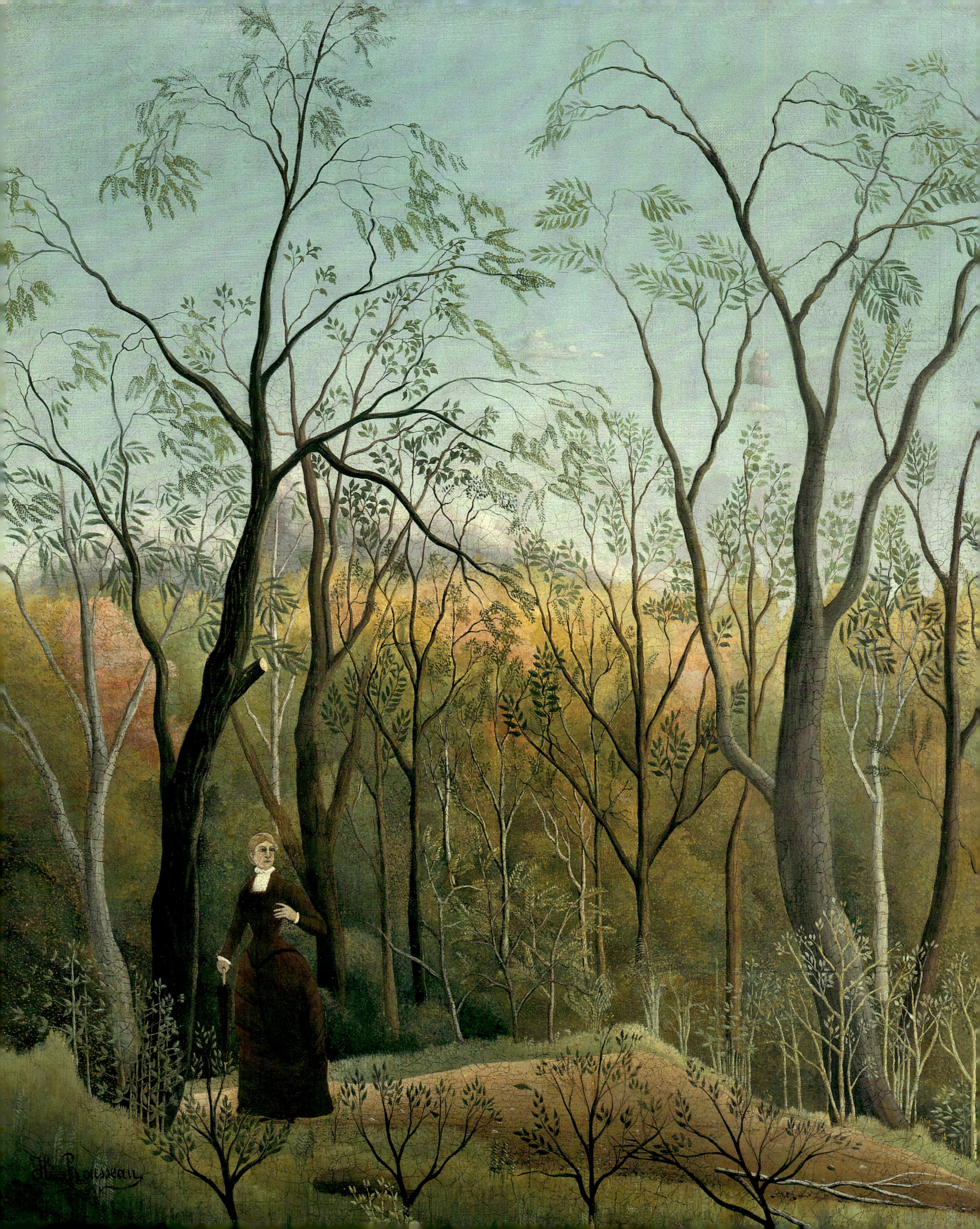
H. Rousseau

7 Incidents in the Landscape

The examples of Poussin and Claude stood for more than order and the ideal. Their landscapes often couched scenes from classical mythology, history or the Bible. For whatever reason they may have been chosen by artist or patron, whatever associations they may have had for their audience, such stories or events required the painter to exercise his imaginative faculties. The landscape setting operated as a stage set on which the figures, large or small, performed with costumes and gestures appropriate to the scene being represented. Landscape served to indicate time and place – generalised Arcadia, perhaps, or specific ancient city – and also to set mood. For instance Poussin's *Four Seasons, Summer* [**133**] shows the felicitous meeting of Ruth and Boaz, with harvesters labouring gracefully under a sunlit sky and in a landscape whose forms are lucid and steady. By contrast *Four Seasons, Autumn* [**134**] represents the fruitpickers moving at more agitated pace in a sparser, rockier landscape over which storm clouds begin to threaten. Thus natural features are subjected to the artist's fantasy and choreographed in conjunction with the figures to evoke a mood in the spectator. For creator and viewer alike, the landscape painting functions as an imaginative experience.

The naturalism so dominant in mid-century French painting had neither banished figures from the landscape nor ceased to use them associatively. The rural populations in Breton's *Blessing the Wheat* or Millet's *Angélus* [**4**, **2**] articulate the virtues of obedience to hierarchy and the Church in the countryside, while Monet's *Cliffs near Dieppe* [**89**] conveys the momentary thrill experienced by urban holidaymakers on their exposure to the sublimity of the Channel cliffs. But such values are, broadly speaking, social, dealing with public concerns about class, community and consumption. Landscape had long served as a vehicle for those matters – Poussin's *Summer*, after all, is also a painting about social hierarchy – and continued to do so throughout the period we are considering here. But one could argue that at the end of the nineteenth and beginning of the twentieth century landscape in varied ways was returned to the painter's imagination. A number of reasons for this can be sketched. An increasingly urbanised and industrialised society, watching its physical environment change around it, developed a taste for a more evocative, nostalgic, timeless landscape free from modern intrusions. An intellectual culture within that society, responsive to Symbolism's fresh emphasis on the evocative and emotive as well as to philosophical and psychological notions about memory and the unconscious, formed an audience for the imaginative and suggestive. And in the visual arts conflicting styles and groupings, from avant-garde Symbolists to Ecole-trained devotees of the *paysage composé*, coalesced in their reaction against naturalism's dominance. The increasing momentum behind the *paysage historique* stressed its imaginative element, thus emphasising it as a somewhat élite idiom quite contrary to naturalism.[1]

Maurice Denis matured in that climate, and by the turn of the century, following an intellectually formative trip to Rome in 1897, his critical writings voiced the values of the 'classical' landscape: disciplined, nationalistic and imaginative. In the early years of the century Denis painted a number of substantial *paysages historiques* with subjects taken from Greek mythology. The two versions of *Eurydice* [**136**] painted in 1906 are typical of these.[2] Denis based his composition on his recent experience of the Mediterranean landscape. Early in 1906 he and Roussel had bicycled along the coast, visiting Cross at Lavandou and Valtat at Agay. Denis's journal recorded his impressions: 'Lovely pine woods along the bay of Agay. Then the Touring route goes along the red rocks, overhung by the Estérel ... The îles de Lérins seem like two virgin islands, scarcely inhabited, legendary.' [3] From the cultural pell-mell of Denis's observations of nature, frank reliance on the guidebook's itinerary, and antique reverie, *Eurydice* emerged. Denis took his subject from classical sources, perhaps Ovid's *Metamorphoses* or Virgil's *Georgics*, both of which tell how Orpheus's young bride was killed by a snake just after their wedding. The landscape recalls quite closely the coastal terrain of the Var, where pine-covered rocks reach down to the waves. Cross frequently painted such sites in a palette which contemporaries compared to that of Denis,[4] using them both for pictures with nudes and

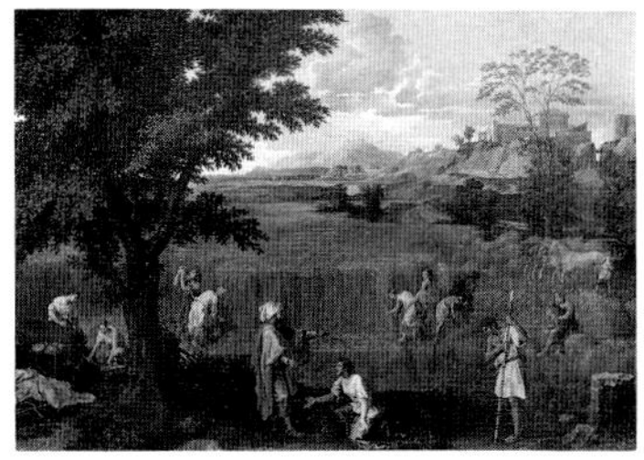

133
N. Poussin
Four Seasons, Summer 1660–4
Paris, Musée du Louvre

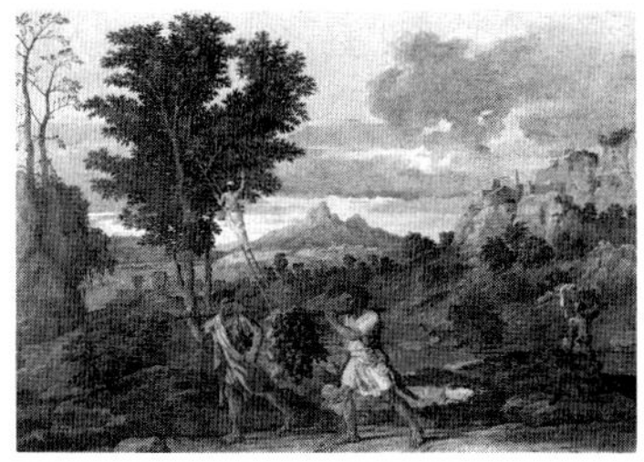

134
N. Poussin
Four Seasons, Autumn 1660–4
Paris, Musée du Louvre

opposite
132
H. Rousseau
Walking in the Forest *c.*1886
Zürich, Kunsthaus

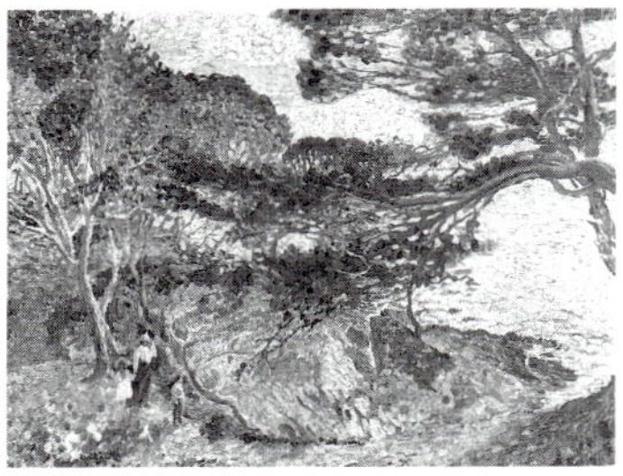

135
H. -E. Cross
Cap Layet 1904
Munich, Neue Pinakothek

136
M. Denis
Eurydice 1906
Berlin, Dauerleihgabe des Ernst von Siemens-Kunstfonds, Nationalgalerie

also for more naturalistic images. Comparing one of the latter – *Cap Layet* of 1904 [**135**] – to *Eurydice* brings home the imaginative transformation Denis wrought on the landscape. Cross's painting is atmospheric and, with its image of a bourgeois family stroll along the wild seashore, alludes to the temporariness of tourism. Denis's composition, by contrast, stages in the simplified landscape a tragic drama. On the one hand the bodies are in the same deep pinks as the soil and trunks, the trees follow the rhythms of the fleeing figures, and there is an overall unity of texture. That sense of harmony is shattered by the incident. The action is spread out, fragmented: tragic protagonists here, snake being clubbed there, disturbed figures everywhere. Paintings such as *Eurydice*, shown at Denis's 1907 one-man show at the Bernheim Jeune gallery, were praised for their imaginative qualities, [5] though *Eurydice* may have had personal associations of which critics could hardly have known. Denis's sister-in-law Eva, to whom he was very attached, had died in 1901 and his baby daughter Noëlle almost succumbed to acute appendicitis two years later, so perhaps for Denis the tragic death of Eurydice was a cathartic meditation on mortality.[6]

Denis's fellow Nabi, Vallotton, whose previous land- and cityscapes had been relatively unexceptional [**75**], turned to the *paysage historique* in 1904, probably in response to the work of his contemporaries. *Pentheus* [**137**] was submitted to the Salon d'Automne in 1905, where the Swiss Vallotton's excursion into the mythological was met with some surprise. 'Is that lad running away Orpheus,' asked the critic Louis Vauxcelles, 'or rather some chap from the canton of Vaud who has surrendered his clothes to some lubricious cow-girls? Oh! no, M.Vallotton is no lyric painter of satyrs, oreads, fauns and sacred groves; it all makes one think of Devambez [**182**] rather than Theocritus'.[7] Even Camille Mauclair, an enthusiast of the return to order, found Vallotton guilty of 'unbelievable ugliness through excess of admirable intentions'.[8] Why did Vallotton's painting arouse such a reaction? It may have been because it was not Poussinesque enough, but closer to his fellow Swiss Böcklin [9] whose work represented a rival, Teutonic, classicism. Certainly Vallotton's landscape has the sombreness of many of his compatriots' settings. The densely packed trees and bushes do not read as the conventional Mediterranean ideal, and

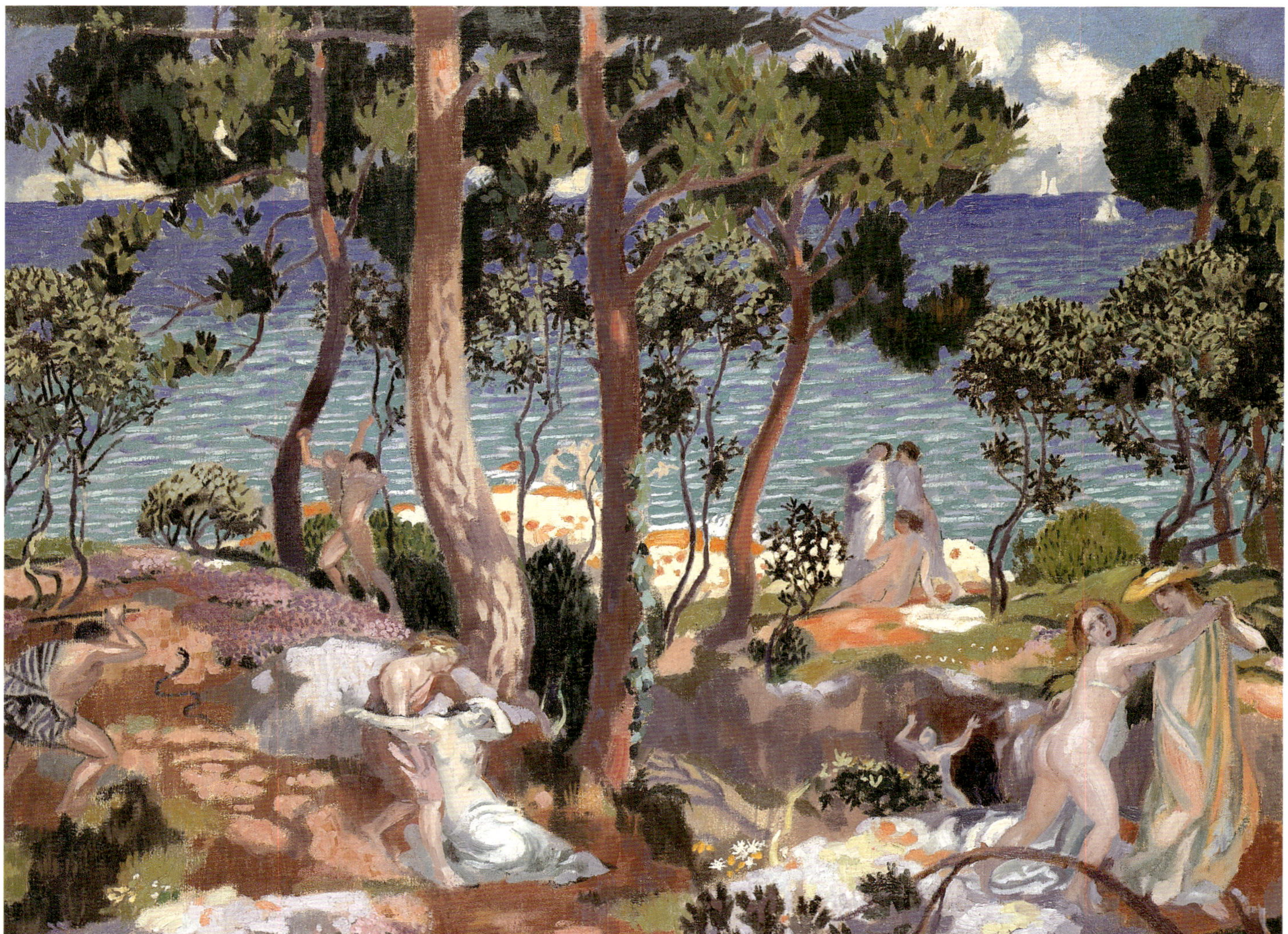

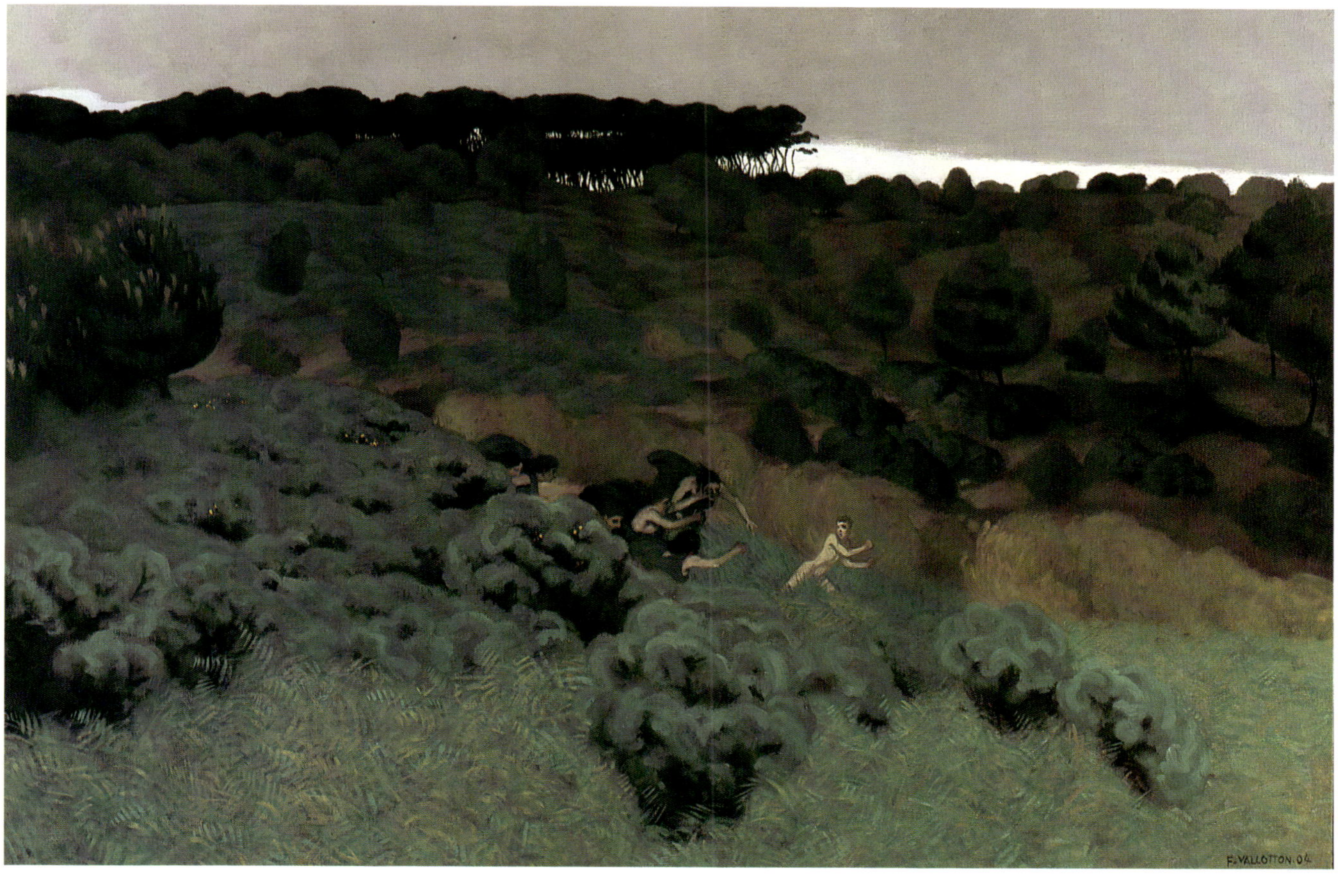

137
F. Vallotton
Pentheus 1904
Switzerland, Private Collection

from them burst figures neither harmoniously pastoral nor sentimentally tragic but telling a story of the most unnatural violence. As told by Ovid in the *Metamorphoses*, Pentheus mocked the followers of Bacchus, who pursued him and tore him limb from limb, his immediate murderers being his aunt and mother. For all its mythological authority Vallotton's theme and manner of representing it – the vicious incident exploding in a flurry of sharply highlit limbs in the centre of a wild scrubland setting – were perhaps too disturbing for his audience. At one level his choice was determined by a desire to experiment with the *paysage composé* that so many of his colleagues were using, but given Vallotton's recent and somewhat uncomfortable marriage it may well also have been impelled by some underlying psychosexual imperative suggested by the story of Pentheus.

If Vallotton upset expectations with his shift of subject and odd but apt composition, René Ménard stood for the conventions. Ménard's credentials as a classicist had been well established by the 1890s. Nephew of a distinguised scholar of the ancient world, well travelled in Italy and Greece, Ménard was 'intimately pagan', as one critic put it in 1899.[10] His work was constantly compared to the classical paradigms – Bouyer called him the 'inheritor of Theocritus and Poussin'[11] – and Ménard was in many ways the successor to Puvis de Chavannes, sustaining the classical idiom in major mural commissions such as the huge panels for the Faculty of Law at the Sorbonne [**140**] painted between 1907 and 1913.[12] Ménard's typical compositions featured generalised landscapes of sea-coast and forest, mountain and pond, which contrived to allude simultaneously to both Aegean and French nature, thus buoying up the notion of French culture as being the continuation of classical civilisation. These strictly planar landscapes, sober in tone yet drenched in an empyrean light, were peopled by nymphs and herdsmen, their draperies and horses recalling the Parthenon frieze. Ménard's subjects were mainly serene and pastoral, rather than representing specific mythological stories. *Hercules and the Lion* [**139**], a pastel made in 1914, is thus somewhat unusual in subject. The landscape is barren heathland, worked in brown, sombre purple, and dark blue-greens, with the valley to the right lit in white and livid yellow. Over this forbidding panorama a storm breaks, and within it man and beast struggle, locked as if in perpetuity both in combat and into the landscape, for their colouration melds with their surroundings. Perhaps the image is more than a powerful evocation of Hercules's labour of killing the Nemean lion. It is a true *paysage historique* in its use of myth in conjunction with landscape to convey grave ideas, the elemental struggle between good and evil which in 1914 carried surely inescapable connotations of Franco-German conflict.

All three pictures by Denis, Vallotton and Ménard indicate the significance of the *paysage historique* in the early twentieth century, and were both formed by and contributed to the broader cultural and nationalistic currents associated with classicism. They demon-

138
L. -O. Merson
St Francis of Assisi Preaching to the Fish 1880
Nantes, Musée des beaux-arts

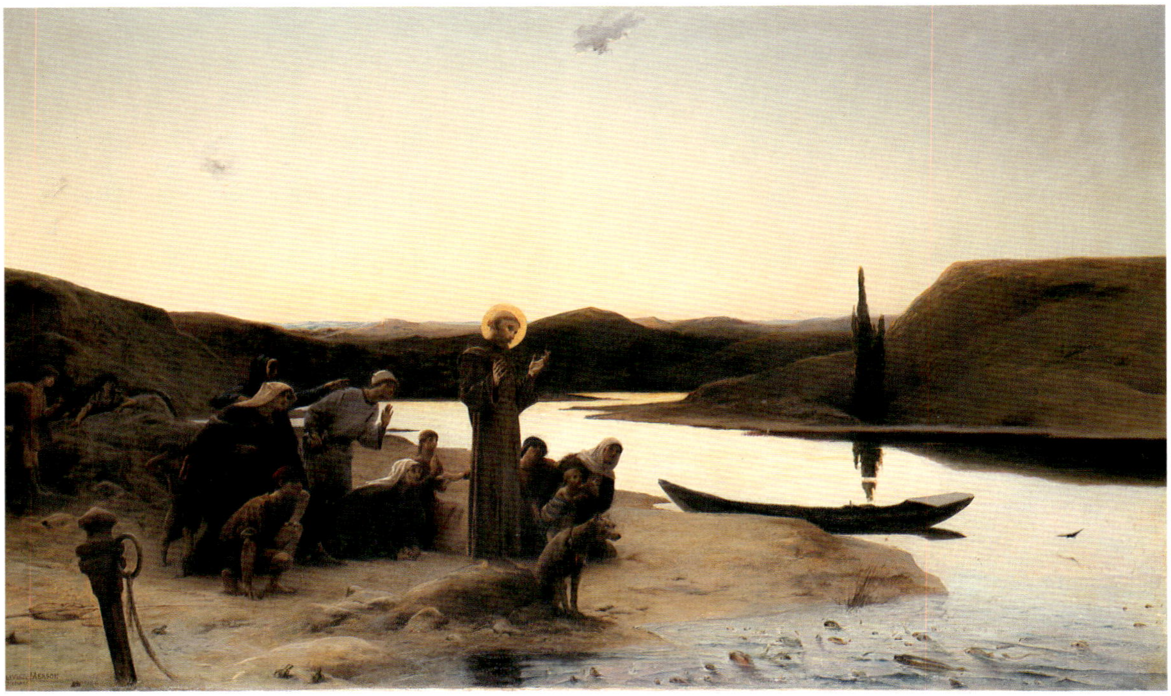

strate how that instinct crossed ideological differences, for Denis's politics were reactionary, Vallotton's anarchist. But, more than that, they show how effectively traditional forms could be reinvented to serve as a vehicle for the imagination, how ancient mythology could be manipulated by the artist's fantasy and skills as a picture-maker into images rich in personal, psychosexual, or patriotic meaning. The possibilities for the interplay of figure and landscape, so deep-seated in the traditions of the genre, may have become increasingly recognised in the classicising climate of the turn of the century, but they had in fact never disappeared from painters' repertoires.

The continuity of tradition can be seen in two canvases painted in the 1880s by artists of traditional training and values. Of different generations, Gustave Moreau and Luc-Olivier Merson had both studied at the Ecole des beaux-arts. Moreau had failed to win the Prix de Rome but had spent a lengthy period in Italy during the 1850s, whereas Merson won the Prix in 1869. Both no doubt saw themselves as history painters, concentrating on the figure, but landscape was nevertheless an integral part of their work. Merson's *St Francis of Assisi Preaching to the Fish* [**138**] was exhibited at the Salon of 1881. Iconographically Merson was in error, as it was not St Francis but St Anthony of Padua who performed that particular piscine miracle.[13] Stylistically the painting is a combination of the compositional structures of Poussin – one might compare it to the Louvre's *Finding of Moses* of 1638 – and the simplicity of the quattrocento painters such as Fra Angelico and Filippo Lippi whose work Merson had so admired when studying in Italy during the early 1870s.[14] The rhythm of the awestruck figures leaning towards the saint is echoed by the distant hills, and only the holy man and the evergreen tree, symbol of eternal life, break the earthly horizon to reach heavenwards. The subdued light and calm scene evoke a mood of contemplation and serenity in the viewer, entirely appropriate in a landscape geared to a human incident of devotion and piety. Whereas Merson's highly finished canvas was an exhibition picture, Moreau's *Tomyris and Cyrus* [**141**] by contrast has an extraordinarily rough and dishevelled surface, much of it crafted with a palette knife, indicative of an experimental painting kept back in the studio. His source was an obscure story by Herodotus, telling of how the Persian Emperor Cyrus invaded the land of the Massagetae, whose queen was Tomyris. After the first battle her son, drunk on wine deliberately left by the Persians, was captured. Tomyris demanded his return, threatening Cyrus with more blood than he could drink if

139
R. Ménard
Hercules and the Lion 1914
Courbevoie, Musée Roybet-Fould

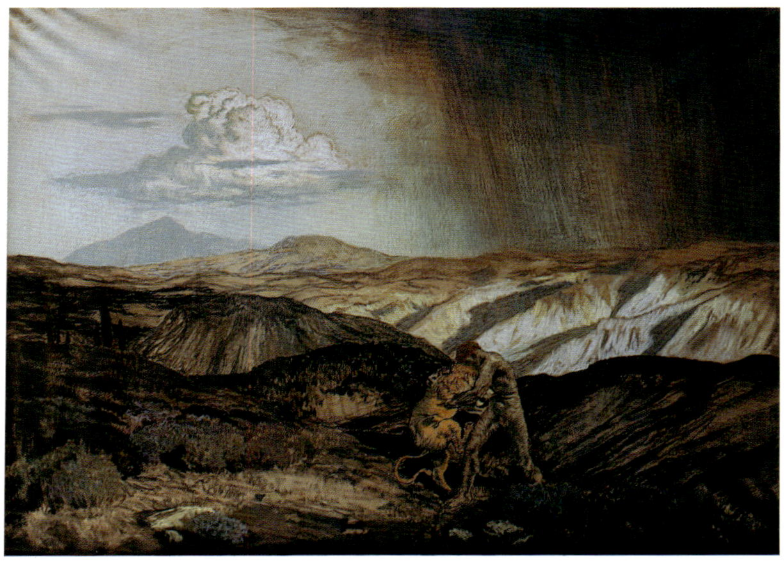

her wishes were not met. But the young man committed suicide. Following a terrible battle in which Cyrus was killed, Tomyris kept her word by ordering his severed head to be placed in a skin full of human blood. This was the incident Moreau represented, but he transformed his source. Herodotus explains that the Massagetae lived not in the Caucasus but to the west on a vast plain, and yet Moreau imagined the grisly scene of Cyrus's posthumous humiliation taking place in rocky, snow-strewn mountains. For all the violent drama of this moment, Moreau did not place it centrally or make the figures dominate; the eye has to find them in the snowscape. The natural environment again establishes the mood, the mountains' wildness an echo of the barbarity of Tomyris's revenge. The fact that the figures are hard to trace, that their tones again bind them into the picture surface, reinforces the equation between the natural and the moral, in addition to adducing an element of shock when the spectator makes out the horrific incident. Moreau's disorderly, trowelled surface, both cold and bloody, is as unconventional as Merson's smooth brushwork is disciplined and calm, yet technically both are as well adapted as the landscapes in which the figures are set to the stories the images tell.

The spectator's response to a representation of a landscape will change according to whether the image includes people or not. A painting of nature alone will evoke feelings and associations both implanted by the artist in the image and brought by the viewer to it. It may read, for example, as hostile or inviting, stirring up atavistic instincts about the ability of the land to provide food and shelter. For if the image is unpeopled, the viewer becomes its staffage. The empty landscape carries implications of the timelessness of pure nature and, unsullied by ties with people and their activities, may instil feelings of calm and tranquillity. French landscape painting of the mid-nineteenth century was often taken to read this way. Victor Fournel argued in 1884 that Daubigny's pictures were moving and restful because they were empty, and that also made them distinct from the *paysage historique*.[15] Viewing the Universal Exhibition's retrospective of the previous ten years in 1900, Paul Flat pointed out that whereas Théodore Rousseau and Daubigny [**229**] had made their landscape paintings poetic by leaving out figures, contemporary painters insisted on putting them in.[16] If there are figures in a painting we will immediately respond to them. We are at once distanced from the landscape, which belongs to 'other people', and yet also drawn in by curiosity, identifying with what they are represented as doing. How the painter sets up the fictive figures, as well as the way the landscape setting is contrived, determines our response, and calls into play associations and values from our social, cultural

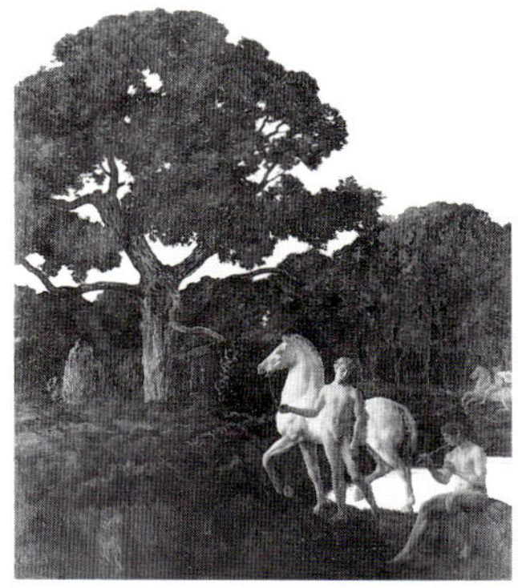

140
R. Ménard
The Golden Age: left panel 1908
Paris, Musée d'Orsay

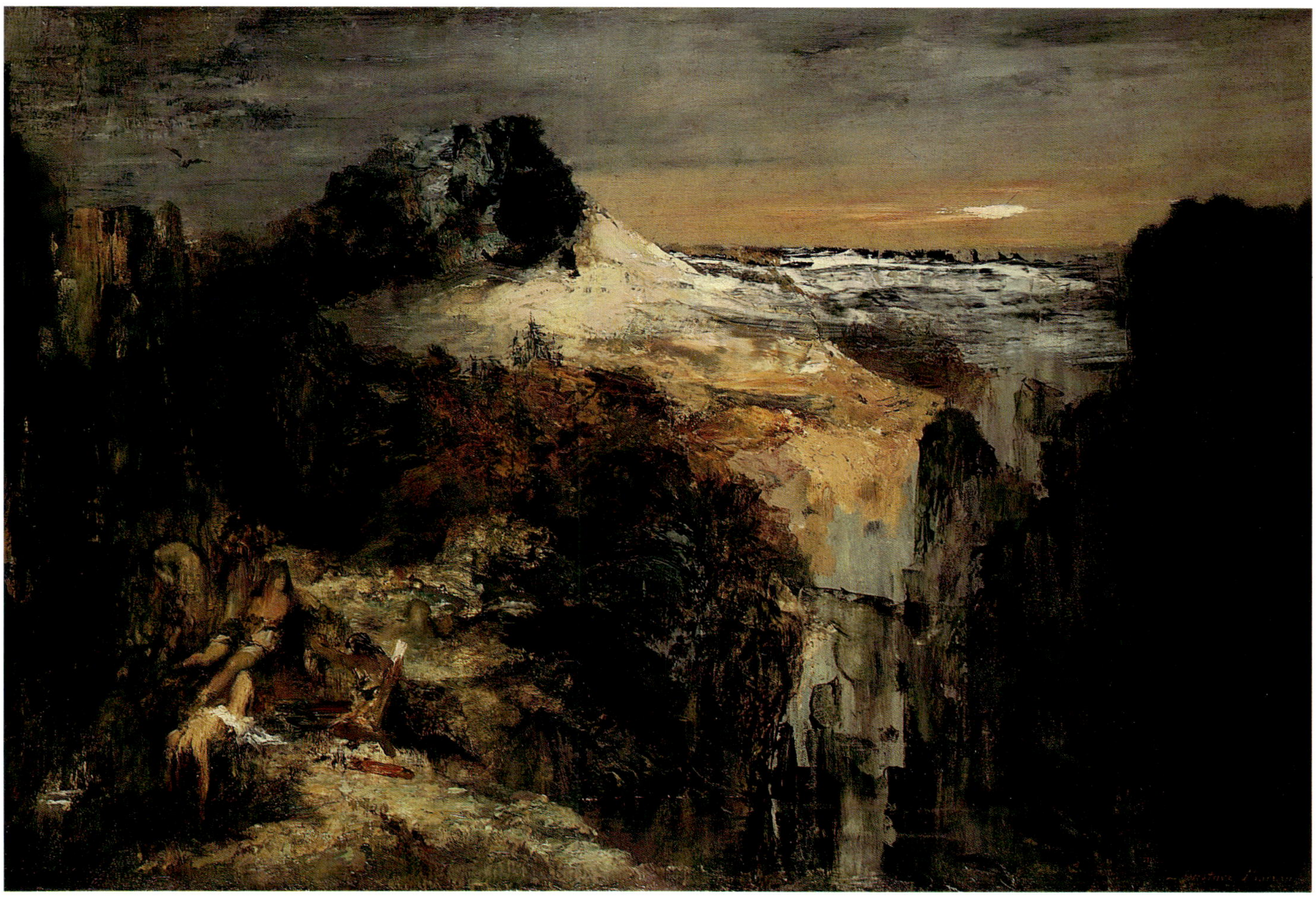

141
G. Moreau
Tomyris and Cyrus *c.*1885
Paris, Musée Gustave Moreau

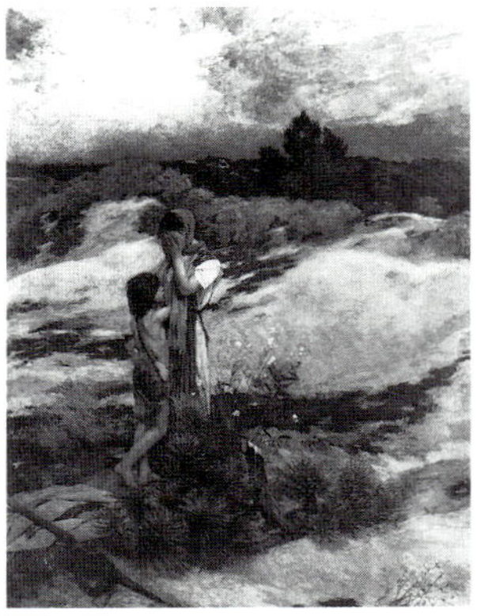

142
J.-C. Cazin
Hagar and Ishmael 1880
Tours, Musée des beaux-arts

143
J.-C. Cazin
Rest Before Nightfall 1883
Washington, Corcoran Gallery of Art, William A. Clark Collection

and historical experience. Flat pointed out that in recent years painters had found it increasingly difficult to leave out the human element. No doubt he referred to pastoral or mythological staffage, but he specifically mentioned how figures necessarily introduced into the landscape *'la signification morale'*, in broad terms social values.

Cazin in particular was expert at suggesting such qualities. He made his reputation at the Salon in 1880 when he exhibited two biblical subjects, *Hagar and Ishmael* [**142**] and *Tobit and the Angel* to critical acclaim.[17] In both paintings pairs of figures are set in the gently undulating landscape of Cazin's native Pas-de-Calais, and dressed in clothes as much contemporary as biblical. Although the paintings depict conventional religious subjects, they are also distinctly accessible, pitched as they are midway between traditional history painting and modern naturalism. Cazin worked variations on this theme throughout the decade. At times his images might discreetly indicate a religious theme, as in a painting of a *septentrional* farmyard where a man leads out a donkey carrying a mother and baby, naturalistic in subject and treatment, except for the unobtrusive haloes that mark it as the commencement of the Flight into Egypt.[18] Other paintings are more ambiguous. The *End of the Day*, shown at the Salon of 1888,[19] represents a labourer turning from his wheelbarrow and tools to greet his wife who has brought their baby out to his workplace in the waterlogged flatlands. While perhaps alluding to the Holy Family, it at least calls into play the bourgeois family values which the Third Republic sought to reinforce in the lower classes. *Rest Before Nightfall* [**143**], painted five years earlier, was something of a prototype for this suggestive approach to reading the figures, although it was not a Salon picture. In costumes at once archaic and plausibly contemporary, a woman adjusts her headscarf as her husband holds their baby. They seem to be readying themselves to move on through the scrubby uninhabited dunes. Cazin gives no indication of their purpose or destination in his image, an ambiguity enhanced by the painting of the landscape itself, with its cool yet luminous tones and soft ambient light. Subtle colour and barren setting conspire to evoke a mood of melancholy, echoed by the parents' slightly bowed heads but mollified by the family's sympathetic cohesion. Whether this picture too alludes to the Flight into Egypt Cazin leaves the viewer to answer. It also recalls Millet's *Angélus* [**2**], that icon of peasant piety. Whatever spiritual associations *Rest before Nightfall* might call up, it is surely a landscape with *'signification sociale'*, for vagrancy was an increasing problem. Between the 1870s and the 1890s arrests for the offence almost doubled, and at the end of the century the Société d'agriculture estimated that there were about 400,000 vagrants in France, over one per cent of the population.[20] Cazin, as a good Republican, may have been drawing attention to such deprivation, as anarchist artists did later in the century.[21] His allusive figure paintings were defined by Paul Desjardins in his obituary of Cazin as distinct from the 'architectural' compositions of the Poussinesque *paysage historique*. Rather, he argued, they were 'musical' in the way that their subdued tones, gently rhythmic landscapes and compositional dispositions worked in harmony.[22] Neither classical nor dramatic, Cazin's use of figures provided a potent example of how the interrelationship of landscape and human incident, however modest, can make a distinctly affective impression on the spectator.

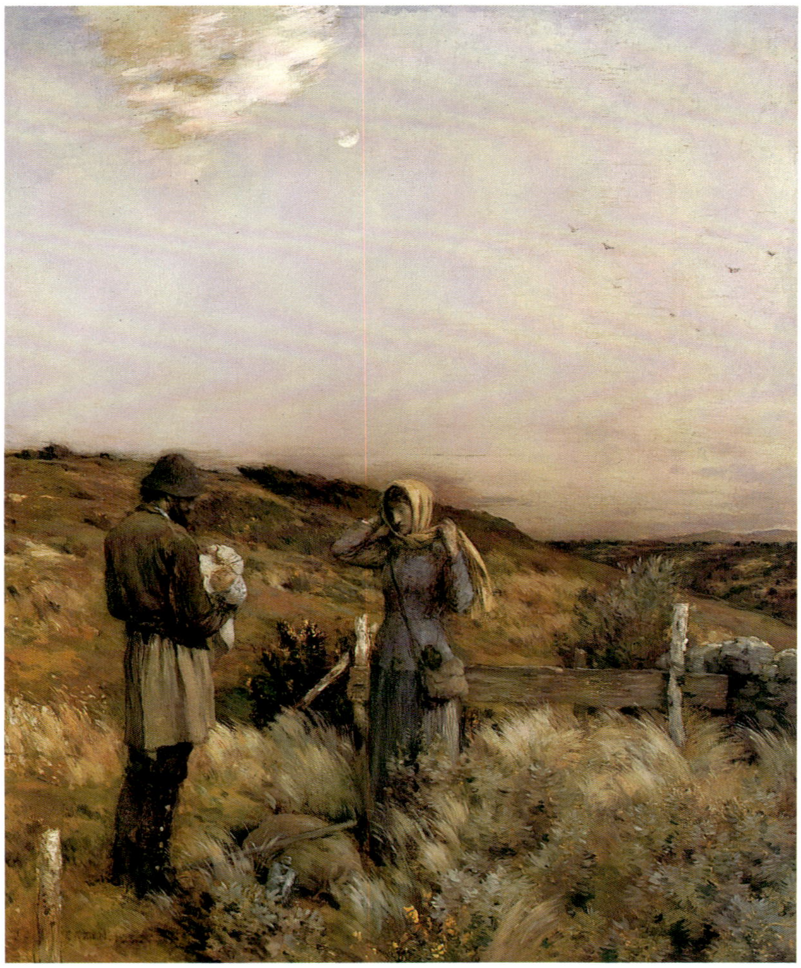

Playing off figures and landscape has of course been a consistent feature in western European painting for centuries. But one can argue that in France during the 1880s artists were increasingly concerned to shake off the clichés of history and genre painting to inject new imaginative possibilities into the combination. If Cazin's initiatives took place in the establishment forum of the Salon, avant-garde painters too demonstrated an interest in using landscape as a theatre for events. The toiling faggot-gatherers of mid-century Barbizon painting or the promenading bourgeois of Impressionist painting of the 1870s were people from daily life. But the 1880s, one might hypothesise, saw the return of the figure as an actor in the landscape. Dramatic incidents on a landscape stage were part of Douanier Rousseau's repertoire from the outset of his career. *Walking in the Forest*

[132], a canvas made about 1886, is constructed on lucid lines. The main tree-line bisects the canvas, and two tall trees frame the shallow foreground area, creating a very theatrical space into which Rousseau places a single female figure, off-centre to the left. Her body language suggests apprehension, and as she looks down the path we feel she is being followed. The threatening atmosphere is enhanced by the density of the woods, confining the protagonist to the front of the stage, as well as by the storm clouds gathering in the distance over her head. Rousseau's ambiguous staging leaves questions open. Is this *bourgeoise* in a wild forest or a domesticated park? Is she alone and frightened by her solitude, or being pursued by another figure visible to her but not to the spectator? Rousseau sets up his fiction so that these questions remain unanswerable. The landscape, at once dense, confining and spiky yet also neatly ordered and smoothly finished, affects our reading of the figure and heightens the drama.

Dramatic incidents and confrontations began to play a part in Gauguin's landscapes in the late 1880s. Before that Gauguin had painted mainly peasant types conventionally going about their bucolic business, but from 1888 his figures took on more imaginative rôles. Whereas Rousseau's apparent isolation from artistic debates obscures his motives for painting scenes such as *Walking in the Forest*, Gauguin's shift of direction is more easily traced. Working at Pont-Aven in Brittany in 1888 he was ambitious to define an identifiable avant-garde style of his own, developing stark delineation and arbitrary colour zones in collaboration with Emile Bernard in particular. Gauguin was concerned to win himself status in the emerging climate of Symbolism, with its rejection of naturalistic description in favour of the evocative and subjective. *Blue Tree Trunks, Arles* [144], painted in late 1888 during his fractious two months with van Gogh, demonstrates the remarkable transformation in Gauguin's landscape practice from the conventional Impressionist canvases that he was still producing earlier that year. But this landscape is not just an index of his deliberate naïvety of drawing and rejection of local colour. Within this rocky landscape lit by a livid sunset, and product surely of fantasy rather than observation, Gauguin enacted an exchange between an Arlésienne and a man in workers' *bleus*. The incident is disguised behind the tree, but the man's firm posture and the woman's flinching movement suggest some disagreeable, even sexual, encounter. But it is not just the figures' poses which imply such tensions. They are small semi-legible elements in the fictive landscape, barren and sourly lit, using imaginative staging of the *paysage* to conjure up a disconcertingly sinister mood.

Gauguin's strategy for achieving prominence in the avant-garde involved not only stylistic change but also the recasting of his own image as an artist. At the end of the decade – genuinely impoverished, struggling for the artistic status he craved, and increasingly estranged from his wife and children – Gauguin consciously played up the painful extremes of his personal circumstances. In 1889 he regularly represented himself as an outsider in the Breton landscape. *Bonjour, Monsieur Gauguin*, painted that autumn, exists in two versions. The first would seem to be the smaller [145] that was used to decorate an overdoor in Marie Henry's inn at Le Pouldu. Gauguin followed it with a larger canvas in which, under a more sombre sky, his figure looms larger and the Breton woman shies uneasily from him, rather than watching him cautiously as in the earlier variant.[23] Gauguin manipulates landscape to indicate the mood of the protagonists. The representation of the stark unsheltered terrain of the south Breton coast, with its squat cottages, sparse trees and narrow lanes, uses unwelcoming nature as a metaphor for the suspicion of the woman secure behind her gate. *Bonjour, Monsieur Gauguin* derives its title from Courbet's *Bonjour, Monsieur Courbet* [146], which Gauguin had seen the previous year on a visit to the Musée Fabre in Montpellier with van Gogh. In Courbet's painting the bland landscape does no more than generalise the site at which the painter was sincerely greeted by his patron Bruyas. Contrarily, Gauguin used the title ironically to show the artist's

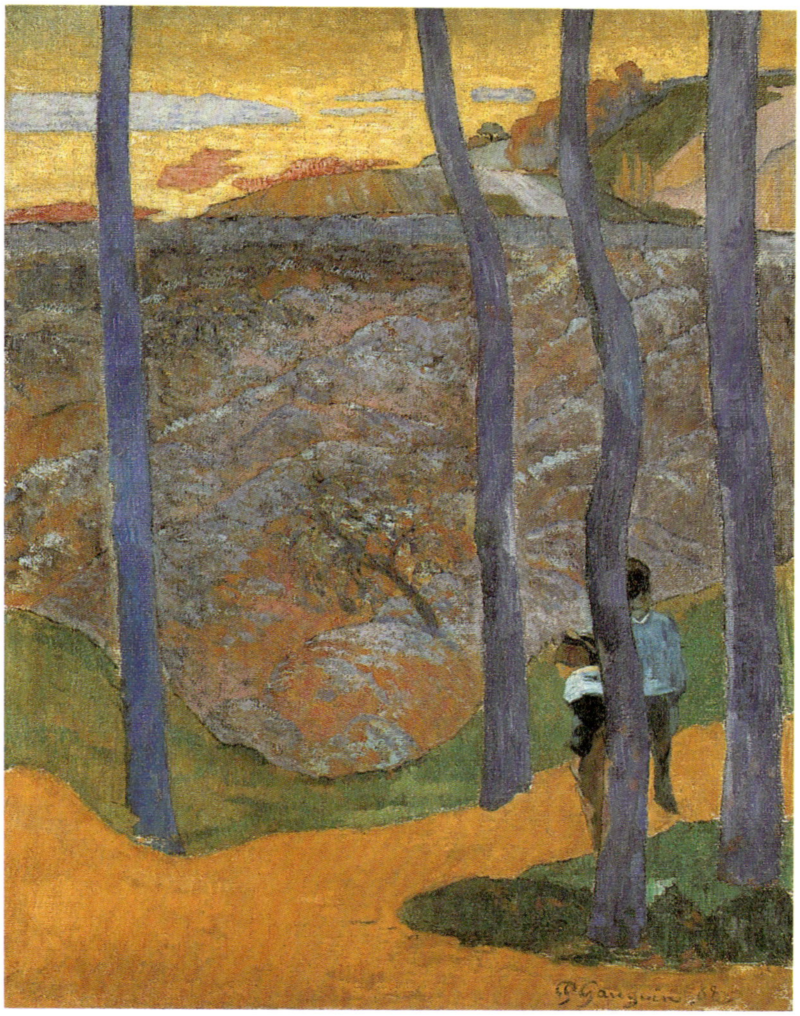

144
P. Gauguin
Blue Tree Trunks, Arles 1888
Copenhagen, Ordrupgaardsamlingen

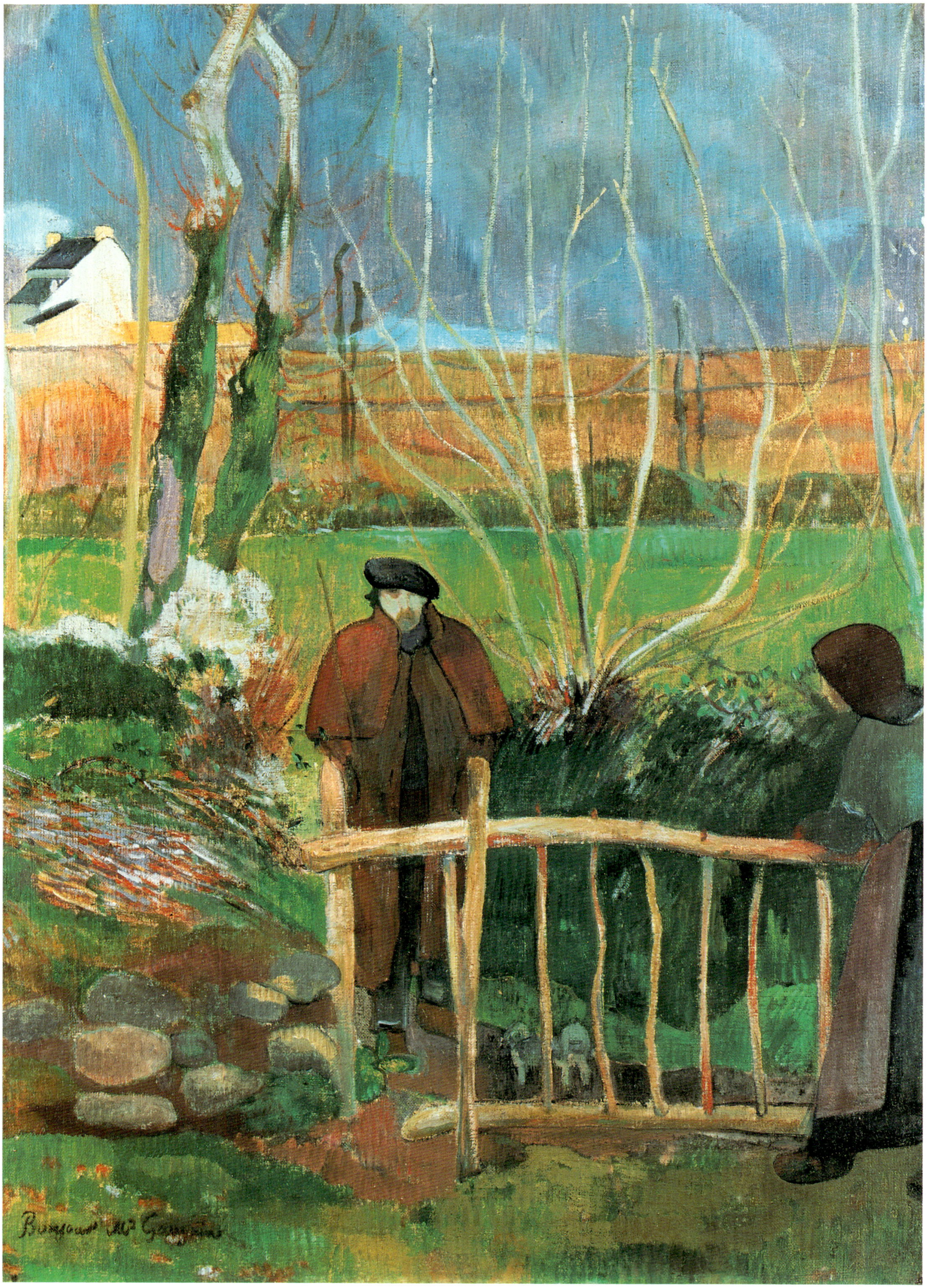

alienation, a state the landscape enhances.

The paintings made by Gauguin in the South Seas after 1891 equally show the use of landscape as a theatre. In *Mata Mua (In Olden Times)* [**147**], painted in the French colony of Tahiti in 1892, the landscape is arranged in lucid planes, the bands of sumptuous tropical colour forming a stage on which the figures perform. No drama is represented here, but rather ritual, with a musician and listener in the foreground and in the middle space three women who dance around an idol. Such a scene was essentially imaginary. European settlers and missionaries had eradicated much of Tahitian religion and culture long before Gauguin's arrival; as the title admits, his painting is a recreation of an imaginary past. *Mata Mua* was as artificial in its genesis as in its subject. The bushy tree in the centre appeared in two smaller paintings also made in 1892.[24] They are 'pure' landscapes in which tiny figures play an insignificant part, and might be said to have acted as studies for *Mata Mua*. In that sense *Mata Mua* was very much a *paysage composé*, a studio confection and thus an ideal vehicle for the scene Gauguin's imagination enacted within it. Peaceful, ritualistic and nostalgic, that scene, for all its arbitrary chromatics and decorative simplification, is in essence a pastoral. If *Mata Mua* integrates elements in the fabrication of landscape imagery which were both traditional and modern, a similar case could be made for Rousseau's jungle paintings. A painting such as the *Tropical Landscape* of 1910 [**148**] is 'modern' in its contrivance of the jungle as *décor*, and yet its staging of an epic combat in elemental nature almost brackets it, one might argue, as a *paysage historique* alongside Ménard's nearly contemporary *Hercules and the Lion* [**139**]. Above all, Rousseau's painting is a work of the imagination, a point brought home forcibly by his confrontation of an American Indian with an African gorilla, geographically absurd but justified as the product of his own fanciful mythology.

Singling out Cazin, Rousseau and Gauguin in an argument about the imaginative use of figurative incidents in landscape paintings is admittedly an arbitrary exercise. One could make the same case with different painters. But those three – operating within the establishment, in semi-isolation, and in the avant-garde – represent a strain in French painting of the period, identifiable with no particular style or grouping, which sought to use landscape as a theatre for figurative incident. All three contrived the 'natural' environment to set the emotional tone of the protagonists. Although in certain respects such images may refer back to past traditions, not least to the *paysage historique* which itself was a force for the imaginative integration of figure and landscape in contemporary painting, they also represent a parallel and fresh initiative to adapt the flexible possibilities of *paysage* to the fantasy of the artist.

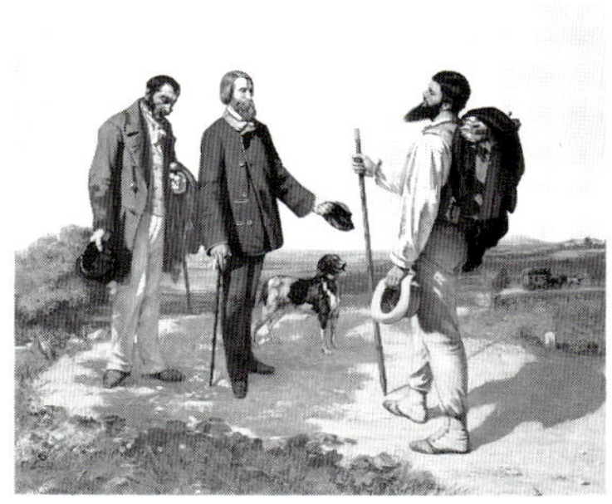

146
G. Courbet
Bonjour, Monsieur Courbet 1854
Montpellier, Musée Fabre

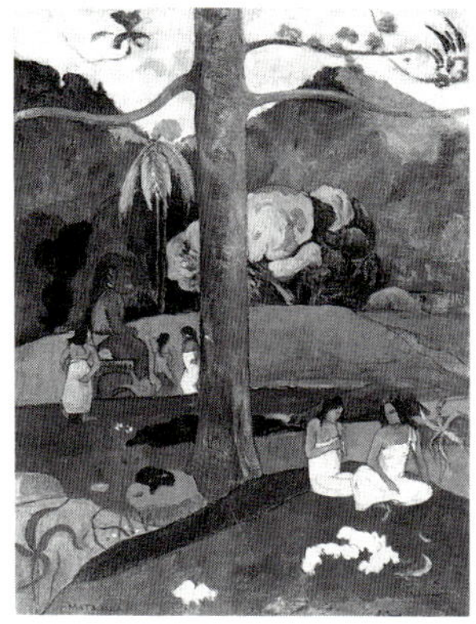

147
P. Gauguin
Mata Mua (In Olden Times) 1892
Madrid, Fundación Colección Thyssen-Bornemisza

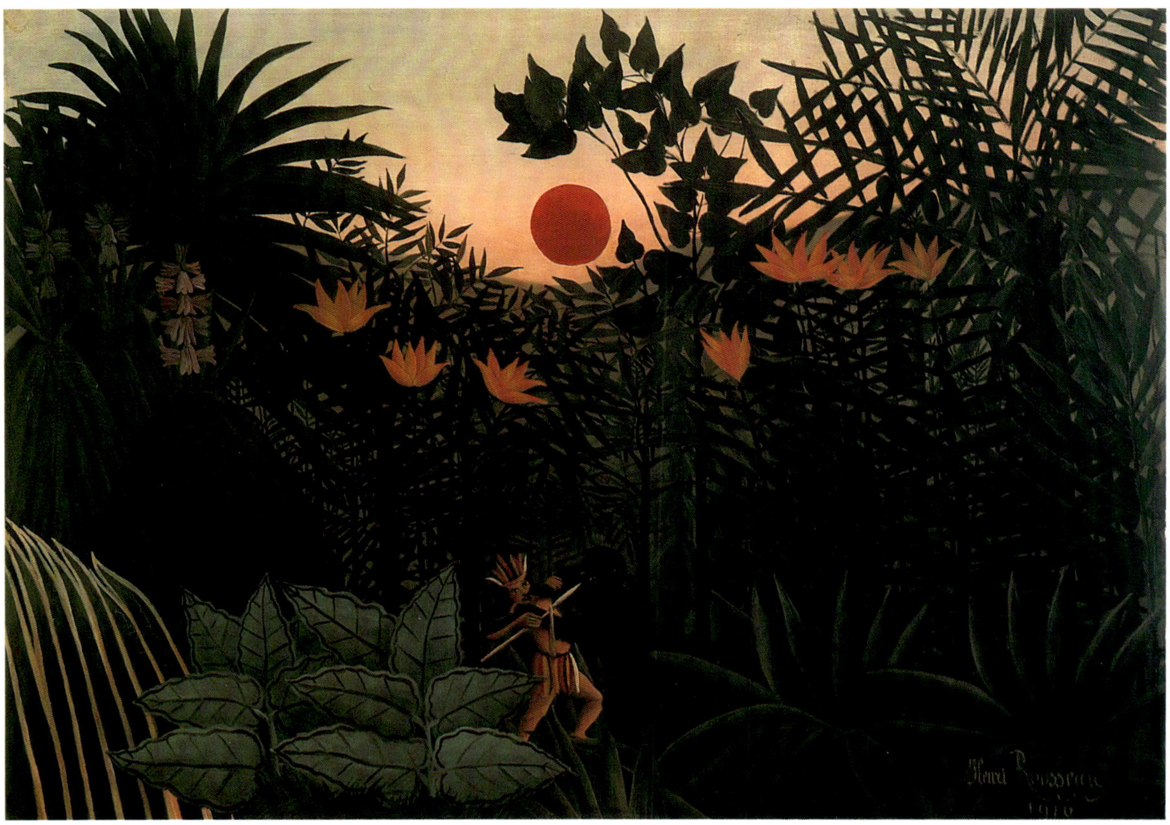

opposite
145
P. Gauguin
Bonjour, Monsieur Gauguin 1889
Los Angeles, The Armand Hammer Collection

left
148
H. Rousseau
Tropical Landscape – an American Indian struggling with a Gorilla 1910
Richmond, Virginia Museum of Fine Arts, Collection of Mr and Mrs Paul Mellon

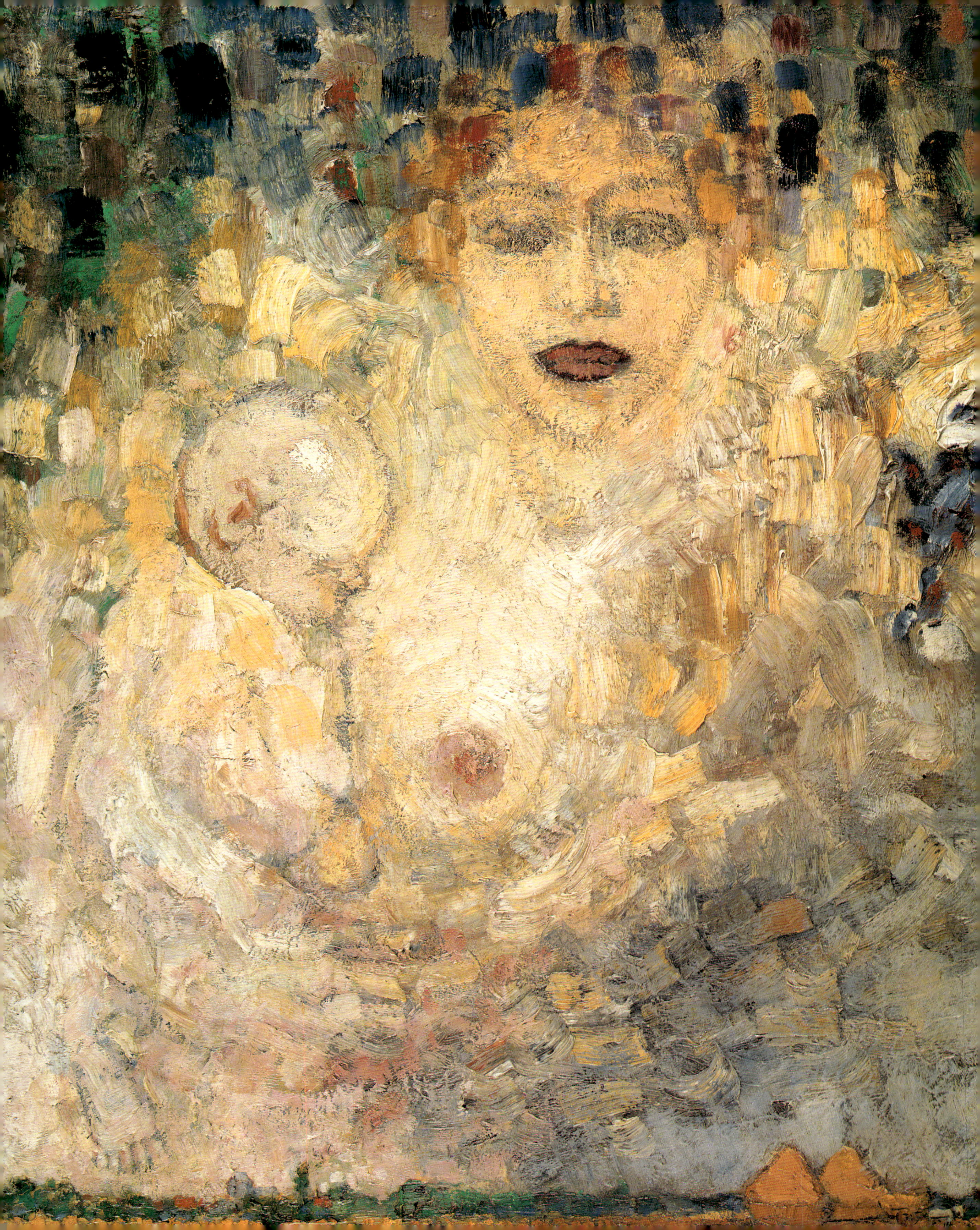

8

Landscape as Vision and Metamorphosis

Landscape painting in France at the end of the nineteenth and the beginning of the twentieth century throws up some fascinating images which are difficult to place within the conventional categories of *paysage*. Some are more or other than mere sites, some even appear to transcend the notion of landscape altogether, and yet they still retain a 'natural' character. How might one explain, for example, Kupka's *Création* [**150**] paintings of about 1911? At first sight they appear entirely non-representational, a tumbling mass of brightly coloured forms. And yet those forms have an organic character, and the configuration and tones suggest a weighty foreground, a horizon, and a billowing upper space. One's sense of some kind of landscape armature within such ostensibly amorphous energy is ratified by the knowledge that Kupka regularly summered in Brittany, sending postcards which show his admiration for the dramatic rock formations on the stormy Breton shoreline.[1] The residual inspiration of landscape in these, some of the most radically 'abstract' paintings produced before 1914, and in particular the presence of natural elements in what is so consciously an imaginative alchemy, leads one to ask whether and how artists prior to Kupka treated landscape with such visionary distortion or submitted landscape to such metamorphic fantasy.

One might best begin by outlining the conditions in which artists might have been encouraged to experiment so imaginatively with natural forms. The later years of the nineteenth century witnessed the emergence of advanced psychological ideas. Doctors such as Jean-Martin Charcot and Hippolyte Bernheim were putting forward influential theories which radically redefined 'the human organism … [as] a sensitive nervous mechanism, prone to suggestion, visual thinking and imagistic projection in dreams'. Their experiments with hypnotism broke down the conventional assumption that the human mind rationally orders the sensations and information it gets from the exterior world, Bernheim in particular advancing the notions that we are highly impressionable in certain mental states and that imaginative interior images have their own validity as 'truth'.[2] Such ideas were in wide currency by the turn of the century and were easily assimilated into the Symbolist aesthetic which had consistently promoted the suggestive and imaginary, seeking *correspondances* between images and emotions, the physical and the psychological. In an intellectual climate which was coming to terms with the blurring of boundaries between the human body and mind and the environments – tangible, visual, emotional, affective – in which they operate, it was inevitable that artists and writers should begin to consider how one's experience of landscape might alter one's external perception or internal vision and conversely how one's state of mind might affect one's experience of landscape. Moréas, a leading figure in Symbolism, jotted in his *carnets* how he associated the shadows of poplar trees with beautiful women such as Dido or Nausicaa, and Desjardins's 1899 Salon review discoursed at some length on how certain material habitats enhance perceptions of people's physical charms, perceptions mediated by art; thus Venice suggestively favours tactile flesh and heavy hair.[3] Obversely, experience of art might evoke images of landscape. This notion lies behind Kupka's *Piano Keys/Lake* [**151**], in which the spectator is shown the pianist's fingers on the keyboard and is asked to share the painter's vision of figures in a lakeside landscape conjured up by the imaginary music.

The artist who could work from a fruitful interior life, imagination unfettered by external reality, won praise in such a climate. Odilon Redon was a particular paragon; he worked in a living room rather than a studio, and 'the noise of the trolley buses passing in the avenue below does not trouble the serenity of his fantasy'.[4] The imagination could be fruitfully affected by mood, and Denis was praised for the way that 'on the days when his state of mind is Franciscan he could paint Umbrian landscapes on the slopes of the [Parisian] fortifications'.[5] Given an intellectual framework encouraging artistic fantasy and imaginative reconstitution of landscape according to the painter's psychological state, one might expect to find images that transport *paysage* into the domain of dream. The very title of Lévy-Dhurmer's *Ma mère, un soir, a vu la ville d'Ys* [**152**] suggests disjunction between reality and fantasy: the artist's mother *saw* the mythic Ys, the

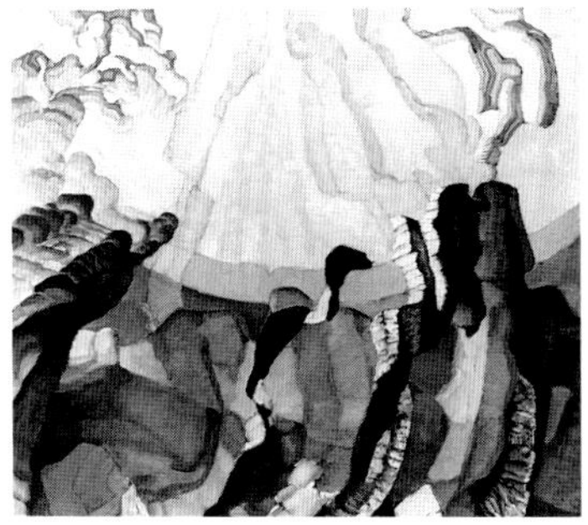

150
F. Kupka
Création 1911–20
Prague, Narodni Gallery

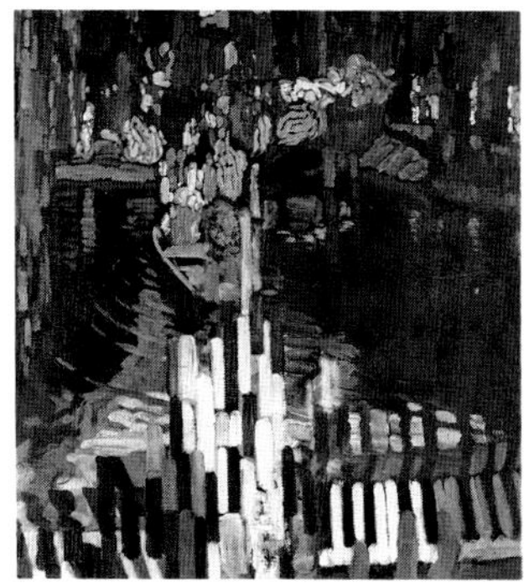

151
F. Kupka ***Piano Keys / Lake*** 1909
Prague, Narodni Gallery

opposite
149
K. van Dongen
Guus and Dolly 1905 (detail)
Private Collection

152
L. Lévy-Dhurmer
Ma mère, un soir, a vu la ville d'Ys
*c.*1898
Brest, Musée municipal

153
C. Monet
Rouen Cathedral: the Portal, Morning Fog 1894
Essen, Folkwang Museum

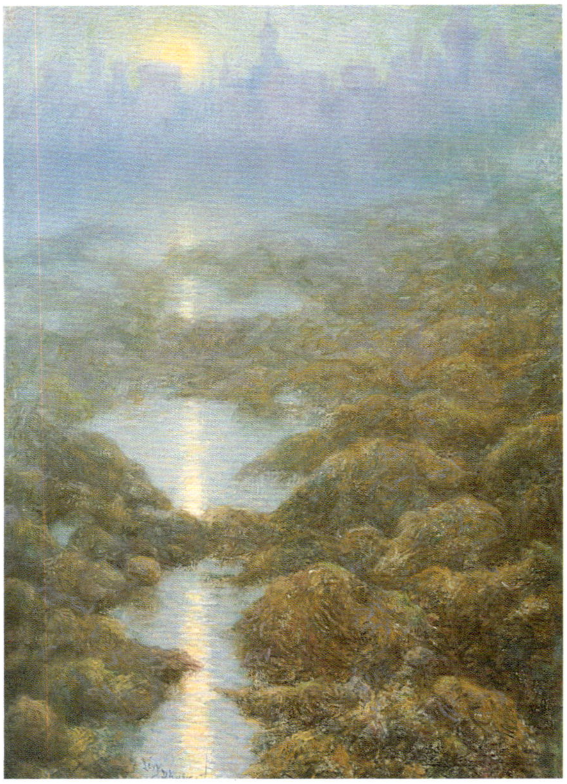

Breton Atlantis. Up to a point Lévy-Dhurmer's exquisite pastel sustains that disjunction, for the seaweed-covered rocks and rippling pools are rendered naturalistically while the lost city wafts scarcely discernible in the soft violet mists. Yet the artist does not allow the eye, as it tracks seawards, to gauge where the real gives way to the dream, and ultimately the image reads as a whole, as a vision rising – distant, impalpable, almost invisible – before us: myth rendered real by the imagination.

If Lévy-Dhurmer's pastel plays with the ambiguities between the naturalistic and the fantastic, that is surely also true of some other images of the mid-1890s. In May 1895 Monet showed at the Durand-Ruel gallery twenty of the thirty canvases of Rouen Cathedral on which he had been working since early 1892. The paintings received a varied, but largely positive, response and continue to be interpreted from a variety of perspectives: as the apogee of Impressionist observation, a flirtation with Symbolist nuance, a meditation on the Frenchness of the Gothic or Monet's own identity as a Norman.[6] Such complex works must be understood within multiple frameworks, but one consistent element in spectators' reactions to them is worth indicating here: the image as dream. Monet's representations of the cathedral involved a number of variables. Light was of course the essential of these, and he also altered his viewpoints. Another, and perhaps less analysed, variable was his treatment of the ground. In none of the paintings of the façade did Monet seek to bring out the street life that surrounds the great church, by including crowds or vehicles, for instance. In a number of the canvases he indicated the floor of the square in front, so it acts somewhat like a discreet plinth for the giant sculptural edifice towering above it. Other paintings may lose the square in the activity of the marks and colours, but the weight of the enormous columns and portals implies the massive bulk of the building pressing down on solid ground. A few others are different again. The canvas now in Essen, *The Portal, Morning Fog* [**153**], was number one in the 1895 catalogue. It is one of the paintings in which the values change most gradually, the range of colours is most circumscribed, and the textures are least dense. The image lightens from bottom to top, the deep blue-violet from which the façade emerges increasingly giving way to a resonant pink, until the left-hand tower is almost exclusively in this tone, with very little blue modulation. The upper pinnacles and higher sections of the two turrets each side of the rose window are modelled in buttery yellows, registering the dawn light rising behind the great structure. In this sense the painting deals with revelation, as the cathedral emerges from the shadows of night into the full light of day. Above all, in this light, Rouen Cathedral appears weightless, floating, like a vision, above ground we cannot see and which it does not touch. It was surely examples such as this which led to a consistent response to the cathedral pictures as dream images. At the time of the exhibition the Neo-Impressionist Angrand wrote to a friend saying that the pictures 'pulse with the atmospheric artifice of dream', using somewhat ironically the word *rêve*, a Symbolist touchstone.[7] André Michel, a critic identified neither with the avant-garde nor the Symbolists but rather with classicising painters such as Ménard, admired the *Cathedrals* as a 'series of *views* or *visions*' in which the 'stone phantom ... has served as a pretext or stimulus for his powerful, arbitrary dream (*rêve*)'.[8] Such an interpretation remained current, for as late as 1910 J.-C.Holl, in his important text on contemporary painting, could still look back on the *Cathedrals* in quasi-Symbolist terms as evocative, as visions.[9] To commentators such as these, of different generations and different aesthetics, Monet seemed to turn reality into dream. One might argue that Lévy-Dhurmer did something similar. His pastel would have been invented in the studio, but by the time he made the *Cathedrals* Monet's practice was so tied to retouchings and harmonisations away from the motif that the quality of direct observation all but disappears; indeed, in these paintings observed reality can hardly be separated from studio activity and the artist's fantasy, his *rêve*. Why was the Essen painting number one? Perhaps the answer is because it represents morning mist disappearing in the dawn light, though maybe too in order to set the tone of the show as one dealing with the painter's visionary imagination. Like Lévy-Dhurmer, though by different means, Monet produced images of dream.

As well as engendering visions which rendered the imaginary visible and the solid ethereal, artists around the turn of the century also exercised a fascination for the metamorphic in landscape. The idea of changing one physical thing into another has always intrigued, and it has been a conceit particularly played with ideas of landscape, drawing as they do parallels between nature and humanity. Painters working in the Mannerist tradition had produced extraordinary landscapes which punningly alternated as bodies or visages, and even artists of more pedagogic character had turned their attentions occasionally to such a fantasy, Valenciennes for one exhibiting *Mount Athos Carved as a Monument to Alexander the Great* at the Salon of 1796 [**154**]. The naming of landscape features to introduce human or animal associations was common, from Claude-François Denecourt's inventively trite mid-nineteenth-century mapping of the Forest of Fontainebleau which called trees the 'Henri IV' or the 'Siamese Twins' to the perhaps more genuinely vernacular naming of the rocky motifs Monet painted on Belle-Ile in 1886 or Friesz at La Ciotat in 1907 as the *Rocher du Lion* and the *Bec d'Aigle*. For physiognomists of man and nature such as Eugène Mouton rocks were considered highly expressive, taking on 'a specific physiognomy and a kind of individuality'.[10] Rocks, of course, do nothing of the kind; it is only the human imagination which imposes such associations upon them. And at the *fin-de-siècle* painters' fantasy did this, and with a diversity of results which bears investigation.

Between 1888 and 1897 Georges Lacombe regularly spent his summers at Camaret, on the extremity of the Crozon peninsula to the south of Brest. Here, where the Atlantic breakers crash against the Breton headlands, Lacombe made a number of dramatic paintings of the cliffs. *Vorhor, the Green Wave* [**155**] shows the same location as another painting, perhaps executed a little earlier and representing the waves breaking more gently in the steep cove.[11] Both demonstrate Lacombe's indebtedness to Japanese prints in the stylisation of the ocean patterns and the abruptly synthetic forms, an economy of outline which enhances the association of the cliff walls with human faces. The great curving shape on the right especially reads as a giant profile of sweeping nose, sour mouth, and jutting chin, giving the landscape a sinister character amplified by the livid yellows and purples of sea and sky. Lacombe and his public would have been attuned to such transmogrifications because metamorphic caprices were embedded in nineteenth-century culture's reading of landscape, perpetuated in texts such as Mouton's and repeated in imagery; in 1899, for example, the popular scientific magazine *La Nature* published a photograph of a cliff [**157**] which seems to have a human profile, using that ostensibly 'objective' medium to prove the

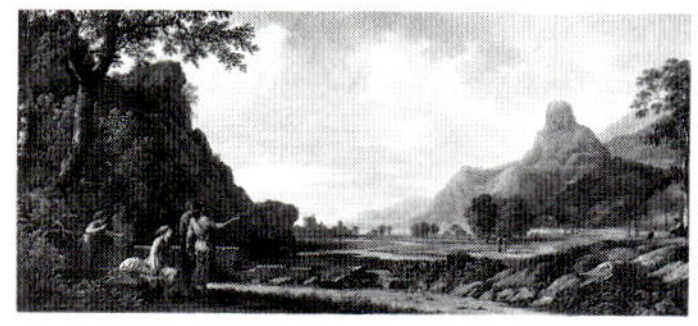

154
P. -H. de Valenciennes
Mount Athos Carved as a Monument to Alexander the Great c.1796
Chicago, Art Institute, Restricted gift of Mrs Harold T. Martin

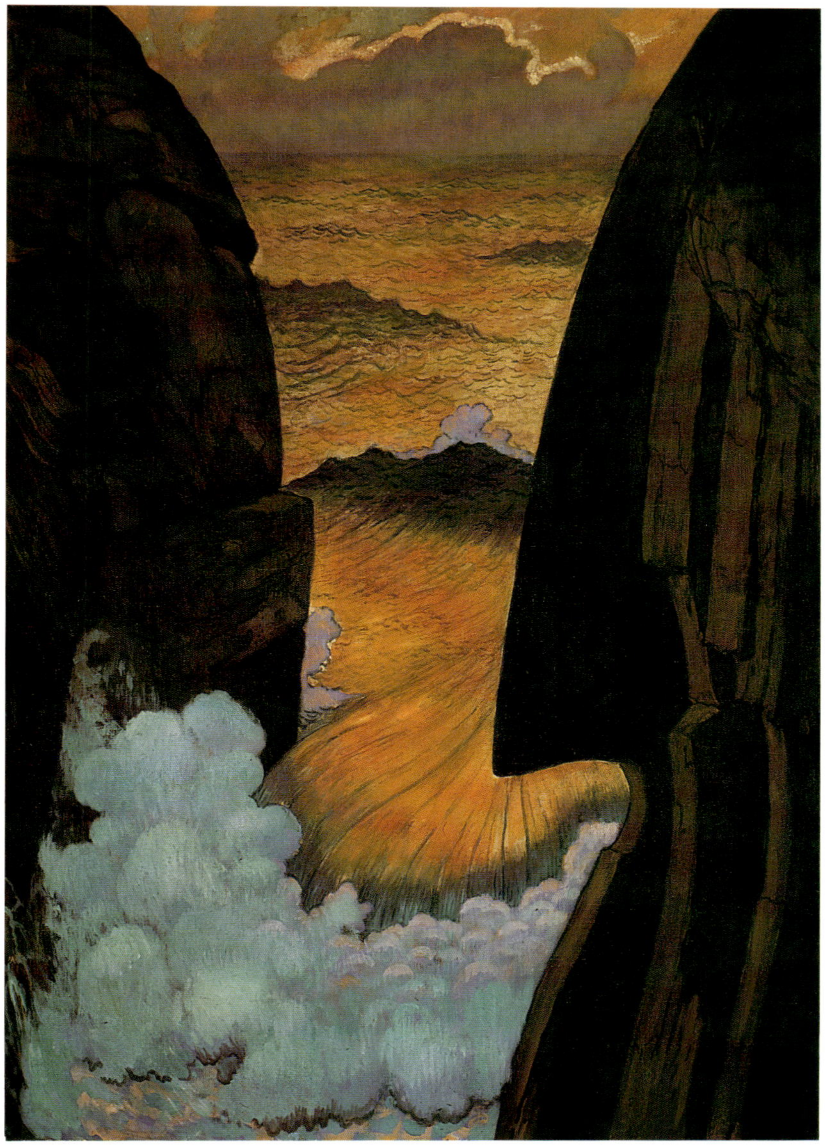

155
G. Lacombe
Vorhor, the Green Wave c.1896–7
Indianapolis Museum of Art, Gift of the Alliance of the Indianapolis Museum of Art

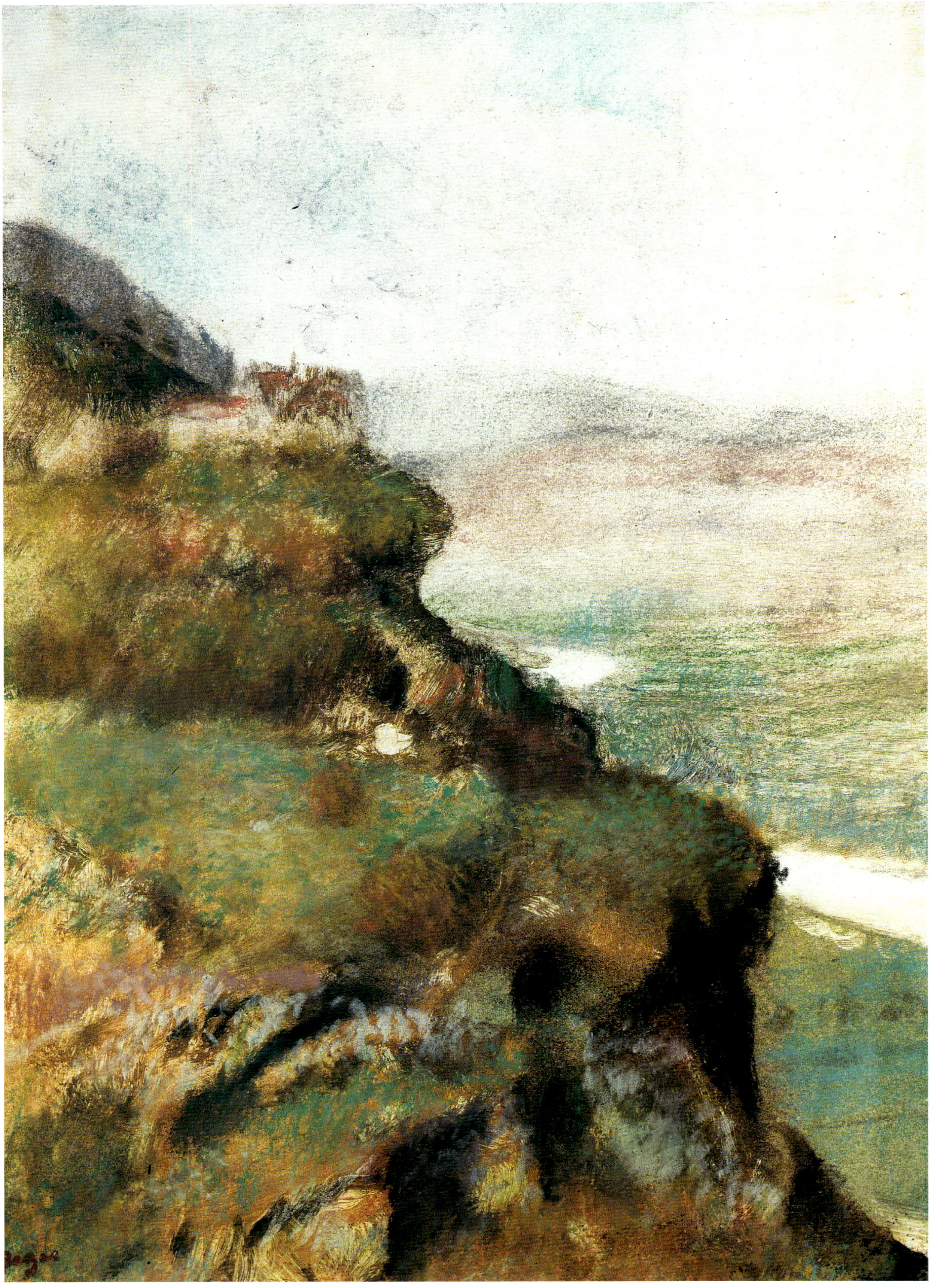

parallel. One wonders whether Degas, who about 1890 began to make extraordinarily adventurous landscape images in monotype and pastel, had visited this site, for his *Landscape with Rocky Cliffs* [**156**] has a similar configuration with features that might imaginatively be read as noses or eye sockets.[12] Degas's landscape, for all its general fidelity to local colour, hardly reads naturalistically, with its buildings perched precariously on the edge of an escarpment, even though it is not as overtly anthropomorphic as Lacombe's *Vorhor*. Many of the mixed media landscapes exhibited by Degas in 1892 had been stimulated by a trip he had made in a tilbury from Paris to Burgundy in September 1890. At his destination Diénay he had made a number of landscape monotypes based not on sketches or direct observation of the countryside through which he had passed but on memory, which he allowed to transform or invent motifs as caprice and imagination dictated.[13] Radical in medium and unconventional in their genesis, these works treat landscape as a vehicle for extraordinary quirks of fantasy, as in the pastel now in Houston [**158**]. Before the eye pans over the distant landscape, an extensive plain patterned by roads or rivers, it has to negotiate the insistent foreground forms. The spectator's high vantage point is shared with massive shapes, one a pinnacle, the other a rock or hummock, which together take on an assertively masculine identity. How Degas's imagination arrived at such forms we cannot easily explain; they perhaps combine transformation of the phallic rock formations or menhirs he may have passed on his Burgundy trip, an openly ridiculous joke about natural phenomena, and unconscious psychosexual fantasy. Whatever the case, Degas established in this lush green landscape, sensuous in tone and extensive in space, an incongruously totemic presence in which human form is metamorphosed by the artist's *rêve* into a dominant natural feature.

Degas's phallic landscape is highly unusual in its masculine allusion, for nature was commonly associated with female metaphors. In Zola's harrowing

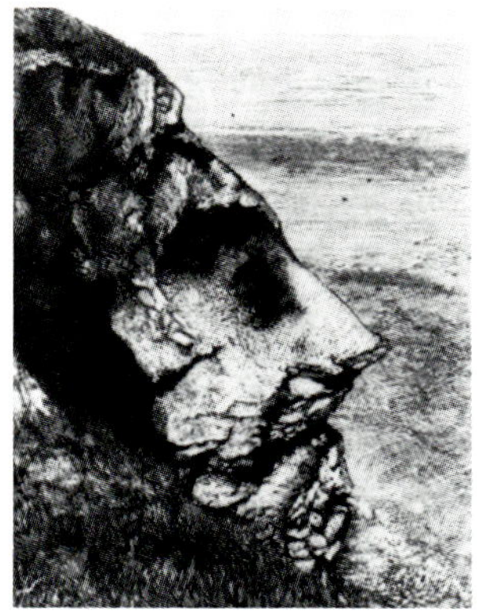

157
Unknown Artist
Cliff-face from *La Nature* 1899

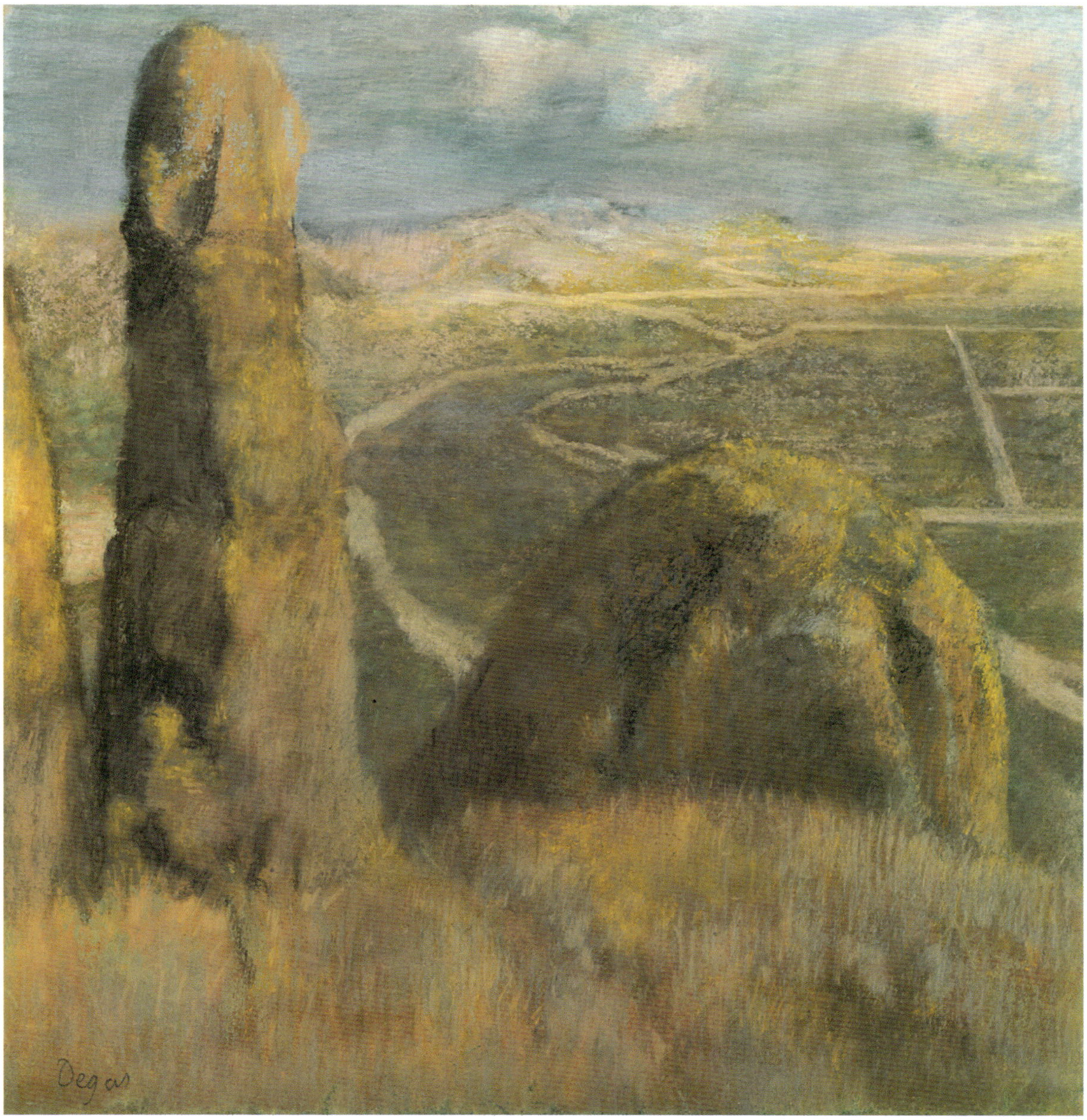

opposite
156
E. Degas
Landscape with Rocky Cliffs 1890
Josefowitz Collection

left
158
E. Degas
Landscape *c.*1892
Houston, Museum of Fine Arts
Purchased with funds provided by the Brown Foundation Accessions Endowment Fund

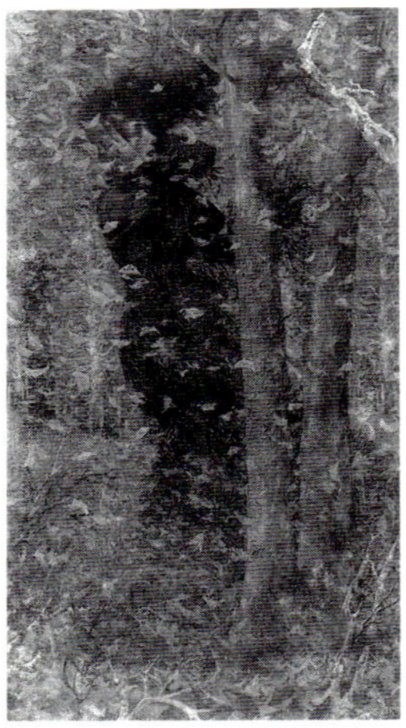

159
L. Lévy-Dhurmer
La Bourrasque (The Gust) c.1896
London, Whitford and Hughes

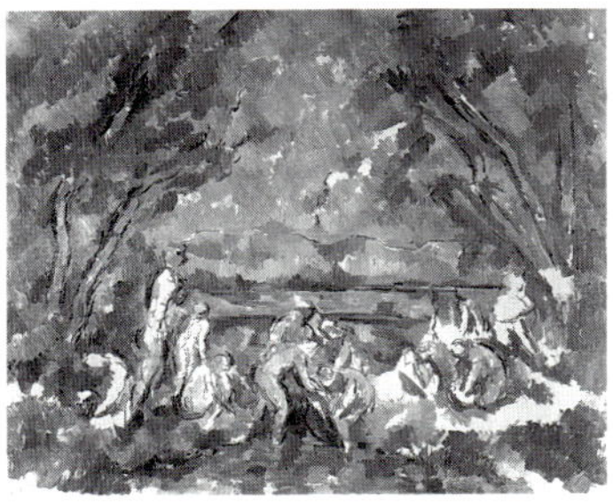

160
P. Cézanne
Study for the Large Bathers c.1902–6
Switzerland, Private Collection

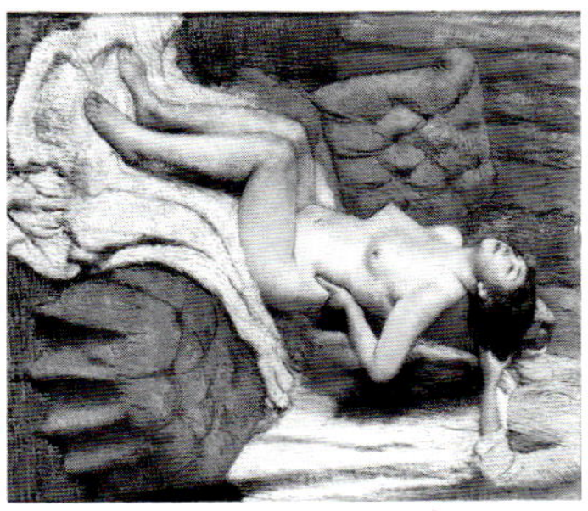

161
E. Degas
Nude Woman Having her Hair Combed [inverted] c.1886–8
New York, Metropolitan Museum, The H. O. Havemeyer Collection

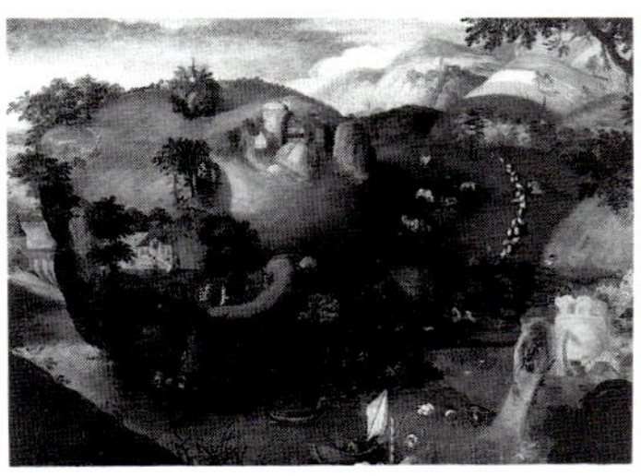

162
Anon (Southern Flemish School)
Anthropomorphic Landscape: Portrait of a Woman late 16th century
Brussels, Musées royaux des beaux-arts de Belgique

novel of agricultural life, *La Terre* of 1887, the farmer Hourdequin thinks of the land he owns as female, to be possessed and inseminated, and André Theuriet's volume of poems *La Vie rustique*, published the following year, celebrated *'la terre maternelle'*, the womb-like soil.[14] That a quasi-socialist novel and reactionary, nationalistic poetry chose the same imagery indicates the currency of the topos, which implicitly set up the polarity of female/nature, male/culture and was just as entrenched twenty years later when Michel Epuy's pantheist excursus *Le Sentiment de la nature* proclaimed that: 'Nature is woman; woman is perfect nature … She is its genuine microcosm; in her soul, as in her body, all nature's metamorphoses are splendidly reflected'.[15] These deep-seated beliefs of a male-dominated culture, difficult as they are to accept today, shaped the imaginations of the predominantly male painters who interested themselves, consciously or not, in the metamorphosis of landscape imagery. Lévy-Dhurmer's embodiment of the autumn wind blowing fallen leaves through the forest in his *Bourrasque* of c.1896 [**159**] evidently elides woman with natural elements, but might one not equally argue that Cézanne's late bather paintings, especially the large multi-figure sketch [**160**] in which landscape and bodies are both graphically and chromatically so interwoven, also articulate – however unprogrammatically – that archetypal metaphor?

Degas deliberately fused the female body and landscape in a number of pastels made during the 1890s. In *Landscape: Steep Coast* [**163**] the coastline hills soon reveal torso, breasts and thighs, with the cliffs formed by tumbling hair, for this 'landscape' was made by tipping on its side a drawing of a seated woman having her hair combed – recognisable from other images [**161**] – and then disguising it under natural textures and tones.[16] Such a transformation is thus both a caprice whose ancestry goes back to Mannerist metamorphoses [**162**] and a conceit on Degas's own work. If Degas lightly disguised a woman's body under a 'natural' veil, van Dongen, in his *Guus and Dolly* [**149, 164**], focuses squarely on the bare-breasted mother and child; indeed, at first sight the painting reads like a portrait. It was made during the summer of 1905 at Fleury-en-Bière, near Fontainebleau, where van Dongen painted conventional *plein air* studies.[17] The painting celebrates the birth of Dolly that April, and it is more than a portrait, for along the lower edge is a simply but quite naturalistically painted landscape, not found at first glance, and painted in contrast to the broad, slab-like touches ranging from sensuous pinks and fleshy yellows to the deeper blues and greens of the figures and clouds. That strip of landscape acts as a visual ambush, jolting the spectator into the realisation that

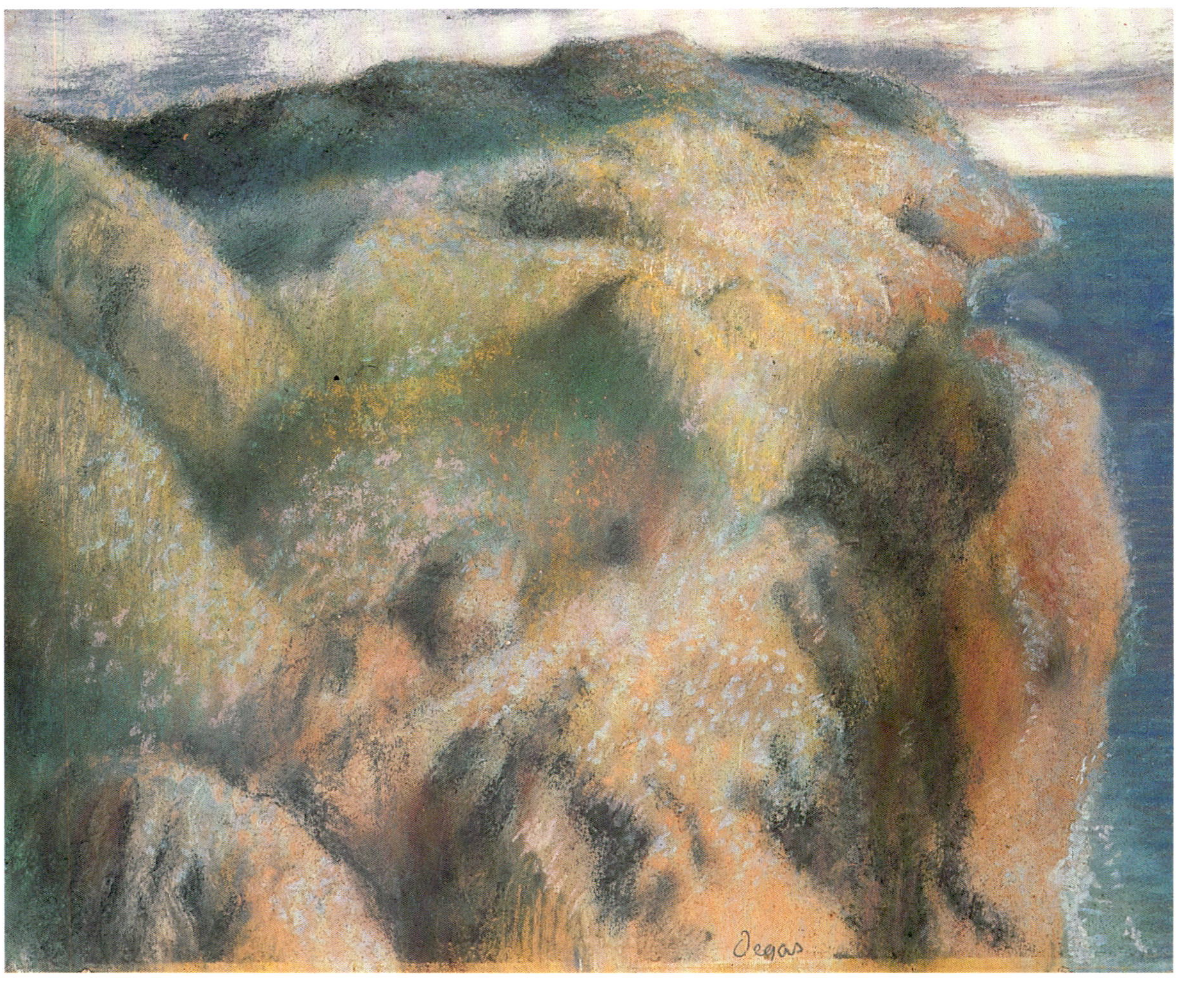

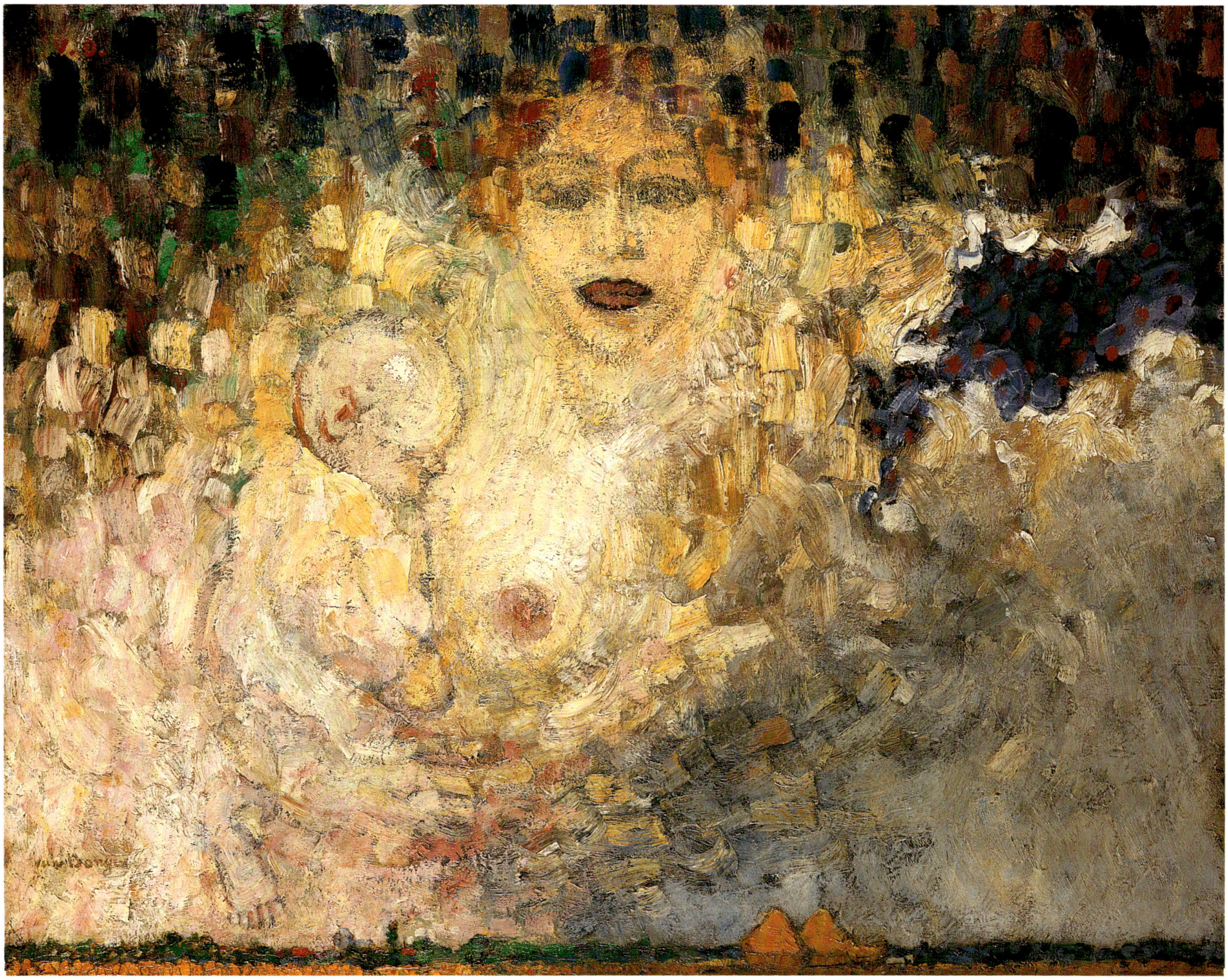

above
164
K. van Dongen
Guus and Dolly 1905
Private Collection

opposite
163
E. Degas
Landscape: Steep Coast c.1890–2
Geneva, Galerie Jan Krugier

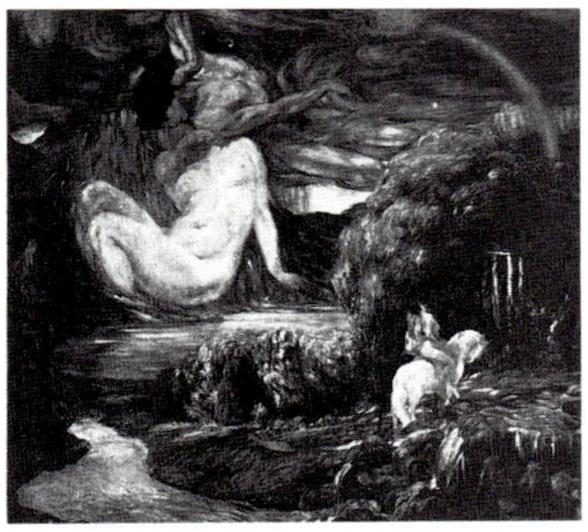

165
C. -H. Dufau
Radioactivity and Magnetism 1908
Paris, Sorbonne

166
O. Friesz
Landscape, La Ciotat 1907
Amsterdam, Fridart Stichting

this is less a portrait than some kind of visionary image; moreover, it is an inventoried summer landscape, with farm buildings and cornfields, haystacks and a horse and cart, the result of deliberation. Landscape and figures act together, the former representing the fertility of the land naturalistically and the latter transforming van Dongen's wife and child into a fantastic cloud-borne apparition, an iconic deification of female fecundity, a visionary fusion of woman and nature. In one of her murals for the Sorbonne, exhibited at the 1908 Salon d'Automne, Clémentine-Hélène Dufau took the sexualisation of the metamorphic landscape further. Commissioned to paint an allegory of *Radioactivity and Magnetism* [**165**] she had no iconographical conventions on which to fall back. To represent these exciting phenomena new to modern science Dufau's solution was to use modern anthropomorphic imagery. Her generalised landscape setting stands in for elemental nature, while the female body is equated with solid matter and the male with invisible forces, their erotic attraction an image of physical power and fusion. This use of the human body to represent scientific phenomena was seen by contemporaries in the larger context of the unifying forces and patterns in nature. Writing of Dufau's mural, the critic of *Art et décoration* used the term *eurythmie*, as did Rudolf Steiner's Theosophy and choreographers such as Emile Jacques Dalcroze who typified the *fin-de-siécle's* fascination with the search for harmony between spirit and matter.[18]

Whereas the human form in Degas's, van Dongen's and Dufau's metamorphic elisions of figure and landscape is decipherable, in other images the relation between the two is more visually ambiguous and metaphorically obscure. A canvas Friesz painted at La Ciotat during the summer of 1907 is a case in point. *Paysage (La Ciotat)* [**166**] is a highly synthetic reduction of the landscape motif into a linear structure, the graphic energy of which is matched by the chromatic force of the complementary reds and greens, blues and oranges, which so animate the canvas, much of which is left blank. One might consider the landscape merely as a pretext for Friesz's

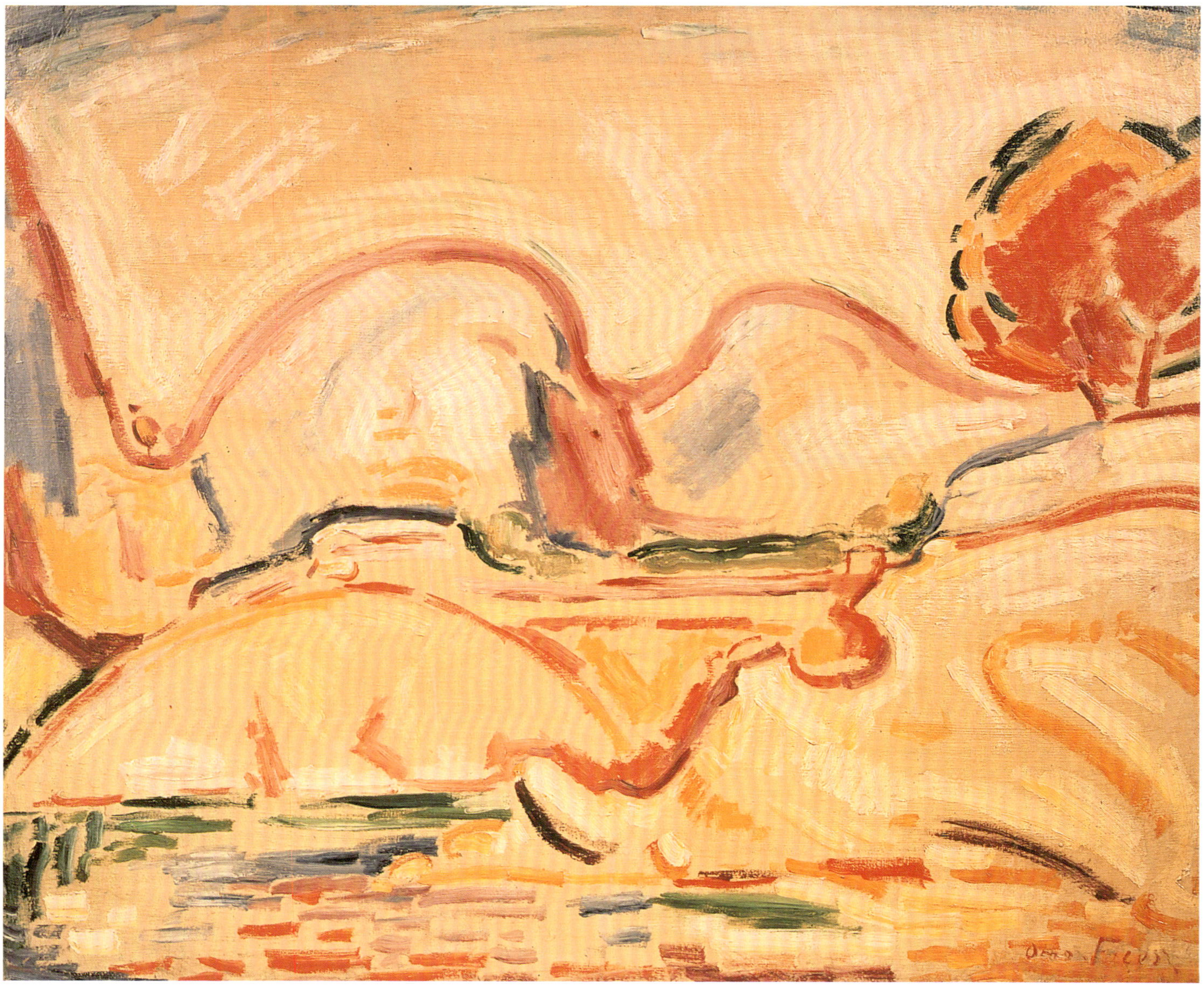

dynamic reduction of his painterly means, but that would not account for a motif which seems to include some curiously human rhythms, the far ridge reading perhaps as a female figure lying on her side. Such a suggestion may be more in the spectator's mind than in the artist's, for we do not know what Friesz's intentions were. Nevertheless, the perception of some kind of clandestine corporeal or organic presence in landscapes of this period remains an insistent one. Eugène Carrière, whose reputation was made with portraits, maternities and scenes of social import rendered in an emotive monochrome *enveloppe*, also painted landscapes. He specifically drew analogies between figure and landscape, telling the *Revue de Paris* in 1899 about his thoughts on a train journey: 'I looked out of the windows at the landscape speeding by, and I admired the undulation of the hills, to which the curves of the foliage were married; I turned around, and in front of me I saw a woman with a proud and pure mouth and in the mouth was clearly repeated all that I had just seen and admired. There is a hierarchy of forms which explain one another; in nature, nothing is isolated from its natural sphere because everything is related, the hill and the plain, the tree, the earth and man. Likewise, a beautiful woman appears in a beautiful landscape, you see only her, but in her you see again all the rest'.[19] The somewhat bizarre promptings of Carrière's imagination affected his landscapes, the metamorphic qualities of which were recognised by contemporaries, Toulouse-Lautrec for one comparing them to 'human masks'.[20] A typical image such as the so-called *Landscape with Twisting Road* [**167**] may not suggest a whole figure, but its thin fluid paint and undulating, folding forms nevertheless have an organic quality which brings to mind Carrière's articulation of current ideas about the unity of humanity and nature. This was not merely a question of physical analogy. He argued in a lecture given in Paris at the Musée d'histoire naturelle in 1901 that 'Man's imagination is exalted by contact with Nature. Visionary of the real, he undertakes his own discovery. Our imaginative power lies in our incessant effort to realize our relationship with Nature, the place we hold there, the significance of our arrival among the crowd of beings'.[21] Carrière's notion of the artist-visionary was couched in a Symbolist rhetoric which would not necessarily have appealed to Monet, Degas or Friesz, but it is characteristic of the *fin-de-siècle's* fascination with the suggestiveness of the imagination and the unifying rhythms of body, mind and nature. With the exception of Monet, none of the artists discussed in this chapter were exclusively devoted to landscape, which perhaps allowed them to take imaginative, metamorphic liberties with nature. All of them exemplify in their different ways the possibilities of the *paysage de rêve*, the elusive but insistent use of landscape as an expression – in Amiel's phrase – of a state of mind.

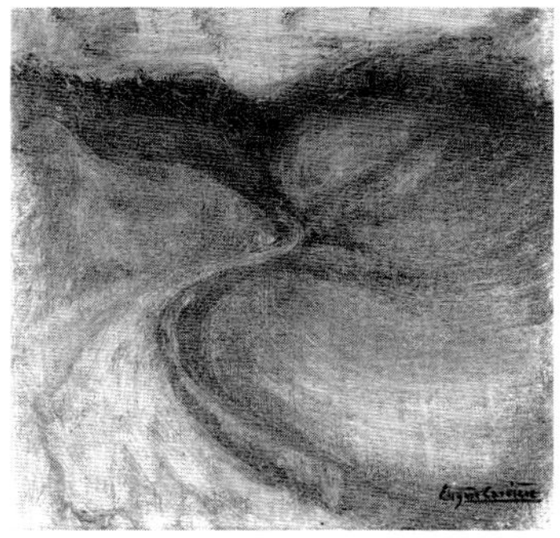

167
E. Carrière
Landscape with Twisting Road
*c.*1900–5
Paris, Musée d'Orsay

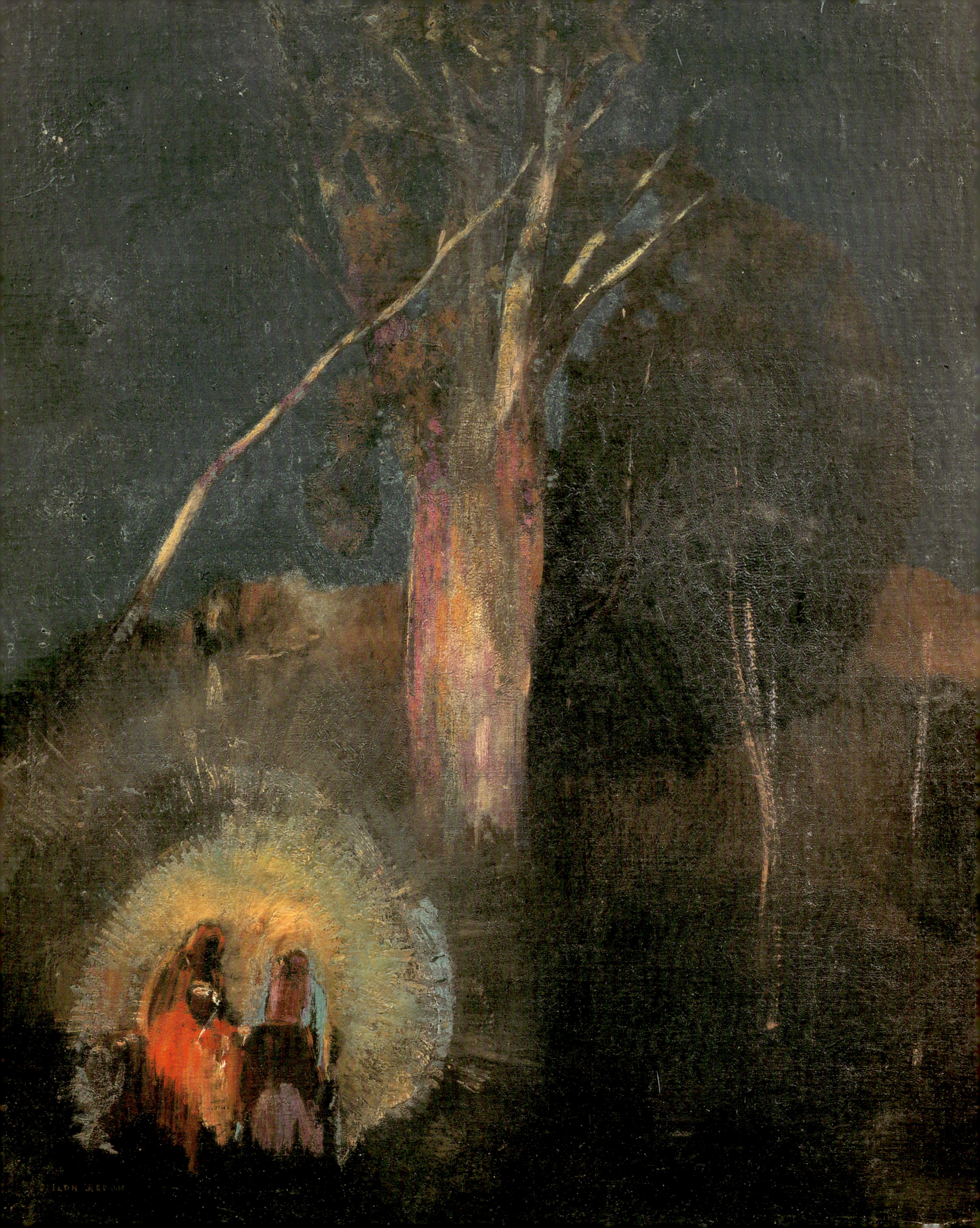
REDON

9 The Nocturne

Painting images of landscape by night has been a challenge and source of perplexity for artists over centuries. It is an exercise fraught with difficulties, not least because of the problems of working directly from nature, but also because of the impossibility of mixing the correct tones in the darkness or by lamp-light. So man's age-old fascination with night, the lost hours of darkness so paradoxically pregnant with both rest and threat, peace and fear, metaphor for the other side of human experience, requires of the painter the use of memory. And memory is such an unreliable faculty, susceptible to the imagination and the subconscious. Artists have long had reason to attempt to paint the nocturnal landscape, either because their subject requires it – the visitation of the shepherds in a Nativity, for instance – or simply due to the enticement of moonlight. At certain times painters have specialised in night subjects – one thinks of seventeenth-century Dutch painters such as Aert van der Neer – but by its very nature the representation of nocturnal illumination in paint on canvas has been uneven in its results. As Burne-Jones testified at the trial in 1878 when Whistler sued Ruskin for offensive remarks about his *Nocturne in Black and Gold – The Falling Rocket*: 'It is one of a thousand failures that artists have made in their efforts to paint night'.[1]

Yet by the end of the nineteenth century the painting of nocturnal scenes, especially landscapes, had become so commonplace that in 1899 Paul Desjardins, reviewing the Salons for the *Gazette des beaux-arts*, felt obliged to title a sub-section of his article '*Les Heures, principalement du soir et de la nuit*', explaining that he could hardly count the number of night and evening pictures on view.[2] A simple account of the apparent proliferation of such images would centre on the Symbolist aesthetic. Generated initially in literary, and especially poetic, circles in the mid-1880s, and finding its first voice in the manifesto published by Jean Moréas in the *Figaro littéraire* on 18 September 1886, Symbolism sought to deny the value of the description of external reality, the ostensible aim of the naturalist aesthetic then dominant in European writing and visual arts, in order to emphasise the Idea, the core of association and emotion that lay beyond physical appearances and which could only be suggested or evoked. This emphasis on nuance and allusion, on the conjuring up of emotion rather than on the detailing of facts, had an increasing influence around the turn of the century, appealing as it did to the Symbolist artist who was, by implication, established as a particularly sensitive and élite conduit for the articulation of the subtlest and most profound human feelings. Such ideas had been disparately voiced before they were publicly codified by Moréas and the subsequent writers who jostled in their rivalry to define the new aesthetic in their own terms. Verlaine's poem *Art poétique*, published for the first time in *Paris moderne* on 10 November 1882, had already insisted:

Car nous voulons la Nuance encore
Pas la Couleur, rien que la nuance!
(For we still want Nuance,
Not Colour, nothing but nuance!)

Such an emphasis on the suggestive inevitably brought into play the imagery of night; it is hardly surprising that Verlaine's collection of verse *Fêtes galantes* contained poems with titles such as *Clair de lune*.[3] Indeed, Symbolism's obsession with the nuanced, emotive and nocturnal had become by the 1890s something of a cliché. Desjardins appreciated the night paintings on show in 1899, but they were only to be expected; from the most established to the tyro, he explained, painters today 'are crepuscular, less from *parti-pris* than by natural affinity. This corresponds to the state of mind of people aged thirty'.[4]

An explanation based on *Zeitgeist* can only be a partial one, and we do well to search for others. Amiel's widely read *Journal intime*, turning as it so often does to nature as a metaphor for feeling, referred regularly to the night. An entry made in July 1877 helps us here. 'A superb night – a starry sky – Jupiter and Phoebe holding converse before my windows. Grandiose effects of light and shade over the courtyard. A sonata arose from the black gulf like a repentent prayer wafted from purgatory. The picturesque was lost in poetry, and admiration in feeling'.[5] Amiel's reflections are more than unpondered musings, and indicate something of the

opposite
168
O. Redon
The Flight into Egypt *c.*1900–3
Paris, Musée d'Orsay, Gift of Mme Arï Redon

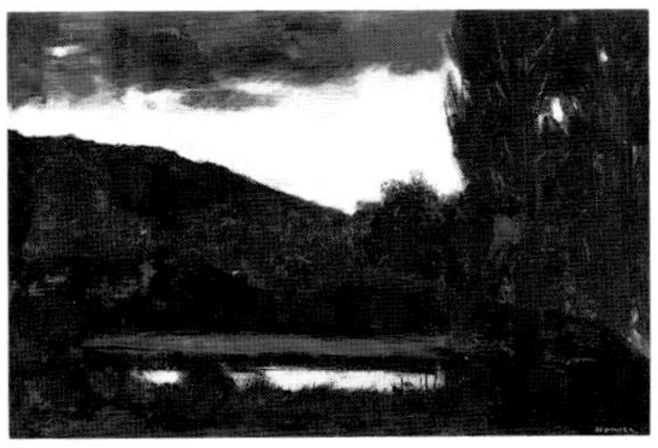

169
J.-J. Henner
Vallée de Munster, Effect Noted after a Storm 1879?,
Paris, Musée Henner

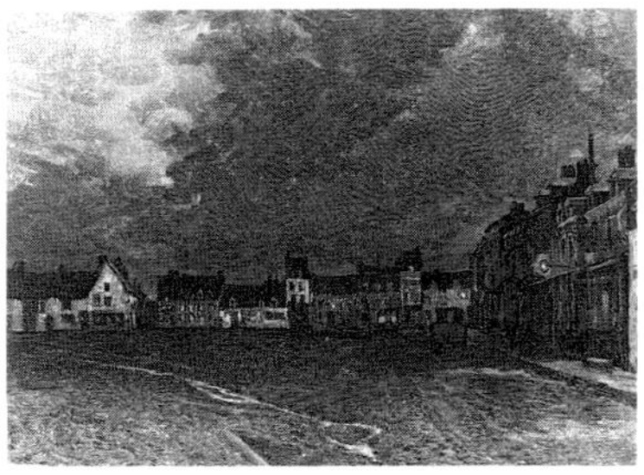

170
J.-C. Cazin
La Ville morte 1883
Location unknown

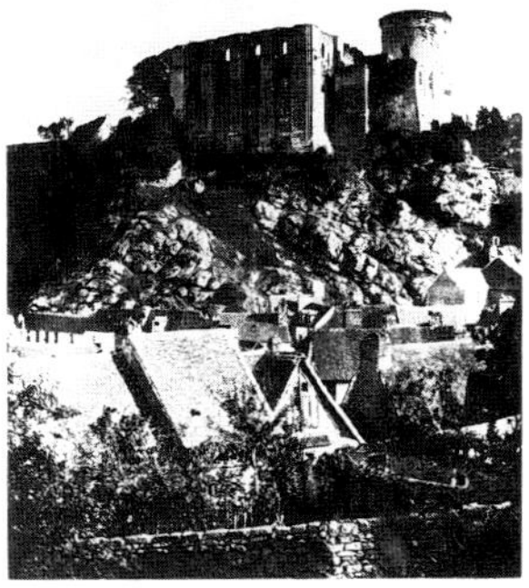

171
L. A. de Brébisson
Ruins of the Château de Falaise 1851
Private Collection

opposite
172
H. Rousseau
The Keep 1889
Santa Barbara Museum of Art
Bequest of Wright S. Ludington

range of associations which the night brings into play, for this short entry touches on mythology, music and religion, borrows notions from the aesthetics of landscape in its inference of the sublime and reference to the picturesque, and associates nocturnal nature with emotion. The associations which Amiel so neatly encapsulated find affiliations elsewhere in contemporary writing. The chic social commentator Octave Uzanne wrote in 1889 that: 'Staying up in the country at night disturbs us and gives us a feeling of mystery, and almost of superstition; this gigantic and inscrutable night surrounding us is filled with strange mysteries, and keeps us awake, as if on the edge of an abyss; we fall asleep weighed down by an obscurity which seems to animate and develop our inward light, and to make it more restless, intense'.[6] If for Uzanne the night was troubling because it stood for something intangible, even intimidating, for Maupassant, boating down the Seine by moonlight a few years earlier, the mood was quite different: 'The air is soft, the pervading charm of the waters envelops and possesses one; one breathes slowly with infinite joy, in utter well-being, in divine repose, in sovereign quietude'.[7] For all these writers – moral philosopher, bibliophile dilettante, naturalist novelist, none subscribing to the Symbolist aesthetic – night produced different responses, but for all of them its otherness was deeply moving, both dwarfing the sense of self and yet simultaneously enhancing it.

While we can only guess whether painters, expressing themselves on canvas rather than with the pen, shared any of the diverse associations articulated by such writers, it is evident that images of the night had a distinct currency and equally varied set of associations prior to and independent from the full flowering of the nocturne as a topos in the Symbolist imagination. Henner, member of the Institut and loyal upholder of the traditions of history painting, made a number of extraordinary canvases of a mountain pond in his native Jura by night, landscapes of such reductiveness that they must have been made from memory. One of these [**169**] was exhibited at the smart establishment Cercle Volney in 1888,[8] where five years before Cazin had shown his *Ville morte* [**170**], an image of the deserted market square of Montreuil at nightfall which had attracted critical acclaim both in the press and in the private journal of Odilon Redon. For Redon the *Ville morte* was 'an incalculable world of reverie and reminiscence', particularly impressive because unlike most contemporary paintings the emotion it evoked lingered with the spectator.[9] Henner's and Cazin's paintings are quite different – the one a broadly brushed oil sketch, the other a carefully crafted townscape – but paintings such as these, made by artists of established reputation, helped set up paradigms of the nocturne for a younger generation, in these instances as a timeless, natural landscape and a human habitat deserted by its population. The imaginative and visual ancestry of Le Sidaner's *The Square at Petit Fort-Philippe* [**92**], for one, can be traced back to Cazin's *Ville morte*.

If the nocturne already had a place by the early 1880s in the careers of Henner and Cazin, artists whose praises were often sung in terms of melancholy and reverie, it was also a significant element in the work of another painter, quite distinct from Symbolist circles and very far from established: Henri Rousseau. His first exhibited work, *Soir du carnaval* [**183**], shown at the Salon des Indépendants in 1886 while he was still working for the *octroi*, the toll-collecting service of Paris, was a nocturne, as was another substantial canvas of this decade, *The Keep* of 1889 [**172**]. Previously unidentified, this impressive canvas seems to represent the château at Falaise, famous as the home of Robert le Diable and birthplace of William the Conqueror. Images of this castle, one of the most impressive fortifications in Normandy, proliferated from the early days of the *voyage pittoresque* tradition into the twentieth century; Corot had painted it in the 1840s, for instance, and Othon Friesz in 1904.[10] Both these painters viewed the château from the heights of Mont Myrrha to the west, looking across the valley of the Ante; Rousseau, on the other hand, painted the view from the valley looking up to the great round tower built by Sir John Talbot in the early fifteenth century. Such a viewpoint silhouettes its powerful structure against the sky, dominating the cottages beneath, and it is one that can be found in early photographs of Falaise made in the *pittoresque* mode. The similarity of Rousseau's viewpoint to, for instance, de Brébisson's photograph of 1851 [**171**] should come as no surprise, for Rousseau was given to working from secondary sources such as prints or reproductions of other paintings. It is highly likely that *The Keep* was painted from an illustration to a guidebook or a photograph similar to de Brébisson's. This lack of direct observation of the motif is borne out by the ambiguities in the painting: a strange diagonal of what would seem to be moonlight runs through the valley along what might be either a path or the top of a wall. Rousseau matched this uncertainty with incidents of precision: the spiky leaves of the foreground plant, the sinister barred window in the cottage above, the exact rendition of the constellation in the night sky. These incongruities are picked out in the light of a moon set in a deep blue sky and shining out over eerie brown, grey and yellow clouds, creating a haunting, even slightly alarming image which recalls one of Amiel's nocturnal sensations: 'The picturesque was lost in poetry'. For in *The Keep* Rousseau used the possibilities of the nocturne to transform a rather trite *pittoresque* motif into an image which stirs the viewer's feelings and imagination.

Recognising that the nocturne was almost on the point of being overplayed, one critic in 1897 took it upon himself to list the painters – Thaulow, Moreau-

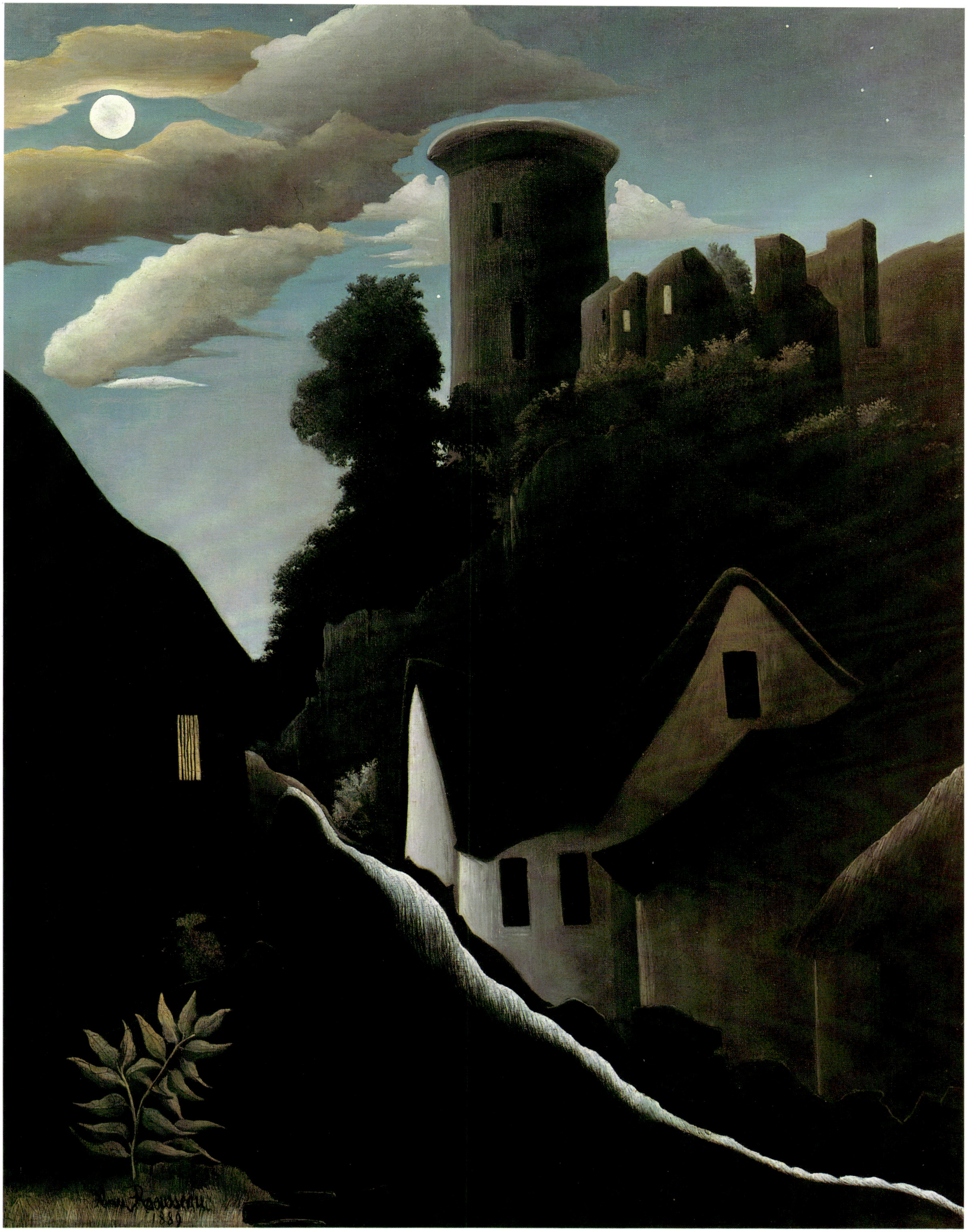

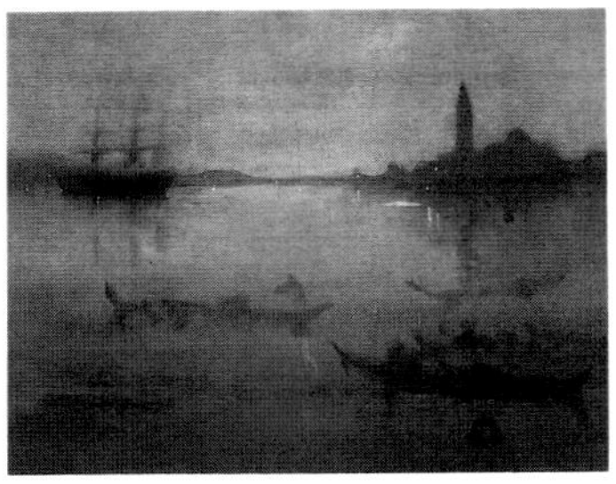

173
J. A. M. Whistler
Nocturne in Blue and Silver: the Lagoon, Venice c.1880
Boston, Museum of Fine Arts, Emily L. Ainsley Fund

Nélaton, Billotte, Dulac and others – who had adopted Cazin's propensity for 'the silence of the evening'.[11] Even old hands such as Harpignies essayed nocturnal landscapes,[12] and it was stock rhetoric in the often over-blown celebrations of that generation of painters 'aged thirty', *vide* Léon Thévenin on Lévy-Dhurmer: 'And if the Night is his constant inspiration, it is the nocturnal side of the soul that he exposes once more to our imagination: restless world of anxious thoughts, garden of nuanced life where infinite dreams blossom, occult universe in which all light is eclipsed, where every vision becomes an enticement!'[13] Why had the nocturne so flourished? In 1899 Desjardins put it down to a contemporary sensitivity which expressed itself in a fascination with the ceaseless fugacity of light and time, citing Monet's *Grainstacks* and *Cathedrals* [**239**, **153**] as salient examples and isolating dusk and dawn, those transient brackets of the night, as contemporary painters' favoured hours.[14] The nocturne, as we have seen, was a highly convenient vehicle for the Symbolist imagination. Moreover, previous generations of artists, attuned to a naturalist aesthetic with its demands for accuracy and observation, had shied from night motifs; the nocturne is extremely rare in the work of Monet and Pissarro and entirely absent from that of Sisley, their conditioning as *plein air* painters all but dismissing night from their repertoire. For a younger generation the nocturnal landscape allowed room for manoeuvre, and for a whole range of light effects and moods relatively unhampered by tradition or recent practice.

One might also seek to explain the nocturne's popularity by turning to evidence from another field: music. Visiting Bayreuth in 1896 Fauré wrote to his wife that he had stayed up all night in the smoking room of his hotel 'watching night disperse and day dawn, ... [over] a veritable forest of fir trees, ... something I really love!'.[15] For a composer the experience of watching the transformation of the landscape under changing light must have unfolded like the development of an extended piece of music. For an artist, whose work does not progress over the passage of time but remains fixed and iconic, the nocturne essentially produces an image different from a representation of the day. A nocturne may also exploit the rhetoric of the night – mystery, awesomeness, alarm – to enhance that essential difference. Painting the night, then, may have been concerned with more than the nuances that contemporaries so vaunted; it was staking out a new territory for painting, probing the other, the imaginative, even the unconscious. Writing to his friend the violinist Eugène Ysaye in September 1894 Debussy compared the composing of his '*trois nocturnes*' to a painter working in a single colour.[16] 'Nocturne' had earlier been applied to some of Chopin's piano music, of course, but the fact that Debussy took it up suggests that he wanted to work on the nuanced and suggestive in his own medium, aware that contemporary painters were actively doing so in theirs and anxious, as one 'aged thirty', to participate in his generation's obsessions.

Too close an association with the more effete and ephemeral aspects of Symbolist literature could be seen to jeopardise the 'new' possibility of the nocturnal landscapes even during the 1890s, when the vogue was at its height. In 1894 Raymond Bouyer, enemy neither of Whistler [**173**] nor of the nocturne, regretted what he saw as the pervasiveness of the inimitable American artist's influence which led to paintings as skimpy, arcane and fugitive as the free verse in the new literary reviews: 'Copying Whistler and Mallarmé is like humming in the evening to imitate wind in the leaves'.[17] A decade later the nocturne was a joke for the younger generation. Braque summed up contemporary landscape practice in two witty drawings on the back of a letter to a Belgian friend in 1905: one shows a cottage with the sun low on the horizon and is annotated *Ecole divisioniste* and *peinture claire*, the other represents a classical portico in a frame marked *hors concours* and is inscribed *Ecole nocturniste* and *peinture noire*.[18] The Fauve Braque was distancing himself from a current which he saw as *retardataire* but was still an active force in French painting; it was in 1905 too that Camille Mauclair lauded Le Sidaner [**92**] as 'the incomparable virtuoso of the nocturnal nuance', the Debussy of painting, and a genius.[19] But by this time the vogue, which had lasted twenty years, was passing.

Yet the avant-garde had initially been quick to seize on the possibility of the nocturne. In the late 1880s the Neo-Impressionists had started to develop its possibilities, urged on no doubt both by their personal friendships with Symbolist poets such as Jules Laforgue and Gustave Kahn and also by the new dimensions that the nocturne opened up for landscape painters of a young generation unconstrained by the etiquette of the *plein air* aesthetic. One of Seurat's major figure paintings, *Parade du cirque*, shown at the Indépendants in 1888, was a nocturne, and he had essayed the genre in one of the landscapes he had made at Honfleur two years earlier.[20] He returned to it at Gravelines in 1890. Of the four times of day Seurat painted there, *The Channel at Gravelines: Evening* [**174**] broadly represents the same westerly view across the canalised river as the morning canvas [**91**], slightly shifting the viewpoint but including the same large building and semaphore mast at the harbour entrance. It is an evocative painting, not of deep night but of the fading light of a summer evening, the sun still faintly illuminating the soft Channel sky. The colour is subtly varied, a ceaseless modulation of pinks and pale violets, oranges and blues, conjuring up the waning light playing on hard quays, marmoreal water and liquid sky. All this is held in a disciplined structure carefully prepared with preparatory studies,[21] for *Gravelines: Evening* is a studio painting contrived to evoke mood by its bal-

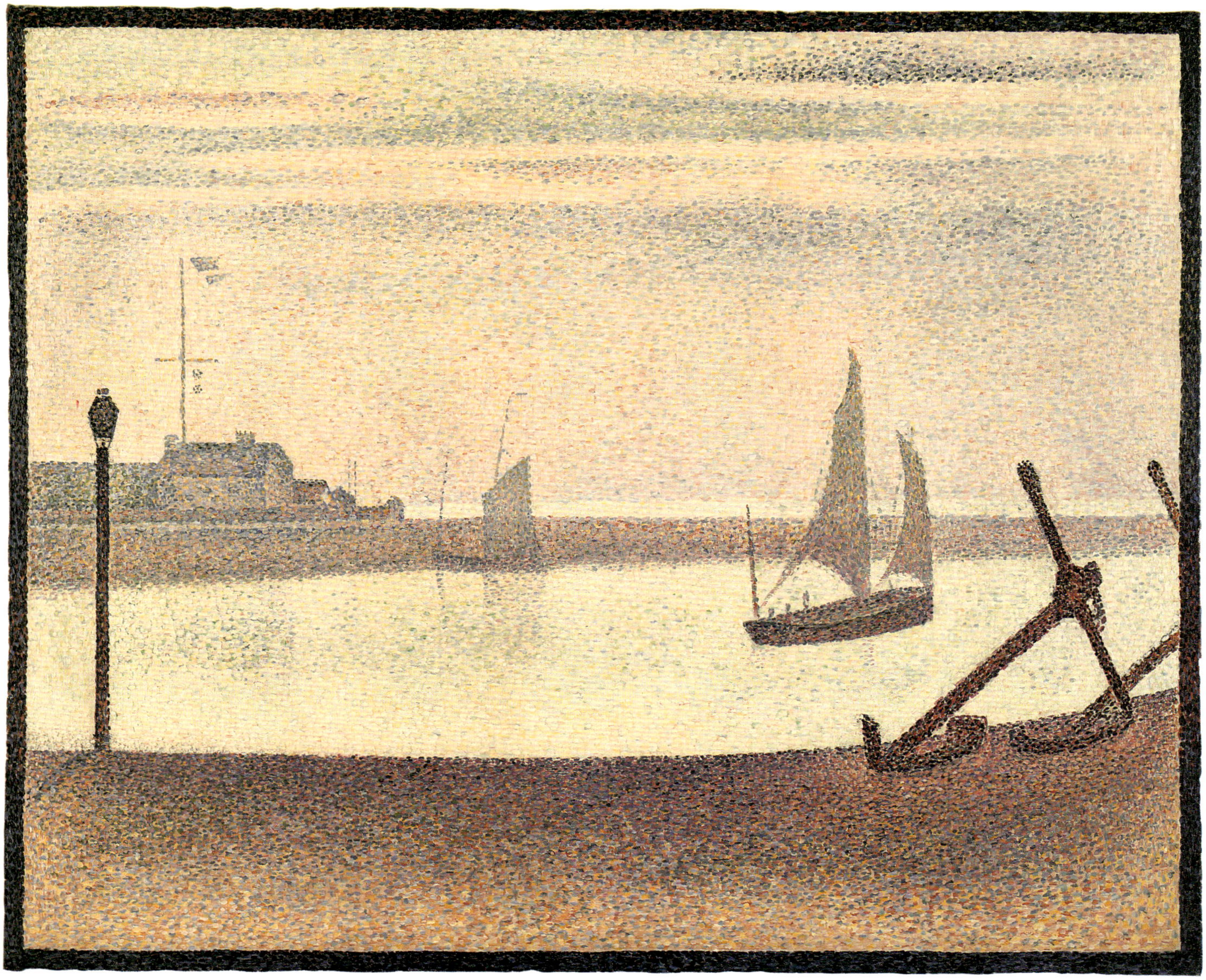

174
G. Seurat
The Channel at Gravelines: Evening
1890
New York, Museum of Modern Art, Gift of Mr and Mrs William A. M. Burden

ance of form and colour. During the summer of 1890 Seurat wrote to the journalist Maurice Beaubourg telegraphically outlining his current aesthetic, explaining: 'Calmness of tone is the equality of dark and light; [calmness] of tint, [the equality] of warm and cool, and the horizontal for line. Sadness of tone is the dark dominant; [sadness] of tint, the cool dominant, and [sadness] of line, downwards directions'.[22] Attuned to Symbolist ideas, Seurat attempted to preordain the spectator's emotional response by his ordering of the formal elements of his picture. His system was not rigid and allowed for nuance, thus *Gravelines: Evening* seems, by Seurat's own account, to be both calm – in its balanced values and horizontal armature of quay and cloud – and sad in its coolly subdued tonality and dipping angles of the sails and silhouetted anchors. But for all the calculation, this is an elusive and poetic image. Nature here is reduced to sky, water and light; even the water is channelled between quays in this landscape where all the 'land' is man-made, marked off with signal masts and gaslamps. Curiously, in this intensely human habitat no people are visible, and even the smack making its way out to sea seems crewless as it plies the channel on which it leaves no shadow. Nature and humanity are both contingent in this nocturne which reads as much as dream as observation.

Seurat's Neo-Impressionist colleagues explored similar effects. In the spring of 1889 Angrand had produced a canvas [**176**] of even more distilled beauty than Seurat's Gravelines nocturne, reducing a motif of the suburban Seine to what he called in a letter 'a grey symphony'.[23] At the turn of the decade, as this group lost interest in the hard-edged suburban motifs on which they had focused in the mid-1880s and shifted towards rural landscapes less harsh in character, the options of dusk, night and dawn appealed to them. During the autumns of both 1889 and 1890 Signac and Luce worked together at Herblay. Signac showed a group of four Herblay paintings under the title *Le Fleuve* at both Les XX in Brussels and the Paris Indépendants in 1891, where they were seen with Seurat's Gravelines canvases. Some twenty kilometres northwest of Paris, Herblay's

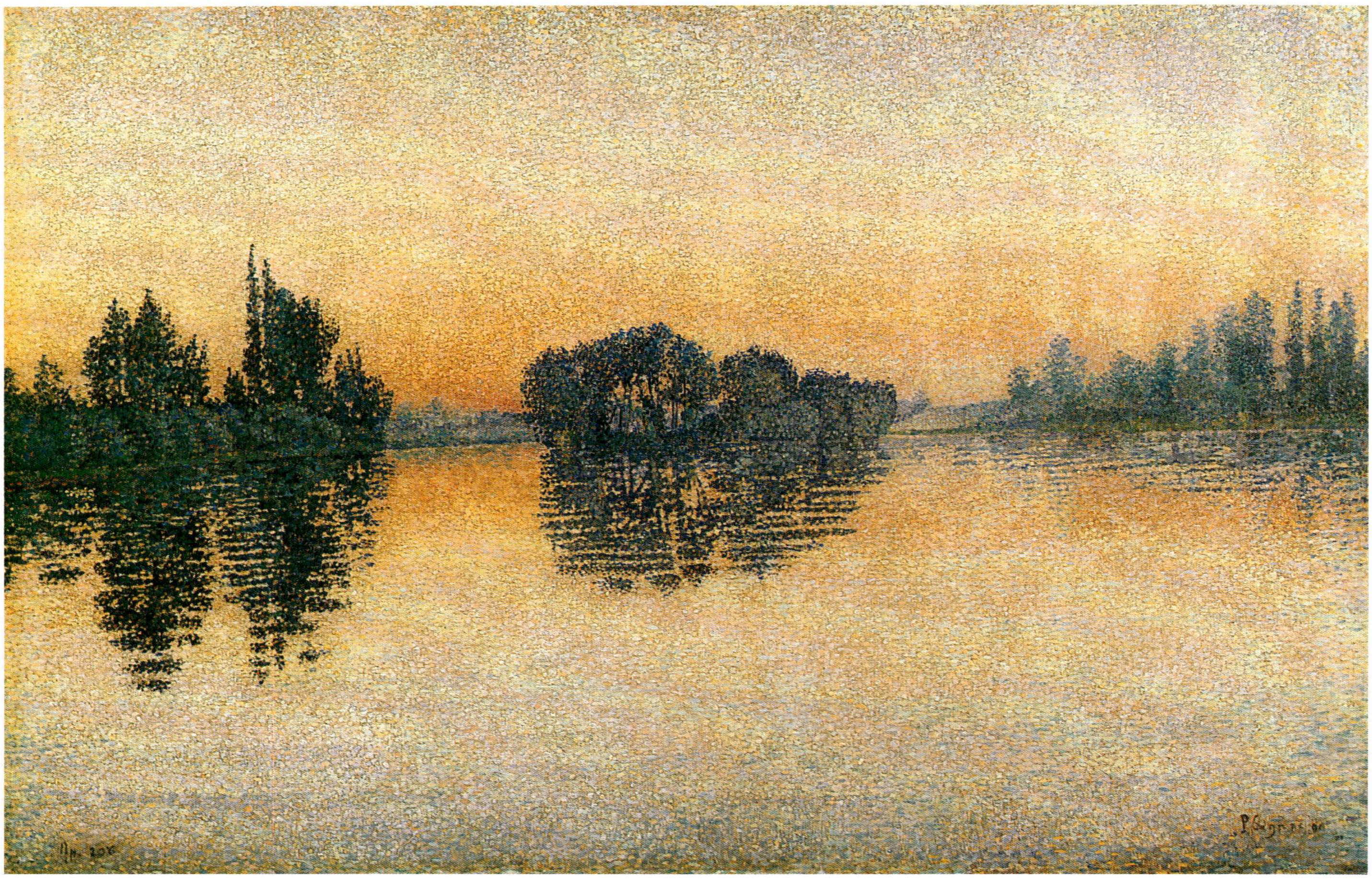

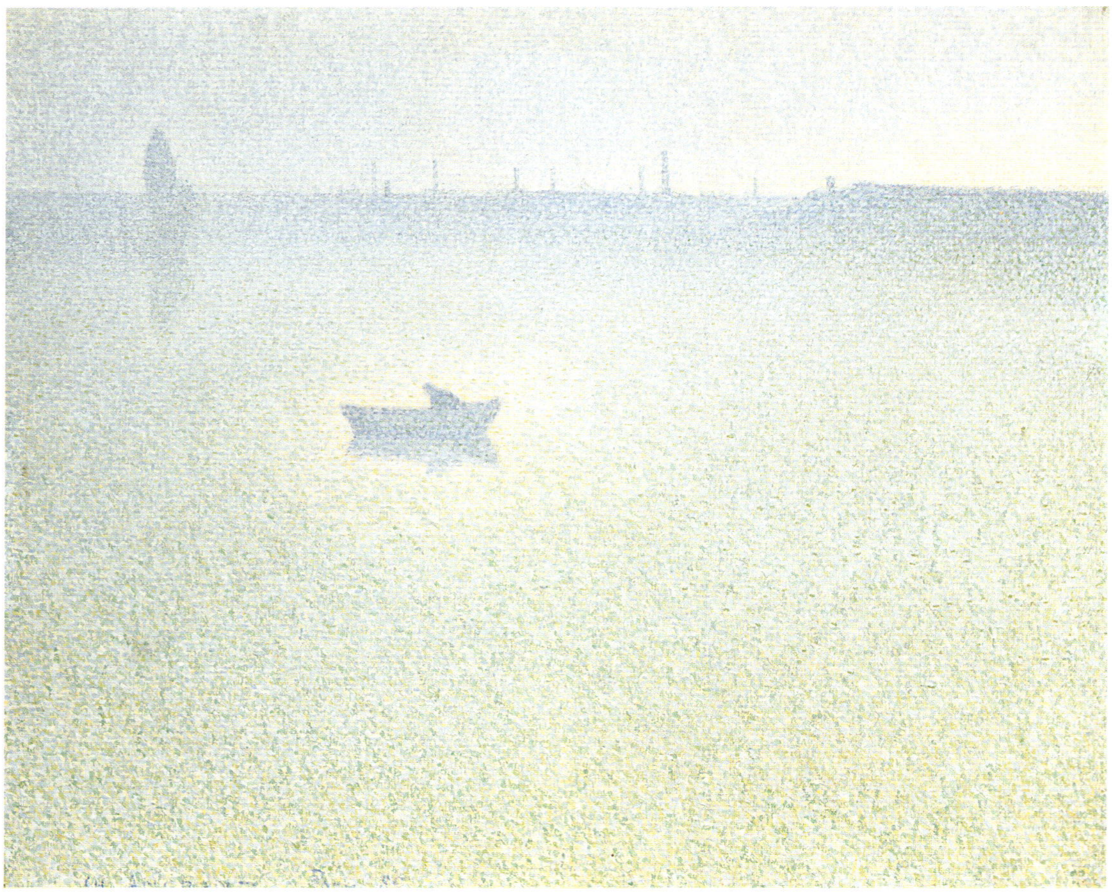

above
175
P. Signac
The Seine at Herblay: Sunset
1890
Glasgow, Glasgow Art Gallery and Museum, Kelvingrove

right
176
C. Angrand
The Seine at Dawn 1889
Geneva, Petit Palais

bucolic riverscape encouraged Signac to apply his divisionist technique to diverse effects and motifs, from Daubignyesque mist [**15**] to flamboyant sunset. Opus 206 [**175**] – at this time Signac numbered his canvases like musical compositions – is the latter, executed not in a doctrinaire pointillist manner but with a varied surface of dabs and patches, quite broad in the lighter zones. Signac probably studied the sunset from a boat in midstream but worked on the painting in his studio, as Seurat had done with *Gravelines: Evening*. The landscape is ordered almost symmetrically, with the central island balancing the two shores and the bisecting horizon more than doubling the motif with its elongation of the dark blue-green trees against the strident sunset tints. Signac's *Herblay: Sunset* is thus a scrupulously contrived image: a 'musical' canvas which counterpoints both the dominant complementaries blue and orange and the formal structure. It is also an exploitation of the timeless poetry of light and water – albeit at its most rhetorical – which does not absolutely exclude the modern, for is that not a riverboat's steam emerging from behind the island's right-hand trees?

Among the first canvases Cross produced after settling at Cabasson in 1891 was the *Pointe de la Galère* [**177**], a vantage point on the île du Levant just off the Mediterranean coast. Again it is strictly organised, with a dark foreground zone, the central reflective waterway and a more softly delineated horizon below a light-filled sky. Yet Cross's painting is even more stylised than those of Seurat and Signac, its spiky, sinuous pines reminiscent of Japanese woodblock prints and its decoratively dotted surface laid over an underlayer applied in flat horizontal bands. Cross played off violet-blue against orange-pink to create an effect which is perhaps more theatrical than atmospheric, and it may be that this early representation of the Mediterranean is indebted to the *japonisant* shadow-plays which Henri Rivière [**178**] was currently staging at the Chat noir cabaret in Paris. For the *Pointe de la Galère* makes no bones about its poetic and decorative artifices: the *broderie anglaise* texture, the hyperbole of sunset, the eerily empty boats. Both the Symbolist aesthetic and the practical difficulties of painting by night freed the artist from the obligation to observe nature closely, an opportunity Cross and his colleagues collectively exploited.

The night could also soften the image of the city. In the years around the turn of the century many painters made nocturnes in which recognisable Parisian sites were rendered mysterious or banal streets enlivened by the envelope of darkness decorated with studs and smudges of gaslight. Artists as different as Le Sidaner, Carrière and Bonnard [**179**] produced pictures in this vein, and the purchase of Ulmann's nocturne *Le Trocadéro* by the State in 1908 indicates how such motifs were well absorbed into established taste.[24] Yet any such image in whatever style stresses the 'otherness' of the nocturne. Cityscapes bring into play the notions of topography, the explanation of where streets and buildings are in relation to each other and what relative status they have; cityscapes, as we have seen with representations of Notre-Dame and the Eiffel Tower, deal in physical certainties and implicit values. But nocturnal representations of the city dissolve these in darkness, which distorts scale, denies detail, and blurs hierarchies in the democracy of the semi-visible. This is evident from Luce's *Louvre and Pont du Carousssel: Night Effect* [**180**], another example of the Neo-Impressionists' fascination with the nocturne in the early 1890s. Here the Pavillon de Flore and the south-west wing of the museum-palace, largest building in central Paris, have no greater identity than the bank of trees and quayside on the left bank; the Louvre remains recognisable but reduced to a silhouette in Luce's medley of sumptuous secondary flecks of violet, orange and green, their velvety textures pricked by the line of gaslights. The veil of darkness which here replaces topographical certainty with an almost sensual strangeness could also be used in a more threatening way, as Luce knew. His *Rue Ravignan, Night* [**181**] represents a Montmartre backstreet, the foreground partially lit by a single gaslamp which fails to illuminate the dark central void towards which the pedestrian makes his way. The city here is grimly shrouded, the stark forms of the tenements creating threatening shadows in a harsh inner city environment. Using the nocturne to stage the sinister theatre of the city was an option not lost on other artists. André Devambez, no avant-garde painter but a previous winner of the Prix de Rome, exhibited his *Charge* [**182**] at the Salon des artistes français in 1902. An image of striking immediacy, the tilted, raking view on to the boulevard gives a sense of the turmoil and violence to which our gaze is directed. Devambez heightened the picture's excitement not only by detailing elements such as the disciplined swathe of *gendarmes* confronting the chaotic arc of rioters but also by immersing the disturbance in darkness and picking out key features: the ranked faces of the police, and the gloriously incongruous cheeriness of the illuminated posters and discs of the café tables. In this politically charged image, dark and light refuse to take sides but throw civil disobedience and crowd control into rather ridiculous relief as a sideshow to the boulevard parade.

Devambez's *Charge* indicates that there was more to the nocturne than merely a pictorial device for imbuing a landscape with mystery or mood. The nocturnal scene could serve as a setting for events in which the fictive darkness created an imaginative environment conducive to allusive meanings. Such an approach to the nocturne is taken by independent painters at least as early as among those of the mainstream. Rousseau's *Le Soir du carnaval* [**183**], his

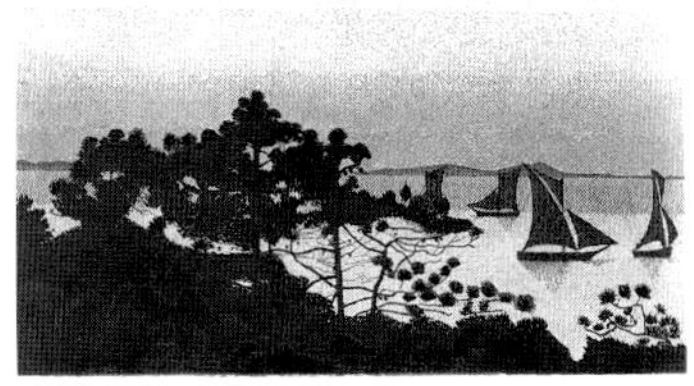

177
H. -E. Cross
The Pointe de la Galère *c.*1891–2
Private Collection

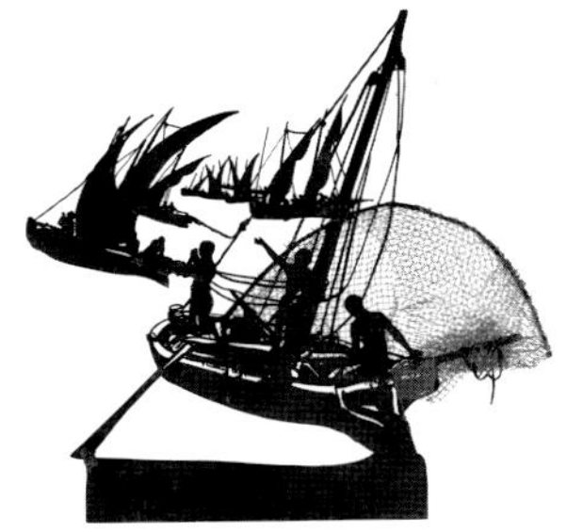

178
H. Rivière ***Following the Star: the Fishermen*** 1890
Paris, Musée des arts décoratifs

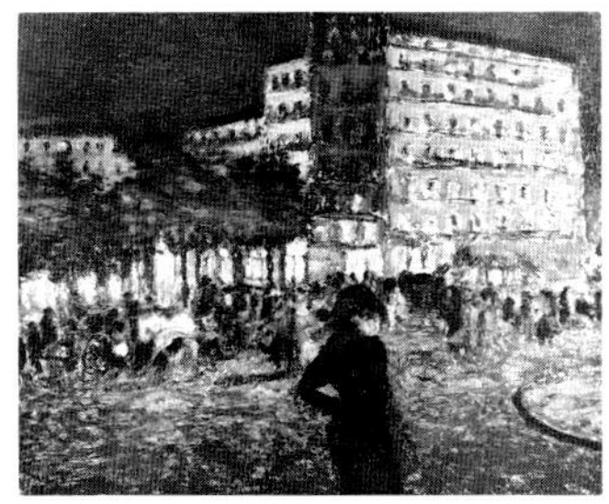

179
P. Bonnard ***Place Pigalle, by Night*** *c.*1905–8
New Haven, Yale University Art Gallery

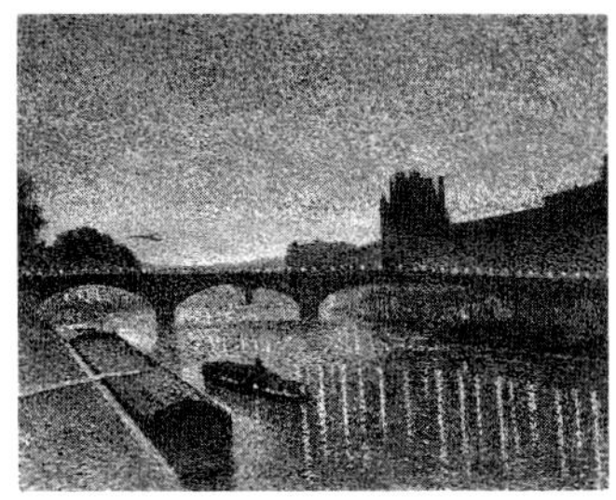

180
M. Luce ***The Louvre and Pont du Caroussel: Night Effect*** 1890
Private Collection

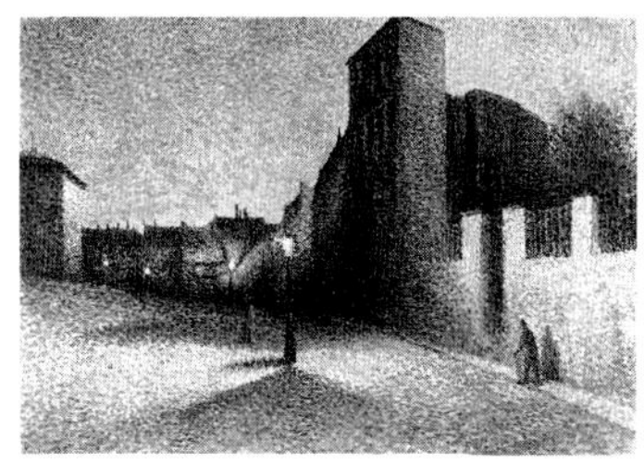

181
M. Luce ***Rue Ravignan, Night*** 1893
Houston, Museum of Fine Arts, The John A. and Audrey Jones Beck Collection

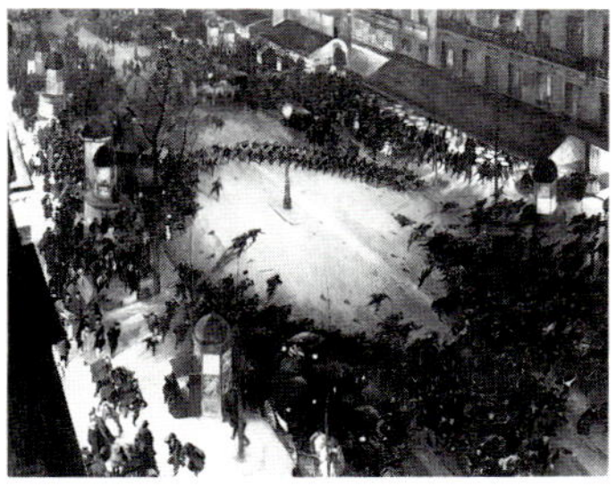

182
A. Devambez
The Charge 1902
Paris, Musée d'Orsay

first submission to the Indépendants in 1886, is an extraordinary compendium of incongruities, with its raffish Pierrot and demure Colombine set against a wretched winter forest, its single grey cloud floating high in the cold sky, its lonely kiosk decorated with a mask and flanked by a gaslight. Whereas the remarkably strange *Soir du Carnaval* was painted by an eccentric outsider and was scarcely noticed on its exhibition, *Cypresses Against a Starry Sky* [**184**] was made by an artist conscious of developments in the avant-garde and determined to stake his claim there – 'a last attempt', as van Gogh put it himself, in a number of essays in painting nocturnes. *Cypresses Against a Starry Sky* was painted in May 1890. Its simply outlined forms and energetic but ordered brushwork clearly indicate radical painterly practice, an intention implied by van Gogh in a letter to Gauguin describing the painting's 'exaggerated' colour.[25] He summed it up as 'very romantic, … but also *Provence*, I think'. It would seem likely that for him the painting conveyed more than mood and locality, not least because of the pivotal importance of the cypress trees, rising like some foliated steeple through the central space and penetrating the upper edge of the canvas. The evergreen cypress, as van Gogh well knew, is planted in cemeteries as a symbol of eternal life in death. This was a stock association. In a volume of 1885 that contains comparisons of human and natural physiognomy the cypress is described as 'a striking image of death, sombre, inflexible and upright, dominating life'. Jean Moréas, travelling through the Midi in the 1900s, thought that they could be considered, 'according to one's spiritual disposition, … as regretting life's passing or as a reassuring symbol of life after death'.[26] Given that the pastor's son van Gogh associated the colour blue, which permeates this painting, with eternity, *Cypresses Against a Starry Sky* may well best be read in spiritual terms, as a landscape invented to convey man's pilgrimage through life,[27] his transit only a humble occurrence alongside the universal truths of death and eternity.

183
H. Rousseau
Le Soir du carnaval 1886
Philadelphia Museum of Art, The Louis E. Stern Collection

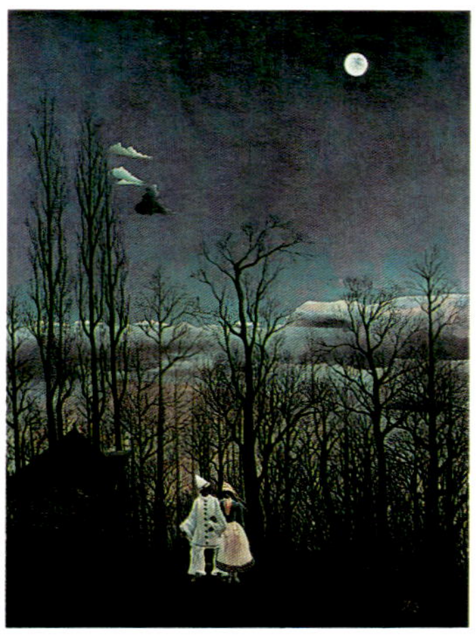

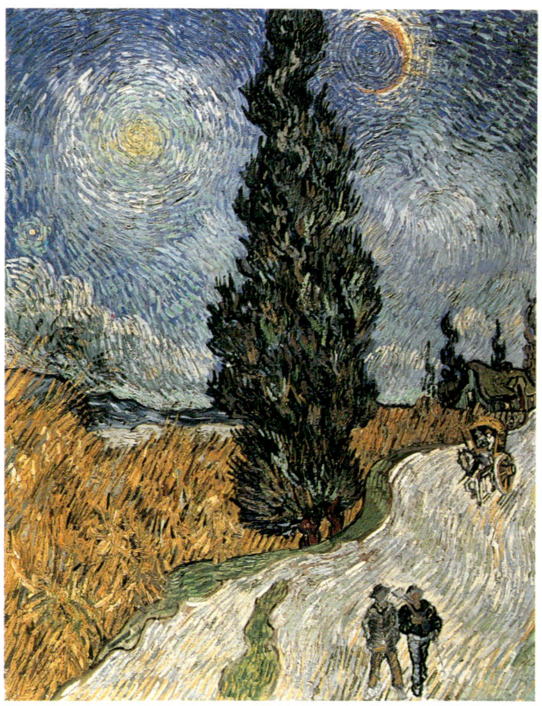

184
V. van Gogh
Cypresses Against a Starry Sky 1890
Otterlo, Rijksmuseum Kröller-Müller

If such an interpretation of van Gogh's painting remains speculative, one is on surer ground with other painters such as Maurice Denis and Charles Dulac. Denis was a devout Roman Catholic, and his *Path Through the Trees* [**185**] – which he kept throughout his life as a kind of icon – was painted about 1891 at a time of self-analysis when the young artist was marking out his position as a member of the Nabis and propagator of the Symbolist aesthetic as well as contemplating taking the sacrament of marriage. This little nocturne, it has been suggested, is thus a '*paysage intérieur*'.[28] The landscape is seen as if we, like the cloaked figures before us, are passing down the road of life, directed by high walls which are there perhaps to keep us on the path of the good life, protecting us from evils beyond, or to suggest the narrowness of human understanding. The road leads us towards the glow cast by some invisible source over the horizon, while Denis's deep harmony of secondary purples and greens throws the emphasis on the pilgrims' passage through the nocturnal landscape towards the light. The spiritual import of this image is evident from its reappearance in a slightly modified form as an illustration to Thomas à Kempis's *Imitation of Christ* published by Denis in 1903.[29] Charles Dulac's piety led him to take the Third Order of St Francis in 1890, and on his early death in 1898 he was buried in his monk's habit. His attitude to landscape was even more overtly religious than that of Denis, as Dulac saw the representation of the natural world not only as a form of worship in itself but also as a means to articulate specifically spiritual metaphors. From mid-December 1897 to mid-January 1898, and then again from March to April that year, he stayed at Villeneuve-les-Avignon on the Rhône.[30] During the first period he painted *Sunset, Avignon* [**186**], which at first sight appears to be a straightforward nocturnal landscape with subtly exaggerated colours, from the petrol-blue of the sky, which gives way to green and then orange just above the horizon, to the sweeping purplish foreground, simple and unblemished by houses or trees, just touched with silvery mauve on the right-hand hills. But Dulac's letters make it quite clear that such landscapes were intended to convey more than mere appearances. He wrote from Avignon in April 1898: 'Isn't this infinitely pure water, this crystalline blue so abundant and living, animating the factories, fertilising the plains, the very symbol of the One who gives life to our souls?'[31] Dulac's contemporaries were quick to realise his intentions, for the 1890s witnessed a period of religious revival in the face of what many Catholics saw as the invidiously secular Republic, and Catholic apologists sought actively to promote Christian art. Dulac's obituary in

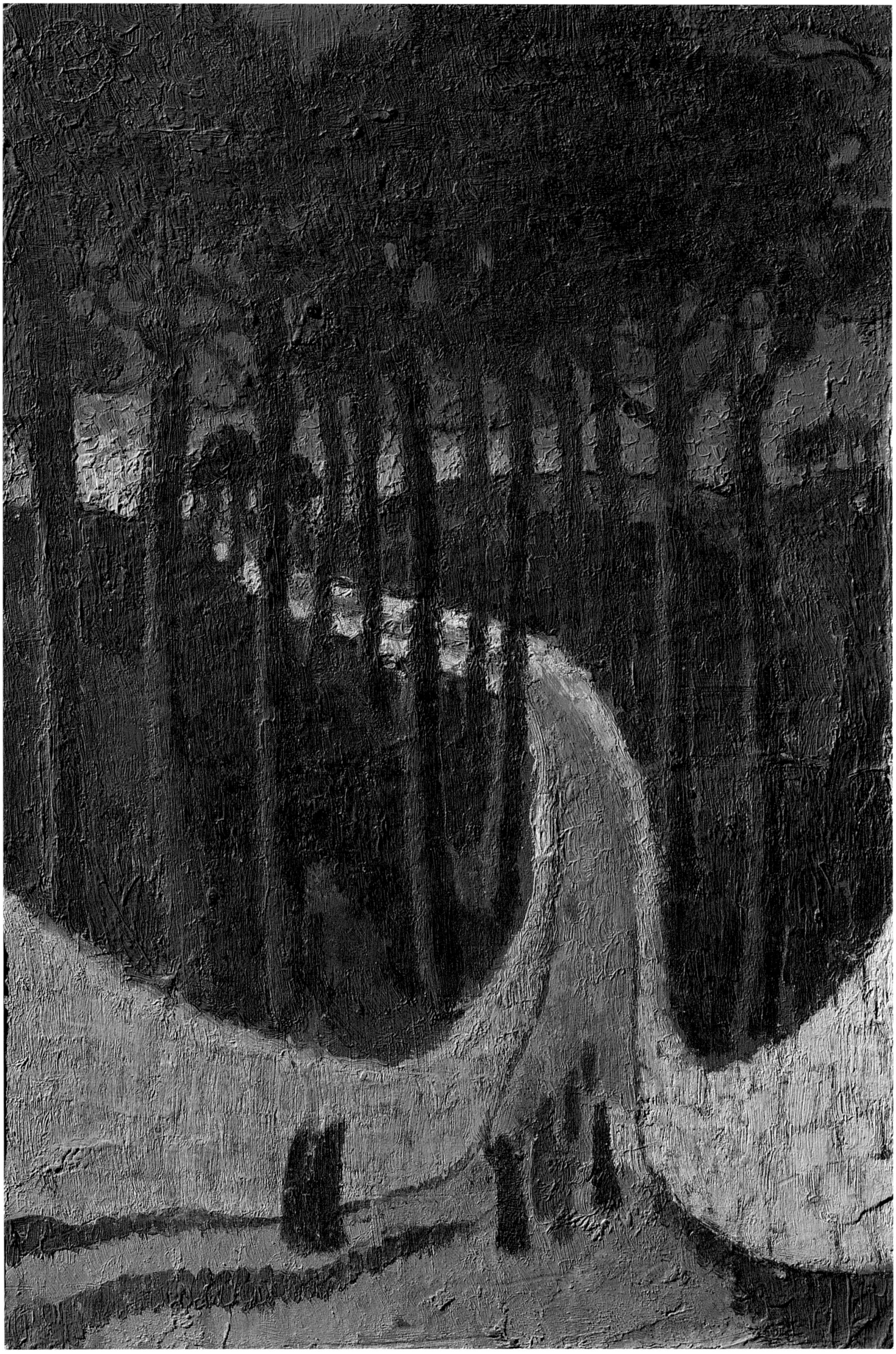

185
M. Denis
Path Through the Trees
*c.*1891
Saint-Germain-en-Laye,
Le Musée départmental du
'Prieuré'

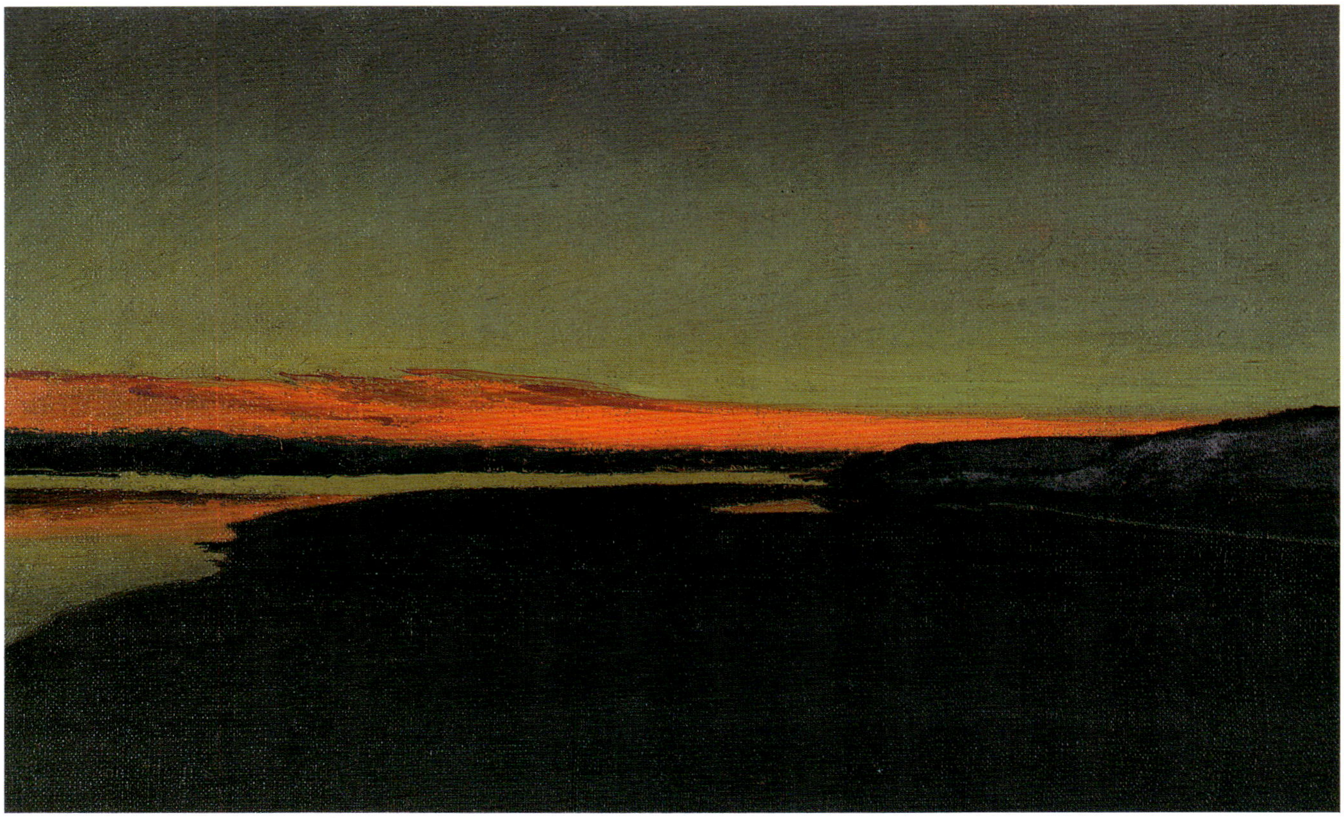

186
C. Dulac
Sunset, Avignon 1898
Reims, Musée des beaux-arts

the *Gazette des beaux-arts* spoke of his piety and linked his landscapes to Amiel's notion of '*états d'âme*'. This idea was expanded by Denis in an article of 1905 which placed Dulac's work within the contemporary arguments of the reactionary art historian Georges Lanoë that 'modern landscape painting had become the sole repository for religious idealism'.[32] Denis's and Dulac's nocturnes are more than just the products of a shared, sincere and somewhat reactionary piety, for despite the differences between the paintings – Denis's naïvety in contrast to Dulac's suavity, one might say – each little picture has a harmonious surface and unified, enveloping sobriety of colour that implies a serene unity of thought and emotion.

Although Denis and Dulac obviously employed Christian associations in their work, other artists of the period were more ambiguous in their approach. Charles Lacoste was a Bordeaux painter who was friendly with writers such as André Gide and Francis Jammes and who, shortly after settling in Paris in 1899, entered into friendly relations with Vuillard, Denis, Vallotton and other Nabi artists. Lacoste's small-scale paintings, executed in simplified areas of matt colour and at this stage of his career usually representing landscapes and urban views, shared the fine tuning of his Symbolist associates. *La Main d'ombre* of 1896 [**188**], painted in 1896 and exhibited at a one-man show in the capital two years later, is typical of his subtle economy. The motif may represent the Gironde in his native town, or possibly London, which he knew well, but the failing light disguises the site's identity, rendering it as the universal modern city, its emphatic man-made structures and artificial lighting softened and minimised by the incipient night. Over this dusk-drowned city and its anonymous populations the sky glows with the rich blue aura of the vanished sun, in front of which project five great fingers of trailing cloud, as if a hand of almost infinite proportions was stretching itself over this spare and melancholy scene. It is a picture rich in ambiguity, for it may be dawn rather than dusk, and the figures may be going to work rather than leaving it. And what of the hand? Is the spectator to take it on trust as some meteorological phenomenon actually observed, or as an image of some superhuman force? It has been interpreted as trying to claw the people back into its clutches, as hinting at the plight of the urban worker.[33] Alternatively it might seem to cover and protect, even to bless, the silent shadowy processions, an account which corresponds to some of Lacoste's writings. One passage runs: 'The word of God created light. Light speaks to us everywhere, spreading so it seems to be inherent in everything, even the night. Light does not only reveal the ordinary appearance of things and beings but also … transfiguring what it illuminates … lets one glimpse that transformation's significance for the soul'.[34] However, these remarks are undated and may have been written after Lacoste's religious conversion following the death of his father in 1915. Prior to this, in 1904, he had spoken to Jammes of how 'I look for what is hidden, the emotion of things, of skies, in order to express the feelings stimulated by objects, the nuances with which they seem to resonate'.[35] Although Lacoste's representations of nature came to be commonly viewed as religious motifs,[36] *La Main d'ombre* may well be interpreted not as an explicitly Christian metaphor for a loving God, but as an image more generally intended to convey a reassuring awe in the presence of the beyond, a feeling of superhuman grandeur best conveyed in a nocturnal landscape.

Similarly Redon's *Flight into Egypt* [**168**], although a biblical subject, cannot perhaps be explained as having unequivocal Christian inspiration. The painting was made about 1900, at a period in Redon's life when, like many other artists and intellectuals with spiritual concerns, he was interested in garnering the best of various world religions and mythologies into a single truth. He therefore made images of Buddha, Orpheus, the Sphinx and other divinities as well as Christian subjects.[37] The Flight into Egypt had been treated by Redon's mentor, the eccentric printmaker Rodolphe Bresdin, and in an appreciation of his work Redon had written of the way Bresdin's imagery dwelt on images of flight and escape.[38] Whether Redon was consciously following Bresdin's example or not, the subject prompts a night motif and as an image of faith in adversity was perhaps a particularly appropriate theme for a devout artist at a time of Republican anti-clericalism. Certainly the Flight into Egypt was visible at the Salons in the work of established academicians; Redon's former teacher Gérôme, for one, had a rather banal processional nocturne at the Salon of 1897.[39] In 1880 Luc-Olivier Merson had added a new dimension to the iconography in a successful canvas soon reproduced in numerous replicas [**187**], in which the Holy Family rests in the lonely desert night, the Virgin and Child couched in the lap of a sphinx, symbolising the passing of the pagan gods in the face of the new dispensation. Redon eschewed such overt iconography for a more personal imagery. In his *Flight* there is little light in the oily blue sky and the landscape cannot be made out in the darkness. The chief light source is the powerful glow emanating from the Holy Family, illuminating the tree trunks with streaks of mid-violet and pale yellow. In the ambient gold and green, edged with duck-egg blue, one scarcely discerns the figures themselves. It is their aura of holiness that lights up nature, a superhuman effect which gathers force from Redon's enthusiastic denial of natural appearances, for the great central tree-trunk is baseless, floating like a vision in the divine illumination.

We have seen how artists discovered in the nocturne rich opportunities to paint nuances of light, ranging from deepest night to the hours of dusk and dawn, when the sense of passage between dark and light is most febrile and evocative. However, it was not primarily such conventional concerns that drew painters to the genre around the turn of the century. Rather it was the licence the nocturne gave to the imagination to conjure up mood and evoke emotion, to act as a theatre of awe, incongruity and otherness, which appealed to painters who, like their public and market, were often directed by the tensions and uncertainties of *fin-de-siècle* culture to meditation on the mysteries of the human condition.

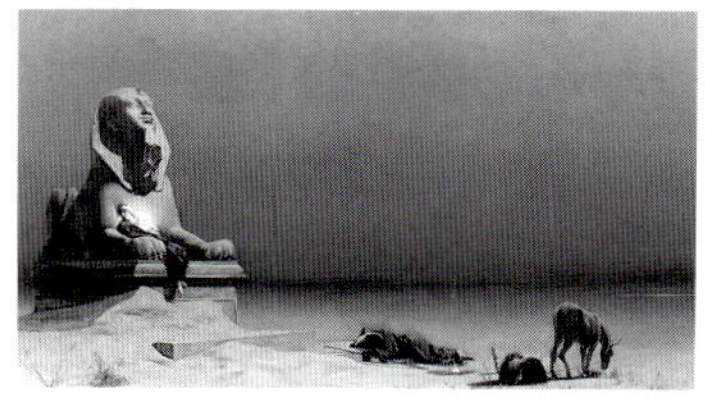

187
L. -O. Merson
Rest on the Flight into Egypt 1879
Boston, Museum of Fine Arts, Bequest of George Golding Kennedy

188
C. Lacoste
La Main d'ombre 1896
Paris, Musée d'Orsay

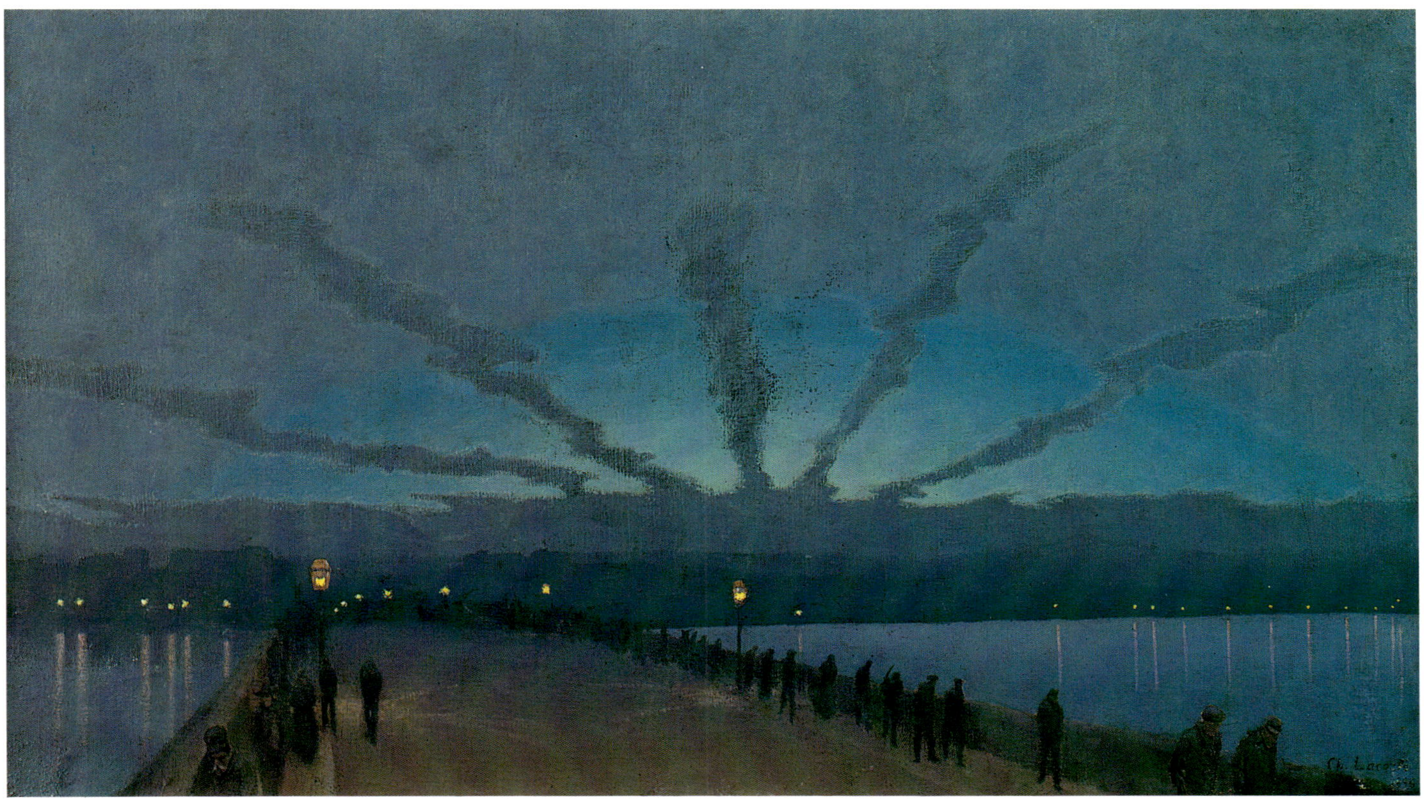

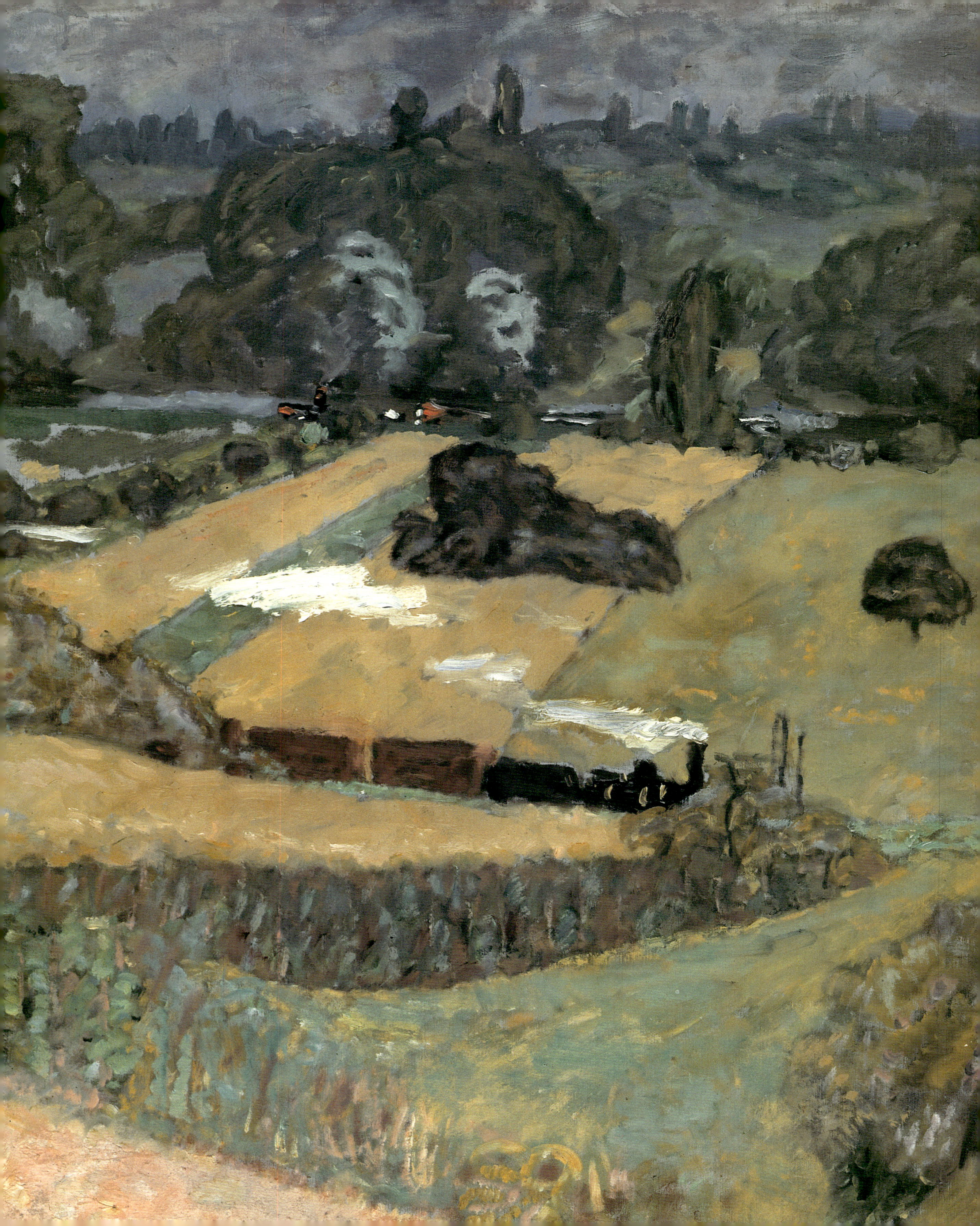

10

The Panoramic Landscape

The panorama has been common in landscape painting since the emergence of the genre in the fifteenth century, when it stretched out behind Van Eyck's *Virgin and Child with Chancellor Rollin* or Piero della Francesca's portraits of the Duke and Duchess of Urbino. So long established, it remained an important format for French painters between 1874 and 1914. The panoramic view challenges the painter to represent space, both laterally and in depth; in terms of categories of *paysage*, it is thus the absolute opposite of the *sous-bois*, the claustrophobic, introverted repesentation of natural space compressed between ground and foliage of the kind that often enticed Cézanne. The ability to depict a panorama was often considered an essential criterion for a *paysagiste*. For instance Emile Michel, a landscape painter who doubled as a critic, picked out Japy's *Plains at Villers-Cotterets* at the Salon of 1880 because it 'allows your eye to penetrate the vast stretch of terrain'.[1] Representing distance implied a high degree of naturalism; by Michel's terms, a painted panorama should allow the spectator's gaze to roam over and into the view as if over a natural vista. Perhaps nowhere were these demands more admirably met than in Chintreuil's appositely titled *L'Espace* [**191**], an immense vista of the Parisian region seen from La Tournelle-Septeuil. First exhibited at the Salon of 1869, it reappeared posthumously at the Universal Exhibition of 1878 and entered the Louvre in 1883, a triumphant talisman of the naturalist landscapist's ability to explore the nuanced lighting and atmospherics of an almost boundless panorama. Contemporary theorists of natural physiognomy believed that a vast space in nature could give a sense of silence and solitude,[2] a notion which accorded with one of landscape painting's conventional purposes: to evoke calm and repose. However, the spacious panorama naturalistically painted could also be boring. One reviewer of the Salon of 1891 regretted the increasing tendency to paint 'immense, huge, flat and banal plains' without any redeeming features.[3]

Given its expanse, the panorama is a convenient medium for giving information about a landscape. Louis Tauzin's *Ile Seguin, seen from Meudon* [**190**], painted about 1900, takes the vantage point afforded by the high ground to the south-west of Paris to inventory the distant city's salient buildings: one can make out the Eiffel Tower, the Ecole Militaire, Les Invalides, the Grand Palais, Notre-Dame and the Pantheon. Such monuments, old and new, are set against the foreground suburbs with their typical combination of houses, factories and leisure facilities. Not long after Tauzin painted this canvas the île Seguin, here part of a still verdant vista, disappeared beneath the Renault works. His panoramic format thus serves both as a topographical exercise and as a record of a moment in the flux of suburban change. The potential of the panorama for representing data seemed to some open to abuse. In 1897 André Michel complained that increasing numbers of projects for

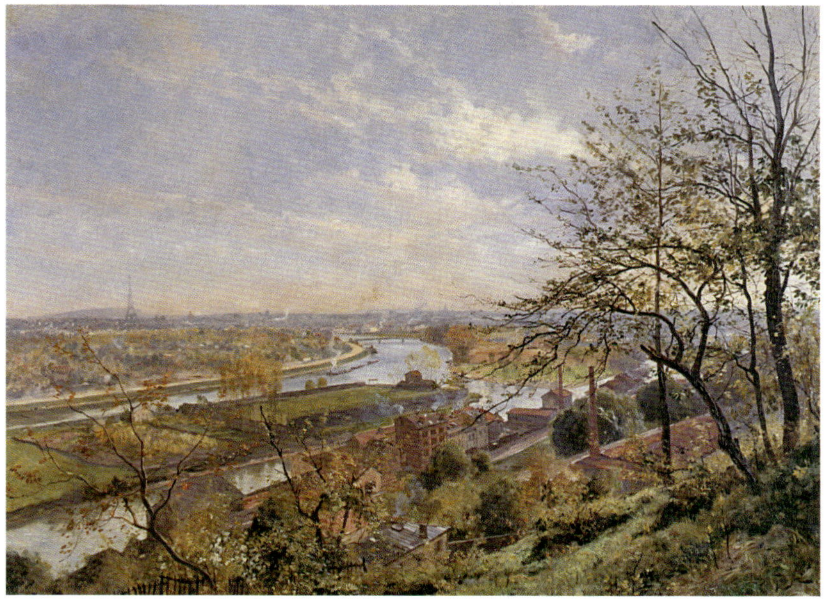

190
L. Tauzin
Ile Seguin, seen from Meudon *c.*1900
Boulogne-Billancourt, Musée municipal

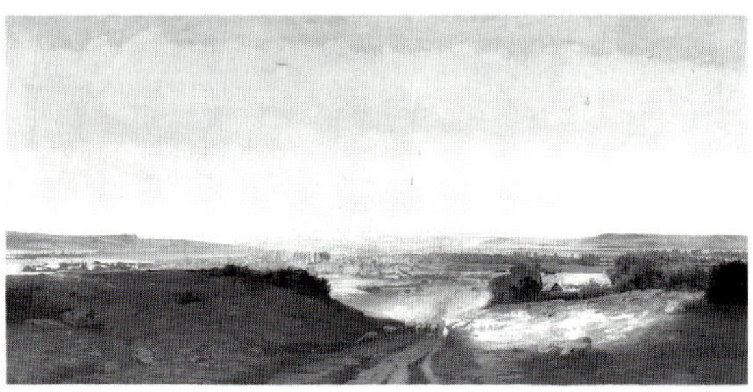

191
A. Chintreuil ***L'Espace*** 1869
Paris, Musée d'Orsay

opposite
189
P. Bonnard
The Train and the Barges *c.*1910 (detail)
St Petersburg, The Hermitage Museum

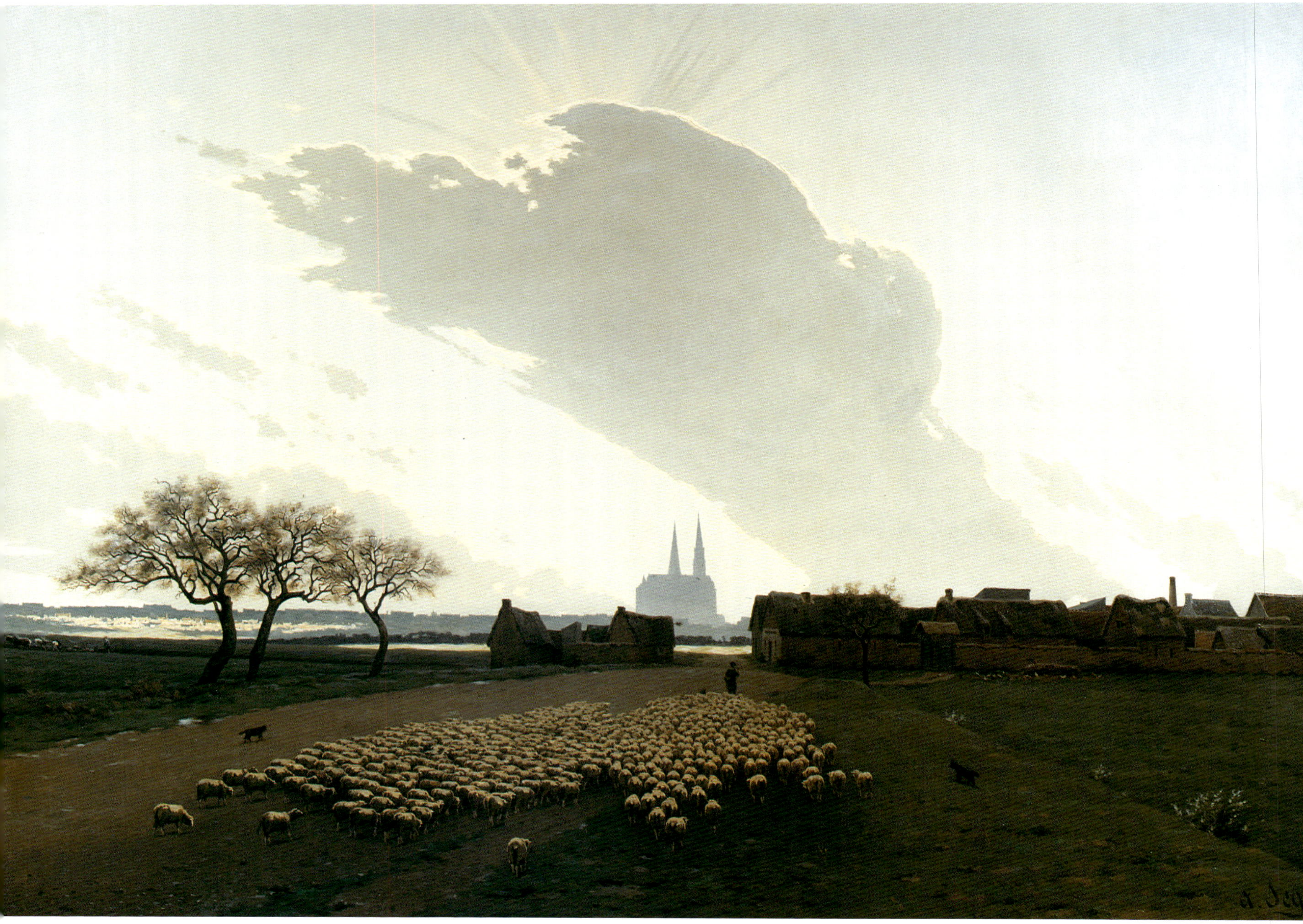

192
A. Ségé
En pays chartrain 1884
Chartres, Musée des beaux-arts

murals in public buildings such as *mairies* were relying on 'simple panoramic views rolled out in long friezes' which neglected decorative obligations for literal realism; he cited a detailed vista of Alfortville by Raoul Arus [**193**] as a particular aberration.[4] A distant view demanded the elimination of detail. This was the opinion of Paul Mantz in his review of the 1877 Impressionist exhibition: 'The painter is at the top of a hill; at his feet he sees an immense plain spread out before him; … he does not see every pebble on the path, every blade of grass in the meadow'.[5] The panorama could be taken to extremes of simplification or of detail; for the landscape painter it was often a question of finding a balance between too much and too little.

An image representing extensive space allows the artist ample opportunity to furnish the landscape, and in so doing use the artifice of the painting to bring values and associations into play. Such is the case in Ségé's *En pays chartrain* [**192**], shown at the Salon of 1884. The panorama was his stock in trade, and the State had bought one of Brittany from the Salon of 1870.[6] *En pays chartrain* has as subject one of the great views of France, the cathedral of Chartres rising above the plains of the surrounding Beauce. The large scale of his canvas, in contrast to conventional landscape formats, was obviously chosen to give the spectator some equivalence to the immensity of the view represented, in which Ségé balances out broad effects and close observation. The cathedral is not made a feature in conventional *pittoresque* manner, but is placed on the horizon a few kilometres away. The eye is led to it down the path along which the shepherd leads his flock and through the village whose clustered cottages part to allow our gaze to travel across the fields streaked by the low sun. One can read the painting simply as a view of a recognisable site, its harmonious light and the untroubled pace of its calm horizon making it an image of peace and changelessness.

But perhaps there is more to it than this. The cathedral is central, a focus for the gaze but also performing in the fiction of Ségé's panorama the function for which it was built centuries before: celebration of the glory of God. Its great shape is close in warm grey tone to the immensity of the sky, and above the cathedral stretches a massive cloud as if in benediction of this peaceful scene. Perhaps, too, the inclusion of a shepherd and flock is more than a rustic likelihood, evoking such evident biblical associations.

Sisley's *Bend in the Seine at Saint-Cloud* [**195**] seems at first sight in great contrast to Ségé's Salon picture, both in its more modest size and its breadth of handling, as if in response to Mantz's injunctions. Sisley used the conventional means to articulate space, organising the painting into bands of differing green tones and using aerial perspective to blur the distant ridge. Although handled with the graphic flourish typical of Impressionist *plein air* work of the 1870s, the *Bend in the Seine* is quite clearly legible as a view, Sisley itemising groups of houses, open fields, and the great sweep of the Seine crossed by bridges. As a representation of the south-western suburbs of Paris it does not stray far from the prototype established by Troyon in his similar vista from the heights of Suresnes, exhibited at the Salon of 1859 [**194**].

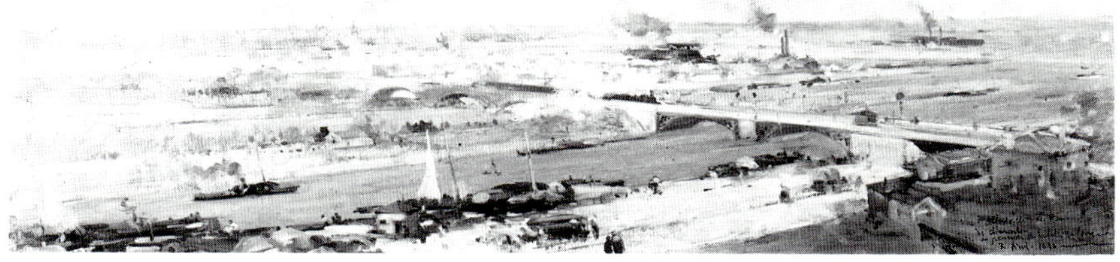

193
R. Arus *View of Alfortville* 1896
Paris, Musée du Petit Palais

Both treat the distant panorama as countryside dotted with distinct communities, minimising the city's proximity; indeed, Troyon's inclusion of steamboats on the river is more 'modern' than Sisley's neglect of them. Both use the foreground to emphasise rurality, Troyon very evidently with his herd of cattle, Sisley with his peasant couple, the man carrying a tool, in the high grass or crop which dominates the first plane. And yet perhaps there are other associations inherent in Sisley's painting, as in Ségé's. To the left of his panorama the pale patch he brushed in among the trees represents, albeit in shorthand, what contemporaries would easily have recognised as the ruins of the *château* of Saint-Cloud. It had been one of Napoleon III's favourite summer residences, and he had commissioned Daubigny to paint the *château* and the celebrated fountains in the park.[7] The *château* was destroyed by fire late in 1870 when the Prussian armies encircled Paris, but the ruins remained as a symbol of the catastrophic demise of the Second

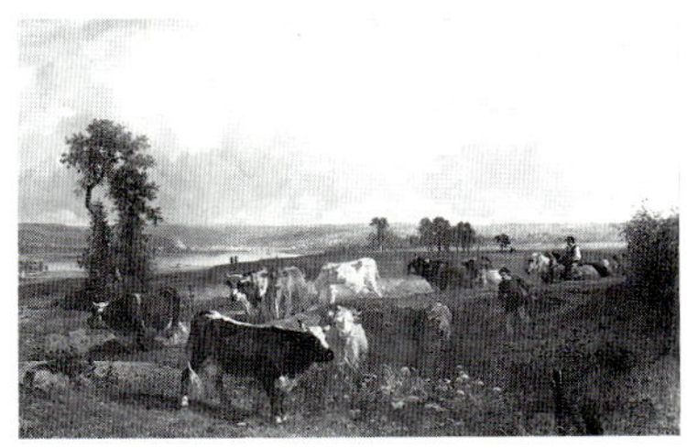

194
C. Troyon
View Taken From the Ridge at Suresnes
1856
Paris, Musée du Louvre

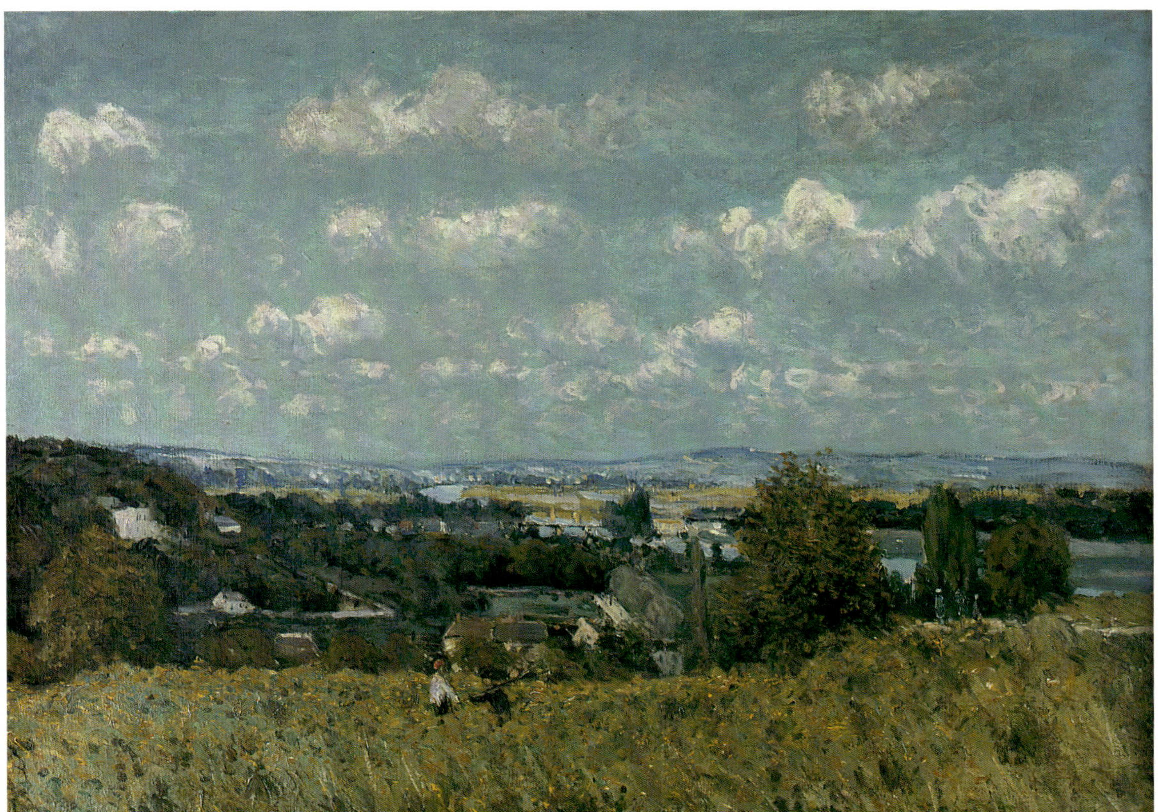

195
A. Sisley ***The Bend in the Seine at Saint-Cloud*** 1875
Rennes, Musée des beaux-arts

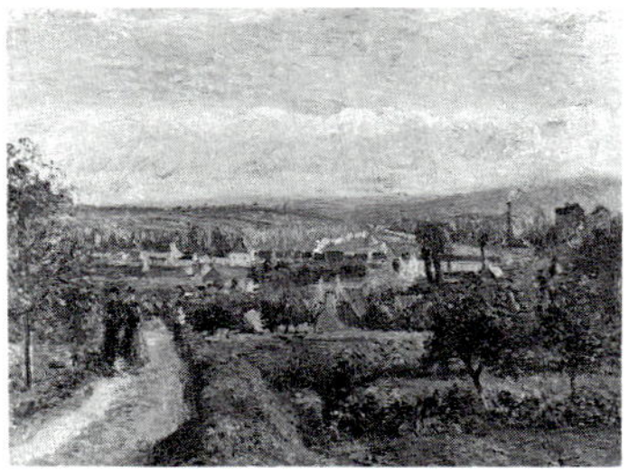

196
C. Pissarro
View of Saint-Ouen-l'Aumône 1876
New Haven, Yale University Art Gallery, Gift of Helen C. Altschul, widow of Frank Altschul, BA 1908

197
C. Pissarro
Banks of the Oise, Pontoise 1873
Indianapolis Museum of Art, James E. Roberts Fund

Empire. Their inclusion, discreet but specific, on the flank of Sisley's panorama may have been an intentional note by the Republican painter. In the cases of Sisley and Ségé very different panoramic vistas seem to have carried allusions – political and spiritual – beyond their mere representation.

Because of its literal capacity to contain so much, the panorama, as both visual experience of nature and category of landscape painting, can call to mind many associations, not least because great space carries with it implications of the passage of time. It was a panoramic view that encouraged Emile Michel in his last book, on the Forest of Fontainebleau, to muse on historical time: 'When the walker on the ridge near Nemours, with his back to the forest, sees the Loing at his feet flowing through the valley, he takes in as it were in shorthand a long historic past and a picturesque horizon which has not much changed in its essentials. Near him, in those piles of rocks strewn on the slopes, would have sheltered the primitive peoples attracted by the habitat which the proximity of both forest and river afforded them. Nowadays locomotives incessantly plough along the tracks below one, while alongside, more rapidly still, the human word is transmitted instantaneously via simple wires'.[8] Michel's meditations on the domestication of nature over the centuries turns our attention to the matter of travelling time. The panorama is, almost by definition, all that the eye can see; it represents the maximum perceptible distance. Faced with a great expanse in either nature or art, humans instinctively compute how long it would take to traverse it. Travelling time, and with it notions of the panorama, had been revolutionised by the railway. 'In a few hours, it shows you all of France,' enthused Jules Claretie in 1865, 'and before your eyes it unrolls its infinite panorama, a vast succession of charming tableaux, of novel surprises. It shows you only the chief outlines of a landscape, being an artist versed in the ways of the masters. Don't ask it for details, only for the living whole. Then, after having charmed you with its painterly skills, it suddenly stops and quite simply lets you off where you want to go.'[9] If this new form of travelling through landscape affected one's perceptions of it, how was the painter to cope with the train journey's perpetuation of the panorama over time, its ceaseless shifting of 'all that the eye can see'?

Artists of Daubigny's generation appear to have been unwilling to have their conventional notion of the painted panorama disturbed by new perceptions of time and space. If his *Fields in the Month of June* [**241**], shown at the Salon of 1874, is an idyllic vista of timeless agricultural labour, younger painters seem to have recognised, perhaps only semi-consciously, the implications of the new technology, and one can even trace something of a consensus about how to represent it in panoramic paintings. Pissarro's *Banks of the Oise, Pontoise* [**197**], contemporary with Daubigny's

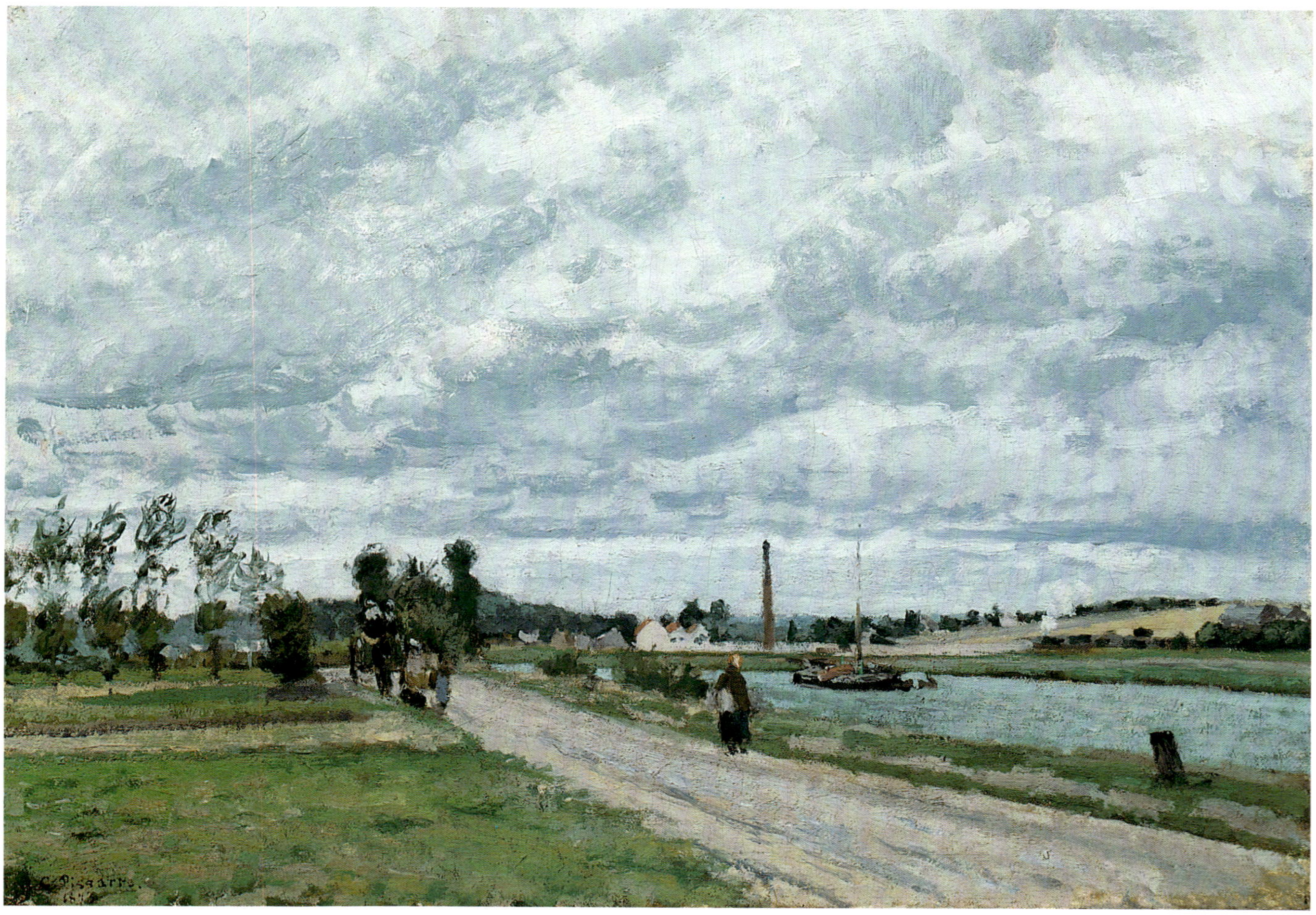

canvas, does not lead the eye across the expansive space but into it along the diagonals of river and tow-path. It does not represent age-old activity but the changing landscape of modern France. During the 1870s Pissarro represented Pontoise, a market town some twenty-five kilometres north-west of Paris, and its environs in a variety of ways. *Banks of the Oise* emphasises the river as a commercial artery and the industrial works which were beginning to line its banks.[10] For all Pissarro's interest in atmospheric effects, in depicting gusty weather under a low cloud-base, this is an image concerned with passage through the panoramic space, by foot, cart, barge or train. Pissarro's occasional use of the panorama's potential for presenting information about a landscape recurred in his *View of Saint-Ouen-l'Aumône* [**196**] of 1876. He represents the community across the river from Pontoise in an almost programmatic fashion, itemising modern and time-honoured elements by showing the factory alongside the village and a train traversing the farmland vista.[11] Monet had done the same four years earlier in his painting known as *The Train* [**198**], which represents the industrial suburb of Déville, outside Rouen. Even more demonstrably than in either of Pissarro's canvases, he uses the image of the railway to identify the landscape as modern not only in style but in subject, for his train almost completely spans the panorama through which it passes and the locomotive's steam partly masks, but also draws attention to, the forest of factory chimneys behind. Significantly, all three paintings include figures on foot, whose presence marks the old way of traversing a landscape, literally confronting the old pace with the new velocity.

That consensus survived into the twentieth century. One finds the same elements appearing in van Gogh's *Summer Evening* [**199**], painted at Arles in June 1888. The artist explained in a letter to his brother Theo that he was trying to represent the *mistral* blowing fiercely.[12] But van Gogh was surely conscious, as Pissarro must have been with *Banks of the Oise*, of painting more than a weather effect. Indeed, the contrivance of the painting is evident from the fact that Arles is seen from the north-east, so the sun 'sets' in the south-west.[13] Two stock modes of representing landscape are evident in *Summer Evening*. Its division of the landscape into banded planes of country, industrial outskirts, and old town is the same procedure van Gogh had used to depict the Parisian suburbs the previous year [**38**]. And its wide view plays off the features Pissarro and Monet had used in their panoramas the decade before. Van Gogh makes a double conjunction of ancient and modern. He silhouettes the modern factories against the Romanesque church of Saint-Trophime and the centrally placed Roman arena, historic sites to which he usually paid little attention. And he juxtaposed strolling figures and the train passing across his

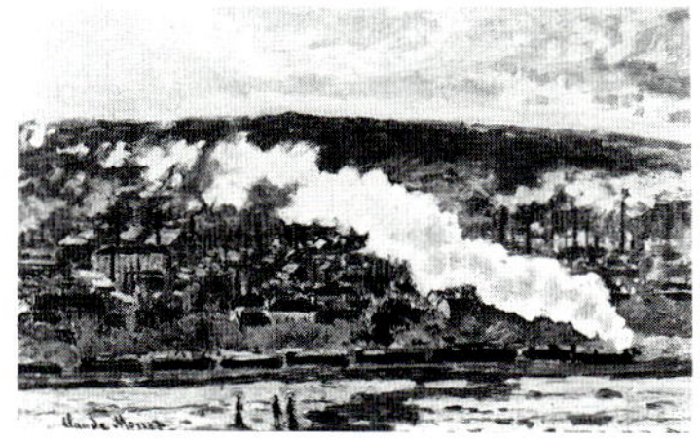

198
C. Monet
The Train 1872
Private Collection

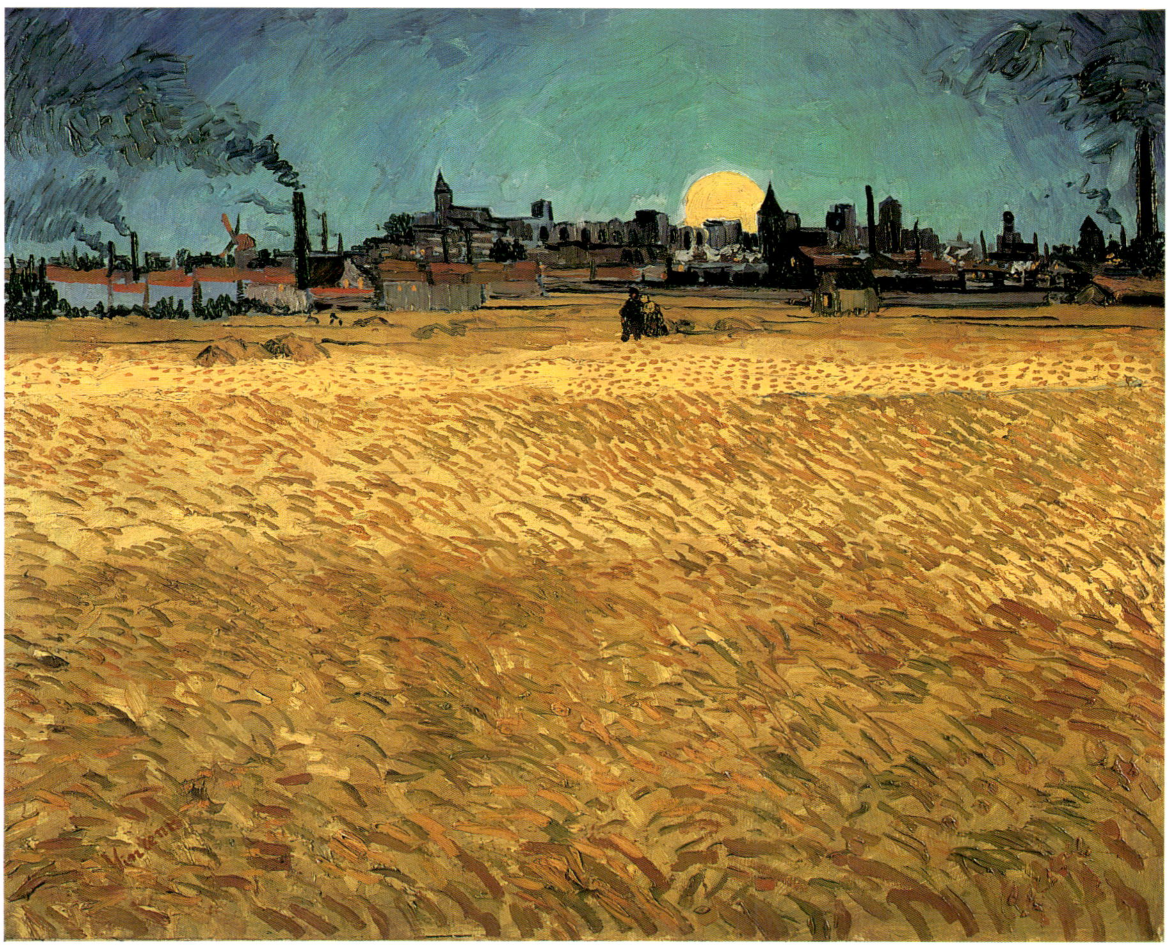

199
V. van Gogh
Summer Evening, Arles 1888
Winterthur, Kunstmuseum, Presented by Dr Emil Hahnloser 1922

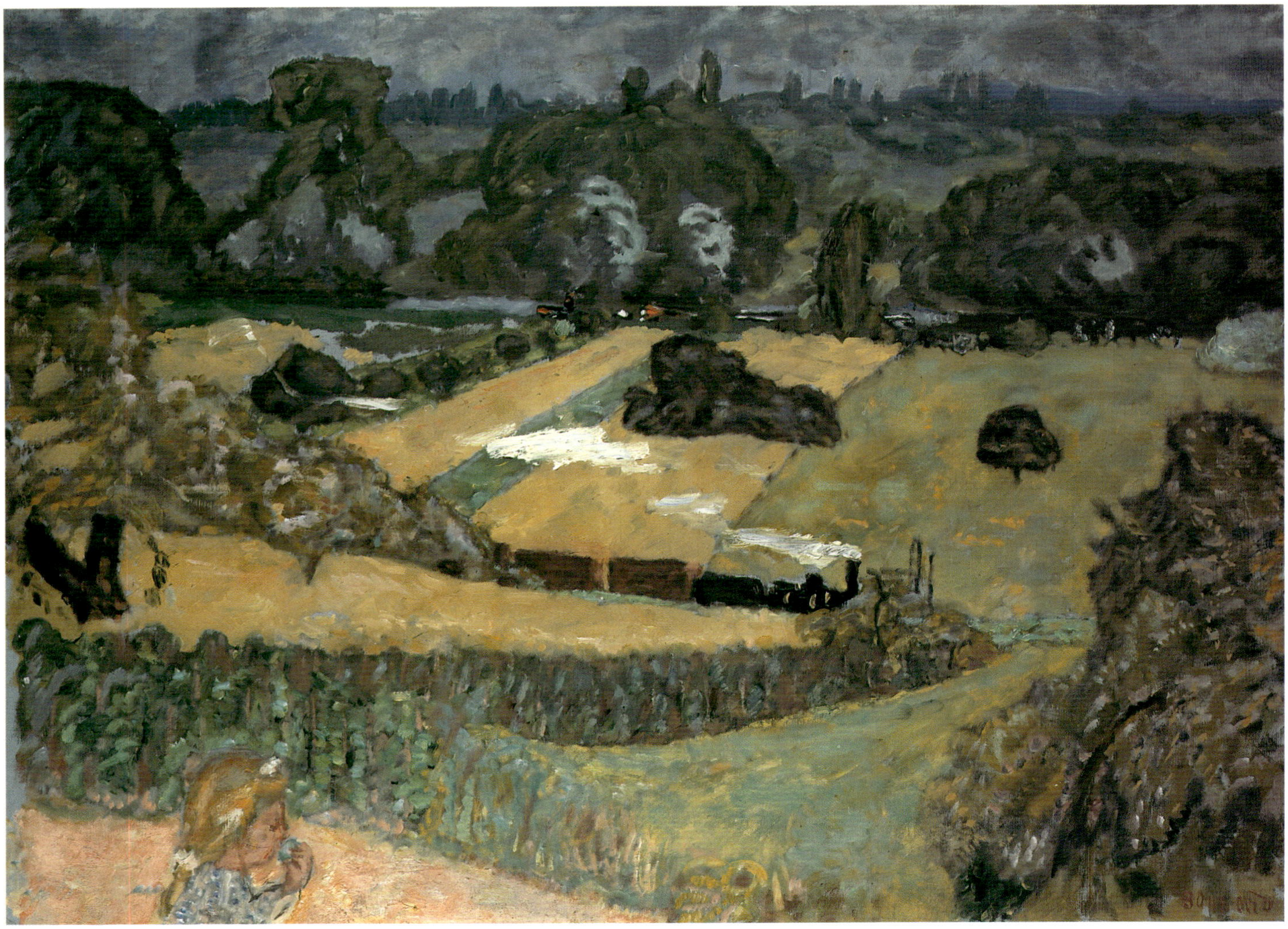

200
P. Bonnard
The Train and the Barges c.1910
St Petersburg, The Hermitage Museum

panoramic view. Over twenty years later Bonnard came up with the same solution. In *The Train and the Barges* [**200**], which impressed Apollinaire when it was shown at Bernheim Jeune in 1910,[14] Bonnard painted a panorama of the Seine valley at Vernonnet, between Paris and Rouen. Within the broadly painted swathes of verdant field and forest one picks out the black accents of locomotive and tug, pulling their carriages and barges in opposite directions across the panorama. Again it is an image of modern momentum, a moment in time seized before both locomotive and tug pass out of the spectator's view to right and to left. Once they have escaped this single field of vision we would have to turn first one way and then the other to see each moving machine; they would become more than the eye can see, not one panorama but the 'succession of tableaux' Claretie defined in 1865. Bonnard holds the train and the barges tight within the fiction of his canvas, where the little girl could encapsulate them both in her field of vision, if she bothered to look. But he represents them straining to get out, recognising that in the age of the machine the panorama is never still.

Younger generations began to relish the disconcerting effect that the train had on one's perceptions of transit. In the 1870s Flaubert had so hated the disturbance of his peace of mind engendered by railway travel that he stayed up all the previous night in order to sleep through the journey.[15] Thirty-five years later Moréas jotted down an account of his rail trip along the Mediterranean coast in a staccato manner which gives the effect of fragmented perception: 'A plain with blue mountains in the distance. Fréjus: a road, a peasant woman in a short red skirt. A muddy river and flash of a pond. On the other side, the sea, pale today under an overcast sky, foamy. The rapidity of our passage made it seem immobile'.[16] Aware of how the machine affected, even distorted, vision, perception and memory, Moréas accepted the panorama not as a unified vista of controlled information but as a dislocated list of fragmentary visual snapshots of colour, topography, climate, humanity. In an intellectual culture geared by the early years of the century to Bergsonian ideas of flux it was not only increasingly possible to relish the disjointed experience of the 'succession of tableaux' that Claretie had described but also, almost forty years on, to find pictorial form for his notion of landscape viewed from the train as unrolling in an 'infinite panorama'. At the Universal Exhibition in 1900 there were attractions which recreated by means of 'architectural copies, murals or dioramas' not only locales, such as the

‘Swiss village’, but also artificial landscapes which allowed the visitor to ‘experience’ a long journey. There was ‘the Tour du Monde, a bizarre catch-all, that took bargain seekers all over Africa, South America and Asia by dioramas and fragmented plaster reproductions of such places as the imperial palace at Peking and a terraced tower of Angkor Wat’. And the Russian exhibit, designed in conjunction with Thomas Cook, took ‘tourists’ on the Trans-Siberian railway. ‘The carriages left “Moscow Station” and rolled east as scenes of the Caucasus, the steppes, and of the wilds (and the riches, to inspire confidence) of Siberia rolled by the windows on a long canvas … The “trip” ended when a Chinese boy went through the cars serving jasmine tea, shouting, “Peking! All change here!”’[17]

Here was Claretie’s unrolling panorama presented as a spectacle, seguing one painted landscape into another and then the next. By now the customariness of the speeding train encouraged such a perception, threatening traditional definitions of the painted panorama as static stocktaking. Such shifts in philosophical, perceptual and social notions about moving through space were bound to have pictorial ramifications. However, although both Marquet and Matisse were in the team that painted the *Transsibérien* panorama,[18] neither showed much interest in finding new ways of representing perceptual flux in their later landscapes. Indeed, the deployment of ‘Claudian’ compositions by Matisse and other painters could be taken as the antithesis of an aesthetic committed to a ‘modern’ articulation of landscape, space and time. It was the Transsiberian spectacle that gave the name to perhaps the most innovatory variant on the panorama produced before the First World War, *La Prose du Transsibérien et de la petite Jehanne de France*. This was a combination of a poem by Blaise Cendrars and Orphic painting by Sonia Delaunay, with words and images printed in parallel on the pages of a fold-out book [**201**].[19] Of Swiss origin, the youthful Cendrars had travelled widely as tramp and sailor, before settling in Paris and befriending Apollinaire, Léger and their circle. His poem is an extraordinary collage of reminiscences of places visited or imagined, lists of names of cities, invocations of the repetitive percussion of the train journey, descriptions of clocks, sequences of pet names and objects and snatched conversations: the careering textures the modern world smears across the senses and the memory. Sonia Delaunay’s contribution is in the rhythmic non-representational arcs and prismatic colours of the Orphism she had developed with her husband Robert [**50**]. At times her shapes distantly recall fields, hills or lakes, and natural colours such as greens and blues also suggest nature. Specific motifs occasionally crop up; there is the Eiffel Tower at the bottom, and spire-like forms emerge from the arcs. It is not so much information that colour and rhythm convey but energy and momentum. Indeed, while the verticality

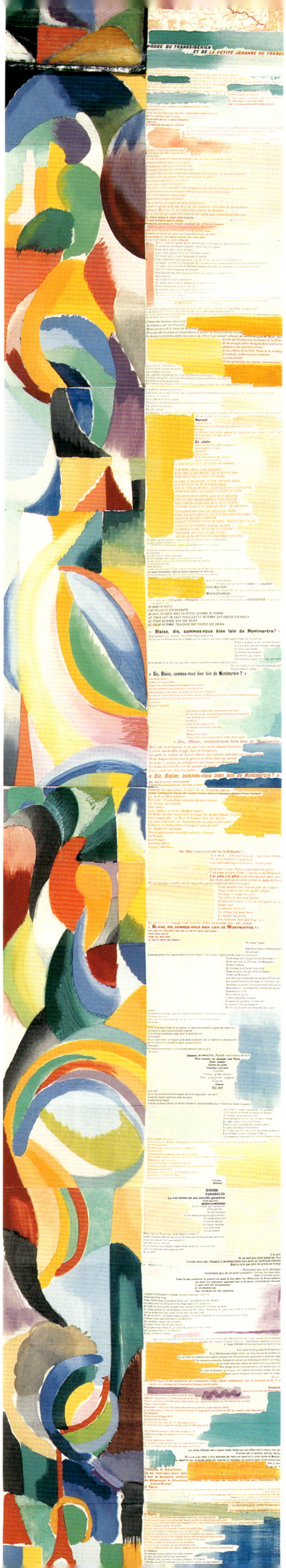

201
S. Delaunay
La Prose du Transsibérian et de la petite Jehanne de France
Paris, Editions des hommes nouveaux, 1913
Edinburgh, Scottish National Gallery of Modern Art

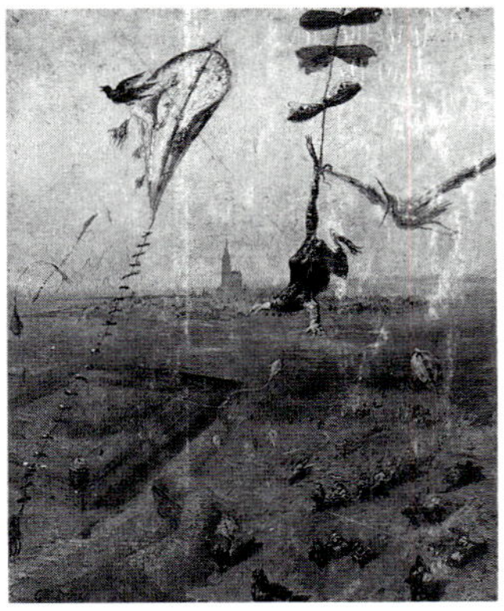

202
G. Doré
Between Heaven and Earth 1862
Belfort, Musée

203
A. Devambez
Avions fantaisistes 1911
Beauvais, Musée départmental de l'Oise

is necessary to accompany Cendrars's long *Prose*, Delaunay's work is not a picture in any conventional mode, not least because one cannot see it all at once. In that sense it is like a journey: a matter of incidents, passing visual signs and colours, the perception of dynamic movement, and of jumbled impressions of sight and sound – Delaunay's and Cendrars's contributions respectively. As a series of visual effects, her chromatic forms need – like the text – to be experienced over a passage of time, to assist in the building up of perceptions, sensations and memories, again like a journey.

However much the railway changed the concept of the panorama, there was another revolution in store. 'What! we've just left those people down there? Is it possible?', exclaimed Maupassant on his first balloon flight in 1887. 'Below us now Paris spreads out, a flat bluish patch, striped with streets, from which domes, towers and spires stick out here and there. Then all around the plain, the earth split up by long thin white roads in the middle of green fields.'[20] Flight radically alters the notion of the panorama. Maupassant could see from above Paris the interlocking of city and country in a way far more comprehensive than from the single viewpoint of a landscapist such as Tauzin [**190**]. The view from above distorts. In his excitement Maupassant described the terrain around Paris as flat, which he knew was wrong, a mistake the panoramas of Tauzin and Sisley [**195**] would never have made. As early as the 1860s Nadar had photographed Paris from his balloon and Gustave Doré had painted an imaginary view of Strasbourg from aloft [**202**]. Although Nadar, with his more modern medium, was prepared to look sharply down on the city, both Doré's picture and Navlet's gigantic panorama of Paris shown in 1855[21] represent a horizon, as if they could not escape from the conventional division in a landscape painting between sky and land.

Another step forward came with the aeroplane. The French had long been aviation pioneers, and fascination with aircraft burgeoned following the Wright brothers' first flight at Kittyhawk in 1903. That year Ferdinand Ferber, Gabriel Voisin and Louis Blériot made pioneering flights in the Paris region. By 1909 Blériot had flown across the Channel and 500,000 people had witnessed air races at Reims. Five years later flights linked Dieppe and Deauville, serving the races.[22] Symbol of adventure, spectacle and transport, the aeroplane fascinated painters; Picasso and Braque jokingly compared their Cubist

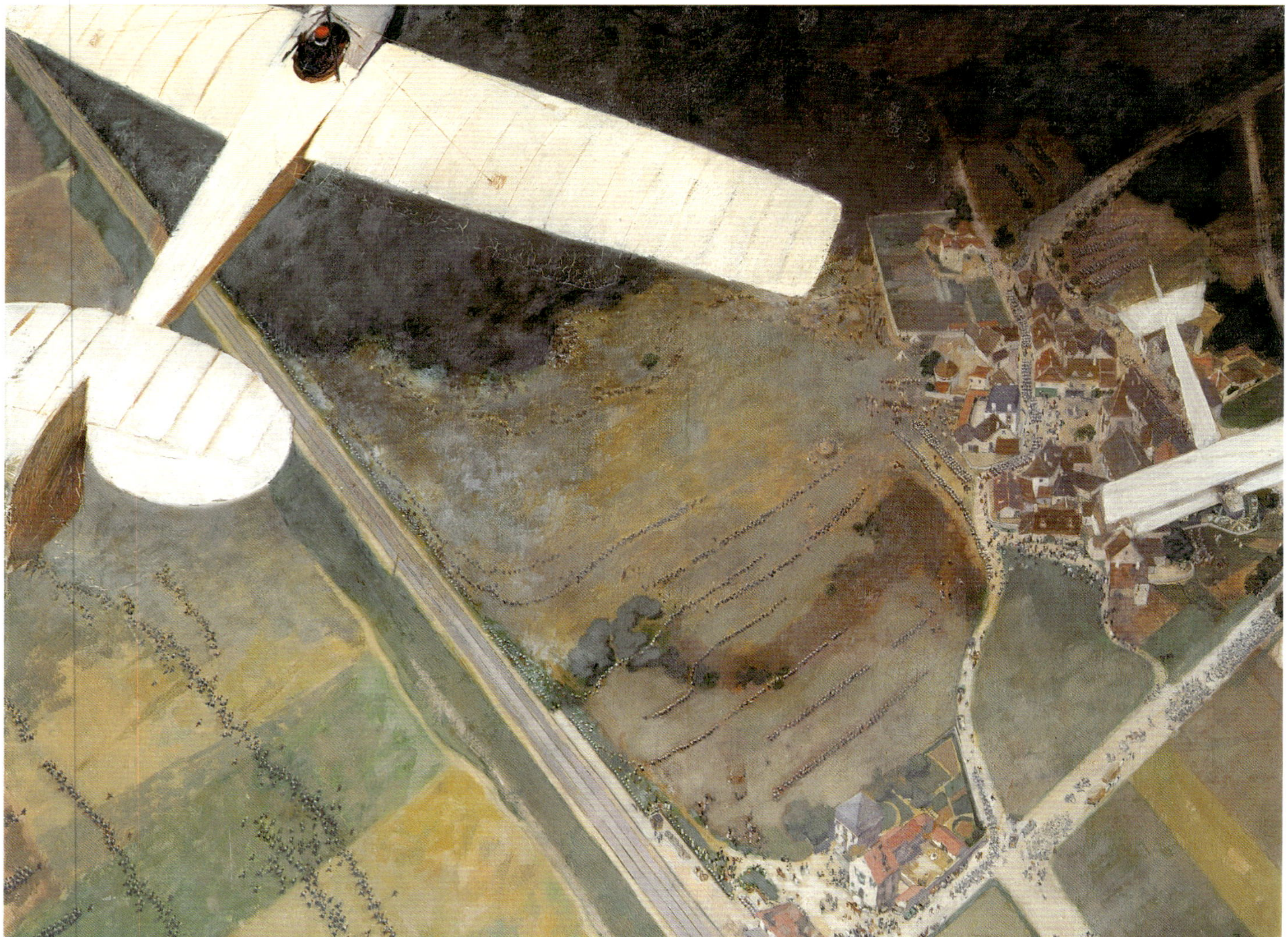

contructions to aircraft by calling each other Orville and Wilbur, Delaunay represented Blériot's biplane, and Georges de Feure even designed a revolutionary monoplane.[23]

The aeroplane revolutionised notions of time and particularly space even more than the balloon had done, because powered flight allowed control of direction and greater speed. Curiously it seems not to have been avant-garde painters who responded most imaginatively to these new technological phenomena. André Devambez, for instance, who had won the Prix de Rome in 1890, soon abandoned historical subjects for scenes of modern life. He was particularly interested in animating quotidian subjects with adventurous compositions, often using a high viewpoint. In his *Charge* of 1902 [**182**] he looks down on an urban riot from a boulevard balcony, and in order to draw the great floods that swamped Paris in 1910 he worked from the top of the Eiffel Tower.[24] Devambez was fascinated by flight, and several of the decorations commissioned from him for the new French Embassy in Vienna and painted between 1909 and 1911 represent motifs with aeroplanes and dirigibles.[25] In 1911 Devambez followed the Army's autumn manoeuvres, and the resulting canvas, *Avions fantaisistes* [**203**], is one of the most remarkable images of early aviation. He probably did not make a flight but relied on photographs taken from the aircraft, as seems to have been his practice.[26] This may explain the imaginary implication of the title, though Devambez might equally have been alluding to how flight requires the artist to imagine the landscape differently. For here he created a new version of the panorama. Horizon, that conventional requisite, is abandoned, for we look down on the landscape as if it were an animated map. Respectably finished and even Corotesque in tone, *Avions fantaisistes* details the files of soldiers and horses, the headquarters and trappings of military manoeuvres. But for all its conservatism of execution and patriotism of subject, it is a composition geared to the modern. The aircraft edge in and out of the canvas, and the sense of passing to and fro is enhanced by the angular criss-cross of fuselage and wing, road and railway. This is exaggerated by the viewpoint. We look down as if from another aeroplane, and the recession, instead of being across space to a distant horizon as it would be in a typical panorama, is here through space down to the solid ground. Monet, Pissarro and Bonnard had used figures in their panoramas to contrast their place in, and perception of, the landscape in relation to the passing train. Here Devambez adds a new dimension, the aircraft, demonstrating yet again the flexibility of the panorama as a format for representing notions about space and time.

The panorama proved itself at this period an adaptable idiom. Its potential to carry information characterising the painted landscape remained a consistency, from the detail of Devambez's *Avions fantaisistes* and Ségé's *En pays chartrain* [**192**], via the more approximate surface of an Impressionist canvas, to the dynamic simultaneity of Sonia Delaunay's *Prose du Transsibérien*. If Ségé's image of vast space implied continuity and eternal spiritual values, other paintings treated the panorama as a fictive space to be traversed, implying discontinuity. Delaunay, on the other hand, rejected a fixed image of a landscape through which the eye passes for a multiplicity of fluid images which flow out beyond the artificial confines of the picture. The panorama thus served as a vehicle for articulating ideas about passage through time and space which developed in parallel with philosophical and perceptual notions as well as technological progress. In this sense one might argue that as a landscape format it stood for certain of the opposite values to the *paysage composé*. The *repoussoir* feature, the restricting of the eye's field, the slowing of its passage through and into the imaginary space are antithetical to the true panorama. The ideal Claudian composition stands, by contrast, for stability and is thus against velocity. To limit momentum in a landscape, one might say, is to render it 'decorative', a category which will be examined in the next chapter.

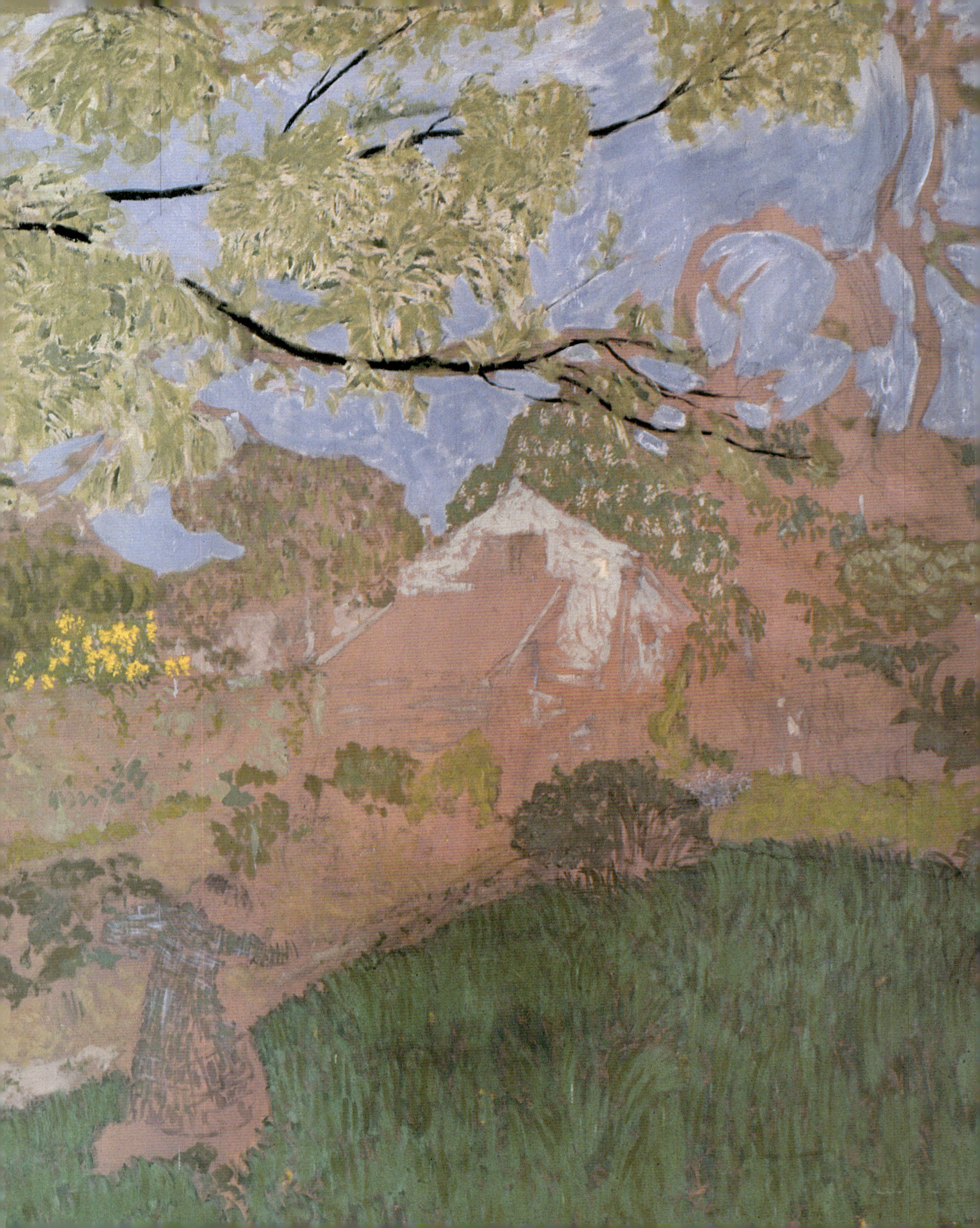

11 Landscape as Decoration

Decorative painting was of extreme importance not only aesthetically but politically in French art between 1874 and 1914. The decoration of the Pantheon in the 1870s was intended to demonstrate the vitality of the nation's art in the wake of the Franco-Prussian war, and the iconographic scheme – the life of Ste Geneviève – was selected not only because she is the patron saint of Paris but because she brought hope and succour to the city when fifth-century Gaul was invaded by northern hordes. The commissions went only to the most prestigious painters, including Alexandre Cabanel, Elie Delaunay, Jean-Paul Laurens and Puvis de Chavannes. It was Puvis who became the dominant decorator of the early Third Republic, producing between 1870 and his death in 1898 mural paintings (executed in his studio in Paris and stuck on to the walls of their intended site) for the town halls of Paris and Poitiers, as well as for the museums of Lyon, Amiens [**208**, **210**] and Rouen. Decorators of younger generations such as Besnard, Martin or Denis [**206**, **213**, **216**] were measured against Puvis's example, for many contemporaries looking back from 1914 over forty years of French art would have argued that he had been the nation's greatest recent artist.

There was lively debate about how to define the 'decorative'. Decorative paintings, most contemporaries agreed, needed to have an overall effect, a harmonious integration of pictorial means to achieve unity. Whatever the subject, decorations should give a general impression, pleasing but not blandly unmemorable, appealing to the eye but not intrusive. Whereas grand historical themes such as the Pantheon decorations inevitably necessitated these requirements to be ordered around dominant figures, in many cases they could be happily, if not perhaps entirely, met by landscape. Appreciation of the decorative in painting was not restricted to major public decorations or figure subjects. Reviewing the first Impressionist exhibition Armand Silvestre characterised the broad handling and approximate effects that he found in the landscape paintings of Monet, Sisley and Pissarro as '*décorative*' because they sought an overall '*effet d'impression*'.[1] Some critics found similar virtues thirty years later in the very different paintings of the Fauves. 'Our young landscapists see truthfully "because they see decoratively",' wrote Louis Vauxcelles in 1906. 'The site is for them a pretext, a décor in which the figures are to be enclosed by arabesques.'[2] The terms might have changed, from emphasis on painterly *effet* to synthetic arabesque, but the general notion that a landscape painting benefited from a decorative unity was consistent. Crucially, that unity had to be achieved by economy and harmony of means. A decorative work, it was agreed, needed to be taken in at a glance, although the eye should also be able to enjoy its constituent elements in more leisurely manner. Arus's *View of Alfortville* [**193**], as we have seen, was condemned as a decorative project because it was a catalogue of disjointed details, the antithesis of the genuinely *décorative*.[3]

Within this broad consensus there were debates and disputes. In the 1890s Impressionist painters were concerned with the distinction between *décor* and *décoration*, as Virginia Spate has pointed out. If the former meant only appealing ornamentation, the latter involved a finely wrought and emotionally charged harmonisation of observation of nature and pictorial organisation on the painter's part. By such criteria Monet's paintings of Rouen Cathedral [**153**], exhibited in 1895, qualified as decorative because they were 'an interrelated group of easel paintings derived from "research" into nature'.[4] That raised another issue. Could a free-standing, portable picture qualify as decoration, or was such a rubric only applicable to a work intended for and installed within a specific architectural location? Degas was firmly of the view, as he told Pissarro in 1892, that the '*tableau-décoration* is absurd'. And in his important survey of recent decorative painters published in 1914 Achille Segard agreed, arguing that to be counted as decorative work had to be subordinate to its architectural context.[5] Such dogmatic views ran against the more liberal usage of the term current among critics from Silvestre to Vauxcelles.

It is little wonder that discussion of the decorative was so prevalent at this period because there were so many opportunities for painters to produce such work. The State and other institutions, from munici-

opposite
204
E. Vuillard
Cottage at L'Etang-la-Ville c.1899
(detail)
Beauvais, Musée départmental de l'Oise

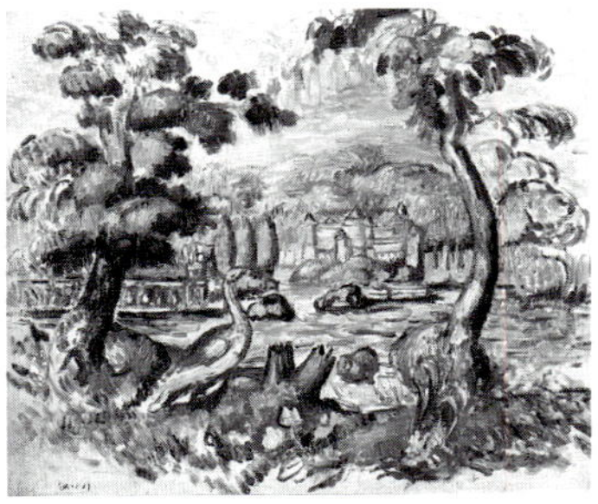

205
A. Renoir
Landscape: Project for a Tapestry 1900s?
Paris, Musée d'Orsay

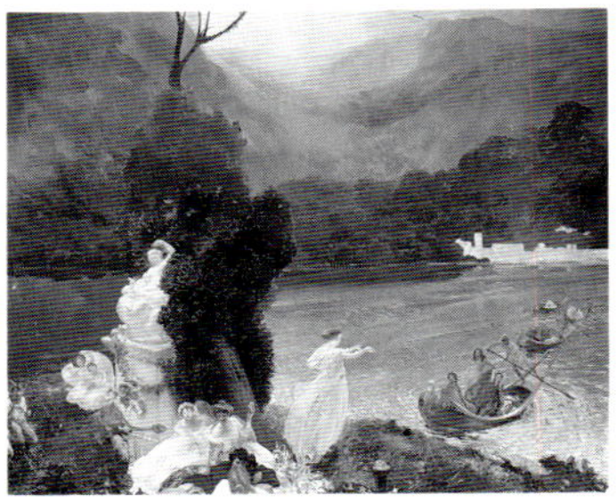

206
A. Besnard
The Island of Contentment 1900
Paris, Musée des arts décoratifs

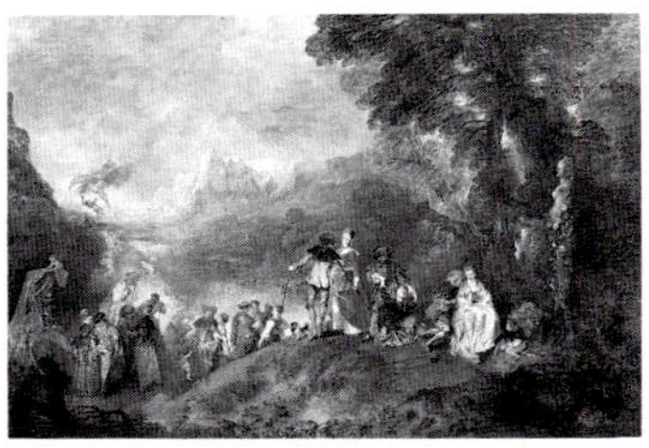

207
A. Watteau
Disembarkment from Cythera 1717
Paris, Musée du Louvre

pal authorities to commercial organisations such as banks, hotels and railway companies, frequently commissioned decorations, and such projects formed the core of many painters' careers and reputations. Inherent in the traditions and possibilities of landscape were qualities particularly suited to decorative projects. Take schemes as different as Puvis's for the museum in Lyon from the mid-1880s or Ménard's for the Sorbonne just before the First World War, Darien's for the *mairie* of Vanves in 1902 or Martin's for the Capitole in Toulouse the following year [**208**, **140**, **31**, **213**]. They are very different images, the first pair designed for cultural institutions and evoking a mythological past, the second pair for municipal buildings and describing specific locales. Yet all use landscape's capacity to stimulate in the spectator feelings of calm amd well-being, for which Puvis was particularly admired,[6] and all use landscape as a stage on which to play out scenes – be they mythological, pastoral, modern or bucolic – which convey the ideology such public decorations were intended to promote.

We will see how the decorative landscape articulated ideological values, notably by analysing Martin's Toulouse scheme, but at this point it should be emphasised how closely decoration was identified as a central element in defining French culture. Decorative painting has a long and sustained history in French art. Looking back from our period, the cultured French person could trace two strands in the national tradition. One was the grandiose depiction of mythological and historical subjects stemming from the School of Fontainebleau in the sixteenth century, passing through Le Brun in the seventeenth, to Delacroix's achievments in the Louvre and Palais Bourbon in the mid-nineteenth century. The second was the more delightful and sensual current associated with rococo painters such as Boucher and Fragonard. In the climate of nationalism so dominant at this period, writers on art frequently cited France's traditional distinction (as they saw it) in decoration and sought evidence for its continuity in the present. As Henri Mazel put it bluntly in 1890: 'Today decorative painting is the glory of France'.[7] The two currents that made up the decorative 'tradition' can broadly be defined as classical and rococo. Each stylistic trend could be characterised in its own way as particularly French: the classical because of its associations with order, balance and the Mediterranean tradition; the rococo because it alluded to the intellectual distinction of the Enlightenment and the aristocratic delights of the *ancien régime*. The former clearly interlocks with the fascination with the Mediterranean and the return to centre stage of the *paysage historique*. The considerable revival of interest in the rococo at the end of the nineteenth century was no less culturally and politically based. Its élitist connotations need to be linked to the revival of the Right in French politics; indeed, traditions of fine craftsmanship and eighteenth-century taste were points of contact between the apparently divergent French Republic and Russian Empire, which signed an alliance in 1894.[8] Rococo influence can be discerned in a wide variety of decorative landscapes of this period. Renoir's ambitious *Baigneuses* was subtitled '*essai de peinture décorative*' when it was exhibited in 1887, and its use of poses derived from Girardon's sculpture is evident together with its more general allusion to Boucher in form, palette and placing of the female nudes in a sensual landscape.[9] Painting a tapestry design [**205**], probably in the 1890s, Renoir turned to the rococo again, creating an *ancien régime* concoction of rosy chromatics, fluffy forms and aristocratic *château*. The rococo was as consistent an undercurrent in the flamboyant and successful work of Besnard as it was in Renoir's at this period. Commissioned by the Central Union of the Decorative Arts to produce a large decorative painting for their pavilion at the 1900 Universal Exhibition, Besnard produced the *Island of Contentment* [**206**], clearly

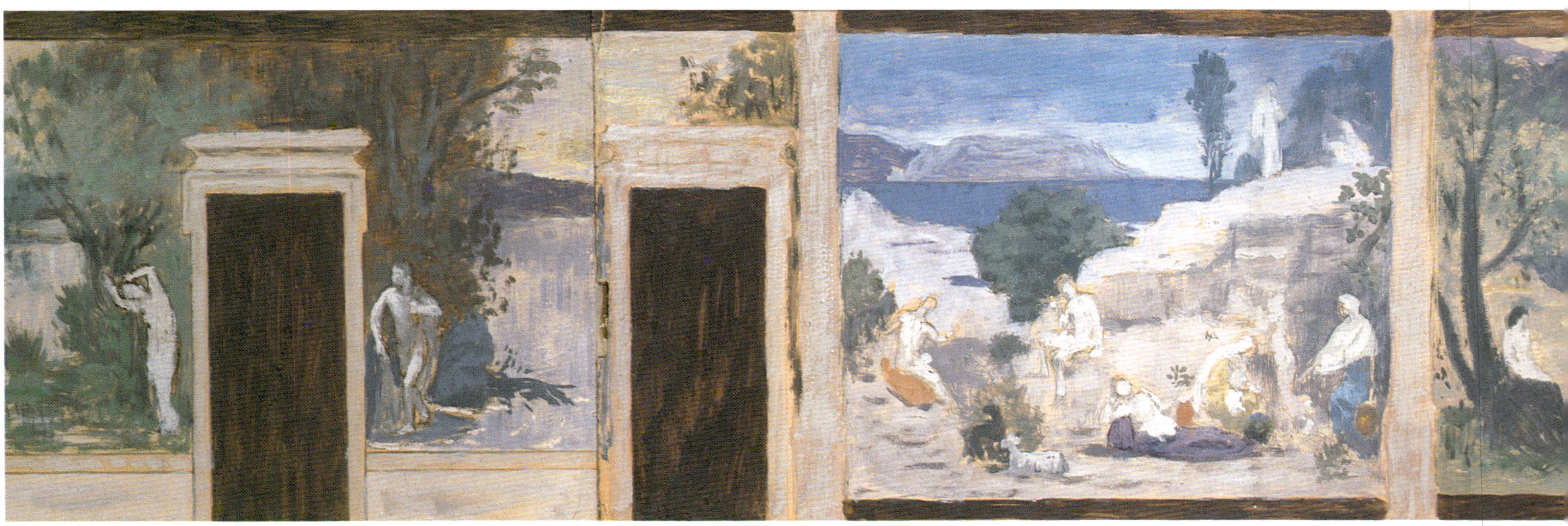

intended as a modern caprice on Watteau's *Disembarkment from Cythera*, the rococo paradigm of the genre [**207**].

From this it may seem that the decorative was promoted by conservative forces of nationalism and traditionalism. However, there was substantial encouragement from the direction of the avant-garde also. Many of the desiderata of decoration – repudiation of detail and promotion of an overall sense of unity and harmony reflecting inner states of mind – closely matched the new aesthetic of Symbolism. And as painters began to develop means to achieve Symbolist qualities in their two-dimensional work, their pictures became, almost by definition, more decorative. The general impulse to simplify forms and draughtsmanship, the ideal of *synthèse*, which became so important from the 1880s, as well as the unified pointillist surfaces of the Neo-Impressionists and the flat zones of colour of the Nabis, all served the decorative purpose. And the rise of Art Nouveau, with its emphasis on breaking down the barriers between the fine and the applied arts, encouraged painters to undertake work which crossed those hitherto definite frontiers.

Maurice Denis is perhaps the ideal example linking these trends. In the 1890s he produced not only painted decorations but designs for tiles, wallpaper, ceramics and stained glass. By the following decade he had achieved international standing, based on prestigious commissions for decorative paintings. When Segard came to account for this career in 1914 he saw Denis as fusing disparate influences, both from the Renaissance past and from modern painting such as Gauguin and the Neo-Impressionists, into a style based on Symbolist premises.[10]

Another important inspiration for Denis was Puvis de Chavannes, who by the 1880s was recognised by avant-garde and conservative voices alike as the leading decorative painter in France. Puvis's decorative schemes were essentially history paintings. To a public servant such as Léonce Bénédite, curator of the Musée du Luxembourg, this was how it should be: 'No subject lends itself more appropriately to decoration than history. We want to find ourselves in front of a sort of ideal, heroic world, distanced from ours by time or a light veil of abstraction. That way … we attach an idea of moral mission to the decoration of public walls.'[11] A discreet moral programme underpins the paintings Puvis made for the stairwell of his home-town Lyon between 1883 and 1886 [**208**].[12] Puvis chose the programme himself; it was outlined both in his contract and on a long canvas [**209**] on which he sketched out the scheme. The central panel at the head of the stairs represents the sacred grove of the muses, and the panels facing each other from the adjacent walls show 'the two essential elements of art: form and feeling'. These took the form of *Vision antique*, an image of draped and nude figures in a classical pastoral, and *Inspiration chrétienne*, representing the painter-monks of early Renaissance Italy. In all three panels landscape plays a crucial rôle. Puvis himself described how in the *Bois sacré* 'the landscape, bathed by the silent light of evening, is constrained by high mountains which close off access to this favoured place, only allowing a band of sky to be seen. From the earth, strewn with shrubs and flowers, grow the trees of the epic heights: laurel,

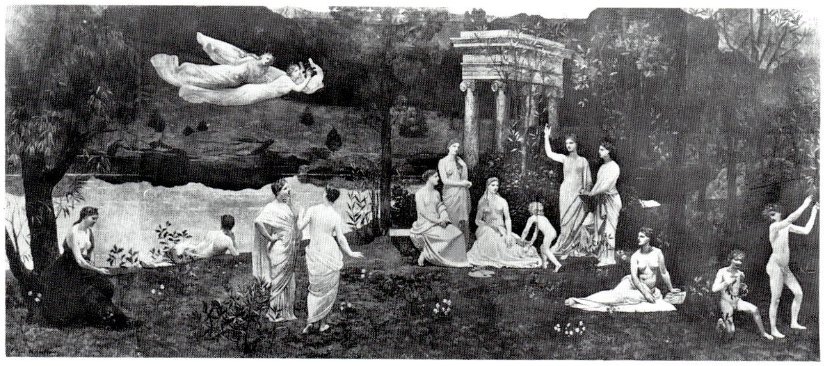

208
P. Puvis de Chavannes
Stairwell at Musée des beaux-arts, Lyon, centring on *Le Bois sacré* 1884

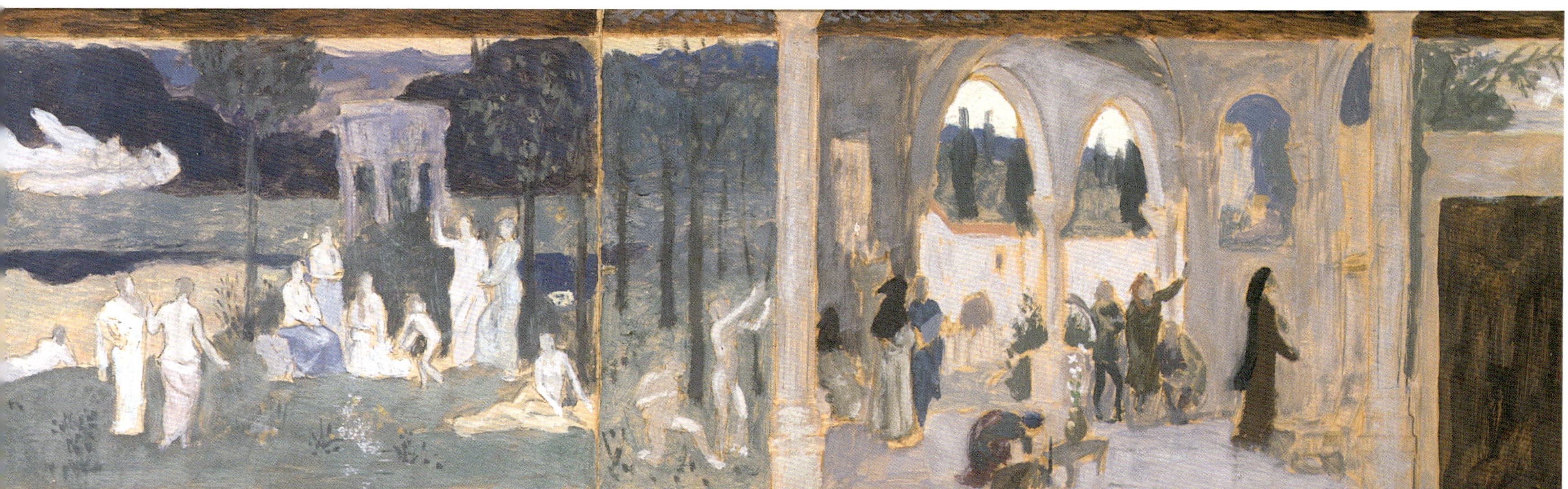

209
P. Puvis de Chavannes
Sketches for the Lyon decorations: 'Inspiration chrétienne', 'Le Bois sacré', 'Vision antique' c.1883–4
Lyon, Musée des beaux-arts

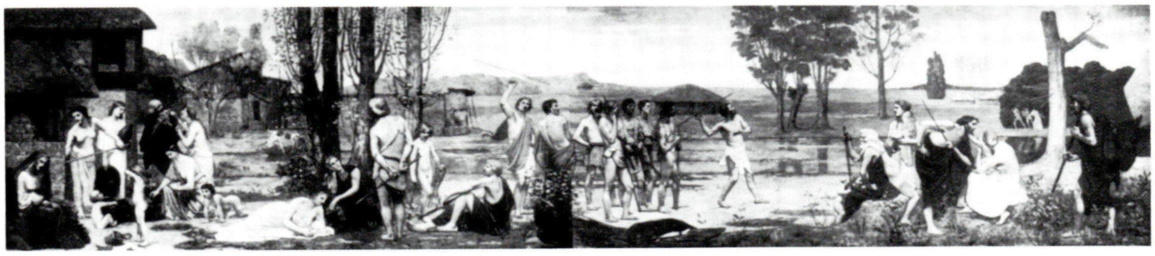

210
P. Puvis de Chavannes
Ludus pro patria 1880–2
Amiens, Musée de Picardie

pine, oak'.[13] Landscape was thus as essential as the white-draped figures for setting the ideal tone, calm and empyrean. In *Vision antique* the arid shoreline and blue sea identify the Mediterranean of the mythological past, while in *Inspiration chrétienne* beyond the monastery walls is glimpsed a cemetery punctuated by cypress trees, as Bénédite pointed out,[14] an intimation of mortality in lives given up to devotional creativity. Puvis's Lyon decorations articulate the notion that French culture is a continuation of classical art and its values, mediated by Christianity, sustaining ideas of untroubled order, dutiful work and social harmony in tune with the ideology of the Third Republic. Although these virtues are only tangentially conveyed and Puvis preferred his work to be allusive, his imagery could at times be more demonstrably nationalistic. In *Ludus pro patria* [**210**], painted for the museum of Amiens between 1880 and 1882, his frieze of villagers from some unspecified Gallic past represent the men practising their martial skills, watched by the older and younger generations whom they will be charged to defend in time of war. However generalised, the landscape inevitably recalls the flat terrain of Picardy, the region around Amiens which had seen heavy fighting between the armies of Faidherbe and von Manteuffel during the Franco-Prussian war. A decade on, however innocuously pre-Roman Puvis's decoration appeared on the surface, it was bound to suggest nationalist notions about the need for a strong army both for defence and even *revanche*. Indeed, *Ludus pro patria* conspired to give 'ancient' justification for the policy of conscription which the Third Republic had made law in 1872.

In 1900 Henri Martin was commissioned to decorate a room in the Capitole, the city hall of his native Toulouse. He exhibited half the scheme, the rustic scenes including *Men Scything* [**213**], at the Salon des artistes français in 1903, where the jury's failure to give them the medal of honour led to a public outcry. Three years later the whole scheme, now including the half representing Toulouse as well as a large number of preparatory studies, was shown at the Salon in the privileged conditions of a separate room.[15] Writing in *Art et décoration*, a prestigious journal founded a decade before to promote decorative work, Henry Marcel argued that Martin's ensemble was the most significant mural programme since Puvis's work at Amiens and Lyon. For Segard in 1914 the *Men Scything* in particular represented the paradigm of decoration; it could be taken in at once, it

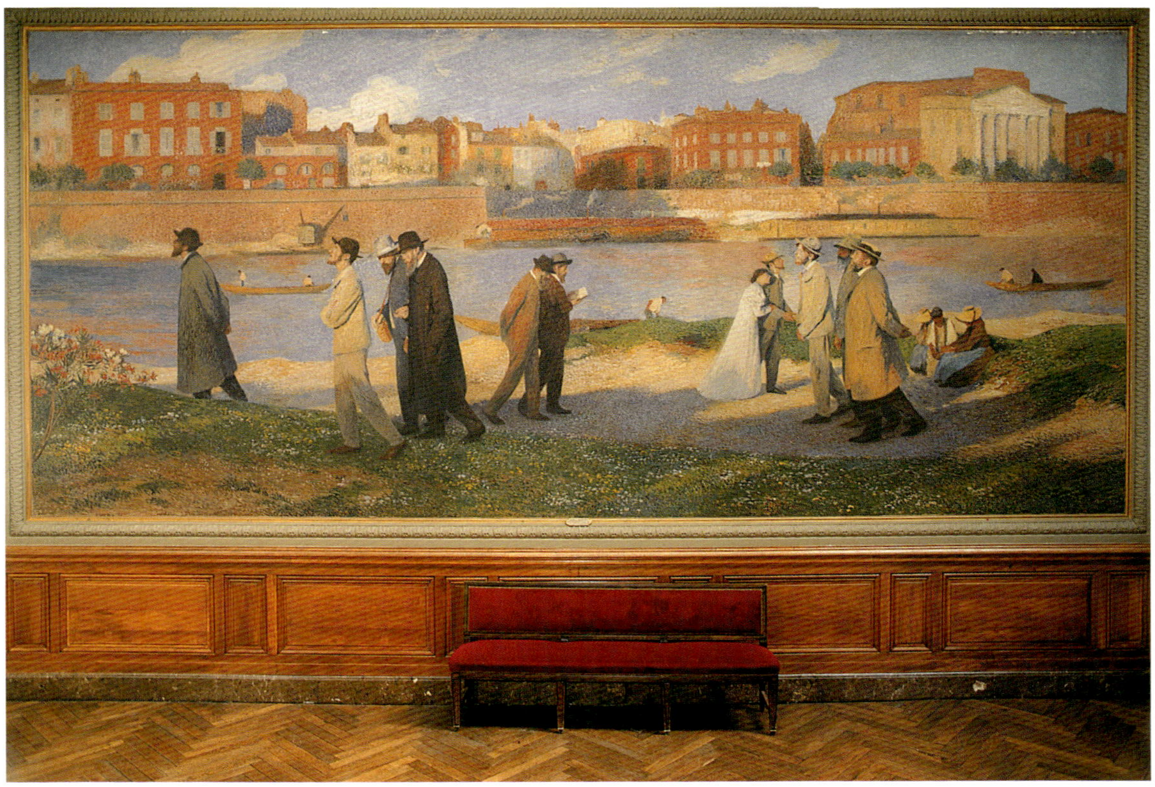

211
H. Martin
The Banks of the Garonne 1906
Toulouse, Capitole

was visually lucid yet rich enough to satisfy prolonged appreciation, and the memory of the image and its 'moral lesson' stayed with one.[16] Martin had begun with the idea of having a poet and his muse in the foreground watching the peasants at work, but had dropped the plan.[17] Such a decision concurred with a growing school of thought that found heavy historical and allegorical subjects in decorations overbearing, 'lessons in high political philosophy', preferring images drawn from nature, which could be understood by everyone.[18]

Martin's Capitole scheme ingeniously infiltrated an ideological programme into subjects that were democratically simple to read. The two halves of the room are divided into country and city, the former based on the valley of Labastide-du-Vert, near Cahors, where he had bought a house in 1900, and the latter on the banks of the Garonne as it flows through Toulouse [**211**]. Shown to the Parisian public in 1906, the ensemble – representing the verdant, sun-flooded meadows of the Lot and the red brick typical of Toulouse – must have seemed strikingly southern, a reminder of the old *septentrionaux-méridionaux* polarity. Indeed, critics were quick to point out that Martin's material was his *terre natale*,[19] respecting the panels' regional identity vis-à-vis other painters closely associated with their *pays*, such as Lhermitte and the Marne [**249**]. Martin's city/country dichotomy makes conventional distinctions. The city is constructed as a distinctly urban environment, with its domestic and public buildings and its commercial waterway, as well as a place of leisure and intellectual life. For along the banks of the Garonne stroll artists such as Martin's teacher Jean-Paul Laurens and his close friend Henri Bellery-Desfontaines, as well as the great socialist orator Jean Jaurès, wearing a boater: men of the region all. The rural panels represent the valley floor, the surrounding ridges flattening out the space just as the buildings do in the Toulouse paintings. The meadows of Labastide-du-Vert, in *Men Scything*, are the site of physical labour, the sweeping actions of the peasants echoing each other across the long shadows of the evening light. Labastide-du-Vert is imagined as a bucolic paradise, almost a vast *hortus conclusus*, in which Martin could rehearse other legible themes. The main rural panels follow the four seasons, centring on the great summer scything scene. *Spring* represents a peasant lad courting a shepherdess among blossoming cherry trees, *Autumn* a bent old woman with her goats under the golden leaves, and *Winter* the village under snow. By including the dancing girls and the baby in *Men Scything*, Martin also managed to contrive within the seasons another cycle, that of human life: childhood, youth, maturity and old age. Thus the ensemble set up the country as a place of feeling and the city as one of thought. The masterpiece is *Men Scything*, and it is especially clear from the preparatory oil study in monochrome [**212**] that Martin arrived at a solution which is both pictorially lucid and ideologically adept. The repetition of the labourers' rhythmic poses and of the noble poplars, as well as the elision of their shadows, suggests a timeless harmony between man and nature, within the seasonal cycle. The willingness of these individuals to pursue their goal in common, the similarity of the men's stances and costumes, the sharing of their communal task, surely evoke the Republican values of

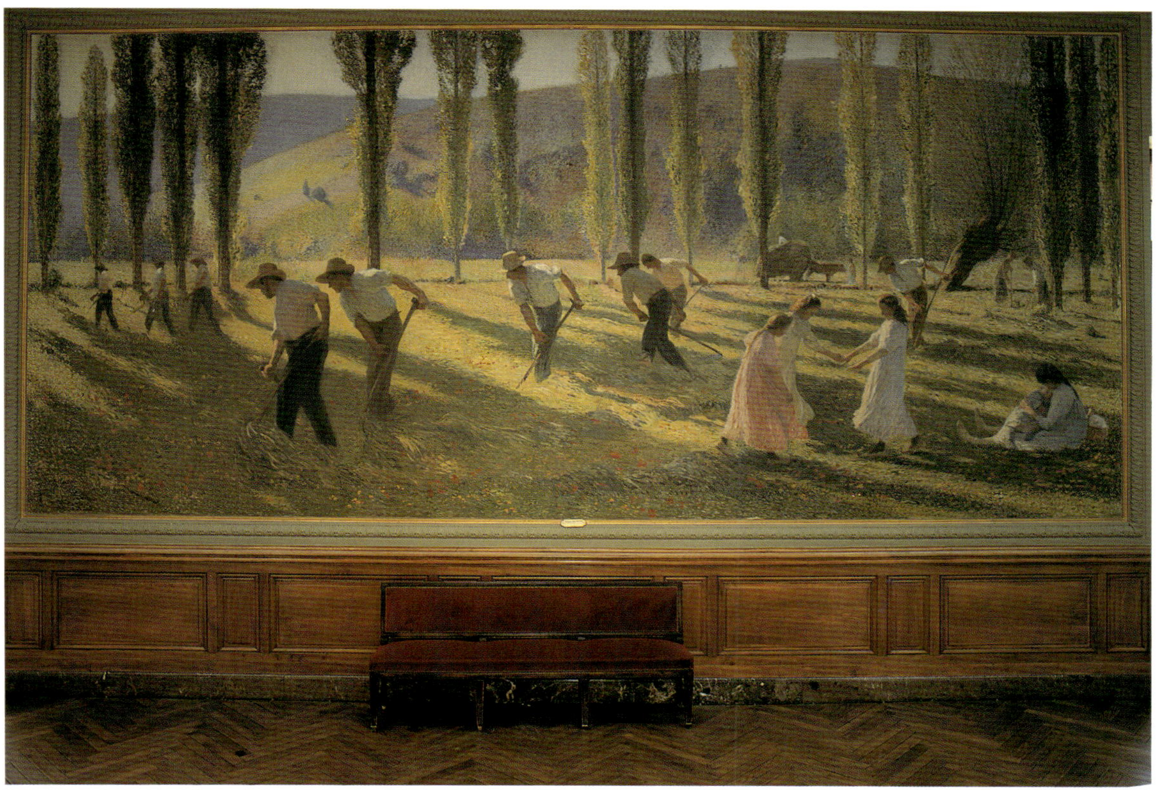

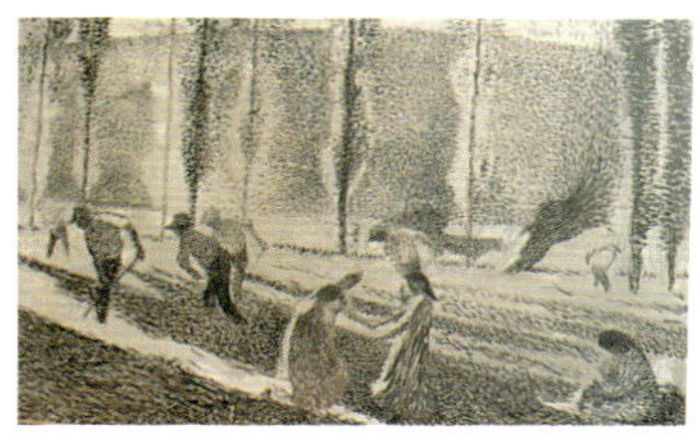

212
H. Martin
Study for 'Men Scything' *c.*1902–3
Private Collection

213
H. Martin
Men Scything 1903
Toulouse, Capitole

214
K. -X. Roussel
Study for 'The Cortège of Bacchus'
*c.*1912
Private Collection

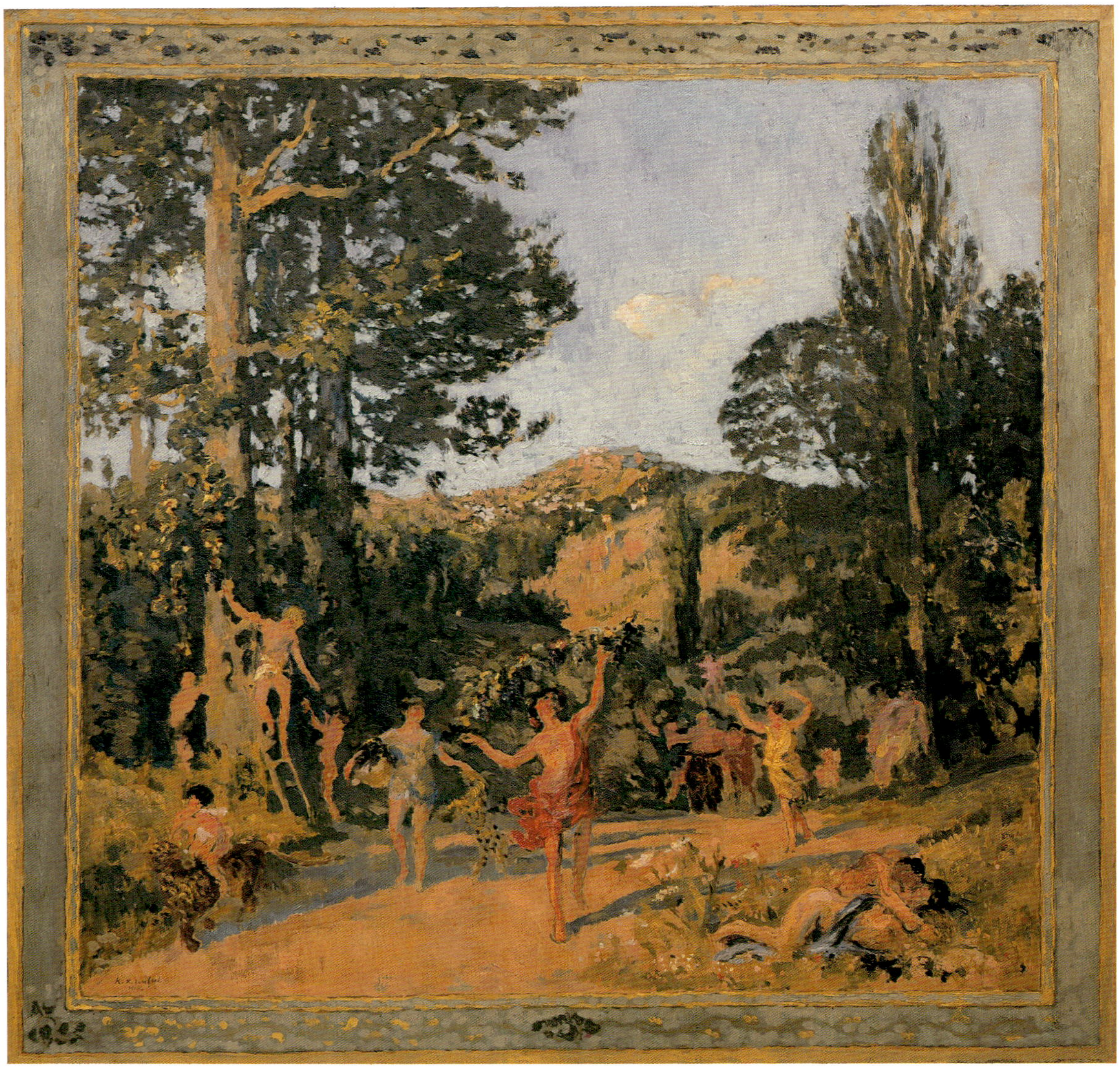

Liberty, Equality and Fraternity, as does the *Banks of the Garonne*, with its brotherhood of freedom of thought. Critics commonly referred the bucolic *Men Scything* and other rural motifs to Virgil,[20] praising Martin's grand scheme simultaneously for its allusions to the classical and for the Frenchness of its celebration of *terre natale*. No other decorative scheme of this period managed to combine such rich associations of meaning with such a high quality of pictorial expression.

Opportunities for grand public decorations did not come only from State or municipal patronage. One of the most remarkable of the commercial organisations to provide an important series of commissions was the Théâtre des Champs-Elysées, built between 1906 and 1913 on the avenue Montaigne in the fashionable heart of Paris. The theatre was designed by several architects, and its decoration was shared by a number of artists. René Lalique designed a glass dome and Antoine Bourdelle sculpted friezes for the balcony. Maurice Denis painted the cupola surrounding the dome with allegories of the great musical forms and Vuillard decorated the foyer of the adjacent studio-theatre with scenes from comedies old and new.[21]

Ker-Xavier Roussel was commissioned to paint the enormous drop-curtain, measuring seven-and-a-half by over eight metres. With over a decade's experience of painting mythological and pastoral scenes, Roussel was no doubt expected to choose such a theme for this ambitious project. He selected the *Cortège of Bacchus*, which he developed via at least four oil sketches. One of these [**214**] differs only slightly from the final curtain – which includes a glimpse of the sea in the rear space, making it more explicitly Mediterranean – thus giving a good indication of Roussel's final scheme. In the centre is the prancing Bacchus, draped in red and brandishing a garland. To each side are his acolytes, a couple making love on the right, a boy on a leopard to the left, while behind them trail the remainder of this delightful gang, cavorting and picking fruit as they go, with Silenus bringing up the rear unsteadily on his donkey. These antics take place within an idyllic landscape drenched with golden light and filled by two great clumps of trees which frame the scene, holding the vast composition in place.

Once the curtain was installed Roussel had to retouch it due to the effect of the theatre's electric light on the colours.[22] The decorator always has to integrate the work with the environment; where Puvis had had to be scrupulous about matching his tones to the surrounding stone, here Roussel had to adapt his painting to the latest technology. Roussel's choice of imagery may appear at first sight to typify the classicism that had pervaded the work of younger French painters for almost two decades and was by 1913 tinged with reactionary ideals. However the *Cortège of Bacchus* is not without a subversive streak. Roussel was keen on Nietzsche's ideas, owning a volume of his work.[23] Nietzsche argued that Christianity had harmfully suppressed man's natural pagan energy, and called for a return to this source of dynamism and joy, a force which had both regenerative and destructive powers. Such ideas were appealing to young intellectuals around the turn of the century, suspicious of the Catholic revival; Derain and, as we have mentioned, Cross were among the initiates. In 1905 Ernest Seillière had published an essay specifically on the imagery of the dance in Nietzsche's writing, in which the Dionysian dance was held up as an expression of self, at once energetic, bestial and divine.[24] These were notions exactly in tune with Roussel's imagery and they may have lain behind the roistering sensuality which he appropriately attributed to Bacchus's band. How ironic that his celebration of the pagan should hang immediately below Denis's cupola, in which Lyric Drama is represented by Parsifal holding up the Holy Grail!

During the 1890s there was an increasing feeling that decorative painting had a place not only in public spaces but, importantly, in the private home environment. Whether such decorative works should be permanently installed, as Degas insisted, or could be free-hanging paintings of decorative character, as the critic Gustave Soulier argued in 1897,[25] was a continuing debate. Another supporter of the idea of domestic decoration was Bénédite who argued that: 'One senses nowadays that increasingly our daily habits are infiltrated by the need to arrange everyday things with taste, order, discernment, harmony'.[26] He seems to have been articulating obliquely a complex of ideas. Art Nouveau sought to combine the fine and applied arts into a unified whole, and the domestic interior filled with decorative paintings and exquisite objects fulfilled that modern aesthetic ideal. It was an élitist one, of course, but there was a bourgeois clientele with the taste and funds to satisfy it. The dining-room of Bellery-Desfontaines, who was an artist and cabinet-maker, is an apt example [**215**]. The room was designed as an ensemble, the furniture in harmony with the decorative paintings of Mediterranean pastorals by his friend Henri Martin. In the same year, 1908, Matisse published his 'Notes of a Painter', advocating decorative precepts for which the Bellery-Desfontaines room, so very different from his own work, also stood. Matisse's concept of decoration meant 'an art of balance, of purity and serenity, devoid of troubling or depressing subject matter, an art which could be for every mental worker, be he businessman or man of letters, for example, a soothing, calming influence on the mind, something like a good armchair in which to rest from physical fatigue'.[27] The decorative canvas or interior, then, was designed to act as 'social restorative'[28] to the French bourgeoisie, a purpose to which landscape, with its conventional associations of tranquillity and escape, was well suited.

Matisse's reference to the mind suggests another dimension. Debora Silverman has explained how at the *fin-de-siècle* French psychologists were especially interested in the relationship between the domestic interior we inhabit and our interior mental life.[29] An idealised domestic environment such as Bellery-Desfontaine's, with its serene landscapes representing a healthy outdoor life and people in harmony with each other and with nature, was by this account a psychologically positive one. And one should not forget the social and political climate of the turn of the century, with the Dreyfus Affair, the rift between Church and State over education, colonial confrontation with Britain, increasing pressure for *revanche* against Germany, the rise of the organised Left and the proliferation of strikes. With a public life of such division, turmoil and uncertainty, it is no wonder that the French bourgeoisie turned to the decorative landscape to bring into its private sphere a sense of peace, pleasure and order.

The diverse initiatives of Art Nouveau were effectively packaged up for this market by entrepreneurs such as Siegfried Bing. In 1895 Bing commissioned from Maurice Denis decorations for a girl's bedroom. Denis took as a theme Schumann's *Lieder* cycle *Frauenliebe und Leben*, producing seven long thin panels as well as designing the furniture. By the turn of the century the paintings belonged to the German Count Kessler at Weimar; these originals have since been lost, but at that time Denis copied them for his own bedroom.[30] They represent motifs of

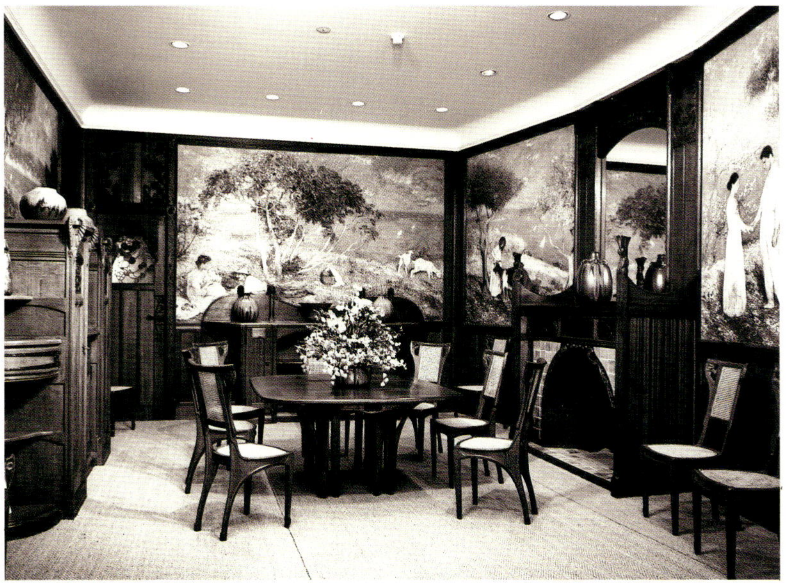

215
H. Martin
Dining-room Decorations for Henri Bellery-Desfontaines 1908
Beauvais, Musée départmental de l'Oise

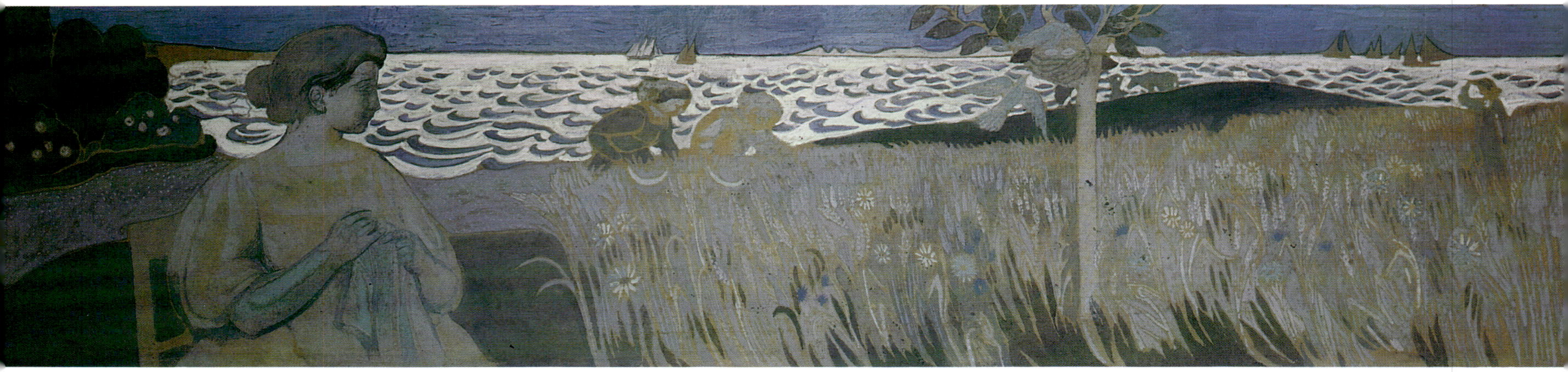

216
M. Denis
Embroidery by the Sea
designed 1895; replica, 1901–22,
Saint-Germain-en-Laye, Musée
départmental du 'Prieuré'

romance and maternity, beginning with a scene of engagement, and including marriage, birth, childhood and so on. *Embroidery by the Sea* [**216**] is typical, with its elongated format, graceful linearity and subdued crepuscular tones of blues and greys with which Denis unified his scheme. The subject represents the woman in that brief, idyllic phase between marriage and childbirth; whether pregnant or hoping to be, she looks towards the off-centre tree where doves are nesting. Typically of Denis's work, it is autobiographical. He married Marthe Meurier in 1893, and they spent their honeymoon at Perros-Guirec on the north coast of Brittany, the landscape of which he echoed in *Embroidery by the Sea*. Their first child was born in October 1894, although he tragically died early the following year. This panel is more than just a personal image of waiting for the first-born. Another typical feature of Denis's work is the way it served to convey his devout Catholicism. The doves were surely intended to suggest not only the maternal instinct but also the Holy Spirit, making this painting something of an oblique Annunciation. For Denis, to find parallels between daily life and the New Testament was to reassert the presence of biblical truth in everyday experience. Writing about these decorations in 1907 Denis's friend Adrien Mithouard praised them as 'very gentle images of discreet innocence and maternal emotion',[31] an unsurprising response from a politician and writer whose periodical *L'Occident* gave voice to far Right views shared by Denis. But the decorations cut no ice with Pissarro when he saw them at Bing's Gallery in 1895. He found the 'lugubrious' tones in 'goose-shit grey' utterly inappropriate for a girl's room.[32] This response may have been due to Pissarro's ideological differences with Denis, but it is more likely because of a different attitude to decoration. As we have seen, the old Impressionist conceived of the decorative as involving an intense response to nature. The young Symbolist's highly synthetic landscape ordered around pleasing arabesques rather than grounded in observation presented a concept of *décoration* antithetical to Pissarro.

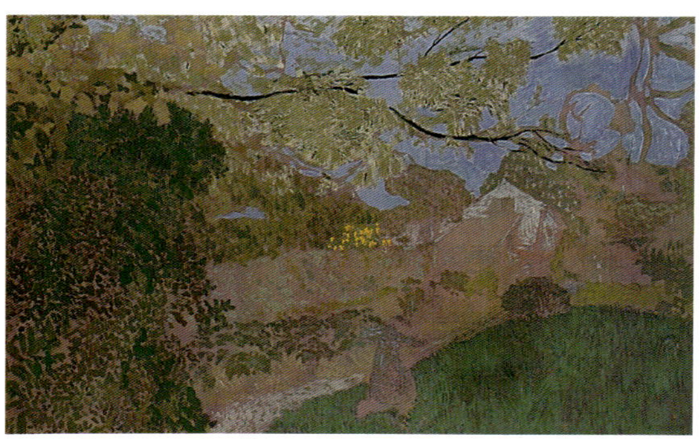

217
E. Vuillard
Cottage at L'Etang-la-Ville c.1899
Beauvais, Musée départmental de l'Oise

During the 1890s Vuillard produced half a dozen substantial decorative schemes for bourgeois friends and clients, only two of which do not have landscape settings. About 1899 he started another large decorative panel which he did not completely finish, perhaps because it was uncommissioned.[33] Where Puvis's decorations and even, by somewhat stretching the point, Martin's arguably fell within the classical tradition of French decoration, Vuillard's unfinished *Cottage at L'Etang-la-Ville* [**204, 217**] could be interpreted as belonging within the rococo. While not harking back to the eighteenth century so deliberately as Besnard's contemporaneous *Island of Contentment* [**206**], Vuillard's fluffy forms and pastel palette are loosely reminiscent of Fragonard's decorations of the 1770s. The unresolved state of the large panel allows one to see how Vuillard worked. He first covered the whole surface with the rich pink tone, building up on it, the darker colours first. Thus in the foliage on the left the black branches preceded the olive leaves, over which successive paler greens were placed. The yellow accents at the centre were applied late. Although Vuillard used recession in his composition, placing the garden and cottage on a diagonal, the whole image reads decoratively – generalised, harmonious and relatively flat – because the pink base gives it unity. L'Etang-la-Ville, where Vuillard's brother-in-law Roussel lived and whose daughter is represented in the garden, lies between Versailles and Paris. It is a suburb, and in his decoration Vuillard adopted the stock notion of the suburb as a rural retreat, untainted by the city. Contemporary critics noted the tendency of his decorations to produce an artificially idyllic image of the countryside, understandable, suggested

Segard, in paintings made by a city-dweller for the apartments of city-dwellers.[34]

Whereas artists such as Denis and Vuillard had formed their work around ideas of the decorative from the outset of their careers, for an older painter like Monet the adaptation of his instincts as an observer to the requirements of decoration was a long drawn out process. Although Monet had been brought up in a naturalist tradition, his painting had sporadically but regularly come to terms with the decorative, and in certain respects provides an index of different possibilities for adapting natural motifs to such purposes. In 1876 he had produced four large panels for the country residence of his then patron Ernest Hoschédé.[35] These canvases do not stray far from his typical style during that period, the slightly greater attention to broader, quite uniform handling and a certain consistency in the chromatics of each panel in accordance with their function. Nevertheless, critics reviewing them at the 1877 Impressionist exhibition were happy to consider them as decorations.[36] Between 1882 and 1885 he worked on and off on painted door-panels for his dealer Durand-Ruel's Paris apartment.[37] These motifs of fruit and flowers vary from conventional floral still-lifes to close-up images of blooms derived from the example of Japanese woodblock printmakers such as Hiroshige. By the following decade his notion of the decorative had shifted ground again, and was centred on the series of paintings of the same motif harmonised in colour and touch and exhibited as an ensemble.

His water garden at Giverny, which he had begun to cultivate in 1893, provided further new opportunities for him to develop his decorative ideas. The early canvases of the garden, frequently motifs of the Japanese bridge of the kind he showed at Durand-Ruel's gallery in 1900, adhered to the conventional landscape structure with a horizon bisecting the motif. In the paintings that he made between 1906 and 1909 he abandoned that traditional armature. Instead, the artist looks down diagonally from his vantage point on the bank to the waterlily pads floating on the surface, which itself reflects the trees and clouds above the pond.[38] Monet had attempted views down on water before, notably when working in the bleak moorland of the Creuse valley in the Massif Central in 1889. These close-ups of the rushing torrent had been a challenge to his virtuosity in translating what he observed into a vivid painterly analogue of reality, and to the capacity of his *sensation* to document nature's dynamic.[39] These paintings were loyal to the typical horizontal landscape format (however untypical a view down across a mountain stream), the canvas shape which most closely corresponds to the elongated oval of the human field of vision. In 1907–8 Monet painted a number of motifs of the waterlily pond in a circular format [**218**]. The tondo is very unlike our field of vision, thus distinctly artificial and decorative. All the tondos exclude the banks of the pond or the overhanging trees. Foliage and the sky above are discernable only as reflections in the painted surface. In other words those quintessential staples of landscape painting – trees, clouds, even land itself – are systematically excluded from Monet's canvases, except as reflections. This abolition of the horizon and exile of the conventional features of the genre, or at least their double demotion to reflections of the unseen, render these paintings among Monet's most suggestive, even Symbolist, images. Their great distance from naturalist convention was recognised when the waterlily pond paintings were shown *en masse* in 1909, Roger Marx noting that Monet had broken the last links that tied him to the Barbizon tradition in which he had been schooled.[40] Detached so from naturalism, the waterlily canvases were distinctly decorative, as the Manufacture nationale des Gobelins recognised when in 1911–12 it used one of the tondo motifs as the basis for a tapestry.[41]

Underlying the *fin-de-siècle*'s fascination with the decorative were distinct paradoxes. The branch of painting that was intended to be soothingly harmonious and easy on the eye nevertheless provoked differences of opinion and purpose. Whether designed to promote Republican values in a public place or to give an aura of tranquillity in a private space, the decorative still stood for a discernible and celebrated trait in national culture. And for all that decorative work was meant to be generalised and its broad effects swiftly taken in, paintings as different as Martin's *Men Scything* or Monet's waterlily gardens were founded on close observation.

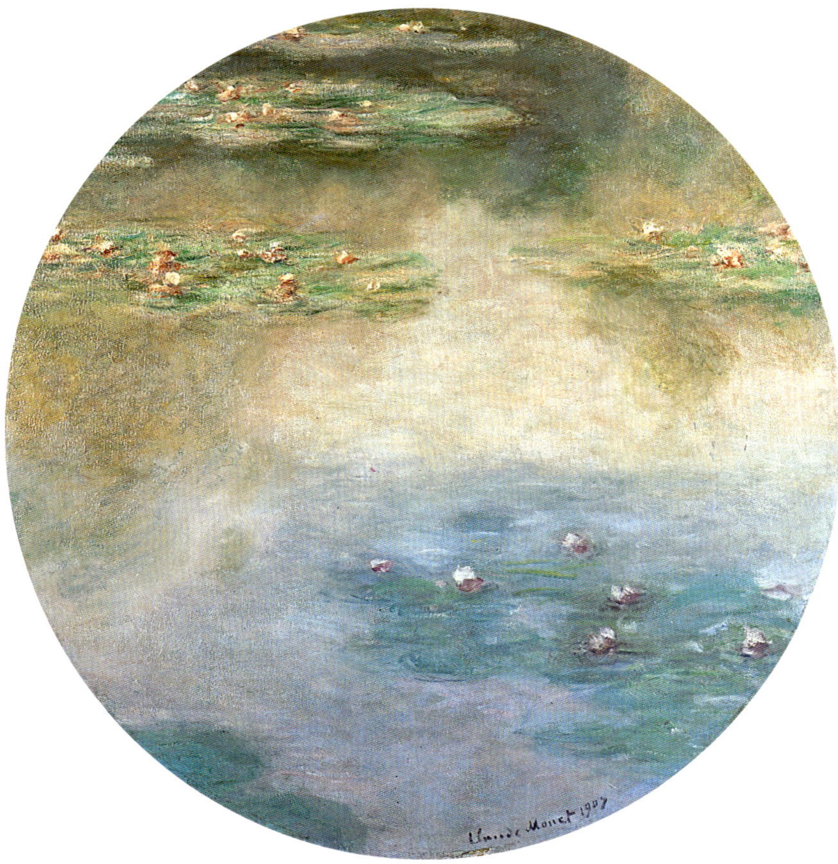

218
C. Monet
Waterlilies 1907
Saint-Etienne, Musée d'art moderne

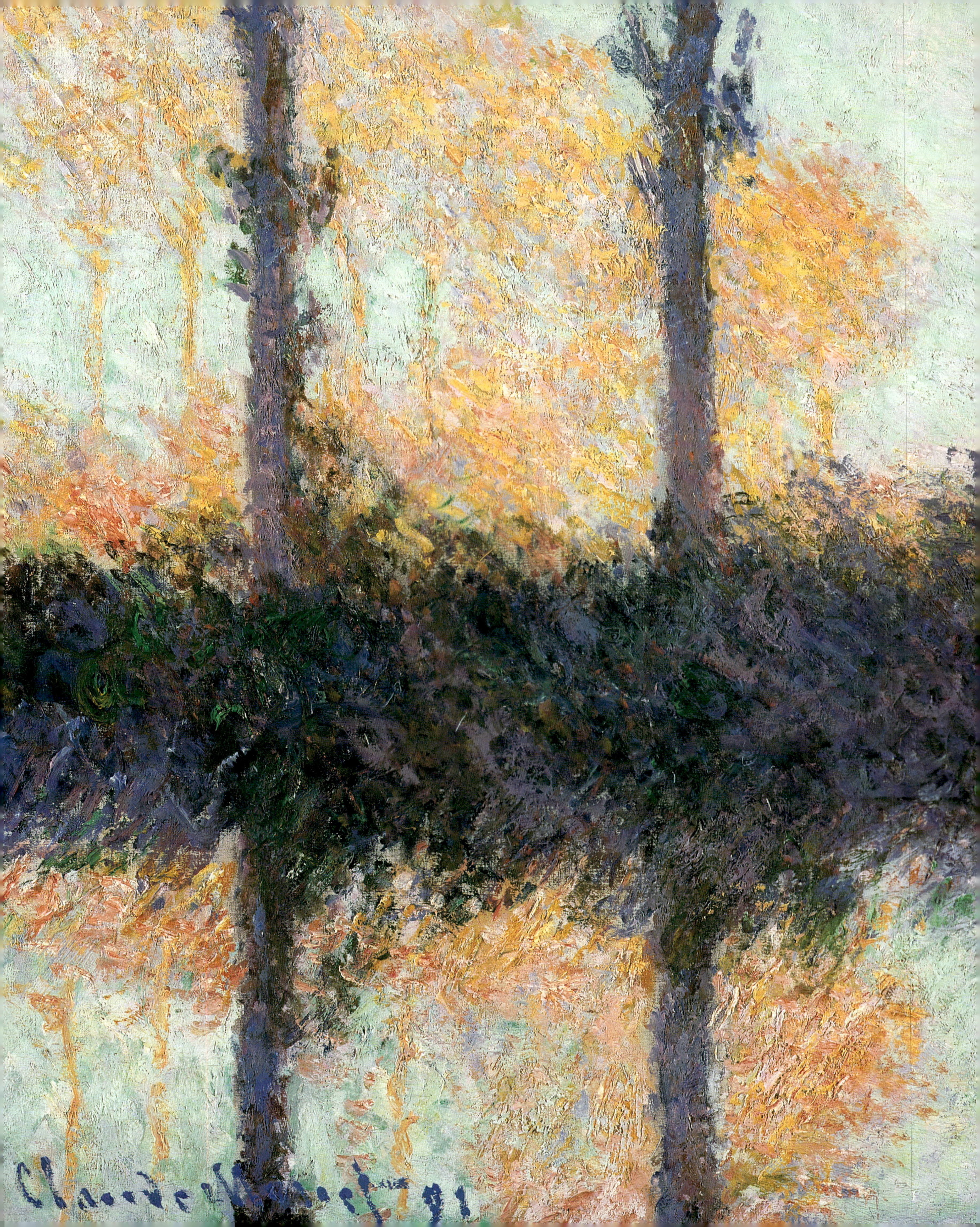
Claude Monet 91

12 Landscapes in Series

In May 1891 Monet exhibited fifteen *Grainstack* paintings [**239**] at the Durand-Ruel gallery. Less than a year later, in February and March 1892, he showed the same number of canvases of poplar tree motifs at the same dealer's. These were followed in May 1895 by twenty paintings of Rouen Cathedral [**153**], again at Durand-Ruel's. Defecting temporarily to the rival gallery of Georges Petit, in June 1898 a number of serial groups were displayed, among them eighteen *Mornings on the Seine* and again seven canvases of Rouen Cathedral. In 1900, back with Durand-Ruel, Monet exhibited thirteen paintings of the Japanese footbridge in his Giverny garden. This extraordinary catalogue of five major shows within a decade, all based on pictures which formed series, had a cumulative and dominating effect on both contemporary and current thinking. By forming his career in his fifties on the concept of the series, Monet gave the impression of having forged the idea. That hegemony has lodged in our understanding of landscape painting at this period, and in the most exhaustive account of Monet's activity as a painter of series no consideration is given to the contemporaneous and even precedent groups and serial images of artists as diverse as Sisley, van Gogh and Signac.[1] The account that follows, by no means an exhaustive catalogue of serial painting at this period, is intended to demonstrate how current such possibilities were and to sketch some distinctions between different initiatives.

The idea of creatively repeating the same landscape motif, rather than merely painting a replica, did not easily accord with the nineteenth-century imagination. Writing of Jan van Goyen in his 1881 monograph on seventeenth-century Dutch painting Henry Havard dismissed his images as too uniform. Havard's decision to reproduce two examples which showed the same site with minor changes was presumably to highlight their monotony rather than to show up nuances of variation.[2] The positivist philosophy which had given birth to naturalism, the dominant aesthetic of the mid-nineteenth century, emphasised the scientific study of the physical world. By this token the repeated representation of a motif was an understandable means of registering factual material about external reality. Caillebotte, for example, was only one of many artists who did this, painting probably in the mid-1870s a group of oil sketches of the same motif at different times of day, all of approximately the same size.[3] Pissarro used watercolour for such exercises, and in 1890 produced a substantial number of sheets, again usually of the same size, representing the view from his studio window under different weather conditions. Frequently these were annotated with the day's date and even the particular *effet*.[4] Systematic accumulation of data was thus one motive for repeating images of the same landscape. Another was convenience. For the landscape painter on a campaign in the countryside, working out of doors, it was practical not to have to shift one's equipment too often but to focus on views which, if not exactly identical, were at least familial. All the Impressionist *plein-airistes* did this, and Monet in particular had produced pairs and informal clusters of paintings since the 1860s.[5]

The group of eight pastels that Sisley exhibited at the Durand-Ruel gallery in the summer of 1888 thus fit into a pattern of established practice. Unfairly neglected by recent art historians,[6] they may be the first instance of an artist publicly displaying a consciously grouped series of landscapes. Sisley represented a view from his house at Moret, a small town to the south-east of Paris, looking over the railway yard [**220, 221**]. They are winter scenes, showing different conditions of snow and frost under varied light effects, which Sisley identified in a list he sent to his dealer.[7] He also characterised them as a unit, referring to a '*Suite de 8 pastels*', and together they catalogue a sequential span of 180 degrees from his window vantage. At once practical – made indoors during inclement weather – and naturalistic in their charting of climate and site, the suite had a commercial potential which Sisley also seems to have recognised. Made in a concentrated bout of observation, they required no inconvenient travel to produce a saleable body of work, which suited the recent market revival of the pastel medium. Monet for his part was not slow to exploit the inherent commercial advantages of serial work.

It is surely also true that representing the same site over and over again in the name of naturalistic

219
C. Monet
The Four Trees 1891 (detail)
New York, Metropolitan Museum, The H. O. Havemeyer Collection

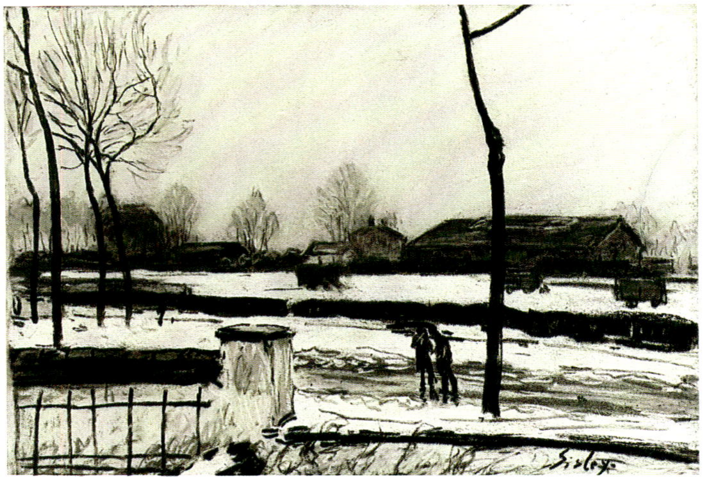

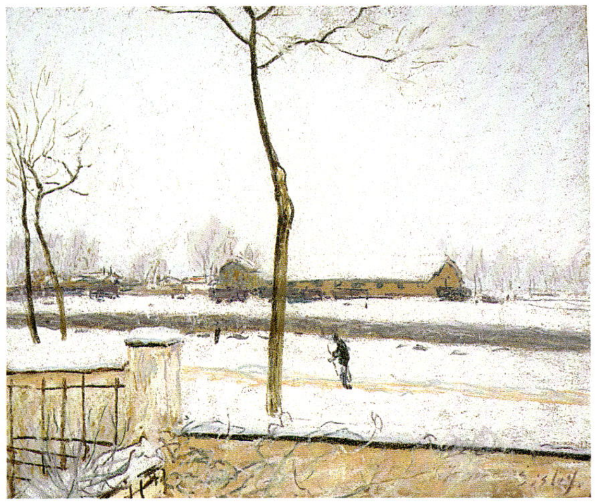

left
220
A. Sisley
Railway Station at Moret 1888
Wuppertal, Von der Heydt Museum

right
221
A. Sisley
Railway Station at Moret 1888
Edinburgh, National Gallery of Scotland

observation was not merely a matter of objective study. It also gave the painter a sense of coming to grips with a landscape and its *effets*; as Paul Tucker has suggested of Monet's closely related representations of Belle-Isle in 1886, the artist seems to have wanted 'to know a place so intimately that he could feel a certain mastery over it'.[8] As we have seen in the case of Monet's images of Rouen Cathedral [**153**], serial representations of a motif could be used both to evoke a range of feelings, stimulated by varied light, colour or weather, or to concentrate on conjuring up a single emotion by cumulative impact. That the series had affective import for the viewer is suggested by Félix Fénéon's reaction to Sisley's pastels in 1888, in which he spoke of the 'powerful sensation' made by the repetition of this 'desolate' motif.[9] The preparedness of this young critic to respond to serial imagery not just as naturalistic data but in emotional terms is itself indicative of an aesthetic shift. Coincidentally 1888 saw the publication of a new novel by Francis Poictevin, titled as it happens *Paysages*. The review by Fénéon's colleague Gustave Kahn explained how the novel was constructed unconventionally, diminishing narrative but instead using 'the juxtaposition of *sensations* to evoke, by their series' the passage of a banal year spent in different places. Kahn praised Poictevin's handling of 'slight and infinite variations of *décor*', comparing this to the skills of Impressionist painters, by whom he may have meant friends attuned to the Symbolist aesthetic such as Seurat and Signac rather than Monet or Sisley.[10] Symbolists emphasised the suggestive and emotive qualities of a work of art. This downgrading of the representation of the material world in favour of the evocation of some inner core of intangible meaning encouraged artist and writer to look to method and technique to conjure up such meaning. By the late 1880s, then, within the avant-garde repetition was increasingly recognised as an oblique means of suggesting emotion.

In 1889 van Gogh's landscapes became increasingly clustered into variants on particular motifs. There are several reasons for this. Restricted to the Saint-Rémy asylum and its immediate environs, his choice was limited, circumstances which perhaps provided a welcome certainty. He seems also to have been concerned to build up a body of pictures which established his *oeuvre* and justified his work.[11] Among these might be considered some of the paintings of olive groves which he made during the second half of the year. There are about fifteen of these, many measuring 70 by 90 cm, the standard size 30 canvas. Although they do not strictly qualify as a series – they were neither planned as a sequential group nor harmonised for display as an ensemble – their common subject and composition alone register them as a group. Van Gogh considered the olive groves in a typical landscape painter's way, explaining to Bernard in a letter of early December that painting them was 'a hand-to-hand struggle with nature … I am working at present among the olive trees, seeking after the various effects of grey sky against a yellow soil, with a green-black note in the foliage; another time the soil and the foliage all of a violet hue against a yellow sky; then again a red-ochre soil and a pinkish sky'.[12] Even while responding to nature by working *en plein air* he was aware of the exaggerations to which he was subjecting nature, listing his chromatic distortions of local colour. Van Gogh's brushwork emphasised that exaggeration. Smaller canvases of olive trees, such as the one in Edinburgh [**222**], have very abrupt, dashing handling, denoting them as exploratory works. The size 30 paintings, for instance the splendid sunset painting from Göteborg [**223**] made in November 1889, have an equally energetic surface but now ordered more into zones of different marks which carry their own colour harmonies, such as the violet and ochre for the soil and yellow, green and vermilion for the sky. That decorative discipline nevertheless has a powerful emotional charge, of which van Gogh was surely aware. At the end of 1889 he was in correspondence with both Gauguin and Bernard, together in Brittany, about their recent work which had tackled religious themes. Paintings such as Gauguin's *Christ in the Garden of Olives*,[13] in fact a self-portrait, infuriated van Gogh who thought of them as a step

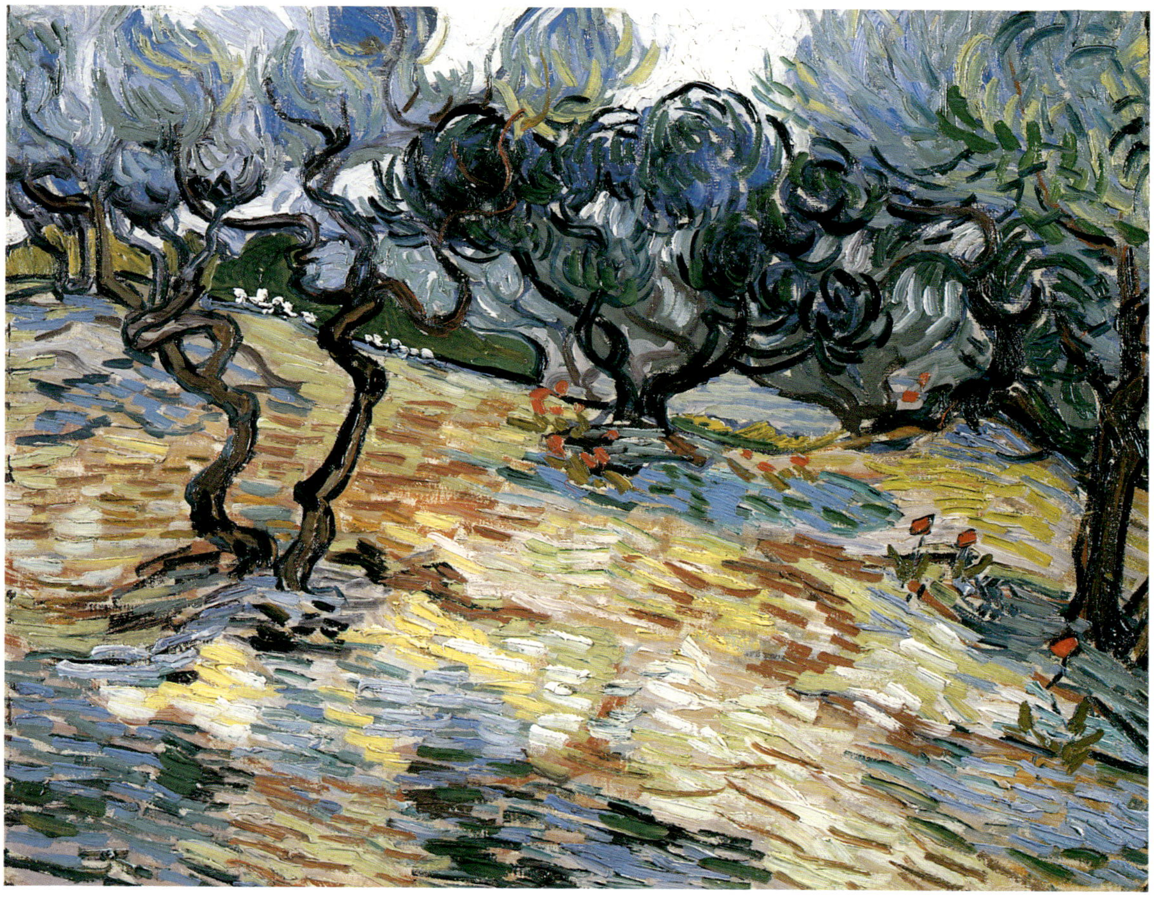

222
V. van Gogh
Olive Trees 1889
Edinburgh, National Gallery of Scotland

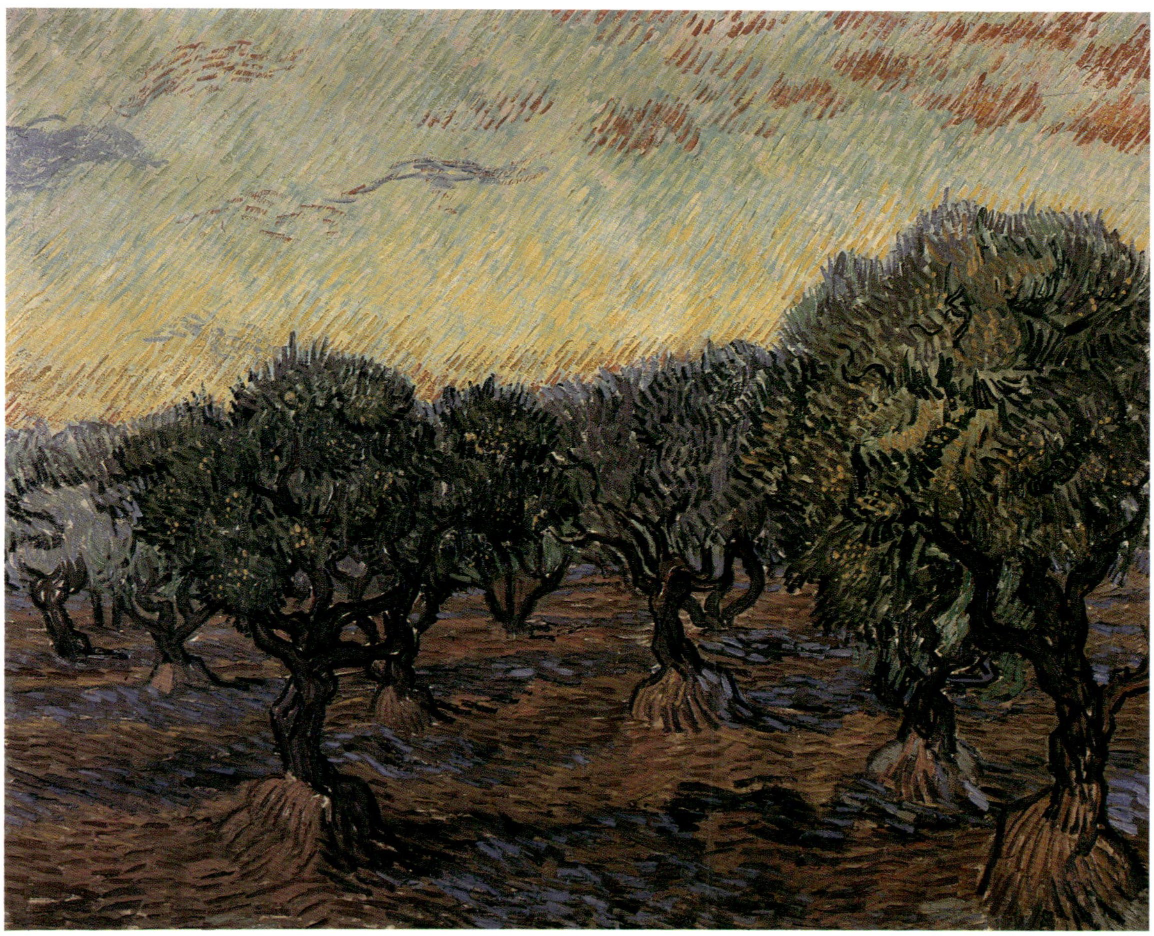

223
V. van Gogh
Olive Grove 1889
Göteborg, Konstmuseum

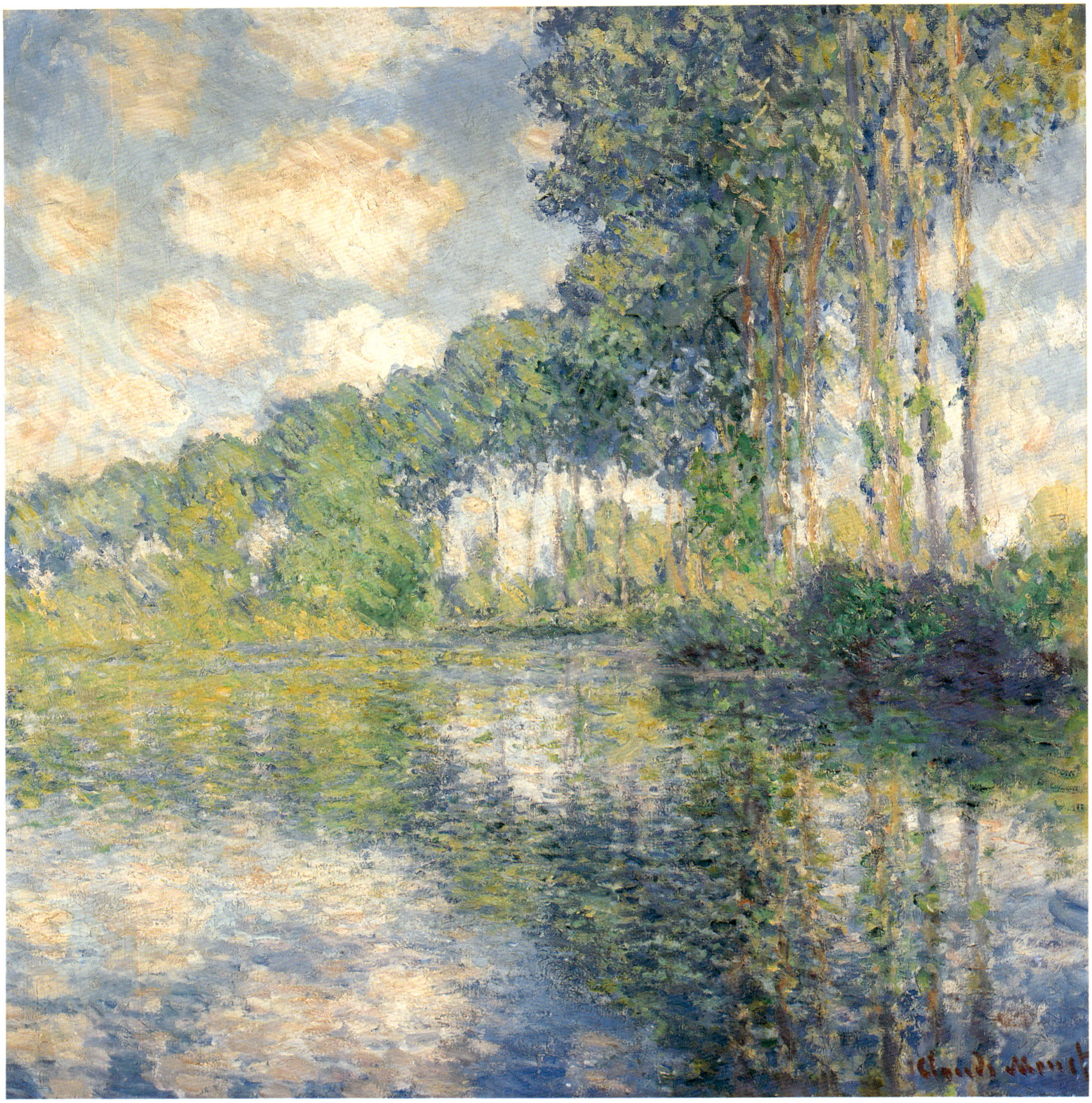

224
C. Monet
Poplars on the Epte 1891
Edinburgh, National Gallery of Scotland

backwards, by implication a reversion to the *paysage historique*, although he did not put it in such terms. In the same December letter to Bernard he argued that 'one can try to give an impression of anguish without aiming straight at the historic Garden of Gethsemane'.[14] Emotions can be evoked, he was insisting, by painterly means, and his olive grove paintings demonstrate that Symbolist ambition, the variations of colour and brushwork through the group stimulating different affective responses.

Monet's practice was more systematically serial. By the time he started his second conscious series, the *Poplars*, in the spring of 1891 he had a clear idea of how he would execute and display the paintings.[15] Although he would have begun by blocking out each motif *en plein air*, selecting the atmospheric conditions, fixing the composition, and choosing the basic chromatics, each canvas would be developed in the studio. There he would build up the complex layers that encrust the surfaces of these gorgeous paintings, and ensure that the pictures harmonised with each other. In that way when they were shown together in a single room they would work as a series not only because of a common subject but also due to a degree of coordination in their colouring. There are nevertheless evident differences between the paintings.

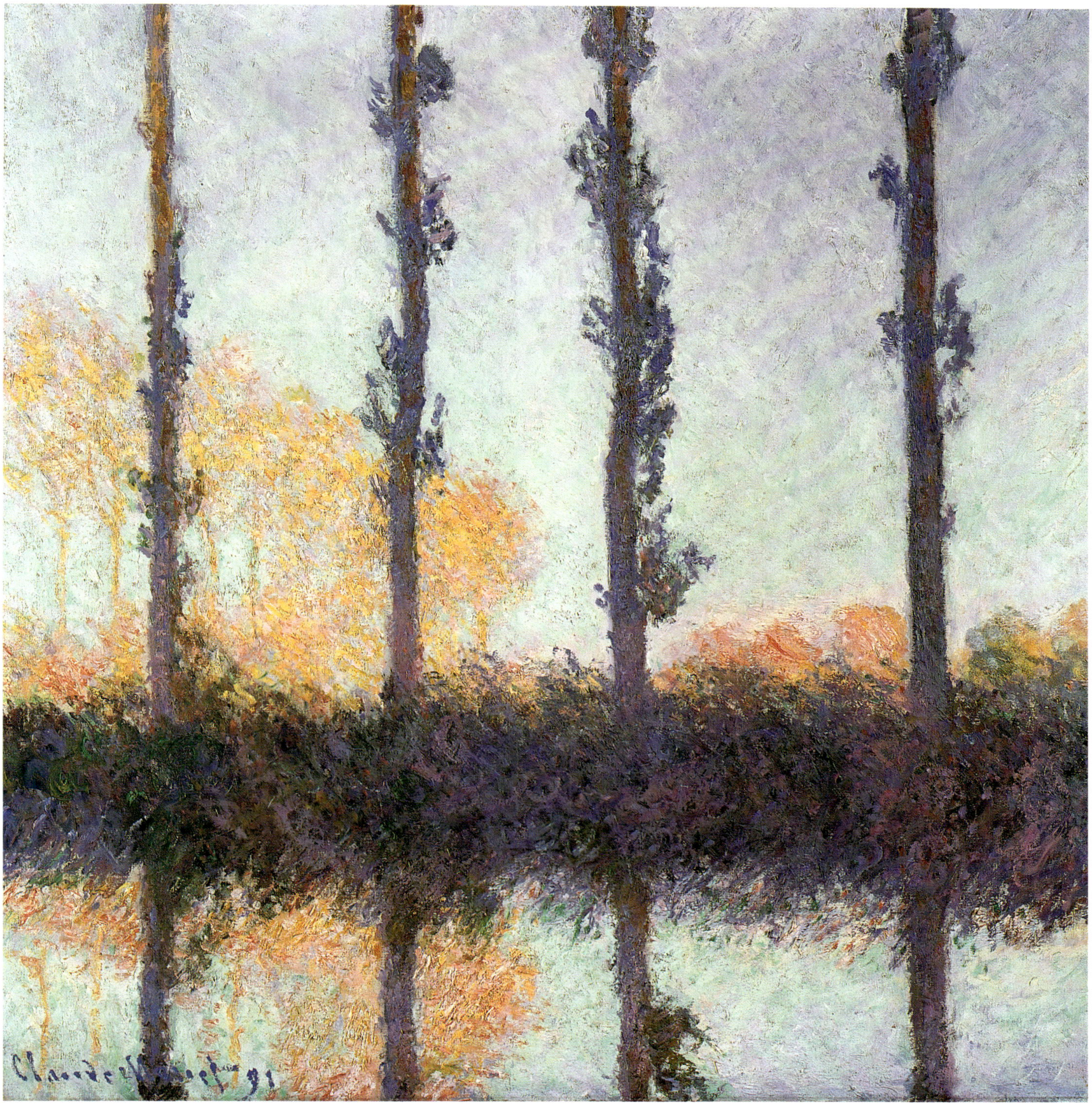

Some show stormy or cloudy weather while others are soaked in sunshine [**224**]. And Monet varied his canvas formats, at times opting for a vertical shape to echo the height of the trees, at others going for the emphatic square. The paintings of course show off Monet's skill in portraying weather effects, but also his craft as a pictorial organiser. Monet stresses the repetition of the vertical poplars, their trimmed trunks acting like a colonnade in the fictive architecture of his paintings. And even when he focuses on trees close to the picture plane, in some cases placing them, the bank, and their reflections almost like a grid near the surface [**225**], Monet never fails to show the line of poplars snaking into recessive space along the line of the Epte. So for all the apparent naturalism of his *effets* he artfully employs repetition and the arabesque, two defining features of the decorative. For both collectively and integrally the *Poplars* function as a decorative series.

The same year as Monet exhibited the *Poplars* Signac showed a group of five paintings, first at Les XX in Brussels and then at the Salon des Indépendants in Paris, giving them slightly different titles at each venue.[16] He had spent the previous summer in Brittany, and the group was called *La Mer. Les barques (Concarneau 1891)*. These paintings

225
C. Monet
The Four Trees 1891
New York, Metropolitan Museum,
The H. O. Havemeyer Collection

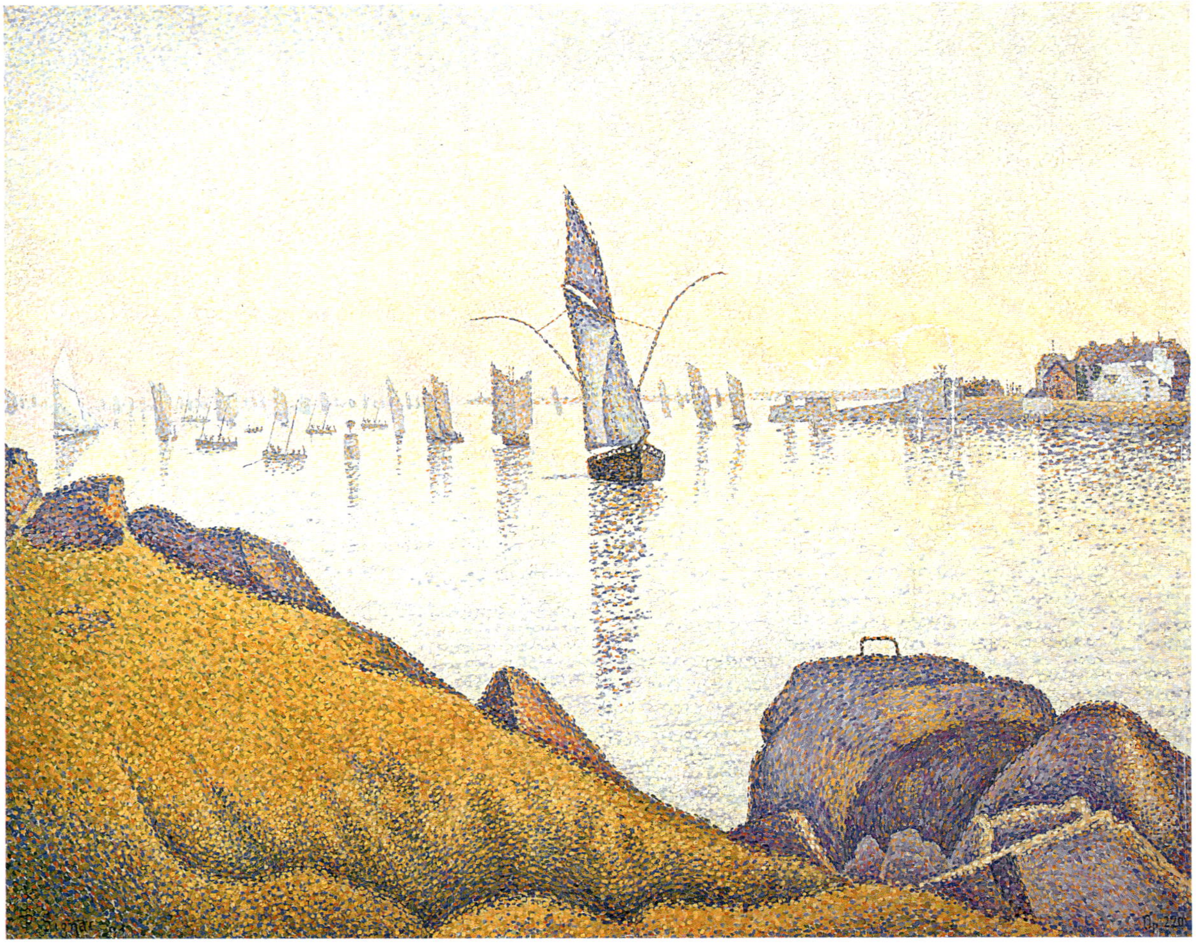

226
P. Signac
Concarneau, the Fishing Boats (Allegro maestoso, evening) 1891
New York, Metropolitan Museum, The Robert Lehman Collection

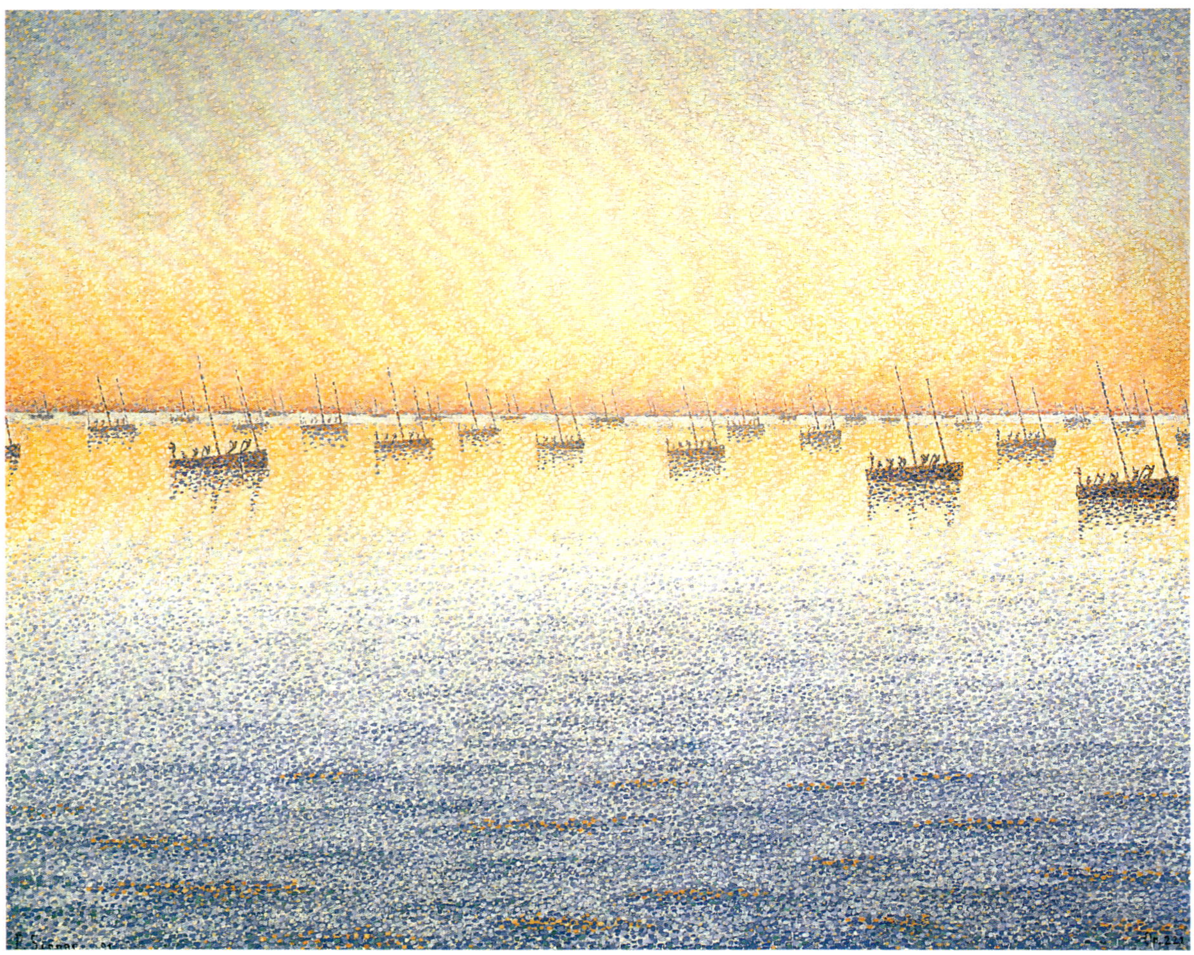

227
P. Signac
Concarneau, the Fishing Boats (Adagio, sunrise) 1891
Mrs John Hay Whitney

have none of the consistency of motif that the *Poplars* or van Gogh's *Olive Groves* have, nor were they made from the same vantage point, as Sisley's pastels were. The Concarneau fishing fleet is represented entering [**226**] and leaving port, out at sea in windless conditions [**227**] and blown along in a gusty squall. In addition Signac depicts diverse times of day, the calm painting of the open sea, for instance, showing sunrise behind the far-flung fleet. Signac employs several means to give these paintings a coherence. He uses standard size 25 canvases, and deploys in them all a dotted Neo-Impressionist touch which not only maintains textural consistency but also has a fluidity appropriate for representing space, sky and water. The repetition of the fleet of sailing boats both within each canvas and across the group again sets up a resonance, which caused Fénéon in his review to refer hintingly to Egyptian art with its decorative hieraticism.[17] This visual harmonisation was intended to serve the thematic unity Signac had imagined for his canvases. He gave them musical titles, so the calm painting of sunrise is *Adagio* and the evening picture of boats returning to harbour is *Allegro maestoso*, while the others are titled *Larghetto*, *Scherzo*, and *Presto (finale)*. At this time Signac, sharing his Symbolist colleagues' fascination with music as an art form which is non-representational but capable of provoking profound emotions, gave all his canvases opus numbers; the Concarneau quintet are Op. 218 to 222. And inevitably such friends responded positively to these associations, Comte Antoine de la Rochefoucauld, first owner of *Allegro maestoso*, writing in his review that Signac's precise accents and magisterial spacing reminded him of the music of Bach or Wagner.[18] These beautiful paintings, once again, are not strictly serial as they do not represent the same site, but they are consciously symphonic in form. They are not repetitive, but logical in their internal development and cumulative in their emotional effect. As Debussy was to attempt for the orchestra a few years later, Signac essayed in his canvases the construction of a symphonic form around that elemental force, the sea.

Painting groups or series of motifs is a way of ordering one's responses to nature. In terms of establishing a typology of, say, weather or light effects, such practices can be seen as naturalistic. On the other hand, the business of rendering those effects harmonious and decorative might best be viewed as closer to the Symbolist aesthetic. Significantly, painters' interest in working on landscape subjects in terms of groups or series was chiefly concentrated in the few years between about 1888 and 1892, a phase of crucial and productive dialogue between those two creative currents. As debate subsided away, as distinctions between naturalist and Symbolist ideas became less relevant to the *paysagiste*, so did this attention to the series. If Monet's continuation with series right into the twentieth century might seem – ironically – somewhat repetitious, it was perhaps forced on him because that concept had come to characterise his stock in trade. Although the canvases Derain painted in London in 1905–6 were intended as a direct challenge to yet another of Monet's great serial groups, the Thames paintings he had worked on for several years and finally showed at Durand-Ruel's in 1904, the Fauve did not proceed by repeating representations of the same site. Derain's dynamic and diversely handled paintings of different motifs can be seen as a younger generation's repudiation of a procedure developed to suit an aesthetic of nuance and suggestion which had now, fifteen years on, become somewhat stale.

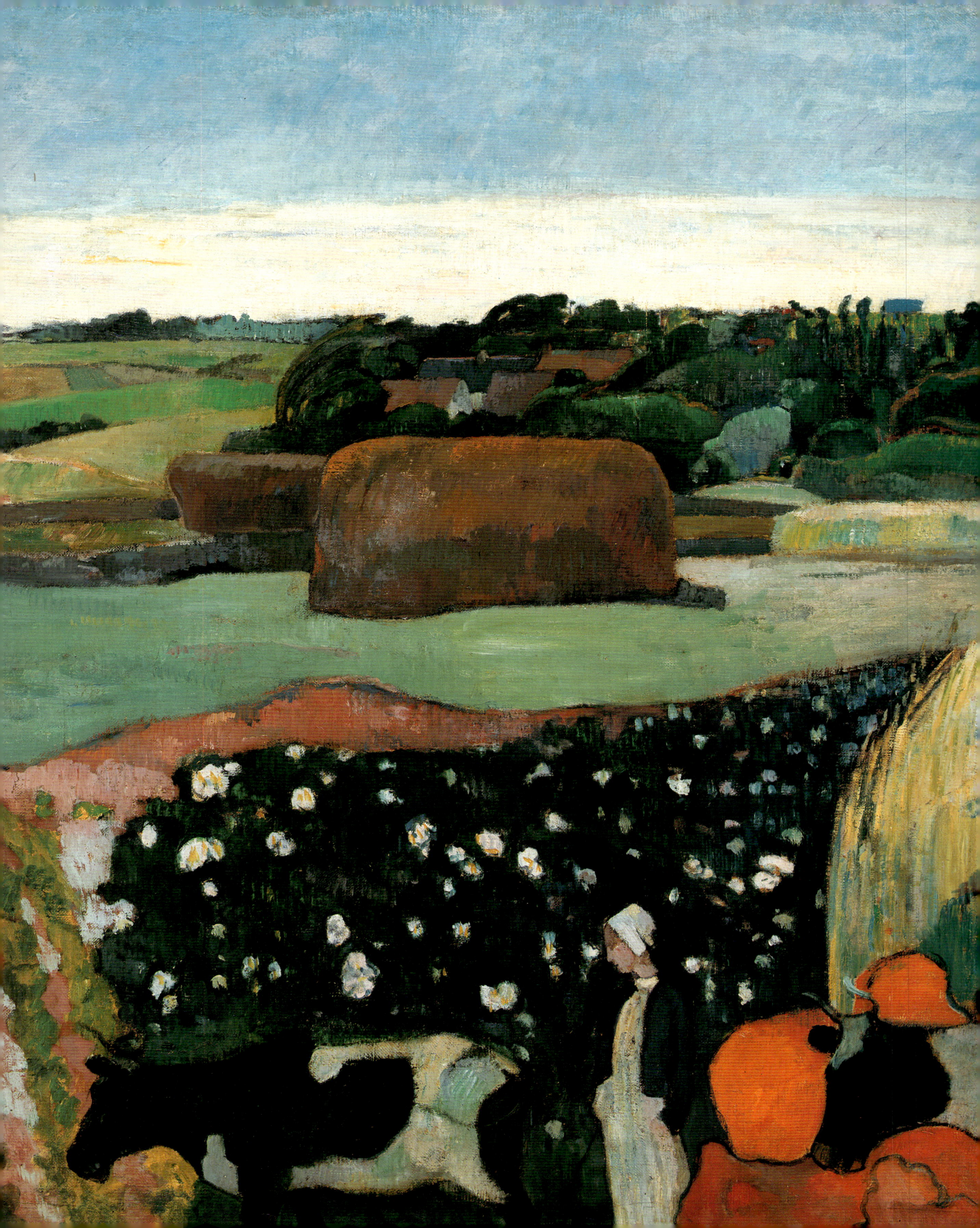

13 The Seasons

The represention of the seasons in western art dates back to ancient times, and in French landscape painting to the books of hours of the Middle Ages. The categorisation of nature's cycle into four distinct and consecutive units simplifies natural change in a comprehensible manner, reducing the complexities and irregularities of nature into a cultural code easily understood in human exchange. That typology is helpful to us all – farmer, traveller or whoever – in conversation and description, but it is also easily adaptable to visual imagery, the motif of blossom immediately connoting spring, as that of falling leaves does autumn. And as Paulhan reminded us in his 1913 *Esthétique du paysage*, the seasons have human no less than astronomical meanings; we have long associated spring with morning, youth and love, summer with day and physical maturity, autumn with dusk and age, and winter with night and death.[1] These were conventional associations, and as we have seen Martin used them in his decorations for the Capitole of Toulouse [**213**]. Not all artists adhered to the typology. Certainly in his paintings of the four seasons of 1892 Maurice Denis did not follow the standard pattern, but left out winter to focus on four months – April, July, September and October – which do not follow the cycle. If three of them, with their staffage of young women, do not accord with the associations Paulhan attributed to each season, at least *April* does, representing virginal girls picking spring flowers.[2] The rhythm typical of landscape painters' practice was itself seasonal. To break the round of their studio work, both specialist *paysagistes* and figure painters commonly painted landscapes in the spring and summer months, returning to the *atelier* with the onset of inclement weather to prepare their canvases for the opening of the Salon the following spring. The *plein air* painter, not tied to the studio, would work out-of-doors in every season, as attested by the paintings of Pissarro at Eragny, Monet at Giverny or Sisley at Moret. While such spontaneous representations did not directly bring into play the conventional associations of the different seasons, inevitably artists' responses were conditioned by the ideas and assumptions they brought to the seasonal motif. Pissarro, for example, disliked the summer 'with its fat green monotony'.[3] However, for the painter of the *paysage composé* or the rapid *impression*, the grand decorative commission or the canvas scaled for the domestic market, the fiction of finite seasons continued to provide a convenient structure for landscape pictures. Taking my cue from Puvis de Chavannes, whose murals for one of the entrance halls of the Paris Hôtel de Ville represent Summer and Winter,[4] I will confine my discussion to these two seasons.

WINTER

As a subject for the landscape painter winter, particularly the snowscape, had the advantage of relative freedom from restrictive convention. The winter scene had no significant place within the Italianate tradition; indeed, the frosty pastoral is unthinkable! Even in Dutch art it was not associated with great figures such as Ruisdael or Hobbema but with bumptious images of rural life and winter games by less familiar names. It had not been much favoured by French painters such as Huet, Troyon, Dupré or Théodore Rousseau prominent earlier in the century. One can see the challenging freedom offered by the winter scene being enjoyed to the full by Pissarro in his painting *Hoar Frost* [**230**]. His design is notably free of conventional landscape devices such as *repoussoirs*, so much so that it provoked a caricatural response from one critic when it was hung in 1874 at what came to be known as the first Impressionist exhibition. In *Le Charivari*, the contemporary equivalent of *Private Eye*, Louis Leroy imagined visiting the show with a former pupil of Bertin, stalwart of Neo-Classical landscape. The old artist describes *Hoar Frost* as 'palette scrapings applied uniformly on a grubby canvas. It's got neither head nor tail, top nor bottom, foreground nor background'.[5]

That freedom had been enjoyed by painters before Pissarro, notably Courbet who had used the palette knife to great effect in snowscapes. In mid-century Millet and Daubigny too had produced occasional but impressive winter paintings. A canvas such as the latter's *Snow* [**229**], shown at the Salon of 1873 and re-exhibited to great acclaim at the Universal Exhibition of 1900, made no attempt to idealise

opposite
228
P. Gauguin
The Haystacks, Le Pouldu 1890 (detail)
Washington, National Gallery of Art, Gift of the W. Averell Harriman Foundation in memory of Marie N. Harriman

top
229
C. Daubigny
Snow 1873
Paris, Musée d'Orsay

centre left
230
C. Pissarro
Hoar Frost 1873
Paris, Musée d'Orsay

centre right
231
C. Monet
Vétheuil in the Fog 1879
Paris, Musée Marmottan

bottom
232
C. Monet
The Break-up of the Ice at Vétheuil 1881
Madrid, Fundación Colección
Thyssen-Bornemisza

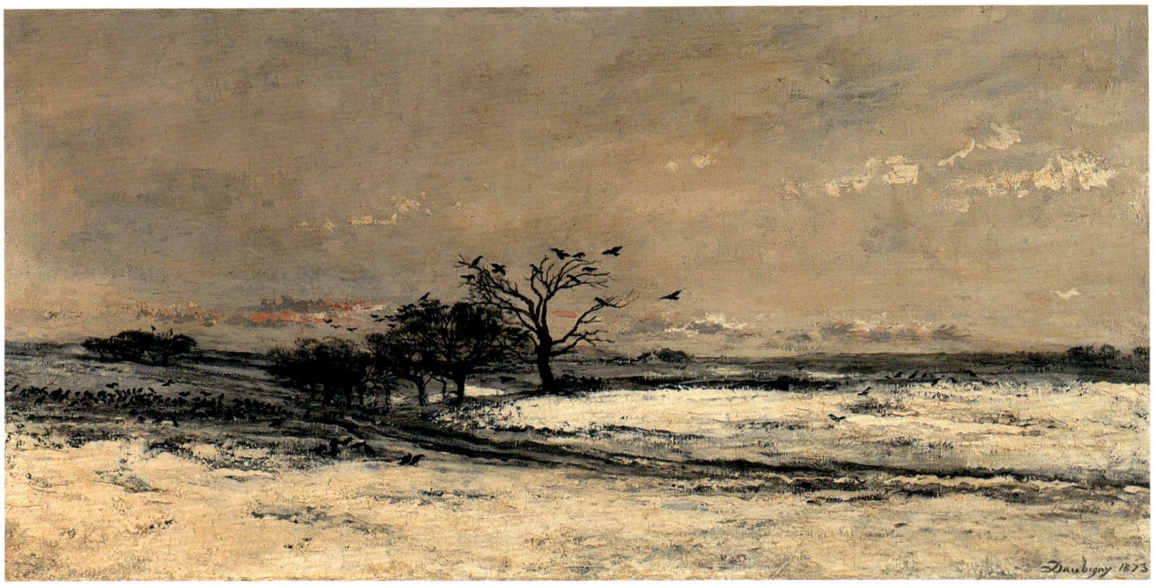

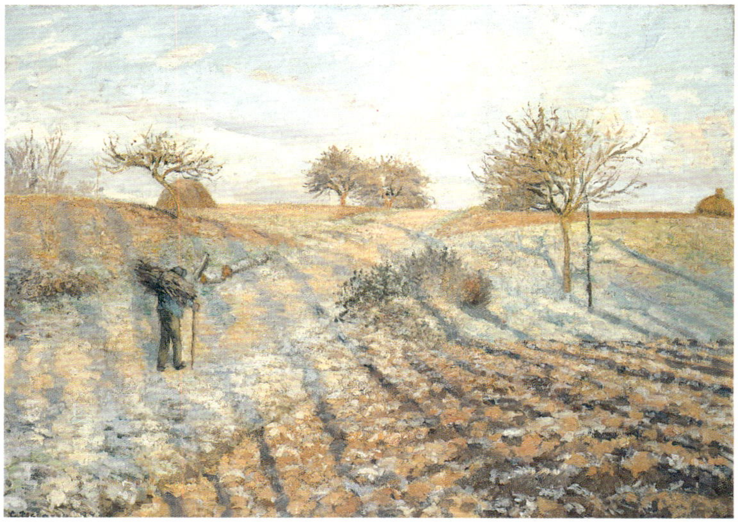

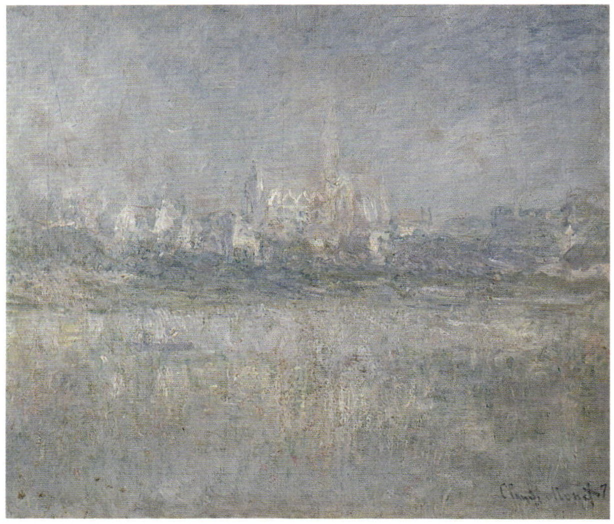

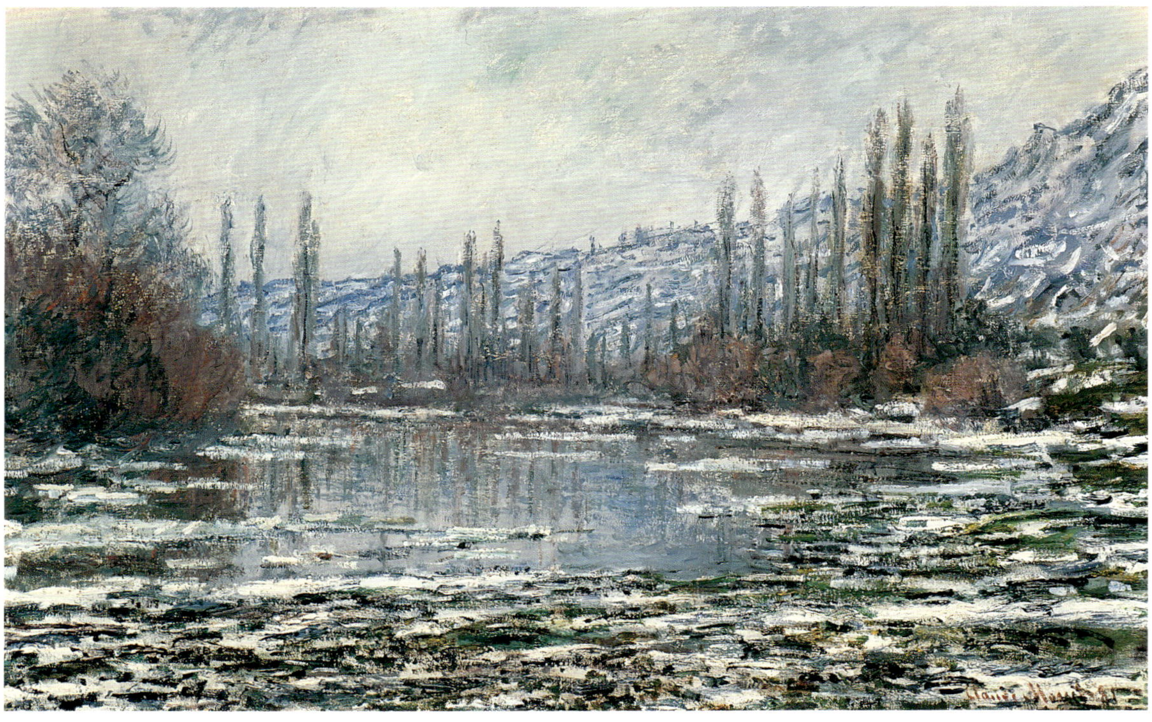

the scene. The barrenness of the snow-covered plain is made more stark by the silhouetted trees and the clustering crows, and Daubigny's broad effects, created by knife, brush and scratchings, give a vivid sense of the scruffy combination of snow and mud. In such a case we see a naturalist painter relishing his freedom from the restraints of ideal conventions in order to focus on a more democratic ideal of representing the widest possible range of natural effects. This was the rule for the *plein air* painter. Commencing and perhaps completing a canvas *sur le motif* with the aim of achieving the maximum accuracy of *effet* was one of the most finely tuned naturalist techniques, and it insisted on evenhandedness in the choice of effect and motif. The search for the furthest frontiers of atmospheric conditions, the desire to test one's abilities to transcribe the worst vagaries of nature often led artists to work in the extremes of winter weather. Monet's painting of *Vétheuil in the Fog* [**231**] of 1879 typifies this kind of experiment, where the wintry conditions so shroud the village that it appears almost indecipherable in the veil of freezing vapour.

For all that winter scenes permitted a significant degree of freedom and experimentation, their gradual proliferation in mid-century established certain orthodoxies. The winter of 1879–80 was especially severe, and both that year and the next Monet painted groups of canvases representing the frozen Seine and the ice breaking up as it thawed. The riverside compositions he chose in the vicinity of Vétheuil generally follow the prototypes established by Daubigny, as is the case with the 1881 painting now in the Thyssen Collection [**232**]. Here the river swings gently into and then out of pictorial space, framed on the left by a clump of trees and balanced across the rear planes by the gradually tumbling ridge punctuated by the towering poplars. Within this restful design the artist set the quiet drama of the thaw, with the reassuring natural colours of brown and green, intimating growth, emerging from the enclosing grasp of the cold violets and whites of the snow. This same playing off of the suggestion of sap and soil against the frozen covering of winter occurs in Lucien Simonnet's submission to the 1893 Salon des artistes français [**234**]. Simonnet's motif is the reservoir at Ville-d'Avray, the suburban town to the south-east of Paris which had been Corot's home and where he had painted so often. The viewpoint is one used on several occasions by Corot [**233**], held in high

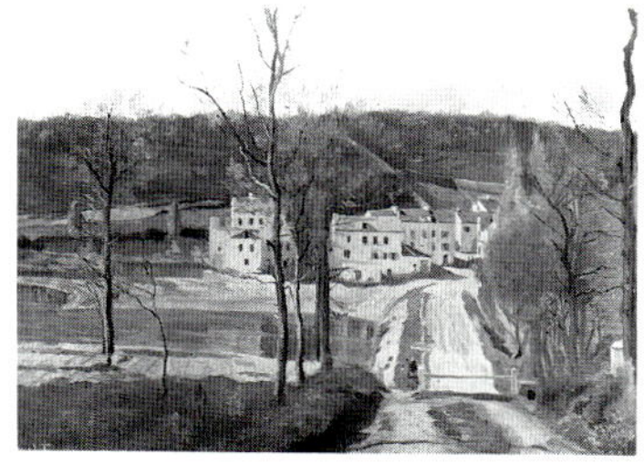

233
C. Corot
Ville-d'Avray, the Cabassud Houses
c.1835–40
Paris, Musée du Louvre

234
L. Simonnet
Ville-d'Avray: Snow Effect 1893
Paris, Musée d'Orsay

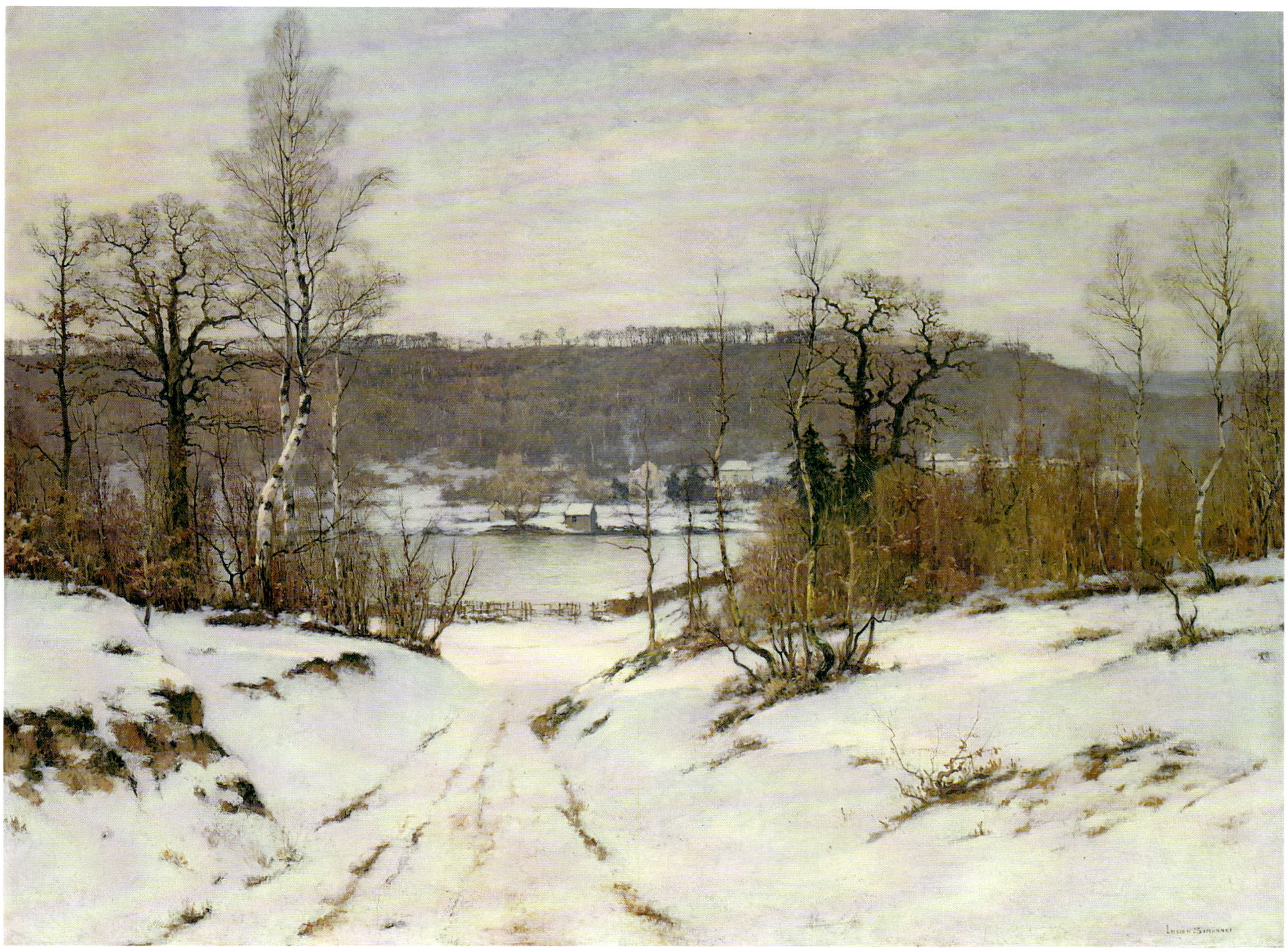

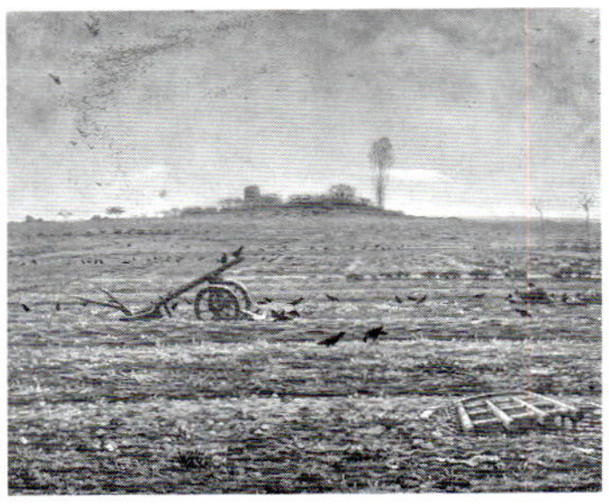

235
J.-F. Millet
Winter: The Plain of Chailly 1862
Vienna, Österreichische Galerie

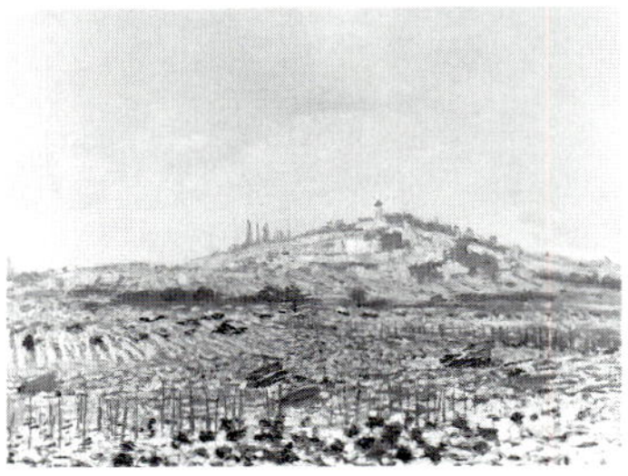

236
C. Monet
Vineyards in the Snow 1873
Richmond, Virginia Museum of Fine Arts, The Adolph D. and Wilkins C. Williams Fund

esteem in the 1890s, and Simonnet must have deployed it knowingly. He used this vantage celebrated in French landscape vocabulary for a precise naturalist rendition, submitting the motif to a wintry *effet* which Corot, perhaps due to his Italianate training, had found unappealing.

If Monet and Simonnet crafted different kinds of naturalist snowscape on to compositions not originally representing winter scenes, at least one mid-century winter motif seems to have created a touchstone to which later landscapists felt required to respond. Millet's *Winter: The Plain of Chailly* [**235**] had been exhibited at the Salon of 1867, where Monet would have seen it, and at the Millet retrospective held at the Ecole des beaux-arts in 1887, which van Gogh visited. It has been convincingly argued that Monet's *Vineyards in the Snow* [**236**], painted in the environs of Argenteuil in 1873, owes its expanse of snow-covered agricultural land to a reminiscence of Millet's canvas.[6] Van Gogh made a more direct citation when he copied an etching after *Winter: The Plain of Chailly* while at the asylum of Saint-Rémy in January 1890.[7] Working from memory and the black-and-white source, van Gogh recast the naturalistic local colour of the original into a harmony of blue-green [**237**]. In places the soil becomes a greyish pink, for instance around the plough, and the horizon line is tinged with pale yellow. The overall effect is one of cold, rendered vibrant by the controlled textures of the brushwork. By imposing his own chromatics on his antecedent's design, van Gogh produced both an homage to Millet's landscape and an imaginative transformation of it.

At one level Monet's *Vineyards in the Snow* and van Gogh's copy after Millet represent two different generations of landscape painting: the Impressionist's direct response to nature and the Symbolists's willingness to exaggerate and suggest. Responding each in their different way to Millet's motif they demonstrate yet again the flexibility of the landscape genre. Inevitably our reading of winter images is affected by our instinctive reactions to winter as a season through which we regularly live and whose discomforts we unenthusiatically endure. The critic Lafenestre brought the spectator's subjectivity into play in 1893 when he recommended Simonnet's *Ville-d'Avray* with the proviso, 'if you don't detest the winter'.[8] Van Gogh's copy is often interpreted as an expression of the loneliness he felt at Saint-Rémy. The plough and harrow indicate human presence, but they have been abandoned in the open fields until they are needed again, potent images of solitude. Indeed, van Gogh rendered an already stark motif even more desolate by adapting Millet's originally autumnal motif into a

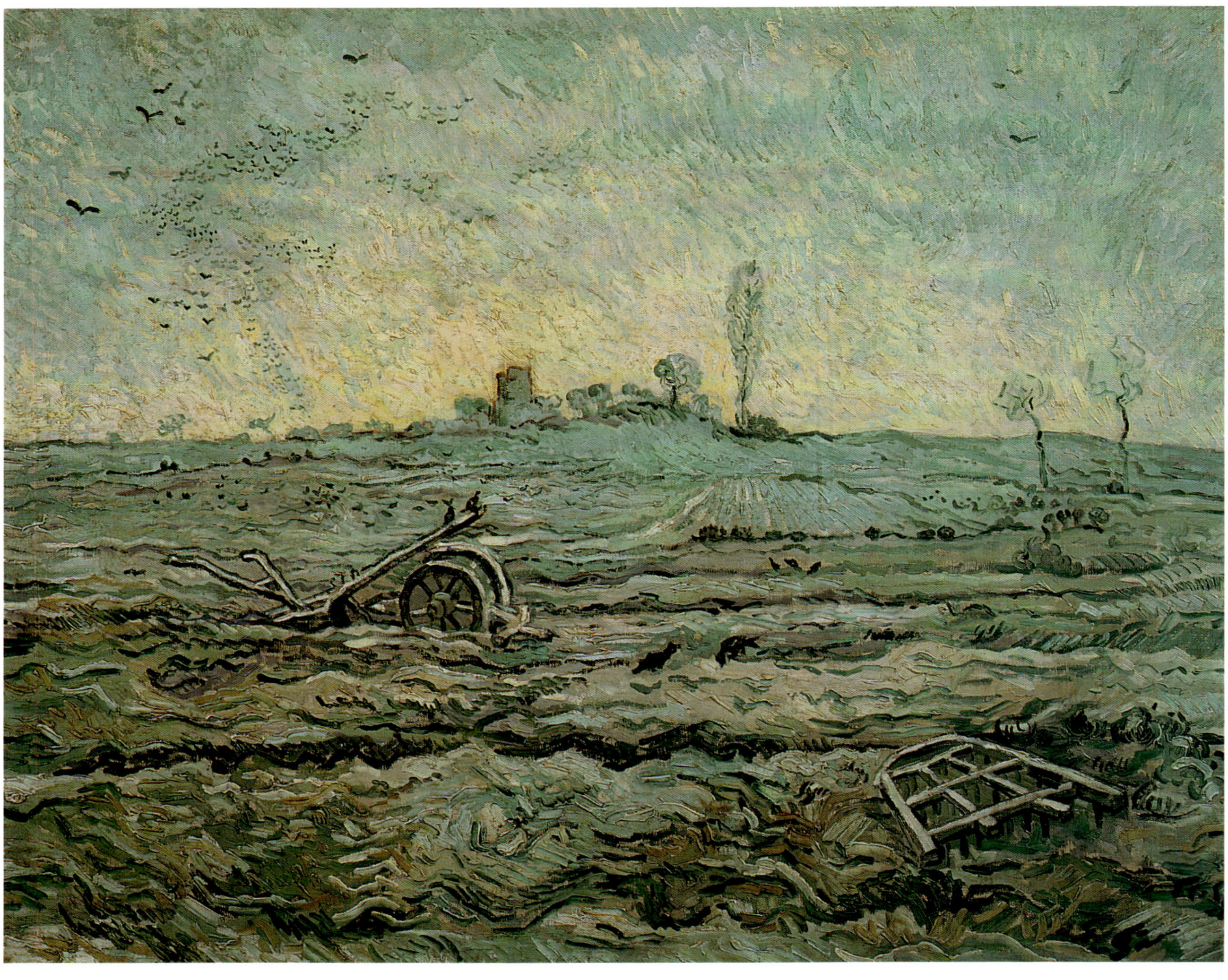

237
V. van Gogh
Winter: the Plain of Chailly (after Millet) 1890
Amsterdam, Rijksmuseum Vincent van Gogh

winter scene. His copy may also be viewed as an expression of the nostalgia for his native Netherlandish countryside which he felt at this period. His letter to his brother Theo of 29 April 1890 which accompanied the Millet copies he had sent to Paris conveyed his 'melancholy', explaining that he had been painting 'memories of the North'.[9] Perhaps Monet's paintings of the thawing ice should also be considered affectively. Certainly they struck contemporaries in that way. Huysmans' review of the 1882 Impressionist exhibition spoke of the 'intense melancholy' of these canvases, and subsequent writers have speculated on whether these sombre images of natural change and decay do not suggest Monet's emotional distress following the death of his wife Camille in 1879 and his ensuing domestic turmoil.[10] Landscape painters, it seems, took advantage of the instinctively negative feelings we generally share about winter to produce images which at least echoed those instincts, if not actively played upon them for expressive or cathartic effect.

Winter motifs challenged the painter's abilities to represent all kinds of weather, from the even light of overcast skies, the reflections on snow which give it perhaps a pink, blue or violet tint, even snowflakes falling in a blizzard. They all attracted landscapists fascinated by nature at her most extraordinary or intractable. And winter motifs, like any other landscape subject, could be ordered to accord with other values and concerns which the artist wished to articulate. Sisley's *Winter at Veneux-Nadon* of 1881 [**238**], for instance, is evidently a canvas in which he was concerned to represent the *effet* of unifying light in a landscape blanketed by snow under a low cloud base. It also reaches back into the picturesque tradition, representing the venerable village houses and the changeless activites of the woman fetching water from the well and the children tobogganing. Yet this image of appealing stability is jolted by the appearance in the distance of the dark accent of a train, its machine-generated steam more blanched than the natural whites of winter. Sisley did not let his fictive village settle into a comfortable image of timelessness, but surely it was precisely that quality of the eternal that Monet sought in his series of *Grainstacks*.

These paintings, fifteen of which were first exhibited at the Durand-Ruel gallery in May 1891, have provoked an almost bewildering range of interpretations, by no means all mutually exclusive. The *Grainstacks* have been read as the apogee of observation of light and its representation, as metaphysical meditations on the passage of time, as a decorative or musical ensemble, as a frankly commercial gambit, and as a motif of stored grain representing the

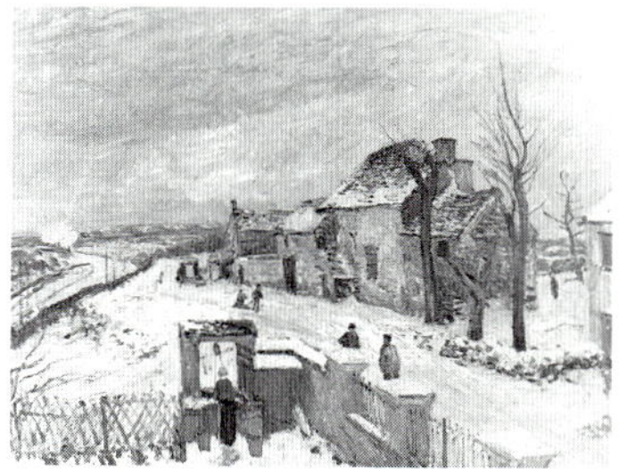

238
A. Sisley *Winter at Veneux-Nadon* 1881
Private Collection

239
C. Monet
Grainstacks: Snow Effect 1890–1
Edinburgh, National Gallery of Scotland

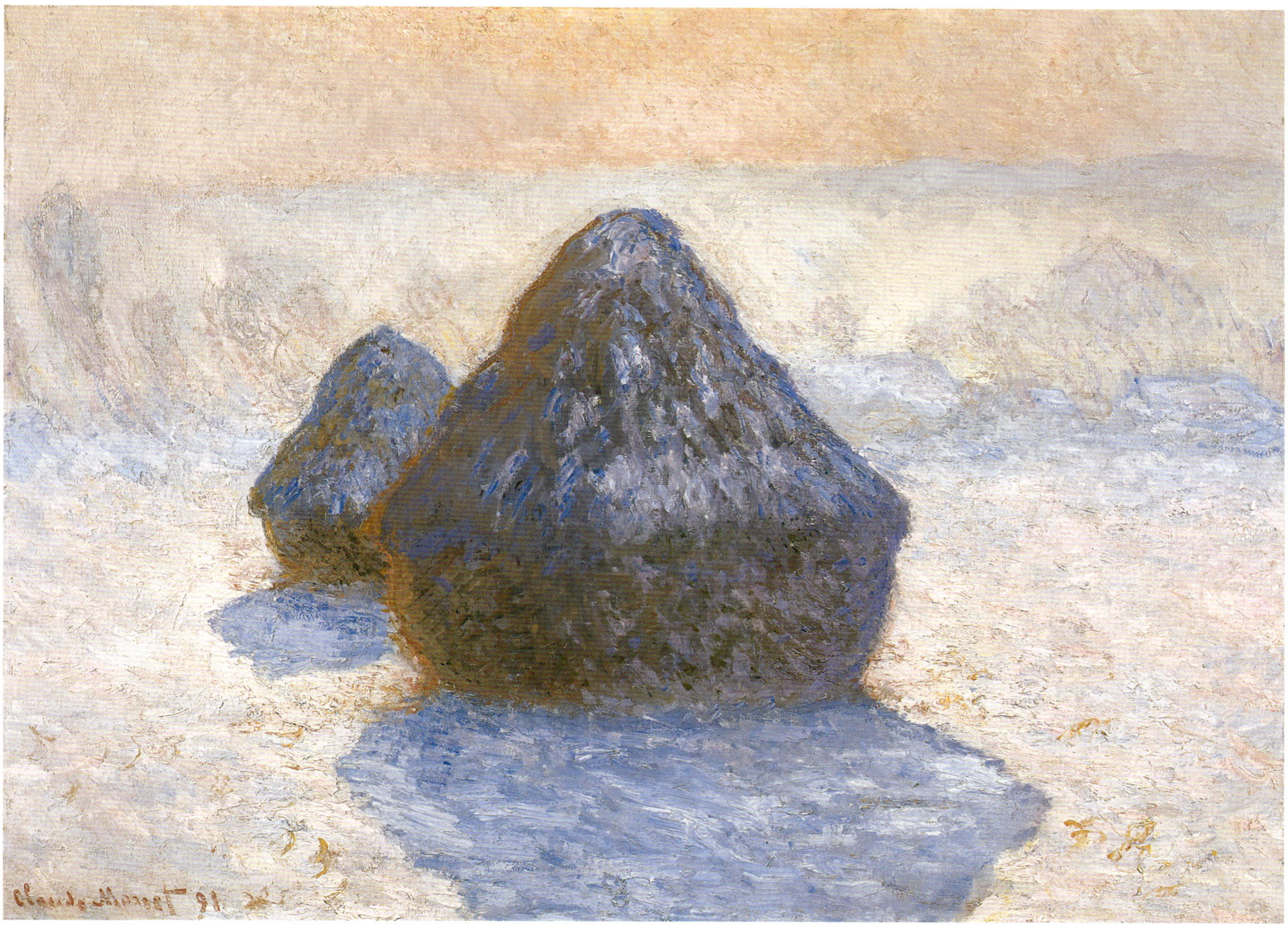

agricultural economy of the Vexin region.[11] Monet himself had a flexible attitude to this body of work. 'I'm hacking away, I've got in mind a series of different effects (grainstacks), but at this time of year the sun goes down so quickly that I can't follow it,' he wrote to his friend the critic Gustave Geffroy on 7 October 1890.[12] To Durand-Ruel the following January he asked forgiveness for delays, explaining: 'I've got lots of things on the go and can't be distracted for a minute wanting above all to profit from these splendid winter effects'.[13] This was the language of the *plein air* painter, the Impressionist obsessed by the *effet* and tormented by nature's vagaries. Yet Geffroy reported at this time that Monet 'does not want to represent the reality of things, he wishes to fix the light between him and the objects [he paints]'.[14] This could be taken as Monet attempting to push Impressionist virtuosity to an extreme pitch by representing ambient light. And yet the willingness to disregard objective reality in order to suggest the intangible, the ambition to paint the unpaintable, is close to the Symbolist aesthetic. Certainly Geffroy's preface to the exhibition catalogue, which Monet must have approved, spoke of the *Grainstack* series in emotive rather than descriptive terms. Geffroy described how in the sunset variants 'Veils of tragedy – the red of blood, the violet of mourning – trail around them on the ground and above them in the atmosphere … Monet unmasks changing portraits, the faces of the landscape, the manifestations of joy and despair, of mystery and fate'.[15] And Monet's own practice of harmonising the paintings in the studio so that each *effet* not only stood on its own but worked off the others and his insistence that they be hung in a room as a series suggest not only a concern for the decorative but also a parallel with music, for the *Grainstacks* act like variations on a theme. In both those senses his position was again analogous to Symbolist notions about art. Whether Monet was in a genuine conceptual muddle about his work at this time or whether he was craftily playing *plein-airiste* to one audience and Symbolist to another, it is apparent that clear distinctions about artists' intentions and between competing if overlapping aesthetics cannot easily be made, as Richard Shiff has so ably demonstrated.[16]

Beginning work in the late summer of 1890 and having the canvases ready for show in May the next year, Monet gave himself the opportunity to paint almost all the seasonal variations. The *Grainstack* series also incorporates the daily cycle, with the light effects indicating morning, midday or evening, as well as different climatic effects such as clear or overcast skies, fog or sunshine. If that seems like an objective index of natural phenomena which Monet could watch reacting upon his static motifs, one should be aware of the artifices he employed in these ostensibly truthful observations. The Edinburgh painting [**239**] represents fog reducing visibility after a hundred yards or so, the early light of day, the sun still low in the sky but strong enough to break through a light overcast and make shadows on the gleaming frost-covered snow. By that account it is an image of atmospheric precision. But Monet took liberties with exactitude; as Paul Tucker has pointed out, the long shadows should be parallel and not diverge.[17] But does one look at these paintings in search of meteorological accuracy, and did Monet intend us to? Surely this painting has a consciously cultivated harmoniousness to it, the gentle violet greys and sonorous purples subtly resonating within a texturally unified surface. Even the motif of two grainstacks places them together in a familial arrangement, and one senses that here Monet orchestrated his painterly means to create an image of soothing unity, just as van Gogh had exaggerated his winter motif to evoke a mood of melancholy. If winter carries with it inhospitable associations, it can also prompt the opposite response, when 'the ground covered with snow, the sky dimmed with mist, and the smooth soft distances combine to form a general scale of colour, and a harmonious whole, which charms the eye'.[18] That was Amiel's reaction to the winter landscape, and it tallies with Edinburgh's *Grainstack* picture which, before we consider it within the complex of Monet's serial practice, surely strikes us first as an image of enchantment.

Winter motifs rarely attracted the Fauve painters. The inherently cool harmony of the snowscape did not suit their bright palettes and busy brushwork, they felt none of the naturalist obligation to respond evenhandedly to the diversity of nature, and their youthful Nietzschean energy, their sense of modernity, and their attraction to the Mediterranean drew them elsewhere. For painters working early in this century and determined to order the images and conventions of landscape to suit their own pictorial concerns, the winter scene was of little interest. Subtle and elusive, the effects of the inhospitable season when the land sleeps need to be closely and patiently observed. Winter's mood, claustral and solitary, transforms most aptly into landscape paintings that are tranquil and meditative.

As the opposite of winter, summer naturally carries contrasting associations. The season of warmth and growth, it brings people out to enjoy the fresh air and to work on the land. The season's character inevitably affects the ways in which it is represented. Whereas winter confines people to their homes – the landscapes we have just discussed are largely unpopulated – summer, on the contrary, prompts images of open terrain and human activity. Surveying a career of half a century as a painter of landscape and rural life, Jules Breton wrote nostalgically in the 1890s about his *pays* of Courrières that he had so frequently represented [4]. 'At harvest-time the plain is moving and superb. Nowhere do I feel more brimming with love for the nurturing soil, for the sun, the great fecund force, nowhere more profoundly, more magnificently splendid or surrounded by an atmosphere of such deliciously irridescent tints; and … I should add that nowhere do I feel more grateful for divine Providence! And one sees the sheaves aligned, the piles of corn mount up, the blocks of haystacks erected; the carts balancing their domes of grain come and go and, at evening, all the strong tanned harvesters travel homewards, while the sun gently withdraws its vermilion rays and, quite scarlet, sets and sleeps in the purple dusk.'[19] To modern taste Breton's prose may seem excessively hyperbolic and sentimental, but it articulates notions about the summer that were commonplace in the nineteenth century, whereby the harvest season in particular is constructed to represent the generosity of the elements, the bounty of the land and the community of the population. At harvest-time in particular, that epitome of summer, man and nature exist in perfect harmony.

Visual imagery shared that topos. *Fields in the Month of June* [**241**], exhibited by Daubigny at the Salon of 1874, could be an illustration to Breton's text by another painter of his generation. Depicting the fertile downlands of the Vexin near Auvers, Daubigny's panorama uses its expanse as a metaphor for the fecundity of the land. Fields, pastures and orchards spread out before the eye, nurtured by the peasants scattered throughout this vista and whose livelihoods, the spectator is assured, will be sustained by the fertility of the soil. In its way Daubigny's painting is as rhetorical as Breton's prose. But does one not find much the same notions articulated in Pissarro's *A June Morning, View from the Heights of Pontoise* [**240**], painted only a few miles from Daubigny's motif and exhibited at the first Impressionist exhibition at the same time that the older artist's June subject was at the Salon? Gauguin's *The Haystacks* [**242**] belongs to a group of landscapes made at Le Pouldu on the rocky south coast of Brittany in 1890. He responded to this windswept terrain, with its compact fields and farms clustered among sheltering trees in shallow valleys, by painting it as a patchwork of zones. While suggesting a sense of distance, these also have an active surface quality enhanced by the regular Cézannesque brushwork and

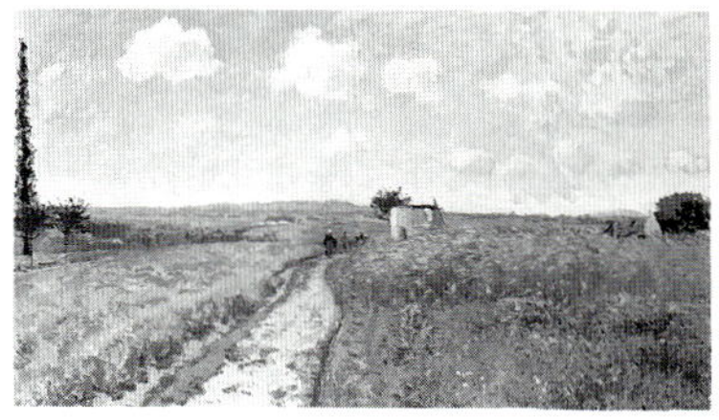

240
C. Pissarro ***A June Morning, View From the Heights of Pontoise*** 1873
Karlsruhe, Kunsthalle

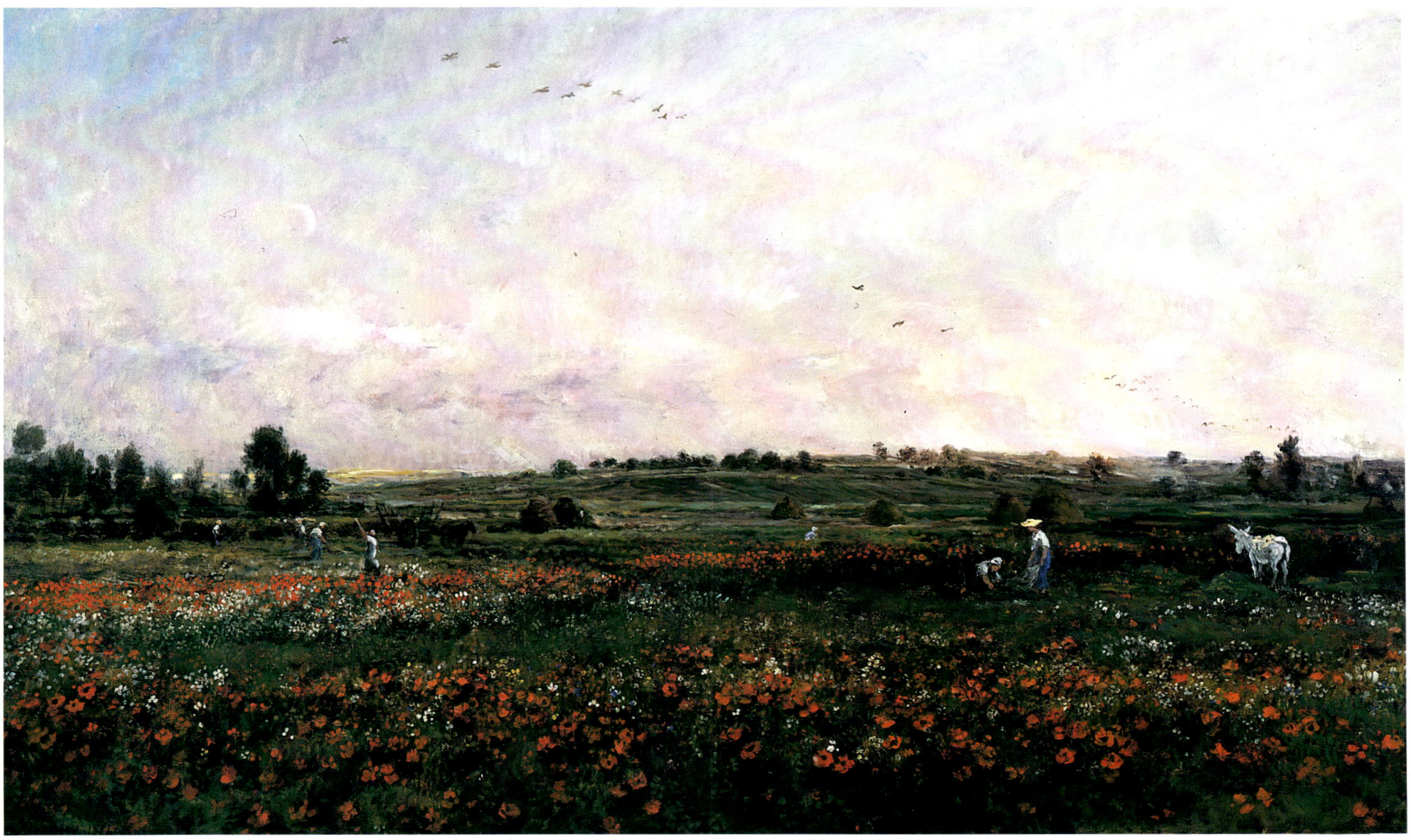

241
C. Daubigny
Fields in the Month of June 1874
Ithaca, New York, Cornell University, Herbert F. Johnson Museum of Art
Gift of Louis V. Keeler (Class of 1911) and Mrs Keeler

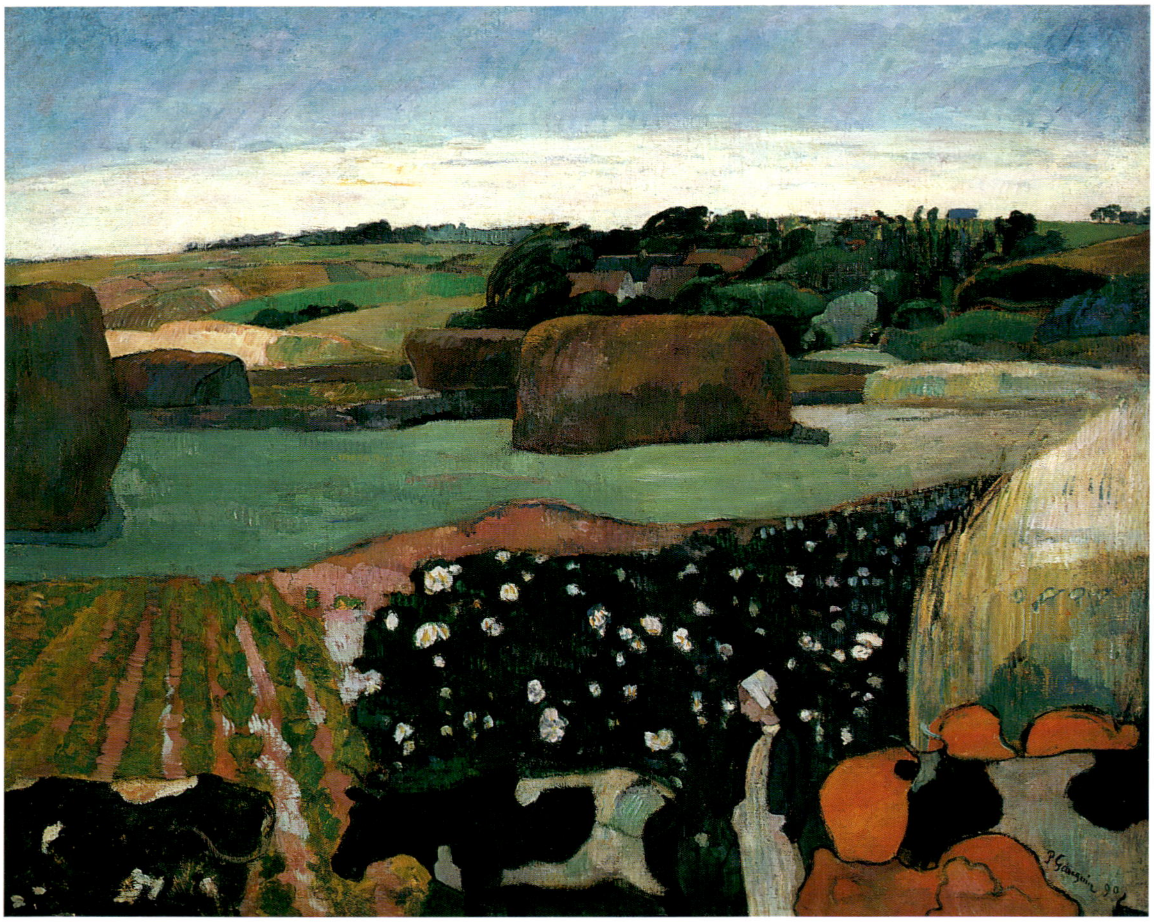

242
P. Gauguin
The Haystacks, Le Pouldu 1890
Washington, National Gallery of Art
Gift of the W. Averell Harriman Foundation in memory of Marie N. Harriman

the oscillation of warm and cool colours, also derived from the Aixois's example. The decorative quality of Gauguin's landscape is furthered by the striped and patterned textures of the foreground plots and by the procession of cows which leads across the first plane. The order Gauguin imposed on this motif gives it a ritualistic quality consistent with his objective of bringing out the 'primitive' qualities of Breton life, backward and unchanging. The ideas that underpinned Gauguin's *The Haystacks* were very different from those behind Angrand's more-or-less contemporary *The Harvesters* [**243**]. In contrast to Gauguin's broad, decorative planes Angrand worked with a flecked touch geared to the Neo-Impressionist division of tone, and was not concerned with the 'primitive' but enunciated his anarchist ideology by representing the ideal of communal rural labour within a harmonious image. Yet despite distinct differences of technique and social values both canvases represent the summer landscape in essentially the same way. In both the figures are bound into the surface of the painting – Gauguin's Breton girl matching her piebald cattle, Angrand's figures elided with the land in touch and tone – thus conveying the indivisibility of peasant and land. Both are images of the repetitive rhythms of agricultural life, from day to day and season to season, and both show the bounty of the land that supports that life. Representing the two dominant avant-garde styles of the 1890s, Gauguin's and Angrand's images of harvest differ little from the reactionary Jules Breton's nostalgic evocation of harvest-time, for the values he articulated were powerful and widely shared.

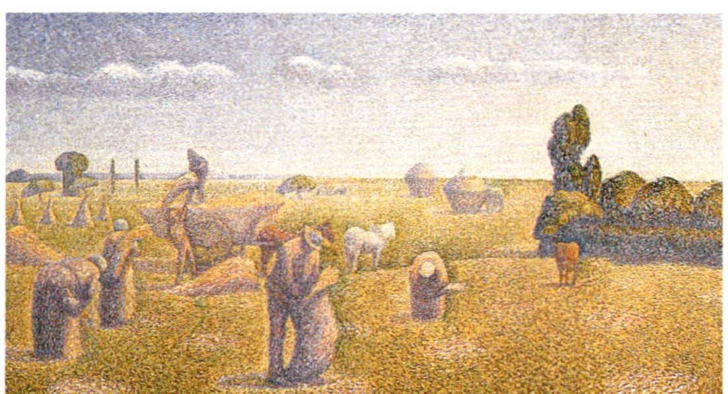

243
C. Angrand
The Harvesters 1892
Houston, Museum of Fine Arts, The John A. and Audrey Jones Beck Collection

Even Monet's *Haystack in a Field* [**244**], although neither an expansive landscape nor including figures, carries many of the same associations. One of a trio of such motifs painted during the summer of 1893, its piles of hay, both in the foreground and glimpsed in the further meadow through the pollarded willows, suggest human labour. That labour has its purpose – collecting fodder for animals – and its allotted time in the seasonal cycle, when the grass has grown tall in the rain and sun. It is not just Monet's representation of the summer conditions, warm blond light and a gentle breeze, but the way he painted them, in soft

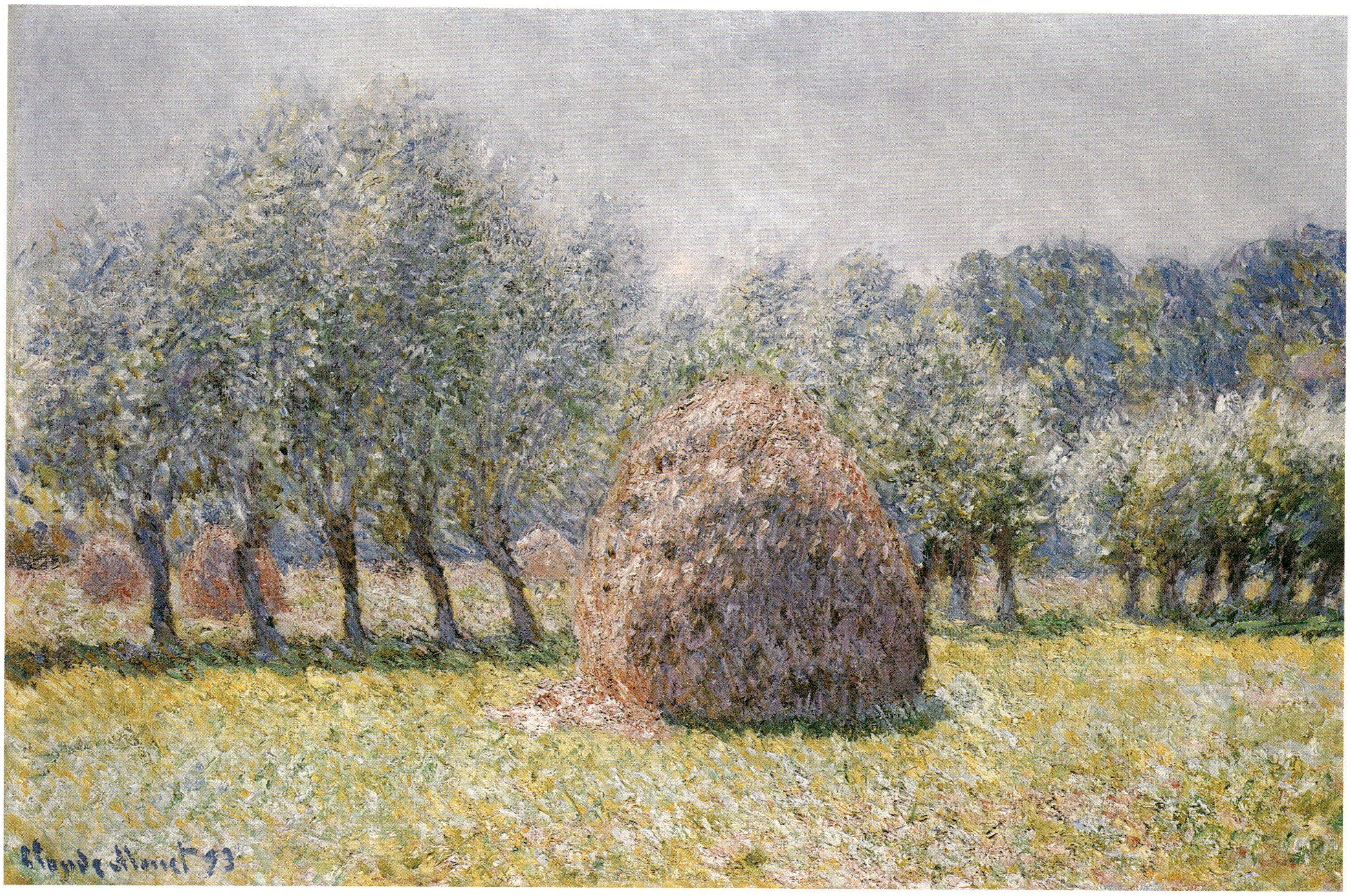

pastel tones and regulated textures, which makes this painting such an effective image. Both motif and its making artfully combine to convey a sense of harmony and rightness in this modest landscape.

In most cases making images of the harvest meant painting not only mid-summer weather and the ripe crops but also figures. Despite the gradual advent of farm machinery in the later nineteenth century the harvest was still a great event in the rural community, involving unanimous effort and the sharing of tasks towards a common goal. As such it made an ideal metaphor for articulating political values, and it is no wonder that it was used by painters such as Henri Martin for major public decorations [**213**]. An oil study by Martin [**245**] for a decorative scheme apparently unused [20] took advantage of the elongated format of the mural to spread more than a dozen figures across the scene, so that under the cornflower-blue sky and amidst the yellow crop peasants are shown drinking, resting, scything and binding the corn into sheaves. Martin was celebrated for producing images that expressed ideas clearly, and whereas for some critics such a picture conveyed the healthy virtues of 'love of life, cult of nature' Apollinaire was more scathing about this ability, calling Martin 'the great painter of primary education'.[21] A less overtly pedagogical way of idealising the community of the harvest and the bonds between peasant and land was by means of a consistency of touch and colour, as we have already seen with Gauguin and Angrand. The

244
C. Monet
Haystack in a Field 1893
Springfield, Massachusetts, Museum of Fine Arts, James Philip Gray Collection

245
H. Martin
The Harvest (Summer) *c.*1900–10
Brest, Musée municipal

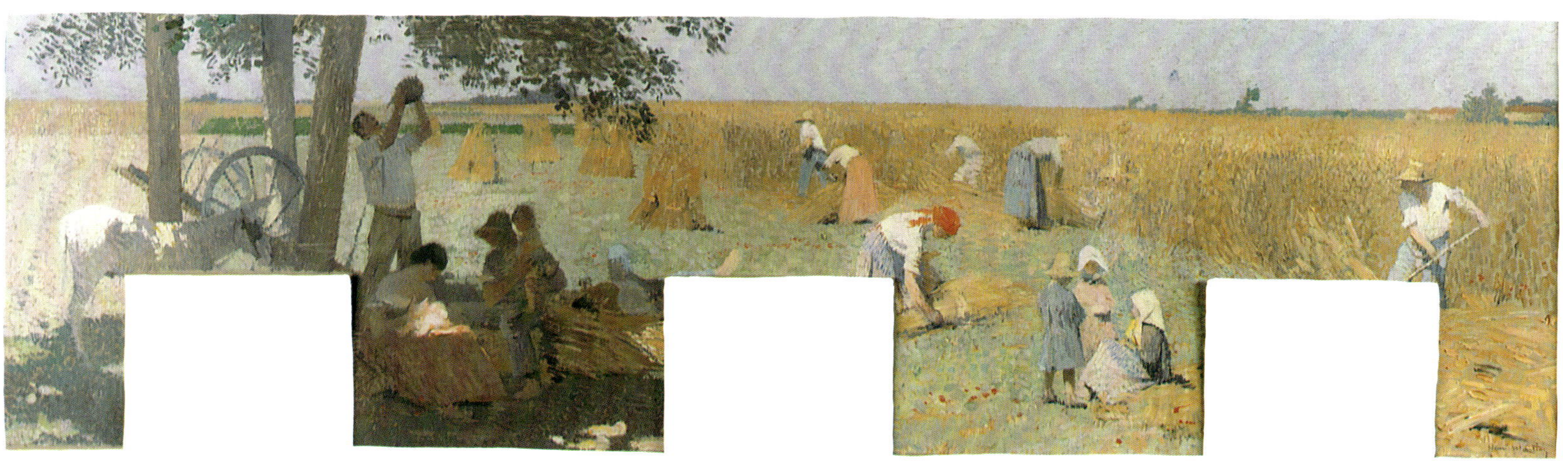

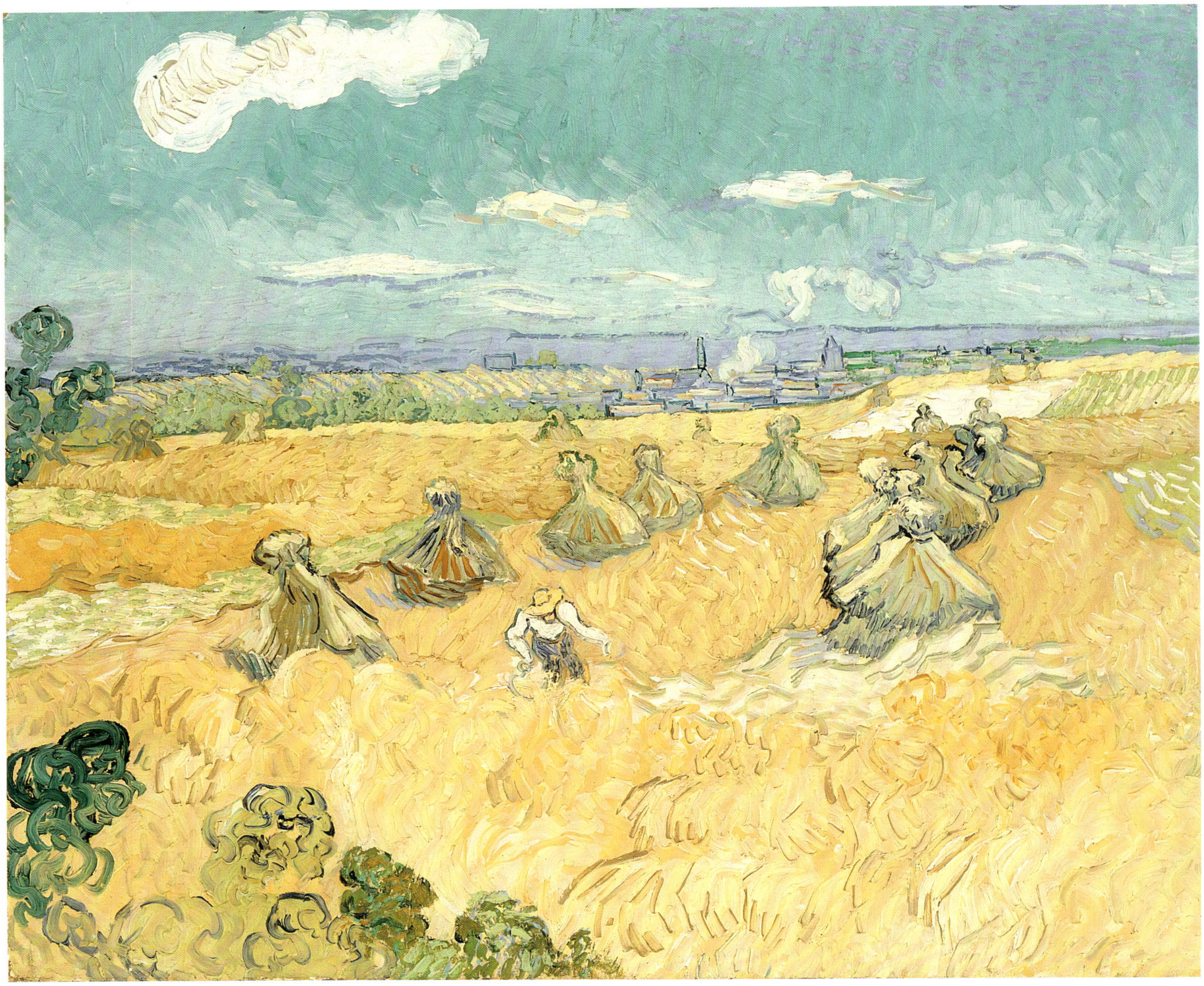

246
V. van Gogh
Wheat Fields with Reaper, Auvers 1888
Ohio, Toledo Museum cf Art, purchased with funds from the Libbey Endowment, Gift of Edward Drummond Libbey

247
R. Seyssaud
Harvest at Sunset c.1895–6
Mr & Mrs J. Benatoff

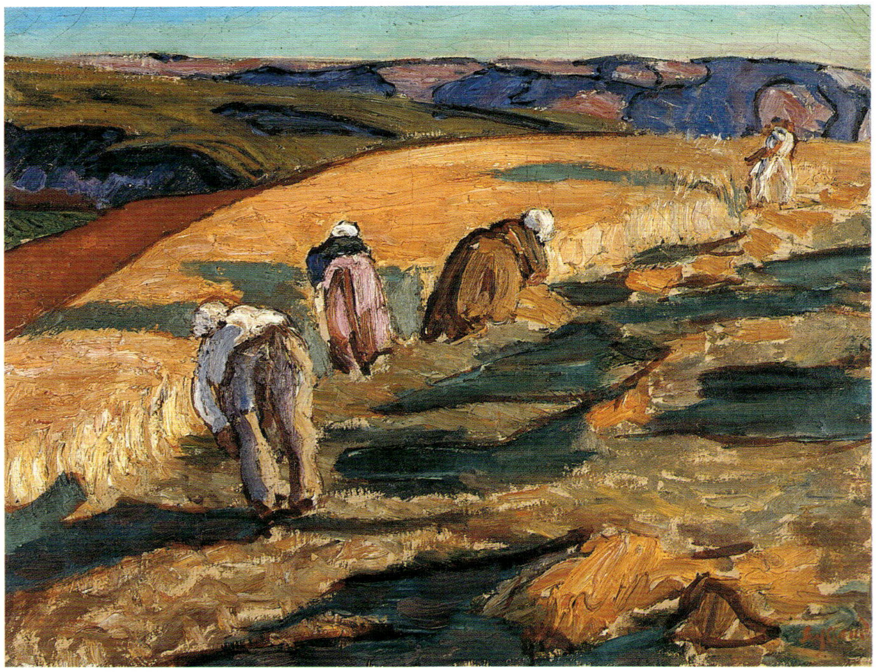

Marseillais René Seyssaud's rich texture and heated chromatics did the same in his *Harvest at Sunset* [**247**], painted during the mid-1890s. Seyssaud not only bound his figures into the surface of his picture, for by cutting out the horizon to look down on the labourers he contrived to give a greater sense of the effort of their task than in Martin's more comfortably spacious rendition.

The figure in the harvest landscape need not always convey community. For van Gogh, that figure's associations changed with his mood. During an extraordinary week between 13 and 20 June 1888 he completed some ten paintings of the cornfields around Arles.[22] At one level he saw these harvest motifs as a colouristic project; they were yellow paintings, he explained in a letter to Theo, compared to the blue marines he had painted earlier that month at Saintes-Maries-de-la-Mer and the pink and white orchards in blossom made in the spring.[23] At another they identified his work as a painter with the peasants' labour. Writing to Emile Bernard at the end of June van Gogh spoke of the group as 'yellow – old gold – done quickly, quickly, quickly and in a hurry, just like the harvester who is silent under the blazing sun, intent only on his reaping'.[24] A painting such as *Wheat Fields with Reaper* [**246**] shows the urgency of his activity in the energetic brushwork and the limited palette. But the chromatic simplicity of this pleasing harmony of yellow and blue does not detract from its subtlety, for the primaries are offset by secondary violet and green, the whole rendered in a remarkably fresh and lucid unity. The reaper fits comfortably into this setting, the rhythms and texture of his body echoing those of his surroundings. This is an image of toil, certainly, but of energy and optimism too. Left to our own devices, that is perhaps the way we would read the *Reaper* image [**248**] which van Gogh made in four versions the following June,[25] as it too shows a single figure sickling corn. But van Gogh told Theo that 'I see in this reaper – a vague figure fighting like the devil in the midst of the heat to get to the end of his task – I see in him the image of death, in the sense that humanity might be the wheat he is reaping'. At the time van Gogh had newly arrived at Saint-Rémy and his spirits were low. Nevertheless, he insisted that his account of the picture was not negative: '...there's nothing sad in this death, it goes its way in broad daylight with the sun flooding everything with a light of pure gold'.[26] Death, then, was to van Gogh as natural as the cycle of the seasons and the peasants' toil on the land.

Another natural association of the harvest is represented in André Brouillet's *Love in the Fields* [**251**], a smaller and more horizontal variant of his exhibit at the Salon of 1888.[27] Showing a snatched, greedy kiss, the painting deals with female sensuality and assertive virility, and in placing the two young peasant figures in front of the cornfield they are harvesting Brouillet frankly associates human sexuality with natural fertility. Once again, such an analogy was drawn by avant-garde artists as well as Salon exhibitors: Gauguin's *Loss of Virginity* of 1890 is also set in a harvest landscape.[28] And the topos lived on. Lhermitte's *The Family* [**249**] of 1908 represents the peasants as tied to the land. Although painted almost a decade into the twentieth century, the ox-drawn cart and traditional tools insist on the timelessness of harvesting. The powerful physique of the scyther dominates the centre, but this splendid specimen of French manhood looks tenderly down on his wife breast-feeding their baby, while the grandmother watches. Yet again the cycle of life is implicitly linked to the cycle of the seasons, for we are encouraged to read the rolling generations alongside the turning seasons, to match the fertility of the peasant with the bounty of the soil. Lhermitte's naturalism may look *retardataire* alongside Gleizes's *Harvest Threshing* [**250**], but paradoxically the Cubist painting articulates much the same ideals. Although Gleizes introduces machinery into his rural scene, the golden-brown tones and the faceting lock the figures into the landscape, and the painting's simultaneism introduces a sense of the past, present and future. Thus by radically different means Gleizes evoked the same notion of *durée* as Lhermitte.

What Gleizes's painting serves to underline is that throughout this period when painters opted to paint a landscape in a particular season they tended, however drastically different were their styles and ideologies, to emphasise the timelessness of the motif. Perhaps the ancient lineage of the typology prompted this. Where modernity introduced notions of change and progress, the cycle of the seasons still implied elemental consistencies in the human condition, above all the pattern of our lives. Rich in such profound associations, the imagery of the seasons continued to offer a challenge both to the eye and to the imagination of the landscape painter.

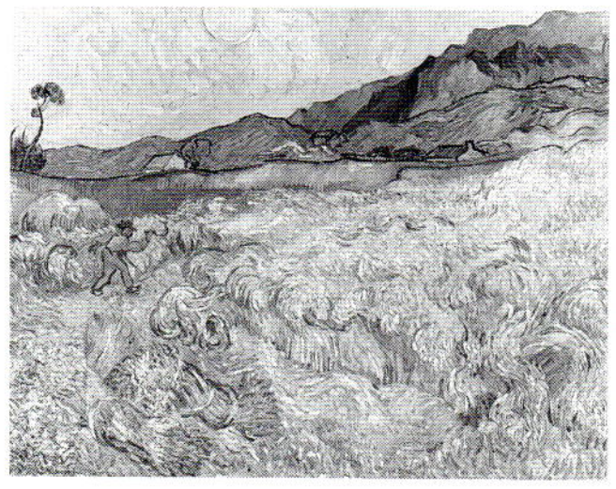

248
V. van Gogh
The Reaper 1889
Amsterdam, Rijksmuseum Vincent van Gogh

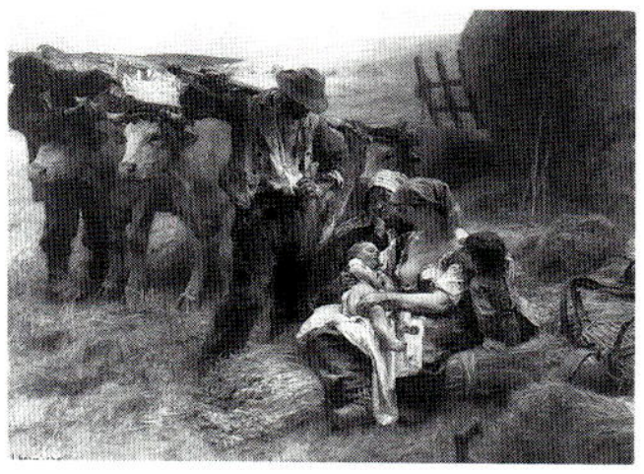

249
L. Lhermitte
The Family 1908
Beverly Hills, Private Collection

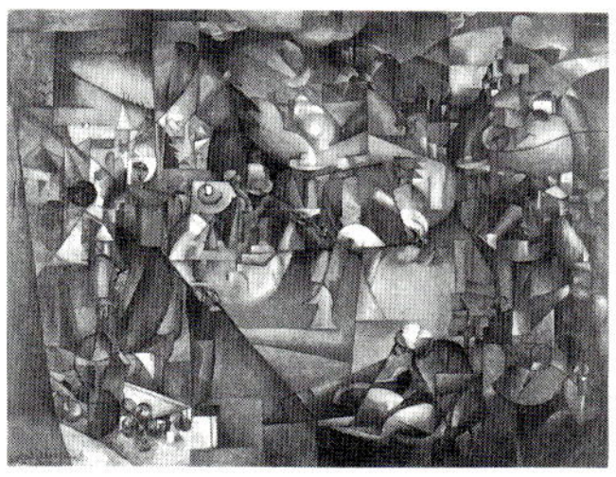

250
A. Gleizes ***Harvest Threshing*** 1912
Location unknown

below
251
A. Brouillet
Love in the Fields *c.*1888
Poitiers, Musées de la ville

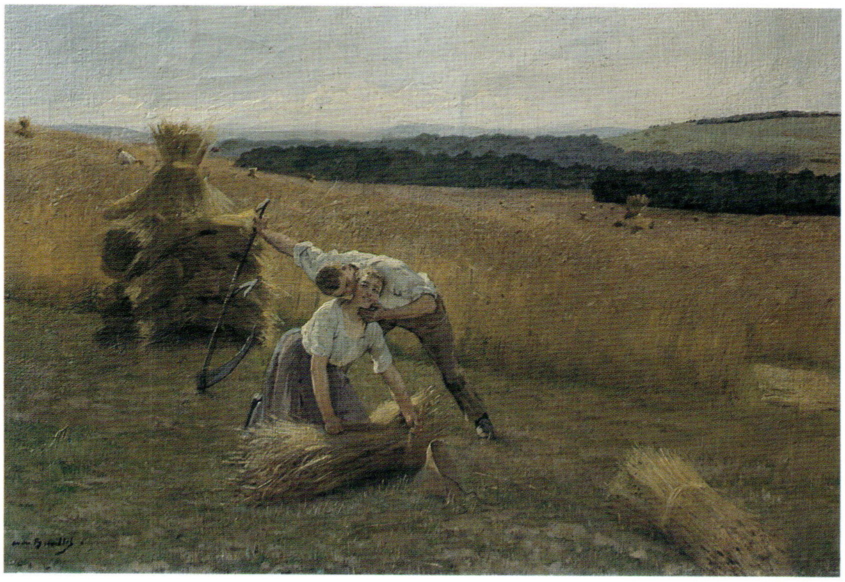

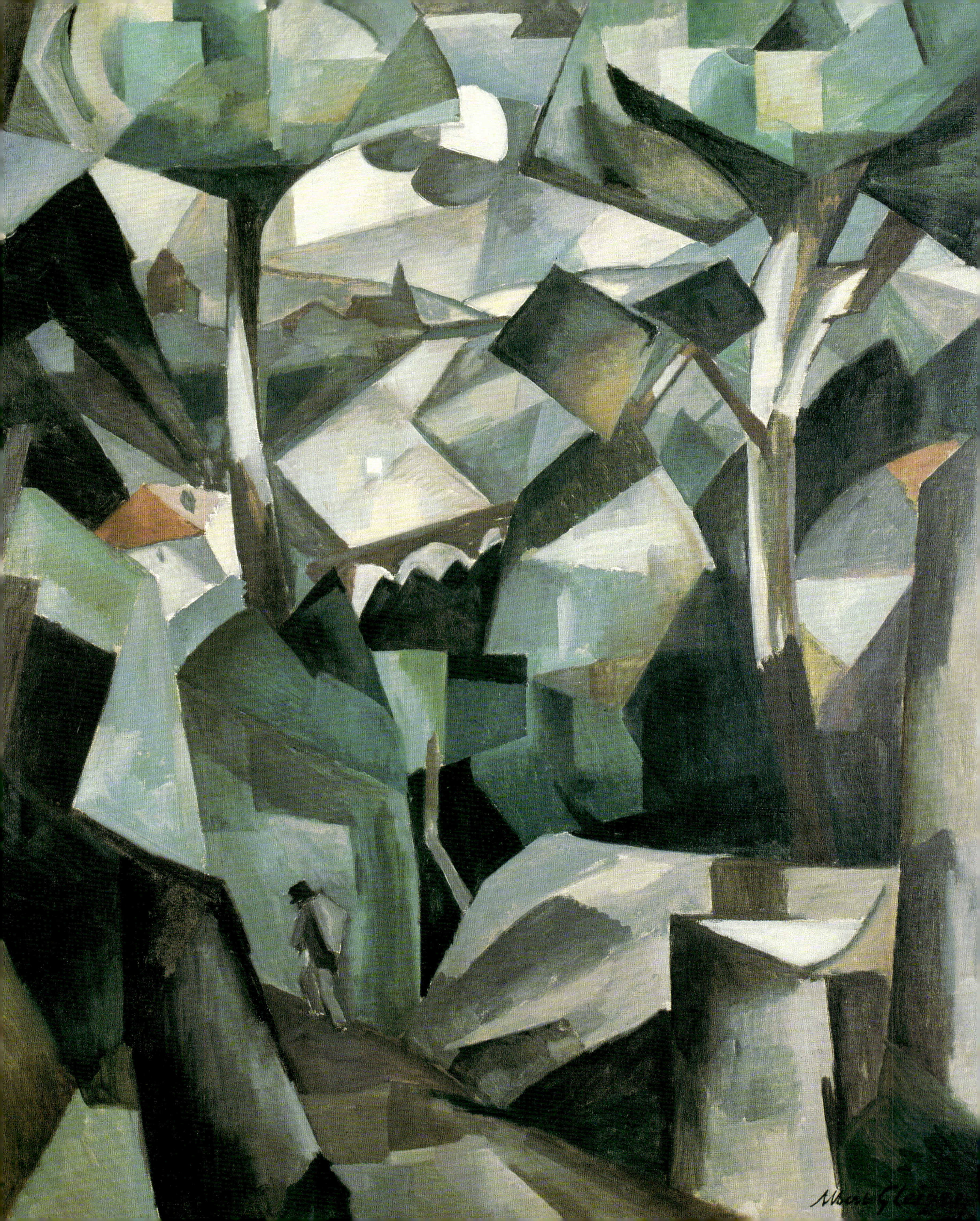

14 Tour d'horizon

The forty years from 1874 to 1914, I hope I have shown, were an intense and exciting period for landscape painting in France. The paths the reader has followed were planned to take in both the customary and the unexpected, to look at famous names and celebrated images as well as forgotten figures and surprising pictures. By plotting out themes to be explored and selecting paintings which seem to me to illuminate them, I have tried to elucidate neglected patterns and stimulate fresh thinking about the representation of landscape at this period. This is not to say that the more conventional method of charting stylistic shifts is invalid. By focusing on the way different generations interpreted a single motif – the Normandy cliffs, for example – one can identify changing aesthetics and artistic methods. Changes took place not only in the means of representation but also in what was represented. Over these four decades we have seen how the nocturne as a subject and the series as a practice developed as exciting possibilities for landscape painters and then faded away. And we have seen change revolve around a continuum, notably in the case of the 'Claudian' composition, used by Corot in 1873 [**116**] and Gleizes in 1911 [**124**] as the armature for paintings extremely different in style but sharing the same instinct for a convention associated with the ideal to articulate notions of harmony in nature.

The momentum of the avant-garde's search for new means of expression was propelled by growing consciousness of a changing world, whose increasing pace was sharply altering perceptions of the physical environment. But within this trajectory were reassuring continuities. Landscape painters still concerned themselves with motifs such as the changing of the seasons which had both a time-honoured history in the *paysage* genre but also spoke of enduring truths and changeless cycles. Classicism, too, had deep roots in French painting, and the vocabulary it offered artists in the ordering of their landscapes remained of continuous value. This was not merely a matter of design, for the classical encouraged fictive touchstones such as the pastoral. In essence fantasy, pastoral could be a matter of sensuality and delight, as in the Mediterranean canvases of Cross [**111**] or Matisse [**128**] and could even be adapted to mollify the modern; there is a case for interpreting some of Monet's Argenteuil paintings [**30**] as imaginative suburban pastorals. Each of these manifestations adapted ancient associations of nature as stable, tranquil and welcoming to modern modes of representation.

Other salient consistencies can be tracked across the themes explored here. The importance of landscape painting as an emotional vehicle for the artist should never be underestimated. This came into play at several levels. It involved artists' reactions to nature and their means of representing it, what the Impressionists understood by that complex term *sensation*. Integral to that private reaction to nature, at once internal and gestural, was the selection of motif. Even the stock subject would suggest a personal response from the painter, perhaps prompted by external conditioning – hence the differences both stylistic and iconographical between Notre-Dame represented by the *dévot* Aman-Jean [**56**] and the anarchist Luce [**57**, **58**]. The landscape motif could even have more deeply personal resonances, as we have seen with canvases as sharply distinct as Denis's *Eurydice* [**136**] and Guillemet's *Wreck at Villerville* [**80**]. Crucially, landscape at this period served as an imaginative as well as an emotional medium. This too could be highly personal, as in the fantastic metamorphoses we have seen wrought on natural forms by artists as different as Degas [**158**, **163**] and Friesz [**166**]. No less emotionally charged in their own way are the imaginative incidents taking their mood from the surrounding landscape, as witnessed in the menacing *Bonjour, Monsieur Gauguin* [**145**] or the meditative *Path through the Trees* by Denis [**185**].

Landscape was widely used to articulate general truths and values about attachment to one's *pays*, about security of habitat, the grandeur of France's natural and architectural heritage and the fecundity of her soil: the forces, therefore, that bind and define the nation. Such ideas could be implicit in relatively conventional landscapes focusing on natural features – we have seen modernity and prosperity suggested in pictures by Monet [**8**] and Pissarro [**197**], for example – although they might be more overt and involve

252
A. Gleizes
Landscape (Meudon) 1911 (detail)
Paris, Musée national d'art moderne, Centre Georges Pompidou

figures playing a substantial rôle in the landscape, as in the grand public decorations of Puvis [**210**] or Martin [**213**]. Indeed, the traditional use of landscape as a theatre for the staging of the great truths of the human condition remained an enduring challenge to the painter, one met at this period by an impressive variety of imaginative solutions motivated by a wide range of ambitions and ideologies.

We see the entwinement of consistency and change once more in the business of making pictures. Painting out of doors remained a constant practice throughout these four decades, from Monet to Matisse, as attested by *the Seine at Petit-Gennevilliers* of 1872 [**42**] and *Acanthus* of 1912 [**213**]. So too did the allegedly reactionary *paysage composé*, for pictures as different as Gleizes's *Landscape, Meudon* [**214**] and Ménard's *Hercules and the Lion* [**139**], both made just before the First World War, belong under that rubric as much as does Corot's 1873 *Pastorale* [**116**]. Indeed, a painter such as Matisse saw no paradox in switching at will from one practice to the other, for if *Acanthus* is a *plein air* painting, *Le Bonheur de vivre* [**128**] is a *paysage composé*. Of course, differences and contradictions existed. Sisley had different reasons for working outdoors than Derain, the former [**195**] subtly attempting the spontaneous record of atmospheric effects, the latter [**107**] dynamically seeking the motif's organic unity. And the use of classical compositions and subjects owed its fresh impetus at the turn of the century not only to burgeoning nationalism's determination to redefine French culture around the ancient values associated with the Mediterranean world, but also in part to the inspiration of Nietzsche.

That fascination with the Mediterranean, whether taking pictorial form in images of nymphs, ancient villages or wild countryside, was rooted in nostalgia, itself symptomatic of a desire for security in a rapidly changing world of class friction, technological advances and international instability. The Côte d'Azur, as well as other coastal and picturesque parts of France, were becoming magnets for tourists, among whom the itinerant landscape painter should be counted. The ability to escape from the city, if only temporarily, for a change of pace and of air, was no longer restricted to an élite but was becoming increasingly possible for wage-earners lower down the social hierarchy. Travel to the countryside was facilitated by the spreading railway network, the craze for cycling, and the launch of the motor car. Part of this pattern was that nature became more hospitable and accessible to women, a development recognised in contemporary landscape imagery from poster to painting [**11**, **89**]. Nature's growing importance as a placebo for a wide range of social classes manifested itself also in the art market, where the centrality of landscape painting indicates the importance of *paysage* as a domestic icon of reassuring values. The artistic effort expended on landscape was not just concerned with stylistic experiment, as was often the case with still-life. Painters' immersion in nature was one manifestation of a desire shared generally among the bourgeoisie to establish nature – whether in the form of holiday or painting, suburban home or picture postcard – as a touchstone of reassurance. As it has been so consistently in European culture, the image of nature was asked to secure many certainties, among them the differences between north and south, the fruitfulness of the land, the progress of industry, the adherence of the regions and rural populations to the values upheld by the bourgeois Republic. Painters used *paysage*, so flexible in composition, so adaptable to different artistic styles, so evocative of emotion and stimulating to the imagination, to fulfil these complex public and personal needs. That these were so adventurously and variously met between 1874 and 1914 proves the enduring challenge and delight that artists find in painting the landscape.

Notes and References

1

LANDSCAPE PAINTING IN FRANCE 1874–1914: PROGRESS, NATIONALISM AND TRADITION

1 Bouyer 1894a, p.91, n.2, n.4
2 'L'Argent' 1913 (Péguy 1961, pp.1101–2)
3 White 1965; Whiteley 1979; Green, N. 1987
4 *Louis Cabat* 1987, n.p.; Bouyer 1897, p.103, n.2
5 Derain 1955, p.60; *Fauve Landscape* 1990–1, p.185
6 *Monet-Rodin* 1989–90, pp.73–99
7 Breton 1890, pp.332–3
8 Michel, A. 1897, p.48; see also de Fourcaud, June 1884, p.492
9 Baudelaire 1965, pp.103–5
10 Duvergier de Hauranne 1873, p.860; Mantz 1878, p.438
11 Lafenestre 1894, p.192; Bouyer 1894a, p.4
12 Paulhan 1913, p.6
13 Shiff 1984, esp. pp.187–9
14 'Proudhon et Courbet', *Le Salut publique*, 26 July 1865 (Zola 1974, p.38); Flat 1893, p.340
15 Amiel 1889; Degas 1947, p.252; Mithouard 1907, p.6; Paulhan 1913, p.73
16 Alain-Fournier 1913, p.2
17 Amiel 1889, p.250 (10 May 1878)
18 Uzanne 1889, p.148
19 *Souvenirs de voyage* 1992, p.53 (letter of 27 July 1874); Guisan and Jakubec 1974, p.45 (letter of 23? July 1900)
20 Michel, A. 1888, p.139; Lafenestre 1889, p.2
21 Champier 1879, p.118; Paulhan 1913, p.20
22 Tucker 1990, p.104
23 *Jean-François Millet* 1975–6, p.106
24 Déroulède 1894, p.i
25 K. 1891, p.117
26 Segard 1914, II, pp.99–100
27 Bouyer 1901, p.396; Thiébault-Sisson 1902, p.34; Vlaminck 1961, pp.79–80
28 Lee 1990, p.51 (letter of 12 June 1914)
29 Salmon, A. 1912, pp.26–7
30 Williams 1973, pp.1, 17; Herbert 1970; Grad and Riggs 1982; Green, N. 1990
31 Van Gogh 1958, III, p.465 (letter W.19)
32 Guisan and Jakubec 1974, p.45 (letter of 23? July 1900); Vlaminck 1961, p.66; *Henri Martin* 1983, p.73
33 Michel, E. 1876, pp.13–14
34 *Jules Breton* 1982–3, p.20
35 Theuriet 1888, p.vii
36 'Petits Voyages en Auvergne', *Gil Blas*, 17 July 1883 (Maupassant 1980, 2, pp.235–7)
37 D'Amat, vol.IX, 1961, pp.1282–3; vol.VIII, 1959, p.1494
38 Hamerton 1892, p.47
39 Thomson 1990, p.44
40 Elwitt 1975, pp.103–16
41 Buzard 1993, p.41
42 Tucker 1982, pp.57–87; Herbert, R. L. 1988, 219–29
43 Schivelbusch 1986, pp.24, 55
44 Vachon n.d., p.146; Degas 1947, p.252; Séailles 1899, pp.162–3 (see Bantens 1990, p.87)
45 Herbert, R. L. 1988, pp.223–6
46 Weber 1986, p.71
47 *Fauve Landscape* 1990–1, p.76
48 *Fauve Landscape* 1990–1, p.82
49 Cazeau 1982, p.117; undated letter from Signac to van Rysselberghe, *c.*1900 (Special Collections, Getty Center for the History of Art and the Humanities)
50 Weber 1986, p.194
51 *Guide Michelin* 1900, p.6
52 *Claude Monet at the Time of Giverny* 1983, p.277 (letter of 1 April 1906)
53 Mirbeau 1908 (see Nathanson 1989, pp.14,18)
54 Marx, R. 1909, p.530
55 *Guide Michelin* 1900, p.6
56 Apollinaire 1965, p.20
57 Michel, A. 1896, p.7
58 *Souvenirs de voyage* 1992, p.63; Marcel n.d., p.27; Pennell 1920, p.363
59 Renard 1887, pp.42–69; 'From Michelangelo to Picasso', *Les Marches de Provence*, February 1912 (Apollinaire 1972, pp.195–6)
60 Holl 1910, pp.39,72,58
61 Wildenstein 1974–92, II (1979), p.223 (letter of 1 February 1883)
62 Hellebranth 1976, nos 39,119
63 Houssaye 1882, p.25; Mabilleau 1890, p.6
64 Monod 1905, p.202
65 Burty 1874, p.3; Monod 1905, p.202; Copeau 1910, p.174
66 Greenspan 1981; *On Classic Ground* 1990; Herbert, J. 1992; Benjamin 1992; House 1993
67 Havard 1879
68 Renan 1961, p.598 (letter of 20 February 1872); Steegmuller 1982, p.220 (letter of 25 September 1875)
69 Michel, E. 1880, p.909; Laforgue 1895 (Dottin 1988, p.132)
70 Michel, E. 1906, p.99; Bouyer 1908
71 D'Indy 1906/9, p.80
72 Reff 1960, pp.164–74; Herbert, J. 1992, pp.112–45
73 Bouyer 1908, p.113
74 Davis Butler 1967, pp.92-3
75 Michel, A. 1896, p.158; Salmon, A. 1912, p.26
76 Vlaminck 1961, p.81
77 20 May 1915 (?) (Special Collections, Getty Center for the History of Art and the Humanities)

2

THE SUBURBS OF PARIS

1 Cherbuliez 1876, p.524
2 D'Haussonville 1881, pp.827–8; Evenson 1979, p.220
3 Périer 1890, pp.9,11; Petit 1939
4 Zeldin 1980, p.291; Herbert, R. L. 1988, pp.196-8
5 Phlipponneau 1956, pp.66–7, 80; Peeters 1886, pp.5,16; Meyeur and Rebérioux 1984, p.250
6 Barron 1886, p.117
7 Tucker 1982, p.61 et al
8 *Triomphe des Mairies*, 1986–7, pp.248–9
9 Bernier 1886, p.9
10 Barron 1886, p.38
11 Lorrain 1911, p.97
12 Paris, Musée d'Orsay; Washington, D.C., National Gallery
13 Peeters 1886, pp.15–16; Tucker 1982, pp.151–2
14 Bigot 1877, p.1046
15 Thomson 1985, pp.94–5; Thomson 1987b, p.20
16 *Georges Seurat* 1991–2, p.224; Thomson 1985, p.64
17 F[orain] 1889, p.2
18 Tucker 1982, p.99
19 London, National Gallery; Chicago, Art Institute
20 *Georges Seurat* 1991–2, p.258
21 Thomson 1985, pp.134–5; Farr/House 1987, no.34
22 *Van Gogh à Paris* 1988, nos 113 and 113a, p.298
23 See also *Emile Bernard* 1990, nos 11,12
24 Barron 1886, p.63
25 Mockel 1895, p.60
26 *Paris-Journal*, 11 May 1914 (Apollinaire 1972, p.380)
27 Herbert, J. 1992, pp.54–5
28 Berkeley Smith 1903, p.313; *Fauve Landscape* 1990–1, pp.128–9,137
29 *Fauve Landscape* 1990–1, p.134

3

NOTRE DAME AND THE EIFFEL TOWER

1 *1889* 1989, pp. 224–6
2 *Lighting up the Landscape* 1986, no. 68; Thomson 1986, p.847
3 Saint-Juirs 1890, pp.153–4
4 Driskel 1992, ch.6
5 Thomson 1985, pp.75, 78
6 *Journal des artistes*, 20 Dec. 1884; quoted in Bazalgette 1976, p.69
7 'Tiphereth' 1893, p.6
8 *1893* 1993, no.25
9 Paris, Musée d'Orsay; Brussels, Musées royaux des beaux-arts
10 Pennell 1920, p.315; see also Vaudevire 1990
11 Bazalgette 1976, pp.58,181; Barr 1951, p.37
12 Gerstein 1989, p.106
13 Gerstein 1989, p.106
14 Bailly-Herzberg 1989, IV, p.282 (letter of 20 October 1896)
15 Pau, Musée des beaux-arts; Monod 1913, p.1
16 St Petersburg, Hermitage
17 Salmon 1912, p.11
18 Holl 1912, p.118
19 Holl 1912, p.119
20 *De Corot aux Impressionnistes* 1991, pp.34–5; a similar painting is repr. p.36
21 Baedeker 1900, p.282
22 Mauclair 1905, p.722
23 De Vogüé 1889, p.200
24 *1889* 1989, pp.220–4
25 Bertaut 1931, pp.190–1; *1889* 1989, p.225
26 Laforgue 1887, p.345; Antoine 1921, pp.149–50
27 Bluysen 1890, p.79
28 *La Vie moderne*, 29 October 1887, p.696; 4 February 1888, p.72
29 Christie's, 1 December 1987, no.101; New York, private collection
30 Thomson 1982, p.84; Mayeur and Rebérioux 1984, pp.133–7
31 Bailly-Herzberg 1890–91, II, p.277 (letter 530; 7 July 1889)
32 Bailly-Herzberg 1890–91, II, p.315 (letter 559; late December 1889); see also p. 319 (letter 561, 29 December 1889)
33 Thomson 1982; Thomson 1990, pp.59–65, 102–4
34 *1889* 1989, p.220
35 Castex and Bellefroid 1968, p.40
36 Rewald 1953, pp.32–3 (13 December 1898)
37 *L'Intransigéant*, 5 March 1912 (Apollinaire 1972, p.207)
38 Green 1980, p.166
39 *L'Intransigéant*, 6 June 1912 (Apollinaire 1972, p.241)
40 Matthews 1987, p.133
41 Spate 1979, pp.187–203
42 Apollinaire 1965, p.45

4

THE CHANNEL COAST

1 *Jongkind and the Pre-Impressionists* 1976–7, p.15
2 Angrand 1988, p.139 (letter of 29 November 1901)
3 'La vie d'un paysagiste', *Gil Blas*, 28 September 1886 (Maupassant 1980, 3, p.287)
4 Proth 1879, pp.56–7
5 Debussy 1980, p.162 (letter of 5 August 1907)
6 Malte-Brun 1882, pp.38, 40
7 *Georges Seurat* 1991–2, p.240
8 Maupassant 1888 (1979, p.49)
9 Bouyer 1894b, p.412
10 Wildenstein 1974–92, II (1979), pp.2–8; nos.708–43, 751–808
11 Wildenstein 1974–92, II (1979), p.216 (letter 255, 15 March 1882); p.218 (letter 270, 11 April 1882)
12 Wildenstein 1974–92, II (1979), p.218 (letter 264, 6 April 1882)
13 Jamot 1906, p.481
14 Hamilton 1992, pp.49, 56; Weber 1986, pp.177–94; Herbert, R. L. 1988, pp.265–302
15 'Les Gares', *La Dernière Mode*, 18 October 1874 (Mallarmé 1945, p.774)
16 Spate 1992, pp.154–6
17 Thomson 1985, pp.158–9, 161–8, 176; *Georges Seurat* 1991–2, pp.244-55
18 Baedeker 1881, p.350; 1900, p.397
19 Gidel 1891, pp.65–6
20 Hare 1895, p.77
21 *Seurat at Gravelines* 1990, p.27
22 St Tropez, Musée de l'Annonciade
23 Mouton 1885, p.547
24 Mitchell 1981, pp.26, 36
25 Wildenstein 1974–92, II (1979), p.214 (Letter 236, 8 February 1882)
26 Herbert, R. L. 1988, p.302
27 De Lostalot 1883, p.343
28 Bénédite 1897, p.165; Desjardins 1901, pp.189–90

5

THE MEDITERRANEAN COAST

1 Soubiran 1993
2 Weber 1986, p.184
3 'The Midi', *Paris-Journal*, 14 June 1914 (Apollinaire 1972, p.406)
4 Chartrain-Hebbelinck 1969, p.95, n.1
5 'Petits Voyages. La Chartreuse de la Verne', *Gil Blas*, 26 August 1884 (Maupassant 3, 1980, pp.10–11)
6 Jones 1988, p.145 (letter 182, 20 April 1912)
7 Wildenstein 1974–92, II (1979), p.232 (letter 388, 12 January 1884)
8 *Souvenirs de voyage* 1992, p.136
9 *Fauve Landscape* 1990–1, p.63; p.116, n.17
10 Wildenstein 1974–92, II (1979), p.233 (letter 394, 26 January 1884); van Gogh 1958, III, p.436 (W.4, June 1888)
11 Wildenstein 1974–92, II (1979), p.243 (letter 438, 5 March 1884)
12 Retté 1894, pp.352–3; Signac, 1949, p.106 (29 September 1894)
13 Derain 1955, p.147
14 Cachin 1971, p.51
15 *Souvenirs de voyage* 1992, p.138 (letter of 23 January 1882)
16 Moréas 1908, p.251
17 Monod 1905a, p.2; *Louis Valtat* 1989, no.3
18 House 1986, p.25
19 Wildenstein 1974–92, II (1979), nos 1158–72
20 Baedeker 1895, p.104
21 'Dix Marines d'Antibes de M. Claude Monet', *Revue indépendante*, July 1888 (Fénéon I 1970, p.113)
22 Special Collections, The Getty Center for the History of Art and the Humanities
23 Marseille 1991–2
24 Dubois et al. 1985, pp.6–15, 38
25 Cézanne 1976, p.146
26 Cézanne 1976, p.292 (letter of 1 September 1902)
27 Paris, Musée d'Orsay; Chicago, Art Institute
28 'Notes d'un voyageur', *Le Gaulois*, 4 February 1884 (Maupassant 1980, 2, p.346)
29 Jones 1988, p.96 (letter 96, 11 August 1900)
30 Derain 1955, pp.147–9
31 Herbert, J. 1992, p.83
32 Stockholm, Moderna Museet
33 *Fauve Landscape* 1990–1, p.93
34 Special Collections, The Getty Center for the History of Art and the Humanities

6

REINVENTING THE PASTORAL IDEAL

1 Boime 1971, p.146
2 Tucker 1990, p.233; Rewald 1949–53 (1949), p.122 (20 May 1895)
3 Lafenestre 1893, pp.670–1
4 Marcel et al. 1908, pp.vi-vii
5 Michel, A. 1896, pp.262–3; Derain 1955, p.107
6 Michel, A. 1896, pp.48, 50
7 'Exposition K.-X.Roussel', *L'Occident*, December 1903 (Denis 1920, p.139)
8 Jamot 1906, pp.458, 464–6
9 Gautier 1865, p.19
10 Special Collections, Getty Center for the History of Art and the Humanities
11 Moréas 1908, p.226
12 Fromentin 1876 (1948, p.151)
13 Soubiran 1993, pp.142, 412–26
14 Sterling and Adhémar 1958, no.393
15 Duvergier de Hauranne 1873, pp.860–1; Claretie 1865, p.186
16 Compin, Lacambre, Roquebert et al. 1990, I, p.224
17 Desjardins 1899, p.448
18 Cézanne 1976, p.209 (letter of 24 May 1883)
19 *Cézanne and Poussin* 1990, p.133, fig.49
20 Gauguin 1984, p.154 (letter of 20 June 1887); p.156 (letter of early July 1887)
21 *Gauguin* 1989, no.31
22 *Post-Impressionism* 1979–80, no.83
23 Monod 1905b, p.202
24 *Matisse in Morocco* 1990–1, p.68
25 *Matisse in Morocco* 1990–1, p.211
26 Robbins 1963–4; Spate 1979, pp.18–22
27 'The Salon de la Nationale before the Opening', *L'Intransigeant*, 13 April 1910 (Apollinaire 1972, p.76)
28 Compin, Lacambre, Roquebert et al. 1990, I, p.500
29 *Places of Delight* 1988–9, pp.183–257; Marx, L. 1992; Strick 1992
30 Mozziconacci 1990, no.28; Lafenestre 1893, p.670
31 House 1985, p.21
32 Denis 1957, II (early February 1906); Angrand 1988, p.158 and n.2 (letters of 26 January and 4 February 1904)
33 Amiel 1889, pp.220–1 (27 January 1875)
34 *Neo-Impressionism* 1968, p.47
35 Greenspan 1981, p.143, n.112; Cross 1922, p.447
36 Whitfield 1991, p.144
37 *Fauve Landscape* 1990–1, p.118, n.132 (letter of 12 May 1906)
38 Compin 1964, no.97 (letter of September 1902)
39 *Roussel* 1993, no.57; also Boucher and Imbert 1983, no.161
40 Cousturier 1927, p.39
41 Leighten 1989, p.107
42 Compin 1964, nos 97, 160, 142, 147, 171

7

INCIDENTS IN THE LANDSCAPE

1 Bouyer 1897, p.97; Marguillier, 1899, p.329
2 The other (private collection) is repr. Bouillon 1993, p.122
3 Denis, 1957, II, p.34 (early February 1906)
4 Monod 1909, p.3
5 Monod 1907, p.4
6 Bouillon 1993, pp.108, 122
7 Vauxcelles 1905
8 Mauclair 1905b, p.523
9 *Félix Vallotton* 1991–2, p.185
10 Desjardins 1899, p.457
11 Bouyer 1897, p.79; Michel, A. 1897, p.84; Migeon 1902, p.102; Bouyer 1914, pp.176–7
12 Compin, Lacambre, Roquebert et al. 1990, II, pp.314–15
13 *Le Moyen-Age* 1980, p.59
14 Saunier 1902, pp.148–9
15 Fournel 1884, pp.344, 346
16 Flat 1900, p.616
17 Tours, Musée des beaux-arts; Lille, Musée des beaux-arts
18 Bénédite 1897, between pp.172–3
19 Paris, Musée d'Orsay
20 Weber 1986, p.46
21 Hutton 1990
22 Desjardins 1901, pp.185–6
23 Prague, Narodni Galerie; *Gauguin* 1989, p.180
24 St. Petersburg, Hermitage; Amsterdam, Van Gogh Museum

8

LANDSCAPE AS VISION AND METAMORPHOSIS

1 *Frantisek Kupka* 1975, nos 79–80
2 Silverman 1989, p.106 and ch.5
3 Moréas 1908, p.214; Desjardins 1899, pp.37–8
4 Salmon, A. 1912, p.6
5 Segard 1914, II, pp.195–6
6 Tucker 1990, pp.143–87; Pissarro 1990, pp.6–35; Spate 1992, pp.224–32
7 Angrand 1988, p.70 (letter of 23 May 1895)
8 Michel, A. 1986, pp.290–1
9 Holl 1910, pp.56–7
10 Mouton 1885, p.537
11 Musée de Brest
12 Thomson 1992, p.154
13 Kendall 1993, pp.145–229; Kendall 1994
14 Zola 1967, p.834; Theuriet 1888, p.55
15 Epuy 1907, p.114
16 Thomson 1987a, pp.110–11; Kendall 1993, pp.214–20
17 *Kees van Dongen* 1989-90, nos 2, 3
18 Norberg 1908, p.34
19 Séailles 1899, pp.162–3; Bantens 1990, p.87
20 Joyant 1926, p.192
21 Carrière 1907, p.26; Bantens 1990, p.89

9

THE NOCTURNE

1 Pennell 1920, p.176
2 Desjardins 1899, p.451
3 Stephan 1974, ch.IV; Balakian 1977
4 Desjardins 1899, p.453
5 Amiel 1889, p.245 (21 July 1877)
6 Uzanne 1889, p.153
7 'De Paris à Rouen', *Gil Blas*, 19 June 1883 (Maupassant 1980, 2, p.221)
8 De Lannoy 1990, no.468
9 Dargenty 1883; Redon, 1961, p.153
10 Private collection; London, Tate Gallery
11 Pératé 1897, p.46
12 Glasgow Art Gallery
13 Thévenin 1898, p.6
14 Desjardins 1899, p.451
15 Jones 1988, p.79 (letter of 4 August 1896)
16 Debussy 1980, p.69 (letter of 22 September 1894)
17 Bouyer 1894b, June 1894, p.412
18 Letter of 13 July 1905 (Special Collections, Getty Center for the History of Art and the Humanities)
19 Mauclair 1905a, p.534
20 New York, Metropolitan Museum; *Evening, Honfleur*, New York, Museum of Modern Art
21 *Georges Seurat* 1991–2, nos 222–4
22 *Georges Seurat* 1991–2, p.382
23 Angrand 1988, p.32 (letter of first week of April, 1889)
24 Paris, Musée d'Orsay
25 Van Gogh 1958, III, p.287 (letter 643, June 1890)
26 Mouton 1885, p.502; Moréas 1908, p.263
27 *Vincent van Gogh* 1990, p.260
28 Destremau 1988, p.156
29 Destremau 1988, fig.2, p.160
30 *French Symbolist Painters* 1972, no.54; Greenspan 1981, pp.359–93
31 Louis 1905, p.127
32 Greenspan 1981, p.360
33 *Charles Lacoste* 1985, no.29, p.18
34 *Charles Lacoste* 1985, p.12
35 *Charles Lacoste* 1985, p.30 (letter of 16 February 1904)
36 Holl 1912, p.146; Salmon, A. 1912, p.104
37 Hobbs 1977, p.110
38 Redon 1961, pp.168–9
39 Ackerman 1986, no.439

10

THE PANORAMIC LANDSCAPE

1 Michel, E. 1880, p.917
2 Mouton 1885, p.532; Appleton 1975, p.149
3 'Mitchi' 1891, p.242
4 Michel, A. 1897, p.60
5 Mantz 1877
6 *Le Musée du Luxembourg en 1874* 1974, no.220
7 Musée de Châlons-sur-Marne
8 Michel, E. 1909, p.249
9 Claretie 1865, p.4
10 Brettell 1990, pp.79–93
11 Thomson 1990, pp.37, 39
12 Van Gogh 1958, III, p.33 (Letter 535)
13 *Vincent van Gogh* 1990, p.126
14 'The Bonnard Exhibition', *L'Intransigéant*, 10 March 1910 (Apollinaire 1972, p.61)
15 Schivelbusch 1986, p.58
16 Moréas 1908, p.235
17 Mandell 1967, pp.64–5, 79
18 Barr 1951, p.40
19 Spate 1979, pp.208–9
20 'De Paris à Heyst', *Le Figaro*, 16 July 1887 (Maupassant 1980, 3, p.318)
21 Paris, Musée d'Orsay
22 Wakeman 1992, pp.771–2; Weber, 1986, p.187
23 Millman 1992, pp.217–19, 227–31, 234–5
24 *André Devambez* 1988, no.26; Strasbourg, Institut d'histoire de l'art
25 *André Devambez* 1988, nos 69–72 (Paris, Mobilier National)
26 *André Devambez* 1988, pp.47–8

11

LANDSCAPE AS DECORATION

1 Silvestre 1874
2 Vauxcelles 1906 (quoted in Benjamin 1992, p.297)
3 Michel, A. 1897, p.60
4 Spate 1992, pp.236–7
5 Bailly-Herzberg 1980–91, III, pp.262–3 (letter of 2 October 1892); Segard 1914, II, p.63
6 Michel, A. 1897, p.57
7 Mazel 1890, p.116; Saunier 1894, p.12
8 Silverman 1989, p.159 and ch.9
9 Philadelphia Museum of Art; House 1992a, pp.581–2
10 Segard 1914, II, pp.150–1, 200
11 Bénédite 1898a, pp.136–7
12 *Puvis de Chavannes* 1976–7, pp.193–200
13 *Puvis de Chavannes* 1976–7, p.193
14 Bénédite 1898b, pp.142, 144
15 *Henri Martin* 1993, pp.49–52
16 Segard 1914, II, p.6
17 Segard 1914, II, p.11, n.1
18 Marcel 1906, p.151
19 Segard 1914, II, pp.8, 15–16
20 Marcel 1906, p.147; Segard 1914, II, pp.18–19
21 *1913* 1987–8, pp.72–103
22 *1913* 1987–8, p.92
23 Stump 1972, p.97 (quoted in Greenspan 1981, p.143, n.112)
24 Seillière 1905, p.234
25 Soulier 1897, p.46
26 Bénédite 1898b, p.129
27 Matisse 1908 (quoted from Flam 1973, p.38)
28 Benjamin 1992, p.299; see also Groom 1993, ch.1
29 Silverman 1989, ch.5
30 Bouillon 1993, p.70
31 Mithouard 1907, p.8
32 Bailly-Herzberg 1980–91, IV, p.147 (letter of 3 January 1896); also p.143 (letter of 27 December 1895)
33 Salmon 1983, p.445; Groom 1993, p.130
34 Segard 1914, II, p.259
35 Wildenstein 1974–92, I (1974), nos 416, 418, 420, 423
36 Bigot 1877, p.1047; Sébillot 1877
37 Wildenstein 1974–92, II (1979), nos 919–60
38 House 1983, pp.150–4
39 Wildenstein 1974–92, III (1979), nos 1239–40
40 Marx, R. 1909, p.524
41 *Hommage à Claude Monet* 1980, p.329

12

LANDSCAPES IN SERIES

1 Tucker 1989
2 Havard 1881, pp.193–4; fig.58, p.192, fig.59, p.193
3 *Gustave Caillebotte* 1989, nos 7–13
4 Thomson 1990, pp.82–4
5 House 1986, pp.194–7
6 Except Shone 1992, pp.153–5
7 Venturi 1939, I, p.62 (letter of 17 May 1888)
8 Tucker 1989, p.29
9 'Quelques Impressionnistes', *La Cravache*, 2 June 1888 (Fénéon 1970, I, p.127)
10 Kahn 1888, pp.283–4
11 Van Tilborgh and van Uitert 1990
12 Van Gogh 1958, III, pp.522–3
13 West Palm Beach, Norton Gallery of Art
14 Van Gogh 1958, III, p.524
15 Tucker 1989, pp.107–41; Spate 1992, pp.218–24
16 Chartrain-Hebbelinck 1969, p.72, n.3
17 'Au Pavillon de la ville de Paris. Société des artistes indépendants', *Le Chat noir*, 2 April 1892 (Fénéon 1970, I, p.213)
18 De la Rochefoucauld 1893, p.4

13

THE SEASONS

1 Paulhan 1913, p.81
2 Otterlo, Rijksmuseum Kröller-Müller; Bouillon 1993, pp.36–8
3 Bailly-Herzberg 1980–91, III, p.368 (letter of 15 September 1893)
4 *Triomphe des Mairies* 1986–7, pp.379–80, 382–3
5 *Centenaire de l'Impressionnisme* 1974, pp.259–60
6 Tucker 1982, pp.37–8
7 *Van Gogh and Millet* 1988–9, pp.115–19
8 Lafenestre 1893, p.679
9 Van Gogh 1958, III, pp.260–1
10 Huysmans 1883 (1975, p.267); *Hommage à Claude Monet* 1980, p.212
11 Herbert, R. L. 1979, pp.106–7; House 1986, pp.197–201; Tucker 1989, pp.71–104; Spate 1992, pp.203–18
12 Wildenstein 1974–92, III (1979), p.258
13 Wildenstein 1974–92, III (1979), p.260 (letter of 21 January 1891)
14 Geffroy 1892, p.186 (quoted in House 1984, p.133)
15 Tucker 1989, p.101
16 Shiff 1984
17 Tucker 1989, p.80
18 Amiel 1889, pp.264–5 (7 February 1880)
19 Breton 1896, p.37
20 *Images du travail* 1985, p.168
21 Copeau 1910, p.173; 'The Salon des Artistes Français', *Paris-Journal*, 1 May 1914 (Apollinaire 1972, p.368
22 *Van Gogh in Arles* 1984, p.93–4
23 Van Gogh 1958, II, p.599
24 Van Gogh 1958, III, p.499
25 *Vincent van Gogh* 1990, pp.220–5
26 Van Gogh 1958, III, p.202
27 Chavanne and Gaudichon 1988, p.120
28 Norfolk, Virginia, Chrysler Museum

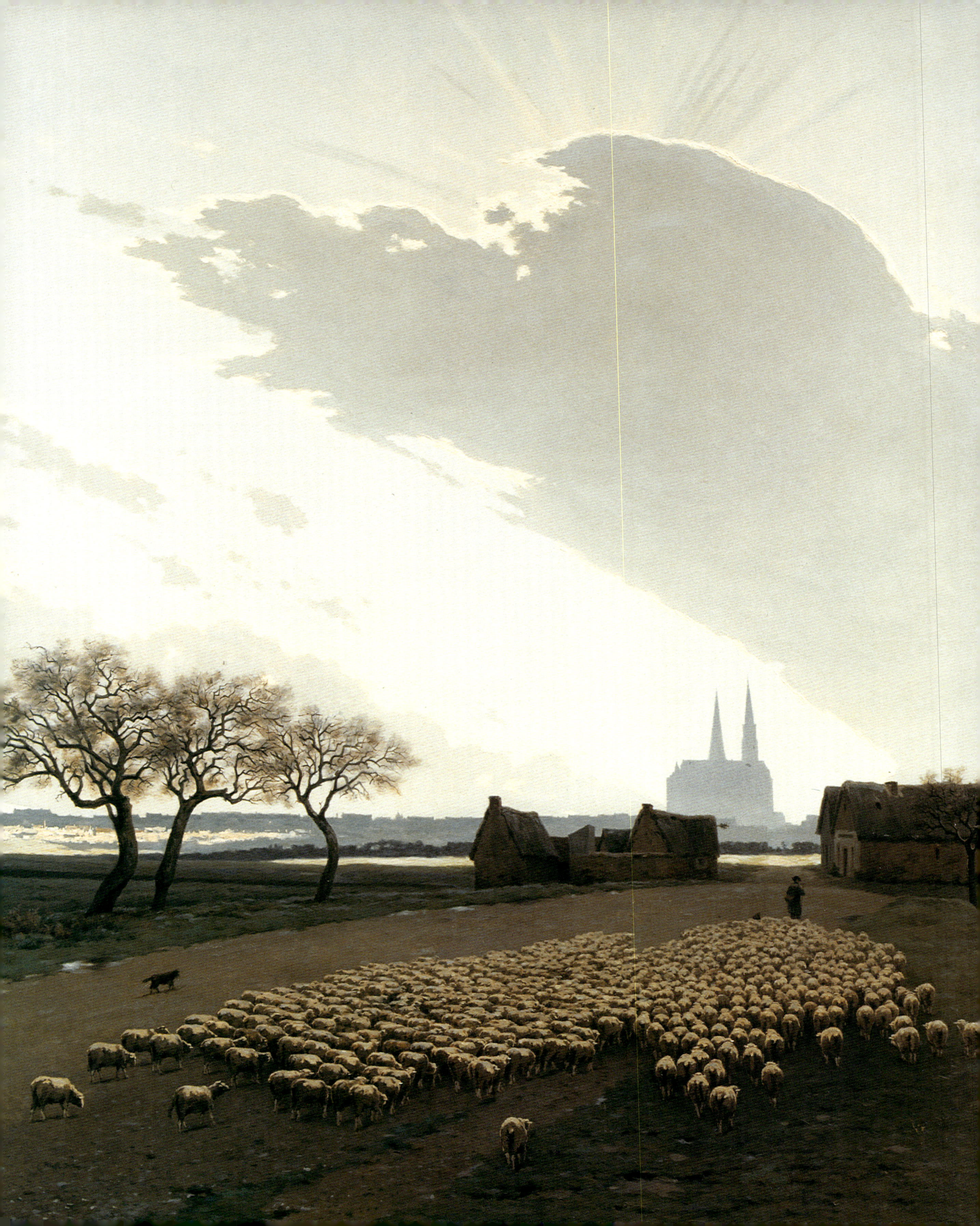

Explication de texte: Critical Writings on Landscape 1874–1914

MICHAEL CLARKE

Naturally it is through landscape that the majority of artists struggle to fix their impressions. The landscape, that model which is immediately available to us with every step we take, and which permits us to extract the poetry of things more readily than any other subject, is found here transposed across a thousand different temperaments.

Alcanter de Brahm, 'Le Salon des Indépendants' *La Critique* 1906[1]

The nineteenth century in French art has been described as 'the century of landscape'[2] and its critical concerns spilled over into the twentieth. This extract from a Parisian exhibition review uses critical terminology, such as 'impression' and 'temperament', that embodies many of the issues of debate concerning landscape painting in the period under consideration.

Landscape was probably the most widely practised, if not most respected, genre of painting in the later nineteenth century in France. Its subject matter had been expanded from the arcane classicism of the historical landscape to include not only the forest clearings of Barbizon, but also the Impressionist iconography of the suburbs and factories of Paris, the seaside resorts of Normandy. It had therefore become, to a much greater extent than hitherto, 'available'. The immediacy of its recording by the Impressionists in their rapidly brushed, highly coloured canvases led many artists and commentators to react against this apparent spontaneity and to search for seemingly more profound expressions of the painter's relation to nature, and to question and examine this subjective / objective relationship between man and nature, the artist and his painting. Zola, famously in 1865, defined a work of art as 'a corner of creation seen through a temperament'[3] and Maurice Denis later praised Cézanne in 1907 for achieving a 'reconciliation between the objective and the subjective'[4] in his mighty struggles before nature. The various reactions to and developments from Impressionism included Neo-Impressionism and Symbolism in the 1880s and 90s, and Fauvism and Cubism in the early twentieth century. In addition, a desire for a return to order and balance placed increasing emphasis, one might argue, upon the 'decorative' in landscape as a successor to the *paysage historique* or *composé* – 'nature as she ought to be' – that had been developed from the art of Poussin, especially by the Neo-Classicists in the early nineteenth century.

However, the theoretical history of landscape has no neat beginning or ending, is in some respects cyclical, and contains many surprising contradictions as well as unsuspected alliances. Through listening to the 'voices from the past' of contemporary criticism a richer understanding emerges of a period in which French painting was fundamentally transformed, particularly through the depiction of the landscape.

The first 'Impressionist' exhibition, held in 1874 in the studio of the photographer Nadar on the boulevard des Capucines, is generally considered to have been brought about as a result of discrimination at the official annual Salons against the young painters who went on to form the Impressionist group. Further alternative exhibiting societies followed, incuding the Salon des Indépendants (associated with the Neo-Impressionists) established in 1884, and in 1903 the Salon d'Automne (at whose 1905 exhibition the term 'Fauve' was first coined by the critic Vauxcelles). In 1881 the French state withdrew from organising the official Salons, handing them over to a society of artists. This in turn split in 1890 and a rival body, the Société nationale des beaux-arts, was set up. In addition there were many other groupings such as the extraordinary Ordre du Temple de la Rose+Croix (associated with an esoteric, mystical aspect of Symbolism), the Union libérale des artistes français, and the Société nouvelle de peinture et de sculpture. The dealers also contributed to the exhibition scene. The Durand-Ruel gallery played a major role in the promulgation of Impressionism and also periodically presented commercially successful shows of the preceding generation of landscape painters, the masters of Barbizon. There was the Goupil Gallery, its successor Boussod et Valadon, and the Georges Petit Gallery. Other prominent individual dealers included Ambroise Vollard and Daniel-Henri Kahnweiler. This is just a cursory listing of the better-known names. The important point is that there was

opposite
253
A. Ségé
En pays chartrain 1884 (detail)
Chartres, Musée des beaux-arts

an enormous amount of artistic production in the period under review and the appearance of so many venues often had as much to do with the necessary expansion of Paris's exhibiting capacity as with ideological differences between artistic groups, though understandably more progressive artists tended to gravitate towards the newer exhibiting venues.

Allied to this enormous growth was a vast industry of critical writing ranging from what amounted to little more than tedious listings in the daily newspapers to longer, more polemical articles in the monthly journals. The craft of the Salon critic or *salonnier* had developed greatly since the eighteenth century, to the extent that the late nineteenth-century reader was confronted with a plethora of informed and informing comment. This did not pass unnoticed by the artists themselves. Monet, for instance, kept his own extensive collection of press clippings about his work.

Recent histories have concentrated on particular aspects of this vast upsurge in artistic activity: for example on the importance of specific sites to artists and movements, and on the underlying social and economic factors. In the background, of course, lie the late John Rewald's two magisterial chronicles of the histories of Impressionism and 'Post-Impressionism'.[5] These concentrated on the perceived avant-garde: Monet, Pissarro, Seurat, van Gogh, Gauguin and so on. This was a partial view, conceived in a modernist climate, that was unconcerned with the vast majority of art produced at that time.

In the realm of landscape one finds that most artists, certainly in the 1870s and 80s, were working in styles derived from their predecessors. The classical balance of scenes by Harpignies [**120**] harks back to the achievements of Corot who, it should be remembered, only died in 1875 and had been taught by pupils of Valenciennes, author of the most important treatise on Neo-Classical landscape painting (first published in 1800).[6] The popularity of the rural ideal of a sanitised French peasantry, as depicted by an artist such as Jules Breton, continued unabated until the end of the century. The masters of Barbizon or the 'School of 1830' – Rousseau, Diaz, Dupré and their associates – had innumerable followers and imitators whose dark forests and woodland glades regularly populated the various Salons.

A benign, pastoral view of 'the landscape painter' was conjured up by the artist and writer Frédéric Henriet in 1876 in his study *Le Paysagiste aux champs*: 'But nevertheless, of all artists, the most balanced still, – at least I shall be forgiven for so believing, – are the landscape painters. Placed closer to nature, in the fields they acquire taste, a simple way of life and independence of character. In communion respectively with the life of the dream and the life of reality, they are the most reasonable of all the insane and the least morose of all the wise.'[7]

Mainstream landscape painting, then, of the type that had earlier caused Baudelaire to complain that landscapists were 'too herbiverous in their diet',[8] was safe, sane, mildly escapist and, interestingly, capable of inducing gentle reverie. Indeed, a passage such as this could well be illustrated by photographs of the aged Corot, seated on his painting stool, dressed in his carter's smock, a canvas on the easel in front of him and a verdant landscape beyond. This was the 'folk' image of the landscape painter, unthreatening, a worshipper of nature.

Conservative critics were soon to mourn the apparent passing of the 'great' era of French landscape. Millet, Corot, Troyon, Daubigny and Huet had all died in the 1860s and 70s. Reviewing the 1881 Salon, J. Buisson asked '... has the fatal hour come for landscape? It is permitted to ask the question despite the importance, the number and the size of the landscapes at this year's exhibition.'[9] Of the previous year's Salon the former Directeur des beaux-arts (he resigned his post in 1878), Philippe de Chennevières, had reflected: 'Yes, it was good, this year, to honour with a special occasion, the slightly failing glory of French landscape, if only to comfort the last survivors of this art which ten years ago still occupied such a great place in our school [of painting] and was practically at its head. The 1880 Salon shows it to be really ill, sick from this malady of exhaustion which afflicted Holland after its famous age of great men, the Ruisdaels, Hobbemas, Dujardins, Cuyps, Van Goyens, Paul Potters, Rembrandts and Van de Veldes. The great generation is burnt out and has only survived through Jules Dupré, whose works are seen rarely, and by Français who has become a veritable patriarch.'[10]

De Chennevières continued with a survey of the landscape section, praising many including Henriet and Ségé [**192, 253**], and concluding that there was much that was fine and professional which, '...if architects knew how to use them in the manner of the seventeenth century would serve as charming panels for the decoration of our modern *hôtels*'.[11] As has already been observed, the decorative function of landscape became an increasingly discussed topic in the late nineteenth century. Although de Chennevières's suggestion was slightly condescending, his proposed decorative use for landscape was one which had distinguished antecedents in Roman wall painting, Renaissance and Baroque villas and French interiors of the eighteenth and nineteenth centuries. However, decoration was no substitute, in de Chennevières's eyes, for the individual easel landscape of originality: 'But, alas, where are the small canvases, so powerful and so personal, of our masters of ten years ago? Where are the Corots? Where are the Paul Huets? Where are the Cabats? Where are the Th. Rousseaus? Where are the Millets? Where are the Troyons and the Courbets? Where are the landscapes of yesteryear?'[12] [*Où sont les paysages d'antan?*, a play on the famous refrain of a ballade by the late medieval poet François Villon, *Où sont les neiges d'antan?*].

A more stringent view was provided by J.-K.

Huysmans, reviewing the same Salon: 'This truth: that the landscape painters have now attained a facility without equal, becomes evident every day ... No individuality with the majority of these painters: an identical and singular vision of a site arranged according to the predilection of the public ... Alas! I sense that these landscapes are botched together in a studio, in a few sessions, at a great gallop.'[13] The majority of landscape production was therefore an unthinking industry, pandering successfully but with little honour or achievement to the popular taste.

Huysmans successfully combined the career of civil servant with those of novelist and critic. In his early writings he championed Impressionism, whose 'triumph' he saluted in 1882: 'It is with joy that I can now eulogise M. Monet, for it is to his efforts and those of his fellow Impressionists of landscape that is certainly due the redemption of painting; happier and more gifted than the poor Chintreuil [**191**], very much the type of pastoral painter described by Henriet who was a trailblazer of his time and who died in sorrow, without having succeeded in expressing those sunlit and moist effects which he strove so desperately to render. MM. Pissarro and Monet have finally emerged victorious from the terrible struggle. It can be said that the problems, which are so difficult, of light in painting, have been finally solved in their canvases.'[14]

Impressionism was therefore perceived by Huysmans essentially as a technical achievement, the introduction of light into painting. Dark grounds were banished, a heightened colouring was deployed and to varying degrees a knowledge of contemporary theories of the complementary laws of colour contrast was displayed. In the 1880s and 90s an increasing number of artists would lighten their palettes under the influence of Impressionism. As Maurice Denis later noted in 1906, many Salon painters from around 1885 onwards borrowed the 'easy secret' of Impressionism with the result that, 'one saw nothing else but "luminous" pictures and violet shadows'.[15] The term itself came to be used rather loosely, sometimes in a pejorative sense, of artists who unthinkingly followed its basic precepts in pursuit of fashion.

'Impressionism' had, of course, first been coined as a term of satirical abuse by Louis Leroy in his review of the original 1874 exhibition, in particular with reference to Monet's *Impression: Sunrise*.The implied point of Leroy's satire was that the term 'impression' was too personal and should not have been used in a picture title. One might perhaps have used instead 'effect' (*effet*), for effects, according to the then prevailing academic orthodoxy, could be found in nature – for example, effects of sunrise, mist or rain. The 'impression' was internalised within the artist. As Richard Shiff has explained,[16] the term had an inherent duality – on the one hand it could mean the reception by the artist of the impression of the scene presented to him, on the other the subjective trace of the artist's own nature or temperament in the resulting work of art.

In this context it is instructive that one of the most important reviews of the first Impressionist exhibition showed awareness of just these critical distinctions. Jules Castagnary had been a particular supporter of Courbet and the Realists and also admired what he termed in his 1866 Salon review 'the great army of landscape painters',[17] men such as the Dutch painter Jongkind. But he discerned a new development in the Impressionists' treatment of landscape: 'They are *impressionists* in the sense that they depict not the landscape but the sensation produced by the landscape. The word itself has passed into their language; it is not *landscape*, it is *Impression* that the *Sunrise* of M. Monet is called in the catalogue. In this way they leave reality behind and enter into full idealism.'[18]

Castagnary continued by retreating somewhat from the bold assertion made in his last sentence – an interpretation which anticipates the Symbolist aesthetic. Instead he went on to stress that the differences between the Impressionists and their predecessors were not that great. It was really just a question of 'finish', or lack of it as far as the Impressionists were concerned. But other artists such as Courbet, Corot and Daubigny had already been accused of this fault. The Impressionists would not, in Castagnary's opinion, found a 'school' because that would require new ideas and not just a new manner of painting. This rather contradictory claim should not obscure the significance of Castagnary's observation on landscape, however. By designating the 'sensations' produced by the landscape, rather than the landscape itself, as the true subject of Impressionist painting, Castagnary signalled a decisive move away from the traditional categories of landscape, indeed the emphasis on 'landscape' as suitable subject matter. Paradoxically, of course, an art that was concerned with 'sensations' rather than 'landscape' had free licence as to where to find its subject matter: scenes of urban leisure or horticultural labour, motifs as diverse as railway station interiors, grainstacks or cathedral façades.

Shiff, again, has correctly directed attention to the inherent subjectivity of the artist as implied in Castagnary's account of 'sensations'. The Impressionists were both recorders of 'modern life' and of their individual 'impressions'. The latter quality would commend both Monet and Cézanne to the Symbolists, who were otherwise hostile to Impressionism in general, which they perceived to be merely factual and materialistic. Monet's great series of *Grainstacks* near Giverny, fifteen of which were exhibited at the Durand-Ruel gallery in May 1891,[19] were viewed as a significant step in the development of landscape by a broad spectrum of critics. In one sense Monet was partially following traditional landscape theory which encouraged the sketching of the same site at different times of day and at different seasons. But he regarded these pictures as finished works of art that went far beyond any concept of 'seizing nature as it is'.[20] They represented a highly personal search, in semi-abstract form, for the surrounding *enveloppe* or atmosphere of landscape via repeated examination of a relatively banal motif. In a different sense, Cézanne's distinction, reported by Denis,[21] between mere 'reproduction' and 'representation' of nature, was certainly analogous to the Symbolists' search for 'equivalents' in art.

The same charge against Impressionism, that of factual materialism, was also made, though for different reasons, by the right-wing critic and historian Georges Lanoë in his two histories of French landscape painting, published in 1901 and 1905 (the former in collaboration with T.Brice),[22] which were doubtless coloured by the conservative, Catholic climate of the 1890s. For Lanoë, 'The landscape painters à la *Monet* are all materialists'.[23] Their work lacked imagination, the very faculty which Baudelaire had praised in his mid-century accounts of the Barbizon artists and Théodore Rousseau in particular.[24] Furthermore, according to Lanoë, the Impressionist style suffered grievously on account of its secular nature. Great landscape painting, according to Lanoë, should be infused with religious sentiment: 'The only religious painting of our epoch can be landscape painting – because it is in contemplating eternal Nature that man is most firmly convinced of the greatness of God.'[25] Denis, having read Lanoë, proposed Marie-Charles Dulac [**186**] as the embodiment of the ideal, religious landscape painter (though he painted mainly Italian scenes).[26]

Impressionism was further condemned by Lanoë for its concentration on 'seizing the effects of nature in a moment' and reducing the art of landscape to 'rendering an impression as quickly as possible'.[27] The Impressionists were mere *plein-airistes* who failed to compose their pictures properly. They represented not the start of a new tradition but the degenerate end of the old one. Biased and misguided though Lanoë may appear to the present-day reader, important evidence does emerge from his testimony.

Firstly, he was one of a small number of writers who around this time considered the whole history of French landscape painting. In conservative circles, therefore, the traditional concept of 'landscape' was still very much held to be valid. Secondly, although one might well disagree with his conclusion, Lanoë was able to provide a historical context for the Impressionists. To a certain degree they were indeed *plein-airistes*. Traditional Neo-Classical landscape theory had approved the making of on the spot sketches in oils, but as preparation for the considered studio painting that was to follow. Such sketches were the means to an end but they should not become the end itself. This distinction was well known throughout the nineteenth century and had informed the debate between the two protagonists of Leroy's famous and derogatory review of the first Impressionist exhibition. Indeed one of them had been a pupil of the Neo-Classical landscape painter 'Vincent'.

A more balanced review than Lanoë's of the history of French landscape had been provided by the historian and critic Raymond Bouyer. Relatively little known and described by a contemporary as solitary and mild-mannered,[28] Bouyer was a regular contributor to the periodical *L'Ermitage.* His most lasting contribution, however, was a series of six articles entitled *Le Paysage dans l'art* which appeared in the ailing and ultra-conservative journal *L'Artiste* in 1893 and was republished in book form the following year.[29] Underlying Bouyer's series was his proposal for a historical and comparative museum devoted to landscape. His enthusiasm for this would have been encouraged by a number of recent exhibitions which had provided historical surveys of the subject. Just as, Bouyer claimed, the history of music could be traced from Palestrina through Beethoven to Wagner, so could landscape be followed from its beginnings in Flanders, on to Ruisdael and finally to the modern school. The parallel between music and landscape painting, both of which were perceived to have non- or indefinite subjects, was commonly cited in the nineteenth century.

Bouyer's analysis of contemporary landscape is particularly instructive and, for all its apparent conservatism, reveals a great deal about the state of landscape painting at that time. According to Bouyer, after the landscape of France itself (as opposed to classical Italy) had been rediscovered by the masters of the nineteenth century it was necessary to master light and atmosphere: '...and landscape, after the timidities of classicism, romanticism with its bitumen and the minute detail of Pre-Raphaelitism enters, around 1870, into a new era which claims *to forget*, confronted by the open air, all the experience of centuries: Manet overturns Courbet. Amidst insults or laughter, Impressionism imposes itself, *pure tone* reveals itself, the fashion is for *grey*, sites are brought up to date, canvases become lighter, the fever to innovate complicates the desire *to be truthful*, ... and delicate painting aspires to the fluid semi-transparency of diffused light in the peasant scenes of Bastien-Lepage, of Roll and of Ulysse Butin, in the modern eulogies of Cazin, in the agitated notations of René Billotte, in the coloured sensations, similar to those of the English, of Lepère and of Lebourg, in the joyful suburbs of Claude Monet or the suffering ones of J. Fr. Raffaëlli...; finally in the arcadian solitudes of Puvis de Chavannes, neo-Poussin of fresco, who has silently prepared the hour, as logical as it is unforeseen, where one can, without blushing, admire Wagner and bring back the Ideal.'[30] This long but abbreviated extract provides a general survey of the types of contemporary landscape that concerned Bouyer and is representative of the varieties that were on offer to the public at the main exhibiting venues between 1880 and the mid 90s. Impressionism is understood to be as much about the grey, light-toned landscapes of Bastien-Lepage and his associates as it is with Monet who, in this particular context, is noted mainly for his contribution to the cosmopolitan landscape. Waiting in the background are the large, decorative and mythological landscapes of Puvis – modern classical landscapes that appealed to middle-of-the-road taste and to civic functionaries when they came to commission decorative schemes for public buildings.

Elsewhere, however, Bouyer singled out what he perceived to be the major defect of Monet and Impressionism: 'But through the brutal decomposition of tone the Impressionist comes up against all the eccentricities of the prism'.[31] Evidently he still preferred the tonal balance of Corot and like-minded artists of the preceding generation to the highly coloured canvases of the Impressionists. Equally at fault was Neo-Impressionism which, according to Bouyer, had the 'uniformity of a recipe'.[32] This, of course, was exactly not what Seurat and his followers had intended. The system of coloured dots, unveiled to the public with Seurat's *La Grande Jatte* at the last Impressionist exhibition in 1886, was meant to liberate rather than restrict artists. The technique that Seurat developed was based on contemporary theories of the contrast of complementary colours. Thus the intensity of the primary colours of red, yellow and blue could be heightened by the juxtaposition of their respective complementaries green, violet and orange. These should be applied in unmixed touches to set up a vibration of colour in the eye of the beholder. This optical ordering in Neo-Impressionism, or chromo-luminarism as the artist-theorist Paul Signac preferred to call it, in practice went hand in hand with increasingly ordered, almost classical, compositions [**254**]. Seurat's major compositions were invariably preceded by a series of oil-sketches or *croquetons*. Signac wrote in 1899 that, 'The Neo-Impressionist … will not begin a canvas without having decided on the arrangement. Guided by tradition and by science, he will harmonise the composition to his conception.'[33] Whereas, according to Signac, the light and colour of the Impressionists was determined by 'instinct and instantaneity', that of the Neo-Impressionists derived from 'reflection and permanence'.[34] The concerns here exhibited could almost be those of the old, traditional, Neo-Classical landscapists for whom order and balance had been paramount.

At the third exhibition of mainly Nabi and avant-garde art organised by the enterprising dealer Le Barc de Boutteville in 1892 Bouyer had remarked on an interesting juxtaposition: 'And, 47, rue Le Peletier, in a simple shop, Neo-Impressionists and Symbolists were cohabiting, as it were, represented by the most advanced bizarreries, what one sees and what one dreams, Light and Style.'[35] These two categories of

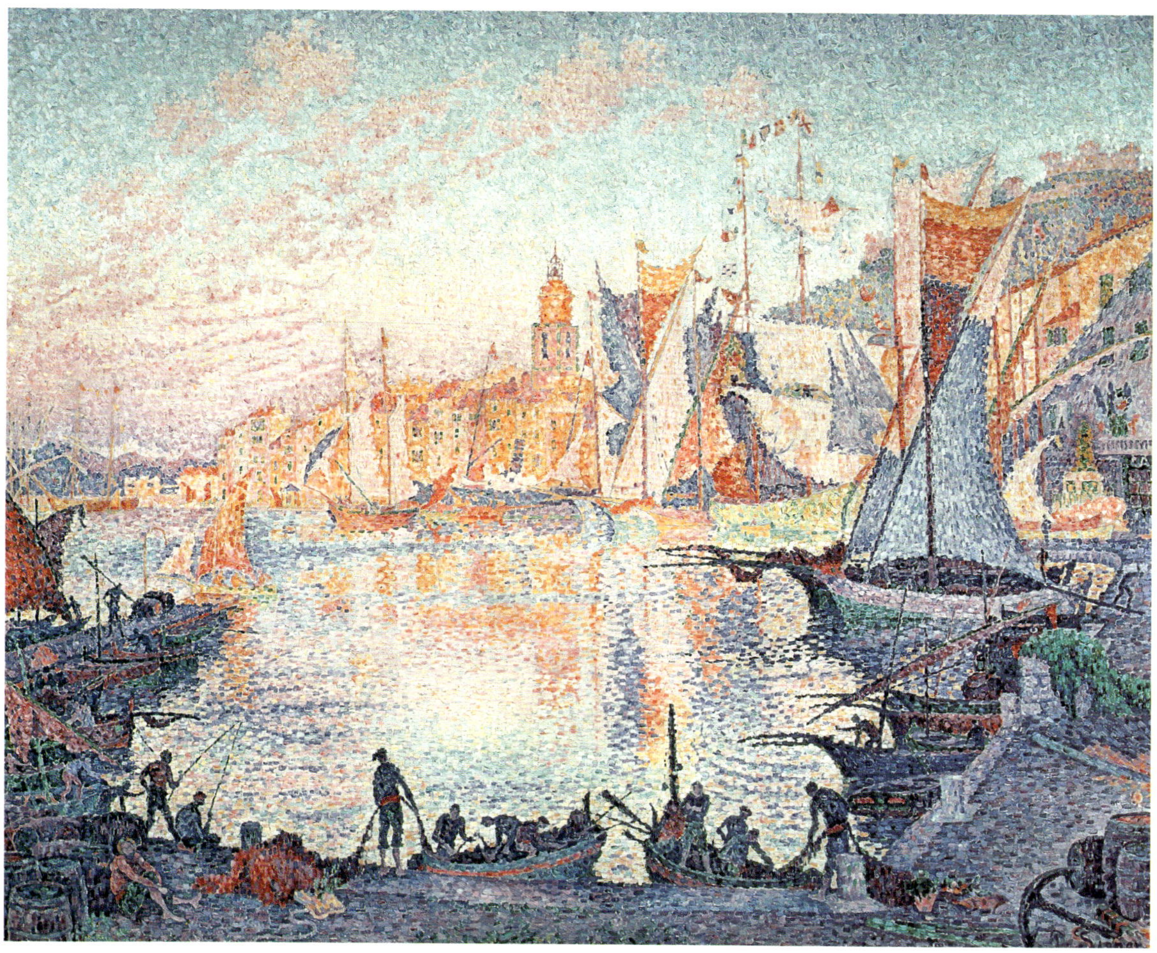

254
P. Signac
The Port of Saint-Tropez *c.* 1901
Tokyo, National Museum of Western Art

255
T. Rousseau
The Massacre of the Innocents
The Hague, Mesdag Museum

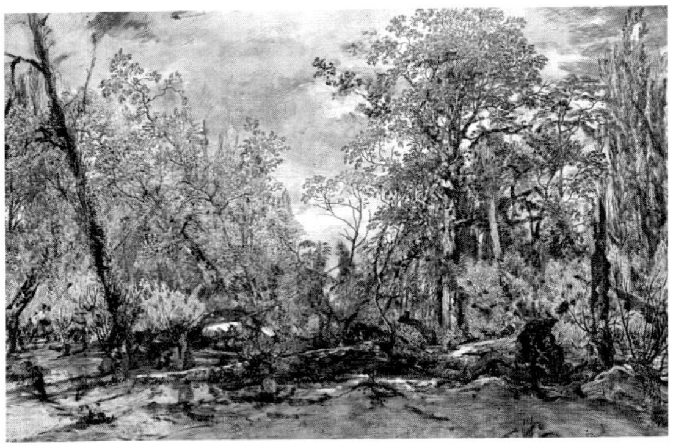

Light and Style informed Bouyer's historical survey of landscape. Light was instinctive and concerned the execution of a painting. It had replaced 'little by little dark landscapes with light landscapes, and the history of which is none other than the very history of rustic sincerity'.[36] That phrase, 'rustic sincerity', derives from traditional theory and was used as early as 1708 by Roger de Piles to describe the Dutch school of landscape, generally perceived as offering an alternative tradition to the classical and basing itself on an observation of nature as it is, rather than as it ought to be.[37] Style, according to Bouyer, was deliberate and expressed the Idea of a painting. Jean Moréas's *Symbolist Manifesto* had been published in 1886. Symbolist painters and poets were particularly concerned with art expressing the Idea, albeit an abstract one. Gauguin wrote to his friend Schuffenecker in 1888: 'Art is an abstraction; derive this abstraction from nature while dreaming before it, and think more of the creation which will result than of nature.'[38] This represents a Symbolist elaboration of Henriet's 'traditional' painter, 'In communion respectively with the life of the dream and the life of reality'.[39]

To his considerable credit, Bouyer had been able to locate approximately both Neo-Impressionism and Symbolism within his historical scheme of landscape. In a more general sense the two movements have been linked with two different strands in French philosophical thought. Neo-Impressionism, a quasi-scientific manner of representation could, like Impressionism, be related to the philosophy of Positivism which limited knowledge to the immediately observable. A reaction to this severe empiricism produced a deliberately irrational school of philosophy, whose most famous exponent was Bergson, which offered new interpretations of consciousness and intuition and found its closest equivalent in the arts in Symbolism. Symbolist landscape was not intended to be imitative of reality but expressive of the Idea. In explanation of this Gauguin wrote from Tahiti to his friend Charles Morice in 1901: 'Puvis explains his idea, yes, but he does not paint it. He is a Greek while I am a savage, a wolf in the woods without a collar. Puvis would call a painting 'Purity', and to explain it he would paint a young virgin holding a lily in her hand – a familiar symbol; consequently one understands it. Gauguin, for the title 'Purity', would paint a landscape with limpid waters; no stain of the civilised human being, perhaps a figure.'[40]

As it happens, Gauguin's concept of the landscape being expressive in itself of an idea, is not wholly unrelated to the art of Théodore Rousseau, whose great, melancholy, cut-down oaks of the Forest of Fontainebleau had been intended by the artist to symbolise loss, destruction, and have titles such as *The Massacre of the Innocents* [**255**]. Both types of landscape required the imagination to extract meaning or an idea from an image of nature. Maurice Denis would later correctly link Gauguin's attitude to nature back to Baudelaire's stress on the primacy of imagination in the act of creation, and Baudelaire had been the prime advocate of Rousseau. Denis observed: 'Art is no longer only a visual sensation which we record, only a photograph, however refined it may be, of nature. No, it is a creation of our spirit of which nature is only the occasion. Instead of "working with the eye, we search in the mysterious centre of thought" as Gauguin said. This imagination again became, as Baudelaire wished, the queen of the faculties.'[41]

Among the most eloquent critical spokesmen of Symbolism was the poet and novelist Albert Aurier (he died in 1892). In opposition to naturalism and Impressionism he proposed 'an idealist reaction, mystical even'.[42] Painting should not concern itself with a direct representation of objects, but rather, with Ideas, expressed in a special language. Art for Aurier became a superior and élitist form of semiotics. Ideas were to be expressed through signs: 'These are the letters of an immense alphabet which only the man of genius can spell out.'[43]

In the context of landscape painting, nature was represented not realistically but through the 'synthesis' achieved by the artist. This was defined by Maurice Denis as a simplification of forms to express an idea, to 'render intelligible'.[44] Gauguin's explanation of how he would paint a landscape expressing 'Purity' is a good example. In practical terms accurate observation of nature, such as the Impressionists had attempted, was undesirable. Ideas could be expressed through irreducible essentials. Thus Gauguin advised Sérusier in 1888: 'How do you see this tree? Is it really green? Use green, then, the most beautiful green in your palette. And that shadow, rather blue? Don't be afraid to paint it as blue as possible.'[45] Basic shapes and colours were the signs of the Symbolist landscape painter, but mediated through the personality or temperament of the artist-creator to evoke beauty, poetry or dream.

The flat, coloured patterning of much Symbolist painting could be read as decoration. The adjective 'decorative' was frequently used in the 1890s in the context of painting, particularly with regard to landscape. It was a term with a wide and often loosely applied range of meaning, sometimes pejorative, at others laudatory. Thus Fénéon, champion of the Neo-Impressionists, could claim in 1889 a kind of mindless decorative potential in Monet: 'A landscape by Monet never develops fully a theme of nature and seems to be one of some twenty or other rectangles one would cut out from a panoramic canvas of a hundred square metres.'[46] Other commentators, writing of Monet's *Grainstacks* and *Poplars* series, genuinely admired what they perceived to be an increasingly decorative quality. For example Bouyer, whilst admitting that in the past, '... the excess of lively colouring has encouraged one to think of the severities of the decorative line ...' continued, 'but already brightness revives the décor; décor evokes the style; style evokes the symbol. Increasingly, the orientation is towards the *Decorative Landscape*, that is to say towards composition, full of attractions, nobility, ... and pitfalls'.[47] As Denis put it, the word 'decorative' was becoming 'the *tarte à la crème* [buzzword] among artists and even among fashionable laymen'.[48]

Roger Benjamin, in a recent article, has traced the various historical paths which lead back from the decorative landscape.[49] There is, quite literally, the landscape as domestic décor, a tradition already alluded to in this essay; there is the decorative landscape as a reformulation of the historical or composed landscape; there is the decorative landscape as a 'staged' landscape, an artifice of the composed landscape, found in artists from Poussin to the Cubists; and there is the concept of the 'arabesque', the voluptuous curve of form, often found in historical decorative art, and which Benjamin rightly perceives as informing the aesthetic of a picture such as Matisse's *Bonheur de vivre* [**128**] of 1906.

The decorative represented a return to some sense of order and balance, albeit with a degree of relaxation. Louis Vauxcelles, whose review of the 1905 Salon d'Automne gave rise to the use of the term 'Fauve' to describe the art of Matisse and his associates, took a positive and encouraging view of the decorative: 'Our young landscapists see truthfully "because they see decoratively". The site is for them a pretext, a décor in which the figures should be enclosed by arabesques. They all seem to be preoccupied with balancing volumes and masses. And this is apparent even among those whose errors are most disconcerting.'[50]

Matisse's *Bonheur de vivre* is, as many have observed, a celebration of Mediterranean lyricism. Its composition and subject combine to produce an updating of the classical tradition, into which it fits surprisingly easily. Matisse himself expressed his desire for, 'an art of balance, of purity and serenity, devoid of troubling or depressing subject matter, an art which could be for every mental worker, be he businessman or man of letters, for example, a soothing, calming influence on the mind, something like a good armchair in which to rest from physical fatigue'.[51] In his many, sometimes contradictory, writings Matisse revealed a deep familiarity with the art of the recent past. According to him the Impressionists had succeeded merely in capturing fleeting impressions, and he did not consider the theory of complementary colours to be absolute. Above all he believed in the primacy of the picture as an independent work of art: 'I cannot copy nature in a servile way; I am forced to interpret nature and submit it to the spirit of the picture. From the relationship I have found in all the tones there must result a living harmony of colours, a harmony analogous to that of a musical composition.'[52] The latter part of this passage could almost have been written of the nineteenth-century master Corot, considered by many to have attained an equilibrium, a balance in his landscapes that was neglected by his successors. Both Corot and Matisse (who frequently mentioned Corot), it could be argued, achieved in their historical contexts a balance between tradition and innovation, between art and nature.

Matisse sought the 'essential character' of a landscape and was prepared to 'risk losing charm in order to attain greater stability'.[53] This he achieved through a painterly conception of space. By contrast, the Cubists – the name derived from Vauxcelles's remark that Braque had sent landscapes 'with little cubes' to the 1908 Salon d'Automne – viewed space in a plastic sense, sculpturally. Whilst they, too, sought to depict the 'essential character' of the subject of a painting (be it a portrait, still-life or a landscape), the allusion was primarily through increasingly abstracted form. Space and time were fragmented, conventional pictorial reality could be reassembled in a seemingly random but in fact rigorously composed manner. Gleizes's and Metzinger's text *Cubism* of 1913 included an enthusiastic section on landscape and the apparently limitless possibilities of Cubist art: 'Without employing any allegorical or symbolical literary artifice, merely by inflections of lines and colours, a painter can show, in the same picture, a Chinese city, a French town, together with mountains, oceans, fauna, and flora, and nations with their histories and desires – all that separates them in external reality. Distance or time, concrete fact or pure conception, nothing refuses to be uttered in the language of the painter, as in that of the poet, the musician, or the artist.'[54]

Benjamin has likened Cubist landscape to the *paysage composé* and one finds just this terminology, but transferred to an urban context, in the Cubist painter André Lhote's recollection of the immediate pre-War years. 'The Cubists, between 1911 and 1914, had a passion for the *paysage composé*. One knows the *Eiffel Towers* of Delaunay, and the *Rooftops* of Léger, these dramatic visions of the City of cities [Paris], where the smoke of the factories' chimneys unites unreal images.'[55]

Lhote, however, was writing a quarter of a century after the event. His *Traité du paysage* was published in 1939 and one of the fascinating aspects of his text was its attempt to link or compare different periods and styles in the history of landscape painting. However, Lhote's use of the term *paysage composé* seems perfectly apt in this context, for these were highly composed, artificially staged images. Furthermore, he evidently saw the factory smoke achieving the same effect as aerial perspective had in traditional landscape painting, or the *enveloppe* of mist and diffusion of shapes that Corot had sought in his mature work.

The rest of this passage from Lhote surveys the landscape activities of other members of the Cubist group: 'Metzinger constructed curving harbours in harmony with the bulging shapes of full sails, Gleizes and Villon stylised leafy scenes where hunters, harvesters passed by and where chaste female bathers posed motionless. De la Fresnaye, finally, attempted in his direct studies to reconstruct this historiated mosaic of walls, chimneys, labours, rivers and clouds which the countryside offers to "simultaneous" vision. His direct studies are more than studies: they suggest heroic compositions. But de la Fresnaye, who would have made a great landscape painter, is dead and his comrades, except for Villon, have deliberately rejected landscape for their "orphic" or "decorative" concerns.'[56]

Cubism, understandably, in many instances rejected landscape as a suitable subject. The subtleties of time, space and composition that characterise mature Cubism are far better suited to the portrait, interior or still-life than they are to landscape. They are more concrete, less nuanced, less atmospheric, less vague. Cubist landscape often appears disparate, confused by comparison. Whereas Cézanne, from whom the Cubists took so much, had succeeded in constructing a 'closed', almost sculptural landscape, he had always preserved his 'vibrations' of atmosphere so that his creations, whilst they are not reproductions of nature, exist in parallel to it. He had never presented a 'simultaneous' view of nature or 'historiated mosaic' as Lhote termed it.

The period under review in this exhibition closes with the advent of the First World War. This cataclysmic event in France's history was followed, in the visual arts, by a period of reaction against the modern (which some took to be represented by Cubism), the mechanistic and by implication, the German.[57] The production of landscape painting flourished anew, its links to the great French 'past' of Claude, Poussin and, more recently, Corot vouchsafed its respectability. A former Fauve such as Derain worked in the 1920s and 30s in a landscape style that was in many ways more traditional, *retardataire* than his landscapes of his Fauve period had been. Lhote, in his treatise, praised Pierre Bonnard as the greatest living exponent of landscape and in many ways this was just because Bonnard had remained true to his vision and because his career had been one of long, slow, steady development. Landscape was no longer consistently at the forefront of the avant-garde, however. One would never claim, as Bouyer correctly had of the nineteenth, that the twentieth century was the 'century of landscape'.

1 De Brahm 1906, p.23
2 Bouyer 1893, March, p.201
3 Zola 1974, p.38
4 Denis 1913, p.239
5 Rewald 1946; 1978
6 Valenciennes 1800
7 Henriet 1876, p.141
8 Baudelaire 1965, p.201
9 Buisson 1881, p.72
10 Chennevières 1880, p.52
11 Chennevières 1880, p.56
12 Chennevières 1880, p.56
13 Huysmans 1883, p.139
14 Huysmans 1883, p.238
15 Denis 1913, p.211
16 *New Painting* 1986, pp.70–1
17 Castagnary 1869
18 Castagnary 1874, p.3
19 See especially Tucker 1989
20 Valenciennes 1800, p.404
21 Denis 1913, p.404
22 Lanoë 1905; Lanoë and Brice 1901
23 Lanoë 1905, p.254
24 Baudelaire 1965, pp.108–9, 196
25 Lanoë and Brice 1901, p.14
26 Denis 1913, p.233
27 Lanoë and Brice 1901, p.233
28 Mazel 1894, pp.35–6
29 Bouyer 1893, 1894
30 Bouyer 1893, January, p.28
31 Bouyer 1893, January, p.29
32 Bouyer 1893, January, p.29
33 Signac 1899, p.65
34 Signac 1899, p.63
35 Bouyer 1893, January, p.23
36 Bouyer 1893, August, p.114
37 De Piles 1708
38 Malingue 1949, p.134
39 Henriet 1876, p.141
40 Malingue 1949, pp.300–1
41 Denis 1913, pp.259–60
42 Aurier 1893, p.213
43 Aurier 1893, p.213
44 Denis 1913, p.251
45 Sérusier 1942, pp.42–4
46 Fénéon 1970, p.172
47 Bouyer 1893, August, p.117
48 Denis 1913, p.165
49 Benjamin 1993
50 Vauxcelles 1906
51 Flam 1973, p.38
52 Flam 1973, p.37
53 Flam 1973, p.37
54 Gleizes and Metzinger 1913, pp.59–60
55 Lhote 1939, p.13
56 Lhote 1939, p.13
57 See especially Green 1987

Catalogue Section

Bibliography

This bibliography includes works cited in the footnotes and those of general importance to the study of this subject. It is by no means exhaustive.

ACKERMAN 1986
G. Ackerman, *The Life and Work of Jean-Léon Gérôme*, London 1986

ALAIN-FOURNIER 1913
Alain-Fournier, *Le Grand Meaulnes*, Paris 1913

D'AMAT 1959
G. d'Amat (ed.), *Dictionnaire de biographie française*, VIII, Paris 1959; IX, Paris 1961

AMIEL 1889
H. -F. Amiel, *Amiel's Journal. The Journal Intime of Henri-Frédéric Amiel*, ed. Mrs Humphry Ward, 2nd edn, London 1889

ANDRE DEVAMBEZ 1988
André Devambez (1867–1944). Présentation d'une donation. Beauvais, Musée départmental de l'Oise, June–October 1988

ANGRAND 1988
C. Angrand, *Correspondances, 1883–1926*, ed. F. Lespinasse, Rouen 1988

ANTOINE 1921
A. Antoine, *Mes Souvenirs sur le Théâtre Libre*, Paris 1921

APOLLINAIRE 1965
G. Apollinaire, *Selected Poems*, trans. O. Bernard, Harmondsworth 1965

APOLLINAIRE 1972
___, *Apollinaire on Art: Essays and Reviews, 1902–1918*, ed. L. C. Breunig, London 1972

APPLETON 1975
J. Appleton, *The Experience of Landscape*, London 1975

AURIER 1893
G. A. Aurier, *Oeuvres posthumes*, Paris 1893

BACOU 1984
R. Bacou, *Donation Arï et Suzanne Redon*, Paris 1984

BAEDEKER 1881/1900
K. Baedeker, *Paris and its Environs. Handbook for Travellers*, Leipzig and London 1881 and 1900

BAEDEKER 1895
___, *Northern Italy*, London 1895

BAILLY-HERZBERG 1980–91
J. Bailly-Herzberg (ed.), *Correspondance de Camille Pissarro*, I, *1865–85*, Paris 1980; II, *1886–90*, Paris 1986; III, *1891–94*, Paris 1988; IV, *1895–98*, Paris 1989; V, *1899–1903*, Saint-Ouen-l'Aumône 1991

BALAKIAN 1977
A. Balakian, *The Symbolist Movement. A Critical Appraisal*, New York 1977

BANTENS 1990
R. J. Bantens, *Eugène Carrière. The Symbol of Creation*, New York 1990

BARBIZON 1992
Barbizon et l'Ecole de la Nature, Paris, Brame et Lorenceau, and London, Agnews, October–December 1992

BARR 1951
A. Barr, *Matisse: his Art and his Public*, New York 1951

BARRON 1886
L. Barron, *Les Environs de Paris*, Paris 1886

BAUDELAIRE 1965
C. Baudelaire, *Art in Paris, 1845–1862*, ed. J. Mayne, London 1965

BAZALGETTE 1976
L. Bazalgette, *Albert Dubois-Pillet, sa vie et son oeuvre (1846–1890)*, Paris 1976

BENEDITE 1897
L. Bénédite, 'Jean-Charles Cazin', *Art et décoration*, II, July–December 1897, pp. 161–75

BENEDITE 1898A
___, 'La Peinture décorative aux Salons', *Art et décoration*, III, January–June 1898, pp. 129–47

BENEDITE 1898B
___, 'Puvis de Chavannes', *Art et décoration*, IV, July–December 1898, pp. 129–53

BENJAMIN 1993
R. Benjamin, 'The Decorative Landscape, Fauvism, and the Arabesque of Observation', *Art Bulletin*, LXXV, no. 2, June 1993, pp. 295–316

BERKELEY SMITH 1903
F. Berkeley Smith, *How Paris Amuses Itself*, New York and London 1903

BERNIER 1886
R. Bernier, 'Un poète impressionniste. Jean Ajalbert', *Revue moderne*, no. 25, 20 January 1886, pp. 7–14

BERTAUT 1931
J. Bertaut, *L'Opinion et les moeurs. La Troisième République, 1870 à nos jours*, Paris 1931

BIGOT 1877
C. Bigot, 'L'Exposition des impressionnistes', *Revue politique et littéraire*, 2me sér., 28 April 1877, pp. 1045–8

BLUYSEN 1890
P. Bluysen, *Paris en 1889. Souvenirs et croquis de l'exposition*, Paris 1890

BOIME 1971
A. Boime, *The Academy and French Painting in the Nineteenth Century*, London 1971

BOUCHER AND IMBERT 1983
M. -C. Boucher and D. Imbert, *Palais des beaux-arts de la ville de Paris. Catalogue sommaire illustré des pastels*, Paris 1983

BOUILLON 1993
J. -P. Bouillon, *Maurice Denis*, Geneva 1993

BOUIN-LUCE AND BAZETOUX 1986
J. Bouin-Luce and D. Bazetoux, *Maximilien Luce. Catalogue de l'oeuvre peint*, 2 vols, Paris 1986

BOUYER 1893
R. Bouyer 'Le Paysage dans l'art', *L'Artiste*, nouv. pér., V, January 1893, pp. 19–35; February 1893, pp. 113–29; March 1893, pp. 194–211; VI, July 1893, pp. 29–48; August 1893, pp. 99–126; September 1893, pp. 195–214

BOUYER 1894A
___, *Le Paysage dans l'art*, Paris 1894

BOUYER 1894B
___, 'L'Art et la vie au Salon du Champ de Mars', *L'Artiste*, nouv. pér., VII, June 1894, pp. 401–21

BOUYER 1897
___, *Les Artistes aux Salons de 1897*, Paris 1897

BOUYER 1901
___, 'Jean-Charles Cazin, 1841–1901', *Revue universelle*, no. 17, 27 April 1901, pp. 393–6

BOUYER 1902
___, 'Le Déclin du paysage', *Revue bleue*, 11 October 1902, p. 467

BOUYER 1908
___, 'Nicolas Poussin (1594–1665)', in *Histoire du paysage en France*, ed. H. Marcel, Paris 1908, pp. 100–16

BOUYER 1914
___, 'René Ménard', *Art et décoration*, XXXV, June 1914, pp. 173–88

DE BRAHM 1906
A. de Brahm, 'Le Salon des Indépendants', *La Critique*, 12, March 5–20, 1906

BRETON 1890
J. Breton, *La Vie d'un artiste. Art et nature*, Paris 1890

BRETON 1896
___, *Un Peintre paysan. Souvenirs et impressions*, Paris 1896

BRETTELL 1990
R. Brettell, *Pissarro and Pontoise. The Painter in a Landscape*, New Haven and London 1990

BUISSON 1881
J. Buisson, 'Le Salon de 1881', *Gazette des beaux-arts*, pér. 2, XXIV, 1881, pp. 29–81

BURTY 1874
P. Burty, 'Exposition de la société anonyme des artistes', *La République française*, 25 April 1874, pp. 2–3

BUZARD 1993
J. Buzard, *The Beaten Track. European Tourism, Literature and the Ways of Culture*, Oxford 1993

CACHIN 1971
F. Cachin, *Paul Signac*, Paris 1971

CARRIERE 1907
E. Carrière, *Ecrits et lettres choisies*, Paris 1907

CASTAGNARY 1869
J. Castagnary, 'Salon de 1866', *Le Nain jaune*, 30 May 1869

CASTAGNARY 1874
___, 'Exposition du boulevard des Capucines, les Impressionnistes', *Le Siècle*, 29 April 1874, p. 3

CASTEX AND BELLEFROID 1968
P. Castex and J. -M. Bellefroid (eds), *Nouvelles Reliques de Villiers de L'Isle-Adam*, Paris 1968

CAZEAU 1982
P. Cazeau, *Maximilien Luce*, Lausanne and Paris 1982

CENTENAIRE DE L'IMPRESSIONNISME 1974
Centenaire de l'Impressionnisme, Paris, Grand Palais, September–November 1974

CEZANNE 1976
P. Cézanne, *Letters*, ed. J. Rewald, 4th edn, Oxford 1976

CEZANNE AND POUSSIN 1990
Cézanne and Poussin. The Classical Vision of Landscape, Edinburgh, National Gallery of Scotland, August–October 1990

CHAMPIER 1879
V. Champier, *L'Année artistique. Année 1878*, Paris 1879

CHARLES LACOSTE 1985
Charles Lacoste, 1870–1959. 60 ans de peinture entre symbolisme et naturalisme, Paris, Mairie du XVIe arrondissement; Beauvais, Musée départemental de l'Oise; Bordeaux, Galerie des beaux-arts, April–November 1985

CHARTRAIN-HEBBELINCK 1966
M. -J. Chartrain-Hebbelinck, 'Les Lettres de van Rysselberghe à Octave Maus', *Bulletin, Musées royaux des beaux-arts de Belgique*, 1/2, 1966, pp. 55–130

CHARTRAIN-HEBBELINCK 1969
___, 'Les Lettres de Paul Signac à Octave Maus', *Bulletin, Musées royaux des beaux-arts de Belgique*, 1/2, 1969, pp. 52–102

CHAVANNE AND GAUDICHON 1988
B. Chavanne and B. Gaudichon, *Catalogue raisonné des peintures des* XIX *et* XX *siècles*, Poitiers, Musées de la ville, 1988

CHENNEVIERES 1880
P. de Chennevières, 'Le Salon de 1880', *Gazette des beaux-arts*, pér. 2.1, XXII, pp. 41–70

CHERBULIEZ 1876
V. Cherbuliez, 'Le Salon de 1876. I. Les impressionnistes, les tableaux de genre et les portraits', *Revue des deux-mondes*, pér. 3, XV, 1 June 1876, pp. 513–33

CLARETIE 1865
J. Claretie, *Notes d'un parisien*, Paris 1865

CLAUDE MONET AT THE TIME OF GIVERNY 1983
Claude Monet at the Time of Giverny, Paris, Centre Culturel du Marais, April–July 1983

COMPIN 1964
I. Compin, *H. -E. Cross*, Paris 1964

COMPIN, LACAMBRE, ROQUEBERT ET AL. 1990
___, G. Lacambre, A. Roquebert et al., *Musée d'Orsay. Catalogue sommaire illustré des peintures*, 2 vols, Paris 1990

COPEAU 1910
J. Copeau, 'Henri Martin', *Art et décoration*, XXVII, June 1910, pp. 173–80

COUSTURIER 1927
L. Cousturier, *K. -X. Roussel*, Paris 1927

CROSS 1922
H. -E. Cross, 'Inédits d'Henri-Edmond Cross', *Bulletin de la vie artistique*, 3me année, no. 19, 1 October 1922, pp. 447–9

DARGENTY 1883
G. Dargenty, 'Chronique des expositions. Exposition du Cercle de la rue Volney', *Courrier de l'art*, no. 5, 1 February 1883, p. 54

DAVIS BUTLER 1967
J. Davis Butler, *Jean Moréas. A Critique of his Poetry and Philosophy*, The Hague and Paris 1967

DE COROT AUX IMPRESSIONNISTES 1991
De Corot aux Impressionnistes. Donations Moreau-Nélaton, Paris, Grand Palais, April–July 1991

DEBUSSY 1980
C. Debussy, *Lettres, 1884–1918*, ed. F. Lesure, Paris 1980

DEGAS 1947
E. Degas, *Lettres*, ed. M. Guérin, Oxford 1947

DENIS 1913
M. Denis, *Théories, 1890–1910. Du Symbolisme et de Gauguin vers un nouvel ordre classique*, Paris 1913

DENIS 1920
___, *Théories*, 1920 edn

DENIS 1957
___, *Journal:* I, *1884–1904;* II, *1905–20*, Paris 1957

DERAIN 1955
A. Derain, *Lettres à Vlaminck*, Paris 1955

DEROULEDE 1894
P. Déroulède, *Chants du paysan*, Paris 1894

DESJARDINS 1899
P. Desjardins, 'Les Salons de 1889', *Gazette des beaux-arts*, pér. 3, XXI, 1899, pp. 441–58

DESJARDINS 1901
___, 'En mémoire de Jean-Charles Cazin', *Gazette des beaux-arts*, pér. 3, XXVI, 1901, pp. 177–91

DESTREMAU 1988
F. Destremau, 'Le *Chemin dans les arbres* de Maurice Denis, 1891–2', *Gazette des beaux-arts*, pér. 6, CXII, no. 1467, 1988, pp. 155–62

DRISKEL 1992
M. P. Driskel, *Representing Belief. Religion, Art and Society in Nineteenth Century France*, Pennsylvania 1992

DUBOIS ET AL. 1985
P. Dubois et al., *L'Estaque au temps des peintres, 1870–1914*, Marseille 1985

DUVERGIER DE HAURANNE 1873
E. Duvergier de Hauranne, 'Le Salon de 1873. Le paysage et la sculpture', *Revue des deux mondes*, pér. 2, CV, 1 June 1873, pp. 859–92

ELDERFIELD 1979
J. Elderfield, 'The Garden and the City: Allegorical Painting and Early Modernism', *Bulletin, Museum of Fine Arts, Houston*, VII, no. 1, Summer 1979, pp. 3–21

ELWITT 1975
S. Elwitt, *The Making of the Third Republic. Class and Politics in France, 1868–1884*, Baton Rouge 1975

EMILE BERNARD 1990
Emile Bernard, 1868–1941, Mannheim, Städtliche Kunsthalle, and Amsterdam, Rijksmuseum Vincent van Gogh 1990

EPUY 1907
M. Epuy, *Le Sentiment de la nature*, Paris 1907

EVENSON 1979
N. Evenson, *Paris: A Century of Change, 1878–1978*, London and New Haven 1979

FARR AND HOUSE 1987
D. Farr and J. House, *Impressionist and Post-Impressionist Masterpieces: The Courtauld Collection*, London and New Haven 1987

FAUVE LANDSCAPE 1990–1
The Fauve Landscape, Los Angeles County Museum of Art, New York, Metropolitan Museum, and London, Royal Academy, 1990–1

FENEON 1970
F. Fénéon, *Oeuvres plus que complètes*, ed. J. U. Halperin, 2 vols, Geneva 1970

FLAM 1973
J. Flam, *Matisse on Art*, London 1973

FLAT 1893
P. Flat, 'La Peinture au Salon des Champs-Elysées', *L'Artiste*, nouv. pér., v, May 1893, pp. 326–41

FLAT 1900
___, 'Les Beaux-arts à l'Exposition Universelle. I. La Décennale française', *Revue bleue*, sér. 4, XIII, no. 20, 19 May 1900, pp. 613–19

F[ORAIN] 1889
J. -L. F[orain], 'Souvenir', *Le Fifre*, no. 3, 9 March 1889, p. 2

DE FOURCAUD 1884
L. de Fourcaud, 'Le Salon de 1884', *Gazette des beaux-arts*, pér. 2, XXIX, 1884, pp. 377–90; 1884, pp. 465–92; XXX, 1884, pp. 50–63; 1884, pp. 105–21

FOURNEL 1884
V. Fournel, *Les Artistes français contemporains. Peintres. Sculpteurs*, Tours 1884

FRENCH SYMBOLIST PAINTERS 1972
French Symbolist Painters, London, Hayward Gallery, June–July 1972

FROMENTIN 1876
E. Fromentin, *Les Maîtres d'autrefois*, Paris 1876 (English edn, London 1948)

GAUGUIN 1984
P. Gauguin, *Correspondance. Documents. Témoignages*. I. *1873–1888*, ed. V. Merlhès, Paris 1984

GAUGUIN 1989
Gauguin, Paris, Grand Palais, January–April 1989

GAUTIER 1865
T. Gautier, *Quand on voyage. Loin de Paris*, Paris 1865

GEFFROY 1892
G. Geffroy, *La Vie artistique*, I, Paris 1892

GEORGES SEURAT 1991–2
Georges Seurat, 1859–1891, Paris, Grand Palais, and New York, Metropolitan Museum, 1991–2 (English edn)

GERSTEIN 1989
M. Gerstein, *Impressionism. Selections from Five American Museums*, New York 1989

GIDEL 1891
P. Gidel, 'La Normandie maritime', *Photo-journal*, I, 1891, pp. 65–70

GLEIZES AND METZINGER 1913
A. Gleizes and J. Metzinger, *Cubism*, London 1913

VAN GOGH 1958
V. van Gogh, *The Complete Letters of Vincent van Gogh*, 3 vols, London 1958

VAN GOGH IN ARLES 1984
Van Gogh in Arles, New York, Metropolitan Museum, October–December 1984

VAN GOGH IN SAINT-REMY AND AUVERS 1986–7
Van Gogh in Saint-Rémy and Auvers, New York, Metropolitan Museum, November 1986–March 1987

VAN GOGH A PARIS 1988
Van Gogh à Paris, Paris, Musée d'Orsay, February–May 1988

VAN GOGH AND MILLET 1988–9
Van Gogh and Millet, Rijksmuseum Vincent van Gogh, December 1988–February 1989

VAN GOGH AND EARLY MODERN ART 1990
Van Gogh and Early Modern Art, Essen, Folkwang Museum, August–November 1990

GRAD AND RIGGS 1982
B. Grad and T. Riggs, *Visions of City and Country. Prints and Photographs of Nineteenth Century France*, Worcester (Mass.) and Washington, D.C. 1982

GREEN, C. 1980
C. Green, 'Cubism and Abstract Art' in *Towards a New Art. Essays on the Background to Abstract Art, 1910–1920*, London, Tate Gallery, 1980, pp. 156–77

GREEN, C. 1987
___, *Cubism and its Enemies*, New Haven and London 1987

GREEN, N. 1987
N. Green, 'Dealing in Temperaments: economic transformation of the artistic field in France during the second half of the nineteenth century', *Art History*, X, no. 1, March 1987, pp. 59–78

GREEN, N. 1990
___, *The Spectacle of Nature. Landscape and Bourgeois Culture in Nineteenth Century France*, Manchester 1990

GREENSPAN 1981
T. Greenspan, *'Les Nostalgiques' Re-examined: The Idyllic Landscape in France, 1890–1905*, Ph.D., City University, New York 1981

GROOM 1993
G. Groom, *Edouard Vuillard, Painter-Decorator. Patrons and Projects, 1892–1912*, London and New Haven 1993

GUIDE MICHELIN 1990
Guide Michelin pour les chauffeurs et les vélocipédistes, Paris 1900

GUISAN AND JAKUBEC 1974
G. Guisan and D. Jakubec (eds), *Félix Vallotton. Documents*. II, *1900–1914*, Lausanne and Paris 1974

GUSTAVE CAILLEBOTTE 1989
Gustave Caillebotte, 1848–1894. Dessins, études, peintures, Paris, Galerie Brame et Lorenceau, February–March 1989

HAMERTON 1892
P. G. Hamerton, *The Present State of the Fine Arts in France*, London 1892

HAMILTON 1992
V. Hamilton, *Boudin at Trouville*, London 1992

HARE 1895
A. Hare, *North-Western France*, London 1895

D'HAUSSONVILLE 1881
O. d'Haussonville, 'La Misère à Paris. I. La Population indigente et les quartiers pauvres', *Revue des deux mondes*, pér. 3, XLV, 15 June 1881, pp. 812–49

HAVARD 1879
H. Havard, 'L'Exposition des artistes indépendants', *Le Siècle*, 27 April 1879, p. 3

HAVARD 1881
___, *Histoire de la peinture hollandaise*, Paris 1881

HELLEBRANTH 1976
R. Hellebranth, *Charles-François Daubigny, 1817–1878*, Morges 1976

HENRI MARTIN 1983
Henri Martin, 1860–1943. Etudes et peintures de chevalet, Toulouse, Palais des Arts, and Paris, Mairie du 5e arrondissement, February–May 1983

HENRI MARTIN 1993
Henri Martin, 1860–1943, Cahors, Musée Henri Martin, September–October 1993

HENRIET 1876
F. H. Henriet, *Le Paysagiste aux champs*, Paris 1876

HERBERT, J. 1992
J. Herbert, *Fauve Painting: The Making of Cultural Politics*, London and New Haven 1992

HERBERT, R. L. 1970
R. L. Herbert, 'City versus Country: the Rural Image in French Painting from Millet to Gauguin', *Art Forum*, VIII, February 1970, pp. 44–55

HERBERT, R. L. 1979
___, 'Method and Meaning in Monet', *Art in America*, LXVII, no. 5, September 1979, pp. 90–108

HERBERT, R. L. 1988
___, *Impressionism. Art, Leisure and Parisian Society*, London and New Haven 1988

HOBBS 1977
R. Hobbs, *Odilon Redon*, London 1977

HOLL 1910
J. -C. Holl, *Après l'Impressionnisme*, Paris 1910

HOLL 1912
___, *La Jeune Peinture contemporaine*, Paris 1912

HOMMAGE A CLAUDE MONET 1980
Hommage à Claude Monet (1840–1926), Paris, Grand Palais, February–May 1980

HOUSE 1983
J. House, 'Monet's Water Garden and the Second Water Lily Series (1903–1909), in *Claude Monet at the Time of Giverny*, Paris, Centre Culturel du Marais, April–July 1983, pp. 150–65

HOUSE 1984
___, 'Monet in 1890' in J. Rewald and F. Weitzenhoffer (eds), *Aspects of Monet*, New York 1984, pp. 124–39

HOUSE 1985
___, 'Renoir and the Earthly Paradise', *Oxford Art Journal*, VIII, no. 2, 1985, pp. 21–7

HOUSE 1986
___, *Monet. Nature into Art*, London and New Haven 1986

HOUSE 1992A
___, 'Renoir's *Baigneuses* of 1887 and the Politics of Escapism', *Burlington Magazine*, CXXXIV, no. 1074, September 1992, pp. 578–85

HOUSE 1992B
___, 'Time's Cycles', *Art in America*, LXXX, no. 10, October 1992, pp. 126–35, 161

HOUSE 1993
___, 'Cézanne and Poussin: Myth and History' in *Cézanne and Poussin. A Symposium*, ed. R. Kendall, Sheffield 1993, pp. 129–49

HOUSSAYE 1882
H. Houssaye, *L'Art français depuis dix ans*, Paris 1882

HUTTON 1990
J. Hutton, '*Les Prolos vagabondent*': Neo-Impressionism and the Anarchist Image of the *Trimardeur*', *Art Bulletin*, LXXII, no. 2, June 1990, pp. 296–309

HUYSMANS 1883
J.-K. Huysmans, *L'Art moderne*, Paris 1883 (ed. H. Juin, Paris 1975)

IMAGES DU TRAVAIL 1985
Images du travail, Biot, Musée national Fernand Léger, July–October 1985

D'INDY 1906/9
V. d'Indy, *César Franck*, Paris 1906 (English edn 1909)

JAMOT 1906
P. Jamot, 'Le Salon d'Automne', *Gazette des beaux-arts*, pér. 3, XXXVI, 1906, pp. 456–84

JEAN-FRANÇOIS MILLET 1975–6
Jean-François Millet, Paris, Grand Palais, October 1975–January 1976

JONES 1988
J. B. Jones, *Gabriel Fauré: A Life in Letters*, London 1988

JONGKIND AND THE PRE-IMPRESSIONISTS 1976–7
Jongkind and the Pre-Impressionists, Northampton (Mass.), Smith College Museum of Art, and Williamstown, Clark Art Institute, 1976–7

JOYANT 1926
M. Joyant, *Henri de Toulouse-Lautrec, 1864–1901*. I. *Peintre*, Paris 1926

JULES BRETON 1982–3
Jules Breton and the French Rural Tradition, Omaha, Joslyn Art Museum; Memphis, Dixon Gallery; and Williamstown, Clark Art Institute, 1982–3

K. 1891
K., 'Les Envois des peintres français à Berlin', *La Vie parisienne*, 28 February 1891, pp. 116–17

KAHN 1888
G. Kahn, 'Chronique de la littérature et de l'art', *Revue indépendante*, n. s., VI, no. 16, February 1888, pp. 282–6

KAHN 1904
___, 'L'Exposition Claude Monet', *Gazette des beaux-arts*, pér. 3, XXXII, 1 July 1904, pp. 81–8

KEAR 1991
J. Kear, 'Making Hay with Monet: Monets of the '90s', *Art History*, XIV, no. 4, December 1991, pp. 593–9

KEES VAN DONGEN 1989–90
Kees van Dongen, Rotterdam, Boymans-van Beuningen Museum, December 1989–February 1990

KENDALL 1993
R. Kendall, *Degas Landscapes*, London and New Haven 1993

KENDALL 1994
___, 'A little mystery, some vagueness, some fantasy: Degas's anthropomorphic landscapes', *Apollo*, CXXXIX, no. 384, February 1994, pp. 39–45

FRANTISEK KUPKA 1975
František Kupka, 1871–1957, New York, Guggenheim Museum, 1975

LAFENESTRE 1889
G. Lafenestre, *Le Salon de 1889*, Paris 1889

LAFENESTRE 1893
___, 'Les Salons de 1893. I. La Peinture au Salon des Champs-Elysées', *Revue des deux mondes*, pér. 3, CXVII, I June 1893, pp. 658–79

LAFENESTRE 1894
___, 'Les Salons de 1894, II', *Revue des deux mondes*, pér. 4, LXIV, 1 July 1894, pp. 174–99

LAFORGUE 1886
J. Laforgue, 'A propos des toiles', *Le Symboliste*, 30 October 1886, p. 14

LAFORGUE 1887
___, 'Chronique parisienne', *Revue indépendante*, n. s., II, no. 5, March 1887, p. 344–5

LAFORGUE 1895
___, 'Notes sur le Musée du Luxembourg en 1886', *Revue blanche*, X, 15 June 1895, pp. 556–62

LAFORGUE 1988
___, *Textes de critique d'art*, ed. M. Dottin, Lille 1988

LANOE 1905
G. Lanoë, *Histoire de l'école française de paysage depuis Chintreuil jusqu'à 1900*, Nantes 1905

LANOE AND BRICE 1901
___ and T. Brice, *Histoire de l'école française de paysage (depuis le Poussin jusqu'à Millet)*, Paris 1901

DE LANNOY 1990
I. de Lannoy, *Musée national Jean-Jacques Henner. Catalogue des peintures*, Paris 1990

LECLERCQ 1900
J. Leclercq, 'Le *Bassin aux nymphéas* de Claude Monet', *Chronique des arts et de la curiosité*, 1 December 1900, p. 363

LEE 1990
J. Lee, *Derain*, Oxford 1990

LEGER 1973
F. Léger, *Functions of Painting*, ed. E. Fry, London 1973

LEIGHTEN 1989
P. Leighten, *Re-Ordering the Universe. Picasso and Anarchism, 1897–1914*, Princeton 1989

LEROY 1874
L. Leroy, 'L'Exposition des impressionnistes', *Le Charivari*, 25 April 1874, pp. 2–3

LHOTE 1939
A. Lhote, *Traité du paysage*, Paris 1939

LIGHTING UP THE LANDSCAPE 1986
Lighting up the Landscape. French Impressionism and its Origins, Edinburgh, National Gallery of Scotland, August–October 1986

LORRAIN 1911
J. Lorrain, *Du Temps que les bêtes parlaient. Portraits littéraires et mondains*, Paris 1911

DE LOSTALOT 1883
A. de Lostalot, 'Exposition des oeuvres de M. Claude Monet', *Gazette des beaux-arts*, pér. 2, XXVII, 1883, pp. 342–8

LOUIS CABAT 1987
Louis Cabat (1812–1893), Troyes, Musée des beaux-arts, July–October 1987

LOUIS 1905
R. Louis (ed.), *Lettres de Marie-Charles Dulac*, Paris 1905

MABILLEAU 1890
L. Mabilleau, 'Le Salon du Champ de Mars. II', *Gazette des beaux-arts*, pér. 3, IV, 1890, pp. 5–29

MALINGUE 1949
M. Malingue (ed.), *Lettres de Gauguin à sa femme et à ses amis*, Paris 1949

MALLARME 1945
S. Mallarmé, *Oeuvres complètes*, eds H. Mondor and J. Jean-Aubry, Paris 1945

MALTE-BRUN 1882
V. -A. Malte-Brun, *Calvados. Géographie. Histoire. Statistique. Administration*, Paris 1882

MANDELL 1967
R. Mandell, *Paris 1900. The Great World's Fair*, Toronto 1967

MANTZ 1877
P. Mantz, 'L'Exposition des peintres impressionnistes', *Le Temps*, 27 April 1877

MANTZ 1878
___ , 'Exposition Universelle. La Peinture française', *Gazette des beaux-arts*, pér. 2, XVIII, 1878, pp. 417–40

MARCEL N.D.
H. Marcel, *Chassériau*, Paris n.d

MARCEL 1903
___ , 'Salons de 1903. Henri Martin', *Art et décoration*, XIII, May 1903, pp. 141–8

MARCEL 1906
___ , 'Les Peintures d'Henri Martin pour le Capitole de Toulouse', *Art et décoration*, XIX, May 1906, pp. 145–52

MARCEL ET AL. 1908
___ et al., *Histoire du paysage en France*, Paris 1908

MARGUILLIER 1899
A. Marguillier, 'Charles Dulac', *Gazette des beaux-arts*, pér. 3, XXI, 1899, pp. 325–32

MARSEILLE 1991–2
Marseille au xix. Rêves et Triomphes, Musées de Marseille, November 1991–February 1992

MARX, L. 1992
L. Marx, 'Does Pastoralism have a Future?', *Studies in the History of Art, National Gallery of Art, Washington. Symposium Papers* XX. *The Pastoral Landscape*, Washington 1992, pp. 209–25

MARX, R. 1909
R. Marx, 'Les *Nymphéas* de M. Claude Monet', *Gazette des beaux-arts*, pér. 4, I, 1909, pp. 523–31

MATISSE 1908
H. Matisse, 'Notes d'un peintre', *La Grande Revue*, LII, no. 24, 25 December 1908, pp. 731–45

MATISSE IN MOROCCO 1990–1
Matisse in Morocco. The Paintings and Drawings, 1912–13, Washington, National Gallery; New York, Museum of Modern Art; Moscow, Puskin Museum; Leningrad, Hermitage, 1990–1

MATTHEWS 1987
T. Matthews, *Reading Apollinaire. Theories of Poetic Language*, Manchester 1987

MAUCLAIR 1905A
C. Mauclair, 'Le Salon de la Société nationale des beaux-arts', *Revue bleue*, sér. 5, III, no. 17, 20 April 1905, pp. 532–6

MAUCLAIR 1905B
___ , 'Le Salon d'Automne', *Revue bleue*, sér. 5, IV, no. 17, 21 October 1905, pp. 521–5

MAUCLAIR 1905C
___ , 'Le Style de la rue moderne', *Revue bleue*, sér. 5, IV, no. 23, 2 December 1905, pp. 719–22

MAUPASSANT 1888
G. de Maupassant, *Pierre et Jean*, Paris 1888 (English edn 1979, trans. L. Tancock)

MAUPASSANT 1980
___ , *Chroniques 2, 1 March 1882–17 August 1884; Chroniques 3, 26 August 1884–13 April 1891*, ed. H. Juin, Paris 1980

MAYEUR AND REBERIOUX 1984
J. -M. Mayeur and M. Rebérioux, *The Third Republic from its Origins to the Great War, 1871–1914*, Cambridge 1984

MAZEL 1890
H. Mazel, 'La Peinture et la sculpture en 1890', *L'Ermitage*, n. 3, June 1890, pp. 116–17

MAZEL 1894
___ , 'Raymond Bouyer' in *Portraits du prochain siècle*, Paris 1894, pp. 35–6

MELLERIO 1900
A. Mellerio, *L'Exposition de 1900 et l'impressionnisme*, Paris 1900

MICHEL, A. 1888
A. Michel, 'Le Salon de 1888', *Gazette des beaux-arts*, pér. 2, XXXVII, 1888, pp. 441–54; XXXVIII, 1888, pp. 21–31; 1888, pp. 137–53

MICHEL, A. 1896
___ , *Notes sur l'art moderne*, Paris 1896

MICHEL, A. 1897
___ , *Les Salons de 1897*, Paris 1897

MICHEL, E. 1876
E. Michel, *Du Paysage et du sentiment de la nature à notre époque. Discours de réception prononcé dans la séance publique du 11 mai 1876*, Nancy 1876

MICHEL, E. 1880
___ , 'Le Salon de 1880. II. Le paysage, la sculpture, l'architecture', *Revue des deux mondes*, pér. 3, XXXIX, 15 June 1880, pp. 908–42

MICHEL, E. 1906
___ , *Les Maîtres du paysage*, Paris 1906

MICHEL, E. 1909
___ , *La Forêt de Fontainebleau*, Paris 1909

MIGEON 1902
G. Migeon, 'Réné Ménard', *Art et décoration*, XI, April 1902, pp. 101–12

MILLMAN 1992
I. Millman, *Georges de Feure*, Courbevoie 1992

MITCHELL 1981
P. Mitchell, *Jean Baptiste Antoine Guillemet, 1841–1918*, London 1981

'MITCHI' 1891
'Mitchi', 'Autour du Salon', *La Vie parisienne*, 2 May 1891, pp. 242–3, 246

MITHOUARD 1907
A. Mithouard, 'Maurice Denis', *Art et décoration*, XXII, July 1907, pp. 1–12

MOCKEL 1895
A. Mockel, *Emile Verhaeren*, Paris 1895

MONET-RODIN 1989–90
Claude Monet/Auguste Rodin. Centenaire de l'exposition de 1889, Paris, Musée Rodin, November 1989–January 1990

MONOD 1905A
F. Monod, 'Le 21e Salon des Indépendants', *Art et décoration*, XVII, May 1905, Supplément, pp. 1–2

MONOD 1905B
___ , 'Le Salon d'Automne', *Art et décoration*, XVIII, December 1905, 198–210

MONOD 1906
___ , 'Supplément. Chronique. Salon des Indépendants', *Art et décoration*, XIX, May 1906, pp. 2–3

MONOD 1907
___ , 'Supplément. Chronique', *Art et décoration*, XXI, May 1907, p. 3–4

MONOD 1909
___ , 'Supplément. Chronique', *Art et décoration*, XXV, January 1909, pp. 2–3

MONOD 1913
___ , 'Supplément. Chronique. Le 29e Salon des Indépendants', *Art et décoration*, XXXIII, April 1913, pp. 1–3

MOREAS 1908
J. Moréas, *Esquisses et souvenirs*, Paris 1908

MOUTON 1885
E. Mouton, *La Physionomie comparée. Traité de l'expression dans l'homme, dans la nature, et dans l'art*, Paris 1885

LE MOYEN-AGE
Le Moyen-Age et les peintres français de la fin du XIXe siècle, Cagnes-sur-Mer, Château-Musée, May–June 1980

MOZZICONACCI 1990
J. -F. Mozziconacci, *Répertoire des peintures du XIXe siècle*, Carcassonne, Musée des beaux-arts, 1990

LE MUSEE DU LUXEMBOURG EN 1874 1974
Le Musée du Luxembourg en 1874, Paris, Grand Palais, May–November 1974

NATHANSON 1989
R. Nathanson (ed.), *Bonnard. Sketches of a Journey. From Octave Mirbeau's Journal 'La 628-E8'*, London 1989

NEO-IMPRESSIONISM 1968
Neo-Impressionism, New York, Guggenheim Museum, February–April 1968

NEW PAINTING 1986
The New Painting: Impressionism 1874–1886, San Francisco and Washington 1986

NORBERG 1908
P. Norberg, 'La Peinture aux Salons', *Art et décoration*, XXIV, July 1908, pp. 21–36

ON CLASSIC GROUND 1990
On Classic Ground. Picasso, Léger, de Chirico and the New Classicism, 1910–1930, London, Tate Gallery, June–September 1990

PAULHAN 1913
F. Paulhan, *L'Esthétique du paysage*, Paris 1913

PAYSAGES DE LA REGION CENTRE 1985–8
Paysages de la Région centre, 1800–1914, ou la conscience d'une identité régionale, Blois, Musée des beaux-arts et al., December 1985–April 1988

PEETERS 1886
E. Peeters, *La Culture maraichère aux environs de Paris. Rapport adressé à M. le Ministre de l'Agriculture, de l'industrie et des travaux publics*, Brussels 1886

PEGUY 1961
C. Péguy, *Oeuvres en prose, 1909–1914*, Paris 1961

PENNELL 1920
E. R. and J. Pennell, *The Life of James McNeill Whistler*, revised edn, London 1920

PERATE 1897
A. Pératé, *La Peinture aux Salons de 1897. Paris et Londres*, Paris 1897

PERIER 1890
E. Périer, *Notes sur la ville d'Asnières*, Asnières 1890

PETIT 1939
J. Petit, *Asnières*, Nanterre 1939

PHLIPPONNEAU 1956
M. Phlipponneau, *La Vie rurale de la banlieue parisienne*, Paris 1956

DE PILES 1708
R. de Piles, *Cours de peinture par principes*, Paris 1708

PISSARRO 1990
J. Pissarro, *Monet's Cathedral. Rouen, 1892–1894*, London 1990

PLACES OF DELIGHT 1988–9
Places of Delight. The Pastoral Landscape, Washington, National Gallery, and Phillips Collection, November 1988–January 1989

POST-IMPRESSIONISM 1979–80
Post-Impressionism. Cross-Currents in European Painting, London, Royal Academy, November 1979–March 1980

PROTH 1879
M. Proth, *Voyage aux pays des peintres. Salon universel de 1878*, Paris 1879

PUVIS DE CHAVANNES 1976–7
Puvis de Chavannes, 1824–1898, Paris, Grand Palais, November 1976–February 1977; Ottawa, National Gallery of Canada, March–May 1977

REDON 1961
O. Redon, *A Soi-même. Journal, 1867–1915*, Paris 1961

REFF 1960
T. Reff, 'Cézanne and Poussin', *Journal of the Warburg and Courtauld Institutes*, XXIII, 1960, pp. 150–74

RENAN 1961
E. Renan, *Oeuvres complètes*. X. *Correspondance, 1845–1892*, ed. H. Psichari, Paris 1961

RENARD 1887
G. Renard, *Croquis champêtres*, Paris 1887

RETTE 1894
A. Retté, 'Notes de voyage', *La Plume*, no. 129, 1 September 1894, pp. 351–3

REWALD 1946
J. Rewald, *The History of Impressionism*, New York 1946

REWALD 1948
___, *Paul Cézanne. A Biography*, New York 1948 (1968 edn)

REWALD 1949–53
___ (ed.), 'Extraits du journal inédit de Paul Signac. I, 1894–5', *Gazette des beaux-arts*, pér. 5, XXXVI, 1949, pp. 97–128; 'II, 1897–98', XXXIX, 1952, pp. 265–84; 'III, 1898–99', XLII, 1953, pp. 27–57

REWALD 1978
___, *Post Impressionism from van Gogh to Gauguin*, New York 1978

REWALD AND WEITZENHOFER 1984
___ and F. Weitzenhofer (eds), *Aspects of Monet*, New York 1984

ROBBINS 1963–4
D. Robbins, 'From Symbolism to Cubism: the Abbaye de Créteil', *Art Journal*, XXIII, no. 2, Winter 1963–4, pp. 111–16

DE LA ROCHEFOUCAULD 1893
A. de la Rochefoucauld, 'P. Signac', *Le Coeur*, I, no. 2, May 1893, pp. 4–5

ROUSSEL 1993
K. -X. Roussel, Saint-Tropez, Musée de l'Annonciade, July–October 1993

SAINT-JUIRS 1890
Saint-Juirs, *La Seine à travers Paris*, Paris 1890

SALMON, A. 1912
A. Salmon, *La Jeune Peinture française*, Paris 1912

SALMON, M. -J. 1983
M. -J. Salmon, 'Beauvais, Musée départmental de l'Oise. Impressionnistes et post-impressionnistes', *Revue du Louvre*, 5/6, 1983, pp. 443–5

SAUNIER 1894
C. Saunier, 'Le Paysage dans l'art', *L'Ermitage*, no. 7, 1894, pp. 12–13

SAUNIER 1902
___, 'Luc-Olivier Merson', *Art et décoration*, XII, November 1902, pp. 146–60

SCHIVELBUSCH 1986
W. Schivelbusch, *The Railway Journey. The Industrialization of Time and Space in the 19th Century*, Leamington Spa 1986

SEAILLES 1899
G. Séailles, 'Eugène Carrière: l'homme et l'artiste', *Revue de Paris*, III, 1899, pp. 147–92

SEBILLOT 1877
P. Sébillot, 'Exposition des impressionnistes', *Le Bien Public*, 7 April 1877

SEGARD 1914
A. Segard, *Peintres d'aujourd'hui. Les Décorateurs*, 2 vols, Paris 1914

SEILLIERE 1905
E. Seillière, 'Le Symbole de la danse chez Nietzsche', *Revue bleue*, sér. 5, III, no. 8, 25 February 1905, p. 231–5

SERUSIER 1942
P. Sérusier, *ABC de la Peinture*, Paris 1942

SEURAT AT GRAVELINES 1990
Seurat at Gravelines. The Last Landscapes, Indianapolis Museum of Art, October–November 1990

SHIFF 1984
R. Shiff, *Cézanne and the End of Impressionism. A Study in the Theory, Technique, and Critical Evaluation of Modern Art*, Chicago 1984

SHONE 1992
R. Shone, *Sisley*, London 1992

SIGNAC 1899
P. Signac, *D'Eugène Delacroix au Néo-Impressionnisme*, Paris 1899 (1911 edn)

SILVERMAN 1989
D. Silverman, *Art Nouveau in Fin-de-siècle France. Politics, Psychology and Style*, California 1989

SILVESTRE 1874
A. Silvestre, 'Physiologie du refusé. L'Exposition des révoltés', *L'Opinion nationale*, 22 April 1874

SOUBIRAN 1993
J. -R. Soubiran, *Le Paysage provençal et l'école de Marseille avant l'impressionnisme, 1845–1874*, Paris and Toulon 1993

SOUCY 1972
R. Soucy, *Fascism in France. The Case of Maurice Barrès*, California 1972

SOULIER 1897
G. Soulier, 'Conclusion sur la peinture aux Salons', *Art et décoration*, II, July–December 1897, pp. 43–8

SOUVENIRS DE VOYAGE 1992
Souvenirs de Voyage. Autographes et dessins français du XIX siècle, Paris, Louvre, February–May 1992

SPATE 1979
V. Spate, *Orphism. The evolution of non-figurative painting in Paris, 1910–1914*, Oxford 1979

SPATE 1992
___, *Claude Monet. The Colour of Time*, London 1992

LA STATUE DE LA LIBERTE 1987
La Statue de la Liberté. L'Exposition du centenaire. Paris, Musée des Arts décoratifs, October 1986–February 1987

STEEGMULLER 1982
F. Steegmuller (ed.), *The Letters of Gustave Flaubert, 1857–1880*, London 1982

STEPHAN 1974
P. Stephan, *Paul Verlaine and the Decadence, 1882–1890*, Manchester 1974

STERLING AND ADHEMAR 1958
C. Sterling and H. Adhémar, *Musée national du Louvre. Peintures. Ecole française, XIXe siècle. I. A-C.*, Paris 1958

STRICK 1992
J. Strick, 'Notes on some Instances of Irony in Modern Pastoral', *Studies in the History of Art, National Gallery of Art, Washington. Symposium Papers* XX. *The Pastoral Landscape*, Washington, D.C. 1992, pp. 197–207

STUMP 1972
J. Stump, *The Art of K. -X. Roussel*, Ph.D., University of Kansas 1972

THEURIET 1888
A. Theuriet, *La Vie rustique*, Paris 1888

THEVENIN 1898
L. Thévenin, *La Renaissance païenne. Etude sur Lévy-Dhurmer*, Paris 1898

THIEBAULT-SISSON 1902
Thiébault-Sisson, 'J. -C. Cazin', *Les Arts*, no. 1, February 1902, pp. 30–4

THOMSON 1982
R. Thomson, 'Camille Pissarro, *Turpitudes sociales*, and the Universal Exhibition of 1889', *Arts Magazine*, LVI, no. 8, April 1982, pp. 82–8

THOMSON 1985
___, *Seurat*, Oxford 1985

THOMSON 1986
___, 'Edinburgh, National Gallery: *Lighting up the Landscape*', *Burlington Magazine*, CXXVIII, no. 1004, November 1986, pp. 847–8

THOMSON 1987A
___, *The Private Degas*, London 1987

THOMSON 1987B
___, 'Van Gogh in Paris: the fortifications drawings of 1887', *Jong Holland*, no. 3, September 1987, pp. 14–25

THOMSON 1990
___, *Camille Pissarro: Impressionism, Landscape and Rural Labour*, London 1990

THOMSON 1991
___, 'Young Man's Painting' (review of *The Fauve Landscape*), *Times Literary Supplement*, no. 4604, 28 June 1991, p. 16

THOMSON 1992
___, 'On Narrative and Metamorphosis in Degas' in *Dealing with Degas*, eds R. Kendall and G. Pollock, London 1992, pp. 146–58

VAN TILBORGH AND VAN UITERT 1990
L. van Tilborgh and E. van Uitert, 'A Ten Year Career. The *Oeuvre* of van Gogh', in *Vincent van Gogh. Paintings*, Amsterdam, Rijksmuseum Vincent van Gogh, March–July 1990, pp. 15–26

'TIPHERETH' 1893
'Tiphereth', 'Le Salon du Champ-de-Mars', *Le Coeur*, I, no. 3, June 1893, pp. 5–8

TRIOMPHE DES MAIRIES 1986–7
Le Triomphe des Mairies. Grands décors républicains à Paris, 1879–1914, Paris, Petit Palais, November 1986–January 1987

TUCKER 1982
P. Tucker, *Monet at Argenteuil*, London and New Haven 1982

TUCKER 1989
___, *Monet in the '90s. The Series Paintings*, Boston, Museum of Fine Arts, February–April 1989

UZANNE 1889
O. Uzanne, *The Mirror of the World*, London 1889

VACHON N.D.
M. Vachon, *Puvis de Chavannes*, Paris n.d

FELIX VALLOTTON 1991–2
Félix Vallotton: A Retrospective, New Haven, Yale University Art Gallery, October 1991–January 1992

LOUIS VALTAT 1989
Louis Valtat. Paysages de l'Estérel, Saint Tropez, Musée de l'Annonciade, July–October 1989

VALENCIENNES 1800
P. H. de Valenciennes, *Elémens de perspective … pratique à l'usage des artistes*, Paris 1800

VAUDEVIRE 1990
C. Vaudevire, 'Joseph Pennell (1857–1926) et la France: les Dessins du Louvre', *Revue du Louvre*, 2, 1990, pp. 129–35

VAUXCELLES 1905
L. Vauxcelles, 'Le Salon d'Automne', *Gil Blas*, 17 October 1905

VAUXCELLES 1906
___, 'Le Salon des Indépendants', *Gil Blas*, 20 March 1906

VENTURI 1939
L. Venturi, *Les Archives de l'impressionnisme*, 2 vols, Paris 1939

DE VERNEILH 1983
B. de Verneilh, 'Maximilien Luce et Notre-Dame de Paris', *L'Oeil*, no. 332, March 1983, pp. 24–31

VINCENT VAN GOGH 1990
Vincent van Gogh. Paintings, Amsterdam, Rijksmuseum Vincent van Gogh, March–July 1990

VLAMINCK 1929/1961
M. Vlaminck, *Tournant dangereux*, Paris 1929 (English edn 1961, intro. D. Sutton)

DE VOGUE 1889
M. de Vogüé, 'A travers l'Exposition, I: Aux portes, la Tour', *Revue des deux mondes*, CIX, I July 1889, pp. 186–201

WAKEMAN 1992
R. Wakeman, '*La Ville en vol*: Toulouse and the Cultural Legacy of the Airplane', *French Historical Studies*, XVII, no. 3, Spring 1992, pp. 769–90

WEBER 1986
E. Weber, *France fin-de-siécle*, Harvard 1986

WHITE 1965
H. and C. White, *Canvases and Careers: Institutional Change in the French Painting World*, New York 1965

WHITELEY 1979
L. Whiteley, 'Accounting for Tastes', *Oxford Art Journal*, no. 2, April 1979, pp. 25–8

WHITFIELD 1991
S. Whitfield, *Fauvism*, London 1991

WILDENSTEIN 1974–92
D. Wildenstein, *Claude Monet. Biographie et catalogue raisonné*, 5 vols, Lausanne and Paris 1974–92

WILLIAMS 1973
R. Williams, *The Country and the City*, London 1973

ZELDIN 1980
T. Zeldin, *France, 1848–1945. Taste and Corruption*, Oxford 1980

ZOLA 1967
E. Zola, *La Terre: Oeuvres complètes d'Emile Zola*, ed. H. Mitterand, V, Paris 1967

ZOLA 1974
___, *Le bon combat. De Courbet aux impressionnistes*, ed. J. -P. Bouillon, Paris 1974

1889 1989
1889. La Tour Eiffel et l'Exposition Universelle, Paris, Musée d'Orsay, May–August 1989

1893 1993
1893. L'Europe des peintres, Paris, Musée d'Orsay, February–May 1993

1913 1987–8
1913. Le Théâtre des Champs-Elysées, Paris, Musée d'Orsay, October 1987–January 1988

Chronology

1870
July France declares war on Prussia
September Collapse of Second Empire
Foundation of Third Republic
Siege of Paris commences

1871
January Capitulation by France
May Treaty of Frankfurt, ceding Alsace and a part of Lorraine to a united Germany
Bloody suppression of Paris Commune, established in March

The 1870s saw the Right Wing gain control of national politics, the division or dispersion of the Left, and a widespread desire for stability in which to restore national prosperity.

1872
July Military conscription made law
Jules Verne, *Around the World in Eighty Days*

1873
September Last occupying German forces leave French soil

1874
April Société anonyme des artistes peintres … (first Impressionist exhibition)

1876
Edmond Duranty, *La Nouvelle Peinture*

1878
Universal Exhibition
Public holiday to celebrate success of the Exhibition 30 June

1879
January Election of the Republican, Grévy, as President

The election of a Republican as President initiated a period of reform with, for example, the legalisation of trades unions and the introduction of new divorce laws in 1884. However, in the 1880s unstable administrations and a fragile economy slowed reform and the Left gained ground, capitalising on the failure of the Republic to solve 'La Question sociale'. Through the 1890s French agriculture endured a slump, exaggerated by inefficient land division, rural depopulation and foreign competition.

1880
July Amnesty for Communards
Bastille Day inaugurated as national holiday

1881
State abandons control of Salon to Société des artistes français

1884
August First Salon des indépendants

1885
Emile Zola, *Germinal*

1886
May Eighth and last Impressionist exhibition
September Jean Moréas, 'Manifeste du symbolisme', *Figaro littéraire*

1887
May Millet exhibition at Ecole des beaux-arts, Paris

1889
April General Boulanger, former Minister of War, whose political support had gathered considerable strength, abandons coup and flees to Brussels
May Opening of Universal Exhibition
Inauguration of Eiffel Tower

The 1890s was a decade of increasing polarisation in French politics. In November 1890 Cardinal Lavigerie launched the Ralliement, *rallying Catholics to the Republic. Religious revivalism combined with militarist agitation for* revanche *(revenge) against Germany and anti-semitism and created a resurgence of the Right. On the far Left the anarchist terror campaign of 'propaganda by deed' was enacted against the establishment.*

1890
May Division of the Salon into Salon des artistes français and Société nationale des beaux-arts (Salon du Champ de Mars)
August Maurice Denis, 'Définition du Néo-traditionnisme', *Art et critique*

1891
Moréas founds L'Ecole romane to promote Latin tradition in poetry
May Monet's series of *Grainstacks* exhibited at Durand-Ruel
December The first Exposition des peintres impressionnistes et symbolistes staged by Le Barc de Boutteville at his gallery in Paris

1892
February Monet's series of *Poplars* exhibited by Durand-Ruel
November Degas's pastel and monotype landscapes exhibited by Durand-Ruel

1894
June Assassination of President Carnot by anarchist
July Repressive laws against anarchism
December Captain Dreyfus condemned for spying for Germany

1895
November Cézanne exhibition staged at Vollard's gallery

1897
February Part of Caillebotte (+1894) bequest of Impressionist paintings hung at the Musée du Luxembourg

1898
January Zola's *J'accuse* exposes the cover-up of Dreyfus's innocence

1899
Publication of Signac's *D'Eugène Delacroix au Néo-impressionnisme*
February Failure of right-wing coup by Déroulède
August–September Retrial of Dreyfus

1900
April Opening of Universal Exhibition
July First section of Paris *métro* opened

The 1900s witnessed much social and industrial agitation in France, with miners', electricians' and postal workers' strikes in 1904–7, as well as agricultural unrest in the Hérault and Languedoc. In foreign affairs growing fears of German colonial expansion and central European hegemony fired nationalistic anxieties.

1901
March Van Gogh retrospective at Galerie Bernheim Jeune

1903
July First Tour de France cycle race
October First Salon d'Automne

1904
April Entente Cordiale with Britain

1905
March Seurat and van Gogh retrospectives at the Indépendants
October Vauxcelles's review of works by Matisse and others at the Salon d'Automne gives rise to the term 'Fauves'

1906
October Gauguin and Carrière retrospectives at the Salon d'Automne

1907
July Picasso completes *Les Demoiselles d'Avignon*
October Cézanne retrospective at the Salon d'Automne

1908
November Braque exhibition at Kahnweiler gallery; Vauxcelles's review gives rise to the term Cubism
December Matisse, 'Notes d'un peintre', *La Grande Revue*

1909
May Monet's *Nymphéas, Paysages d'Eau* exhibition at Durand-Ruel gallery
July Blériot flies the Channel

1910
Cubist paintings increasingly in evidence at the Indépendants and Salon d'Automne

1911
April Cubist painters show as a group in *salle 41* at the Indépendants
June Crisis over German gunboat *Panther* at Agadir

1912
October Cubist *Section d'Or* group exhibition at Galerie de la Boétie
December Cubism attacked in Chambre des Députés

1913
March Appearance of Orphist paintings at the Indépendants
May Stravinsky's *Rite of Spring* at Théâtre des Champs-Elysées
Alain-Fournier, *Le Grand Meaulnes*
Guillaume Apollinaire, *Alcools*
Blaise Cendrars and Sonia Delaunay, *Prose du Transsibérien*
Marcel Proust, *Swann's Way*

1914
June Assassination of the Austrian Archduke at Sarajevo
August Germany declares war on France

Artists' Biographies and List of Works included in the Exhibition

The **bold** number before each work refers to the illustrations in this book.
All works are oil on canvas unless otherwise stated; dimensions are given in centimetres, height preceding width.

EDMOND AMAN-JEAN
1860–1936

Like Seurat, with whom he shared a studio, *c.* 1881–2, a pupil of Lehmann at the Ecole des beaux-arts. In the 1880s his work was influenced by Puvis de Chavannes and Cazin. He exhibited regularly at the Salons, and at the Salon de la Rose+Croix, 1892–3. Painter of portraits and decorative projects.

56
Sainte Geneviève before Paris 1885
74 × 101 cm
Musée de Brest

EMILE BERNARD
1868–1941

Born in Lille, Bernard studied for a time in the studio of Cormon – a contemporary Salon painter. There he met Toulouse-Lautrec and van Gogh. In the search for his own style, he experimented with *Pointillisme*, but subsequently quarrelled with Signac and destroyed all his own work of this period. In 1886 he went to Pont-Aven where he met Gauguin. They developed *Synthetism* or *Cloissonisme* for which Gauguin was later to take the credit. Eventually Bernard abandoned these new developments to travel in the Orient and Egypt and to paint in the more traditional manner of his earlier training.

46
Quai de Clichy 1887
39 × 59 cm
Musée d'Orsay, Paris (on deposit to the Musée départemental du Prieuré, Saint-Germain-en-Laye)

PIERRE BONNARD
1867–1947

Trained as a lawyer, but by 1890 was involved with the Nabis group which included Denis, Roussel and Vuillard. In the early 1890s he worked in a patterned decorative style under Japanese influence. After 1895 he moved increasingly into more tonal and loosely brushed painting.

189, 200
The Train and the Barges c. 1910
77 × 108 cm
The Hermitage Museum, St. Petersburg

ANDRE BROUILLET
1857–1914

Pupil of Gérôme and Jean-Paul Laurens at the Ecole des beaux-arts. Made a reputation in the Salons of the 1880s for modern life subjects of both rural and urban themes treated in the *peinture claire* of middle-of-the-road naturalism. In 1902–3 he painted murals for the Nouvelle Sorbonne.

251
Love in the Fields c. 1888
54.8 × 73.5 cm
Musées de la ville de Poitiers

JEAN-CHARLES CAZIN
1841–1901

Student of Lecoq de Boisbaudran, who stressed the cultivation of visual memory. Worked in London during the early 1870s. Returned to France and made a substantial reputation during the 1880s with figurative subjects often on biblical themes set in his native Pas-de-Calais. His later work is dominated by melancholy landscapes.

143
Rest Before Nightfall 1883
123.19 × 106.05 cm
Corcoran Gallery of Art, Washington, William A. Clark Collection

82
Mesnilval c. 1894
73.5 × 92 cm
Musée du Petit Palais, Paris

PAUL CEZANNE
1839–1906

Of bourgeois stock from Aix-en-Provence. Moved in the circles of his friend the novelist Zola and painters such as Pissarro and Guillemet in Paris during the 1860s, showing at the Salon des refusés in 1863. In the early 1870s he was introduced by Pissarro to *plein air* painting, and he exhibited with the Impressionists in 1874 and 1877. He became increasingly solitary, working chiefly in Provence. His public reputation grew after the dealer Vollard organised his first one-man show in 1895.

102
View of Mont Marseilleveyre and the île de Maire c. 1878–82
54 × 64 cm
Memorial Art Gallery of the University of Rochester (Rochester, New York), Anonymous gift in tribute to Edward Harris and in memory of H.R. Stirlin of Switzerland

121
The Sea at L'Estaque c. 1885
72.9 × 59.5 cm
Private Collection on Loan to the Fitzwilliam Museum, Cambridge

MARC CHAGALL
1887–1985

Born in Vitebsk and studied first in St Petersburg under the designer Léon Bakst. In 1910 he travelled to Paris, and was soon drawn to the possibilities of Cubism and Orphism. He was supported by Apollinaire, but his first one-man show was held in Berlin at Der Sturm gallery in 1914. Cut off on a visit to Russia by the outbreak of war, he remained there until 1922, returning to settle in France the following year.

76
The Pont de Passy and the Eiffel Tower 1911
60 × 80 cm
The Metropolitan Museum of Art, Robert Lehman Collection, 1975

CAMILLE COROT
1796–1875

Trained by Bertin and Michallon in Neo-classical landscape conventions. Spent 1825–8 in Italy, then travelled in France before returning to Italy in 1834 and 1843. During the 1830s and 1840s his work included Poussinesque figure compositions for the Salon as well as landscapes in a variety of styles, but after *c.* 1850 his work became characterised by a silvery tonality and a mood of pastoral nostalgia.

116
Pastorale: Souvenir d'Italie 1873
172.7 × 144.4 cm
Glasgow Museums: Art Gallery and Museum, Kelvingrove

HENRI-EDMOND CROSS
1856–1910

Exhibited at the Indépendants from 1884 in a naturalistic vein, and then adopted Neo-impressionism *c.* 1890. He settled on the Mediterranean coast in 1891, producing landscapes and, after 1900, imaginative nude subjects with an increasingly decorative touch and unnaturalistic palette. Contributed illustrations to anarchist periodicals in the 1890s.

111
The Beach at Saint-Clair 1901
68 × 92 cm
Private Collection, Paris

EDGAR DEGAS
1834–1917

Trained as a history painter in the 1850s, then, during the following decade, gradually converted to scenes of modern life. His submissions to the Impressionist exhibitions in the 1870s and 1880s centred on portraits and innovatively composed scenes of urban entertainment. During the 1890s his longstanding if discreet interest in landscape burgeoned, and his only one-man exhibition was of landscape pastels held at the Durand-Ruel gallery in November 1892.

156
Landscape with Rocky Cliffs 1890
oil monotype and pastel on paper
40 × 29 cm
Josefowitz Collection

158
Landscape c. 1892
pastel on paperboard
52 × 50 cm
The Museum of Fine Arts, Houston; Museum purchase with funds provided by the Brown Foundation Accessions Endowment Fund

PAUL-LOUIS DELANCE
1848–1924

Pupil of Gérôme at the Ecole des beaux-arts. Became a regular exhibitor at the Salon and, later, at the Société nationale des beaux-arts. An extremely versatile artist, he essayed most genres of painting, including landscape.

68
The Champ-de-Mars, Paris in January 1889
1889
126.5 × 192.5 cm
Musée Carnavalet, Paris

ROBERT DELAUNAY
1885–1941

Pupil of the theatre designer Ronsin. Turned to painting in 1904. Having passed through Impressionist and Cézannesque phases, by 1910 he had begun to experiment with Cubism. However, his interest in colour, and especially simultaneous contrast, led Apollinaire to dub his work – with the loosely related paintings of Kupka and Léger – Orphic Cubist. By 1912 he was painting abstract canvases in coloured and circular forms in collaboration with his wife Sonia.

50
The Windows, No. 3 1912
79 × 64.5 cm
Kunstmuseum Winterthur, Bequest 1973 of Clara and Emil Friedrich-Jezler

SONIA DELAUNAY
1885–1979

Born in Russia, Sonia Terk. Trained initially in Karlsruhe before going to Paris in 1905. Her work at this period was flatly painted and brightly coloured, but after her marriage to Robert Delaunay in 1909 their work developed in a parallel exchange. She was not only a painter but a designer of clothes, books, etc.

201
La Prose du Transsibérien et de la petite Jehanne de France, Editions des hommes nouveaux 1913
pochoir and text on paper in hand-coloured leather folder (no. 26); with separate pochoir announcement of the edition
open 199 × 35.5 cm, announcement 9.1 × 34 cm
Scottish National Gallery of Modern Art, Edinburgh

MAURICE DENIS
1870–1943

In the 1890s a central figure in the Nabis group, which included Bonnard, Roussel and Vuillard. He operated both as a painter of imaginative Symbolist subjects and, in the applied arts, as a designer of stained glass, wallpaper, etc. By the end of the decade his devout Catholicism and right-wing views led him to a more classicising style, and after 1900 he made a substantial reputation with decorative schemes for public and private patrons. He was also an important aesthetic theorist.

185
Path through the Trees c. 1891
28 × 19 cm
Musée départemental du Prieuré, Saint-Germain-en-Laye

216
Embroidery by the Sea, designed 1895, replica 1901–22
distemper on canvas
53 × 232 cm
Musée départemental du Prieuré, Saint-Germain-en-Laye

136
Eurydice 1906
85 × 111 cm
Staatliche Museen zu Berlin Nationalgalerie, Dauerleihgabe des Ernst von Siemens-Kunstfonds

ANDRE DERAIN
1880–1954

Born at Chatou in the Parisian suburbs, and developed as a key Fauve painter after his military service (1901–4). His campaign at Collioure with Matisse in 1905 introduced him to the Mediterranean, and in 1905–6 he painted in London. After essays in Cubism, his pre-1914 style settled down into a deliberately sophisticated naïvety, often based on landscape.

107
Collioure, the Village and the Sea 1905
60.2 × 73.5 cm
Scottish National Gallery of Modern Art, Edinburgh

ANDRE DEVAMBEZ
1867–1944

Had a sound academic training and was winner of the Prix de Rome in 1890. On his return from Italy he worked as an illustrator as well as a painter. His subjects in both fields were frequently scenes of the modern city and of new forms of transport such as the automobile and aeroplane.

203
Avions fantaisistes 1911
55 × 72.2 cm
Musée départemental de l'Oise, Beauvais

KEES VAN DONGEN
1877–1968

After studying at the Academy of Fine Arts in Rotterdam he settled in Paris in 1900. An anarchist sympathiser, he was friendly with both older painters such as Luce and the avant-garde circle of Picasso. Worked also as an illustrator. His paintings usually tackled urban themes and nudes in bright colours. In 1905 his paintings hung with the Fauve canvases at the Salon d'Automne, but before long his reputation was chic rather than controversial.

149, 164
Guus and Dolly 1905
73 × 92 cm
Private Collection

RAOUL DUFY
1877–1953

Studied first at his native Le Havre and in 1900 at the Ecole des beaux-arts under Bonnat with Friesz. His early manner was Impressionist, but by 1904 he was in contact with Marquet, with whom he went on painting campaigns in Normandy from 1904–6, also travelling to the Mediterranean for the first time in 1905. After a Cézannesque phase with Braque at L'Estaque in 1908 he developed a more linear, fluid style which enjoyed great popular success.

87
Old Houses Along the Honfleur Basin 1906
60 × 73 cm
Fridart Stichting, Amsterdam

MARIE-CHARLES DULAC
1865–98

Began his career in a wallpaper factory and as a scene-painter, then exhibited with the Indépendants from 1890. He also showed at the Salon de la nationale from 1894 and with the Nabis at Le Barc de Boutteville's gallery in 1896. Converted to Catholicism *c.* 1892 and illustrated St Francis's *Song of Creatures* in 1894. After his death a retrospective was organised at Vollard's gallery by friends such as Aman-Jean, Denis and Carrière.

186
Sunset, Avignon 1898
27.2 × 46 cm
Musée des beaux-arts, Reims

ANDRE DUNOYER DE SEGONZAC
1884–1974

Studied under Luc-Olivier Merson and Jean-Paul Laurens. From 1909 he exhibited at both the Salon des Indépendants and the Salon d'Automne. Called up in 1914, he had a distinguished war career, ending as chief camouflage officer for the 3rd Army. His early paintings were frequently in a densely worked facture, though his later reputation rested rather on fluid watercolours, often of Mediterranean landscapes.

63
Notre-Dame 1913
73.3 × 100 cm
Columbus Museum of Art, Ohio, Gift of Howard D. and Babette L. Sirak

OTHON FRIESZ
1879–1949

Student at the Ecole des beaux-arts of his native Le Havre and then of Paris. In 1901 he met Pissarro and Guillaumin, and in the following year shared a show at Berthe Weill's gallery with Matisse, Marquet, Manguin and Dufy. He travelled widely, visiting the Mediterranean for the first time in 1904, and again in 1906 with Braque after their trip to Antwerp. In the following years he produced figurative scenes as well as landscapes.

166
Landscape, La Ciotat 1907
64.8 × 80 cm
Fridart Stichting, Amsterdam

PAUL GAUGUIN
1848–1903

Began as a collector and amateur painter in the Impressionist circle, and was encouraged by Pissarro. From 1886–90 he evolved an independent manner based on simplified flat areas of sometimes non-representational colour. He worked chiefly in Brittany, with an interlude in Martinique in 1887. In 1891 he settled in Tahiti, returning to France briefly from 1893–5, and finally moving to the Marquesas Islands in 1901.

122
Martinique Landscape 1887
115 × 89 cm
National Gallery of Scotland, Edinburgh

145
Bonjour, Monsieur Gauguin 1889
74.9 × 54.6 cm
The Armand Hammer Collection,
The Armand Hammer Museum of Art and Cultural Center, Los Angeles, California

228, 242
The Haystacks, Le Pouldu 1890
74.3 × 93.6 cm
National Gallery of Art, Washington,
Gift of the W. Averell Harriman Foundation in memory of Marie N. Harriman

ALBERT GLEIZES
1881–1953

Trained as a textile designer, and was involved in the Utopian socialism of the Abbaye de Créteil community *c.* 1906–8. In his early painting he experimented with various styles, but by 1911 had developed a personal variant of Cubism, exploring pictorial equivalents for his intellectual and social concerns. He spent much of the First World War in New York. His later work sought abstract expression for his religious faith.

124, 252
Landscape (Meudon) 1911
146 × 114 cm
Musée national d'art moderne,
Centre Georges Pompidou, Paris

VINCENT VAN GOGH
1853–90

Son of a Dutch pastor, devoting himself to art *c.* 1880. For five years he worked in the Netherlands, moving via Antwerp to Paris, where he worked for two years, 1886–8, absorbing new pictorial possibilities. From February 1888 he worked for fifteen months in Arles, spending the last two months of 1888 in the fractious company of Gauguin. From May 1889 he lived voluntarily at the asylum in Saint Rémy for a year, after which he returned north, committing suicide at Auvers, outside Paris, in July 1890.

246
Wheat Fields with Reaper, Auvers 1888
73 × 93 cm
The Toledo Museum of Art, Ohio,
Purchased with funds from the Libbey Endowment, Gift of Edward Drummond Libbey

222
Olive Trees 1889
49.2 × 62.9 cm
National Gallery of Scotland, Edinburgh

223
Olive Grove 1889
74 × 93 cm
Göteborgs Konstmuseum

237
Winter: the Plain of Chailly (after Millet) 1890
72 × 92 cm
Vincent van Gogh Foundation,
Rijksmuseum Vincent van Gogh, Amsterdam

ANTOINE GUILLEMET
1841–1918

Taught by Corot and encouraged by Daubigny. Made his début at the Salon of 1865. In the late 1860s he entered the circle of Manet and Zola, who became lifelong friends. His broadly handled naturalism was more acceptable than the work of his Impressionist friends, and by 1874 one of his large Paris cityscapes had been bought by the State. In 1882 he used his position as a Salon juror to get a painting by Cézanne exhibited.

80
Wreck at Villerville 1889
55 × 74 cm
Private Collection, USA,
courtesy of John Mitchell & Son

GEORGES LACOMBE
1868–1916

Comfortably off and academically trained. His work followed a varied path. During the 1890s he belonged to the Nabis group with Denis, Bonnard and Vuillard, painting highly simplified landscapes and carving wooden sculptures often with elemental themes. After 1900 his landscape painting was in a Neo-impressionist manner.

155
Vorhor, the Green Wave c. 1896–7
egg tempera on canvas
100 × 72 cm
Indianapolis Museum of Art, Gift of the Alliance of the Indianapolis Museum of Art

CHARLES LACOSTE
1870–1959

Established a lifelong friendship, at school in Bordeaux, with the poet Francis Jammes. Through him he established himself in an impressive circle of intellectuals and collectors in Paris in the 1890s, among them André Gide and Arthur Fontaine, patron of Redon and Vuillard. He contributed to *L'Estampe originale* in 1894 and held his first one-man show at the Salon des cent in 1898. He worked in a simplified, discreet manner similar to the Nabis.

188
La Main d'ombre 1896
40 × 68 cm
Musée d'Orsay, Paris, Don de la Société des Amis du Musée d'Orsay, 1980

HENRI LE SIDANER
1862–1939

Trained at the Ecole des beaux-arts under Cabanel. His early Salon exhibits were cool-toned figure subjects often on religious themes. Following a trip to Bruges in 1898, and under the influence of writers such as Camille Mauclair and his artist friend Henri Martin, he painted mainly figureless views of towns and gardens in a still Symbolist ambience.

92
The Square at Petit Fort-Philippe 1902
58 × 78 cm
Hugh Lane Municipal Gallery of Modern Art, Dublin

MAXIMILIEN LUCE
1858–1941

Of proletarian origin, and an early member of both the Salon des Indépendants and the Neo-impressionist faction there. A committed anarchist, he painted an important group of canvases in the late 1880s depicting the mining regions and heavy industry of northern France and Belgium. He also worked in London and by the Mediterranean, with Pissarro and Signac respectively, and extensively in Paris and its environs.

57
Notre-Dame 1900
116 × 81 cm
Private Collection

58
Notre-Dame c. 1900
81.3 × 60.6 cm
San Diego Museum of Art, Gift of Ambassador and Mrs Maxwell Gluck

ARISTIDE MAILLOL
1861–1944

Like Le Sidaner, a pupil of Cabanel at the Ecole des beaux-arts. Became a member of the Nabis in the early 1890s, with Denis, Vuillard, Bonnard and others. His paintings often feature the landscape of his native Roussillon, but by the late 1890s his failing eyesight forced him to concentrate on sculpture.

106
Village in the Pyrénées orientales c. 1895
49 × 68 cm
Ashmolean Museum, Oxford

ALBERT MARQUET
1875–1947

Native of Bordeaux, and met Matisse, Manguin and Camoin in Moreau's studio at the Ecole des beaux-arts in 1897. In 1902 he exhibited with Matisse, Friesz and others at Berthe Weill's gallery and in 1905 in the Fauve 'cage' at the Salon d'Automne. However, his straightforward landscape motifs and tonal handling avoided controversy, and following his 1907 one-man show at the Galerie Druet he pursued a steadily successful career.

84
The Beach at Fécamp 1906
50 × 60.8 cm
Musée national d'art moderne,
Centre Georges Pompidou, Paris

60
Notre-Dame under Snow c. 1910
81 × 65 cm
Musée Carnavalet, Paris

HENRI MARTIN
1860–1943

Studied at the Ecoles des beaux-arts of his native Toulouse and then of Paris, under Jean-Paul Laurens. In the 1880s he exhibited conventional history paintings at the Salon, shifting in the 1890s to large canvases on Symbolist themes combining the classicism of Puvis de Chavannes with Neo-impressionist chromatics. After 1900 he abandoned mystical allegory, making a major reputation as a decorator of public buildings such as the Capitole at Toulouse and the Palais de Justice in Paris.

245
The Harvest (Summer) c. 1900–10
60.2 × 160 cm
Musée de, Brest

212
Study for 'Men Scything' c. 1902–3
56 × 126 cm
Private Collection

HENRI MATISSE
1869–1954

Pupil of Gustave Moreau at the Ecole des beaux-arts in the 1890s and the leading figure in the controversy over Fauvism at the Salon d'Automne of 1905. He was based in Paris but frequently worked on the Mediterranean coast after 1904 when he stayed with Signac at St Tropez. He first visited north Africa in 1906, returning several times prior to 1914.

59
Notre-Dame c. 1900
43 × 37.5 cm
Tate Gallery, London

123
Acanthus 1912
115 × 80 cm
Moderna Museet, Stockholm

RENE MENARD
1861–1930

Son of an art historian and nephew of a distinguished Hellenist, and trained under Bouguereau and Baudry. However his admiration for Jean-François Millet and Théodore Rousseau, whom he had met at Barbizon as a youth, also marked his painting. His early Salon submissions were conventional history paintings, but by the 1890s he had established the frieze-like pastoral style which won him the reputation of successor to Puvis de Chavannes and decorative commissions at the Sorbonne (1906) and Law Faculty (1909).

139
Hercules and the Lion 1914
pastel on beige paper
84 × 121 cm
Musée Roybet-Fould, Courbevoie

LUC-OLIVIER MERSON
1846–1920

Pupil of Lecoq de Boisbaudran and Pils. He won the Prix de Rome in 1869 and a distinguished establishment career ensued. His Salon paintings, usually on religious or medieval themes, were renowned for their fine draughtsmanship. He also painted a number of important decorative works in Paris, including the *Life of Saint Louis* for the Palais de Justice and the *Escalier des Fêtes* for the Hôtel de Ville.

138
St. Francis of Assisi Preaching to the Fish
1880
88.5 × 152 cm
Musée des beaux-arts, Nantes

CLAUDE MONET
1840–1926

Encouraged to paint as a youth on the Normandy coast by Boudin and Jongkind. Made his début at the Salon of 1865. His controversial fortunes at subsequent Salons led him to become one of the initiators of the Impressionist exhibitions. From 1872–8 he worked at Argenteuil, concentrating on the landscape of the modern city and its environs. Moving to Vétheuil, then Poissy, and finally settling at Giverny in 1883, he devoted the 1880s to working on varied sites in France and northern Italy. During the 1890s he produced successive serial groups, mainly of landscapes in the Giverny region, and after 1900 specialised in paintings of the water garden he had created there.

28, 42
The Seine at Petit-Gennevilliers 1872
47.9 × 62.9 cm
On Loan from the John M. and Sally B. Thornton Trust

88
The Museum at Le Havre 1873
75 × 100 cm
National Gallery, London

232
The Break-up of the Ice at Vétheuil 1881
60 × 100 cm
Fundación Colección Thyssen-Bornemisza, Madrid

83
Cliffs at Pourville 1882
60 × 81 cm
Rijksmuseum Twenthe, Enschede

100
Antibes Seen From the Salis 1888
65 × 83 cm
Philadelphia Museum of Art, Bequest of Charlotte Dorrance Wright

239
Grainstacks: Snow Effect 1890–1
64.8 × 92.1 cm
National Gallery of Scotland, Edinburgh

224
Poplars on the Epte 1891
81.5 × 82 cm
National Gallery of Scotland, Edinburgh

219, 225
The Four Trees 1891
81.9 × 81.6 cm
The Metropolitan Museum of Art, New York, Bequest of Mrs H.O. Havemeyer, 1929. The H.O. Havemeyer Collection

244
Haystack in a Field, 1893
66 × 101.6 cm
Museum of Fine Arts, Springfield, Massachusetts, James Philip Gray Collection

218
Waterlilies 1907
circular, diameter 80 cm
Musée d'art moderne, Saint-Etienne

GUSTAVE MOREAU
1826–98

Trained at the Ecole des beaux-arts under Picot, and remained loyal to history painting when friends such as Degas turned to modern subjects. In the 1860s and again in 1876 Moreau exhibited an ambitious sequence of mythological pictures at the Salon, but their failure to win him substantial status led him to retreat to the privacy of his studio, sustained by private means and the support of a few patrons. In 1889 he became a professor at the Ecole, proving an inspirational teacher to pupils such as Matisse and Marquet.

141
Tomyris and Cyrus c. 1885
57.5 × 87 cm
Musée Gustave Moreau, Paris

PABLO PICASSO
1881–1973

Studied chiefly in Barcelona where he was a youthful colleague of the artists connected with the El Quatre Gats café. He first visited Paris in late 1900, and then sporadically in the following years, settling there in 1904. By then his 'Blue' period of Symbolist scenes of proletarian dereliction was giving way to lighter colours and livelier circus subjects. After 1906 and his meeting with Georges Braque his increasingly experimental work developed into Cubism.

131
Landscape with Two Figures 1908
60 × 73 cm
Musée Picasso, Paris

CAMILLE PISSARRO
1830–1903

Born in the Danish West Indies and settled in France in 1855. Encouraged by Corot, he made his Salon début in 1864. By the early 1870s, however, he was involved with painters seeking alternative outlets and exhibited at all eight Impressionist exhibitions, from 1874–86. After 1880 the figure played a larger role in his landscapes, and in the later 1880s he experimented with Neo-impressionism.

197
Banks of the Oise, Pontoise 1873
38.1 × 55.2 cm
Indianapolis Museum of Art, Presented to the Art Association by James E. Roberts

RAPHAEL PONSON
1835–1904

Pupil in Loubon at the Ecole des beaux-arts in his native Marseille. He then worked briefly in Paris from 1855–6 and visited Italy before settling in his home city. He specialised in marines painted along the Mediterranean coast, submitting large, highly resolved canvases regularly to the Salons, while producing smaller paintings in an increasingly loose handling.

96
The Calanque de Port-Pin near Cassis, 1873
123 × 202 cm
Musée des beaux-arts, Béziers

PIERRE PUVIS DE CHAVANNES
1824–98

With a patchy academic training, his career as a history painter was slow to take off. However, the purchase in 1863 by the Musée de Picardie, Amiens, of two works and the commissioning of another the following year launched his career as a painter of mural decorations for public buildings. His work for the Panthéon, Paris (1874–6 and 1896–8) confirmed his status, and he soon acquired critical recognition. This burgeoned in the 1880s and 1890s when his disciplined classicism appealed to conservatives and his simplified drawing and subtle colours to the Symbolist generation.

209
Sketches for the Lyon decorations: 'Inspiration chrétienne', 'Le Bois sacré,' 'Vision antique' c. 1883–4
30.5 x 171.5 cm
Musée des beaux-arts, Lyon

JEAN-FRANCOIS RAFFAELLI
1850–1924

Had an eclectic and unsuccessful start before moving to suburban Asnières in 1879. His representations of the area's lower classes and dismal landscapes were shown at the Impressionist exhibitions of 1880 and 1881 and with great success at his one-man exhibition of 1884. Thereafter he showed at the Salon, choosing subjects to please the progressive Republican faction. After 1890, his reputation secured, he turned to land- and cityscapes.

33
The Gipsy Woman c. 1880–4
38 x 45 cm
Musée Marmottan, Paris

ODILON REDON
1840–1916

Began as a reluctant pupil of Gérôme at the Ecole des beaux-arts. Learnt much about print-making techniques and fantasy images from Rodolphe Bresdin. In the 1870s he devoted himself to charcoal drawing, producing between 1879 and 1899 a series of albums of lithographs which spread his reputation as an image-maker of the extraordinary. By the mid–1890s he returned more and more to painting, and his oils and pastels became increasingly highly coloured.

168
The Flight into Egypt c. 1900–3
45 x 38 cm
Musée d'Orsay, Paris, Legs de Mme Arï Redon, en exécution des volontés de son mari, 1982

AUGUSTE RENOIR
1841–1919

Met Monet and Sisley at Gleyre's *atelier* in 1862. A painter of portraits, landscapes and modern figure subjects, he was an important member of the Impressionist circle in the 1870s. By the 1880s, following a visit to Italy in 1881, he turned increasingly to timeless images of the female nude, painted first in a Raphaelesque and later a Rubensian style. By 1902 he had settled on the Mediterranean coast, where his work was typified by an idealised richness and light.

94, 98
Rocky Crags at L'Estaque 1882
66.5 x 81 cm
Museum of Fine Arts, Boston, Juliana Cheyney Edwards Collection

HENRI ROUSSEAU
1844–1910

Served in the French army in the 1860s. From 1871–93 he held a lowly post in the Parisian toll-gate service, which gave him the nickname *le douanier* (customs officer). Perhaps beginning to paint *c.* 1880, he made his début at the Indépendants of 1886. Despite ridicule from many, he won the respect of younger avant-gardistes, notably Picasso, Apollinaire and Robert Delaunay.

132
Walking in the Forest c1886
70 x 60.5 cm
Kunsthaus Zürich

172
The Keep, 1889
90.2 x 70.5 cm
Santa Barbara Museum of Art, Bequest of Wright S. Ludington

KER-XAVIER ROUSSEL
1867–1944

Brother-in-law of Vuillard, and, like him, a member of the Nabis in the 1890s. By the turn of the century he had arrived at his mature style, painting sensuous mythological and pastoral subjects in loosely brushed landscapes of rich colour. These themes were ideally suited to decorative schemes, such as the Théâtre des Champs-Elysées (1912–13) and the Kunstmuseum, Winterthur (1916–18).

130
The Embrace c. 1900–5
78 x 104 cm
Musée de l'Annonciade, Saint-Tropez

214
Study for 'The Cortège of Bacchus' c. 1912
72 x 74 cm
Private Collection

ALEXANDRE SEGE
1818–85

Trained by Cogniet and Flers, and made his Salon début in 1844. A devoted landscape painter, he favoured panoramic views. He travelled widely, discovering Brittany in 1838 and working as far apart as the Pas-de-Calais and Corsica. He only achieved modest official recognition in the 1870s, following the purchase of a Breton landscape by the State from the Salon of 1870.

192, 253
En pays chartrain, 1884
134 x 201 cm
Musée des beaux-arts, Chartres

GEORGES SEURAT
1859–91

Student of Lehmann at the Ecole des beaux-arts with Aman-Jean. He privately developed a new manner of tonal drawing and an interest in the systematic application of colour prior to exhibiting his work publicly. The appearance of *La Grande Jatte* at the 1886 Impressionist exhibition established him as the leading painter of the Parisian avant-garde. He upheld this position with pictorially experimental paintings of urban entertainment until his early death.

37
Field of Alfalfa, Saint-Denis c. 1884–5
64 x 81 cm
National Gallery of Scotland, Edinburgh

81
Le Bec du Hoc 1885
64.8 x 81.6 cm
Tate Gallery, London

174
The Channel at Gravelines: 'Evening' 1890
65.2 x 81.7 cm
The Museum of Modern Art, New York, Gift of Mr and Mrs William A.M. Burden, 1963

78, 91
The Channel of Gravelines, Grand Fort-Philippe 1890
65 x 81 cm
The Berggruen Collection, on loan to the National Gallery, London

RENE SEYSSAUD
1867–1952

Trained at the Ecole des beaux-arts in Marseille and worked chiefly in his native Provence. His brightly coloured and aggressively brushed canvases were shown by Vollard in 1899 and Bernheim Jeune in 1901. He exhibited regularly with the Indépendants from 1892 and later at the Salon d'Automne.

247
Harvest at Sunset c. 1895–6
59 × 81 cm
Mr and Mrs J. Benatoff

PAUL SIGNAC
1863–1935

Largely self-taught, and involved with Seurat in the development of Neo-impressionism in the mid–1880s. Although in 1892 he moved to St Tropez, and throughout the decade concentrated on Mediterranean landscapes and figure subjects, he was an important focus for the Neo-impressionist painters and a key figure in the Indépendants. After 1900 he encouraged younger painters such as Matisse and Valtat, and began to travel further afield. He was a committed anarchist.

1, 72
Seine, Grenelle 1899
62 × 78.5 cm
Amos Andersonin Taideomuseo, Helsinki

44
Quay de Clichy 1887
46 × 65 cm
The Baltimore Museum of Art,
Gift of Frederick H. Gottlieb

175
The Seine at Herblay: Sunset 1890
57.1 × 90.2 cm
Glasgow Museums: Art Gallery and Museum, Kelvingrove

226
Concarneau, the Fishing Boats (Allegro maestoso: evening) 1891
64.8 × 81.3 cm
The Metropolitan Museum of Art,
Robert Lehman Collection, 1975

227
Concarneau: the Fishing Boats (Adagio: sunset) 1891
62 × 78 cm
Mrs John Hay Whitney

LOUIS-LUCIEN SIMONNET
1849–1926

Pupil of Boulanger and Nozal. Exhibited at the Société des artistes français from 1887 onwards, and was also a regular contributor to the annual exhibitions in Lyon and Nantes. His very traditional landscape style, in both oil and pastel, was based on a study of masters such as Corot, Daubigny and Harpignies.

234
Ville-d'Avray: Snow Effect 1893
151 × 201.5 cm
Musée d'Orsay, Paris

ALFRED SISLEY
1839–1899

Born in Paris of British parents. Sisley entered the studio of Gleyre in 1862, where he met and became friends with Monet, Renoir and Bazille. Almost exclusively a landscape painter, Sisley's early work was influenced by the Barbizon painters. Having developed his own style he exhibited at the First Impressionist Exhibition (1874) and several of the later ones. Sisley retained his British citizenship, spending time in England during the Franco-Prussian War and returning in 1874 to paint the suburbs of South London. In 1897 he visited Wales and many of his last paintings are Welsh seascapes.

195
The Bend in the Seine at Saint-Cloud 1875
66 × 91 cm
Musée des beaux-arts, Rennes

221
Railway Station at Moret, 1888
pastel on brown paper
45.7 × 54.6 cm
National Gallery of Scotland, Edinburgh

LOUIS TAUZIN
1842–1915

Native of Bordeaux, making his Salon début in 1867. At that period he settled at Meudon in the south-western suburbs of Paris, which he used as a base for painting cityscapes and anecdotal landscapes animated by small figures.

190
Ile Seguin, Seen from Meudon c. 1900
73 × 100 cm
Musée municipal de Boulogne-Billancourt

FELIX VALLOTTON
1865–1925

Of Swiss origin, and trained in Paris. Around 1892 he moved away from a fastidious naturalism into a flatter, more synthetic manner and drew into the orbit of the Nabis. Of anarchist sympathies, he made stark woodcuts as well as paintings, which often caricature bourgeois life. From *c.* 1900 he showed a growing interest in landscape, and around 1905–6 painted a number of canvases in the tradition of the *paysage historique*.

137
Pentheus 1904
93 × 142 cm
Private Collection, Switzerland

LOUIS VALTAT
1869–1952

Pupil of Moreau at the Ecole des beaux-arts. He developed a strongly coloured style in the 1890s when he was on the fringes of the Nabis group. Settling on the Mediterranean coast in 1899 he was encouraged by Signac and connected with the Fauves, as well as being friendly with Denis and Roussel. By *c.* 1905 his work fell increasingly under the influence of Renoir.

99
The Estérel 1903
81 × 100 cm
Musée de l'Annonciade, Saint-Tropez

MAURICE VLAMINCK
1876–1958

Racing cyclist, night-club musician and soft-porn writer. Taught himself to paint, probably after seeing the van Gogh exhibition at the Bernheim jeune gallery in 1901. He had met Derain the year before, and after Derain's military service they formed a fruitful partnership in the suburbs of Paris developing emphatic Fauve styles. He rejected the Midi and Cubism, and by 1914 his work had become parochial and repetitive.

47
Barges at Le Pecq c. 1905–6
50.5 × 65.7 cm
The Museum of Fine Arts, Houston;
Gift of Oveta Culp Hobby

EDOUARD VUILLARD
1868–1940

Passed through the Ecole des beaux-arts before becoming a member of the Nabis, with Denis, Bonnard, Roussel and others. In the 1890s he made a reputation for decorations and small paintings in intricate patterns and subdued tones. After 1900 his work, like that of Bonnard, reverted to naturalism, albeit distinguished by remarkable skills of execution and observation.

204, 217
Cottage at L'Etang-la-Ville c. 1899
distemper on canvas
157 × 255 cm
Musée départemental de l'Oise, Beauvais

Illustration Acknowledgements

PHOTOGRAPHIC CREDITS

Jack Abraham 71

Per-Anders Allsten 123

Courtesy of Apollo Magazine 149, 164

Martin Bühler, Basel 77

© 1993. The Barnes Foundation 128

Studio Basset 41, 208, 209

© Jean-Louis Bouché, Beauvais 203

Jörg P. Anders, Berlin 136

Jean Bernard 20, 101

© 1994. Museum of Fine Arts, Boston 55, 98, 173, 187

Jacques Bocoyran 245

© Jean Brasille 114

© Fitzwilliam Museum, University of Cambridge 121

Christie's Images 53

© The Cleveland Museum of Art 40

© Musée des Années 30 – P. Codiou 190

A. C. Cooper 12

M. Coppens 125

Witt Library, Courtauld Institute of Art 45, 170

Louis Deschamps 195

C. Devleeschauwer 186

Walter Drayer 160

P. J. Gates 80

Christian Poite, Geneva 70

© Glasgow Museums 116, 175

Tom Haartsen 184

Luiz Hossaka 97

© 1994. Indianapolis Museum of Art 105, 155, 197

Frédéric Jaulmes 146

C. Kempf 14

Walter Klein 117

Pascal Lemaitre 36, 49

E. Vila Mateu 21, 99, 130

© Musée Marmottan 33, 35, 93, 231

A. Mewbourn 181

Scott Mclaine, 1994 172

Ville de Nantes 138

Scott Bowron, New York 110

© 1994. Museum of Modern Art, New York 62, 126, 174 (H. Matisse, Notre-Dame, 1914, illus. no.62 : Acquired through the Lillie P. Bliss Bequest, and the Henry Ittleson, A. Conger Goodyear, Mr and Mrs Robert Sinclair Funds, and the Anna Erickson Levene Bequest given in memory of her husband, Dr Phoebus Aaron Theodor Levene.)

© 1993. Claus Orstead 52

Fotostudio Otto 235

H. Plessis 18

Eric Pollitzer 227

© Musée départemental du Prieuré 46, 185, 216

Antonia Reeve 37, 95, 107, 122, 201, 221,222, 224, 239

© Réunion des Musées Nationaux 2, 4, 5, 15, 17, 22, 24, 39, 67, 113, 118, 120, 131, 133, 134, 140, 141, 167, 168, 182, 188, 191, 194, 205, 207, 214, 229, 230, 233, 234

Courtesy of Sotheby's 238

L. Sully-Jaulmes 178

© Cliché Tiziou 207, 217

Malcolm Varon 219, 225

© 1994. National Gallery of Art, Washington 30, 242

© Ole Woldbye 144

COPYRIGHT CREDITS

© ADAGP, Paris and DACS, London 1994

Albert Besnard 206

© ADAGP/SPADEM, Paris and DACS, London 1994

Pierre Bonnard 12, 179, 200

Georges Braque 104, 109, 110, 125

Marc Chagall 76

Robert Delaunay 50, 77

Sonia Delaunay 201

André Derain 48, 107, 127

Kees van Dongen 149, 164

Othon Friesz 166

Albert Gleizes 13, 41, 124, 251

František Kupka 150, 151

Albert Marquet 40, 60, 8

Louis Valtat 99

Maurice de Vlaminck 47

© DACS, London 1994

Maurice Denis 25, 185, 216

André Devambez 182, 203

Raoul Dufy 85, 87

Charles Lacoste 188

Léon Lhermitte 250

Henri Le Sidaner 92

Maximilien Luce 6, 57, 58, 180, 181

Aristide Maillol 106

Henri Charles Martin 211, 212, 213, 215, 245

René Ménard 139, 140

Pablo Picasso 131

Ker Xavier Roussel 130, 214

René Seyssaud 247

Paul Signac 15, 21, 44, 72, 112, 175, 226, 227

Edouard Vuillard 204, 217

© Succession Henri Matisse / DACS 1994

Henri Matisse 27, 59, 61, 62, 108, 117, 118, 123, 126, 128, 129

Index of People and Places

Aiguier, Auguste 78
Ajalber, Jean 37
Alain-Fournier 16
Alfortville 122
Aman-Jean, Edmond 39–40, 189
Amiel, Henri-Frédéric 16, 85, 109–10
Angrand, Charles 53, 113, 156
Antibes 69–70
Apollinaire, Guillaume 22, 50, 51, 65, 84, 157
Argenteuil 20, 28, 29, 30, 32, 152
Arles 125–6, 159
Artois 19
Arus, Raoul 122, 131
Asnières 27–8, 32, 34, 37
Aurier, Albert 174

Baldus, E. 20
Barrigue de Fontainieu, F. de 24
Barron, Louis 28, 29, 37
Bartholdi, F.-A. 22
Barzun, Henri-Martin 84
Bastien-Lepage, Jules 172, 173
Baudelaire, Charles Pierre 15, 170, 172, 174
Bazille, F. 53
Belle-Isle 142
Bellery-Desfontaines, Henri 137
Bénédite, Léonce 133, 137
Benjamin, Roger 175
Béraud, Jean 47
Bergson, Henri 21, 174
Bernard, Emile 32, 34, 35, 37, 95, 132–3, 189
Bernheim, Hippolyte 99
Billotte, Réné 21, 37, 112
Bing, Siegfried 137
Bonnard, Pierre 21, 115, 126, 176, 189
Boucher, François 132
Boudin, Eugène 54, 59, 61
Bouyer, Raymond 13, 15, 24, 112, 172–4, 175
Braque, Georges 53, 73, 75, 85, 112, 129
Brébisson, L.A. de 110
Bresdin, Rodolphe 119
Bretegnier, Georges 85
Breton, Jules 14, 18–19, 89, 155, 170
Brice, T. 172
Brouillet, André 159, 189
Buisson, J. 170

Cabanel, Alexandre 131
Cabat, Louis 14
Caillebotte, Gustave 141
Cals, A.-F. 53
Carrière, Eugène 20, 107, 115
Castagnary, Jules 171
Cazin, Jean-Charles 17, 63, 77, 189
  Channel coast 55–6, 59, 61, 63
  incident in landscape 94
  nocturnal landscapes 110
Cendrars, Blaise 127–8
Cérét 75
Cézanne, Paul 16, 171, 172, 176, 189
  classicism 80, 87
  imagery 104
  Mediterranean coast 67, 71–2, 80
  Mont-Sainte-Victoire paintings 20, 24–5
Chagall, Marc 49–50, 189
Champier, Victor 17
Channel coast 53–63
  see also names of specific locations
Charcot, Jean-Martin 99
Chartres 122–3
Chassériau, Théodore 22
Chauchard, Alfred 17
Chennevières, Philippe de 170
Chintreuil, A. 121, 171
Claretie, Jules 124, 126
Claude Gellée (Claude Lorraine) 15, 16, 17, 24, 25, 78, 89
Clermont, Raoul de 19
Clichy 34, 35
Collioure 75
Concarneau 147
Contini, Joseph 69–70, 78
Coppée, François 37
Corot, Camille 25, 77, 161, 170, 175, 190
  Channel coast 53, 110
  pastoral landscapes 78, 85
Courbet, Gustave 16, 96, 149
Courbevoie 32, 34, 35–6
Courrières 19, 155
Cousturier, Lucie 37, 86
Creuse valley 139
Cross, Henri-Edmond 25, 190
  Mediterranean coast 65, 85, 86, 89–90, 115, 161
  nocturnal landscapes 115
  pastoral scenes 85, 86, 87
Curzon, Alfred de 24

Dalcroze, Emile Jacques 106
Darien, Henry 29, 132
Daubigny, Charles 17, 23, 124, 149–51, 155
Debussy, Claude 112
Dégas, Edgar 20, 103–4, 131, 190
Delance, Paul-Louis 46, 190
Delaunay, Elie 131
Delaunay, Robert 50–1, 127, 190
Delaunay, Sonia 127–8, 129, 190
Denecourt, Claude-François 101
Denis, Maurice 14, 25, 190
  commentary 15, 77, 169, 171–2, 174, 175
  decorative painting 133, 136, 137–8
  imagery 99, 116, 118
  incident in landscape 89–90
  nocturnal landscapes 116, 118
  seasonal paintings 149
Derain, André 14, 17, 77, 162, 176, 190
  Mediterranean coast 67, 75, 85
  series paintings 147
  suburban landscapes 37
Desjardins, Paul 99, 109, 112
Devambez, André 21, 115, 129, 190
Diénay 103
Dongen, Kees van 104–6, 191
Doré, Gustave 128
Drölling, Michel-Martin 22
Dubois-Pillet, A. 40
Dufau, Clémentine-Hélène 106
Dufy, Raoul 53, 59, 61, 191
Duhem, Henri 53
Dulac, Marie-Charles 112, 116, 118, 172, 191
Dunoyer de Segonzac, André 43, 191
Dupré, J. 15
Durand-Ruel, Charles 169

Epuy, Michel 104
Espagnat, G. d' 23
Estérel 68
Etretat 23

Falaise 110
Fauré, Gabriel 65–6, 73, 112
Fécamp 59, 61
Fénéon, Félix 69, 142, 147, 174–5
Flandrin, Paul 24
Flat, Paul 16, 93–4
Flaubert, Gustave 126
Fort-Philippe 61–2
Fournel, Victor 93
Fragonard, Jean Honoré 15
Français, François-Louis 14
Friesz, Othon 17, 53, 85, 106–7, 110, 191

Galerne, Prosper 30

Gauguin, Paul 73, 87, 95–7, 155–6, 159, 174, 191
Gautier, Théophile 78
Geffroy, Gustave 154
Gennevilliers 30, 32
Gérôme, J.-L. 119
Gide, André 118
Giverny 139
Gleizes, Albert 19, 21, 176, 191
classicism 84, 87, 161
seasonal paintings 159
suburban landscapes 32, 37, 84
Gogh, Vincent van 18, 191
imagery 116
Mediterranean coast 66
nocturnal landscapes 116
panoramas 125–6
seasonal landscapes 152–3, 159
series paintings 142–4
suburban landscapes 32
Goyen, Jan van 141
Grandcamp 54–5
Granet, François-Marius 65
Gravelines 61–2, 112–13
Gray, Henri 20
Gris, Juan 75
Guillaumin, Armand 19
Guillemet, Antoine 54, 61, 63, 192

Hamerton 19
Harpignies, Henri 65, 80, 112, 170
Haussmann, Georges Eugène 27
Havard, Henry 24, 141
Hayet, Louis 46
Heidbrink 45
Helleu, Paul 40
Henner, J.-J. 110
Henriet, Frédéric 170, 174
Herblay 23, 113, 115
Holl 22
Honfleur 53, 61, 112
Hoschédé, Alice 21, 63
Hoschédé, Ernest 139
Huet, Paul 53, 65
Huysmans, Joris Karl 37, 153, 171

Indy, Vincent d' 24
Isabey, Eugène-Gabriel 53, 54
Issy-les-Moulineaux 30

Jammes, Francis 118
Jamot, Paul 77
Japy, L.-A. 121
Jongkind, Johan Barthold 39

Kahn, Gustave 112, 142
Kahnweiler, Daniel 169
Kupka, František 99

Labastide du Vert 135
La Ciotat 75
Lacombe, Georges 101, 103, 192
Lacoste, Charles 118–19, 192
Lafenestre, Georges 15, 17, 152
Laforgue, Jules 24, 45, 112
La Fresnaye, Roger de 176
Lanoë, Georges 118, 172
Laurens, Jean-Paul 131
Laval, Charles 80
La Voulte 20
Le Barc de Boutteville, 173
Leclerq, Louis-Antoine 53
Léger, Fernand 37
Le Havre 61
Lehmann, Henri 40
Le Pecq 37
Lepère, Auguste 37, 44
Lépine, Stanislas 39, 40, 46
Le Pouldu 155
Le Prince, Xavier 53, 61
Leroy, Louis 149, 171
Le Sidaner, Henri 53, 61–3, 110, 112, 115, 192
L'Estaque 67, 70–2, 73, 80
L'Etang-la-Ville 138
Lévy-Dhurmer, Lucien 40, 99–100, 101, 104, 112
Lhermitte, Léon 19, 159
Lhote, André 176
Loiseau, G. 23
Lorrain, Jean 29
Loubon, Emile 65, 71
Luce, Maximilien 19–20, 41–2, 113, 115, 192
Lumière, Auguste and Louis 21

Maillol, Aristide 73, 75, 192
Mallarmé, Stéphane 59
Manguin, H.-C. 21, 85–6
Mantegna, Andrea 15
Mantz, Paul 122
Marcel, Henry 134
Marquet, Albert 32, 43, 59, 61, 127, 192
Marseille 71, 72
Martin, Henri 18, 132, 134–6, 137, 157, 192
Martinique 80
Marx, Roger 21
Matisse, Henri 25, 162, 175, 192
classicism/pastoral scenes 78, 84, 85, 87
on decorative painting 137
Mediterranean coast 66, 75, 78, 161
Notre-Dame 42, 43
panoramas 127
Mauclair, Camille 45, 112
Maufra, M.-E.-L. 23
Maupassant, Guy de 19, 20, 53, 55, 65, 73, 110, 128
Mayrevieille, Fernand Cros 19
Mazel, Henri 132
Mediterranean coast 65–75, 78
see also names of specific locations
Méliès, Georges 21
Ménard, Réné 25, 91, 132, 193
Merson, Luc-Olivier 92, 119, 193
Mesnilval 55–6
Metzinger, Jean 176
Meurier, Marthe 138
Michel, André 17, 24, 37, 77, 121–2
Michel, Emile 18, 24, 121, 124
Millet, Jean François 89, 149, 152
Mirbeau, Octave 21
Mistral, Frédéric 24
Mithouard, Adrien 138
Monet, Claude 14, 15, 21, 170, 193
Argenteuil 20, 28, 29, 30, 32, 161
Channel coast 22–3, 56–8, 59, 61, 63
decorative painting 131, 139, 175
imagery 100–1
incident in landscape 89
Mediterranean coast/Midi 65, 66, 69–70
panoramas 125
seasonal paintings 151, 152, 153–4, 156–7
series paintings 141–2, 144–5, 147: Creuse valley 139; grainstacks 153–4, 171–2, 175; poplars 144–5, 175; Rouen Cathedral 100–1, 131, 142; waterlilies 139
Monfried, Gabriel de 73
Monticelli, A. 67
Mont-Saint-Pierre 19
Mont-Sainte-Victoire 20, 24–5
Moréas, Jean 24, 68, 78, 99, 109, 116, 126, 174
Moreau, Gustave 92–3, 193
Moreau-Nélaton, Etienne 44–5, 110
Moreno, Louis 46
Moret 141
Moret, H. 23
Morisot, Berthe 30
Mouton, Eugène 101

Nadar 128, 169
Neer, Aert van der 109
Nice 65
Nietzsche, Friedrich Wilhelm 85, 137
Normandy 53–63
see also names of specific locations

Paris
Eiffel Tower 39, 45–51
Notre-Dame 39–45
panoramas 121, 123
suburbs 27–37, 123
Théâtre des Champs Elysées 136–7
see also names of individual suburbs
Paulhan, Frédéric 16, 17, 149
Péguy, Charles 13
Pelouse, L.-G. 54
Pennell, Joseph 41
Perros-Guirec 138
Petit, Georges 169
Picasso, Pablo 86–7, 129, 193
Pissarro, Camille 15, 16, 19, 138, 193
Eiffel Tower 47
panoramas 124–5
seasonal paintings 149, 155
series paintings 141
Poictevin, Francis 142
Ponson, Raphäel 67, 193
Pont-Aven 95
Pontoise 125
Pourville 58, 63
Poussin, Nicolas 15, 16, 17, 24, 25, 77, 78, 89
Puvis de Chavannes, Pierre 20, 174, 194
decorative painting 131, 132, 133–4
pastoral paintings 77
seasonal paintings 149
Pyrénées 73, 75

Raffaëlli, Jean-François 28–9, 30, 41, 194
Redon, Odilon 99, 110, 119, 194
Rembrandt 15
Renan, Ernest 24
Renoir, Auguste 14, 23, 65, 67–8, 85, 132, 194

Retté, Adolphe 66
Rewald, John 170
Rivière, Henri 47–8, 115
Rochefoucauld, Comte Antoine de la 147
Rodin, Auguste 14
Romain, Jules 21, 84
Rouen Cathedral 100–1, 131, 142
Rousseau, Henri (le Douanier) 47, 94–5, 97, 110, 116, 194
Rousseau, Jean-Jacques 16
Rousseau, Théodore 15, 172, 174
Roussel, Ker-Xavier 86, 87, 136–7, 194
Rubens, Peter Paul 15

Saint-Cloud 32, 123–4
Saint-Denis 30, 32
Saint-Siméon 53
Saint-Tropez 53, 78
Salmon, André 17, 24
Sauzay, A. 23
Schiff, Richard 171
Schivelbusch, Wolfgang 20
Segard, Achille 17, 131, 134–5
Ségé, Alexandre 122–3, 124, 129, 194
Seillière, Ernest 137
Seurat, Georges 173, 194
  Channel coast 54–5, 59, 61–2, 112–13
  Eiffel Tower 47
  nocturnal landscapes 112–13
  suburban landscapes 30, 32–5, 37
Seyssaud, René 159, 194–5
Signac, Paul 14, 15, 21, 23, 25, 51, 173, 195
  classical landscapes 78
  Eiffel Tower 47–9
  Mediterranean coast 65, 66–7, 70, 78
  nocturnal landscapes 113–15
  series paintings 145–7
  suburban landscapes 33, 34, 35, 37
Silverman, Debora 137
Silvestre, Armand 131
Simonnet, Louis-Lucien 151, 195
Sisley, Alfred 123, 124, 141, 153, 162, 195
Soulier, Gustave 137
Steiner, Rudolf 106
Steinlein, T. 21

Tahiti 97
Tanconville 78
Tauzin, Louis 121, 195
Taylor, Baron 53
Thaulow, F. 40, 110
Theuriet, André 19, 104
Toulouse 135
Trouville 59
Troyon, Constant 53, 123
Tucker, Paul 154

Ulmann 115
Uzanne, Octave 16, 110

Valenciennes, P.-H. de 16, 22, 77, 101, 170
Vallotton, Félix 25, 47–9, 90–1, 195
Valtat, Louis 23, 65, 68, 195
Vanves 29
Vauthier, Pierre 32
Vauxcelles, Louis 131, 175
Verhaeren, Emile 37
Verlaine, Paul 109
Vernet, Joseph 53
Vernonnet 126
Vétheuil 151
Ville-d'Avray 151–2
Villeneuve-les-Avignon 116
Villerville 54
Villiers de l'Isle-Adam, Auguste 47
Villon, Jacques 176
Vlaminck, Maurice de 17, 18, 25, 37, 195
Vogüé, Melchior de 45
Vollard, Ambroise 169
Vuillard, Edouard 17, 18, 136, 138, 195

Watteau, Antoine 15
Whistler, James Abbott McNeill 22, 112
Williams, Raymond 17–18
Willumsen, J.F. 40

Ziem, Félix 66
Zola, Emile 16, 40, 63, 103–4, 169